The Wilson Era

Years of War and After—1917-1923

WOODROW WILSON

"For I tell you, my fellow citizens, I can predict with absolute certainty that within another generation there will be another world war if the nations of the world do not concert the method by which to prevent it."—Woodrow Wilson, Omaha, September 8, 1919.

The Wilson Era

Years of War and After

1917-1923

BY JOSEPHUS DANIELS

SECRETARY OF THE NAVY, 1913-1921

"These things I saw and part of them I was."
—Virgil

CHAPEL HILL: *The University of North Carolina Press*

1946

TO

MY WIFE, MY BEST COUNSELLOR

ADDIE WORTH BAGLEY DANIELS
1869–1943

"The truest and tenderest and purest wife ever man was blessed with. To have such a love is the one blessing, in comparison of which all earthly joy is of no value; and to think of her is to praise God."

FOREWORD

"But now, how trowe ye? Such a fantasye
Fell me to mynd, that ay me thought the bell
Said to me, 'Tell on, man quhat the befell' "
—THE KINGIS QUAIR

THE WOODROW WILSON ERA, covering a dozen of the most momentous years in the life of the American republic, may be said to have begun when Wilson responded to the call to doff the scholastic cap and gown and enter the arena of politics in 1910. It moved into high gear as the legislation known as the New Freedom cut athwart old narrowing traditions, dethroned privilege, gave labor its Magna Charta, opened new highways for all the people, and made preparation for victorious participation in the war Wilson sought to avert. It reached its climax when all the free nations approved "Wilson's League of Nations" pact at Versailles, following such world manifestations of hero worship of Woodrow Wilson as were never before given mortal man by the peoples of the whole earth.

In a former volume, *The Wilson Era—Years of Peace, 1910-1917,* I undertook to give some of the sidelights through the period up to Wilson's second inauguration, when the world shook with the echoes of the feet of marching men in the most terrible war that had ever challenged civilization. The present volume, *The Wilson Era—Years of War and After, 1917-1923,* covers the passing of this country from neutrality to war, Wilson's successful master strategy in the direction of the successful fighting of three million Americans under arms, his statesmanship manifested in the discharge of difficult domestic tasks, his consecrated and heroic fight for the peace for which he led the youth into war, his falling with the flag of peace pressed to his heart as his sacrifice made him the great casualty of the holocaust, and his dying in supreme confidence that the Covenant he had brought home would one day bless mankind and destroy forever the curse of war.

In the period treated, I held the portfolio of Secretary of the Navy and, with the aid and stimulation of the most efficient and loyal associates with whom a public official was ever blessed, directed the operation of the web-footed branch of war-making; was a member of the regular Cabinet, the War Cabinet, the Council of National Defense, the Committee of Public Information, which gave out news instead of censoring it, and various committees looking to shipping, war supplies, health, and the protection of the men in the armed forces from the harpies that appear in war days. When, "broken at the wheel," Wilson retired in semi-invalidism, the close ties that had existed between us in official life continued. This personal relation puts upon me the compulsion of revealing the story behind the scenes.

If, in the interest of making history speak the truth, some self-placed auras, undeserved, are removed, and there follows the de-flation of pumped-up reputations, I can truly say that no line has been written in malice. Privileged to enjoy the confidence of the noble man who was the great central figure and light-fountain of the high days of war as the prelude to peace, I have felt it a solemn responsibility, as the last surviving member of his original Cabinet, to give the inside story as his great leadership unfolded, from the day he summoned the people to a war against war until he died in the holy passion of undeviating consecration to lasting peace. In this duty I have sought to correct some of the assumptions in auto-biographies and biographies written to exalt Wilson's trusted associates who, owing all to him, failed him in the supreme hour.

These sidelights of history reveal Wilson as one of the greatest minds of his age, with the noblest passion for unselfish public service and rarest devotion to loyal associates whom by adoption he had tried and proved. They make him no plaster saint, for upon rare occasion he could and did lose his temper exhibiting what Dr. Eliot called "a fierce and unlovely side," which the Harvard president attributed to "most reformers and pioneering folk."

The Wilson Era marked the rejuvenation of the Navy, which had been allowed to lapse to a poor second when Wilson was inaugu-rated. He declared for: "The most adequate Navy in the world," and Congress provided for such a Navy in its Three-Year Program. Any picture of the Wilson days that does not depict the carrying out of Wilson's Naval policy would be incomplete. Naturally, from the Navy Conning Tower I have set down in permanent form the high-lights with some detail, the story of Navy administration with illustrative incidents, stressing its great achievements in World War I. With less detail I have shown the decisive contribution the American Army made on the Western Front where the enemy was vanquished.

There is no attempt to write the full history of those epic days. Volume after volume has made that story familiar. I have essayed rather as a reporter "taking notes" to record the sidelights of that era, with emphasis on what "me befell" as Wilson's Secretary of the Navy and personal and political friend.

> "A chiel's amang ye takin' notes
> And, faith, he'll prent it"—

I have sought to retell incidents that illustrate the central figure of the Era with pen pictures and just appraisement of a few of the great and near-great at home and abroad who figured at the Peace Conference and in the stormy days that preceded and followed that first peace assize of all the nations of the earth

This is no chronological history. It is a personal narrative based on my observation and some participation in the events of those years. What I have written are my recollections, aided by my sketchy diary with borrowings from others.

In this labor of love and duty I have tried to tell the story of an epic era. All the while I have felt that I was "looking back to glory."

Josephus Daniels

CONTENTS

PART FIVE

"The Army Won the War"

PART SIX

Sidelights and Highlights

PART SEVEN

Franklin Roosevelt

PART EIGHT

Politics

PART NINE

"Thus the War Comes to an End"

PART TEN

Peace the Goal in Paris

PART ELEVEN

Epic League of Nations Fight

PART TWELVE

Smearing the Army and the Navy

PART THIRTEEN

Seeking to Oust Wilson

PART FOURTEEN

Aftermath of War

PART FIFTEEN

The Blue and the Gray

PART SIXTEEN

Woodrow Wilson

ILLUSTRATIONS

CARTOONS

MAPS

Part One

WOODROW WILSON

UNDERSTANDING WOODROW WILSON

THERE WAS NO touch of the mysterious or of the mystic about Woodrow Wilson. He was the easiest man to comprehend and understand of all the presidents who have occupied the White House.

When he was alive there were those who would say, "Yes, he is gifted beyond all others in felicity of expression and he knows how to fight, but he is an enigma."

"He lives in a sublimated atmosphere, lacks good-fellowship, and moves in a mysterious way his wonders to perform," said others.

When the "ashes to ashes" was said, the same thought was expressed by a score of writers. Some called him "the inexplicable," the "great unknown," the "scholar who emerged from the cloister to make dramatic plays," the "self-contained idealist who lived in a water-tight compartment apart from his fellows," and the "man whose inner life and thought were impenetrable."

As "Wilson died without having revealed himself, he goes in history, the unknown and unknowable to his generation," was one of the final estimates a Washington correspondent made of the dead President.

Those near Wilson never had the least trouble in understanding him perfectly. Those who knew him only in his words and deeds and public utterances were unerring in their appraisement. Why did his intimates never doubt what he would do, and why did the great body of the people read his transparent public life, while the myth of a not-understandable Wilson was created and grew like the fabled gourd watered by sedulous cultivation?

ALWAYS MEANT WHAT HE SAID

The answer is easy. It has been so rare for a public man to be utterly frank and genuine, to mean wholly what he says, and to carry out his public pledges regardless of all obstacles, that when a new kind of simplicity and directness appeared in a leader, the Washington politicians looked for some reservation he had made for escape from his frank avowals. "If a diplomat says 'Yes,' he means 'No.' If he says 'No,' he means 'Perhaps.'" Hence the accepted notion that other public men besides diplomats use words to conceal thought. Wilson did not understand such use of words. If he did, he did not so employ them. Never was man freer from misleading anyone as to his real meaning and intention.

"This one thing I do," was his self-given mandate. He said he had "a single-track mind." Certainly there was no misunderstanding him. You might disagree with him, and you doubtless did at times. You might deplore his going at things without circumlocution. He never learned that in public business the longest way around is the nearest way through. That's why the idea grew up that Wilson was a "queer" man. He was "queer" to those who expect a President to use public office to pay private debts, to sacrifice the public good to reward a friend, and to those who boast of what is often both a virtue and a failing, that they "never go back on a friend," which means giving that friend something belonging to the public, which it is not for the public good he should have.

Most of the ills of public business come from paying private debts with public office. It is a very natural feeling for a chief executive to reward his supporters by giving them office. He is a wise executive who surrounds himself with men of like conviction, men who have a passion of coöperation to carry out the policies upon which they are agreed. But when some political associate is given an office or contract or concession or lease as a "plum" or an "apricot" (see the Teapot Dome investigation) by a President, that chief executive is an embezzler of power. Are these hard words? If so, the time has come when they need to be said. Even more, there is demand that the Woodrow Wilson principle of risking the love of friends, and of being called ungrateful, rather than making public office a matter of personal friendships, should become the Eleventh Commandment.

SOME WHO FAILED TO "UNDERSTAND"

It was not only in Washington that the myth of "a mysterious Wilson" was entertained. It was found wherever there was difficulty in recognizing the exact meaning of words. Have you observed how difficult it is to make people believe that you mean what you say, even your best friends, when they are trying to circumvent you or persuade you to do something different from your announced purpose?

"We cannot understand him," said the pedants and worshippers of rich donors at Princeton. They stated the truth backward. They understood him perfectly. That was the trouble with the man. He determined to make Princeton a democratic institution, to produce scholars who would feel the compulsion that men with education must be servants of mankind. Could anything be plainer? But your scholastic worshippers at the shrine of the dollar knew that what Wilson proposed was condemnation of themselves. That was what hurt. Wrapped in an academic gown, wishing an aristocratic institution, they were ready to trade the character of an institution of learning for large gifts. Their plan was to give lip service to Wilson's democratic creed while practicing the policy of conserving what they called "the responsible elements of society." It was because Wilson pulled the mask off educational snobbishness that they hated him. It was not because they didn't "understand" him. It was because men "understood" all too well that if his policy succeeded they would stand exposed for what they were—trucklers and flunkies to rich donors.

When Wilson declared, "I have dedicated every power there is within me to bring the colleges that I have anything to do with to an absolutely democratic regeneration of spirit," all hats were in the air! That was a fine sentence, and those who were far from being democratic in spirit said, "The parents of Princeton boys will rejoice that Princeton has a President with such true American spirit." There was no dissent. But when Wilson undertook to put the doctrine in practice, there went up a great cry: "We cannot understand him." When he wished to replace social clubs with study homes, he was proclaimed worse than an enigma. Couldn't understand? Of course not. He was doing exactly what he said he would do. Those who wanted Princeton to be "the most charming Country Club in the world" moaned, "We cannot understand Wilson."

GAVE THE BOSSES NO PLEDGES

"We cannot understand this man Wilson," said former Senator Jim Smith and the other political bosses of New Jersey. "He will not play the game." They said, "See here, we took him up. We nominated him for Governor of New Jersey and elected him. Then he throws us down. We cannot understand such a man."

Again, the political bosses, like the pedagogical snobs, were putting the cart before the horse. It was not that they did not understand him. It was that they understood him too well for their purposes. When the suggestion came to Wilson of becoming the Democratic candidate for Governor of New Jersey, he said he would accept if it implied no promises or pledges. The speaker of the organization who placed Wilson in nomination said Wilson would accept "without any private obligations or undertakings whatever." Later, when he defeated the bosses who were trying to overrule the mandate of the primary, the machine politicians wailed, "We cannot understand this man Wilson." That wasn't their complaint. It was that they understood him too well as they landed on the pavement. It suited their purpose to disguise his disapproval of their adherence to machine methods by attributing something "strange and mysterious" to Wilson.

Then Wilson came to Washington. There was some perturbation on the part of the Old Guard in his party. His Staunton speech on December 26 gave them cold shivers. That was increased when, the day after his inauguration, Wilson announced that he would give no audience to those desiring office. Shades of the immortals! Had not the great Lincoln bemoaned the necessity of giving up much time to talking to office-seekers? Here was the schoolmaster in the White House locking the doors against men desiring public office. They united in one jeremiad, "We cannot understand this man." That wasn't what they meant. They understood only too well. He was doing something they did not like. They couldn't help themselves. They did not wish to cry out the condemnation they felt. So they added some snow to the enlarging snowball myth that Wilson did things nobody could make out.

In all the precedent-breaking days in Washington, the corridors whispered that the man in the White House had such a surprising manner of approach and such different ways of doing things that a glossary was needed to enable the folks to get what he was driving at. This reached a crescendo when, discarding a custom of over a century, he went up to the Capitol and delivered his message in person. "Actually, he seems to think he can look us in the eye and hypnotize us to do his will," said a Congressman—one who admitted that he could comprehend what Wilson was driving at.

Wasn't Wilson a Democrat? Was he not the heir of Jefferson, the original Democrat? Had not Jefferson discarded the practice of speaking his recommendations to Congress established by Washington? Had not Jefferson's party criticized even the "Father of His Country" for aping royalty and delivering a message "from the throne"? Was all this Jeffersonian precedent to be scrapped by the New Jersey schoolmaster? They couldn't understand.

WASHINGTON PUZZLED WILSON

Wilson set about breaking precedents in Washington and was proclaimed "a queer person." On the other hand, he was mystified about Washington. He could not understand it. "Every time I wish to be perfectly natural," he said, "and every time I do the things that I want to do and which seem all right, I am told they are the very things I must not do." But if he did not understand Washington, nobody heard about that. Everybody heard that Washington could not "understand" Wilson. Though a golfer, he did not wish to join the most exclusive country club. What was the matter with the man? Was there a screw loose? Other presidents had even felt honored to come into the most aristocratic club and putt with its members. He must be a sort of inexplicable man who preferred to stay by himself, or select his own friends, rather than mingle with the best society of the national capital. The job of getting this into the heads of social Washington would require a surgical operation. The White House had a man who wasn't like other folks. What sort of creature was he anyhow? They didn't give it up. No, they talked about it over their tea. That was in the days when "Wilson—That's All," taken with ice and the accompaniments, was the only thing they could understand with a Wilson in it. And they haven't quit talking to this day about the golf player who didn't select his associates and appointees from his companions in the golf games. Couldn't they "understand" him? Rather they understood him perfectly. It did not flatter them, and it was more consoling to their self-esteem to discuss the "strange" mind of this new occupant of the White House.

For a century the people of Washington looked to the long-drawn-out days when a tariff was in the making as a harvest time. People who wished to see that the schedules did not fail to help their particular business were in the habit of moving over to Washington. They came with retainers in 1913, as formerly. It was the quadrennial onslaught on the Capital. Hotels were filled, champagne popped, there were dinners galore, and a merry time. This army of lobbyists—they called themselves by a higher sounding name—had hardly become warm in their nests before Wilson issued an order for them to leave Washington. In some way they have never yet understood, he had a roster of the whole outfit. He knew their whole program, could tell what interests they had come to serve and what members of Congress they had approached and were entertaining. It was a sad day for the hotels and the taxis and the social swim, when that queer man in the White House said, "Go."

What did Wilson know? He knew their names, their aims, their methods, and their employers. One thing is known. The tariff lobby hurried from Washington in posthaste. Did they tell those back home what Wilson knew and why they had so suddenly changed their plans? They did not. They added themselves to the poison squad which increased the army spreading the report far and near that "You can't understand Wilson," and they added: "A mysterious man in the White House is a dangerous man." For once they were right. The man was "dangerous" to those who wished to write tariff schedules to put money in their own pockets.

When currency legislation was up, Wilson was beyond the understanding of the big bankers, who had been accustomed to exercise great influence in all government fiscal matters. They thought the bankers ought to have representation in the Federal Reserve Board, since they put up the money. Their position seemed plausible. Wilson told them that the new system was to control and regulate banks, and he could not consent for men who were going to be regulated to be themselves the regulators. Did they "understand" him? Only too well. They understood him so well that they organized to fight the Federal Reserve legislation. Senator Aldrich was summoned from his retirement to show that Mr. Wilson's proposed currency legislation was "an important step toward changing the Government from a democracy to an autocracy." It was a conflict of giants, though not as sensational as the big battle over the National Bank when Andrew Jackson and Nicholas Biddle locked horns. The country understood Wilson, if the opponents of currency reform had failed to do so.

They couldn't "understand" Wilson all through the long and difficult Mexican situation, though his course was as plain as a pikestaff.

This was particularly true of those, like Henry Watterson, who issued a demand that every foot of land from the Rio Grande to the Panama Canal should be brought under the American flag. Exploiters who held Díaz's concessions of his country's patrimony most of all pretended not to understand Wilson. Others were mystified. To be sure, there was wide division of opinion in America as to the wisdom of Wilson's program of "watchful waiting." But no excuse for misunderstanding. He stated it a score of times with the greatest clarity, perhaps never more succinctly than when he said, "So long as the power of recognition rests with me the Government of the United States will refuse to extend the hand of welcome to any one who obtains power in a sister republic by treachery and violence." He made that declaration early in 1913 and never altered his position. And yet the air was full of, "We cannot understand Wilson's Mexican policy."

WILSON'S COURSE IN THE WAR

The European war offered the widest door to the inability to "understand" Wilson. There was never any doubt of his position from the assassination in Serbia to the Armistice. It was: Neutrality just so long as it was consistent with the protection of American rights and the preservation of the just rights of humanity. Those zealous to enter the war and those eager to help the Central Empire failed to "understand" his consistent and difficult course of action. Their own partisanship blinded them, not Wilson's plain course. He navigated between Scylla and Charybdis with a firm hand. He was never uncertain of the port toward which he was steering. If others were doubtful, it was made plain in the note of May 13, 1915, to the Imperial German Government that he would not "omit any word or any act necessary," and in the resignation of Bryan because the Secretary of State felt that Wilson's vigorous policy might lead to war.

And yet in America there were those who said they couldn't "understand" his plain language. Great Britain didn't seem to "understand." Even Ambassador Walter Page, an authority in the use of good English, permitted his zeal for the United States to hurry and enter the war to becloud his mind. Because of Wilson's patience, Germany had taken the cue and acted as if it did not "understand." For weary months the Germans proceeded as if they had not read the "omit no word or act," and could not comprehend the clear import of those words in the *Lusitania* note:

> "The Government of the United States is contending for something much greater than mere rights of property or privileges of commerce. It is contending for nothing less high and sacred than the rights of humanity, which every Government honors itself in respecting and which no Government is justified in resigning in behalf of those under its care and authority."

There was plenty of room for disagreement as to whether Wilson did not exercise too much patience. Some believed he should have asked Congress to declare war sooner. But there was no possibility of doubt that war would follow unless the Imperial German Government kept the pledges it made. If people did not "understand," it was because they deliberately shut their eyes to the fixed policy of President Wilson. They refused to look through plain glass. It was not that Wilson was not understandable. It was that he was not taken at his word.

The Armistice was signed upon the acceptance by the Allies and the Central Government of Wilson's Fourteen Points with his additions in two other addresses. It was as plain as it could possibly be. And yet when Wilson reached Paris there were assertions by some that they didn't "understand" him when he contended that peace should be made according to the faith pledged in the acceptance of his terms. The British Admiralty claimed they didn't "understand" "Freedom of the Seas." They understood only too well that it would end any one country's being the "mistress of the seas." Even in the body of the American Peace Commission there was voiced a lack of ability to comprehend that the League of Nations must be bound up in the Treaty, one and inseparable. But Wilson made it plain, and later in a way that did not admit of any misunderstanding.

The lack-of-understanding myth persisted when Wilson returned home and made the fight for the Convenant. He had accepted the Taft, Root, and Hughes suggestions, and they had been incorporated. Wilson made his attitude so plain on the League that the wayfaring man might read him aright. He did not believe any reservations were needed. If, however, friends of the measure wished to add interpretive amendments, he had no objection.

They did not "understand" Wilson when, in 1919, in the face of the warning of his physician that the strain of speaking for the League from Washington to the Golden Gate might cost him his life, without affectation he calmly said, "I don't care if I die the next minute after the Treaty is ratified." They couldn't "understand" that no man truly believes in a cause he would not die for.

They couldn't "understand" Wilson when as an inspired prophet he said at Omaha:

"I can predict with absolute certainty that within another generation there will be another world war if the nations of the world do not concert the method by which to prevent it."

And the dim of vision couldn't "understand" that he was able to pierce the veil and look a quarter of a century into the future as he said in an address at San Diego:

"I do not hesitate to say that the war we have just been through, though it was shot through with terror of every kind, is not to be compared with the war we would have to face next time.... What the Germans used were toys as compared with what would be used in the next war."

When the Senate adopted thirteen reservations, which Wilson declared were "nullifications," he was dead set against them. Still there were those who were continually telling us—in 1941 they saw his prophecies of Nazi frightfulness fulfilled—that they could not "understand" Wilson. The critics and the doubters and the blind of that period could not gaze through a prism and see the colors. It is hard to give "understanding" to those who will not "understand."

For twenty-five years the League, lacking the practical vision of Wilson, failed to understand and carry out its great purpose and permitted the imperialistic aspirations of some members, and the stupidity of others to prevent action while the Axis powers armed for World War II. Worse than that: There sprang up—even in America—apologists for the Nazis, who invented the fiction that the peace of Versailles was a hard one and that because of its harshness, the blame of Germany's re-arming was laid at the door of Wilson. That propaganda of misunderstanding poured water on Germany's war wheel. André Tardieu truly said that "the Versailles Treaty was a hundred thousand times better than the way it was carried out."

Lastly they could not then "understand" the uplifting faith of "the lame lion of S. Street" as, sensing that the "old machine has broken down," he was able to say to me, "Do not trouble about the things we have fought for. They are sure to prevail. And I will make this concession to Providence—it may come in a better way than we provided."

But in 1945 there came the tragic reaping of what had been sown by those who though "having eyes, see not," in millions of casualties in World War II, because a former American generation did not "understand" and did not follow Woodrow Wilson into the League of Nations.

They "understand" now that the United Nations, highly resolved to make a sure way to the peace Wilson envisioned and fashioned at Versailles, signed the Covenant of World Peace at San Francisco on June 26, 1945. "The stone which the builders refused is become the head stone of the corner." The whole world today has come to hold the view expressed by Jan Christiaan Smuts, who, after the Versailles Treaty, said, "It was not Wilson who failed but humanity itself. . . . Americans of the future will yet proudly and gratefully rank him with Washington and Lincoln and his fame will have a more universal significance than theirs."

Part Two

THE WAR CLOUDS GATHER

II

THE IDES OF MARCH

I T WAS A very different world which confronted Woodrow Wilson on March 4, 1917, as he took his second oath of office, from the one of 1913 when he summoned all forward-looking men to his side. Then there was not a war cloud as big as a man's hand on the world horizon. In 1913 it was domestic problems that pressed for solution. In his first term these had been solved.

War clouds lowered as Wilson quietly took the oath in the President's Room in the Capitol on Sunday, March 4, and repeated it in the presence of a great gathering of people at the Capitol on Monday. Then as in 1913 the oath was administered to the Presbyterian elder as chief executive by the Catholic chief justice.

Behind lay the victories of peace, the building of the New Freedom. Wilson had secured a new Magna Charta for labor, achieved sound policies of taxation, created a system of finance far removed from Wall Street, provided credit for agriculture and business, set up agencies for ending monopoly, brought into being a great Navy and Merchant Marine—setting the chart for free enterprise and prosperity. Would these reforms be lost in the maelstrom of war? He feared a nation could not put its strength into war and keep its head level. Could free assembly and free speech survive? These fears and questions pressed upon him as his carriage passed down Pennsylvania Avenue.

Roof tops bristled with guns and a cordon of police made a hollow square around the carriage of President and Mrs. Wilson. Secret Service men were vigilant. The inaugural address did not partake of the martial spirit. While there pervaded a feeling that war could not be avoided, Wilson addressed many members of Congress who were hoping against hope that the cup of conflict would not be pressed to their lips. On that day, if a vote had been taken, a fourth of the Congressmen would not have voted for a declaration of war. "Will Wilson be borne along upon the rising tide and make a war declaration?" was the question. His hearers listened intently for the

answer. Some hoped to hear the call to battle. Others prayed that
a way might be found to keep us free of the holocaust. While others
cheered, the sense of the troubled days ahead made the President
serious. Oppressed as he was with these reflections, the holiday appearance along the avenue seemed incongruous. And I shared these
forebodings, for my mind was centered on hastening preparations
to end U-boat warfare, then at its height. The tone of the address
heartened many who still hoped the war could be averted, when
Wilson said that if America remained true to herself the "shadows
that lie dark upon our path will soon be dispelled and we shall
walk with the light all about us." Did he still believe we could keep
out of war in the hope that Germany would not commit the "overt
act"? Or was he relying upon Ambassador Page's earlier assurance
that the entrance of the United States into the war would in itself
insure peace without the employment of large armed bodies of
American troops?

There was no hint in his inaugural of foreboding or doubt as he
declared, "Nothing will alter our thought and our purpose, whether
in war or peace." He declared for freedom of the seas and the equality
of all nations; he foreshadowed the League of Nations when he
said, "Peace cannot securely or justly rest upon an armed balance
of power." He called for unity, pledging that "Nothing will alter
our thought and purpose to maintain American rights upon the seas,"
even if "we may be drawn on by circumstances to a more immediate
association with the great struggle itself." People saw resolve in his
declaration: "This is no time for retrospect. It is rather a time to
speak our thoughts and purposes concerning the present and the
immediate future." Briefly he stressed American principles of the
foundation of peace, and gave a measure of hope to those still unwilling to accept war, as he spoke in tones that were almost convincing to himself and those who hung on his words.

Though the day opened bright, as it wore on, a raw and chilly
wind made it very different from the halcyon day in 1913 which
seemed an augury of domestic tranquillity. I was never so nearly
frozen stiff, standing with the President and Mrs. Wilson and the
Cabinet reviewing the long parade. I recall to this day the rigor of
the biting wind and how I rushed to a boiling hot bath to recover
from the chill. But if the President felt the cold as others did, there
was no evidence of such feeling. He stood until the end of the line

passed, believing if men could march and salute, he could do no less than return the salute of those he feared might be making their last greeting before they stood on the firing line. Was the chill in the air a portent of the coldest winter (1917-1918) the world had known since the weather bureau recorded the temperature, and a prophecy of the icy battlefields that stretched before the armed forces? If the wind was icy, the people were hot with resentment toward Germany for its threat to return to unrestricted U-boat warfare; their indignation flamed over Zimmerman's offer to Mexico "to reconquer the lost territory in Texas, New Mexico, and Arizona"; and they were still seething with wrath because a senatorial filibuster against the bill to authorize the arming of merchant ships by "a little group of willful men" had caused Wilson to declare that they had "rendered this government helpless and contemptible."

THE VALLEY OF DECISION

Following his inaugural address, Wilson lived in what Ray Stannard Baker said was the "Valley of Decision." For more than a week, far from well, he remained aloof in his private quarters; the usual Cabinet meetings were not held, and he saw only a few callers. On the evening of March 9, when I called to discuss plans for arming merchant ships, I never saw him so grave. He said he would approve the plans. But, in a letter sent me later, he emphasized that no announcement of arming the ships was to be made. Urging secrecy, he wrote: "I would be very much obliged if you would give the most emphatic orders that no part of any of this is to be given even the least publicity. I should feel justified in ordering a court-martial for disobedience to such orders."

He talked solemnly of what war might imply. Was he still hoping the cup would not have to be drained? I think so. That opinion is strengthened by the view of Ambassador Gerard, who, leaving the White House, said, "Wilson was in a most serious mood. He said he had done everything to preserve peace and even yet he hoped that the Germans would abandon their ruthless submarine war." Further proof of Wilson's seeking to find a way of escape is seen in the statement of Frank Cobb, editor of the *New York World,* upon whom Wilson often depended for counsel. A few hours before he took the plunge, he and Cobb had a long and heart-to-heart talk in the White House. Cobb relates that Wilson, sad beyond thought, told him that for nights he had been lying awake going over the whole situation and over the consequences if we entered the melee, saying he had tried every way he knew to avoid war. Wilson asked Cobb, "Is there anything else I can do?" Cobb answered that his hand had been forced by Germany and he didn't see how he could keep out. While Wilson was rent within himself, groping for a way to keep out with honor, Theodore Roosevelt was writing to Lodge, "If Wilson does not go to war, I will skin him alive." But if Wilson had known what was being said, none of this talk would have moved him, not any more than the impotent pressure of selfish economic groups which declared that the international condition was most alarming and was "causing a cessation of foreign trade," or than Page's appeal that "France and England must have a large credit to prevent collapse of world trade."

THE OVERT ACT THAT CARRIED US INTO WAR

From the day the Kaiser issued his decree for unrestricted warfare I did not doubt that we were headed for war, but, like Wilson, I hoped against hope that there would be no "overt act." I clung to this slender thread until U-boats sank American ships on lawful missions in the Eastern Atlantic. The Kaiser's fateful order was in these words:—

General Headquarters
January 9, 1917

I order that the unrestricted submarine war be launched with the greatest vigor on the 1st of February. You will immediately take all necessary steps, taking care, however, that this intention shall not prematurely come to the knowledge of the enemy and the neutral powers.

WILHELM, I. R.

After reading the text of the Kaiser's declaration of unrestricted U-Boat warfare to the listening ten Cabinet members, the President asked, "What is the concrete suggestion? What shall I propose? I must go to Congress. What shall I say?"

One member of the Cabinet— I think it was Lane—asked, "Which side do you wish to see victorious?" That question recalled Wilson's speech on "peace without victory."

"I do not wish to see either side win. What I most earnestly desire is to see all neutrals unite to bring an end to the killing," replied the President.

After unanimous agreement that Bernstorff should be given his papers and that the break of relations with Germany must come, there were several suggestions that were foreign to the question at issue. For example, Lane, who always loved to speculate, expressed the opinion that after the war it was probable there would be an alliance between Germany, Japan, and Russia, to which Wilson replied that the Russian peasants could be relied upon to prevent such a catastrophe. "If this war results in great destruction of the white race, there may come the threat of domination by the yellow race," was another speculation. Wilson did not think the danger serious.

Within a few days after the inauguration, eight American vessels were sunk by U-boats. In only three of the sinkings were lives lost. These were the *Vigilantes,* on March 16, in which fifteen lives were lost, the tanker *Healton,* with twenty-nine lives lost, and the *Aztec,* with the loss of twenty-eight lives. They were sunk after Wilson had hoped Germany would refrain from the "overt act."

CABINET TALKS OF GERMAN PLOTS

Of a Cabinet meeting before the decision, I quote from my Diary:

"Wilson said he was very far from being too suspicious as to Germany's policies, but so many things are happening that we cannot afford to let Cuba be involved by German plots. Lansing had reported such plots and had asked for the Navy to make demonstrations. The Navy had planned periodical manoeuvres of naval ships and the demonstration would break up the plan. I said to Lansing: 'You are never happy except when you are breaking up naval operations.'

"President Wilson, continuing to talk about reports of German plots, some of them related by members of the Cabinet, related a remark which he said that Gerard, our Ambassador to Germany, had made to von Jagow. The German Minister had said to Gerard: 'If there is a war between Germany and the United States, you will find that there are 500,000 German Reservists in your country ready to take up arms for their mother country and the United States will be engaged in a civil war.' To which Gerard was quoted as replying: 'I do not know whether there are 500,000 German Reservists in the United States, but I do know there are 500,000 lamp-posts in my country and that every German residing in the United States who undertakes to take up arms against America will swing from one of those 500,000 lamp-posts.'

"Lansing reported that rumors had reached him that 500 German Reservists had gone to Mexico to make trouble. McAdoo said he had heard that 250 Japanese had gone to Mexico to make munitions. Wilson (W. B.), who evidently took no stock in these rumors, dryly commented: 'It is strange that Germany and Japan are both going to Mexico, seeing that they are at war with each other.' "

PROPAGANDA REBUKED BY WILSON

Before the final plunge was taken, Wilson rebuked Lane one day for believing unsupported reports and wishing to act upon them. My Diary records:

"Hardly had the Cabinet members taken their seats when Lane said he had heard that the wives of American Consuls on leaving Germany had been stripped naked and subjected to other gross indignities. Lansing, who should have informed the Cabinet earlier if such outrages had been committed, answered as unfeelingly as if it were not a shocking thing, that the report was true. He volunteered nothing else and when asked for more particulars, since his evidence was vague, said he would have to examine the reports to find the evidence."

MEMBERS OF CABINET HOT

Before we entered the war the President and the Cabinet boiled over because the British carried American ships and cargoes, bound to neutral countries, into their ports. That they were willing to pay for the contents did not lessen the condemnation. Writing to Colonel House, Secretary Lane voiced the feeling:

"You would be interested, I think, in hearing some of the discussion around the Cabinet table. There isn't a man in the Cabinet who has a drop of German blood in his veins, I guess. Two of us were born under the British flag. I have two cousins in the British Army, and Mrs. Lane has three. The most of us are Scotch in our ancestry, and yet each day that we meet we boil over somewhat at the foolish manner in which England acts. Can it be that she is trying to take advantage of the war to hamper our trade?"

As the war went on, German ruthlessness was so much worse than British interference with our trade—the one murdered our seamen while the other hit our pockets—that the sentiment expressed by Lane changed into alliance with Britain against the common enemy. From that time on (April 6, 1917), American and British seamen revived the spirit of sea-captains whom Nelson called his Band of Brothers.

COLLEGE MEN EAGER FOR WAR

The collegians, as a rule, sensed that the United States ought to enter the war sooner than others. From the institutions of learning came the earliest advocacy of a declaration of war. That sentiment was voiced in the Cabinet by Secretary Houston, who went from the presidency of two universities to become Secretary of Agriculture. He was more influenced by the Harvard point of view than by that of agriculture. I recall that when the question of the attitude of the country toward war was under discussion Houston read the following extract from a letter (March, 1917) from Edwin A. Alderman, President of the University of Virginia, devoted friend of Wilson, who had advised the Trustees of that institution to select Alderman as its President:

"I believe it to be our duty, as a nation now, as a matter of self-interest, as a matter of national honour, as a matter of future world influence, and as a matter of keeping quick and vital the national spirit and the national conscience, to go to war with Germany, unless the present control of the German Government sees fit to cease its methods of crime and aggression.

"Of course, we are at war with Germany, or rather, they are at war with us. You know my admiration and confidence and affection for the President. In the first place, his knowledge of the real facts goes far beyond anything we outsiders can appreciate; and, in the second place, he has great power of analysis, calmness of judgment, coolness of mind, and a great background of knowledge and understanding. I never permit myself to criticize him, even as a friend, because I have a feeling that in the end it will be shown that he is right. I can understand his aversion to carrying a nation into war that does not want to be carried into war. But he never said a truer thing than when he said that no great war could hereafter occur without our participation. In my judgment that applies to 1917 as well as to some future date....

"It is time now, I believe, to sound the tocsin, and no man can sound it, if he so wills, so effectively as the President."

III

THE DAY OF DECISION

S O FAR AS I can discover, Tuesday, March 20, 1917, is not found in war chronologies as the Day of Decision. That was, however, the time of the great decision that carried the United States into World War I. Eleven days earlier, President Wilson had called Congress to meet in special session on April 16 to "receive such communications as may be made by the Executive." The debate in the Cabinet was whether, in view of the "overt act" having been committed by German U-boats, the Congress should not be convened earlier and asked to make a declaration that a state of war existed between our country and the Imperial German Government. In the Cabinet meeting on March 20, Wilson sketched the steps our country had taken to avert war while giving protection to Americans in their right to sail the seas. He was disinclined to make the final break. With a sort of detachment, after he had finished, he invited the views of his Cabinet associates.

It was a supreme moment. Some of us, fully in harmony with the President's patient and long-successful efforts to protect American rights by peaceful means, had at last, like himself, lost hope of world and national safety without resort to war. Others, approving of steps taken, had earlier wished entrance into the struggle. It is interesting, even when the matter is one of life and death, as was this determination, to observe how ten men with the same objective will differ in the presentation of their views or the reasons for their conclusions. No two of the Cabinet on that day gave expression to precisely the same reasons, or rather, I should say, aside from the impelling reason, each had been influenced by some incident or argument he presented. But all were convinced that the character of the warfare being waged by the Central Powers could no longer be tolerated and that no course was open but for America to throw the weight of its great power into the scales against Germany.

Only once did the President interrupt a Cabinet member. It was when Burleson—no war advocate in these trying months—exhibited

Top, Wilson's first Cabinet. Around the table, clockwise, are President Wilson, and Messrs. McAdoo, McReynolds, Daniels, Houston, W. B. Wilson, Redfield, Lane, Burleson, Garrison, and Bryan. *Center,* the war Cabinet. Lansing has succeeded Bryan; Gregory has succeeded McReynolds; Baker has succeeded Garrison. *Bottom,* the last Cabinet, with Colby succeeding Lansing, Payne succeeding Lane, Houston succeeding Carter Glass, who took McAdoo's place, Palmer succeeding Gregory, Meredith succeeding Houston, and Alexander succeeding Redfield.

PRESIDENT WILSON AND HIS WAR ADVISERS

Standing, left to right, Herbert Hoover, Food Commissioner; Edward N. Hurley, chairman Shipping Board; Vance McCormick, chairman War Trade Board; Harry A. Garfield, Fuel Commissioner. *Sitting, left to right,* Benedict Crowell, Assistant Secretary of War, representing Baker, absent at the war front; William G. McAdoo, Secretary of the Treasury, President Wilson, Josephus Daniels, Secretary of the Navy; Bernard M. Baruch, chairman of the War Industries Board (Underwood and Underwood).

a sheaf of telegrams saying that many people were demanding a declaration of war. Wilson said with much feeling, "We are not governed and cannot be rushed into action by public opinion. I want to be right whether it is popular or not."

WE ARE AT WAR NOW

"You and Burleson and Wilson have not spoken, Daniels," said the President turning to us as the others had urged a war declaration. Burleson said, "We are at war. I am in favor of calling Congress at the earliest moment." W. B. Wilson said, "I have reluctantly made up my mind that action must be taken. We are at war. Congress should be called to declare that it exists."

I answered that in view of Germany's broken promise to cease sinking American ships and assumption of the right to lay off the lanes of the sea, I saw no course except to declare war to preserve the rights dearest to the cherished principles of the American people and to uphold our national honor. I referred to the fact that two days before, on March 18, word came that the American steamships *Memphis, Vigilencia,* and *Illinois* had gone down under submarine attack, the *Vigilencia* without warning. I also stated that what had stung the sea-going men most was the Kaiser's assertion of the right to lay off the lanes of the sea, saying to the American sailors where they could voyage and what part of the ocean was *verboten.* That order sought to establish a war zone around Britain and France and Italy and sink any ship found in that zone. It was unthinkable that Americans who wished to go abroad should be confined to travel in those ships which had a certificate from the American Government that it carried no contraband. I added it was an insult that the Germans directed those ships to carry three alternate stripes of red and yellow, displaying at each mast a large insigne in white and red, with the added provision that such American ships should arrive on Sunday and depart on Wednesday under peril of being sunk by a U-boat. "No American proud of the doctrine of freedom of the seas could fail to resent the denial of that freedom." I added that I had hoped and prayed that the hour when war was our honorable portion would not come, but that the attitude of the Imperial German Government left us no other course. I gave my voice and vote for war after a long conflict that had torn me for months. It was my Gethsemane.

I wrote in my Diary that night:

"If the American people possessed television and a dictaphone and could have seen and heard the President as he spoke of the gravest issues our country had faced, they would have felt a confidence in him and an admiration which nothing else could have imparted. . . ."

DISCUSSION IN CABINET

During the frequent debates in the long days of neutrality, Lane and I had often clashed. He accused Baker and me of holding back. He believed, as secretaries of the military departments, we ought to have been the first to advocate retaliation. We both agreed with Woodrow Wilson, as did Secretary W. B. Wilson, Postmaster General Burleson, and Attorney General Gregory. In the long months of discussion in the Cabinet, we had stood with the President, six to five, against early participation while Lansing, McAdoo, Lane, Redfield, and Houston wished to declare war before the Germans repudiated their promise not to employ U-boats against our merchant ships. The others had urged earlier entrance into the war, but Lansing had made no open declaration. He had early signed vigorous notes demanding that Britain abandon its policy of preventing American ships' reaching neutral ports. Later I learned that these notes were written by Solicitor Cone Johnson. None of his colleagues suspected, as Lansing read vigorous demands on the British Government, that, as he said later in his Memoirs:

"In dealing with the British Government there was always in my mind the conviction that we would ultimately become an ally of Great Britain and that it would not do, therefore, to let our controversies reach a point where diplomatic controversies give place to action. . . ."

EXPECTATION NOT WELL FOUNDED

In the early days of March, Lane and Houston were intimate associates of Spring-Rice, British Ambassador, and Jusserand, the French Ambassador, and were in communication with Walter H. Page—our Ambassador to England. At the Cabinet meeting of the Day of Decision, March 20, Houston quoted the view of the French Ambassador that if we entered war there was no expectation that the United States would need to send an army to France. He quoted

Jusserand as saying what the French Ambassador had already said to me:

"I do not know whether you will enter the war or not, but if you do, we shall not expect you—and I am sure that I am speaking the sentiments of my government—to send any men to France except a detachment for sentimental reasons, to return the visit of Rochambeau. We shall want you to aid us mainly on the sea and with credits and supplies."

That oft expressed view of some Cabinet members who had for months favored a declaration of war was not shared by the Secretary of War or the Secretary of the Navy. Their view and that of the generals and admirals was that once we made a declaration of war, it would be our war and would demand millions of men and billions of dollars. Perhaps their joining Wilson in seeking to secure our rights without going to war was influenced by their knowledge that the French and British Ambassadors were more sentimental than practical. History proved that no mere "Lafayette we are here," or "Return the visit of Rochambeau"—gestures of friendship and a few men—could avail.

THEY WANTED TO SWAP JOBS

After a rather heated debate on the Day of Decision, as we went to the usual weekly Cabinet lunch, Lane proposed that he and I swap jobs and Baker change with Houston. I replied that he would have precipitated us into war before we were well enough prepared to insure victory. As a matter of fact, it is generally the officials and officers upon whom the chief responsibility will rest in case of war, who, understanding what war means, are more anxious to avert it than are civilians, who urge hurried entry. That was true in 1917-1918. It was true in the Spanish American War and in the War of the Sixties.

Secretary Houston, who was a master strategist (he had walked over part of the terrain over which Lee's army passed and had been a student of the Napoleonic Wars) laughingly said to Secretary Baker and me, "I admit that I am a military strategist of the first order."

WILSON SENSED GERMANS WOULD BLOW UP SHIPS

Late Saturday afternoon, March 24, the President and Mrs. Wilson called at the Navy Department. It was the first time Mrs. Wilson had been there, and she was interested in the large and distinguished room occupied by the Secretary of the Navy. "This is the most beautiful office in Washington," she said.

The President told me he had been thinking about the interned German ships and had come to the conclusion that we should put Marines aboard to prevent German sabotage. He felt that the ships were now derelicts. Long before we entered the war, quite a number of German ships were interned in our waters. Some of our officers trusted the German officers and they were received socially by Naval and other families. I told the Chief of Operations that they ought to be kept under surveillance. "They are Naval officers, and officers of every nation can be trusted," he said.

EXPLOSIVES LEFT ON GERMAN SHIPS

At Philadelphia several interned ships were anchored at the Navy Yard. The officers and men were given the run of the city, and some of the officers were social favorites. A Philadelphian who did not trust the interned German officers told me that it was extremely dangerous to leave these ships with none but German crews aboard. Why? It would be easy to blow them up and do serious damage to the Navy Yard. I saw that it might mean danger, and I directed the recall of liberty granted German officers and the removal of all Germans from the ships. I did not trust them, particularly after the President's visit to me. When our officers went aboard the interned ships, without notice to any German officer or enlisted man, they found the Germans had left behind explosives so placed that the ships and a portion of the Navy Yard could easily be blown up. After that discovery at Philadelphia no more trust was placed in the so-called honor of German officer internees.

A GERMAN LOTHARIO

In one Navy Base city where the German officers were welcomed into the homes of American officers, some were very agreeable. In one case the wife of an American officer became infatuated with a German officer. Her infatuation so possessed her that when the German officer was sent to Atlanta and held as a prisoner of war, she turned up in Atlanta to the humiliation of the Navy. That was the only case on record.

A NORTH CAROLINA STORY

On her visit to the Navy Department Mrs. Wilson was much interested in a case containing the sword of John Paul Jones, which had been presented to him by Willie Jones, an early patriot of North Carolina and leader of the Jeffersonian party in that State. She was interested, and so was I, in a story the President told, which I am quoting from my Diary of that day:

"When Benedict Arnold was given a roving commission to destroy, he went South, met and talked with a man from North Carolina, who did not recognize Arnold.

" 'What,' asked Arnold, 'would the North Carolina people do to Arnold if they captured him?'

"The unsuspecting North Carolinian replied: 'They would cut off the leg injured when Arnold was bravely following Washington and give it honorable burial. Then they would hang the balance of the damn rascal.' "

"This story was apropos, as I pointed out to the President and Mrs. Wilson when they were looking at John Paul Jones's sword in a case in the Secretary of the Navy's office. It had been given by Willie Jones, foremost patriot of North Carolina, from whom John Paul took the name of Jones when he was in hiding. The sword had been presented to the Navy by Admiral Nicholson.

"Mrs. Wilson hangs on the President's stories and conversation with enthusiasm. 'Sweetheart,' he calls her."

WILSON'S FORESIGHTEDNESS

Nothing escaped Wilson. He read all the dispatches from abroad and kept up with Army and Navy preparations. My Diary of March 6 records:

"The President called at the Navy Department to talk over arming ships and the danger of submarines in American waters and about bringing the fleet North. He thought in addition to arming ships we ought to have three motor boats on each ship to be lowered in smooth seas to hunt submarines. 'When in England,' he said, 'I saw the annual occasions when a shepherd would stand in a circle and by calls and whistles herd the sheep distant from him.' He drew a like parallel. It wasn't difficult to manage two but it was difficult with three. The submarine would expect a boat on each side of the ship but the presence of the third boat would confuse it."

A WHITE HOUSE HUNCH

Deeply interested, Wilson, in the White House, would mull over the ways to meet the submarine menace and think out plans to outwit the U-boats. Then he would convey his plans to me, sometimes calling late in the afternoon at the Navy Department (he knew I was always there till time for a late dinner), or he would ask me to come to the White House. I would then communicate his views ("I am an amateur," he would always say by way of preface to his suggestions, many of which were adopted) to the Chief of Operations or the Navy Council and say, in Wilson's expression: "This is a White House hunch."

From my Diary of March 8, I quote:

"At night I had a message from Hoover at the White House saying Mrs. Wilson wished me to call. Upon my arrival she said she was a blind—that the President was declining to see anybody and that was why she called. He was suffering from a cold. After the exchange of greetings, we discussed arming ships. He wished it kept secret. Decided to arm ships. The Navy Department had prepared regulations in event we armed and I had sent them to him that afternoon. He suggested changes and particularly to omit: 'No ships shall go to the rescue of the ship attacked.' That seemed inhuman to the President. Upon returning, I called up Benson and Palmer, and Benson went that night to New York to see P. S. B. Franklin of American lines and arrange to have guns and armed guard put on all ships. He saw Franklin, who thought visit and search should be permitted outside of zone. Franklin called me up by telephone and wanted to know if he should arm the *Manchuria,* ready to sail."

NAVY TAKES OVER WIRELESS

It was decided that the Navy should take over all wireless stations operated in the interests of the Germans as well as those operated by Americans, and, at least for the war, make wireless a government monopoly. When I made that proposition Burleson said, "I serve notice that when communication becomes governmental, it must be under the Post Office Department." The President asked, "Is that a threat or a prophecy?" I answered, "It is a bluff or a boast."

INSTRUCTIONS TO THE ARMED GUARD

On March 13, 1917, after consultation and exchange of letters with the President and the Secretary of State, I issued "Regulations Governing the Conduct of American Merchant Vessels on Which Armed Guards have Been Placed," beginning with the declaration that they were placed on vessels "for the sole purpose of defense against any unlawful acts of the submarines of Germany or any nation following the policy announced by Germany." Every possible situation was outlined in the twenty-eight sections of the instructions, including: "No offensive action outside the zones prescribed by Germany" unless the submarine is guilty of an unlawful act that jeopardizes the vessel, her passengers, or crew, or unless the submarine is submerged." I wrote the President, pointing out that the presence of the U. S. Navy personnel on merchant ships would probably be considered an act of war from the German viewpoint, but that Germany's note saying it would sink without warning justified the course we were taking. Some naval officers feared we were in danger of violating old-time rules of the sea, forgetting that rules that apply to surface craft could not be carried out against under-sea assassins.

NAVY PREPARES FOR "FULL SPEED AHEAD"

I was engrossed in the early days of March with preparation for the eventuality of war. I announced publicly that if it became necessary the Navy would commandeer shipbuilding plants to expedite the construction of fighting ships; I held conferences with shipbuilders who had contracts and urged them to cut time for construction of swift motor boats for coast control; awarded contracts for sixteen non-rigid Navy dirigibles; placed orders for six scout cruisers and five other cruisers to be built at once in private yards; gave directions for the construction of one hundred submarine chasers and fifty destroyers; ordered construction of the *Idaho* to be rushed, and announced that the *New Mexico* would be completed in April. I gave myself day and night to conferences that made possible the policy of "Full Speed Ahead," when war was declared on April 6.

WHO IS MR. BONE?

From my Diary of March 2:

"I dined with Burleson and we then went to the Senate to endeavor to secure an early vote on the postoffice bill. It contained a bone-dry provision and one authorizing the use of tubes for mail delivery in the big cities. Burleson, a consistent opponent of prohibition, didn't want the new tube or the dry provision (either). 'I really want Wilson to veto those provisions, but I have consented not to oppose them.' I wanted the bone-dry provision."

Everybody was talking about Bone Dry legislation. I met the Japanese Naval Attaché, and he asked, "Who is this Mr. Bone, who makes Washington Dry? He must be a very influential man."

IV

DECLARATION OF WAR

A PRIL 2, 1917, was to go into history as the highlight, not only of American entrance into war, but of an oration that stirred its distinguished audience to an enthusiasm that swept the country, though no radio enabled the people of the world to hear the voice of the orator. It was on that day—the hour not fixed—that the President was to go before Congress and ask a declaration of war.

In the afternoon as I was closing the daily press conference I looked up and saw President Wilson quietly sitting in one corner of the large room. I closed the conference, at which the correspondents had asked questions which could not be properly answered upon the eve of war. Unknown either to me or the correspondents, Wilson had listened to the exchange. He asked, "Do you have to go through this ordeal every day?" I replied, "Twice every day, but being a newspaper man, I am only taking some of my own medicine."

Wilson, his war message ready, and waiting a summons from Congress, called on me and then on the Secretary of State and the Secretary of War, all three offices being in the War, State and Navy building. Lansing advised a strong military force to guard the President going to and coming from the Capitol. Wilson, always irked by Secret Service or other guards, scoffed at Lansing's fears. However, as a measure of precaution, Baker provided a cavalry squadron and other armed protection that night.

LIKE SAUL AMONG THE PROPHETS

On the floor of the House, seated in a half circle just in front of the Speaker, sat the Justices of the Supreme Court, the figure of Chief Justice White towering like Saul among the prophets. The presence of the distinguished Justices in the hall of the House of Representatives was unprecedented. But, for that matter, the occasion was without precedent. I observed that the Chief Justice seemed to be laboring to conceal his satisfaction that the hour had arrived for the declaration he had long believed to be inescapable. For months he had not concealed his zeal for entrance into the war with the Allies. Shortly after English troops were in action in France he had said to one of my Cabinet colleagues: "I wish I were thirty years younger. I would go to Canada and volunteer." And he knew what war was, having as a youth shouldered a musket in the Confederate Army.

As Southerners saw his towering figure enter, they gave an old-time rebel yell that resounded through the chamber, and it was repeated when they saw him rise at the conclusion of Wilson's address and throw his hat to the ceiling as he led the cheering.

THE PRESIDENT COULD DO "NO OTHERWISE"

With my Cabinet colleagues I was early in my seat. Soon the Senate was received in the usual formal way, the members were in their seats, Vice President Marshall and Speaker Clark were standing expectant.

The hour for the arrival of President Wilson grew nearer. The clatter of the cavalry horses on the pavement could be heard, a regiment from Fort Myer escorting him from the White House to the Capitol. Every person jammed in the hall of the House stood as President Wilson entered the brilliant chamber. He was given a spontaneous and sustained ovation.

"The President of the United States," said the Speaker as Mr. Wilson ascended to the place appointed. As the echo of the gavel died away the distinguished company, hushed by appreciation of the solemn hour, resumed their seats. Any stranger would have chosen Wilson as the leader if he had looked down upon that gathering of the great. Erect, with stern sense of responsibility, his face marked by determination, with confidence born out of long battle before decision, there was a gravity and distinction in his bearing which made him the voice and inspiration of a great people about to embark on what he and his hearers alike regarded as a noble struggle. He looked inches taller in his immaculate dress. A spirit of serious apprehension of all that lay before him seemed to dwell upon his countenance. He was pale, for he had come to that moment through great travail of mind and heart. He bowed his thanks for the evidence that those present were ready to hold up his hands and go all the way with him even unto death. That consciousness of the unity of his countrymen imparted new faith and strength. His eyes took in the scene, rested a moment on the faces of his Cabinet comrades, with knowledge of their affection and admiration, paused as the glamour of diplomatic and military uniforms gave color to the scene, and then rested for a brief period upon the gallery where encouragement and love beamed from his noble wife and his adoring daughters. From that intimate and reassuring glance, he turned to the manuscript he held in his hands and an air of calm and confidence settled upon him. He faced the Congress, which he was asking to join with him in a noble adventure. The spirit of the seer and prophet and fighter was upon him. He spoke clearly and solemnly as befitted the gravity of his recommendation. The great audience seemed hushed as the chosen leader, in sentences so vascular they would have bled if cut, recounted the tragic events which had culminated in the necessity for war. The spirit of the Covenanter flashed from his eyes as he proclaimed: "The world must be made safe for democracy." It was to be a war "without rancor and without selfish object" and without revenge. Why did he counsel war—why must we fight? He answered: "For democracy, for the right of those who submit to authority to have a voice in their own governments, for the rights and liberties of small nations, for a universal dominion of right by such concert of free peoples as shall bring peace and safety to all nations and make the world at last free."

The chamber breathed its approval and consecration. When he came to the climax: "There is one choice we cannot make, we are incapable of making. We will not choose the path of submission," all observed the tall and commanding and venerable Chief Justice rise to his feet—he looked ten feet high—and lead the cheering with which the chamber rang. As he applauded, his face moved convulsively and great tears rolled down his cheeks. There were not many dry eyes. The Chief Justice was not alone in giving vent to patriotic emotion.

The memorable address ended with the inspiring prayer, borrowed from the immortal Luther, as Wilson spoke for America "privileged to spend her blood and her might for the principles that gave her birth and happiness and the peace which she has treasured"—

"God helping her, she can do no other."

The die had been cast. Four days later Congress declared that a state of war existed between the United States and the Imperial German Government. Soon the youth were hurrying to find glory or the grave where poppies waved in France and all Americans were soon mobilizing to win victory.

If I should live a thousand years, there would abide with me the reverberation of the fateful ominous sound of the hoofs of the cavalry horses as they escorted Mr. and Mrs. Wilson back to the White House.

CHEERING A MESSAGE OF DEATH

The next day Private Secretary Tumulty told me that as the President returned to the White House, speaking of his war message and its reception, he said: "Tumulty, think what it meant, the applause of the people at the Capitol and the people lining the avenue as we returned! My message tonight was a message of death to our young men. How strange to applaud that!" Tumulty added that, "after dwelling upon the tragedies inseparable from war, President Wilson let his head fall on the cabinet table and sobbed as if he had been a child."

VOTING AGAINST WAR

The debate on the war resolution in the Senate consumed a whole day, with a vote near night of 82 for and 6 against. There was more opposition in the House and two whole days were spent in debate before, at three o'clock in the morning of April 6, the resolution passed by a vote of 373 to 50. Both North Carolina Senators strongly supported Wilson, and only one North Carolina member of the House of Representatives voted against the declaration of war. (Page was no longer in Congress and Webb was paired.)

FIRST WOMAN CONGRESSMAN VOTED "NO"

The crucial hour came to Jeanette Rankin, of Montana, the first woman to be elected to Congress. The dramatic moment came when her name was called on the final vote. She was torn by conflicting appeals. Some suffragists told her she had been called to the kingdom for such a time to voice woman's opposition to war. Other suffragists urged that if she voted against the declaration she would hurt the cause. I watched her closely. Her emotion was visible. There were tears in her eyes. Four times the Clerk of the House called her name before she responded on the final vote. She clutched her throat as she faintly said, "No," and drooped forward in her seat, at three o'clock in the morning. "I want to stand for my country, but I cannot vote for war," she managed to say. She later told reporters: "In urging suffrage, we women had declared that war was stupid and futile and destroyed the best of the race. I have never felt at any time that war could settle anything." There was sympathy for her as she became the target for abuse and ridicule. One critic said, "Your vote did not represent five per cent of the people. They are not yellow or members of the petticoat brigade." It cost her a reelection, but she said in later years she "would do it again." She was reëlected to Congress a score of years afterward.

HIGHLIGHT OF OPPOSITION

The highlight in fervid eloquence in opposition to the declaration of war was the speech of the Honorable Claude Kitchin, of North Carolina, Chairman of the Ways and Means Committee, who voiced in deep sincerity the feeling of the minority of fifty and of others who could not go with the President and the majority of his colleagues. He had agonized before reaching that hour and that decision. All his desire was to vote with the majority of his party who had honored him by choosing him as leader of the House. His speech, delivered with the eloquence of deep sincerity, was called by those who opposed war as "the chief speech of the night." He got the floor after midnight, when the proponents had spoken with such power as to cause an overwhelming majority to feel that national honor and duty called for participation in the war. The House was crowded and the feeling was tense, most of those present favoring war. But Kitchin had not spoken long before the tribute to courage in a cause the speaker knew was lost won the respect of the great gathering, particularly when he said:

"I cannot leave my children lands and riches—I cannot leave them fame—but I can leave them the name of an ancestor, who, mattering not the consequences to himself, never dared to hesitate to do his duty as God gave him to see it."

Kitchin began his address thus:

"Profoundly impressed with the gravity of the situation, appreciating to the fullest the penalties which a war-mad moment will impose, my conscience and judgment, after mature thought and fervent prayer for rightful guidance, have marked out clearly the path of my duty, and I have made up my mind to walk it, if I go barefooted and alone. I have come to the undoubting conclusion that I should vote against this resolution. If I had a single doubt, I would with profoundest pleasure resolve it in favor of the view of the Administration and of a large majority of my colleagues, who have so recently honored me with their confidence. I know that I shall never criticize any Member for advocating this resolution. I concede—I feel—that he casts his vote in accordance with sincere conviction. I know that for my vote I shall be not only criticized, but denounced from one end of the country to the other. The whole yelping pack of defamers and revilers in the nation will at once be set upon my heels."

He closed with these words, which he followed with deeds by leading in legislation to finance the war, thus showing his devotion to his country:

"I can conceive of a brave, loyal, devoted son of a father who contemplates a personal difficulty with another begging and persuading him to refrain, even condemning, and protesting in vain against his proposed step, but when the final word is spoken and blows are about to be given, taking off his coat and struggling with all of his soul and might in defense of that father.

"When this nation, as it doubtless will today, speaks the final word through the Congress, I trust I will be found in relation with my Government and my country emulating the example of that son."

PAGE RETIRED UNDER CRITICISM

I had known that three of the best members of the House from North Carolina—Kitchin, Webb, and Robert Page—had been sweating blood over the question of going to war. They had stood with Wilson in his long attempt to preserve neutrality, but could not agree when he was impelled to ask a declaration of war. They walked on hot ploughshares. When the attitude of Page was made known to some of his constituents, a number telegraphed him that if he could not stand with Wilson, he ought to retire from Congress. These messages, one from his brother Henry, cut him to the quick, and he announced that he would not run for reëlection in 1916 since some of his constituents felt so strongly about his attitude. When I heard he was taking that course I went to see him—he had been a groomsman at our wedding and our wives were good friends. I told him that he ought to take the course Kitchin was taking— vote his convictions and remain in Congress where, as the most influential member of the Appropriations Commttee, he could render great service. But he had already made his announcement. Having sworn to this, which I thought was to his own hurt, nothing could cause him to withdraw his announcement of his purpose to retire. The House lost one of its ablest members. The bitter telegrams to him showed the temper of the times. Afterwards, when there was need for the appointment of an able man at the head of the Farm Bank for the Carolinas, I asked the President to name Page, the fittest man for the position. He would not do so, saying that at a critical time Page had failed, adding, "Suppose all had done likewise in that critical period!"

WEBB DEFIES KITCHIN'S CRITICS

Though the House respected Kitchin, his attitude was strongly condemned by many. His mail was deluged with letters. "Go to Germany" was the type of not a few. Kitchin also got many letters of "Thank God for Claude Kitchin." He whipped one bitter critic. He seldom retorted in kind to critics, but on the train going home he heard a passenger who recognized him standing in the doorway, abusing him and saying, "Kitchin ought to be sent to Germany." Sensing that the man wished to be offensive, Kitchin seized his critic by the collar and shook him until he cried for quarter.

Immediately after his speech, some members, led by the dynamic Tom Heflin, demanded that Kitchin be deposed from the leadership of the House, to which he had been unanimously elected. Nothing came of it. Honorable E. Y. Webb of North Carolina, Chairman of the Judiciary Committee, later appointed Federal Judge, denounced the attempt to demote Kitchin and declared, "You can call your caucus, and while you are going to vote for the war resolution, we defy you to harm Claude Kitchin or attempt to remove him as our floor leader." The caucus was never called, and Kitchin in the days to come, as head of the Ways and Means Committee, piloted through the House the biggest tax measures in the history of the country and served as patriotically as those who had voted for the war resolution. He sought to make the profiteers pay the cost of the war and did not always agree with the recommendation of Secretary McAdoo, and with characteristic frankness differed over some means, but never over the raising of enough money for war purposes.

At first the Treasury leaders felt that because Kitchin had voted against the war resolution he would balk at raising the revenue to carry it on. Doubting Kitchin's coöperation, McAdoo asked me to go with him to present the Treasury plans. I was glad to do so and we found Kitchin as concerned to obtain all the revenue needed as Wilson, who wrote him asking his aid. He needed no urging. He wanted the main cost of the war paid by those who profited from it. He opposed transferring most of the cost of war upon future generations by paying for the war by bond issues. During the conference McAdoo, who had the bad habit of interlarding his conversation, when he wished to be emphatic, with a number of "hells" and "damns," used these expletives to press his argument. Kitchin didn't like that and turned and asked me: "Have you learned to cuss since you became a member of the Cabinet?" I told Kitchin that Southerners who went to New York to live—like Walter Page and Bill McAdoo—said that in New York you had to use a "damn" to convince New Yorkers you were in earnest.

When authorization of tax bond issues was approved, I suggested to Wilson that there should be omitted the usual provision that the bonds be exempt from taxation. He was interested and said, "See McAdoo and try to convince him to take that course." I did so and told McAdoo that under the impulse of patriotism the people would buy the bonds without the tax exemption provision. I stressed that to exempt bond-holders from taxation would build up a class free from bearing their part of the cost of the war. "But," McAdoo said, "the Treasury can float the bonds at a lower rate of interest and get more money if we put in the usual tax-emption provision." I agreed, but said Uncle Sam could better afford to get less than to have a favorite class free from taxation. But I could not convince him of what Kitchin and I urged. Failing, Kitchin put through the measure as desired by the Treasury. That was the time to end tax-exempt bonds. When some Senators wished to favor big business, Robert Page wrote, "They seem utterly unable to get the veiwpoint of the

MRS. WOODROW WILSON

From a portrait painted by A. Muller-Ury, soon after Mrs. Wilson
went to the White House in 1916 (Brown Brothers).

CONGRESSIONAL OPPONENTS OF DECLARATION OF WAR

Upper left, Robert M. La Follette, Governor of Wisconsin and U. S. Senator (Brown Brothers). *Upper right,* George W. Norris, U. S. Senator, 1913-43 (Brown Brothers). *Lower left,* Jeannette Rankin, first woman elected to U. S. Congress, 1917-19, 1941-43 (Brown Brothers). *Lower right,* Claude Kitchin, of North Carolina, chairman of House Ways and Means Committee in Wilson's administration.

mass of the folk, and always have an ear for the representatives of special interests."

THE PRESIDENT SIGNS THE DECLARATION OF WAR

Ordinarily when the President signed an important measure there were present leaders of Congress who had guided its passage through Congress, Cabinet members, press representatives, and photographers. Not so this most important of important measures. Without any escort of the resolution, it reached the White House while the President was at lunch. Nobody was present except Rudolph Forster, I. H. Hoover, and Officer Starling of the Secret Service, Miss Helen Bones, and Mrs. Wilson. "Wait a minute," said Mrs. Wilson, and handed the President a gold pen he had given her. That pen could relate world history. As soon as the signature, "Woodrow Wilson," appeared on the resolution, which bore the autograph of Vice President Marshall and Speaker Clark, by pre-arrangement Usher Hoover pressed a button which notified my Naval Aide, Byron McCandless, who was waiting in the Executive Office for the signal. Receiving it, McCandless wigwagged that the resolution had been signed. Within five minutes I caused this message to be sent to every ship and shore station:

"The President has signed act of Congress which declares a state of war exists between the United States and Germany.
"Secretary of The Navy"

THE NAVY READY

Flashed from the towers at Arlington, in a few minutes it was received by the Atlantic and Pacific fleets, by vessels and stations all along the coast. To the Commanders of all the five flag-ships the following message was sent that afternoon:

"Mobilize for war in accordance with Department's confidential mobilization plan of March 21st.
"Josephus Daniels"

That plan had been approved the day after the Cabinet and the President had made the war decision. There was no delay. Admiral Mayo, Commander-in-Chief, said, "I did not have to give a signal of any kind or description to pass the Fleet from a peace to a war basis. The Navy was ready and on its toes." Admiral Wilson said,

"If we had engaged the enemy on the way north, the victory would have been ours," and Admiral Strauss declared, "We could have gone out at once in mid-ocean and engaged the German fleet and come out successfully."

On the other side of the War, State and Navy building, Secretary Baker and his staff busied themselves making ready for the mobilization of the great army which gave the deciding strength that won the war.

V

WILSON THE STRATEGIST

T HE WORLD KNOWS President Wilson as scholar, teacher, and historian; as executive and statesman. But it does not know him as we did, as a master of military strategy. His grasp of the whole situation, his clear conception of Army and Navy policies and operations, and his rare judgment were demonstrated in important decisions, and his personal interest and influence had a marked effect on the conduct of the war.

Always interested in the Navy, he kept up with all that was being done and planned, and his suggestions and directions proved of the utmost value to officers and officials. "We shall take leave to be strong upon the seas," he said not long after the beginning of the European war. In his address at St. Louis, early in 1916, he declared that ours should be "the most adequate navy in the world." At the next Cabinet meeting a member expressed surprise at the President's advocacy of so vigorous a Naval policy, and asked if he had been correctly quoted in the newspapers.

"Yes," replied the President, "and it is one thing I said in my swing around the circle that I absolutely believe."

He strongly urged the big construction program presented several months before, and exercised a potent influence in putting through Congress the "three-year program," which authorized the building of 157 Naval vessels.

Long before we entered the war, when the Allied navies seemed impotent before the onslaughts of the submarines, President Wilson pointed to the vigorous policies which later proved so successful.

ADVOCATED CONVOYING SHIPS

"Daniels, why don't the British convoy their merchant ships and thus protect them from submarines?" he asked me early in the war. As sinking increased, he pointed out that their practice of sailing ships separately had proved a failure, and asked, "Why, now, with their distressing experiences, do they hesitate about adopting the convoy system?"

He could not comprehend why the British, as soon as Germany declared war, had not mined the English Channel so that no submarines could pass through it. As a matter of fact, strange as it seems, the channel from Dover to Calais never was a complete barrier to submarines, though the Dover Patrol did brilliant service, and the United States Navy insisted that closing this channel was one of the first steps toward defeating the U-boats.

WILSON VISITS THE FLEET

In the spring of 1917, I directed Admiral Mayo to assemble the Atlantic Fleet in the protected waters near Yorktown for intensive training and practice. No dreadnaughts had been sent to European waters at that time. While the fleet was in practice on the York River, I requested President Wilson to make a visit and speak to the assembled officers and men. He hesitated at first, but upon my repeated urging he said he would go and speak if I would guarantee nothing about his visit or speech got into the papers. Admiral Mayo and I made the promise—and not a word of the visit or of one of the most remarkable speeches in history was printed until I was permitted to release it a year after the Armistice. It showed such grasp of what was needed and pointed out British failures so candidly and breathed such faith in the Navy that when it was made public by me in a hearing before Congress, it created something of a sensation. Eagle-eyed newspaper correspondents were aghast that so notable a trip could be made by the President and he could make so dynamic an address without the knowledge of a single Washington correspondent. It revealed Wilson, not only as a commander-in-chief with mastery of strategy but also as a militant leader when audacity was the price of victory.

The setting was perfect. On the previous day, Mr. and Mrs. Wilson sailed down the Potomac on the *Mayflower* for a week-end voyage. Later, as we often did, my wife and I left for a week-end trip to Hampton Roads on the *Dolphin*. The next morning on a beautiful summer day, both ships sailed past the fleet of scores of ships in formation. Every honor was done the President with 21-gun salutes from all the ships; officers and sailors, all in white uniforms, standing attention as the Commander-in-Chief received the salutes.

Standing on the quarter deck of the flagship, the *Pennsylvania,* welcomed by Admiral Mayo, in command of the American Fleet, the President was introduced by me: "Your Commander-in-Chief, the President of the United States," and he caught the attention and admiration of the men of the service.

That visit to the Fleet, August 11, 1917, was a notable occasion. It was the first time, I believe, that a President has, in the midst of war, gone to the chief naval rendezvous and gathered the officers about him for a heart-to-heart talk. Standing on the quarter deck, surrounded by admirals, captains, commanders, and other ranks, he could see all around him the dreadnaughts which are the embodiment of Naval power. In the background was Yorktown, where Cornwallis's surrender marked the culminating victory of the Revolution. And in this historic spot American forces were again making history.

THE PRESIDENT'S DYNAMIC SPEECH

Wilson's address, informal and confidential as it was, deserves a place in Naval history. Disclaiming any idea that he had come "with malice prepense to make a speech," he told the officers that he had come to have a look at them and say some things that might be best said intimately and in confidence. "One of the deprivations which any man in authority experiences," he exclaimed, "is that he cannot come into constant and intimate touch with the men with whom he is associated and necessarily associated in action." In part his speech was as follows:

"Here are two great navies, not to speak of the others associated with us, our own and the British, outnumbering by a very great margin the navy to which we are opposed and yet casting about for a way in which to use our superiority and our strength, because of the novelty of the instruments used, because of the unprecedented character of the war; because, as I said just now, nobody ever before fought a war like this, in the way that this is being fought at sea, or on land either, for that matter. The experienced soldier,—experienced in previous wars, —is a back number so far as his experience is concerned; not so far as his intelligence is concerned. His experience does not count, because he never fought a war as this is being fought, and therefore he is an amateur along with the rest of us. Now, somebody has got to think this war out. Somebody has got to think out the way not only to fight the submarine, but to do something different from what we are doing.

"We are hunting hornets all over the farm and letting the nest alone. None of us knows how to go to the nest and crush it, and yet I despair of hunting for hornets all over the sea when I know where the nest is and know that the nest is breeding hornets as fast as I can find them. I am willing for my part, and I know you are willing, because I know the stuff you are made of—I am willing to sacrifice half the navy Great Britain and we together have to crush that nest, because if we crush it, the war is won. I have come here to say that I do not care where it comes from, I do not care whether it comes from the youngest officer or the oldest, but I want the officers of this Navy to have the distinction of saying how this war is going to be won.

"The Secretary of the Navy and I have just been talking over plans for putting the planning machinery of the Navy at the disposal of the brains of the Navy and not stopping to ask what rank that brains has, because, as I have said before and want to repeat, so far as experience in this kind of war is concerned we are all of the same rank. . . .

"Every time we have suggested anything to the British Admiralty the reply has come back that virtually amounted to this, that it had never been done that way, and I felt like saying, 'Well, nothing was ever done so systematically as nothing is being done now.' Therefore, I should like to see something unusual happen, something that was never done before; and inasmuch as the things that are being done to you were never done before, don't you think it is worth while to try something that was never done before against those who are doing them to you? There is no other way to win, and the whole principle of this war is the kind of thing that ought to hearten and stimulate America.

"America has always boasted that she could find men to do anything. She is the prize amateur nation of the world. Germany is the prize professional nation of the world. Now, when it comes to doing new things and doing them well, I will back the amateur against the professional every time, because the professional does it out of the book and the amateur does it with his eyes open upon a new world and with a new set of circumstances. He knows so little about it that he is fool enough to try the right thing. The men that do not know the danger are the rashest men, and I have several times ventured to make this suggestion to the men about me in both arms of the service: Please leave out of your vocabulary altogether the word 'prudent.' Do not stop to think about what is prudent for a moment. Do the thing that is audacious to the utmost point of risk and daring, because that is exactly the thing that the other side does not understand, and you will win by the audacity of method when you cannot win by circumspection and prudence....

"I am not discouraged for a moment, particularly because we have not even begun and, without saying anything in disparagement of those with whom we are associated in the war, I do expect things to begin when we begin. If they do not, American history will have changed its course; the American Army and Navy will have changed their character. There will have to come a new tradition into a service which does not do new and audacious and successful things."

Wilson had in mind that I had requested Edison and other inventors and scientists to aid in new ways to win in new kinds of wars and had called upon every man in the Navy to send suggestions, when he emphasized that he did not care whether the method of crushing the U-boats "comes from the youngest officer or the oldest."

STOOD FOR EXECUTIVE RIGHTS

As a student of history Wilson knew how a Congressional Committee hamstrung Lincoln in his prosecution of the war. He knew that the conduct of the war was his responsibility, and from the first he put his foot down on any and every suggestion that would encroach upon his constitutional duty as Commander-in-Chief or divide responsibility.

When certain Republican Senators introduced resolutions to appoint a Miltiary Committee on the prosecution of the war, Wilson called it an Espionage Committee. He vigorously protested to Senaator Simmons, upon whom he came more and more to rely, that, "Congress not saddle me with a legislative committee with the proposed purpose of assisting me to control the vast expenditure of government." He felt very strongly that it was a partisan hobbling device. At a Cabinet meeting he inveighed against it and detailed some of the hobbling of effort in the sixties. His mastery of history of that period gave weight to his argument; the legislation was defeated.

NO SUPER WAR CABINET

These extracts are from my Diary (January, 1918):

"Talked with Swanson about bill to create a Super War Cabinet and Minister of Munitions. We went to see Baker. We agreed to see President and to fight the propositon. The President has his blood up and in a veto message could say some things. He has all the nerve any man needs."

After the meeting of the Cabinet on January 22 my Diary recorded:

"W. W. said he told Senators that proposed War Cabinet could not be established until he was dead. He said Republicans were conspiring to make political capital by attacks on the conduct of the war. They want, he said, a Cabinet in which representatives of privilege will have seats and be in intimate touch. They do not think as we do because they wish to act for a class."

COÖPERATION OF THE STATES

From its creation the Council of National Defense was the clearing-house before and during the war for whatever would affect the country's policies or strengthen the hands of America—particularly during the war. One of its best services was securing the perfect coördination of the forty-eight States with Federal efforts. Presided over by Secretary Baker, it brought unity of effort from Coast to Coast. As illustrating its value I quote from my Diary (April 4, 1918):

"Members of the State Council of Defense met with the National Council in Secretary of Navy's office. I made a brief address on how State and Federal Governments had worked in harmony. The Selective Draft had been administered by local authorities in a manner as nearly perfect as possible. When plans for the draft were in the making most of the Generals wished the military to be in charge. Wilson and Baker wisely decided that the important and new method should be administered by civilians. I congratulated state officials upon the wonderful success. I touched upon some treasonable movements in our country and urged that treason must end but only by law."

Upper left, Byron McCandless, aide to Secretary Daniels, semaphores "D" for "Declared," from White House to Navy Department as Wilson signs declaration of war. *Upper right,* Admiral Taussig leaving *U.S.S. Wadsworth,* flagship of first American force to take part in the war, at Queenstown, May 4, 1917 (U. S. Navy). *Below,* "The Return of the Mayflower," commemorating arrival of U. S. ships to aid British in World War. From painting by Bernard Gribble in the Navy Department in Washington (U. S. Navy).

PRESIDENT WILSON AND SECRETARY OF THE NAVY DANIELS
Taken in the presidential box of an Army and Navy Football Game in New York.

WILSON WORE MANTLE OF WASHINGTON

The two greatest civilian Naval strategists America has produced are George Washington and Woodrow Wilson, but they never navigated a ship or wore a Naval uniform. Their names appear in no Hall of Fame. Captain Dudley Knox in his book, *The Naval Genius of George Washington,* points out that as early as 1780 Washington stated this doctrine that is universally accepted: "In any operation, and under all circumstances, a decisive naval superiority is to be considered as a fundamental principle, and the basis upon which every hope of success must ultimately depend." He said, "The Navy must have the casting vote." It "compelled surrender at Yorktown." Admiral de Grasse "subordinated his judgment as a naval tactician, and even his orders from his government, to the far broader strategic concepts of Washington." Thus was brought the "campaign at Yorktown, and with it the war of Independence, to a successful conclusion." Admiral Hilary Jones claimed Washington as "our first great Admiral." History will give Wilson a like place in modern Naval history. He was the first to see that if America should be drawn into World War I, the United States must have "incomparably the most adequate Navy in the world." Congress heeded his recommendation for a three-year program, the largest in time of peace in history. Wilson ordered armed guard on merchant ships before we entered the war. He was the first to see the necessity of adopting the convoy system. He gave instructions for the construction of the North Sea Barrage, wondering before 1917 why the powerful British Navy did not "shut the hornets up in their nest." In Paris he stood adamant in a hard-fought contest for American Naval equality and for a strong American merchant marine which he had greatly strengthened early in his administration. As a boy his ambition was to enter Annapolis but his father had other ideas. He knew Naval history and became the foremost Naval strategist of his era, as Washington was when he likewise was Commander-in-Chief of the Army and Navy.

VI

COÖPERATION WITH ALLIED NATIONS AND RUSSIA

Hardly had the declaration of war been signed before delegations—called missions—began to come to Washington to discuss plans for participation and to secure money to carry on the war. The British delegation arrived on April 23 and a state dinner was given at the White House that night for fifty-two guests. As Mr. Balfour had been First Lord of the Admiralty, I was seated next to him and he told me of the seriousness of the U-boat destruction and the importance of American aid in every way. He had mastered Naval lore but preferred philosophy and economics and direction of government more than direction of the building of ships and their disposition. Before I met him, a journalist friend who had gone abroad as a correspondent in 1915 told me of this experience with Balfour in London:

"I wished very much to see him and learn about a matter of importance. It wasn't easy. Finally I was told that on a certain day Balfour would give me fifteen minutes, not a second more. As he greeted me I remarked that I had just finished reading his latest book and it had intrigued me greatly. I thought it was a good opening. It was too good, for Mr. Balfour launched upon his favorite philosophy and was so interested in his theme, as I was also, that my fifteen minutes expired before I had been given the opportunity to obtain the information I was seeking. The secretary gave me two minutes. I asked my question, but the brevity of the time made the interview disappointing. It is a bad thing to become so interested in the theories of the man you are interviewing that you neglect your job."

MRS. JOFFRE GETS A HAM

As the White House party was slow to break up, Mrs. Wilson confided to me that the President had a splitting headache and expressed the hope the guests would leave early. I told her I knew a certain way to bring it about. "How?" she asked. I told her that in our home when guests stayed late, my young brother would say, "Mother, let's go to bed so the company can go home." She did not think that would be proper hospitality to foreign guests. Sixty-two plates were laid for the dinner to the French mission. Joffre, sitting next to Mrs. Wilson, quietly enjoyed the Smithfield (Virginia) ham and said he wished Mrs. Joffre could have some of that delicious ham. Mrs. Wilson replied that she would send her one, and she did, the next day.

WAR FINANCES LOW

The French and British had been fighting nearly three years and their finances were depleted. There was but one source to draw upon —the new ally, Uncle Sam. Ambassador Page had cabled early in March that Britain lacked the means to contract purchases in the United States, and R. H. Brand, an expert, suggested that the British Government was at the end of its tether. With this information the President knew that the chief object of the coming of missions was to obtain financial aid sorely needed. With this knowledge, Wilson did not wish to receive the members of the missions until his country had matured its plans. But their necessities made them importunate and Wilson, whole-heartedly in the war, agreed to receive them, and when the British and French missions arrived in the early spring of 1917, Viviani and Joffre for France and Balfour and his able staff for Britain, they were enthusiastically hailed, particularly Joffre. This was because he was the hero of the Marne and because of his democratic ways and personal charm. Viviani headed the French mission.

HUMAN SIDE OF JOFFRE

On the day I took both missions on the *Mayflower* to Mount Vernon, where they placed wreaths on the grave of Washington and spoke briefly, it made me happy to see the comradeship between the great Frenchman and my two youngest sons, who were dressed in sailor suits. He left the company of the great for a while to give the boys the delight of knowing a famous soldier, who was as simple and sweet in association as he was able and distinguished. He had skin like a baby and the merriest eyes; he didn't look as if he could take delight in war. When I saw him in playful talk with my young sons, there came to my mind:

"The bravest are the tenderest,
The loving are the daring."

I asked Joffre one day if he was nervous or frightened as he went into battle. He gave no direct answer but told me this story:

"Early in war, a French officer, who had long been retired, returned to active service. He had grown fat and soft in retirement, but nothing could dissuade him from donning the uniform and going to the front. When the first call to battle came, he found he was frightened and was trembling like an aspen leaf. It distressed him greatly because his body was shaking as he prepared to go where the fighting was fiercest. He struck himself on his breast and said: 'What do you mean, you miserable carcass, to tremble so and disgrace me in the presence of my troops!' And then, caressing his body, he said in tender tones: 'But forgive me for my harshness. If you knew where I was going to take you today, you would tremble more than you do.'"

JEALOUS OF GENERAL JOFFRE

The head of the French Mission was Viviani, who was the real Prime Minister, an able and eloquent man. He was not only jealous of Joffre's popularity but of the more cordial reception he thought Balfour received. Balfour spoke English while few officials could converse with Viviani, who spoke only French. The jealousy reached the height after both Balfour and Viviani had been invited on separate days to address Congress, Balfour coming first. President Wilson and the Cabinet members attended to hear Balfour. When the day came for Viviani to make his address, the report reached the French Embassy that President Wilson would not attend. This was construed by Viviani as an affront and he was furious. I heard he said he would not speak if the President did not show him the same honor he had shown Balfour. Hot-footed, Ambassador Jusserand went to the White House to ascertain the President's intention. "I am overwhelmed with important affairs," Wilson said, "and cannot go. Moreover, I do not understand French and am looking forward with pleasure to reading Viviani's address later in English." However, when acquainted with the construction that would be placed on his absence, Wilson attended with members of his Cabinet, and the French statesman spoke in his most eloquent manner of perfervid oratory. When Viviani's book appeared some years later, I was interested to read what he had to say about the visit of the French Mission to Washington. He did not mention it.

BORROWED OVER EIGHT BILLION DOLLARS

In a period of eighteen months, so Secretary McAdoo reported, the greatest diplomats of Europe were almost literally camped on the doorsteps of the Treasury. Funds were supplied on the same basis that the United States borrowed for itself. Our country loaned more than eight billion dollars to Britain, France, Belgium, Greece, Italy, Rumania, Russia, Liberia, Serbia, and Cuba. Secretary McAdoo consulted me about establishing an arrangement which would make certain that the money obtained from us would be wisely expended in buying supplies in this country for our allies and our own use. I had already approved the plan which later was taken over by the board headed by Mr. Baruch. It was important that the loans should be used for new purchases for war, but in July the J. P. Morgan Company asked the Treasury to care for an overdraft due by Britain for loans before we entered the war. McAdoo firmly declined and saw to it that loans were used for new materials needed for war purposes. Moreover in every loan made to allied governments, those countries pledged repayment at the same rate of interest which Uncle Sam paid for his loans. They never were paid. But that does not reflect upon McAdoo's wise arrangements.

NO SECRET AGREEMENTS

There was a report that secret arrangements as to peace were made, but Wilson denied this. However at a private dinner Wilson, Balfour, and House informally discussed probabilities of the postwar needs, and Wilson let Balfour know that he looked to an international organization for peace. But the military situation was so desperate that it was uppermost. Reporting his conversations with Balfour and Viviani at a meeting of the Cabinet, Wilson said: "England and France have not the same views with regard to peace," and added that no plans could be perfected now, but later "we can bring them to our way of thinking."

JOFFRE WANTED FIGHTING MEN

To come back to the visit of the French and British missions—it is worth remembering that General Joffre was the only member of these missions who sensed that Uncle Sam's fighting men must fight on French soil. While Balfour and Viviani pressed for financial aid and minimized the probability that America must send millions of its youth into the trenches, Joffre made a quiet call on the Secretary of War and frankly told him of the serious situation following an unsuccessful major offensive by the French, and pointed out the need of American troops. I do not know that he told of the recent mutiny of French troops, but he urged: "It will cheer our people if you will show your flag and send over some of your troops." Welcomed at the War College, Joffre, talking as one soldier to another, said that France was convinced that the "military effort of the United States will be considerable and in proportion to your power." He declared, "The need is so pressing for Americans on the battlefields of France that the training could be done in the field of operations." He said there was nothing the Germans so dreaded as the sight of American soldiers at the front. "The sooner you get American troops fighting alongside the French the better," he said. Joffre also asked Secretary Baker to send at once artisans, engineering regiments, and troops of a technical character and hospital units, nurses and doctors. They were soon on the way.

General Bridgers, of Britain, saw no need of an American Army in France. He said it would make two more joints in the trench line and it had been found that joints were always weak spots. Colonel Fabre, of France, thought that the United States could contribute very little to the military effort, but instead should give large financial aid.

DINNER WITHOUT WINE

Writing of social events when the missions were in Washington, Dr. Franklin Martin, head of the Medical War Services, included in his book accounts of a state dinner at the White House for forty; a reception at the Army and Navy Club, given by the Secretary of War and the Secretary of the Navy, to meet Marshal Joffre and the Army and Navy officers of the French and British missions, and a dinner given by Mrs. Daniels and me at our home:

"This dinner, given for the heads of the English and French Commissions with their distinguished accompanying naval representatives, was one of the most unique and interesting social affairs of the time. Secretary and Mrs. Daniels received their guests in the drawing room of their charming home on Wyoming Avenue, much as they would have received their neighbors and family connections at a gathering in their home in North Carolina.

"Through the partially opened doors could be seen in a capacious adjoining dining room a large oval mahogany table with seats for about forty guests. The service was elaborate and artistic. To the astonishment of some of us who knew Secretary Daniels' views on prohibition, we observed a row of glasses much resembling wine glasses of a conventional dinner. Would the entertainment of guests from the governments of Europe induce him to desert his colors?

"Led by Mrs. Daniels with the distinguished guests, we entered the dining room and found our places. As we were about to be seated, Secretary Daniels at the head of the table advanced a step, raised his hand, and, bowing his head, asked an old-fashioned blessing. An electric spark of surprise and admiration flashed through the circle of guests. Several of the French group silently made the sign of the cross.

"We then assumed our places, and the fine dinner was served. The row of wine glasses maintained their virginity, as they were filled throughout with Apollinaris water, White Rock, red and white grapejuice; and we were also served with a delicious fruit juice cup.

"The guests entered into the spirit of the occasion. The dinner was the admiration of all who attended, and one of the most remembered functions of a long series of formal dinners and receptions, notwithstanding the fact that not a few at the table that night were for the first time in their lives at a formal dinner without spirits and wine."

WHEN JAPAN WAS AN ALLY

The Japanese mission, headed by Admiral Ishii, was the most colorful. I invited the Admiral to go with my wife and myself and Senator and Mrs. Pittman to the launching of the *Nevada*.

When the Japanese mission laid a wreath on the tomb of Washington I welcomed them in a brief address in which I recalled that it was a Secretary of the Navy from my state, Hon. William A. Graham, who began the negotiations that opened the then hermit nation, Japan, to the world. Graham sent Commodore Matthew Galbraith Perry, who was a diplomat as well as a navigator, and began relations between the two countries which made them allies. I said the successful mission proved Graham had the wisdom to adopt the faith of Lord Palmerston who said: "When I wish an important duty performed in any part of the world, calling for a cool head and a steady hand, I always send a Captain of the Navy," and I added:

"Today, with stronger ties than ever, woven out of the threads of our mutual participation in the world-wide struggle to insure to all mankind the right to live their own lives and pursue their own national ideals, Japan and America pause at the tomb of Washington, in the hope that there may fall upon us all a double portion of his spirit of faith in the triumph of the right and his readiness to make the supreme sacrifice for the principles for which America, Japan, and their allies are now contending in the arena of war. They have drawn the sword to end military feudalism. They will sheath it only in a victory that will guarantee permanent peace."

In his address, Admiral Ishii said:

"Japan claims entrance in this holy circle. She yields to none in reverence and respect: Nor is there any gulf between the ancient East and the new-born West too deep and too wide for the hearts and the understandings of her people to cross.... Japan is proud to place herself beside her noble allies.... She reaffirms her devotion to securing for the world the blessings of liberty, justice and lasting peace."

From my Diary (September 2), I quote:

"Viscount Ishii is a delightful companion. He has an engaging twinkle in his eye, and in manner and conversation is more like an American than an oriental. He had kept in close touch with all matters that led up to the war and talked out of large knowledge. As a side interest he was familiarizing himself with the meaning of American slang. He was more familiar with our popular slang than I could claim to be. 'Exactly what do you mean when Americans say...' and he would quote current slang. He loved to use it and told my wife that he had made it a fad to master American slang. 'It is so expressive and peculiarly American,' he said.

"I asked him for his photograph. He replied, 'Will you exchange?'"

Above, King Albert and party on a visit to the Naval Academy. *Left to right,* Prince Leopold (in overcoat), Secretary of the Navy Daniels, King Albert, of Belgium, a Secret Service man, Captain P. W. Foote, and Admiral A. H. Scales, Superintendent of the Naval Academy. *Below,* the Prince of Wales at Annapolis. Four central figures, *left to right,* are Assistant Secretary of the Navy Roosevelt, Secretary Daniels, the Prince of Wales, and Admiral Scales (U. S. Navy).

WHEN JAPAN WAS AN ALLY

Upper left, Viscount Kikujiro Ishii, Ambassador to Paris. *Upper right,* Count Sutemi
Chinda, Ambassador to the United States, 1911-16 (Brown Brothers). *Lower left,*
Admiral Baron Tomosaburo Kato, Minister of the Japanese Navy. *Lower right,*
Admiral Shimamura, Chief of Staff Japanese Navy Department.

In my Diary of September 7 is this entry:

"Lansing called to talk about what Japan could do in the war. He said that the Vice Admiral was authorized to treat on what part Japan should take in prosecuting the war. Japan is willing to patrol on the Pacific and release English and American ships in that area. Would they send ships or troops to Europe? Lansing thinks they are not thinking about taking part except in the Pacific. Benson to see Vice Admiral and also the British Naval Attaché and ascertain more fully Japan's willingness to contribute to the war. Ishii and the civilian members of the Mission have not gone into details."

THE ITALIAN MISSION

Not long after the British and French missions returned, we were all set to welcome the Italian mission. It was a distinguished body, headed by Marconi, Udine, cousin of the King, and military officers. After a White House banquet, official Washington dined with Ambassador Cellari to meet them at the Italian Embassy.

While Udine was of royal blood, the member of the delegation most sought after was Marconi. The Navy and Army specialists in radio talked much with him. Inasmuch as the Navy was the pioneer in developing wireless in America, I was glad to sit at the feet of the master of the science and glad for our experts to obtain the benefit of his great knowledge and experience. He imparted it graciously, and in answer to my questions recounted the steps that led to his famous discovery.

NAVY COÖPERATION

Assistant Secretary Roosevelt and I had several conferences with the Navy members of the missions. They were familiar with the agreements reached immediately after the declaration of war and happy at the complete coöperation already begun. The French requested us to send small ships to take the place of their losses.

PREDICTED A UNITED STATES OF THE WORLD

Representatives of more than thirty nations, composing the International Labor Conference, were taken by me on the *Mayflower* to Mount Vernon. They placed a bunch of chrysanthemums and roses beside a cluster of flowers still marvellously fresh which had been placed there by King Albert of Belgium. Leon Jouhaux, French labor delegate, recalled these words of Washington, which he characterized as a "prophetic phrase":

"We have sown the seeds of liberty and union, which will sprout little by little throughout the earth. One day on the model of the United States of America will be formed the United States of the world. The United States will be the legislator for all nations."

Mr. Jouhaux, after quoting Washington, commented:

"Our presence today at this place attests that this prophecy, profoundly human, taking the form of the society of nations, is in a fair way of being realized, for the great good of humanity."

OTHER ALLIED MISSIONS

As time passed on missions from all the Allied nations, headed by distinguished military leaders, were received in Washington in the same way as the French and British missions. The arrangements were the same—a state dinner at the White House, reception at the Pan American Building, conferences with Washington officials, a round of dinners, and a trip on the *Mayflower* to Mount Vernon where with stately ceremony wreaths were placed on Washington's tomb. My wife and I were hosts on these voyages which brought the hosts and guests close together. The conferences touched every phase of joint action, but McAdoo, Secretary of the Treasury, was the favorite official. All returned home with large loans and solemn commitments to repay the loans after the war. Some, however, had their fingers crossed.

WILSON'S PROPHETIC UTTERANCE: RUSSIA "A FIT PARTNER"

The news in the spring of 1917 that Russia had thrown off totalitarian government and was headed for a democracy was received in Washington with rejoicing, and Wilson made an utterance which was prophetic of the years 1943-1945 when he said that Russia was "a fit partner."

From the moment the Czar was deposed, Wilson showed the deepest interest in and desire to help the Russians in their attempts to set up a democratic government. This is illustrated by extracts from my Diary (March 23, 1917):

"When the Cabinet met, the President, grave within, told several stories before proceeding to business. He expressed the hope that the Russian revolution would be permanent. 'It ought to be good,' he said with a smile, 'because it has a professor at its head.' He seemed—in fact—stated his pleasure that America was the first nation to recognize the new Russian Government. He added that Charles R. Crane knew well the leading spirits and said they were men of ability, and had the confidence of Russia."

There was a general feeling, led by Wilson, that we ought to show our interest in Russia's new democratic regime. It was, therefore, decided to send a Commission to Russia to carry greetings and "convey to the Russian government the friendship and good will of this nation and to express the confident hope that the Russian people, having developed a political system founded on the principles of democracy, would join the free people of America in resisting with firmness and fortitude the ambitious designs of the German government."

THE ROOT MISSION

It was deemed important that the Commission should be composed of men of ability and sympathy with the new order in Russia. Lansing suggested that the Commission be headed by the distinguished and able Elihu Root, saying, "I wish we could do something to prevent the socialistic element in Russia from carrying out any plan which would destroy the efficacy of the Allied Powers." When the suggestion was made in the Cabinet meeting that Root head the commission, I ventured to advise that it would be a mistake to send him. I hastened to add that there was no abler man in America or one more sincerely interested in the objects of the mission.

"I do not think we ought to consider politics in selecting members of the mission," said Wilson rebukingly, thinking I did not approve Root because he was a Republican.

I replied that it was not because Root was a Republican that I doubted the wisdom of letting it be the Root Commission, and said I thought Theodore Roosevelt and William Jennings Bryan should be members of the mission because they were known in Russia as liberals. I added:

"My reason for doubting that Root should head the Mission is not because in every way he is not fitted or would not deserve to be well received. But as soon as the name of Root is mentioned, the Russians living in New York will send word to Russia that Root is "a little brother of the rich" and is in sympathy with government controlled by those who enjoy special privilege. Before Root arrives in Russia these reports, unjust to him, will close the ears of Russian revolutionists to his arguments and appeals. He will not have a chance to do the things he sincerely wishes to do."

Neither Wilson nor any member of the Cabinet agreed with me. Lansing and McAdoo rebuked me, and Wilson agreed with them.

Lansing had suggested Root, but Wilson also selected others he knew and trusted—Charles R. Crane, John R. Mott, Cyrus McCormick, S. R. Berton, James Duncan, Lehman (who took the place of Gompers), Charles Edward Russell, a Socialist, General Hugh L. Scott, of the Army, and Admiral James H. Glennon, of the Navy. The papers said that Lansing cabled the American Ambassador to Russia that Root was "a most distinguished statesman, who is devoted to the cause of political liberty and to the sovereign rights of the people." Wilson named Russell, a Socialist, to offset the criticism of Root. Wilson admired and esteemed Russell.

However, at first Wilson had to be convinced, when Lansing suggested Root to head the Russian mission, that Root was in perfect sympathy with the aims that actuated our government in sending a mission to Russia. Wilson appreciated his ability, but when Root opposed his shipping bill and other New Freedom measures (1915), Wilson had spoken of Root and Lodge as men who would stoop to "twist the truth" and who used "insincere and contemptible methods." When Root rang clear on war measures and advocated world peace, Wilson changed his former harsh opinion made in the heat of conflict. When he talked with Root, he found, in the matter of helping a democratic regime in Russia, that their minds ran in the same channel. He wrote that Root was "genuinely and heartily in sympathy with the revolution in Russia."

OBJECTIONS TO ROOT

The Mission was therefore headed by the great New Yorker and was called "The Root Commission," and Root in eloquence and sincerity lacked nothing. However, before he reached Russia, his way was blocked. He had no chance, and the Mission of patriotic men failed of its high purpose.

When I warned that Root's association with Big Business would be heralded and would defeat his objective, I did not know that others had advised against his selection. Rabbi Stephen S. Wise wrote Wilson urging him not to appoint Root, saying:

"Why should a man be singled out for this great opportunity of service to a fellow democracy in the making who is not of your mind, who is not a sharer of your own spirit touching the fundamental issues of democracy?"

The President made this reply (April 28) to Rabbi Wise:

"Before your letter about Mr. Root came, I had already asked him to serve as the head of the Commission we are about to send to Russia. Before doing so I convinced myself that he was genuinely and heartily in sympathy with the revolution in Russia, and his experience such, his tact so great, and his appreciation of the object of the Commission so clear that I cannot but feel that he will prove to have been an admirable choice."

Mrs. Carrie Chapman Catt, head of the World Women Suffragists, wanted Wilson to aid the women of Russia in securing the full realization of their rights under the new order of things. Wilson wrote her that the Commission was not going "to give or offer advice or to attempt guidance, but only to express the deep sympathy of the United States," and said that he had tried "to put men in the Commission whose popular sympathies and catholic views of human rights will be recognized."

NO DRINKS FOR ROOT COMMISSION

Secretary Lansing gave a luncheon (May 14) to the members of the Commission to Russia, attended by Cabinet members and others. Root was in happy mood and had high hopes of success. At the close of his able address, Root laughingly turning to his colleagues and with a glance at me, said: "Due to the orders of the Secretary of the Navy, we can have nothing to drink on the voyage." Charles Edward Russell, turning to me, said, "We thank you for all you are doing for righteousness," and John R. Mott added, "All mothers bless you for your practical temperance."

RUSSIAN MINDS POISONED

Perhaps it was because Russians in America did not believe Root would stand for an end of the old order in Russia—a belief that did Root grave injustice—that he failed to catch the ear and inspire faith in the revolutionary Russians. Many causes operated to prevent success—perhaps the greatest was the coming uprising of Communists. But when the members of the Mission returned without having achieved what Root and his associates ardently desired, I learned that prejudice against Root had become so widespread that he could not win over the masses in Russia. Admiral Glennon, recommended by me as the Navy member of the Mission, told me later that he had "never heard more patriotic or wiser utterances in support of the true democratic spirit than were found in the addresses of Root." But, he added, men who were to make Russia bolshevist had so poisoned the mind of Russians that the good seed sown by Root fell upon stony ground.

SAVED RUSSIAN ADMIRAL'S LIFE

It was while in Russia that the Naval member of the Mission, Admiral Glennon, showed he was a diplomat and a life-saver. When the sailors on a Russian ship took charge, murdered a hundred officers, and took Admiral Kolchak a prisoner, Glennon, unaware of the situation that had developed, set out for Sebastopol to visit Admiral Kolchak, accompanied by our Naval attaché, Admiral McCully, master of the Russian tongue and beloved of Russians. When they found their host a prisoner and liable to be shot, Glennon asked to speak to the sailors. He was a very large man. Smiling down on the crew from his towering height, Glennon won them as he requested that he be permitted to take Kolchak with him to Petrograd and to America. That alone would save his life. Naturally Kolchak had affection and gratitude for Glennon. I saw something of him in Washington. He had great admiration for Farragut and journeyed to place a wreath on his grave. He loved his country and had the saddest eyes into which I ever looked. Upon the eve of his departure from Washington to return to his country, where he met death in Siberia, leading the forces against the Bolsheviki, he gave a banquet to friends. I spoke optimistically of the great future of Russia, which he thought was facing its doom. "Do you think

Russia can regain its place of greatness?" he asked me in a tone that spoke his own despair. I predicted that, after the fever of war and revolution, Russia would emerge greater than ever. He smiled sadly, but lacked faith. He had belonged to the old order and it was dead. He was to die with it.

In July, 1918, I was one of a large company of officials at a dinner given by the Russian Ambassador. He was of the governing class and a close friend of the Czar. The dinner over, the men repaired to the drawing room to smoke and hear a distinguished engineer recently returned from Russia, where he had spent a number of years. The engineer saw a great development for Russia, and I distinctly recall his saying, "The two great countries in the world are Russia and the United States, and it is manifest destiny that they must be partners in the coming great development—"

The engineer never finished that sentence, for at that moment Ambassador Bakhmeteff entered, his face as white as a sheet and his whole body shaking. He told the company the news had just come that the Czar had been assassinated.

RUSSIA PROPOSES IMPRACTICAL THINGS

From my Diary, reporting a Cabinet meeting in July:

"Discussing the advice of the War Council on Russia, W. W. said the Russians proposed such impractical things to be done immediately, that he often wondered whether he was crazy or whether they were. Once, he said, after reading a page of an examination paper and making no sense of it, he handed it to Mrs. W. and asked her to read it, asking after she had read it: 'Is there any sense in it?' She said 'No,' and he was overjoyed because that convinced him he was not crazy.

" 'My father,' said W. W., 'thought all sin came from Ego. Some men make themselves the centre of the universe instead of making God the center, and that gives them a wrong outlook on the world.' Everything was for self and that made sin."

When I had spoken so optimistically to Kolchak, I did not foresee that in the 1940's the two biggest countries in the world would unite their strength to fulfill the prophecy of the great engineer made in the Russian Embassy on the night the news came of the assassination of the Czar.

Part Three

NAVY FIRST LINE OF DEFENSE

VII

OUR FIRST STEPS TOWARD WAR

EVERY NOW AND then after the Day of Decision—occasionally before—President Wilson, unannounced, would drop in on an afternoon at the Navy Department. On March 23 a cable had been received from Ambassador Walter Page, and the next day, instead of my going to the White House as was the custom, Wilson came to the Navy Department to discuss Page's cablegram, in which he conveyed Balfour's statement that "the British Government will heartily fall in with any plan we propose as soon as coöperation can be formally established. . . ." Page stated:

"Knowing their [British] spirit and their methods, I cannot too strongly recommend that our Government send here immediately an Admiral of our own Navy who will bring our Navy's plans and inquiries. The coming of such an officer of high rank would be regarded as a compliment and he would have all doors opened to him and a sort of special staff appointed to give him the results and methods of the whole British naval work since the war began. . . . Many things of the greatest value would be verbally made known to such an officer which would never be given in a routine way nor reduced to writing. Admiral Jellicoe has privately expressed the hope to me that our Navy may see its way to patrol our coast and possibly relieve the British cruisers now on our side of the Atlantic. He hopes, too, in case more German raiders go out we may help capture them in waters where they prey on shipping from Mexico or South America."

We had formerly suggested that course through the British Naval Attaché. Captain McDougall, our Naval Attaché in London, was given access to all records which were not confidential, and his intimate association with the officers of the Admiralty enabled him to keep the Navy Department in constant touch with the situation and to give us data bearing on many phases of Naval effort. But there were many things kept secret, unrevealed to any neutral. Our break with Germany brought about new conditions and made possible a more intimate exchange of views between the American and British navies. Ruthless U-boat warfare was sinking shipping by the million tons, and the British naturally concealing their losses and their plans, it was important for us to secure the fullest information as to the exact situation, and what steps were being taken to meet it. In case war was declared, it was desirable for us to have in London an Admiral to advise close coöperation with the Allies.

THE PRESIDENT GAVE APPROVAL

That afternoon I discussed Ambassador Page's cablegram and the whole matter with the President and he approved the plan. Then the question arose as to what officer should be selected for this important mission. The choice was Admiral Henry B. Wilson, later Commander-in-Chief of the Atlantic Fleet, then commanding the battleship *Pennsylvania*. We were creating a strong patrol force in southern waters, and Admiral Wilson was regarded as the best man to organize and command it.

Following oral approval, the President wrote me:

"The main thing, no doubt, is to get into immediate communication with the Admiralty on the other side (through confidential channels until the Congress has acted) and work out the scheme of cooperation. As yet sufficient attention has not been given, it seems to me, by the authorities on the other side of the water to the routes to be followed or to plans by which the safest possible approach may be made to the British ports. As few ports as possible should be used, for one thing, and every possible precaution thought out. Can we not set this afoot at once and save all the time possible?"

Admiral Jellicoe was, as Ambassador Page said, particularly anxious that our Navy might "see its way to patrol our coast and possibly relieve the British cruisers now on our side of the Atlantic," and also, in case more German raiders got out, as was feared, to "help capture them in waters where they prey on shipping from Mexico or South America." This was in line with the policy we had already adopted. Formally organized on March 28, this force was put under the command of Admiral Wilson, and it accomplished just what Admiral Jellicoe suggested. This was the first request made, after war was declared, by Admirals Browning and

Grasset. It was determined, with the President's approval, to assign Wilson to that duty and Admiral William S. Sims was then chosen for the London mission.

WHY SIMS WAS SELECTED

Admiral Badger, President of the General Board, told me that in view of Sims's close association with British officers and his birth in Canada, the Board agreed he was the best man to send on that important duty. Franklin Roosevelt also favored selecting Sims. On Monday, March 26, I telegraphed Sims to come to Washington. He arrived on the 28th and came to the Navy Department in the afternoon. Showing him Page's telegram, I told him the President had decided to send an admiral to England, and he had been selected. Informing him, in confidence, of our belief that the time was near at hand when the United States would enter the war, I told him that in that event we must prepare for the fullest coöperation with the British Navy. But his immediate duty, I pointed out, was to secure all possible information as to what the British were doing, and what plans they had for more effective warfare against the submarines.

In the course of the conversation, I said, "You have been selected for this mission not because of your Guildhall speech, but in spite of it." In that speech Sims had said, "If the time ever comes when the British Empire is seriously menaced by an external enemy, it is my opinion that you may count upon every man, every dollar, every drop of blood of your kindred across the sea." (President Taft had reprimanded Sims for that utterance.) Impressing upon him the fact that the United States was still neutral, and that until Congress should declare war his mission must be a secret and confidential one, I informed him that it had been decided not to issue written orders detaching him from his duties at Newport, but for him to go quietly as a civilian passenger, and report to Ambassador Page personally before any public announcement was made.

SIMS TOLD OF WILSON'S STRATEGY

Among the matters discussed was the extent of the sinkings by submarines. Ambassador Page had written me confidentially that the situation was more serious than the British admitted. I told Admiral Sims that the President believed the British had not taken the necessary vigorous offensive to prevent destruction of shipping by the U-boats and that he strongly believed two things ought to be done:

First, that every effort should be made to prevent the submarines' getting into the Atlantic—that the "hornets," as he called the U-boats, ought to be 'shut up in their own nests," or some method should be found to prevent their ingress and egress.

Second, that all ships ought to be convoyed. The President had been of this opinion for a long time, and had insisted that it was essential to give protection to shipping. The General Board had strongly recommended convoy, and I favored it. But, as I told Admiral Sims, I had taken this matter up with Naval officers in the Department, and there was division of opinion, most of them seeming to agree with the British Admiralty, which apparently opposed the convoy system at that time. It had not been adopted abroad.

On the last day of March, a week before war was declared, Admiral Sims and his aide, Commander J. V. Babcock, boarded the steamship *New York,* entered upon the passenger list as "S. W. Davidson" and "V. J. Richardson." Their fellow voyagers had no idea that "Mr. Davidson" was an admiral of the United States Navy going abroad on an important mission, and that "Mr. Richardson" was his aide.

Reaching Liverpool April 9 after an uneventful voyage, the *New York,* as it approached the outer harbor, struck a mine. Though the ship was not damaged beyond repair, it was crippled, and the passengers were transferred to another vessel and taken ashore. At the dock the American officers were welcomed by Rear Admiral Hope, and they found that a special train, provided by the Admiralty, was waiting to take them to London. Admiral Sims, on arrival there, at once conferred with Ambassador Page and the British Naval authorities, and was admitted to the confidence of the Admiralty.

COÖPERATION WITHOUT A PARALLEL

Since his departure from America, there had been a radical change in the situation. The United States had declared war against Germany, and we were free to deal with the Allies as associates in the great conflict. While Sims was having his first interview with the authorities in London, we were in conference in Washington with the ranking British and French Admirals in the Western Atlantic. In fact, a working agreement was perfected, and orders had been issued to send destroyers to Europe before we received Sims's first dispatch. Thus Sims in London and our authorities in Washington carried out with the utmost cordiality that splendid coöperation between the British and American navies which continued throughout the war and which has hardly a parallel in naval history.

GRAVITY OF SUBMARINE SINKINGS

In his first cablegram from London, April 14, 1917, Sims reported:

"The submarine issue is very much more serious than the people realize in America. The recent success of operations and the rapidity of construction constitute the real crisis of the war. The morale of the enemy submarines is not broken, only about fifty-four are known to have been captured or sunk and no voluntary surrenders have been recorded. . . .

"Supplies and communications of forces on all fronts, including the Russians, are threatened and control of the sea actually imperiled.

"German submarines are constantly extending their operations into the Atlantic, increasing areas and the difficulty of patrolling. Russian situation critical. Baltic fleet mutiny, eighty-five admirals, captains, and commanders murdered, and in some armies there is insubordination.

"The amount of British, neutral and Allied shipping lost in February was 536,000 tons, in March 571,000 tons, and in the first ten days of April 205,000 tons. With short nights and better weather these losses are increasing."

The Germans, he said, had seventy mine-laying submarines, and were building new ones at a rate approaching three a week.

LOOKED AS IF GERMANS WERE WINNING

What were the British doing to meet this perilous situation? What plans did they have to defeat the U-boats? That was what we particularly wanted to know, and were surprised when it was not stated in that dispatch.

Describing his first interview with Lord Jellicoe (they had been friends in China in 1901) Admiral Sims says, in his book, published three years later:

" 'It looks as though the Germans were winning the war,' I remarked.
" 'They will win, unless we can stop these losses—and stop them soon,' the Admiral replied.
" 'Is there no solution for the problem?' I asked.
" 'Absolutely none that we can see now,' Jellicoe announced.

This grim news was in striking contrast with the buoyantly optimistic reports appearing in the British newspapers which misled the British and the Americans. There was an atmosphere of cheerful ignorance on both sides of the Atlantic which no officials felt it was wise to disturb. Even Sims was astonished when I told him in Washington before he left how desperate the situation was and Page had not painted it in its full blackness if he knew. Purposely the British Admiralty gave out figures of losses three or four times smaller than they were, for fear the people would be panic-stricken if they realized the true situation. When informed that U-boats were being multiplied and ship sinkings were on the mount, with 800,000 to 900,000 tons per month, Page solemnly said, "We are facing the defeat of Great Britain." Sims said the British had been sowing mines near Heligoland but the Germans swept them up about as soon as they were planted. To his consternation Sims found that Britain was not mistress of the seas. He told me later that if the Germans could have kept fifty U-boats constantly at work, they could have sunk two or three million tons of shipping instead of 850,000 a month. Sims thought it was this danger that caused Balfour to go to Washington soon after Sims reached London. It was that, but Britain's dire need of money hastened his trip. Britain was scraping the bottom of its money barrel.

What the British were doing in regard to protecting ships was set forth clearly in Sims's letter of April 19, in which he said:

"After trying various methods of controlling shipping, the Admiralty now believes the best policy to be one of dispersion. They use about six relatively large avenues or areas of approach to the United Kingdom and Channels, changing their limits or area periodically if necessity demands."

Allied Commission at Mount Vernon. *Above, left to right,* Robert Lansing, René Viviani, French statesman, Lord Balfour, head of British Mission to the United States, and (behind Balfour) General Joffre. *Below,* Viviani speaking at the tomb of Washington. On the left are Lord Balfour, French Ambassador Jusserand, and Secretary of the Navy Daniels. (Both pictures Harris & Ewing.)

Above, Allied French Commission at Mount Vernon. *Center*, General Joffre; *right*, Colonel Remon. *Below*, Secretary of the Navy and Mrs. Daniels going aboard the *Mayflower* as hosts to the British and French Missions en route to Mount Vernon to lay wreaths on the tomb of Washington. (Both pictures Harris & Ewing.)

THE ADMIRALTY CRITICIZED

There was considerable criticism of the Admiralty, he said, "for not taking more effective steps," and one of the principal demands was for "convoys of merchant shipping, and more definite and real protection within the war zone." However, not only officers but ship owners and captains opposed convoy, favoring the arming of merchant vessels and independent sailings, he informed us, saying:

"The Admiralty has had frequent conferences with merchant masters and sought their advice. Their most unanimous demand is: 'Give us a gun and let us look out for ourselves.' They are also insistent that it is impracticable for merchant vessels to proceed in formation, at least, in any considerable numbers, due principally to difficulty in controlling their speed and to the inexperience of their subordinate officers. With this view I do not personally agree but believe that with a little experience merchant vessels could safely and sufficiently well steam in open formations."

Later, the convoy system President Wilson had long advocated, which shipping interests and many Naval officers had opposed, proved not only practicable, but a very effective measure.

CARIBBEAN COAST THREATENED

Urging that the maximum number of destroyers and antisubmarine craft be sent to Europe, Sims in his first cablegram informed us:

"It is very likely the enemy will make submarine mine-laying raids on our coasts or in the Caribbean to divert attention and to keep our forces from the critical areas in the Eastern Atlantic through effect upon public opinion."

We had to expect this and to provide against it; and at the same time extend all possible aid to our Allies in Europe. We did both and rushed construction of scores of destroyers, submarine chasers, and other small craft.

"FIT OUT FOR LONG AND DISTANT SERVICE"

"Fit out for long and distant service!" was the order the Eighth Destroyer Division received from the flagship of the Atlantic Fleet the night of April 14, 1917. It was then 9:30 P.M., and they were directed to sail at daylight. At five o'clock next morning they started for their home Navy Yards.

Speeding to New York and Boston, the ships went into drydock, made repairs, tuned up machinery, and took aboard three months' stores and provisions—all in ten days.

FIRST WAR ORDER

Sailing from Boston April 24 under sealed orders, it was not until midnight, when they were fifty miles at sea, that the officers of the flotilla knew its destination. Breaking the seal, the Commander read the following, the first operating order issued to any American force in World War I:

"Washington, D. C., April 14

"Secret and Confidential.

"To: Commander, Eighth Division, Destroyer Force, Atlantic Fleet; U. S. S. Wadsworth, flagship.

"Subject: Protection of commerce near the coasts of Great Britain and Ireland.

1. The British Admiralty have requested the cooperation of a division of American destroyers in the protection of commerce near the coasts of Great Britain and France.

2. Your mission is to assist naval operations of Entente Powers in every way possible.

3. Proceed to Queenstown, Ireland. Report to senior British naval officer present, and thereafter cooperate fully with the British Navy. Should it be decided that your force act in cooperation with French naval forces, your mission and method of cooperation under French Admiralty authority remain unchanged..

"Route to Queenstown: Boston to latitude 50 N., Long. 20 W., to arrive at daybreak, then to latitude 50 N. Long. 12, W., thence to Queenstown.

"When within radio communication of the British naval forces off Ireland, call GCK and inform the Vice Admiral at Queenstown in British general code of your position, course, and speed. You will be met outside of Queenstown.

4. Base facilities will be provided by the British Admiralty.

5. Communicate your orders and operations to Rear Admiral Sims at London and be guided by such instructions as he may give you. Make no report of arrival to Navy Department direct.

"JOSEPHUS DANIELS."

Issued only three days after the conference with British and French Admirals in Washington, this put into effect the verbal orders given the moment they requested that one or two destroyers be sent. Six were on the way—the *Wadsworth, Conyngham, Porter, McDougal, Davis,* and *Wainwright.* They were the first of the United States forces despatched to Europe, the pioneers of the large forces we sent across the Atlantic.

THE RETURN OF THE MAYFLOWER

It was no smooth voyage they had in that long trip. Caught in a southeast gale which lasted for seven days, they were so tossed about by the heavy seas that they could not even set the mess-tables. "We ate off our laps," one officer remarked. But the welcome received when they reached port more than made up for these hardships. Nearing the coast, the ninth day out, they sighted a British destroyer, the *Mary Rose,* flying the international signal, "Welcome to the American colors!"

"Thank you, we are glad of your company," the Americans replied.

Next morning, Friday, May 4, they reached Queenstown. Though efforts had been made to keep secret their coming, the American flag floated from public buildings, business houses, and residences, and from vessels in the harbor. Crowds assembled on the hills and along the shore, cheering as the ships from over the sea hove in sight.

It was a brilliant scene, flooded with sunshine—an historic day, marking the arrival of the first American forces to take part with the Allies in the struggle against the Central Powers. Through cheering crowds the Navy boys proceeded to the American Consulate, where the lord mayors of Queenstown and Cork extended a formal welcome. Sir John Jellicoe, First Sea Lord-of the British Admiralty, in a letter to Commander J. K. Taussig, in command of the flotilla, offered the "warmest welcome possible in the name of the British nation and the British Admiralty," concluding: "May every good fortune attend you, and speedy victory be with us." The arrival of these American ships was commemorated in an historic painting by a British artist, Bernard F. Gribble. It was called "The Return of the Mayflower," the ship which, nearly three hundred years before, had brought British settlers to the New World. I caused the original to be purchased and it was hung in the Navy Department.

"WE ARE READY NOW, SIR"

Vice Admiral Sir Lewis Bayly was Commander-in-Chief of the Naval forces of his country on the coast of Ireland, with headquarters at Queenstown. I met that sterling officer when in England in 1919 and again in 1937. Admiral Bayly called at the American Embassy in London, where I was staying, to talk over Navy coöperation in 1917-18 and to express his lasting admiration for his American Naval shipmates. He was accompanied by his daughter, whose hospitality had won the hearts of the American Naval forces based in Queenstown. It was recalled that on the day of their arrival in 1917 he had invited the destroyer commanders to dine with him that evening, closing his invitation with the characteristic note: "Dine in undress; no speeches." Able and energetic, he was known as a "hard driver"; a man of few words who hated talk and demanded results.

"When will you be ready to go to sea?" was about the first question he asked. He naturally supposed that, after a long and stormy voyage, the Americans would ask time for rest and repairs.

"We are ready now, sir," Commander Taussig replied; "that is, as soon as we finish refueling."

"I will give you four days from the time of arrival," the Admiral said. "Will that be sufficient?"

"Yes," was the answer, "that will be more than ample time."

Four days later they were all at sea, hunting submarines. Before the month was out they were swearing by Admiral Bayly, and he was calling them "my boys."

That famous reply, "We are ready now, sir," recalled the famous remark, "We've just begun to fight," of John Paul Jones when he was winning victories overseas in the War of the Revolution. When it reached Washington and was printed, it stirred American patriotism.

THINGS WERE LOOKING BLACK

" 'Things were looking black,' Commander Taussig said. 'In the three previous weeks the submarines had sunk 152 British merchant ships. The night before we entered the harbor, a German submarine had planted twelve mines right in the channel. Fortunately for us, they were swept up by the ever vigilant British mine-sweepers before we arrived. The day following our arrival, one of the British gunboats from our station was torpedoed and her captain and forty of her crew were lost. Patrol vessels were continually bringing in survivors from the various ships as they were sunk.' "

The Queenstown "area" comprised twenty-five thousand square miles, and yet this wide zone of trans-Atlantic shipping, west and south of Ireland, had been left almost unprotected. "Sometimes only four or five British destroyers were operating in this stretch of waters," said Admiral Sims, "and I do not think the number ever exceeded fifteen."

OUR DESTROYERS ABLE TO COPE WITH SITUATION

Soon after the Americans arrived, the few British destroyers at Queenstown were withdrawn. The British Admiralty felt the supreme duty was to protect its "fleet in being" and kept a large number of destroyers at or near Scapa Flow, where the mighty British dreadnaughts were in readiness to try conclusions if and when the German fleet should come out.

Urging the sending of all floating craft available, Sims had informed us in his cablegram of April 28:

"Yesterday the War Council and Admiralty decided that cooperation of twenty-odd American destroyers with base at Queenstown would no doubt put down the present submarine activity which is dangerous and keep it down. The crisis will be passed if the enemy can be forced to disperse his forces from this critical area."

Within a month twenty-eight destroyers and two tenders were either in Queenstown or on the way there. On May 17 a second division arrived, followed by two other divisions, and two additional destroyers and the tenders *Melville* and *Dixie*. All but two of the destroyers the Navy had in 1917 were dispatched to foreign waters. The *Melville,* which arrived May 22, was the "mother ship" and became the flagship of the United States forces stationed there. On June 1, Sims wrote to the Navy Department:

"It is gratifying to be able to report that the operations of our forces in these waters have proved not only very satisfactory, but also of marked value to the Allies in overcoming the submarine menace. The equipment and construction of our ships have proved adequate and sufficient and the personnel has shown an unusually high degree of enthusiasm and ability to cope with the situation presented."

SIGNAL INSTANCES OF SACRIFICE

A large volume would be required to detail all the exploits of our destroyers in European waters, or even to give the reports of their contacts with submarines. These accounts are preserved in the Naval archives. American destroyers had been operating in European waters six months with no damage from enemy action, when, on October 15, the *Cassin* (Lieutenant Commander W. N. Vernou) was torpedoed. Her rudder was blown off, a gun blown overboard, and the after part of the ship wrecked; yet by expert seamanship she was kept afloat and taken to port, repaired, and put back into service. Nine men of the crew were wounded, but only one was killed—Gunner's Mate Osmond K. Ingram, who gave his life to save the ship. Off the Irish coast a torpedo was sighted. Ingram, who was at his gun, realized that if it struck among the depth-bombs astern, the explosion might sink the ship. Instantly, he ran aft to strip these charges and throw them overboard. He was blown to pieces when the torpedo struck. The memory of this heroic gunner's mate, who made the supreme sacrifice to save his ship-mates, was preserved in the name of a modern destroyer, the *Ingram*, the first Naval vessel ever named for an enlisted man. There is no rank in sacrifice or honors. Years later I went to Birmingham, Alabama, to tell of Ingram's noble sacrifice when a city park was named in his honor.

There is no more striking example of prompt action and quick results by destroyers than that of the *Fanning* and *Nicholson* when they "got" a German submarine, the U-58, on November 17, 1917. Dropping a depth charge alongside the U-boat, the *Nicholson* fired from her stern gun and the *Fanning* opened fire with her bow gun. At the third shot the German crew came on deck and held up their hands in surrender shouting "Kamerad." As it sank the Germans jumped into the water and swam for the *Fanning*, and all but one got aboard.

On June 16 the *O'Brien* defeated a U-boat which was trying to attack the British steamer *Elysia*. The *Trippe, Warrington, Jenkins,*

Wadsworth, McDougal, Cummings, Parker, Benham, and *Conyngham* all had successful encounters with U-boats in July, and there was evidence that the submarines were damaged if not disabled.

In addition to the sinking of the *Cassin* the Navy lost the destroyer *Jacob Jones* by U-boat fire. The deck was blown clear for twenty feet. A number of men were killed and the officers and men, always under submarine fire, behaved with great courage. They were in a serious position all night in the cold water until they were rescued by the British ship *Camillia*. Admiral Sims, referring to the officers said, "Lieutenant Commander David W. Bagley and other officers did not leave the destroyer until it began to sink and all officers and men bore themselves with great coolness." The report on Lieutenant Kalk, who died of exhaustion and exposure in seeking to save his men, said, "He was game to the last." I named a destroyer the *Kalk* in honor of his sacrifice. Of the commanding officer Sims said, "Bagley's handling of the situation after his ship was torpedoed was everything in the way of efficiency, good judgment and courage and vigorous action."

Serious damage to the *Shaw* could have been averted by Commander Glassford but he elected to suffer serious damage to his own ship in order to save the big troopship *Aquitania*. Some months after this incident I visited the ship at Portsmouth, England, where the *Shaw* was repaired and found that she was again in commission, doing splendid service in the Navy. I named a new destroyer the *Parrott* after a North Carolina officer who bore himself bravely.

We lost the *Chauncey,* one of the old-type destroyers, when it was sunk November 19.

A DOUBTING THOMAS CONVERTED

There were many stories of the destroyers' efficiency, and one told me by a gentleman on his return from Europe impressed me particularly. Making its way across the North Atlantic, a convoy of troop ships was still some three hundred miles from land when a voyager, who was making his first trip across, remarked, "All you can hear about nowadays is the Navy. It is the Navy this, the Navy that; but as far as I can see, the Navy is not doing much in this war."

One of the civilians in the party who had a son in the Navy, rose to his feet, pulled out his watch and said, "In ten minutes six United States destroyers will meet this convoy."

"What are you talking about?" asked the voyager. "How do you know?"

"Well," was the confident answer, "it is now 4:05 o'clock. The destroyers are ordered to meet this convoy at 4:15, and they will be on time."

The party went out on deck to watch, and, on the minute, at 4:15 the destroyers hove in sight. Swinging into line, on each side of the convoy, the saucy little vessels, heaving foam and spray from bow to stern, spanked along through the heavy seas.

"Good heavens!" exclaimed the doubting Thomas, "if these little destroyers can come three hundred miles to sea in any kind of weather, keep their schedule, and locate a convoy on the dot, I will believe anything I hear regarding the Navy." That's just an example of the way our destroyer boys went at the job, and they kept it up until the last signal to cease firing was heard after the Armistice.

NAVAL LOSSES

In addition to the loss of the destroyers, two ships—the *President Lincoln* and the *Covington*—were sunk returning from France as also was the *Antilles,* an Army-chartered transport not manned by the Navy. Two American transports were torpedoed, the *Finland,* manned by a civilian crew, and the *Mount Vernon,* manned by the Navy. Both were successfully navigated to port and repaired. The *Tuscania* and the *Moldavia,* British-chartered vessels, were sunk while carrying American troops to Europe, and the *Dwinsk* was sunk while returning. One of the worst casualties of Naval ships was the *President Lincoln,* under Commander P. W. Foote. With 715 persons on board it was returning to America bringing American soldiers home, and as it was steaming along five hundred miles from land, terrific explosions from three torpedoes fired in a salvo from a submarine sunk the ship. Five minutes after the torpedoes exploded, with her colors flying the *President Lincoln* went down. Three officers and twenty-three men were lost; seven working below decks were either killed by the explosion or drowned by the in-rush of water; sixteen men on a raft alongside were caught by the current and carried under as the ship went down. Admiral Sims cabled that the "small loss of life is due to thorough discipline of the ship's company and excellent seamanship of Commander Foote. This was evidenced by actual results after the ship had been sunk and the

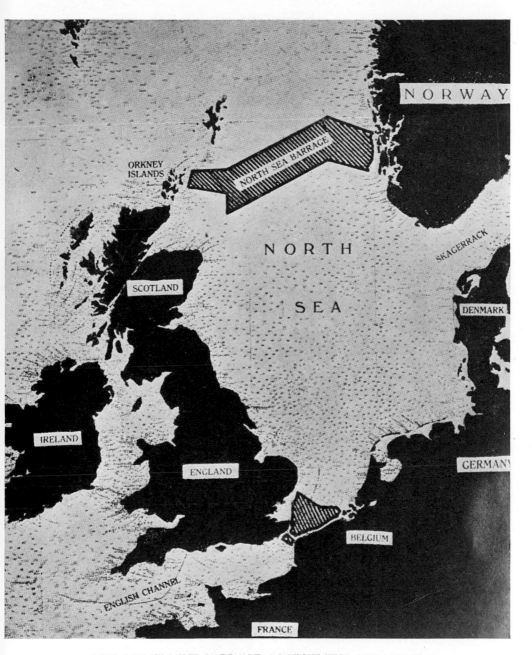

THE GREAT MINE BARRAGE AGAINST THE SUBMARINE

This shows the location of the mine barrage across the North Sea as well as the smaller one across the English Channel. The destruction by this barrage, more than any other single factor, shattered the morale of the German submarine crews (U. S. Navy).

SURRENDER OF THE U-58

The crew of this submarine surrendered to the *Fanning*, after the destroyer's
depth charges had shattered the under-sea boat. This was the first U-boat captured
(U. S. Navy).

personnel was adrift on rafts and in boats." Admiral Gleaves, who directed the operations of these ships, wrote Foote, "Your action and judgment under such trying conditions was in accord with the best traditions of the Navy."

When the *Covington,* under Captain R. D. Hasbrouck, was torpedoed July 1st, the men and officers showed great heroism but were unable to save the ship, which went down with colors flying. The only ship of the cruiser transport force that was sunk, in fact the only Naval vessel of the United States lost during the war, was the armored cruiser *San Diego,* Captain H. H. Christy commanding. It was sunk by a mine or fire in New York Harbor, July, 1918. Captain Christy was the last to leave the ship. Going from the bridge down two ladders to the port deck, he slid down a line to the armor belt, then dropped four feet to the bilge keel, and thence to the docking keel; from there he dropped into the water. The men cheered and clapped as he left the ship, and on the rafts they sang, "My Country, 'Tis of Thee."

COÖPERATION WITH ALLIED NAVIES

Four days after war was declared, Vice Admiral Browning of Britain, and Rear Admiral Grasset of France, by invitation came to the United States to confer about early coöperation with our Navy. Since 1914 they had maintained ships in the Western Atlantic to patrol the waters from Halifax to the Panama Canal. A long conference was held with them by the Secretary and Assistant Secretary of the Navy Roosevelt and high ranking officers of our Navy. I told them that we wished to place our full Naval strength where it could best advance the common cause and the following agreement was reached whereby the United States could best throw its weight into the struggle:

"1. The United States Navy to take over the patrol of the Atlantic coast from Canada to South American waters. They explained the importance of that patrol and why they had felt it essential to preserve it since 1914. They gave three reasons for its continued maintenance: (a) protection of shipping for the Allied armies, including food for their civilian populations, and oil from Texas and Mexico for their fleets and armies; (b) protection against the coming of U-boats, which was deemed not only possible but probable; and (c) readiness to destroy

German raiders. They told us that if we could take over this patrol it would serve the double purpose of protecting shipping on this coast and releasing their ships, which were needed overseas.

At that time both here and abroad there was a general belief that German strategy would dictate the sending of U-boats to our coast. There was a fear, too (and there were many reports), of possible submarine bases at out-of-the-way places on the Atlantic and Gulf. Indeed, from the beginning of the war in 1914 the Navy had been vigilant in sending craft into all places on our coast, from Canada to the Panama Canal, which might possibly enable U-boats to subsist in our waters. That conference agreed that this vigilance should be continued and made more effective, because it was thought the incentive to submarine activity on this side of the Atlantic would be stimulated by the desire to sink transports carrying American troops.

"2. The United States to have in readiness squadrons to operate against any raider in either the North or South Atlantic. That was regarded as of great importance by the French and British conferees, and it was one of the chief duties of our Patrol Squadron. Speaking later of that, Admiral Badger, head of the General Board, said: 'While a discussion of the general subject was had, the British and French Admirals were particularly concerned as to the patrol of the east coast of North and South America, for which their forces were considered inadequate.' The Chief of Naval Operations was directed at this meeting to strengthen the patrol force and to send it wherever it would render the quickest and best service against the enemy. It was later sent to Gibraltar to protect the vast volume of shipping plying between the Mediterranean and northern Europe. A strong force, under Admiral William B. Caperton, was later on duty on the coast of Brazil and other South American countries for the protection of Allied shipping in the South Atlantic.

"3. Recognizing the accepted Naval doctrine of all countries that destroyers should be provided for operation with every dreadnaught, the British and French admirals said they hesitated to request the detachment of any destroyer from the fleet. 'Of course your fleet naturally would not be willing to part with or weaken the screen of destroyers,' said Admiral Browning, but he expressed the hope that we might send at once one or two destroyers to Europe for the moral effect this would inspire, as well as their aid in combating submarines. Though the Commander-in-Chief of the American fleet felt it would be taking desirable protection from his command, it was agreed immediately to send six destroyers overseas. 'We will send a division at once,' I informed the British and French admirals, 'and all other aid in our power.' Admirals Benson and Mayo were then directed to issue the necessary orders for the destroyers to make ready for distant service. In pursuance of the policy of the United States adopted at this conference, the American Navy continued to send destroyers, submarine chasers, yachts and other craft overseas until the number in Europe reached 373.

"4. Our Navy agreed to look after the west coast of North America from Canadian to Colombian boundaries.

"5. It was promised that United States armed government vessels would maintain continuous service to Chile, from which country America and the Allies obtained nitrates indispensable for the manufacture of munitions. All during the war there was fear that the steady flow of nitrates might be interrupted, and every effort was made to transport large quantities as rapidly as possible. It was gratifying when Admiral Browning reported that the British relations with Chile were 'excellent.' While our relations with that country were also cordial, scarcity of ships and hazards of transportation were such that the United States spent many millions to establish nitrate plants within its own borders as the war progressed, at Muscle Shoals, the forerunner of T.V.A.

"6. It was agreed that our Asiatic fleet should be maintained. It was operated in close coöperation with Allied fleets all during the war and they acted together when conditions in Russia became acute.

"7. Our Navy undertook to supervise the Gulf of Mexico and Central American waters as far south as the Colombian boundary and as far east as Jamaica and the Virgin Islands. It was through this area that Allied navies transported their oil, chiefly from Tampico and Port Arthur. The protection of tankers was always of prime importance, and the patrol of those waters, begun before we entered the war, was carried on until its close, first under Admiral Wilson and afterwards by Admiral Anderson. The vigilance of this patrol was never relaxed.

"8. Our Navy assumed the duty of sending submarines to Canadian waters, 'if and when enemy submarines appeared off that coast.'

"9. The French Admiralty was assured that, as soon as possible, we would send patrol vessels to the French coast. This was done, our armed yachts sailing early in June for Brest.

"10. We also undertook to send armed naval transports for carrying needed railway material to France, one immediately, and others as soon as possible."

I am giving this agreement because it summarizes the close co-operation which was begun immediately after our entrance into the war and was carried out with complete unity with Allied navies until victory was won.

This conference and others with our Allies were of the utmost importance because all the large policies and operations were settled in the Navy Department and all important decisions were made by the Secretary of the Navy. Officers abroad were in command of ships assigned them. In emergencies they acted on their own initiative. The ships overseas were never under independent command, but always constituted a "task force of the Atlantic Fleet," of which Admiral Mayo was Admiral-in-Chief. Their orders stated: "The individuality of the United States forces should be such that they may be continuously ready to change their areas of operations as may be made necessary by orders of the Navy Department." Civilian control was never withdrawn.

VIII

HORNETS SHUT UP IN THEIR NESTS

I N THE MONTHS before we entered the war, as the news of the sinkings by U-boats indicated that Germany was winning the war, President Wilson turned to me at Cabinet meetings several times and asked: "Daniels, why don't the British shut up the hornets in their nests?" Without waiting for an answer, he would go on to say that as long as the U-boats were permitted to get into the open sea, their ravages could not be checked. He thought that it was possible to find a way to confine them to home waters. As long as our country was not in the war, we could not advise a course for the allied nations, but the moment war was declared Wilson renewed the question and the Navy Department devised plans to do what Wilson had early seen was the certain way to stop the sinkings. Among those outside of Navy officers, in addition to civilian scientists, who early shared Wilson's belief that U-boats should and could be shut up in German waters, were Secretary of Commerce Redfield and Assistant Secretary of the Navy Franklin Roosevelt. They communicated their opinions to Wilson, and Roosevelt took up with him plans that had been drawn in the Navy Department.

In October, 1916, Franklin Roosevelt received a note from the President, saying, "I am interesting myself in the matter." Roosevelt had sent Wilson a copy of his memorandum on "Prepared Measures To Close English Channel and North Sea Against Submarines by Mine Barrage." Roosevelt had written that "elimination of all submarines from the waters between the United States and Europe must of necessity be a vital factor in winning the war."

PLANS AND BLUEPRINTS

We entered the war on April 6, 1917. On the 15th of that month, Admiral Ralph Earle, Chief of the Bureau of Ordnance, completed plans with blueprints of an antisubmarine barrage for closing the North Sea and the Adriatic. In the discussions Roosevelt and I had with experts, the consensus of opinion was that the barrage should extend from the east coast of Scotland to the Norwegian coast and a short barrage should be constructed across the Dover Straits, which would shut off access to the Atlantic, or at least make the continued operation of enemy submarines exceedingly hazardous. The recommendations of Ordnance having been approved, the next step was to secure the approval of the British Admiralty without which we could not proceed.

BRITISH SAID IT WAS NOT FEASIBLE

Two days after Earle presented the plans, I cabled Sims in London, informing him of our belief that the barrage was the only effective way to end U-boat sinkings and directed him to confer with the British Admiralty and report on its practicability. In the cable I said:

"Is it not practicable to blockade German coast efficiently and completely, thus making practically impossible the egress and ingress of submarines? The steps attempted or accomplished in that direction are to be reported at once.

"DANIELS"

Two days later this answer came:

"To absolutely blockade the German and Belgian coast against the entrance and departure of submarines has been found quite infeasible."

That decision was not accepted. On May 9 Ordnance outlined plans in a memorandum to be submitted to the British Admiralty and I cabled Sims:

"Much opinion is in favor of the concerted efforts by the Allies to establish a complete barrier across the North Sea, Scotland to Norway, either direct or via the Shetlands, to prevent the egress of German submarines. The difficulty and size of the problem is recognized, but if it is possible of accomplishment, the situation would warrant the effort.

"DANIELS"

The Admiral was directed to consult with the Admiralty regarding plans. Two days later he cabled that the Admiralty considered the plan "quite impracticable" and he added: "Project has previously been considered and abandoned." He wrote later:

"It may well be imagined this whole subject has been given the most earnest consideration, as it is, of course, realized that if submarines could be kept from coming out, the whole problem would at once be solved. The Admiralty has concluded that no barrier can be completely effective."

We persisted and finally Sims cabled, saying: "The British Admiralty considers we can more profitably concentrate on other work." That advice was not taken.

WILSON CABLES SIMS

When I informed Wilson of the British Admiralty's position, accepted as a finality by Sims, the President went up in the air and on July 4 (a patriotic letter on a patriotic day) sent a "strictly confidential" cablegram to Sims in which he said:

"From the beginning of the war, I have been greatly surprised at the failure of the British Admiralty to use Great Britain's great naval superiority in an effective way. In the presence of the present submarine emergency, they are helpless to the point of panic. Every plan we suggest they reject for some reason of prudence. In my view this is not a time for prudence but for boldness, even at the cost of great losses.

"In most of your dispatches you have quite properly advised us of the sort of aid and coöperation desired from us by the Admiralty. The trouble is that their plans and methods do not seem to us efficacious. I would be very much obliged to you if you would report to me, confidentially, of course, exactly what the Admiralty has been doing, and what they have accomplished, and, added to the report, your own comments and suggestions, based upon independent thought of the whole situation, without regard to the judgment of any one on that side of the water.

"The Admiralty was very slow to adopt the protection of convoy and it is not now, I judge, protecting convoys on adequate scale within the danger zone, seeming to keep small craft with the Grand Fleet. The absence of craft for convoy is even more apparent on the French coast than on the English coast and in the Channel. I do not see how the necessary military supplies and supplies of food and fuel oil are to be delivered at British ports in any other way within the next few months than under adequate convoy. There will presently not be ships or tankers enough and our shipbuilding plans may not begin to yield important results in less than eighteen months.

"I believe that you will keep these instructions absolutely and entirely to yourself, and that you will give me such advice as you would give if you were handling the situation yourself, and if you were running a Navy of your own.

"WOODROW WILSON."

The reply of Sims did not satisfy Wilson in any particular except that he agreed that ships should be convoyed. The British had been slow in adopting this. In his reply to the President Sims had written: "Depend upon the fact, which I believe to be true, that regardless of any future developments we can count upon the support of the British Navy, I have been assured by important Government officials." Later, writing to Ambassador Page approving the idea of having "some proper history books written for the small Americans and Britishers," the Admiral said, "I have received word, practically direct from the President, that he was much displeased with my reply to his cablegram, that it did not change his opinion at all, and that he regards me as owned by the Admiralty and so pro-British that he considered the advisability of replacing me by some other officer."

AMERICANS NOT GIVEN CREDIT

Sims not only accepted the plans of the British Admiralty as sacrosanct but in the matter of crediting American ships in sinking or damaging submarines, he said in his "Summary of Activities of United States Naval Forces Operating In European Waters": "Report of all attacks by U. S. Navy vessels were submitted to the British Admiralty the same as in cases of British ships and awards of British Admiralty were accepted." The Admiralty, out of 256 attacks on submarines by U. S. Navy vessels, gave credit for only twenty-four "successful attacks," a figure not deemed accurate by American captains who felt that we were entitled to credit for 183.

NEW TYPE OF MINE PERFECTED

After the proposal of a great mine barrage in the North Sea, experts in and out of the Navy concentrated to produce the best and most effective mine. They experimented with mines, firing and anchoring devices, and developed a new type of mine adapted

Upper left, Captain Lyman A. Cotten, Commander of fleet of submarine chasers in European waters during World War. *Upper right,* Rear Admiral Albert Gleaves, in command of convoy operations in the Atlantic, convoyed first A. E. F. to France in June, 1917 (The National Archives). *Below,* twenty-two şubchasers, the *U.S.S. Leonidas,* and the tanker *Maxant* at Corfu, Greece (U. S. Navy).

NORTH CAROLINIANS COMMANDING NORTH SEA DREADNAUGHTS

Upper left, Rear Admiral A. T. Long, Chief of Naval Intelligence, commander, *U.S.S. Nevada* in the North Sea. *Upper right,* Admiral Victor Blue, Chief of Navigation, commander, *U.S.S. Texas. Lower left,* Admiral Thomas Washington, Chief of Bureau of Navigation, commander, *U.S.S. Florida. Lower right,* Admiral A. H. Scales, Superintendent of the Naval Academy, captain, *U.S.S. Delaware.*

particularly to deep waters. It did not have to be struck to explode, but would explode if a submarine passed close to it. This was due to the firing apparatus which was evolved from an electrical device submitted by Ralph C. Browne, of Salem, Massachusetts, to be used on a submerged gun. Naval officers adapted the device to mines. They were an improvement of the old type of mine device, but Admiral Strauss, in command of the mine-laying forces, said the barrage could have been effective without the new devices.

When these new mines were perfected, the job of secretly manufacturing them required the requisition of a hundred plants to manufacture different parts for the needed 100,000 mines. No manufacturer knew in what weapon his product would be utilized. He was asked to manufacture a certain part to be shipped to Norfolk, Virginia. There they were sent to a mine-loading plant of twenty-two buildings which had been erected at St. Julian's Creek, Virginia. I observed when on a visit that it was capable of loading and shipping 1,000 mines a day.

PRECIOUS TIME WAS LOST

April, May, June, and July—precious time for carrying out the barrage project—passed without securing the assent from the British Admiralty. In July the Bureau of Ordnance reported the development of a new-type mine-firing gear which would be suitable. Unable to secure British approval and the essential coöperation, on August 15 Admiral Mayo, Commander-in-Chief, was ordered to London to present in person the amended plan, to point out the excellence of our mines, and to state that the United States Navy would furnish all the mines and deliver them in Scotland and supply the ships and personnel to lay the barrage.

Admiral Mayo upon his return told me that, while he was heard respectfully, at first the Admiralty was skeptical of the plan and not interested in it. The Admiralty, after discussion, concluded that "the distant mine barrage could not be very well undertaken until an adequate supply of mines of satisfactory type was assured." That was a *mañana* policy. When six months of inaction had passed, ·he General Board of the Navy lost patience and on their recomendation on October 20 I cabled Sims to be informed if the plan s the approval of the Admiralty." Finally the Admiralty agreed öperate and the two navies united belatedly in the carrying out of the most stupendous project of the kind ever undertaken. It was not until October 22, after insistent urging, that Sims cabled: "Admiralty has approved mine barrier and now confirms approval."

ENTIRE BURDEN ON UNCLE SAM

In the fall of 1917 I had directed Admiral Benson, Chief of Operations, to go to England and France for conference with our Naval representatives and the Naval authorities of those countries to urge coöperation in the mine barrage then hanging fire. It is significant that in Benson's report he said: "Offensive operations in the air I consider a necessary preliminary to other forms of Naval offensives against enemy bases." In addition to a detailed report, he made these observations, which were the result of his studies of the situation:

> "We can expect no additional Naval assistance whatever from the continental European allies. I have been unable to escape the conclusion that all countries opposed to Germany in this war, except ourselves, are jealous and suspicious of one another. They believe, however, in the sincerity and unselfishness of the United States; and feeling thus, they are not only willing for the United States to take the lead in matters which affect our common cause; but they are really anxious that we should dominate the entire allied situation, both as regards active belligerent operations against the enemy, and economically. . . .
> "I am convinced of the possibility of the burden of the entire war sooner or later devolving upon the United States and Great Britain—and this practically means the United States."

With that view he urged that we render every assistance so that all the burden "would not have to be borne by ourselves."

THE PRESIDENT CONGRATULATES NAVY

Upon Mayo's return from Europe (October 19) I took him to the White House to give the President the story of his negotiations in London and to tell how difficult it had been to convince the Admiralty of the feasibility of the barrage. Mayo related to Wilson:

> "When I arrived in London, I found the Admiralty was not favorable to our proposal and gave me at first only a hearing out of courtesy. They did not think we could produce mines to do the job and were skeptical of the efficacy of the barrage.

They felt the mine barrage was impractical but postponed final answer until they could be assured we could provide an adequate supply of a satisfactory type of mines. At first, I was made to feel that I must be humored as an ally but that they had little faith in the project."

The President told Mayo that even before we entered the war, he had believed that victory over U-boats was possible only by "shutting the hornets up in their nests," and congratulated Mayo and the Navy that at last we had succeeded.

ACCOMPLISHING THE PERILOUS TASK

A fleet of America's mine carriers with twenty-three cargo vessels were assigned to take these mines 3,500 miles to Inverness and Invergardon, where they were inspected and assembled under the direction of Captain O. G. Murfin. An experienced ordnance officer, Admiral Joseph Strauss, was placed in command of mining operations. A mine squadron under Captain Reginald R. Belknap was created. The operations were conducted in conjunction with a British mine-laying squadron under the command of Rear Admiral Clinton-Baker. This Northern Barrage cost eighty million dollars. In all, 70,263 mines were laid, 13,652 by the British and 56,611 by the Americans. There was no more dangerous assignment both in laying the mines and in removing them. When this drab and perilous task was completed, attended with disaster and deaths, I went to New York to welcome the men home and voice the gratitude of the American people to those who had succeeded in this perilous adventure.

EFFECTIVENESS DEMONSTRATED

The result of the barrage demonstrated its effectiveness. After its completion and success this statement was made by Sims: "No such project has ever been carried out more successfully.... As an achievement it stands as one of the wonders of the war."

It was fully completed October 26, 1918. Though in operation only a short time, Admiral Earle reported:

"It has been established that six submarines were lost in the barrage and three more so badly damaged that they never again put to sea. However, for further evidence, the British Admiralty officially credit the barrage with 14 additional, or a total of 23.

... Eight and one-half per cent of the total number of submarines lost during the war were brought into the list of missing by the barrage which existed only six per cent of the period of the war. Such results more than justified the effort and time and funds expended."

ACCELERATED GERMAN NAVAL MUTINY

The mutiny of the German Navy, which began the rout of the Germans and led to the Armistice, was in part caused by the terror the Northern Barrage carried to Naval men who saw their doom in the hidden and deadly mines whose presence could not be guessed. That it was a death trap was affirmed by H. Lutz in his *German Revolution,* in which he gives November 2nd as the beginning of the revolt by U-boat crews in Kiel. He says, "The revolt which began about this time, November 2, 1918, spread and from a successful naval mutiny it became a great revolutionary movement."

Information from Austrian sources was to the effect that two weeks after the arrival of the American vessels it was impossible to compel an Austrian crew to take a submarine through the barrage.

Among other appraisals of the effectiveness of the mine barrage conceived and mainly constructed by the American Navy, Fletcher Pratt in his *The Navy, A History,* concludes his story of the mine barrage as follows:

"September was the month that saw the Great North Sea barrage complete. On the 19th the *UB-104* went down among the North Sea fields, on the 25th *U-102, UB-127* and a new, big cruiser, *U-156,* just back from across the Atlantic. Three in one day; and two days later another came back with her crew in a mutiny and a shattered bow; at Wilhelmshaven neither orders nor cocked revolvers could any longer get men aboard the doomed submarines.

"October; submarines suddenly vanished from the seas like stars at dawn; spy lines hummed with news that the German fleet was coming forth to sink or swim in one tremendous smash, and in the South the allied navies steamed in to destroy the Austrian base at Durazzo, with American S C's on the flank of the movement. October, Austria gave up, there was a mutiny in the German dreadnaught fleet, red flags in Kiel dockyard, machine guns in the streets, the crews would not sail on the last adventure, and the naval war flickered out."

Captain Dudley W. Knox, in his *A History of the United States Navy,* after his account of the mine barrage from the day in April (1917) when it was proposed to me by Admiral Ralph Earle, concludes thus:

"The barrage began to take its toll as early as July 9, when *U-86* was damaged while homeward bound. On August 10th *U-113* sustained such casualties while outward bound as to be forced to return to Germany, and on September 8th another submarine suffered the same fate, and *U-92* was sunk. Additional sinkings during September and October were *U-156, UB-104, UB-127, U-102* and *UB-123*; while *UB-116* was sunk by mines in the vicinity of the barrage or perhaps in it on October 28. Possibly as many as eight submarines were destroyed, and probably more than this were damaged in the maze of mines forming this great barrier requiring several hours for a submarine to pass. The strain on the personnel was very great, and stories of the dreadful crossing soon circulated throughout the German submarine force, undermining its morale and contributing substantially to speed the coming collapse."

The most daring and original naval conception of the World War was the North Sea barrage. Admiral Strauss, after the war replying to an inquiry, declared that had the barrage been completed when first proposed, "it would have ended the submarine menace."

IX

THE NAVY'S FERRY TO FRANCE

W HAT WAS THE greatest thing America did in the World War?"
That is a question I have often been asked, and it is easily
answered. It was the raising and training of an Army of four million
men, who turned the tide of battle in France, and a Navy of over
six hundred thousand; the safe transportation of more than two
million troops to Europe; the North Sea barrage. And all this was accomplished in eighteen months.

When the issue hung in the balance, in the spring of 1918, Lloyd
George said, "It is a race between Wilson and Hindenburg." Could
America land enough soldiers in France in time to check the Ger-
man offensive? That was the vital question.

WHAT THE KAISER THOUGHT

When it looked as if America would enter the war, the Kaiser
stated in substance—so it was reported—"Germany has nothing to
fear for three reasons: The Americans have no trained army and
cannot train one under two years and the war will be won before
that time; if the Americans had an Army ready, they have no transports to bring troops to Europe; and if they could get the ships, we
could sink them and the men aboard by our U-boats."

BIGGEST TRANSPORTATION JOB THE WORLD HAD KNOWN

Carrying the American Expeditionary Force across the Atlantic
and bringing our troops home has been justly termed the "biggest
transportation job in history." Sailing through submarine-infested
seas, our ships constantly faced the menace of attack from an unseen
foe, as well as the perils of war-time navigation. Yet not one American troop-ship was sunk on the way to France, and not one soldier
aboard a troop transport manned by the United States Navy lost his
life through enemy action.

That achievement has never been equalled. It was not only the
most important but the most successful operation of the war. When

Rear Admiral Albert Gleaves, commander of the Cruiser and Transport Force, came to Washington for his final instructions, just before the first troop convoys sailed for Europe, as he was leaving my office, I said to him, "Admiral, you are going on the most important, the most difficult, and the most hazardous duty assigned to the Navy."

That was not overstating it in any particular. No nation in history had ever attempted to transport so huge an army overseas. It would have been difficult enough under the most ideal conditions.

The German Navy could have no greater object than to prevent our troops from getting into France. There could have been no greater victory for them than to have sunk a transport loaded with American soldiers. Words can hardly express the strain of those anxious days when our first transports were running the gauntlet to France; or our relief when we received the news that they had all arrived safely at St. Nazaire.

TROOP SHIPS ATTACKED BY U-BOATS

Sailing in a dense fog on June 14, 1917, the first group arrived on June 26; the last, the cargo ships, on July 2. The first group, Gleaves reported, was attacked by submarines the night of June 22 at 10:15 P.M.; the second group encountered two, and a torpedo was fired at the fourth group on June 28. That they had escaped the submarines was an added cause for rejoicing. Not a ship was damaged or a man injured, and an officer reported: "We didn't lose but one horse, and that was a mule."

"The German Admiralty had boasted that not one American soldier should set foot in France," Gleaves said. "The bluff had been called, and it could not have been called at a more psychological moment."

The question of the hour had been successfully answered; France, as well as America, celebrated the event in a very delirium of rejoicing. This was the beginning of that vast stream of troops and supplies that poured across the Atlantic until the Germans were overwhelmed.

General Pershing and his staff sailed May 28 on the *Baltic* and arrived at Liverpool June 8, reaching France at Boulogne, June 13. Four troop convoys sailed from New York the next day. Admiral Gleaves, on his flagship, the cruiser *Seattle,* was in command. No convoy that ever sailed had a stronger escort or was more closely guarded. Their protection was our supreme duty. Before they left, I cabled Admiral Sims: "I hereby instruct you to furnish escorts, to consist of one division of destroyers for each convoy group from the point of meeting to the point of debarkation."

NAVY'S PARAMOUNT DUTY

The policy of the Department, with reference to the safety of ships carrying troops to France, was laid down in this cablegram which I wrote with my own hand:

"Washington, D. C., July 28, 1917

"ADMIRAL SIMS:

"The paramount duty of the destroyers in European waters is principally the proper protection of transports with American troops. Be certain to detail an adequate convoy of destroyers and in making the detail bear in mind that everything is secondary to having a sufficient number to insure protection to American troops.

"JOSEPHUS DANIELS"

The reason that peremptory order was sent was because Sims had suggested we depend on the French Navy to give protection to our transports en route to French ports. He felt that all our destroyers should be engaged in hunting down U-boats, which were most deadly in the waters around England. I knew that, while the mothers and fathers of our men in the armed forces dreaded the dangers in battle, their greatest fear was lest the boys be sunk by U-boats without a chance for their lives. The sinking of a transport with American soldiers en route to the war zone would have been tragic and the American people would have never forgiven the Secretary of the Navy if he had not made their safe passage as certain as was humanly possible. I did not doubt the French Navy would do all it could to give protection in spite of their naval losses and other commitments, but I regarded it as our job—and most important task—to land American soldiers safely on French soil. And not one soldier was lost en route on our ships!

Submarines were reported operating in the area that had to be crossed. Gleaves cabled: "It is practically certain that enemy knew position of the first rendezvous and accordingly sent a submarine to intercept before juncture with destroyers."

U-BOATS KNEW LOCATION OF SHIPS

When he was in Paris, Admiral Gleaves was shown a confidential bulletin of information issued by the French General Staff, dated July 6, which contained the following:

"Ponta Delgada was bombarded at 9 A.M., July 4. This is undoubtedly the submarine which attacked the *Fern Leaf* on June 25, four hundred miles north of the Azores and sank the *Benguela* and *Syria* on the 29 of June 100 miles from Terceira (Azores). This submarine was ordered to watch in the vicinity of the Azores at such a distance as it was supposed the enemy American convoy would pass from the Azores."

"It appears from the French report quoted above and from the location of the attack that enemy submarines had been notified of our approach and were probably scouting across our route," Gleaves said.

COURAGE GAVE SAFE CONDUCT TO COURAGE

On the evening of July 3 (1917) I had the pleasure of announcing the safe arrival of all our convoys, without the loss of a man. This occasioned general rejoicing in France, England, and Italy, as well as America. For us, the national holiday that followed was truly a glorious Fourth. Secretary Baker wrote the thanks of the Army, adding: "This splendid achievement is an auspicious beginning, and it has been characterized throughout by the most cordial and effective coöperation between the two military services." In replying, "in behalf of the men whose courage gave safe conduct to courage," I said that the Navy "waited in full confidence for the day when the valor of your soldiers will write new and splendid chapters in the history of our liberty-loving land."

BRITISH, FRENCH, AND ITALIANS HELPED

Records show that, in all, 2,079,880 American troops were transported to France before the Armistice—952,581 in American vessels, 911,047 of these in U. S. Naval transports; 1,006,987 in British ships; 68,246 in British-leased Italian vessels; 52,066 in French, Italian and other foreign ships. American vessels carried 46.25 per cent, 43.75 of this in U. S. Naval transports; British vessels 48.25 per cent; British-

"PROUD OF YOU, SON"!

leased Italian ships, 3 per cent; French, Italian, and others, 2.5 per cent.

The purely naval duty was escorting these vessels, guarding them against attack by raiders or submarines. Of this the British Navy performed 14.125 per cent, the French 3.125, and the United States Navy 82.75 per cent, over four-fifths. Of the total number of troops 61,617 were under French escort, 297,903 under British escort, and 1,720,360 sailed under the escort of the United States Navy.

But that is only half the story. When hostilities ended, that vast army had to be brought back from Europe. For this, very little foreign shipping was available. Of the 1,933,156 Americans returned from November 11, 1918, to the end of September, 1919, the Navy brought home 1,675,733; all other vessels, American and foreign, 257,423. During hostilities we had returned 11,211 sick, wounded, casuals, etc.; some were returned after September, so that the total number brought by the Navy from Europe to America ran well over 1,700,000.

Of the total troop and official passenger movement incident to the war, approximately 4,000,000, the Navy transported more than 2,600,000. Not only did the Navy man and operate the United States transports, but provided the food for this vast army of soldiers en route. And during the entire war period, four-fifths of all the American troops who sailed were guarded by American cruisers, destroyers, and patrol craft.

CARRIED MUNITIONS AS WELL AS MEN

Not only did the Navy transport 2,600,000 men, but operating the Ferry to France it carried millions of tons of munitions, guns, goods, fuel, supplies, and materials to our Army and Navy forces abroad through submarine-infested seas. Six million tons of cargo were carried by Navy vessels from May, 1917, to May, 1918. In addition, 1,500,000 tons of coal were carried overseas or from England to France, and 700,000 tons of fuel oil and gasoline were transported.

THE FLEET THE KAISER BUILT FOR US

More than half a million of the troops that defeated the Germans were transported across the Atlantic in interned German vessels. I sometimes wonder if the Kaiser ever dreamed, when his liners came scurrying into American ports before the war, that he was presenting us with the one thing we needed most, a lot of the finest transports that ever sailed the sea.

That could not happen, according to the Teuton mind. They had figured it all out. If America kept out of the conflict, their ships would be as safe here as in their home ports. If we did enter the war, their crews would damage them so badly that we could not use them. Before ruthless U-boat warfare was declared, Bernstorff had issued his orders, and all the interned vessels were disabled, their engines and machinery smashed.

"Some you may get running in a year; some you can never use," boasted the German crews.

"If America can repair this ship, I will eat my hat," said another. He had not yet tested his digestion by a diet of headgear.

But they, like the Kaiser and Admiral von Holtzendorff, underestimated American ingenuity and enterprise. By using new methods, and keeping at the task day and night, in a few months all these vessels were repaired and in service, carrying troops and supplies.

The German *Vaterland,* rechristened the *Leviathan,* alone carried nearly a hundred thousand troops to Europe. When she was performing such prodigies for us, it interested me to recall an occurrence when this great vessel, the largest afloat, reached New York on its first voyage, not long before the war began. Glorying in the attention it evoked, the *Vaterland's* officers gave a dinner, inviting leading American shipbuilders and engineers, as well as prominent citizens, to view this latest creation in marine construction.

"It is a veritable floating palace for voyagers to Europe," remarked one of its officers, "but that is not the best or most important thing about the *Vaterland.*"

"Well, what is it?" asked a visitor.

"Come below," said he, "and I will show you."

Below went the party, and there they were shown how the whole vessel had been planned so that it could quickly be converted into a carrier for ten thousand soldiers. "In a remarkably short time, if need arises," the officer remarked, "it can be turned into a troop transport."

He was right. We proved it in 1917, not only in regard to the *Vaterland,* but the other Teuton liners. The repair of those vessels was a triumph of ingenuity and engineering skill. After war was declared the *Vaterland* was immediately taken over, and the same day the United States seized ninety-one German merchant vessels in various ports, aggregating 592,195 gross tons, Austrian ships, 40,461 tons—a total of 632,656 tons of shipping placed under the United States flag from these two sources.

SOMETHING UNPRECEDENTED

When the German ships interned in American waters were taken over by our country, an examination by Naval experts showed that the damages to their engines were of such a serious character that it was believed nothing short of renewal of the cylinders would make them available for our needs. But by use of electric welding, a new process, at least a year was saved in getting these ships into service for the transportation of troops to France. Thirty-six were soon repaired and were in operation by the Navy and twenty by the Shipping Board. That they were put in action many months earlier than under the old process was due to Captain E. P. Jessup, engineering officer, and Admiral Burd of the New York Navy Yard.

GERMAN NAMES FOR SHIPS

The naming of German ships, which had been interned and were put to use as transports, intrigued Mrs. Woodrow Wilson, who had been asked to suggest suitable names. As they were German-built, she thought it would be fitting to give them names of patriotic Germans who had loved independence and had fought under Washington in the American Revolution. For example the *Kronprinz Wilhelm* was called the *Von Steuben,* and the *Prinz Eitel Friedrich* was given the name of *De Kalb.* When changes in names were announced, a brief story of the patriots of German ancestry so honored was released to the press. This was one more evidence of appreciation of the devotion of the many Germans in America who had come here to find the blessings of full liberty not enjoyed in the Fatherland.

The naming of ships for patriotic Americans of German blood was in keeping with the policy of the Navy in giving high command to men with German names and Wilson's protest when some legislators proposed that the schools in the United States should be forbidden to teach the German language. That shocked Wilson, who

A STAR PERFORMER.

called for appreciation of German music and German literature while condemning German atrocities and imperialistic rule.

The ships whose names were changed, mostly through the suggestion of Mrs. Wilson, were:

GERMAN NAME	AMERICAN NAME
Vaterland	Leviathan
Kaiser Wilhelm II	Agamemnon
Koenig Wilhelm II	Madawaska
President Lincoln	President Lincoln
President Grant	President Grant
Barbarossa	Mercury
Grosser Kurfurst	Aeolus
Hamburg	Powhatan
Friedrich de Grosse	Huron
Prinzess Irene	Pocahontas
George Washington	George Washington
Martha Washington	Martha Washington
Prinz Eitel Friedrich	DeKalb
Amerika	America
Neckar	Antigone
Cincinnati	Covington
Kronprinzessin Cecelie	Mount Vernon
Prinzess Alice	Princess Matoika
Rhein	Susquehanna
Kronprinz Wilhelm	Von Steuben

It was not easy to get people incensed by the savagery in Germany to differentiate between the German of the Von Steuben type and the Huns. This was made more difficult by such things as I recorded in my Diary (May 1, 1917), the day Mrs. Wilson gave German names to transports:

"I dined with Secretary Wilson who had as his guests the members of the British Labor Commission. They told of the crucifixion of English soldiers by Germans and of the finding of French girls in trenches who had been compelled by German soldiers."

A quarter of a century later under Hitler the world learned that his reign had restored and multiplied the brutality by the Nazis. Totalitarian rule and ruthlessness and immorality are inseparable, as World War II has disclosed.

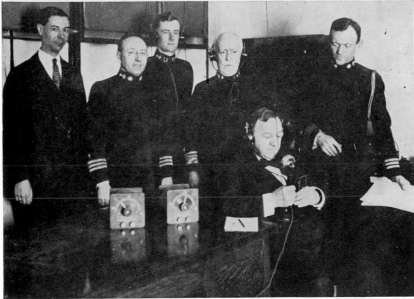

Above, Lafayette Radio Station, France, the most powerful in the world during World War I (The National Archives). *Below,* Secretary of the Navy Daniels sending greetings to President Wilson on board the *U.S.S. George Washington. Standing, left to right,* Haradon Pratt, expert radio aide, Commander S. C. Hooper, Lieutenant A. H. Vanderhoof, Rear Admiral Griffin, Commander Percy W. Foote. *Seated,* Secretary Daniels.

Above, Assistant Secretary of the Navy Franklin D. Roosevelt on his way to review trainees at Navy Radio School (U. S. Navy). *Below*, Lieutenant Commander N. F. Ayer, Commanding Officer, with Sir Montague E. Browning, Vice Admiral and Commander in Chief of British Naval forces in the Western Atlantic and West Indies, with their party, at Navy Radio School (U. S. Navy).

NAVY RADIO GIRDLED THE GLOBE

I F I WERE asked to name the Navy's greatest war contribution
after its service keeping the ferry open to France and ending
the U-boat menace through the courage of the men who manned
the destroyers and constructed the monumental mine barrage, the
answer would be easy. It was the expansion, direction, and use of
the wireless in communications in peace and war. Before the war
I had been intrigued by the possibilities of the wireless and had given
Captain Bullard and Lieutenant Hooper carte blanche in its development. The Navy and Merchant Marine saw in it safety at sea, and
military leaders in war learned to lean on communications as their
strong right arm.

Except for the original Hertz discovery of electromagnetic waves
and Marconi's first conception of their application to practical use
and his invention of the apparatus for producing and detecting radio
waves, the greatest period of advance in radio was from 1913 to
1921, accelerated by the communication demands of the World War.
The United States Navy led in the development. Before the United
States entered the war, Lieutenant S. C. Hooper (now an Admiral)
was sent to Europe as an observer. His report of the value of radio
in war time was so convincing that I ordered a group of officers to
act as a Board of Organization for the United States Radio Service.
It consisted of Captain W. G. Bullard, Lieutenant Commander E. H.
Dodd, and Lieutenant Hooper. On February 20, 1915, I approved
the report which became the backbone of Naval communication.
The pioneer radio beacon was built by the Navy at Point Judith in
Rhode Island in 1916. It automatically transmitted by radio telegraph
warnings to ships from a fixed location.

SOME NAVY FIRSTS

It is of interest that the first remote control of a large radio station
was inaugurated on November 5, 1915, when the control station

controlling the NAA Arlington transmitters was set up and all reception of messages came to the Navy Department.

On November 6, 1915, at 4:10 P.M., I talked by radiophone from my office, wire to NAA, then wireless to Boston Navy Yard. Speaking to Admiral Usher, I gave the following order: "Report as soon as practicable after arrival of the *New York* how soon repairs can be completed." This is believed to be the first Navy Order given over a radio-telephone.

On May 6, 1915, 2:40 P.M., I carried on a conversation with Captain Chandler on the *New Hampshire* in Hampton Roads. This is believed to be the first instance of radiophone work from shore to ship.

The use of radio in the Navy may be said to date from the appointment of the first "wireless officer" in 1912. The first radio control of steering of a Naval unit was designed and applied as a mobile target for the Fleet on the battleship *Iowa,* and shortly radio was protected behind armor. An apparatus developed by the Navy became the pioneer system of commercial broadcasting in 1919. An instrument was developed to locate the enemy by radio and installed on all battleships. This was invaluable during World War I. The first Aircraft Radio Laboratory in the world was established at the Naval Air Station at Pensacola, Florida, in the early days of the Wilson administration and was invaluable in World War I and World War II.

Just before the war the Navy completed a chain of radio stations connecting Washington with all points from Panama to Alaska and Manila and constructed the first Pacific radio circuit ever built. It not only built this vast system on this continent and in the Pacific, but erected in France the most powerful radio station then in existence to which the name La Fayette was given. It was not necessary to say, "La Fayette, we are here," when that station opened. I recall this radiogram:

"Secretary of the Navy:
"This is the first message to be heard around the world and marks a milestone on the road to scientific achievement.
                                        "Lafayette Radio System"

MOST POWERFUL RADIO STATION

Upon the completion and operation of the radio connection with Hawaii, the Navy and the country rejoiced that we were in quick communication with Pearl Harbor. I sent this message:

"Washington, D. C.
September 28, 1917

"Navsta Pearl Harbor.

"Express my gratification to the authorities of Hawaii on this momentous occasion wherein the first exchange of radio messages is made possible between Honolulu and the Atlantic Coast of the United States, also, I congratulate you on the successful completion of the most powerful radio station in the world.

"JOSEPHUS DANIELS"

RADIO IN THE WAR

Upon the outbreak of the war the Navy, upon the President's order of April 6, 1917, took over all private stations and furnished installations in all Naval and shipping board and other ships. Vessels at sea and airships, as well as armies at the front, could be reached almost as easily as if they had been at their docks, and submarine warnings were quickly transmitted.

$43,116 UP TO SIX MILLIONS

Previous to the President's order of April 6, 1917, the Navy, in July, 1915, had taken over the Sayville (N. J.) Radio Station, which was virtually under the control of the German Government (the Telefunken Company), and built after Germany began the war. It was the only direct means of communication with Germany. It was operated under the name of the Atlantic Construction Company. Its value was appraised at $43,116. The Navy at once spent $98,430 on improvements. After the war, the Telefunken Company presented a claim to Uncle Sam for five million dollars for the use of patents and upon the novel theory that during the pre-war exigencies its earnings justified such valuation. Later it abandoned that absurd figure and asked war claims for $900,000. In July, 1931, the War Claims Arbiter awarded the Telefunken Company $5,000,-000 and interest, making a total of $6,875,342.19 as stated in a "Memorandum for the Secretary" signed by J. Frank Staley, Acting Head of the Admiralty Division.

Admiral Hooper, for the Navy, an Army Colonel, and others testified for the Government. Hooper said:

"After all our testimony and opposition the company was given five million dollars plus two or three million dollars interest. This, though the total assets of the company was $283,254.16. In my opinion, it would not have been possible to find a purchaser on July 2, 1921, who would have been willing to pay in excess of the value $43,116 fixed by appraisers in 1918. The Telefunken Company claimed that if we hadn't taken the German radio patents, it would have dominated the sale of Broadcast Receivers and Transmitters in the United States after broadcasting started. We claimed that broadcasting was merely a myth or dream of that in 1919, and the Germans would have gladly sold out for a song. But the Judge knew he had to give them the money 'to prime the pump.' So he did."

Thus was Uncle Sam mulcted out of millions of dollars by a company that had played Germany's game.

GOVERNMENT-OWNED WIRELESS

The Navy having demonstrated the efficiency of government-owned and operated wireless in the days preceding and during the war, in November (1917) I brought to the Cabinet Meeting a request of private companies to construct wireless in South American countries. Instead of approving I suggested that we should seek arrangements with those governments to the end that all wireless in Pan America should be publicly owned and operated for the public good and not by private companies for profit. Wilson approved and directed Lansing to take the matter up with diplomats from the Pan American countries.

As showing the trend for government ownership of public utilities, I quote my Diary on a meeting of the Council of National Defense (October, 1917):

"Logic is: Communication is a governmental function and government must own, control radio, waterways, telegraph and telephone."

Every morning during the war I found on my desk a copy of the only secret daily ever gotten out. It contained everything sent out not only by the Allies but also by the Germans. One dispatch that amused me was picked up from Berlin (November 10) saying that U-boat crews went out in the last days only by offer of bribes.

Seeing that the Naval experts with Uncle Sam's money had developed radio, I early felt that our government ought not to make the mistake of making a present of this priceless means of communication in war and peace to private interests for gain. I recalled how Uncle Sam financed the sending of messages by wire and then unwisely let private monopoly control it. I was later to learn that after the Navy Laboratory had perfected radar, its production was turned over to private companies. The Navy should have held it inviolate.

The genesis of radar, whose success in making air and sea navigation entirely continuous and fool-proof regardless of night or weather, was in the Navy Laboratory established on the Potomac in 1917 upon urgent recommendation of the Edison Navy Aviation Board. The first radio set was developed there by Dr. A. Hoyt Taylor. After radar had saved a ship fighting the Japanese in the Coral Sea, the men streamed down to the radar room to pet and kiss the set. Microwave radar in an airplane changed the antisubmarine warfare to an offensive, Dexter Masters says, and adds, "Radar can penetrate any amount of overcast fog or smoke, which light can't do, and this is its primary distinction. Overcast and night don't exist in the world of radar, which can see through both to guide a plane 25,000 feet up to a spot on the earth's surface many miles away."

With the end of the war private interests, which had been making experiments in wireless, under the cry of "no government in business" resolved to oust Uncle Sam from control and make fortunes for their corporations. At the same time the British were secretly attempting to purchase the patents of the General Electric Company on the Alexanderson transmitter, which would enable England to maintain dominance in international radio. The General Electric Company would have accepted the British offer but for the prompt action of Commander Hooper, who recommended Naval opposition. I protested and the deal was not consummated. Afterwards Admiral Bullard took steps that avoided international entanglements.

A GOVERNMENT MONOPOLY

Realizing that Uncle Sam must control radio in war, I strongly believed it should be a government monopoly, preferably directed by the Navy which had developed it as the best world system of communication. I caused a bill to be drawn up to give Uncle Sam the same relation to wireless messages that he possessed as to mail. My proposal drew opposition from the companies which had been making experiments and owned some patents. They looked to a bonanza from radio if they could force the retirement of the Navy from the field. They didn't want the "just compensation" I offered. They wanted big returns for what they called "risk capital," but as the Navy had spent millions to develop the value of radio, the term "risk" was not correct. They decided to fight. With the approval of President Wilson I addressed a letter (July 19, 1919) to the Speaker of the House urging the passage of the measure that was before the Naval Affairs Committee authorizing "the Use of Radio Stations Under the Control of the Navy Department," in which I said that I regarded the enactment of that measure as "vitally essential" and gave my reasons for this view after reciting a comprehensive history of development of wireless by the Navy with Government funds.

The Committee on Merchant Marine, dominated by men whose creed was "no government in business," would have wished to turn over the transmission of mail to private interests if they had lived when Benjamin Franklin was Postmaster General (Poor Richard was wiser). When I appeared before this committee, I found an atmosphere of antagonism both in the committee and from those who had been experimenting and who had obtained some patents which they deemed valuable. One of them treated me as if I were a pickpocket trying to filch his wealth—wealth he anticipated and afterwards acquired when the Navy lost. I told the committee that since the government must have a high-power radio system for the control of the fleet and governmental business, it would be a needless duplication of capital and effort to permit private stations to operate. I, therefore, urged that the wireless communication be a governmental function, owned and operated by the government. I pointed out that the great bulk of the expenditure for the development of wireless for the United States had been made by the Navy. I suggested that the government return to those private parties such expenditures as they had made in wireless and pay a fair price for their rights and usable patents, and all wireless should be owned by our government and controlled by the communications division of the Navy. But my proposal was received with no favor by the committee.

BEST WIRELESS MESSAGE

During the war I sent and received thousands of wireless messages, and after the war communicated at sea with a ship in mid-ocean (it seemed miraculous); but the one wireless I sent that gave me the greatest thrill and caused most happiness to millions was this:

"VIA ARLINGTON BROADCAST   ARC. 18011
"GOVT. ALNAV #174—
"The signing of the Armistice makes this the greatest day for our country since the signing of the Declaration of Independence. For the world, there has been no day so momentous for Liberty. I send greetings and congratulations to all in the naval establishment at home and abroad. The test of war found the Navy ready and fit, with every man on his toes. Every day, all the men in the service have given fresh proof of devotion, loyalty and efficiency. In America, and in all other countries, people have applauded naval initiative and naval resourcefulness. As we rejoice in the victory for every principle that caused us to enter the war, let us be thankful that when the American people needed a Navy, we were ready with all facilities and were rapidly creating all others that could be employed.

"With warm appreciation for the perfect team work and splendid coöperation."

"JOSEPHUS DANIELS
"Secretary of the Navy"

F.D.R. MADE RADIO HISTORY

"It is against Navy regulations, but I will O.K. it. Go ahead." That permission by Franklin Roosevelt made radio history, according to Bill Stern. He tells how Andy White determined that the prize-fight between Jack Dempsey and George Carpentier in 1921 should be heard all over the world. An officer of the General Electric Company, which had built for the Navy a broadcasting set that could be heard all over the world, agreed to let Andy White use it for the big fight. But he didn't get Navy permission. Two days before the fight, it was found out that their new broadcasting set was to be used without permission. The Navy officers said: "No, we have spent money to get it for the Navy, and its first use cannot be to broadcast a prize-fight. Emphatically NO!"

But Andy White knew a dynamic Assistant Secretary who loved innovations and stunts. He appealed to Franklin Roosevelt, who said: "Mr. White, anybody with your nerve deserves a break. It is against Navy regulations, but I'll O.K. it. Go ahead."

Part Four

———————————

"THE NAVY WON THE WAR"

XI

THE FAR-FLUNG NAVY

WHAT THE NAVY DID

M Y DEDICATION of *Our Navy at War,* to the Six Hundred Thousand Men who served in the United States Navy and Marine Corps in World War I, summed up thus the Navy's war achievements:

"Manning more than two thousand vessels—
Operating with Allied Navies from the
Arctic to the Adriatic—
Transporting troops and supplies across the Atlantic—
Protecting ships from attack and destruction—
Driving off and defeating the murderous submarines,
You made safe the seas, and
Kept open the Road to France, so that,
Of all the vast Army sent overseas,
Not one soldier on an American troop-ship
Lost his life on the way to France.

"Fighting with the Army, your comrades,
The Soldiers of the Sea, won fame in
Hard-fought battles that saved Paris,
Drove back the German hordes, and
Won for Humanity Complete and Glorious Victory.

"In recognition of your splendid service, your dauntless deeds, this work is dedicated by one who was sometime your commander and always your shipmate."

This condensation supplements the stories of some of the strategy and contributions dealt with more fully in other chapters. In addition, the history would be far from complete if there should be omitted in succinct form some of the things that the Navy did in those days when it won tributes from its allies and the gratitude of the American people. Of the Navy's contribution General Pershing, Commander of the American Expeditionary Forces, said:

"We fully realize that had it not been for the Navy, who kept watch and guard night and day over our transport fleet, the American effort in France would never have been successful. The Navy's assistance was whole-hearted and arduous, and was always given in a most generous spirit of coöperation."

"When I was in the United States before the war, I heard severe criticism of your Navy," said Lord Reading, British Ambassador, to me in 1918, "but upon my return I find it is the nation's darling and everybody's praising its forehandedness and efficiency. What have you done to get orchids instead of brick-bats?"

I told the Ambassador that upon his previous visit he had been entertained by rich Americans who had investments in steel, oil, and distilleries, and I had stopped their profiteering and, strange to say, they didn't like it. There had then been no test of naval efficiency, no publicity of the preparedness, and many good people had been misled by the propaganda inspired by selfish interests. "But now," I said, "you have found the critics are proud of the Navy and there are no more knockers in the face of the great service our Naval personnel is rendering."

CINDERELLAS OF THE FLEET

To the Corfu detachment of sub-chasers belongs the honor, among others, of participating in the biggest Adriatic battle of the war after America entered. This occurred at an Austrian port, Durazzo. On September 2, 1918, that port, together with the merchant shipping and men-of-war at anchor there, were bombarded by the Italian and British cruisers which, were screened against submarine attack by destroyers and American sub-chasers.

The submarine chaser fleet was under the command of Captain Lyman Cotten, whose early death after the war was a serious loss. The chasers at Corfu were under the command of Captain R. H. Leigh, and a Mobile Barrage Base was established at Otranto. We called the chaser "The Cinderella of the Fleet" for when she arrived, she was the belle of the ball. They were particularly valuable as "listeners." The submarine detection devices with which they were equipped were vastly superior to those previously in use. We built 440 chasers.

Paraphrasing "The Spider and the Fly," a chaser-seaman wrote:

"Won't you come into my area?" said the Chaser to the Sub,
"I'll treat you just as kindly as I would a tiger cub;
I will listen to your motors, I will catch you without fail,
And then I promise I'll put some salt right on your tail."

THE SUCCESS OF THE CONVOY SYSTEM

From the beginning the convoy system was a great success. It was put into effect gradually and by the end of July, 1917, more than 10,000 ships had been convoyed by the Navy and only ½ of one per cent of them were lost. When the convoy system was applied to the Mediterranean (July, 1917), Gibraltar became the gateway for more traffic than any other port in the world. It was the focus for the great routes to and from the East through the Mediterranean. Under the direction of Admiral Niblack, many convoys were met as far as five hundred miles from the coast and their safety guarded. During the eighteen months when American vessels escorted convoys through the war zone, 183 attacks were made upon them by submarines; twenty-four submarines were damaged and two known to be destroyed. A total of 18,256 ships were escorted carrying vast quantities of freight to the Allies.

THE ARMED GUARD

The first men of the armed forces to see service in the war were the armed guard put on merchant ships before we entered the war. They had more than two hundred encounters with submarines. First in service, they were first in sacrifice. The 384 merchant ships armed made 227 attacks on submarines and only twenty-nine ships carrying armed guards were torpedoed and sunk. They were the sole protection of American shipping until the convoy system was adopted. In many encounters the men showed the highest courage and sacrifice.

THE HALF-WAY HOUSE

Early after we entered the war, the possession of the Azores by the Allies was seen to be important. I sent American ships to Porto Delgado, and on July 4 the *Orion* turned her guns on the German U-boats which had slunk into the harbor thinking they would have no opposition. Our Navy remained in occupation until after the Armistice. Admiral Dunn, who was in command, said:

"The occupation of the Azores is of great strategic value. As our convoy routes passed north and south of the island, if it had been in possession of the enemy, it would have seriously interfered with the successful transport across the ocean of troops and supplies."

COAST GUARD WINS DISTINCTION

With the declaration of war the Coast Guard automatically came under the Navy. It ought to have such status in peace as well. Franklin Roosevelt and I hoped that would follow the Armistice, but Secretary of the Treasury, Carter Glass, was too quick for us and had it returned to the Treasury while I was in Hawaii. No department in Washington surrenders anything voluntarily.

The ships and men of the Coast Guard won distinction. The *Tampa* was destroyed by a torpedo; the *Wellington* was lost. Captain John A. Midgett and crew of the Chicamacomico Station, N. C., were given high commendation for going through a sea of blazing oil to rescue the crew of the *St. Milo*. This was only one of like actions beyond the call of duty.

ANSWER TO THE SEVENTY-FIVE-MILE GUN

In March, 1918, the German long-range guns bombarded Paris; twenty-one shells, weighing about 250 pounds each, fell during the week and seventy-five persons were killed and ninety injured. It began on Good Friday. As the worshippers were at prayer in the Church of St. Gervais, a shell crashed through the buildings and exploded. For five months Paris endured that menace.

The answer to the menace was a fourteen-inch gun operated by the Navy. It got into action, and when the big guns arrived the Germans stopped shelling Paris, though the French had started moving the archives from Paris. The operation of these big guns justified their construction and use.

In 1917 the Bureau of Ordnance had suggested that the Navy build fourteen-inch guns and mount them on trains in France; Admiral Earle felt they might turn the tide of battle. These guns threw a 1400-pound projectile 42,000 yards or nearly twenty-five miles. Five of these immense railway batteries were built at a cost of three million dollars and sent to France. Franklin Roosevelt believed so strongly that the Navy could render great service with these big guns that he planned to resign as Assistant Secretary, don the Navy uniform, and go with Admiral Plunkett to France to direct in the operations. I was so intrigued by their possibilities that I went to the Baldwin Locomotive Works while they were under construction, and the enthusiasm of Admiral Earle and Samuel Vauclain, president of the Baldwin Locomotive Works, was so contagious that I shared their enthusiasm for the undertaking.

"I heard a good story about the big fourteen-inch Naval guns in France," said President Wilson at a meeting of the Cabinet (February 25) on his return from Paris. "They created a great sensation as they were carried about the country to the battle front. One man said: 'They kills everybody within one hundred miles and hunts up the next of kin and kills all of them.'"

DREADNAUGHTS WITH THE BRITISH FLEET

Shortly after we entered the war we proffered as many dreadnaughts to serve in European waters as the British Admiralty thought could operate with their fleet. At that time the chief enemy was the U-boat. We sent destroyers and small craft to pursue them. The British after the Battle of Jutland in order to preserve a "fleet in being" protected their ships in Scapa Flow and both navies agreed that large fleets were not needed at that time. One reason for keeping our dreadnaughts in American waters in the early days of the war was that all the oil was needed for the ships in the submarine chase and for the Army. However, there was never any certainty that the German fleet would not try conclusions again after Jutland, and later in the war it was decided to send a division of dreadnaughts to coöperate with the British Grand Fleet. These dreadnaughts were designated as the Sixth Battle Squadron. The Germans never came out and they had no real battle role, but our dreadnaughts were attacked six times by submarines without damage.

I recall that when the General Board recommended this cruise they added the recommendation of a certain able Naval officer to command the battleship division. When the recommendation reached me, I wrote on it, "Approved, except that Admiral Hugh Rodman be put in command of the Division." Some time afterwards Admiral Badger, Chairman of the General Board, asked, "Would you mind telling the Board why you did not name the officer we recommended and substituted Rodman?" I replied:

"The officer you recommended is one of the most learned in the Navy, but I did not think his experience afloat, and his lack of the spirit of comradeship, made him the ideal man for that service."

"The reason I asked you the question was because all the members of the General Board agreed that you were wise and that Rodman was the man who ought to have been placed in command," remarked the Chairman.

The American dreadnaughts which went over first were the flagship *New York,* commanded by Captain E. L. Beach; the *Texas,* Captain Victor Blue; the *Wyoming,* Captain H. A. Wiley, afterward Captain H. H. Christy; the *Arkansas,* Captain W. H. G. Bullard, afterward Captain L. R. de Steiguer; the *Florida,* Captain Thomas Washington, afterward Captain M. M. Taylor; and the *Delaware,* Captain A. H. Scales. Captain Andy Long was on this duty also.

Later in the war another division was sent over, commanded by Admiral Thomas S. Rogers, and was composed of the *Utah,* Captain F. B. Bassett; the *Nevada,* Captain W. C. Cole; and the *Oklahoma,* Captain C. B. McVay. These had their base on Bantry Bay, Ireland, ready to oppose any German cruisers which might threaten shipping in the waters to the south of Ireland or England and on routes to the ports of Northern France.

These American ships and the British were truly, as they were called, "comrades of the mist." Their service was highly esteemed and at the conclusion of the war Admiral Sir David Beatty, the British Commander-in-Chief, in an address to the Americans aboard the flagship paid high tribute to the officers and men aboard the battleships. He said that he, "had certain misgivings as to when and how the Germans might attack," but he added, "when the Sixth Battle Squadron became a part of the Grand Fleet I knew then that the Germans would throw up their hands. American ships were the "straw that broke the camel's back."

RODMAN'S SHIPS LEAD

When U. S. battleships arrived in the North Sea under Admiral Rodman's command, the Commander-in-Chief, Admiral Beatty, ordered a rendezvous of the combined fleet at a certain time and place. When the day arrived for going to sea to execute these orders, a terrific gale and snowstorm took place. The navigation in the vicinity of Scapa Flow is difficult in the fairest weather, the channels

MEMBERS OF THE NAVAL CONSULTING BOARD

Left to right, Thomas A. Edison, Hudson Maxim, W. R. Whitney (in background), and W. L. Saunders, marching in Preparedness Parade in New York City. (I. N. R.).

The first women ever to wear Navy uniforms. In World War I, without Congressional authority, Secretary of the Navy Daniels enrolled thousands of women as Yeomen (F). He also caused women to be enrolled in the Marines. *Above,* Yeomen (F) at U. S. Naval Station, New Orleans. *Below,* Yeoman (F) at Navy Yard, Portsmouth (both Official Photos, U. S. Navy).

are narrow and tortuous, the currents are strong and there is always grave danger of running on the rocks in these treacherous currents. To handle ships in these channels in a blinding snowstorm with a howling gale puts the commanding officers to the severest test of their skill and ability as seamen. It was the dangers of this kind in the North Sea that made captains get old before their time and the beards of admirals turn gray. With Rodman, however, orders were orders, and regardless of the storm and snow and heavy seas, he was on the scene of the rendezvous with his division of battleships ready for a fight or a drill. His was the only division that arrived on time, and it is said that a little note bearing the signature of Beatty to his Flag Commanders carried the following message:

"On a certain day a rendezvous was ordered in the North Sea. The Commander-in-Chief painfully regrets to say that the only division which arrived promptly at the time and place designated was that of the U. S. battleships."

Needless to say this little billet-doux put the British commanding officers very much on their mettle, and the Commander-in-Chief never had occasion to complain of such tardiness afterwards.

During all his time of service with the British Fleet, Admiral Rodman always maintained the American individuality of himself and of the ships under his command; but he none-the-less heartily and loyally obeyed the orders of Admiral Beatty and so convinced him of his willingness to undertake any task and perform any duties with the ships under his command as to win great affection and admiration of Admiral Beatty and of the British Commanders.

TWO OF ADMIRAL RODMAN'S STORIES

Rodman won great popularity and the King evidenced admiration for him. One of the most popular pictures about Rodman's fleet in British waters showed Rodman, Beatty, Sims, and the King standing on the bridge of a ship looking toward the coast of Scotland. They were all laughing hilariously. I knew that Rodman must be telling them an off-color story and so I preserved the picture and when I saw him I said, "Admiral, what improper story were you telling the King and the others in that picture?" He said, "We were looking at the Edinburgh Castle and the King pointed to a portion of it saying, 'Queen Mary was confined there.' I asked, 'By what suitor?' " Rodman laughed, and then said, "I did not know when I asked that question that I was referring to a relative of the King."

Another of Rodman's good stories was of an occasion when he was visiting at Hopeton overseas, and was introduced to a certain lady. He said he understood her to be Lady Linlithgow or something like that. He did not catch the name and called her successively Lady Lithograph, Lady Linotype and Lady Linoleum. Finally seeing he did not get her name right, the lady said, "Call me Mary," and Mary she was all that evening.

TRIBUTE TO AMERICANS

On the departure of Admiral Rodman's fleet after the Armistice, Admiral Sir David Beatty, paying high tribute to the officers and men, said:

> "There is not much that I have to say, but it comes from the heart, not only my heart, but the hearts of all your comrades of the Grand Fleet. I want to thank you, Admiral Rodman and all in your magnificent squadron, for the wonderful coöperation and loyalty and the assistance you have given in every duty.... The disappointment that the Grand Fleet was not able to strike their blow for freedom of the world is counteracted by the fact that it was their prestige alone that brought about this achievement. ...
>
> "I congratulate you upon having been present upon a day which is unsurpassed in the naval history of the world."
>
> "As somebody said the other day: 'The fighting is now over, the writing is now going to begin.' "

He was a prophet!

XII

THE NAVY THAT FLIES

T HE STORY OF THE Navy that flies in World War I foreshadowed the immensely larger place aviation was to take in World War II. Though most military leaders in the early part of 1917 regarded aviation as little more than the eyes of the Fleet, there were those who even then foresaw that success in war would more and more depend on aviation. From my first flight in 1913 I advanced aviation in the Navy in spite of small appropriations and the absorption in big ships. The first of the armed forces of the United States to reach France were 130 Naval aviators under the command of Lieutenant Kenneth W. Whiting. This group sailed on the *Neptune* and arrived at St. Nazaire on June 9, just fifteen miles from Quiberon Bay, where, on November 30, 1777, the first foreign salute to the American flag was received by the *Ranger,* commanded by John Paul Jones. Nineteen stations were established along the coast of France, and the Navy later had five stations in Ireland and two in England. Before the war ended, the Navy Aviation Corps reached 40,000, equipped with 1,170 flying boats, 695 sea planes, 262 land planes, ten free balloons, and fifteen dirigibles. We aided Italy in fighting the Austrians, with our training school at Lake Bolsena and an operating station at Porto Corsini, on the Adriatic, across from the Austrian naval base at Pola.

VALUE OF COÖPERATION ON LAND, SEA, AND AIR PROVED

Our aviators flew across the Alps and the Adriatic Sea; they patrolled the waters along the French coast, protecting the vast Allied shipping going into and out of the French ports, and guarding the convoys of American troops, munitions, and supplies. Our Northern Bombing Group bombed the German submarine bases and ammunition and supply depots in Belgium. Operating with their British comrades, our aviators flew over Heligoland Bight, almost within sight of the home bases of the German fleet. They took part in the North Sea patrol in connection with the movements of the British

Grand Fleet, and those assigned to the British stations at Felixstowe and Portsmouth had a part in the famous Dover Patrol that kept clear the road from England to France.

The chief task of aviation was patrolling the long coast lines, watching for submarines, and furnishing aerial escort for the convoy of troops, supply, and merchant ships to and from European ports. They sank two submarines and damaged others, downed many enemy planes. No surface craft convoy protected by American Naval craft was successfully attacked by the enemy. The value of the co-operation between aircraft and ships, so signally in evidence in World War II, was demonstrated in many instances. The story of the daring and efficiency of the Naval aviator is one that stands high in the annals of that war.

BUILT AIRPLANE FACTORY

On April 6, when war was declared, though in the preceding months more Naval planes had been provided, there was need for accelerating construction. The few private aviation plants could not supply the pressing need and the Navy in July, 1917, began the construction of an airplane factory at the Philadelphia Navy Yard. It covered forty acres and the value of the planes built before the Armistice was five million dollars. The master mind in that first general plant was Admiral David Taylor. Under the management of Naval Constructor Coburn, this plant set standards for private plants. It continued to make Navy planes as long as I was in office and I recommended its enlargement and continuation so that it could fashion all Naval aircraft. But when Harding became President, the making of war weapons by the government came to a halt and the Navy became dependent upon private construction at increased cost. The plea of profiteers that won was the selfish slogan, "No Government in Business," and the Navy's dependence on private contractors with no real competition cost Uncle Sam many millions of dollars and made possible foreign governments' obtaining inventions and improvements the Navy had brought about.

FIRST LINE OF OFFENSE

I recommended that Congress establish a Bureau of Aeronautics. Anticipating such action, the Army and the Navy created an unofficial joint aeronautical board, and support was given to the Naval

Advisory Committee for Aeronautics. Recommendations were made for the enlargement of the Aviation Base at Pensacola.

In my last annual report I wrote: "Naval aviation will, in the not distant future, possess an importance second only to that of ships."

If I had been able to look into the future I would have said: "... more important than ships or any type of engines of war."

HELIUM GAS

During the war the Navy had developed the production of helium gas and in my last report I recommended its expansion for larger production. At an early Cabinet meeting after the President returned from France there was discussion of a bill which I had caused to be introduced in Congress to prevent any helium from going out of the country. The oil men were very much opposed to that bill, saying that unless they could sell to foreign countries they could not afford to operate because the United States used so little. They had concessions in Mexico, but Carranza had stipulated that if any foreign government had any interest in the concessions they would be forefeited. Therefore, the oil men were very anxious to be permitted to sell helium abroad. The President agreed with me that all helium should be retained in the United States.

Years later in the Roosevelt administration an attempt was made by Germany to obtain helium from this country, and some officials in the State Department favored granting the permission. But Secretary Ickes put his foot down on it strongly and was able to prevent it because Congress had given the Secretary of the Interior the power to control the export of helium.

DID NOT SEE UNITY

At that time the Army sought to separate all "aviation" from land bases "which shall be controlled by the Army, and the Navy shall control all aerial aviation attached to the fleet." The perfect unity of aviation in World War II by all military branches had not yet been foreseen by military leaders.

A MARINE'S BRILLIANT EXPLOIT

While combats in the air were comparatively young in 1917-18 as compared with the victories of airmen in World War II, the history of the exploits of aviators in World War I showed that they pioneered the great advances that distinguish 1941-45. Aviators then did not blast cities and open the way for the landing of millions of troops, but the valor of aviators in the Army, Navy, and Marine Corps helped win the war and brought them glory. It also inspired the vastly greater victories in World War II.

Here is the lead to a typical story that illustrates as brilliant an exploit as flying has seen; it was printed in detail in two full columns of the London *Morning Post* (August 31, 1918):

"First Lieutenant Edwin G. Chamberlain, of the U.S. Marine Corps, has performed wonderful feats as an aviator at the front. He took part in a fight with twelve German planes, smashed five of them while his own machine was badly crippled, shot down two others, enabled his British companions to escape, swooped out of the air and charged headlong into a detachment of Hun infantry, routed it, 'bluffed' his captors with a fake grenade, took one of them prisoner, rescued a wounded French soldier, swam a river under fire while he drove the prisoner before him and carried the other, finally landed right side up with both trophies in the Allied lines—and then wouldn't give his name for fear of being scolded."

A major of the British Army said: "If the Yank had been attached to my squadron, I would have recommended him for the V.C."

TEST BETWEEN DREADNAUGHT AND AIRPLANE

One of my last acts as Secretary of the Navy was to direct a test of whether dreadnaughts can be sunk by bombs from the air. That question was hotly debated in the early days of 1921. In conjunction with the Secretary of War, the Joint Board of the Army and Navy was directed to make the test at Hampton Roads at the historic place of the inconclusive dual between the *Monitor* and the *Merrimac*.

In 1920 the Navy tried experiments bombing the *Indiana,* an antiquated battleship. But the *Indiana* was anchored, had no anti-aircraft guns and there was no fight. The experiments were primarily to determine what destructive effect airplane bombs would have, exploding on a ship. Bombs of various sizes were placed on the deck and exploded one at a time. Some of these, of course, caused considerable damage, as they were loaded with heavy explosives. But the ship did not sink until other bombs, placed under water, blew up with such force that several seams of the ship's bottom were opened. As to the ability of airplanes in flight to hit a vessel, I ventured the prediction then that the time might come when Naval constructors would give all their energies to plan for giant ships of the skies, and then I asked (1921): "But who can venture to say the offensive against air warfare will not be as effective an offensive as has been perfected against every method of warfare since time began?"

"NOT A SINGLE PLANE" CANARD

Daniel Willard, Chairman of the Advisory Committee of the Council of National Defense, wrote me (March, 1921):

"When I hear critics say we spent six hundred millions or a billion dollars and did not produce a *single plane,* the reply ought to be made that the Government's program did not contemplate the production of a *single plane,* but rather the production of 50,000 planes within the shortest space of time. The aircraft program was laid out on a basis sufficiently broad to definitely terminate the conflict. No one, speaking for the Administration, has ever made this matter as clear as it ought to be."

PREPONDERATING ASSAULT

Destruction from the air in World War II was the offensive that terrified the Nazis. In 1917 Brand Whitlock, Ambassador at Brussells wrote to Washington:

"Belgian, English and French officers all write that if America can send over preponderating squadrons of aircraft the scales of battle can be quickly turned. It would terrify Germans to see the air black with American flying machines."

In 1918 we were making ready to do that very thing in overwhelming number when the Armistice was signed ten months before any military leader thought possible. Aviators helped the Army, and Wilson's leaflets broadcast in Germany, hastened the end.

XIII

MAKING SEAMEN OUT OF LANDSMEN

WHEN WAR WAS declared, the Navy was ready with plans approved by Congress to train quickly all the men needed for the great undertaking. Largely the work of Admiral Victor Blue, a Naval Reserve Act enabled the Navy to convert civilian youths into capable seamen and officers. Training stations in all parts of the country were filled as soon as war was declared. There was never a minute from April 6, 1917, to November 11, 1918, when a ship was ready to sail that officers and men were not ready to man the ship, and this was true not only of fighting Naval craft but of troop and merchant ships.

Upon the outbreak of war—even before—old training stations were enlarged and new ones established in both oceans and on the Gulf, and the station at Great Lakes became the largest in the world.

During the war the Navy expanded its personnel until when the Armistice was signed, the Navy contained 217,256 regulars and 271,571 reserve enlisted men, total 488,827 men, and 10,489 regular officers and 20,706 reserve officers—total officers and men 520,022.

High tribute was paid by Sir Eric Geddes, First Lord of the British Admiralty, who, deeply impressed in a visit to America during the World War, said:

> "The dauntless determination which the United States has displayed in creating a large body of seamen out of landsmen is one of the most striking accomplishments of the war. Had it not been effectively done, one would have thought it impossible, and words fail me to express admiration of the feat undertaken and accomplished by your Navy Department, of which Mr. Daniels is the civic chief."

A SLACKERS' PARADISE

Within a few days after the declaration of war, I was besieged by Congressmen and men of influence to enroll with commission rank sons or favorites who had no experience that qualified them for

the duties of a Naval officer. I declined and gave commissions only
to men of demonstrated qualifications. That was not popular with
those who wished to wear gold braid without earning it. It was
necessary to give authority outside of Washington to make enroll-
ments. I soon learned that some Commandants of Naval districts
were giving commissions to young men who had never been to sea.
I therefore sent this telegram to the District Commandants:

"April 10, 1917
    "Suspend enrollment of officers in Class Four until further
orders.

"DANIELS"

At the same time I ordered them to come to Washington. As one
glaring example, the son of a mayor in a big city with a Navy Yard
was given a commission as Lieutenant Commander and assigned
shore duty usually performed by a $1,200 clerk. I gave orders that
applicants should be enrolled in the ranks and no reserve commissions given until by service they had demonstrated fitness for
advancement. I told the officers that the enrollment of reserve officers
of favorites would cause the Navy to be called "the Slacker's
Paradise."

As one illustration of how some enrolling officers "let down the
bars" when I had declined to give a Congressman's secretary a commission, I recall that some days later the Congressman said to me:
"You remember the young man I asked you to commission as an
officer and you said it could not be done until after he had enlisted
and had won it by service?" I remembered. He then said: "The
young man has his commission and is wearing the gold braid. Somebody can give commissions in the Navy if the Secretary does not."
The young man had gone to one of the Naval districts and had
been enrolled. Worse than that, two sons of a very rich man, denied
enrollment in this country, got to London, where they were given
commissions, stuck close to their desks, never went to sea, and
after the war strutted as heroic officers who had served in the war
zone. I had supposed all Naval officers would be keen to enroll only
those who were fit. Most of them insisted upon proof of Naval
knowledge, but a few forgot their duty to the Navy. No man
should wear Uncle Sam's gold braid except by going through the
procedure that makes him efficient.

THE PATRIOTIC SPIRIT OF YOUTH

Such desire for favor was the exception. As a rule the youngsters were ready for any kind of duty. This verse, current at all training stations, showed the good-nature of the youths:

"I never thought I'd be a gob—
You see, dad owns a bank;
I thought at least I'd get a job
Above a captain's rank.
But woe to me, alack! alas!
They've put me in white duds;
They don't quite comprehend my class—
They've got me peeling spuds."

The spirit of most of the youth who hurried from school and college in 1917 was evidenced by this story:

"Captain, I'd like to get a transfer," said a youth to his commanding officer. The captain was surprised for the young man had rendered excellent service in the armed guards and on the cargo transport.

"What is the trouble with your present duty?" asked the captain.

"Well, sir," the young man replied, "I've been going across on merchantmen. I have been torpedoed three times, but I'd like to get on a destroyer or a submarine chaser where I can see a little real action."

VISITORS AT GREAT LAKES

Not only did the First Lord of the British Admiralty visit Great Lakes, but there was welcome for Theodore Roosevelt, who had been Assistant Secretary of the Navy up to the time he resigned to organize the Rough Riders and, as Commander-in-Chief in the White House, had given a great impulse in strengthening the Navy before 1913 and in honor of whose birthday the celebration of Navy Day is held. There was welcome, too, for Secretary Daniels and Assistant Secretary Franklin Roosevelt, who visited it often during World War I.

SPIRIT OF THE WEST

During the campaigns for the selling of Liberty Bonds, I found, on a speaking engagement in Chicago, that not in any seaport was there quite the enthusiasm for the Navy as in the Middle West. On one of my visits when I was to speak I declared that, "It is appropriate that the Secretary of the Navy speak in Chicago for here is the Naval center of the world. The Navy is stimulated by the 'I Can Do It' spirit of the West."

It was on this visit that a prominent Chicago businessman learned that the spirit of America, so much in evidence at Chicago, was found equally in what he regarded as the less progressive South. My train was late from Washington when I arrived in Chicago en route to the Great Lakes Training Station to review a hundred thousand sailors. We then made the trip on a special car with the Governor and other distinguished citizens, including J. Ogden Armour, who from the first had been an ardent supporter of Captain William A. Moffett, Commandant of the Great Lakes Training Station. En route to the station Mr. Armour asked me:

"Is there any naval training station as adequate and which has given you so many well-trained seamen as Great Lakes?"

I told him there was not.

"Is there any officer of the Navy with a greater spirit of enterprise and efficiency than Captain Moffett?"

I told him there was not.

Then he gave me a Chamber of Commerce speech about the breezy West; how when America wanted anything done, and well done, we must look to the Imperial West of which he thought Chicago was the hub. He returned to Captain Moffett, giving him the highest praise, and said:

"Of course you know, Mr. Secretary, no man could have had the enterprise to carry out the enlargement and efficiency of the Great Lakes Training Station unless he were a real Westerner. That's why Moffett has done such great things. He has the blood of the expanding West in his veins."

I asked, "Mr. Armour, do you know where Moffett was born and raised?"

"No," he said, "but somewhere either in Illinois or the adjacent Western States. You can tell that by his spirit and by what he is accomplishing."

I almost floored him when I informed him that Captain Moffett was born in the progressive, militant, up-and-doing Western City of Charleston, South Carolina! It stunned him, and for a time he was what we would say in Southern parlance "flabbergasted." He thought I had made some mistake, that no such breezy, enterprising man as Moffett could come out of old Charleston. I had to have proof to convince him; so I turned to Moffett—the company all listening and most of them as surprised as Armour—and asked:

"Moffett, where were you born?"

He confirmed what I had said by replying: "Charleston, South Carolina."

Not only did Chicago go all out for everything the Navy wanted in military ways and in true Western hospitality, but its people coöperated in every request of the Navy Department. For example: There had been complaints about the immoral and liquor conditions in Chicago and a committee had been appointed to investigate. I took time out to investigate and to confer with Chicago citizens and obtained from all the hotel-keepers in Chicago a promise to organize their employees in anti-liquor squads and see that rooms assigned to men in the service were not accessible to immoral women.

SAVING MANPOWER

When steam replaced sailing ships, the country was told that it would result in needing fewer men to man the ships. When electricity came in vogue, the prediction of reduced complements on ships was made. One of the arguments for the introduction of oil to replace coal, in addition to a cleaner ship, was that fewer men would be needed. Most officers were keen to try the new but slow to part with the old. President Theodore Roosevelt in advocating big ships in 1907 used as an argument that it would reduce the personnel, saying that "though a large ship consumes more coal, a small ship having a large number of guns, actually requires more men and officers than a large one having heavy guns only."

When the *New York* was designed, the complement was fixed at 902 enlisted men. It actually had a crew of 1,444 men in the North Sea, and boards recommended that the regular personnel be 1,410. While Naval boards were demanding an absurdly large number of men on our big ships, how was it in other navies? A British dreadnaught had a crew of 942 when a like American ship was demanding over 1,400. Not only was it an unnecessary expense, but the overcrowding was not sanitary or comfortable. Admiral Rodman, who **commanded the dreadnaughts overseas during World War I,** complained of the lack of sufficient and well-ventilated sleeping accommodations for the large crews and recommended a reduction in the complement on board dreadnaughts. However, he stood almost alone. I gave instructions to boards to study the matter, but they wished at least 25 to 50 per cent more men on a ship than could be wisely used.

In the matter of waste manpower, the Navy and the Army were equally extravagant. In the Army, though trucks and modern machinery were employed and horses were out of date, and there were guns, with bombing for the air, and robots, and the like, the officers made no recommendations for reduced manpower. They continued to demand not only more infantry, but more horses and bigger and stronger cavalry, the spectacle sometimes being witnessed of trucks transporting horses! The criticism of both arms of the military service is that they reach out for all the new methods of warfare and seek to hold on to the outmoded agencies also.

SENATE OVERRULED OFFICERS

Always Admirals and Generals, wishing to be ready for any eventuality, have recommended larger enrollment of men in peace time than is needed. History repeats itself. Early in 1921 the Senate, over the protest of General Pershing, the War Department, and the Military Committee, fixed the Army at 150,000 men. In 1945-46, the Generals, trained in the same school as General Pershing, urged an army far larger than needed for peace-time duty and for the Army of Occupation. The Army leaders also wished the draft law, enacted in the great war, to remain a permanent policy.

XIV

READY TO TRY NEW THINGS

ONE HUNDRED THOUSAND suggestions and inventions were offered the Navy during the war, and it was receptive to all. In 1914 Wilson had told Naval officers, "You must strike out on new paths and be explorers." Speaking at the Navy War College in 1915 I had declared: "Old tactics, old strategy, old theories of Naval warfare are disappearing overnight," and asked, "With what weapon, or what strategy shall we meet the terror of the submarine, the still unrevealed possibilities of the airship?" I told them the Navy looked to them "to assist in the onward march" and called for "the most perfect plans and methods human wisdom can invent." In that same year I wrote Edison that "the imperative need of the Navy is the utilization of American genius to meet the new conditions of war," and asked him to render "a very great service" by organizing the inventive genius of the country. He responded patriotically and soon the Navy had Edison and 100,000 more inventors and scientists seeking new ways to win a new type of war. The story of what Edison and his associates did is a great chapter in Naval history.

WHAT EDISON DID

The Edison Navy Consulting Board, composed of the most distinguished civilian scientists and inventors, won the nation's gratitude by their war service. Mr. Edison gave his time, at Washington and in command of a ship in southern waters, to experiments, devoting himself mainly to work on the detection of the submarine and to the quick turning of cargo boats. He said after the war:

"I was successful in both, building listening apparatus, and while my boat was in full speed I could hear a torpedo the instant it was fired nearly two miles away, and with my turning device, a 5,000-ton cargo boat, fully loaded, going at full speed, was turned at right angles to her original course on an advance of 200 feet."

Among the inventions by Mr. Edison, in addition to what he regarded as his main service to the Navy—the detection of torpedos and the quick turning of cargo boats, there were five outstanding:

1. Smudging the periscope with a special substance on top of the water.
2. Loud-speaking telephones for use on board ships.
3. Glare eliminator for observing periscopes.
4. Preserving submarine boat guns by zinc dust and vaseline emulsion.
5. Silicate of soda for putting out coal bunker and paint fires.

The Edison Board was the inspiration of the Navy Laboratory, where radar was perfected. I always called Mr. Edison "Commodore," and Congress voted him a Distinguished Service Medal. All the members of the Board deserved the gratitude of the country.

When Edison celebrated his seventieth birthday, Wilson in a letter of congratulation said:

"I was an undergraduate at the university when his first inventions captured the imagination of the world, and ever since then I have retained the sense of magic which what he did then created in my mind. He seems always to have been in the special confidence of Nature herself."

A BIRD TO CARRY TNT

My Diary of July 26, 1917, records:

"I talked with W. L. Saunders, Chairman of the Navy Consulting Board, about the bird that will be managed without a pilot and carry TNT. It looks good, will be tried out in Utah on a 75-mile plain."

ELECTRIC DRIVE INNOVATION

The Navy is an organization in which tradition is perhaps stronger than anywhere else. When we had organized the Two-Ocean Navy in 1919 and I went up the Pacific Coast with Admiral Rodman, he recalled the long and hard fight which resulted in equipping the *New Mexico* with the first electric drive which had ever been installed on a battleship. The history of that innovation is not without interest. Up to the construction of the *New Mexico,* all the battleships had the Curtiss or Parsons turbine. There was a division in Naval opinion whether it would not be wiser to equip the dread-

© GREAT LAKES RECRUIT 1917

LIVING FLAG AT GREAT LAKES NAVAL TRAINING STATION

Men in training at Great Lakes Naval Training Station form the American flag.
Inset, Admiral W. A. Moffett, under whom over a hundred thousand seamen were
trained during the World War. Later he was Chief of Aeronautics and lost his life
on the Airship "Akron" (U. S. Navy photo).

FIRST BOARD OF VISITORS TO THE U. S. NAVAL ACADEMY
COMPOSED OF EDUCATORS

Front row, left to right, Benjamin I. Wheeler, President, University of California;
Edwin A. Alderman, President, University of Virginia; Secretary Daniels; Richard
C. MacLaurin, President, Massachusetts Institute of Technology; Kenneth C. M. Sills,
Dean, Bowdoin College. *Back row, left to right,* Albert Ross Hill, University of
Missouri; Charles W. Dabney, President, University of Cincinnati; Alexander C.
Humphries, President, Stevens Institute.

naughts with the electric drive. In long conversations with Mr. Emmet, a graduate of the Naval Academy who was then connected with the General Electric Company, I became convinced that we ought to abandon the old propulsion and adopt the electric drive. This new propulsion had been used in the smaller craft but some engineers doubted the wisdom of putting it in a dreadnaught. One of them said to me, "You cannot risk new equipment with a 25-million-dollar ship." While the debate was going on as to the plans for the *New Mexico,* the collier *Jupiter* was recalled from Mexico. It weathered an unexpected storm, and the prediction was that the electric drive would prove itself to be not as good as other methods of propulsion. With experts, I spent a day on the ship and we found it had weathered the storm perfectly. I gave orders that the dreadnaughts and other big ships should be electrically driven.

Some Naval officers and the manufacturers who were interested in keeping the old types of propulsion sent telegrams of protest to the President and to members of the Naval Affairs Committee predicting a dire fate if the electric drive was installed. They asked for a hearing, which lasted several days. Fortunately for me, Admiral Griffin, Chief of Engineering, and most of his associates testified that the electric drive would be a great improvement. Senator Tillman, Chairman of the Committee, was not convinced, and when the hearing was over turned to me and asked, "What do you advise in view of the wide difference of opinion between the experts?" I answered that my strong recommendation was that dreadnaughts should be electrically driven. Senator Tillman then asked me rather challengingly, "Are you willing to take the responsibility as a civilian to change a method of propulsion? If it fails, you fail. Are you willing to take this responsibility in what so many able men say is an experiment?" I had been brought up in the Andrew Jackson school of "I Take the Responsibility," and I answered, "I am. I know very well that if it is a failure, I will have to bear the condemnation, and I know equally well that if it is a success all the glory will go to the experts."

Admiral Rodman, Commander-in-Chief of the Pacific Fleet, had opposed the electric drive. He was convinced later, after he and I had cruised in the *New Mexico* with Captain Willard and watched the operation of the electric drive on this great leviathan of the sea. Admiral Rodman said to me, "I want to tell you, Mr.

Secretary, that having brought this ship through the Panama Canal and having come through stormy seas with it, I am convinced that it is so great an improvement upon the old method of propulsion that I wonder why we all did not see its superiority and adopt it sooner." Later in 1919 when with our experts I was in England, it was most gratifying to hear British officers express the opinion that the American Navy had made a distinct advance in naval engineering when it adopted the electric drive.

MANY CLAIMED CREDIT

When Uncle Sam joined the Allies, the head of the British Navy said, "the U-boats are winning the war." That danger stimulated efforts on both sides of the Atlantic to end the menace. Naval officers and members of the Edison Board of Civilian Scientists combined to solve the problem of keeping the submarines under. A Special Board on Anti-Submarine Devices was formed with headquarters at New London. In company with Edison I visited that base. Secrecy was essential and the parts were so distributed that a manufacturer of the individual parts would not know the construction of the whole. Even so, when success was obtained and the submarine menace became a thing of the past, it was found that one party had violated a "gentleman's agreement" and filed patent claims for every basic principle involved in detection devices. He sought to patent an idea. So many different people claimed the credit that it was another case of "Who Killed Cock Robin?" There was glory enough for all.

But detection and other devices were not enough. It was found that to use listening devices successfully a special type of vessel and machinery to secure noiseless operation were necessary. This called for the construction of submarine chasers which were effective in British and French waters and in the Mediterranean. I sent an SOS to Henry Ford and at his plant were built a number of the ideal type of submarine-hunting vessels. They were called Eagle boats and were of high speed and noiseless operation.

EXPERIENCE WITH EXCITED INVENTOR

"I have come to tell you that I know you are in collusion with the Steel Trust." These words rang out sharp and clear one morning in the office of the Secretary of the Navy in the early part of 1914.

I was sitting at my desk and looked up to see a very excited gentleman almost running the twenty-foot distance between the door of my office and my desk.

I rose and in a very calm manner said, "Mr. Isham, you would have a very hard time making the members of the Steel Trust believe that statement."

He looked at me as if he were stunned and then around at the people in the office, who saw that something was happening but could not comprehend it all; then he turned and walked out as rapidly as he had entered. Not long after I became Secretary of the Navy, Mr. Isham told me that he and other experts in Ordnance had been studying the methods which should be employed by the Navy to sink an enemy ship better than armor-piercing shells. Shells fired at an enemy ship were constructed to pierce the armor-plate and blow up the ship. The eternal question of making armor-plate thick enough to withstand armor-piercing shells and of making these shells powerful enough to go through the armor-plate was the problem which faced all Ordnance officers. Mr. Isham said the armor-piercing shells were ineffective. He had perfected a shell which, hurled on the side or under a ship, would be much more effective. Admiral Twining, Chief of the Bureau of Ordnance, had very little patience with the Isham shell, intimating that Isham was a crank; that he wanted to make money out of a patent he had; and that the shell he proposed to manufacture would be impotent. However, I directed that an experiment be made on a certain day and gave orders to the Captain of the *Mayflower* to take Isham and Ordnance officers and members of the Naval Affairs Committee down the Potomac where a test would be made. It came near being disastrous. One of Isham's explosives did explode and some members of the Naval Affairs Committee narrowly escaped with their lives and the *Mayflower* was in jeopardy. This accident did not deter Isham. He held that it was such an accident as might have occurred and what was needed was a more comprehensive experiment under better conditions. He offered a bill calling for tests of armor-piercing shells and also tests of the Isham explosives. This would call for an appropriation. The Committee asked my views. Ordnance officers said it would raise expectations that could not be realized, would jeopardize lives, and be a waste of money. In this opinion I concurred and wrote disapproving the bill. Isham was present when my letter was read. Furious about it he rushed to the Navy Department and delivered himself of the denunciation above quoted. I had told him that he had permitted his zeal for his new idea to warp his judgment and that he must not place suspicion upon honorable officers who were doing what they thought right.

MODEST FRENCH SCIENTISTS

Prior to our entrance into the war France sent eminent scientists to Washington to confer with American Naval experts about new weapons with which the French could turn the tide of war. They were disappointed in their expectations, for neither our experts nor the French had then found the answer to the U-boats. Upon leaving they called at the Navy Department to say "good-bye." I told them that the men directing the fighting on the sea looked to men of their profession to devise ways to check the U-boat menace. In a few minutes they returned, saying that they had come back to say that while they hoped to help, they did not wish the fighting branch to depend on their research and discovery. They were prompted by their modesty and the knowledge that in the war then waging, force and force to the utmost would be the determining factor. However, I knew and so did able men in the Navy, that our dependence for modern weapons rested upon civilian inventors and scientists as well as upon men in the service. As a matter of fact, while most of the improvements had originated with those who navigated the ships, there was recognition of the debt of the Navy and Army to Sperry for the gyroscope, to Dr. Gatling for the first machine gun, to the Wrights for the fighting ships that fly, and to other inventors who had no connection with the armed forces.

On one of their frequent visits to the Navy Department, the member concerned with economics said it would be helpful to France if we could be of assistance in securing larger markets in the United States for French wines. That request to me—author of the order abolishing the wine mess on all Navy ships and shore stations—greatly amused Franklin Roosevelt, who said they evidently had not been reading the papers and did not know I "had it in for" the makers of all alcoholic beverages. I told the French visitor that, while eager to aid in any other way, I would not be the suitable American to find customers for that product of La Belle France.

XV

TWO UNSOLVED NAVY MYSTERIES

"I CAN FURNISH A substitute for gasoline at a cost of two cents a gallon which will put every oil company in the world out of business and I have come to offer it exclusively to the Navy."

That was the astounding statement made to me as I sat in the office of the Secretary of the Navy in Washington a short time after the United States had entered the World War. One of our problems was the procurement of oil at reasonable prices. The oil supply had been depleted by the drain made upon American oil companies by the British and French in waging a war in which, as Curzon afterwards said, "The Allies sailed to victory on a sea of oil." It was not long before the big oil companies were demanding that the Naval oil reserves be drawn upon as essential to supply ships engaged in war work. Oil was the main dependence. Franklin Roosevelt, Admiral Griffin, and I had been in a huddle to try to secure an adequate supply at a reasonable price and were up against it. And then a man calling himself John Andrews, saying he was a Portuguese, offered to furnish the Navy's great need with a substitute that would cost two cents a gallon! His offer sounded like manna from heaven.

When I came down to earth, I questioned him about the substitute and proof that it would meet Navy needs. He said: "You need not take my word. All I ask is an opportunity to demonstrate what I claim." About that time Assistant Secretary Franklin Roosevelt and Senator Tillman, Chairman of the Senate Naval Affairs Committee, came into my office and John Andrews repeated to them his offer and his claim. They were intrigued as I had been. Tillman, as he was leaving the office, advised, "Josephus, snap him up. Don't let him get away." Roosevelt, always ready to try anything once, said, "Chief, it is worth trying. I say he should be given the opportunity to prove he can do what he says." The Navy was seeking new weapons and ready to experiment.

The result was that I directed Admiral Burd, Manager of the Navy

Yard at Brooklyn, and Captain E. P. Jessup, senior engineering officer and Captain of the Brooklyn Navy Yard, to provide the facilities for testing the substitute, and talked with them over the telephone and cautioned them—these able officers did not need it—to exercise every care to see there was no trick about the substitute and arrange a demonstration that would prove or disprove the claim of the Portuguese. Shortly after a successful test had been made, the Naval officers, knowing how keen I was about the experiment, telephoned me excitedly that Andrews had succeeded. It seemed a miracle. I directed that a full report be sent to the Bureau of Engineering and that Mr. Andrews be requested to come to see me.

Upon his arrival he asked if the report from the Navy Yard satisfied me. I told him it did and I would like to talk to him about what he would charge the Navy for the exclusive use by our government. My recollection is, and it was confirmed by Admiral Griffin, who was present, and later by Captain Jessup, that he said, "Two million dollars." The amount didn't seem too much, I told him, but before I could ask the President to allocate that sum, he must assure us of two things: (1) that there was a large enough quantity of the chemicals he used; and (2) that the cost would not be prohibitive. To these requests he replied: "You told me if the test was satisfactory, the Navy would buy it. Your officers who saw the demonstration inform me that I did all I claimed. Therefore, I will sell it to the Navy for two million dollars and guarantee it the exclusive possession, but I will not give the secret preparation that propels the engine until I get the money!"

In vain did I tell him that the government could not pay until he met the two conditions—quantity and price. He was adamant. "Give me the money and I assure you that there will be no difficulty about quantity and price." I could not use public money to buy "a pig in a poke." Declaring that I had not kept my word to buy, Andrews departed with his charge that I had not lived up to the agreement. He carried the little bag, which he had held all the time, and, as he left the office, said that if Uncle Sam did not wish to buy, there was a country that would not haggle over price, and he was gone! As soon as I could think or plan, I sent an officer to find out his abode, but he had suddenly disappeared as if in the clouds. The Brooklyn Navy Yard officials could not locate him.

Naval Editor Meriwether, of a New York paper, learning of the experiment, became interested (he had attended the Naval Academy) and set out to find Andrews and get his secret. He finally located him in Pittsburgh, talked with him at a house in the suburbs where he was staying. Andrews said, "Come to see me tomorrow morning at nine o'clock and I will give you the information you want." Bright and early Meriwether was at the cottage, eager for a scoop. But the cottage was empty—not a soul in it. The neighbors knew nothing. No trace was left of Andrews. He had disappeared and all efforts to find him failed. He was never heard of again, nor was his substitute ever employed. It was a mystery of mysteries.

REPORT OF THE EXPERIMENT

At my request, Captain Jessup wrote this account of the successful demonstration:

"One afternoon in the spring of 1917, a Packard car came into the Navy Yard, New York. There were two men in the car, one a Portuguese named John Andrews and the other who introduced himself as a banker from McKeesport, Pennsylvania, whose name I do not remember.

They were directed to me, and Andrews said he had come to demonstrate that he could operate gas engines with water as fuel, and would like an opportunity to make the demonstration on one of our gas engines.

"It happened that I had one of our Navy three-cylinder motor boat engines which we used to build at Norfolk Navy Yard, already connected up on the test block in the laboratory for a test which we were going to make, and I told him we would be glad to let him show us such an interesting experiment. It was arranged that he was to come to the Yard the next morning and make his demonstration.

"He promptly appeared about nine the next morning accompanied by the banker, and we had Admiral Burd, Lieutenant Commander McDowell, Officer in Charge of the laboratory, and Mr. Miller Reese Hutchinson, Secretary of the Naval Consulting Board, there to witness the demonstration.

"The only paraphernalia Andrews had was a small metal can which would hold about a gallon, and a small black satchel such as doctors carry medicine in. The little can was empty, I personally taking it from him to make sure it was empty.

"We gave him a bucket of fresh water and he got into the rear seat of the Packard car with the bucket of water, the little can, and the satchel. The car was an open car but we could not see what he did there. In a few seconds he handed the little can out to me and by its weight I knew it was full. The water to the proper amount was gone out of the bucket and there was no sign of its having been done away with in any manner except by putting it into the little can.

"I carried the can into the laboratory where our engine was on the block connected up for test with a pipe running from an open feed tank to the carburetor of the engine. It is worthy of note that Andrews did not have to make any change in the test setup which we had already prepared for our own test.

"Andrews then poured the liquid from his little can into the open feed tank and it is interesting that he held a lighted cigarette in his fingers, near the stream of liquid flowing into the tank, showing that it was not highly inflammable at that point in the operation.

"Then came the most surprising thing of the whole episode to me. Admiral Burd said, 'Mr. Andrews, while it is true the water is gone from the bucket and we do not see what you did with it if you did not use it in your can, yet we did not actually see you mix the liquid and even if it runs the engine we cannot certify that you used the water in the can.' Mr. Andrews said, 'Give me the bucket.' And he poured from our bucket a full half-gallon of water in on top of the liquid in the feed tank; from this we were sure that at least one-third of the mixture was water.

"He then said, 'Start the engine.' We started it and after a slight adjustment of the carburetor it picked up and developed about 75 per cent of its rated horse-power and used up all of the water and other liquid in the tank.

"The next day he returned and instead of letting him get into his car to mix the stuff, we put him in a little concrete room which had no drain and no place to secrete anything. He did not demur at this and went in with his little can and his satchel and a bucket of salt water, and soon came out with the little can full and repeated his performance of the day before, and the engine acted just as though it were burning gasoline.

"Each time he poured in the extra water, he took out of his pocket a small four-ounce vial and dropped six or seven drops of a greenish colored liquid into the feed tank to compensate for the extra water.

"By this time we were convinced he had something; so we

sent him with Lieutenant Commander MacDowell down to the Navy Department at Washington and he did the same thing for you down there, but when you asked him what he wanted for it, he said, 'Two million dollars.' You said, 'All right, we will place two million dollars in escrow in any bank your banker chooses, that money to be yours as soon as you have taught ten Naval Officers to mix the stuff successfully.' He replied, 'No, two million dollars before I tell you anything,' and that was all you could get out of him.

"His disappearance and the fact that nothing further has been heard of his invention would, on the face of it, suggest that there was some fake about it, but under the conditions which we required and the lack of any special apparatus of his own, coupled with the fact that we saw water to extent of one-third of the total mixture poured into the tank before our eyes, and that the engines consumed this water and developed power commensurate with the careless adjustment of the carburetor, and above all that the water did not come out of the exhaust as steam, which it would have done unless chemically changed by his process, I am convinced Andrews had something, and it is a pity we could not have gotten it out of him."

WILL THE SEA GIVE UP ITS DEAD?

Men who go down to the sea in ships know they face the perils of the deep. In almost every war, and at times in peace, a ship disappears with its crew and the mystery of its fate is never known. In the early part of 1918 the *Cyclops,* carrying a cargo of manganese, sailed from Bahía, Brazil, bound for Baltimore. On March 4 she put into Barbados, British West Indies for coal. When she left the port, she was never heard of again and 309 men met a mysterious fate. In addition to the crew, she was bringing to the United States seventy-two Navy men who had been serving in South American waters, including Maurice Gottschalk, U. S. consul at Rio, and several civilians. Every effort was made to locate the ship, but to this day her fate is a mystery. There were many rumors. One that persisted was that the German-born Captain and members of the crew with German names had turned traitor to their adopted country and taken the *Cyclops* to Germany. Nobody in the Navy believed that gossip. The Captain, G. W. Worley, had come to America when a boy and had rendered excellent service for twenty years in the Naval Auxiliary Service with no suggestion of lack of loyalty.

The only theory that seemed tenable to the Navy was that the *Cyclops* was caught in a sudden West Indies hurricane, that her cargo of manganese shifted, listing the vessel, which turned turtle and went down. Colliers of that type were built with high steel beams, like cranes, with chains of buckets to load and unload coal. If she went down bottom side up, those high steel fingers may have pinned down everything on deck, allowing nothing to float to the surface. "Fate unknown," was the inscription beside the name of the *Cyclops* on the Navy list. Her fate will probably remain a mystery until the last Day when waters are rolled back and the sea gives up its dead.

XVI

WHEN U-BOATS CAME TO OUR COAST

A DMIRAL BENSON, Chief of Operations, and other able Naval officers always believed—as did many British and French officers —that U-boats would try to sink oil tankers from Port Arthur and Tampico. It was from these ports that the Allies received most of the oil that "floated them to victory." This successful transportation of oil was largely due to the vigilance of the fleet in the Caribbean and the Gulf and to the efficiency of the destroyers kept on this side of the Atlantic. When it looked as if the U-boat sinkings would win the war for Germany, we sent nearly all our good destroyers to England and hastened work on the construction of two hundred new ones. We diminished the usual number of destroyers assigned to protect our dreadnaughts, while the British Navy kept three- or fourscore of their destroyers locked up at Scapa Flow to protect their dreadnaughts.

U-BOATS OFF OUR COAST

Twice U-boats entered the Atlantic near our coast and sank some merchant ships, although Naval officers in England had assured us that there was no danger of submarines' crossing the ocean.

Early in the summer of 1918, German submarines appeared off our coast in the Pennsylvania area and sank fifty-two merchant vessels. That news disturbed the American people, and the *Public Ledger* and other papers were severe in criticism of the Navy. Papers and politicians voiced the demands that the Secretary do two things: (1) recall the destroyers from European waters to protect our coast which was endangered; and (2) discontinue sending American troops abroad until assured they would not be attacked by German submarines on this side of the Atlantic. The Navy declined to be moved by the excited clamor. I knew that when most destroyers were sent into the worst-infested zone around England we were leaving our coast largely unprotected. But we had to take that risk. No authority in Washington was influenced by the excited demand that no more soldiers be sent to France when the large flow of troops from this country alone could win the war. The biggest job of the Navy was to use its destroyers to protect hundreds of thousands of fighting men en route to France. And not one soldier on the voyage to France during the entire war lost his life on an American transport!

When the violent denunciation of the Navy was bitterest—led by those who had been most vocal that every destroyer be sent to England—Senators Penrose and Brandegee, leading Republicans, unloosed tirades of abuse of the Navy. I made no answer, but invited Senator Swanson, Chairman of the Naval Affairs Committee, and Senator Lodge, the ranking Republican member, to a conference. They were given then—as always—all the Department information. Returning to the Senate after fully acquainting himself with the facts, Senator Lodge, leading Republican—and no friend of Woodrow Wilson—said:

"Mr. President, the Navy and the Navy Department have necessarily anticipated a submarine attack from the very beginning of the war. They have had it constantly on their minds. They have tried to make every preparation to meet it. I think they have. It would be most injurous for me to stand here and follow down the map of the coast and tell the Senate and the public exactly what those preparations are—tell them where the submarine chasers are, where the destroyers are, where the signal stations are, what arrangements they have made for meeting the danger when it came, as they were sure it would come. No human mind can possibly tell when out of the great waste of waters of the Atlantic Ocean a submarine, which travels by night and submerges by day, will appear. As soon as the Navy had any authentic news to indicate the presence of submarines on this coast they acted. They will do everything that can be done. They have the means to do it. That is all that I feel at liberty to say in a general way.

"Mr. President, for four years the greatest Navy in the world has been devoting its strength to the destruction of German submarines. They were operating in what are known as the narrow seas, where the commerce of the world, we may say, comes together in a closely restricted area; and even there, with the knowledge for years of the presence of the German submarines, it is not going too far to say that many of these submarines escaped them. They are diminishing now, with our assistance. A larger control is being established over the narrow seas, and the work against the submarines at the point of the greatest danger—what we may call the naval front of this war—is succeeding more than any of us dared to hope. It is done by the multiplication of vessels and the multiplication of methods, and there is the great center of the fight.

"One or two submarines have appeared suddenly on our coast, as was to be anticipated. In my judgment, we are doing all that can be done. I have taken the pains to go to the department, where everything has been laid before the members of the Naval Affairs Committee who cared to investigate the subject, and I am entirely satisfied that they are doing everything that is possible. But the chase of the submarine is something like searching for the needle in the haystack. You can not tell in which particular wisp of hay it will come to the surface; but that the defense will be effective I have no sort of question....

"We have a patrol along the coast, which is composed chiefly of what is known as the Life-Saving Service, or the Coast Guard, as it is now known. We also have an organized system for procuring information from fishermen and others on the coast, extending from Maine to the Gulf. Those sources of information were organized and in operation through the Navy Department at least two years before we entered the war; so I believe that so far as our own coasts are concerned the chances of a base there are almost negligible....

"I did not rise to go into the details to describe to you the different naval districts of the country and what has been done in each one of them, but simply to tell you what my opinion is after having examined all the arrangements with the utmost care of which I was capable and with the most intense interest and give my word for what it is worth, that in my judgment the Navy and the Navy Department, the Secretary and Assistant Secretary, and all the officers, the Chief of Staff, and every head of a bureau has done everything that human foresight could suggest....

"I want the Senate also to remember that when newspaper editorials ask what the Navy is doing, I should like to have them consider why it is that we have sent all the troops we have sent—and we have sent a great many thousands—why it is that they have gone to Europe without the loss of a transport, thank God, as I do. How is it that that has happened? It has happened because of the American Navy, which furnishes the convoys, and no other cause.

"I wish I could go on and tell you what the American Navy has been doing in the narrow seas. I can not. The Navy has remained largely silent about its work and its preparation, and it is one of the best things about it, but it has been doing the greatest possible work everywhere. It has not failed in convoying the troops. It has not failed in its work in the Baltic and the Channel and the coast of France and the Mediterranean, and it will not fail here. It will do everything that courage and intelligence and bravery can possibly do."

LODGE UTTERLY DEMOLISHED CRITICS

Senator Lodge's testimony and defense utterly demolished the critics. The foray did the German cause no good and proved a waste so far as its object—terrifying the American people so that they would stop transports' carrying soldiers overseas—was concerned. Secretary Baker continued to speed efforts to send overseas his two million men whose contribution was responsible for the victory, and the Navy gave them safe escort.

XVII

THE MARINES SAVED PARIS

"If the Army and the Navy ever look on
Heaven's scenes
They will find the streets are guarded by
United States Marines."

M R. PRESIDENT, did you know that you have a writer of fiction in
your Cabinet whose works rival those of Rider Haggard?"
was the question Secretary Houston asked, looking at me banteringly, at a Cabinet meeting after the Armistice. The President asked
what member had taken to writing fiction.

"If you read the story of how the Marines won the war in the
report of the Secretary of the Navy, you will think you are reading
fiction, because it reads as if the Marines with little aid won the
war," said Houston. The President said he was glad Daniels had
given a graphic account of the courage of the Marines at Château-
Thierry and Belleau Wood but he had not observed any claim that
the Marines won the war alone. Wilson added: "But I said after visiting the scenes of the terrific fighting that the Second Division,
made up of Army troops and Marines, closed the gap the enemy
had succeeded in opening for their advance to Paris, and, driving
back the Germans, began the rout that was to save Europe and the
world."

WOODS NAMED FOR MARINES

My annual report was a recital of the bloodiest fighting of the
war, when the Marines suffered the largest casualties in the war at
Belleau Wood, where the fighting was literally from tree to tree.
Fighting in that forest of horror for eighteen days, the Marines on
June 25, following a tremendous barrage, took that German nest by
the bayonet, with the heaviest percentage of losses, 1,062 killed and
3,615 wounded. General Foch and General Pershing sent congratulations, and the French officially changed the name from Belleau

Wood to "Bois de la Brigade de Marine." I added that the ablest reporter in France, Melville E. Stone, Manager of the Associated Press, after visiting the area said the operations in and around Château-Thierry did three things: (1) They saved Paris; (2) They seriously injured the morale of the best German troops; (3) They set a standard for American troops that none other dared tarnish.

It was the evening of Memorial Day, May 30, 1918, when Paris was threatened more severely than at any other time since the Battle of the Marne. Archives were packed and preparation made to move the seat of government from Paris. To the rescue came the Second Division composed of Marines and soldiers, commanded by General Harbord, with elements of the Third and Twenty-eighth Army Divisions. When they arrived, the Marines were told to "dig in." General Catlin (Colonel then) commanding the Sixth Regiment of Marines, showed his men the map, indicating the points to be held, so that they would have all possible information. Thus spoke that truly democratic officer: "I hold that men like ours fight none the worse for knowing just what they are fighting for." The secret of Marine efficiency is the comradeship between officers and men. The marines reject the old dogma, "Theirs not to reason why." General Catlin, when wounded, was succeeded by Colonel Harry Lee. After the war Catlin wrote a book entitled, *With the Help of God and A Few Marines*. Colonel Wendell C. Neville was in command of the Fifth Regiment.

When war was declared I tendered, equipped and ready, two regiments of Marines to be incorporated in the Army. Some Army officers were not keen to accept them. However, Secretary Baker was happy to do so and they sailed in June. During the war 30,000 Marines were sent overseas. Their record was glorious.

At the end of their participation in the Meuse-Argonne operation, and of their achievements in the last battle of the war, the commanding officer of the Fifth Army Corps said: "This feat will stand among the most memorable of the campaign," and Pershing referred to their "brilliant exploits in battle." When the war was over, I reserved the highest promotion for the men who faced the enemy in battle, rejecting recommendations of higher rank for men who had not participated in the fighting. Brigadier General Logan Feland led his troops to victory.

On July 2, General John A. Lejeune, ablest Marine officer, suc-

BATTLE OF BELLEAU WOOD

Where the Marines stopped the Kaiser on the way to Paris (U. S. Navy photo from painting by Frank E. Schoonover).

OFFICERS OF THE MARINES IN THE BATTLE OF BELLEAU WOOD

Upper left, Brigadier General Logan (Marine Corps photo). *Upper right*, Major General W. C. Neville (The National Archives). *Lower left*, Brigadier General Albertus W. Catlin, author of "With the Help of God and a Few Marines" (Marine Corps photo). *Lower right*, Brigadier General Harry Lee (Marine Corps photo).

ceeded General Harbord in command of the Second Division, which, among other achievements, took Blanc Mont Ridge and St. Etienne. The official account said: "This victory freed Rheims and forced the entire German Army between that city and the Argonne Forest to retreat to the Aisne."

After the battle, the boys added another stanza to the "Hymn of the Marines," which they sang with zest:

"As we raised our flag at Tripoli
    And again in Mexico,
    So we took Château-Thierry and
    The forest of Belleau.

"When we hurled the Hun back from the Marne,
    He said we fought like fiends,
    And the French re-christened Belleau Wood
    For United States Marines."

A LASTING SATISFACTION

The French lines had been beaten and separated and broken at Château-Thierry. Against the protest of the French, who thought our men were inviting destruction, and against the wish of our remote commanders, the Americans dared to declare by their daring and courage, to quote Wilson:

" 'What did we come over here for? We did not come over to go back. We came over here to go forward.' And their very audacity, their very indifference to danger changed the morale of the battlefield. There were never crusaders who went to the Holy Land in the old ages that we read about that were more truly devoted to a holy cause than these gallant unconquerable Americans."

To my dying day, one of my greatest satisfactions will be that I was privileged to be head of a department that directed these Marines. And among the war memories Newton Baker cherished was that he had granted my request to send these Marines to be bivouacked with like men of the Army to set new high standards of courage unto death.

When I was present (August 3, 1937), at the dedication of the monument at Blanc Mont Ridge, William R. Matthews, of Arizona, who had been in the fight there as a lieutenant, gave me a description of the battle, and said, "the taking of this grand strong point by the Marines of the Ninth and Twenty-third Infantry cracked the final German resistance in this wide plain of the Champagne."

HEAVIEST CASUALTIES IN HISTORY

The casualties by the Marines in the fighting at Belleau Wood were the greatest in World War I. Not only so, but they were also larger than in any fighting in World War II. The impression prevailed for a time after the bloody fight that the Marine losses on Iwo Jima were larger than Belleau Wood. They were tragic. The percentage of casualties by the Marines at Iwo Jima was a little under 39 per cent whereas the percentage at Belleau Wood was about 52 per cent. Shortly after the heavy losses of Marines at Iwo Jima, whose ghastliness shocked the people, Editor Ward, in an article in the *New York Sun* gave the historical record of the bloodiest battles in other historic wars. Going back to the Napoleonic wars, here is the record as he compiled it:

"In the month from early June to early July of 1918, in which the Second Division's Fourth Marine Brigade, led by Brig. Gen. James G. Harbord (now lieutenant general United States Army, retired), bore the brunt of the victorious attack through the incredibly difficult undergrowth and fortified boulders in Belleau Wood, it had about 52 per cent casualties. With an authorized oversea strength of about 8,299 officers and men, the brigade reported 4,391 killed and wounded. The 52 per cent of casualties probably reduced by the fact that some replacement in regiments, depleted during the fighting, enlarged beyond the initial strength the number of men who actually fought with the brigade. Still it appears to be beyond question that the percentage of Marine casualties at Belleau Wood was higher than on Iwo."

The Americans lost 25 per cent at Bunker Hill and the British 35 per cent. At Gettysburg the Confederates lost 40 per cent of their 75,000 men, while the loss of the Federal forces was 28 per cent of the 82,000 men engaged. The highest percentage on record of a one-day battle was that day when Napoleon lost 54 per cent of his army of 74,000 men while Wellington lost 14 per cent of his 50,000. In an area of three square miles of fighting at Waterloo 45,000 men lay killed or wounded. Most people were surprised to find that the

Marine casualties at Iwo Jima had been surpassed by those at Belleau Wood following the severe fighting at near-by Château-Thierry.

COURAGE AT BELLEAU WOOD COMMEMORATED

In the early part of 1919, accompanied by marines and soldiers who had taken part in the Belleau Wood fighting, I went through the wood before the evidences of the struggle and the destruction of trees had been removed. It still bore marks of the terrible fighting. In 1937, as a member of the Commission to Dedicate the Monuments and Cemeteries in honor of Americans who fought and lie buried in the sacred soil of France, I found little of the ravages of war. Instead, in Belleau Wood, at the entrance, was an American Cemetery, where white crosses mark the graves of our dead heroes. And in near-by Château-Thierry rises one of the noblest monuments erected by the American Government, which tells the story of how the Second Division composed of soldiers and Marines stopped the drive on Paris. It was the nearest to Paris reached by any German troops. After that, though the cost was heavy, to quote Woodrow Wilson's report to Congress of how the war came to an end, it was "henceforth back, back, back, always back for the enemies, always back, never again forward."

MARINES GIVEN HIGHEST HONORS

The Marines, under General Lejeune, comprised part of the Army of Occupation, which imposed the terms of the Armistice on the Germans and did not return to the United States until August, 1919, when the highest honors were given them. They were reviewed in Washington by President Wilson, and Secretary Baker wrote me:

"The whole history of the Brigade in France was one of conspicuous service. Throughout the long contest the Marines, both by their valour and their tragic losses heroically sustained, added an imperishable chapter to the history of America's participation in the World War."

LARGEST EMBARKATION CAMP

After the first American troops reached France, Brest was made the chief port by which the armed forces entered France and embarked for home. Under the command of the resourceful and dynamic Brigadier General Smedley Butler, commanding the Thirteenth Regiment of Marines, it became the largest and the best managed embarkation camp in the world, through which 1,600,000 men passed. Two North Carolinians were on duty with General Butler—General Hal Turnage, who won his spurs in action in both world wars and became head of the Personnel Division and Assistant Commandant of the U. S. Marine Corps in World War II, and Captain Josephus Daniels, Jr., who served in the Marines in both world wars.

A MARINE ABOVE AN AMERICAN

Secretary Houston was not the only man who thought I gave too much honor to the Marines. At a War Bond Rally in Baltimore, after the Armistice, I recited the part played by the Navy and Marine Corps in winning the war, emphasizing the heroic and historic fighting in Belleau Wood, saying little about the Army's greater contribution, except that the men of the Army, Navy, and Marine Corps were made of the same stuff and America was proud of all the men whose devotion had won the war. When I had finished, the noted surgeon, Dr. Finney, who was a General in the Army, brought down the house when in his happy address he said, substantially:

"As I listened to Secretary Daniels telling graphically and with pride of the exploits of the Marines in France, saying little about the Army fighters, if I had not been familiar with the facts, I would have supposed that almost alone the Marines had won the war. But I reflected that there were only thirty thousand fighting Marines in France and there were over two million soldiers in the Army and the soldiers must by preponderance of numbers and equality of courage have made the largest contribution to German defeat.

As Secretary Daniels extolled the Marines, and I join him in praise of their courage even if they had only thirty thousand men to our over two million, it recalled an incident after one of the bloodiest battles of the war. It was the custom for the nearest surgeon to give first aid to the wounded in the field hospital and then for a home surgeon to visit them in hospitals. I went into the hospital to give aid and cheer to Americans who had been first treated by French surgeons. As I stopped by the cot of a wounded man, so bandaged I could not recognize his nationality, I leaned over the cot of the badly wounded man and asked: 'Young man, are you an American?' That question roused him. He replied: 'No; I am a Marine.' You see, Daniels and that Marine believe the title 'Marine' is a nobler one than 'American.' "

MARINE CORPS COMMANDANT DEFIANT

During the World War, though I had previously pursued the policy that no man on important duty in Washington could hold the position longer than four years, I felt that the experience of these heads of departments called for their retention during the war. They were reappointed with the full understanding that upon the termination of the struggle their resignations would be accepted. All chiefs of bureaus wrote their resignations "to take effect at the pleasure of the President." When I conveyed to General Barnett, Commandant of the Marine Corps, my policy and asked him to sign the resignation as all others had done, he asked permission to consider it and return the next day. Upon his return he said he would prefer not to sign the resignation, and added, "I am a gentleman, and no gentleman would remain a day after his resignation was desired. I will tender it if you desire as soon as the war is over." When I told an Admiral of this, he said, "You understand, don't you?" I did not and he explained, "If Barnett lived among Indians and was given the name that fitted him, he would be called The-Man-Afraid-Of-His-Wife."

With the end of the war, in which General Lejeune in command of the Second Division had won distinction by ability and courage, the consensus of opinion among the Marines was that he was entitled to more than the Distinguished Service Medal and ought to be elevated to the head of the Marine Corps. I decided to recommend him for appointment as Major General Commandant to succeed Barnett, who had not seen active service in the war. Barnett thought his war appointment was for four years and that the President was without authority to remove him. I looked up the law and found that it read: "Four years unless sooner relieved." That was the law enacted in December, 1913. I asked Barnett if he intended to keep his word. He was defiant in spite of his pledge. "Very well. Good Morning," I said, and he withdrew in confidence that he had killed the Single Oak Policy. The law was invoked, the President removed him and appointed General Lejeune, who entered upon his duties early in the summer of 1920. Barnett and his friends appealed to the President without avail. And then they declared that they would—and they did—prevent the confirmation of Lejeune by the Republican Senate and predicted that General Barnett would be reinstated when Harding became President. I feared that wrong to the ablest Marine might be done in the name of politics.

HOW DENBY WAS INFLUENCED

But the most partisan Republicans and Barnett were riding for a fall. The House Naval Affairs Committee, then having a majority of Republicans, unanimously favored Lejeune. On the day before Harding's inauguration, Chairman Butler, a grand Old Guard Republican from Pennsylvania, who was resolved to go to any length to keep Lejeune in the position he was filling so well, and other members of the Committee, called at the Navy Department and asked me what I thought they could do to prevent the removal of Lejeune. One member suggested that they go in a body to see Mr. Denby, who was to become Secretary in the Harding Administration, and tell him that the one thing they desired above all others was to see Lejeune retained. They took that course. Later Denby called to see me, told me of the earnest request, almost a demand, that Lejeune be reappointed. He asked, "If you were coming into office with such an insistent request from the Naval Affairs Committee, what would you do?" I replied that whatever of success I had been able to achieve was due to the help and coöperation of that committee, members of the two parties, and added, "I'd hate to start in by turning down a request for the retention of an able officer they were unanimously urging." Denby had been a Reserve Marine in the war and upon his recommendation Lejeune was reappointed March 5, 1921, and confirmed and remained as Commandant of the Marine Corps until his retirement. Then he was elected President of the Virginia Military Institute, where he won new distinction. But for the insistence of Butler and the House Naval Affairs Committee, he might have been sacrificed.

I relate this incident because it was the only one of its kind in the eight years I was Secretary of the Navy.

Part Five

<hr>

"THE ARMY WON THE WAR"

XVIII

MASTERLY WAR STRATEGY

NATURALLY, I am not as familiar with the President's part in the strategy of the Army as in that of the Navy, but I know he was as keen to advise and uphold the hands of Secretary Baker as he was concerned with Naval policies. He sensed that the first blows must be struck by the Navy, but that the winning of the war chiefly depended upon a mighty Army fighting with Allies in France, with America giving the decisive blow which was essential to victory. Here are some evidences of his strategy and team work with the Secretary of War:

1. Wilson early saw the necessity of a selective draft law and lent his powerful influence to its employment to raise quickly what he called a democratic army. The weight of his influence defeated the opposition.

2. Wilson shared with Baker the selection of Pershing as Commanding General of the American Expeditionary Force and upheld his wise policy of an American Army, separate from all others, though working in close coöperation.

3. He put his foot down hard on the British and French insistence that American troops as they arrived overseas should be fed into companies commanded by French and British officers. He knew that infiltration would be fatal to the morale of American troops, and would be bad strategy. He would not permit it and results proved his wisdom as a military strategist.

4. When the United States entered the war there was not unity of command of Allied forces. Wilson proposed it and urged it until Foch was made Supreme Commander of the Allied Armies.

5. He showed he was a courageous fighter by going to bat for Baker when Senator Chamberlain said the Army had fallen down. He never failed to uphold any officer who was true to the course charted.

6. When the Germans accepted his Fourteen Points and asked

for an armistice he accepted their surrender though some military leaders wanted to go "on to Berlin."

7. At Paris in all military matters he leaned on General Bliss, statesman as well as general, and on his able and patriotic Naval adviser, Admiral Benson.

My birthday (May 18) occurred simultaneously with two of the most important events of the war. On that day Wilson signed the Selective Draft Act and announced he had "directed an expeditionary force under the command of Major General John J. Pershing to proceed to France as soon as practicable."

The question of organizing an army by drafting every man of given ages was a radical departure from the American volunteer system. It was widely debated. The President said that in war it was the only democratic way to mobilize the manpower of the country. There was difference of opinion in the Council of National Defense at first about whether it was necessary, and more differences in Congress. My good friend, Lemuel Padgett, Chairman of the House Naval Affairs Committee, and most of the Tennessee Congressmen were not favorable. Chairman Padgett said to me, "Tennessee has always been called 'the Volunteer State' and it would be inconsistent for us to vote that we had repudiated a policy by which Tennessee is known." He strongly supported Wilson's pre-war and war policy, but hesitated about voting to end the volunteer system of raising an Army.

There was comparatively little non-compliance with the draft. Baker arranged that Quakers and other conscientious objectors not be required to fight but to be put to work in places where their labor was needed. We did not need a draft to secure all the enlistments necessary for the Navy, but in a war calling for millions I became convinced that all citizens ought to serve and not rely only on the most ardent patriots who would volunteer.

I felt a thrill when the first numbers were drawn, in accordance with the new draft law, on July 20, 1917. With President Wilson, I went to the Senate Office Building, where Secretary Baker was blindfolded and drew the first capsule. Afterwards somebody blindfolded others of the group, and we also drew out numbers.

THE DUNKARD'S PRAYER

"The Lord has placed a heavy burden upon thee, son," said a tall, white-haired leader of a delegation of Dunkards who called on Baker to ask for the exemption of Dunkards from the draft.

ARE THEY LIARS OR SLACKERS?

There was a great divergence in some States between population and registration under the draft. The Massachusetts Senators protested that the Bay State was called upon for too many by considering population. Why? Because so many of the foreign-born living in that State, and their children, had not been naturalized. Discussing what registration disclosed I quote from my Diary notes of a Cabinet meeting (June, 1917):

"Baker read figures of registration, showing more enlistments than census figures indicated were eligible. Out of an expected 100, North Carolina registered 106. The registration in Washington and Oregon showed less than 60 per cent. Why? Baker stated that one army officer accounted for it because those States had prohibition. Wilson commented, 'Baker likes to start something'—looking at Baker and me. I said, 'If prohibition cuts down registration, how about North Carolina, which registers 106 when 100 was expected? North Carolina has long had State prohibition.' Baker quoted the Governor of Washington as saying that the population of Washington was padded at the last census. One Cabinet member said, 'They are either liars or slackers. Between the two I prefer liars.'"

THE FOURTH MADE GLORIOUS

The news that the first troops had landed safely in France made July 4, 1917, a day of rejoicing and thanksgiving second only to that when the Liberty Bell in Philadelphia pealed out at the birth of American independence. It is difficult for one not living at that time to conceive the deep anxiety over the sailing of transports carrying the first American troops to France. Every parent with a son under arms lived in suspense. Each one felt sure that his son would give a good account of himself on the field of battle, but the main apprehension was lest he become the victim of U-boats and be helpless as, crossing the ocean, he found a watery grave. The Kaiser believed that his U-boats would sink the transports, and many Americans feared he was right. Every precaution was taken by the Army and the Navy. It had been suggested from London that the French destroyers meet our transports and escort them into port. I felt that the supreme duty of our Navy was to see that the soldiers were safely landed, and cabled Admiral Sims: "I hereby instruct you to furnish escorts, to consist of one division of destroyers for each convoy group from the point of meeting to the point of debarkation."

Nothing was left to chance or dependence upon allies. No news was given out at the time of sailing or the route. Transports were protected by convoy and were met near the shores of France by American and French destroyers and escorted into port. The sinking of merchant ships had become so terrible in the spring and early summer of 1917 that all were nervous as the first transports were due in France. When the news that the ships, though submarines made an unsuccessful attack, had safely landed their precious cargoes, the satisfaction and happiness in America were deeper than any words can convey.

The exchange of messages between the Secretary of War and the Secretary of the Navy indicates the feeling of both services. Baker wrote:

"July 3, 1917

"MY DEAR MR. SECRETARY:

"Word has just come to the War Department that the last ships conveying Gen. Pershing's expeditionary force to France arrived safe today. As you know, the Navy assumed the responsibility for the safety of these ships on the sea and through the danger zone.

"The ships themselves and their convoys were in the hands of the Navy, and now that they have arrived, and carried, without the loss of a man, our soldiers who are the first to represent America in the battle for democracy, I beg leave to tender to you, to the Admiral, and to the Navy, the hearty thanks of the War Department and of the Army.

"This splendid achievement is an auspicious beginning, and it has been characterized throughout by the most cordial and effective coöperation between the two military services.

"NEWTON D. BAKER

"HON. JOSEPHUS DANIELS,
"*Secretary of the Navy.*"

I made this reply:

"July 4, 1917

"MY DEAR MR. SECRETARY:

"The Navy accepts the thanks and gratitude of the Army as an expression of fraternal esteem rather than as any acknowledgment of sole achievement. The movement of the expeditionary forces, carried out with such complete success, was planned in joint conferences, and goes to the people as a proof of the effectiveness that lies in intimate coöperation between the two great military branches of the Government.

"This generous concentration of activities is as thrilling a thing to me as the safe passage of our transports through the ocean lanes. With Army and Navy thinking as one, planning as one, fighting as one, the great purpose of America is expressed in terms of invincibility. In behalf of the men whose courage gave safe conduct to courage, I send to you the greetings of the Navy, awaiting in full confidence the day when the valor of your soldiers will write new and splendid chapters in the heroic history of our liberty-loving land. You, who have shared with me the anxiety of these days of intolerable suspense, will know the full and happy heart out of which I write.

"JOSEPHUS DANIELS

"HON. NEWTON D. BAKER,
   "Secretary of War."

AN AMERICAN ARMY OR NONE

A convincing proof of civilian ability in directing the war came when Wilson and Baker upheld Pershing in his determination that the Amercan Expeditionary Force should be independent and officered by Americans.

"We will have an American Army or none," said Woodrow Wilson with set jaws at a meeting of the Cabinet when Secretary Baker disclosed General Pershing's indignant rejection of the British and French proposal to sift American troops as replacements into British and French companies or regiments as they arrived in France. Ambassador Walter Page and Admiral Sims, both in London, were in accord with the desire to infiltrate soldiers from the United States into the armies of the European Allies. Their advocacy of such a course was resented by the President, who on more than one occasion had felt that when he asked Sims and Page for their opinion, they had given him the British opinion and not what they might think themselves. Hoover took the same position as Page and Sims; their minds ran in the same channel about that time. Losses had reduced the original complements of the British and French armies and it was desired to restore them to their original size by fresh American soldiers as they reached France. Pershing was ready to coöperate fully, but demanded an American Expeditionary Force. Baker was fully in accord with Pershing.

I wrote in my Diary:

"President Wilson, with a show of resentment at the very suggestion of putting American soldiers to fill up the ranks of the armies of other countries, said: 'We will have an Amercian army or none,' and pointed out the serious objections to the proposed infiltration, adding: 'Moreover, it is entirely possible before this war comes to an end, we may have to fight it out as the chief army in the field.' He already sensed the danger of flagging tired soldiers who had been long in the front lines.

"President Wilson and Secretary Baker were doubtless familiar with the orders of the French ruler who, when Rochambeau and Lafayette and French soldiers came to the aid of the colonies in the American Revolution, declared 'on the King's wishes,' that 'there shall be no dispersing of the French troops and that they shall always serve as an army corps and under French generals, except in the case of temporary detachments which should rejoin within a few days the principal corps.' I do not know whether Pershing knew of the precedent. I rather think he acted on his own sound judgment and knowledge of American soldiers, whose morale would have been lessened if not destroyed if they had been placed in French or British regiments and under officers not of their nationality.

"Baker told me that when General Joffre was in Washington in the early days of the war, he had asked the fine old Marshal if he believed it wise for America to build up an Expeditionary Force of its own, and Joffre emphatically agreed with Baker that the United States should equip, train, officer, and direct its own Army, adding: 'It is hard to direct an Army.' So that military expert did not agree with Hoover, Page, and Sims."

When the matter of infiltration of our men into Allied companies came up, after church one Sunday night Baker and I went to the White House at the call of the President. He wished to decide, before Baker went to Europe, some important matters. After they were disposed of, there was Pershing's objection to infiltration to be discussed. I noted in my Diary (February 24, 1918):

"Lord Reading had been told by the President that unless the allied countries agreed upon a Commander-in-Chief we would not consent for our troops being under any but American command. Baker was told to say that to Lloyd George and Clemenceau. W. W. said Lloyd George removed Robertson and made Parliament believe it was as result of the Allied War Conference and due to a paper written by General Bliss. Believes Lloyd George is playing politics and does not tell the truth. Petain also criticized Pershing because he would not merge American soldiers with French commands. Will not stand for that. An English General objected because orders agreed upon at Versailles Council were sent direct by General Foch and not through British Commander. W. W. expressed hatred of red tape. He related story of a colored soldier who was told to 'Obey nobody but men with stripes on their shoulders.'"

BAKER READY TO RESIGN

Abusive criticism, as unjust as it was vicious, thundered in the early days of the war. I had experienced a literal barrage in my first term when opposing the plans of big oil and steel companies and the big distilling concerns. The Republicans when war was declared demanded a Coalition Cabinet, with Elihu Root in place of Baker and Theodore Roosevelt as Secretary of the Navy, though I never heard that either of them desired the post. When a concert of criticism of Baker was organized and the papers viciously and without cause roasted him, the criticisms greatly incensed his wife. And they troubled him for a time, as this excerpt from my Diary (January 23, 1918) shows:

"Newton Baker came over to confer about a letter he had written to the President saying that he had but one purpose— to have the country united to win the war—and in view of the criticisms he was ready to tender his resignation so the President could name a man as Secretary of War who would unite the country. I told him the President would not permit it, that the opposition would be satisfied with nobody except T. R., Root, or Wood, and the President would not name either, and instead of composing or uniting, his resignation would have the opposite effect. He looks five years older. I told him that within a few months his critics would see how unjust they were."

While Baker was straining every nerve and the Army was steadily becoming so fit that the enemy was feeling its weight, there came the most unjust attack upon the military establishment, which aroused Wilson's hot resentment. Senator Chamberlain, Chairman of the Committee on Military Affairs, at a luncheon in New York declared:

> "The military establishment of America has fallen down; there is no use to be optimistic about a thing that does not exist; it almost stopped functioning. Why? Because of inefficiency in every department of the Government of the United States. I speak not as a Democrat but as an American citizen."

As I read it, I wondered if Chamberlain had suddenly lost possession of his senses. I said as much to Baker, who was astonished at so false and wanton a slander, calculated to give aid and comfort to the enemy. What caused the violent outburst in New York City? Ray Stannard Baker at the time wrote in his Diary:

> "The attack is largely traceable to the great business interests of the country, which resent government control of the railroads and the mines, chafe under taxation, fear the growing power of labor. . . . Several New York papers which supported Wilson's re-election, now in a rampaging mood of hostile criticism."

Coming from the Chairman of the Military Committee, the criticism could not be ignored. Wilson's wrath flamed. He knew it was false, and his resentment was heightened because it reflected upon Baker, who had his affection as well as his confidence. Wilson wrote at once to Chamberlain, quoted the above extract from the luncheon address, and asked if the paper had "correctly quoted" him. The quotation was accurate. Thereupon Wilson publicly branded it as "an astonishing and absolutely unjustifiable distortion of the truth," and proved its falsity by showing what had been done. A little later, Baker went before the Military Committee and for five hours told the story of preparedness and what the Army had done. Backed up by facts, and approved by every responsible officer in the Army, it utterly destroyed Chamberlain's false tirade. As one

GENERAL PERSHING AND SECRETARY OF WAR BAKER IN FRANCE

Upper left, Honorable James F. Byrnes, now Secretary of State, who in World War I piloted appropriations for the Army and Navy through the House and blasted critics of the armed forces. *Upper right,* Harry S. Truman as First Lieutenant in Battery F, 129th Field Artillery in World War I (Press Association Inc.). *Lower left,* Lieutenant General Hunter Liggett, who as commander participated in the Marne, St. Mihiel, and Meuse-Argonne operations and commanded the 3rd Army on the Rhine. *Lower right,* Herbert H. Lehman, who served in the Army and Navy in World War I and as Director General of the United Nations Relief and Rehabilitation Administration in World War II.

example: Chamberlain said the Army had not been able to put 500,000 men in the field. Baker showed that we had a million and a half and they were going to France, fully trained and equipped, at the rate of 250,000 a month, with steady acceleration. No such speech, restrained and fortified with logic and evidence, had been heard in the Capitol in a generation. I was as happy at Baker's victory as I was enraptured by his unstudied eloquence. The aspersions upon his administration had aroused my anger quite as much as they had called forth Wilson's denunciation. Day by day I had been in touch with what Baker was doing and knew the monumental achievement.

Stirred by indignation at the violent and untruthful attacks on Baker and the war effort, Wilson was as happy and proud of Baker's perfect vindication as if he had been his own son, as he was in spirit and in fine quality. Wilson never failed to risk all and dare all for an associate who stood true to the cause for which he professed allegiance. Never!

Big Senator Ollie James, a master of debate, listened entranced during Baker's defense, his hands resting on the top of his cane and his chin in his hands. As the noon recess came, James rushed for a taxi, hurried to the White House, and literally running into Wilson's office, exclaimed: "Jesus, you ought to see that little Baker. He's eating 'em up." And he finished the job that afternoon. Chamberlain had no real comeback though he spoke three hours in the Senate. He made an impotent gesture of introducing a bill providing for a war cabinet "of three distinguished citizens of demonstrated executive ability" given "full control of the war under the direction and supervision only of the President." The bill "died a-bornin'." Already there was a war cabinet functioning under the President.

Chamberlain's attack on Baker ended his influence, and at the next election, despite some Republican support because of his tirade against the administration, he was defeated and never was heard of again. It was a sad ending of a career which in the early years gave promise of distinction.

NO MINISTRY OF SUPPLY

Wilson understood how many crimes and how much lost motion come from the multiplicity of agencies, on the one hand, and the proposals to coördinate, on the other. In the early days of the war, the Army and Shipping Board were temporarily at a disadvantage because, having a three-year program, the Navy had preëmpted the shipbuilding yards, and had given orders that utilized a large portion of the private munition works. Senator Chamberlain, Chairman of the Committee on Military Affairs, wished to take the procuring of munitions from the heads of the War and Navy Departments, which had found ways without legislation through the Baruch War Industries Board to meet their needs. Wilson strongly opposed the creation of a munition ministry patterned after Britain, and pointed out that "so far as the Navy is concerned, it would bring about a dislocation of activities which would cause delay" and so far as the Army is concerned "nothing substantial would be accomplished." He said it would result in "demoralization." He told Chamberlain that the British Ministry of Munitions had not "fulfilled expectations." That letter killed the Chamberlain bill.

WANTED RECONCILIATION

In June I had a call from Governor West, of Oregon, who was seeking to bring about a reconciliation between the President and Senator Chamberlain. The latter had been renominated for the Senate by the Democrats and West told me he could be reëlected if the administration would give him its support. I asked West "What is the matter with Chamberlain?" and told him that no Republican Senator had been so bitter in criticism of the War Department or so embarrassing to the administration in the conduct of the war.

Governor West regretted the whole incident but as a close friend of Chamberlain only said he thought bygones should be bygones. As a quasi-defense of criticism of the administration, he said that enough consideration had not been shown to Democrats on the Pacific Coast and he thought Republicans were given too much weight and Western Democrats, who had made possible Wilson's reëlection, given too little. West was right.

It was the vote of pivotal California, and other western states, which made possible the reëlection of Wilson in 1916. Democratic leaders from the West should have been called to Washington— and I so advised—to fill important posts. Failure to take that course chilled the ardor of men who had supported the Wilson policies. Instead, too many Easterners who had no sympathy with the New Freedom were recognized.

JOINT WAR STRATEGY

Thanks largely to Baker, all matters where joint action was desirable, and indeed all war preparations and movements touching the war, were discussed at frequent meetings of chief officers of the Army and Navy at the War Department, in which Baker and I were often present. Neither he nor I thought our departments were separated but truly one military organization. We, therefore, secured joint war strategy. These conferences were informative and helpful. When any officer returned from the battle zone, we were eager to learn the situation at first hand. I recall one incident that gave me a lesson in French pronunciation. A colonel, just arrived from Rheims, was graphically describing a battle and frequently told of the position at "Rans." I had never heard of such a place and could not follow him. I did not want to disclose my ignorance and so I asked the colonel to please get a map of France and trace the movements so we could get a better picture of what he was relating. I then discovered that "Rans" is the accepted pronunciation of Rheims and could follow him more intelligently. When later I saw the terrible injuries inflicted on the Cathedral there by the Germans, I did not mispronounce the name of the town. The colonel had educated Josephus Daniels—and Newton Baker, who thanked me for calling for the map.

As illustrating what was discussed in these meetings, I give these excerpts from my Diary (August, 1918):

BRITISH PROFITEERING

"It was agreed that the pressing need is cargo ships and Great Britain is to be asked to aid at least to the extent of carrying all supplies intended for her army. She expects to ask us sixty thousand pounds for her big ships if lost. 'You mean dollars, don't you?' I asked the officer. 'No, pounds,' he replied. She also proposes to charge $150 instead of $50 for every person taken over; also desires us to agree to furnish ships equivalent to every day's work done on our ships and every day's docking. Worst of it is, Sims approves."

At one meeting the Army officers stressed that there was great need for horses and trucks and that it was difficult to get enough tonnage. Truck builders had been set back by prevalence of influenza. I opined that trucks were essential but horses were out of date. Army officers dissented. They wanted a mechanized Army and antiquated cavalry, too—horses which ate their heads off and could not keep up.

BAKER ON TRIP TO EUROPE

At a Cabinet meeting after his return from Europe, Baker talked about his visit to the front. He had warm praise of the Naval transport service and the quality of the Marines serving in the American Expeditionary Force. He said he talked incognito with many soldiers and found that all were confident of ultimate victory. He said that Foch was believed to be the greatest military genius, but if the General—very old and a royalist, who helped save the day at the Marne—were younger, he would be the most resourceful. Baker gave a clear insight into the situation at the front, told stories about the service of American soldiers, and related his talks with the war leaders, military and civil in France and England, and the various views as to how long the war would last. Among other incidents, Baker told of an American boy in France, with both legs shot off, who was happy because the lieutenant who had led the charge had been decorated.

On the day Baker arrived in New York, we both spoke at the Southern Society banquet. It was attended by many distinguished men and the directors of the Associated Press. These were rather speech-hardened, but like all others they fell under the spell of Baker's truly great and eloquent speech. I count it among the first half dozen great speeches I have ever heard.

HOPED BAKER WOULD BE DROWNED

Bitternesses ran riot with many people in war days in every way. My Diary (April 13, 1918) says:

"Mrs. Newton Baker was on a train going to Cleveland. Two men who were sitting behind her talked in tones so loud she could not help hearing. One in very vigorous terms expressed the hope that the ship on which the Secretary of War was returning from Europe would be sunk. Mrs. Baker was so indignant she resented it and told the men who she was. The name of the man who wished Baker would be sunk was William E. Lamb, a Chicago lawyer, and bitter Republican partisan.

"I went to see the President about it and he thought the man ought to be punished, and action should be brought here by the Attorney General and the man given the 33rd degree and then the story of his comment overheard by Mrs. Baker given to the public so the man would be forever damned by the people."

EVACUATE FRENCH TRENCHES AT ONCE

Upon his return from Europe, Baker gave us much information that had not gotten in the press or been sent in official reports. I quote from my Diary (June, 1918):

"Baker said that Stettinius, Assistant Secretary, was going to Europe to put business arrangements in good shape and make suitable business adjustments. When in France Baker heard that the French were keeping books and putting down the items they would charge us. They were even going to expect us to pay for the trenches we occupied. 'Then,' said Baker, 'we will evacuate at once. If we were not in those trenches, the Germans would now be occupying them.'"

BAKER NEVER AVOIDED RESPONSIBILITY

In the early rush days after the declaration of war the Army and the Navy busied themselves placing orders for what was needed at once. Fortunately the Congress, in its three-year building program, had made ample provision for the Navy and we were forehanded. The laws forbade appropriations for Army preparedness for more than twelve months at one time. The Army perforce had either to buy without specific authority or lack essential supplies. When Secretary Baker was giving orders for supplies for a coming Army of a million men, General Sharpe said:

"Mr. Secretary, we may all have to go to jail."

Baker replied, "In that case, I hope Mrs. Baker and Mrs. Sharpe will bring us our meals, as I am sure I will not like jail food."

"Buy what you need," Baker said, "I will include it in the emergency appropriation and explain it to the Committee."

When Baker told Chairman Fitzgerald what he had done, he was advised, "Don't put it in the record."

Baker insisted, "I want to be the first to disclose what we have done, and not have somebody else appear later and disclose it."

That was characteristic of Baker. He never did anything except in the open, or anything for which he did not assume full responsibility. He never passed the buck. Once, discussing with General Bliss an act that might be subject to criticism, the Secretary said, "Do not act. I will give the order and let any criticism come to me. That is what a civilian secretary is for, to take the blame."

He understood and so did I that if a career officer made a mistake it might be entered on his record and militate against his promotion, whereas a civilian secretary with no permanent tenure faced no such risk. The motto of Baker was in the practice of Andrew Jackson: "I take the responsibility." It was this acceptance of his duty that first won him the admiration of Army officers, which increased as the years went by—so much so that from Scott, Bliss, March, and Pershing down they all resented what Theodore Roosevelt said of him when Wilson and Baker denied Roosevelt's request to lead troops to France. Teddy then said: "He is exquisitely unfitted for his position." Time and testing proved he was "exquisitely fitted for his position."

SIGNING COMMISSIONS A BURDEN

Early in the war the President found that the signing of commissions required more time than he could find. He issued orders that the Secretary of War and the Secretary of the Navy should sign "by direction of the President." That imposed a heavy duty on Baker—far heavier than on me—and he wrote his name so often without lifting his pen from paper that it was almost involuntary. That and signing thousands of orders and commissions on faith in others caused him to say to me one day: "O, for the time when we will again sign the things we write and write the things we sign."

A TALISMAN'S NAME

Of a good story told by Secretary Baker at a Cabinet meeting in war days, I wrote in my Diary:

"Secretary Baker related how a First Lieutenant in an Army encampment could not get supplies quickly enough. His name is Baker. He sent an urgent telegram for supplies, and the telegram was signed 'Baker,' and they came by express. Now every man who wishes anything in a hurry gets Baker to sign the order and the supplies come because it is thought the Secretary of War is making the order."

WHAT WON THE WAR?

World War I was won by the Allied Armies on the Western Front. That is the considered verdict of history. It could not have been won except for the pouring in of two million American fighting men of valor, whose strength, added to that of the Allies, overwhelmed the German shock troops.

By keeping the Ferry to France open and safe, and defeating U-boat menace, the Navy made possible the transportation of the greatest Army that ever crossed the ocean. And aviation was not only the eyes of the Army, preventing surface attacks, but intrepid aviators protected shipping and won combats in the air which in World War I pioneered its supremacy in World War II. Of the Navy's contribution, General John J. Pershing, reviewing what has been demonstrated to have been the "greatest transportation job in history," wrote (April 21, 1919):

"We fully realize that had it not been for the Navy, who kept watch and guard night and day over our transport fleet, the American effort in France would never have been successful. The Navy's assistance was whole-hearted and arduous, and was always given in a most generous spirit of coöperation."

To be sure there were many contributing forces on sea and land. Among them the arming and equipment made possible by civilian coöperation and by industry, shipping, communications by Navy-directed wireless; the propaganda through dropping leaflets of Wilson's proposals for a just peace all over Germany; and the wisdom of diplomats and intelligence officers and a unity of Allied efforts. But it was the "force, force without stint" on the battlefield which conquered.

CIVILIAN LEADERSHIP

All students of the organization of America's puissant Army have given Woodrow Wilson the place as the foremost civilian strategist of his day. And second only to Wilson's high place, the crowning civilian honor has been given by military experts to Newton Baker, Secretary of War.

Wilson's and Baker's leadership is seen in their selection of Pershing as head of the American Expeditionary Force, their securing of the Selective Draft, their direction of the raising of an army of two and one-half million men and making it ready in an incomparably short time to reach the fighting front, and their appreciation of the whole-hearted joinder in perfect unity of the Navy and Marine Corps. When Pershing was ready to sail for France, Secretary Baker said, "I will give you only two orders—one, to go to France, and the other, to come home after victory. If we do not win, the country will hang you and me on the first lamp-post."

PERSHING'S TRIUMPHAL ENTRY

The military hero of the war was "Black Jack" Pershing and he was hailed by such a reception on September 17, 1919, in Washington, as the capital had never seen. We were in a sense still in "the horse and buggy days." Pershing rode a prancing horse under the triumphal march over the same route Grant had led the victorious Federal Army when it was given an ovation after Appomattox. But while Pershing rode a horse, others used automobiles, and the celebration took only one day, whereas in 1865 it required two days— May 23 and 24. Pershing rode his steed like a veteran who lived in the saddle. Years afterward (1937) when I was in Paris with Pershing as a member of the Monuments Commission, I was present when a model of the equestrian statue of Pershing, which was to be placed at the entrance to Versailles facing a like statue of Pétain, was unveiled. Graciously acknowledging the honor, Pershing facetiously said: "In my country there is a saying that it is bad manners to look a gift horse in the mouth, but I must say I do not think I ever looked as stolid when I was riding in the cavalry." I could testify he was right when I recalled his perfect mastery of his magnificent horse as he rode down Pennsylvania Avenue when his troops were reviewed by the President in front of the White House. Receiving distinguished honors—most deserved—Pershing told Congress:

"The benefits flowing from the experience of our soldiers will be broadly felt. They have returned in the full vigor of manhood, strong and clean. In the community of effort men from all walks of life have learned to know and to appreciate each other. Rich in the consciousness of honorable public service, they will bring into the life of our country a deeper love for our institutions and a more intelligent devotion to the duties of citizenship.

". . . the great achievements, the ideals, the sacrifices of our army and our people belong to no party and to no creed. They are the republic's legacy, to be sacredly guarded and carefully transmitted to future generations."

As he smilingly returned the enthusiastic salutes of the thousands, he looked every inch the hero he was and was all smiles. A reporter of the *Washington Post* wrote: "Watch his smile as he brings his hand down. It's like sunshine after rain. That's the man for you; the man who can smile and who can fight, too."

Pershing wore only one ribbon, the D. S. C., though he had been given enough decorations to beribbon his whole chest and whole body. Naturally the bands played, "And We Won't Come Back Till It's Over, Over There," and that's why they had not returned immediately after the Armistice. A Spanish-American War veteran complained because the band did not render, "There'll Be A Hot Time in the Old Town Tonight," while some wanted "Dixie" and "Yankee Doodle."

BEAT A RETREAT

Pershing had never known how to retreat in his long career in the Army, but that strategy was necessary in Washington, according to a leader of society. She told him: "As you have no wife you are fair game for all the widows and other women who love a celebrity, and unless you capitulate to their advances, you'll have to learn how to beat a retreat." He was the idol and toast, but his heart was never touched after the tragic death of his wife.

LOOKED DOWN ON WHITE HOUSE

When Pershing was made *The* General of the Army, he was quartered in the most beautiful public office in Washington—the office I occupied as Secretary of the Navy until war expansion called for a separate Navy Building. When I called on him he said: "I did not think when I called on you before going to Europe in 1917 that I would fall heir to your palatial official quarters."

I pointed out that he was the only high-ranking official in Washington who could from his perch "look down on the President," referring to the talk that he might become a candidate for President.

He waived the suggestion aside, content to stick to the military career that had brought him fame. I did not then tell him that from that portico Franklin Roosevelt had "looked down on the White House," and I had told him: "You are thinking some day you will occupy the White House." It was twenty years before that prophecy was fulfilled, and I did not pose as a prophet.

TRUMAN DID NOT MAKE THE HEADLINES BUT SERVED IN FRANCE WITH HONOR

Captain Harry S. Truman did not make the headlines like that other distinguished Missourian, General John J. Pershing. Such distinction was reserved for 1945 when, upon the death of Franklin D. Roosevelt, he became Commander-in-Chief of the American Army and Navy. However, after serving in the National Guard in Missouri, he was, on May 22, 1917, commissioned a First Lieutenant of Battery F. When the regiment was called into Federal Service on August 5, 1917, he went with his outfit to Camp Doniphan (now Fort Sill, Oklahoma), where the regiment was redesignated the 129th Field Artillery, part of the 35th Division.

Early in 1918, after taking the examination for his captain's bars, Truman went overseas with the Division School Detail, sailing from New York on March 30 on the transport *George Washington*. He arrived in Brest on April 13, attended the Second Corps Artillery school at Chantillon sur Seine for six weeks, and rejoined his regiment at Angers, as adjutant of the Second Battalion. The outfit was sent to artillery school at Coetquedon for five weeks. Truman was given his first command—of Battery D—at Rennes, capital of Brittany.

One night in the Argonne Captain Truman's Battery D found itself bracketed by enemy fire. It looked as if the whole unit were going to be blown off the map. Leaving guns and equipment the men started to scatter. Suddenly, Truman, whose horse had fallen and thrown him into a shell hole, scrambled to his feet and cut loose with a barrage of his own—a verbal one.

"It was beautiful," a gunner later said. "He called us every name west of the Mississippi. We stopped like whistled-after rabbits and in two minutes were back lammin' it at the Germans."

The enemy batteries were silenced; Battery D lost only one man. Thereafter—even when made a major—the young Missourian was

"Captain Harry," and a sure way to pick a fight was to say anything against Truman.

The last week of the war found Truman and his men in the thick of the Meuse-Argonne encounter with the 60th Field Artillery Brigade in support of the 81st Division. From November 7 to 11, they fired a constant barrage. The long-barreled 75's grew hot enough to fry eggs on, and were cooled with wet blankets.

Even longer than a war, to a homesick soldier, are the months of waiting for demobilization. Battery D stayed in the same sector for a time, then moved to Brest, and finally, on April 9, 1919, set sail for America. Truman has two outstanding memories of the voyage— one of standing at the railing wondering why someone didn't invent a cure for seasickness; the second, of a loving cup presented to him by his men from proceeds taken from shipboard crap games. The thirty-five-year old Missourian was discharged, with the rank of Major in the Reserves, at Camp Funston on May 6, 1919. Recently President Truman said:

> "I can remember that on November 10, 1918, we'd got our orders to move down the following afternoon into the Valley of Verdun. That next morning some units did move down. Some men I knew and thought a lot of got killed that morning. If we had moved down that afternoon, some of us would have got it. Those are the chances of war."

In 1945 Truman was given honors by the Verdun governing body.

XIX

THE SLUR ON BAKER DISPROVED

A LITTLE OVER A year after the end of the World War, the *Encyclopædia Britannica* brought down upon itself the just criticism of the Amercian people by printing a sketch of Newton D. Baker that was so unjust that practically every man who knew of the distinguished service he had rendered demanded an apology from the editors and the exclusion of the sketch from future editions of the Encyclopædia. After a summary of Baker's life the article contained the following:

> "After the outbreak of the World War he endorsed the Administration's peace policy, supported the League to Enforce Peace, and urged that the National Guard be fully tried before compulsory service be decided upon. After America entered the war he recommended moderation toward conscientious objectors and forbade men in uniform to interfere with anti-conscription meetings. The charge of pacifism was often brought against him and his career generally as Secretary was widely condemned throughout the United States as lacking in energy, foresight, and ability, and especially for his failure to prepare adequately in the months immediately preceding the American declaration of war."

Ralph Hayes, who had been close friend and private secretary to Secretary Baker, and who knew perhaps better than anybody of Baker's service as Secretary of War, protested to the publishers of *Britannica* and demanded that in the next edition the true story of Baker's service as Secretary of War should replace the scandalous one. Instead of making the amende honorable promptly, Hugh Chisholm, the Editor-in-Chief of the *Encyclopædia Britannica,* in refusing to make the appropriate corrections, wrote Mr. Hayes, "So far as my knowledge goes this is accurate enough and indeed fairly reflects the prevalent American atmosphere in regard to the former Secretary of War's record."

To Raymond Fosdick, who had protested vigorously, Mr. Hooper, the American editor, wrote, "In the case of Mr. Baker it [*Britannica*] stated what it believed was the fact. Such was the judgment of its editors." The demand that the name of the writer of the sketch of Baker be disclosed was refused, and Hayes was informed that the author was not known. However, the barrage of denunciation got under the skin of the editors and in the edition of the *Britannica* of 1924 the sketch was changed to read as follows:

"After the outbreak of the World War he endorsed the administration's peace policy and supported the League to Enforce Peace. The appointment as Secretary of War was widely criticized on the ground that Mr. Baker was a pacifist. After America entered the war his administration of the department was also widely criticized, especially during the early part of 1918 when a Senate Committee conducted an investigation. Mr. Baker then made certain changes in the department; the result was a considerable improvement. He was largely responsible for the centralization of industrial affairs; he insisted upon the selective draft; and he prevented any political interference with the conduct of the war."

This was most unsatisfactory and then again in 1926 the *Britannica* printed the third version which was little improved upon the original slanderous so-called biography. The third trial of how not to apologize and retract had the following:

"Although an avowed pacifist, immediately after the organization of the 65th Congress in 1917, he submitted a plan for universal military conscription, and remained at the head of the Department of War throughout the whole period of the World War and to the retirement of Wilson in 1921. Administration policies regarding preparedness, conduct of the war and treatment of conscientious objectors became the subject of severe criticism, much of it for partisan ends. In reply to this, he maintained before the Chamberlain Senate Committee early in 1918 that 'no army of similar size in the history of the world has ever been raised, equipped or trained so quickly.' After 1921 he resumed the practice of law in Cleveland. In the Democratic convention of 1924, he made a strenuous but losing fight for a strong League of Nations plank."

CARICATURE OF GREAT OFFICIAL

As soon as I obtained new volumes of *Britannica* and read the sketches of myself and Baker, I wrote to Mr. Cox, president of the Britannica Company in New York City, and said:

"I do not know who wrote them, but I have read them pretty carefully and I should judge that some of them were written by the literary manager of the Republican Campaign Committee. The one about Mr. Baker, I feel like cutting out of my volume. It is a caricature of the service of a man of ability who did a great job and a great work. I shall be glad to hear from you and to know that your Encyclopædia which for so many years has been regarded as fair, intended to make amends for this wholly unjustified biography.

"I do not exactly understand why this Encyclopædia should have emphasized the fact that I am a politician. I do not object to it, because I think a politician of the right kind is rendering quite as important service as a man of any other calling. It happens, however, that neither Mr. Baker nor I is a politician nor has any man in Mr. Wilson's cabinet ever made politics his profession. I am the editor of a newspaper and politics with me has been a side line. Mr. Baker is a lawyer and a politician on the side. By what theory do you label us politicians and label other men who have been more in politics than we have, as statesmen and diplomats? I am asking this for information, not that I care a gnat about being placed as a politician."

Answering my letter, Mr. Cox wrote me on December 16, 1922, as follows:

"The term 'politician' as always used in the Encyclopædia Britannica (and I think I may add in all other encyclopædias) is used in the proper sense of the term without any opprobrious meaning. The meaning is, as given in the Century Dictionary 'One who is versed in the science of government and the art of governing; one who occupies himself with politics.' Whether such person fills the office creditably or the opposite is quite another question. The editors tell me they know no other term in the English language to substitute for it. The word diplomat is limited to one 'officially employed in international intercourse' and statesman to the few who have exhibited unusual ability and sagacity."

In addition Mr. Cox said as regards the biography of Mr. Baker, "Certainly Mr. Ralph Hayes, Mr. Baker's private secretary, has read into it much that the editors did not intend to put in it and which the editors most strongly believe is not there. That Mr. Baker was criticized severely is an historic fact." He undertook to defend the fairness of the *Britannica,* which could not be done, by referring to the fact that when it had been attacked "fiercely" and one editor "was tried and convicted for heresy," it was the policy that all errors that were pointed out were always corrected.

In my letter I had not called the attention of the editor to the fact that while denominating Baker and me as "politicians," in the same edition the editors had called McAdoo and John W. Weeks, Senator from Massachusetts, "American public officials," and Mr. Balfour was denominated a "British statesman." I pointed out that it was a little remarkable that the term "politician" was not used to denominate any political leader in England or any Republican in the United States but was reserved for Mr. Baker and myself who had directed the American armed forces in the World War.

PROTESTS FROM ALL QUARTERS

I joined with General Pershing and a thousand other distinguished men in military and civil life to demand that the *Britannica* recant and repair, so far as it could do so, the wrong it had done Baker—a wrong, however, which by reason of the violent reaction and denunciation had done him no injury. If I should print in this volume the letters of protest written, it would be to call the roll of the most distinguished Americans of that day, including in addition to practically all the officers of the Army and Navy, such illustrious names as Daniel Willard, Julius Rosenwald, Glenn Martin, Dwight Morrow, John D. Ryan, James W. Wadsworth, J. S. Cullinan, Leonard P. Ayres, Edward R. Stettinius, Sr., Harry A. Garfield, F. F. Kappel, John R. Mott, Clarence Howard, Owen D. Young, Bernard M. Baruch, Samuel Gompers, and nearly every president of a college or university in America and most of the social leaders as well as industrialists and men of all professions and callings.

Illustrating the character of the letters I make room only for extracts from three. The first from General Pershing, Commander of the American Expeditionary Force, said:

"It fell to Mr. Baker probably more than any other individual in America, excepting President Wilson, to contribute to or detract from the force and effectiveness of American military contribution to the cause of the Allies. Maligned, misrepresented and scandalously abused by narrow partisans or uninformed, he held consistently to a policy which had for its sole purpose the prompt and effective overthrow of the Central Powers. His support of the Commander-in-Chief of our forces in France was complete, whole-hearted, and unswerving."

Honorable James W. Wadsworth, distinguished Republican and Chairman of the Committee on Military Affairs of the United States Senate, wrote:

"Britannica suffers much more in this matter than does Mr. Baker. It is too bad that such a splendid publication should have made such a mistake. It is utterly false. It is absurd. Mr. Baker had the courage and foresight to advocate and insist upon the selective draft as a means of recruiting the American Army at the outset of the war.

"He had the foresight to plan or direct his subordinates to plan America's participation in the war upon a scale so large as to make the defeat of Germany inevitable."

The third letter I quote, was written by Honorable Dwight Morrow, of the Morgan firm and afterwards Ambassador to Mexico and United States Senator, who said:

"The Encyclopædia Britannica sketch of Secretary Baker is, of course, ridiculous. It must have been written by one who had very little knowledge of the facts. In my mind Britannica is hurt more than Secretary Baker by this kind of article."

BAKER UNCONCERNED

While almost every man who knew anything about the conduct of the war was voicing indignation at the injustice done him, Newton Baker was complacently smoking his pipe and preaching the League of Nations doctrine. To a friend he wrote:

"I am not so concerned as I should be, I fear, about the verdict of history. For the same reason it seems unworthy to worry about myself when so many thousands participated in the

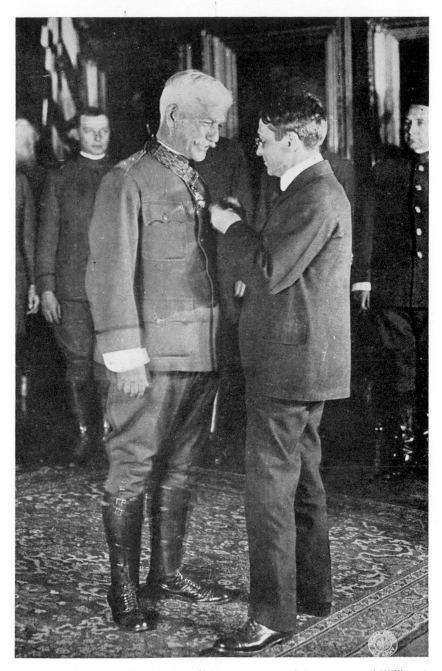

Secretary Baker, on behalf of the French Government, confers upon General William C. Gorgas, Surgeon General of the U. S. Army, the Legion of Honor (Signal Corps photo).

Upper left, Raymond B. Fosdick, Chairman Commission on Training Camp Activities of War and Navy Departments; with Pershing in France. *Upper right,* Rabbi Stephen S. Wise, supporter of Wilson and the League of Nations, to whom Wilson wrote his desire for success of Zion movement (International Film Service). *Lower left,* Dr. Franklin Martin, medical member of Advisory Commission of Council of National Defense. *Lower right,* Admiral Frazier, chief of chaplains of the Navy (U. S. Navy photo).

World War unsefishly and heroically who will find no place at
all in the records we make up and call history."

TRUE PEN PICTURE OF BAKER

It is a loss to history and literature that Secretary Baker did not
live to write his Memoirs. His facility as a writer and his experience
in public affairs, highlighted by direction of the Army in war and
wise counsel where decisions were reached, would have made a
book revealing and illuminating. Asked for his estimate of Baker
as a man and official, his friend and co-worker, Raymond B. Fosdick, in a personal letter (June, 1945) wrote me:

"Newton Baker was one of the most amazing men I ever
met—one of the most modest. I remember coming back from
Europe with him in May, 1919. The ship—it was the *George
Washington*—was held for us in the harbor of Brest for 24
hours, and it carried 4,000 troops. As we came alongside the
ship in a lighter, hundreds of doughboys crowded over to see
the Secretary of War and the whole side of the ship was lined
with faces. The boys were eager to cheer, and all that they
needed was just to have Baker wave his hat at them. We were
piped aboard and Baker made no gesture and there was no
cheer. I said to him afterwards, 'Why didn't you wave your
hand at those boys? They were dying to cheer you.' And Baker
replied, 'That's just what I was afraid of.' He never could see
why people would want to cheer him and always hesitated to
put himself in a position where they might. He was the most
completely self-effacing man I have ever met. Do you remember
the terrific criticism to which he was exposed because General
Leonard Wood was kept back here in the United States? As a
matter of fact, he was kept back at the request of Pershing. I
said to Baker one day: 'Why do you have to stand the gaff for
this? Why don't you tell the public what the facts are?' His
reply was: 'Pershing has got enough on his shoulders, and
what's a Secretary of War for?' "

BAKER DEFINES HIS PACIFISM

When called a pacifist by those who used the term to weaken
his influence, Secretary Baker entered no denial and engaged in no
controversy. Instead he silenced critics by defining his pacifism in
an address to the Reserve Officers Association in these words:

"I am a pacifist. I am a pacifist in my hope; I am a pacifist in my prayers; I am a pacifist in my belief that God made man for better things than that civilization should always be under the blight of this increasingly deadly destruction which war leaves us. And I am a pacifist in believing that the real contribution to that sentiment lies in adequate, sane preparedness on the part of any free people to defend its liberties."

Part Six

SIDELIGHTS AND HIGHLIGHTS

XX

MAKING MEN FIT FOR WAR

WORLD WAR I was the first war in history where civilian and military leaders showed such practical concern for health and morals (they are often twins) as was evidenced by the American government. Early in the war, with the deep interest and active support of President Wilson, the Secretary of War and the Secretary of the Navy appointed Commissions on Training Camp Activities. The purpose was to make men fit for fighting and afterwards to bring them back from war as fine and clean as they went. By a comprehensive recreational and educational program, and by strict enforcement of vice and liquor laws and regulations, the aim was to surround the men in service with an environment not only clean and wholesome but also positively inspiring—the kind of environment which a democracy owes to those who fight its battles. Looking back and assessing the work of the Commission, President Wilson said: "I do not believe it an exaggeration to say that no Army and Navy ever before assembled have had more conscientious and painstaking care given to the protection and stimulation of their mental, moral, and physical manhood."

Uncle Sam was fortunate in securing the acceptance of Raymond B. Fosdick, a man of rare spirit and ability, as Chairman of the Commission. Secretary Baker moved first, and six days after war was declared secured Mr. Fosdick's acceptance as Chairman for the Army work, along with eight men who were leaders in the best humane endeavors. Later when I came to appoint a Navy Commission of eighteen like-minded men and women (I beat Baker in recognizing the need of woman's intuition and direction), I asked Mr. Fosdick to be Chairman so that the Army and Navy could work as one team. He accepted and it was the first unity of direction in the conduct of war.

GRAPHIC WORD PICTURE

A little while ago I requested Mr. Fosdick to refresh his memory and give me some of the highlights of the achievements of a Commission which set a standard to be followed in all future wars. He replied that Newton Baker after the war had asked him to write the history, Baker saying it was his "moral responsibility," but other pressing matters caused him to disobey the order of his chief. However (June, 1945) at my request, in a personal letter, Mr. Fosdick gave a graphic recollection of the spirit of the Commission and some of those who were his associates and (without his knowledge or asking his consent) I am quoting it as a piece of illuminating war history:

"Dick Byrd was made the executive officer of the Commission, and my long friendship with him began at that time. I had never seen him until you appointed him. You will perhaps recall that he had been injured in some gymnasium work and was on inactive service; consequently he was available for our Commission. He did a gallant and effective job on a fulltime basis and was one of the most enterprising members that we had. However, his heart yearned for active service and he hated to have a swivelchair job in war time. Finally, as you will perhaps recall, he succeeded by dint of great perseverance in getting himself passed by the doctors and was assigned to air training at Pensacola. It was a sad day for us when he left, and I felt that the spirit had gone out of the work. But it was toward the end of the war and the better part of the job had already been done.

"John J. Egan served as acting chairman of the Commission during my long absences in Europe. He was a great organizer and he brought to the Commission a spirit of selfless devotion that was indeed rare. I became very fond of him and I used to say to him that the best thing that could happen to the Navy Commission was to have me go to Europe, because it left the Commission in better hands than mine.

"Perhaps the best-known member of our Commission was Walter Camp, who was in charge of athletics. Lee Hanmer was in charge of camp music, and John J. Egan was head of our section on entertainment. Joseph Lee of Boston headed up the work of organizing the communities in the neighborhood of naval stations through the organization known as the War Camp Community Service.

"For the work of law enforcement, i.e., keeping the camps and stations and the adjoining areas free from the evils of prostitution and alcoholism, we used the same personnel that we used in the Army Commission and this section was headed up by an Army man, Major Bascom Johnson, whom I had borrowed from the American Social Hygiene Association. The function of this division was outlined in Sections 12 and 13 of the Military Draft Act, which I had had some share in phrasing.

"To take care of our library service we used the American Library Association, which provided books both at home stations and abroad, as well as battleships.

"I wish I could throw some highlights on the situation. It is curious what odds and ends of memories one carries over a quarter of a century. For example, I remember that after the first meeting of the Navy Commission on Training Camp Activities in July, 1917, we all went to lunch at your house. During lunch, Mrs. Daniels, with that irrepressible Southern sparkle that always made her so charming, told me a story which I have always cherished. It had to do with a joint G.A.R. —Confederate veterans meeting that had recently been held in Washington. The old boys had had a parade which President Wilson had reviewed from a low stand in front of the White House. During the parade one of the Confederate veterans broke line and hobbled over to the stand. President Wilson leaned down to shake his hand, and the old veteran said: 'I'd never thought I'd live to see the day when I'd shake hands with a son of a bitch of a Yankee President!'

"May I say that my relations with you were always understanding and affectionate. I remember so well your big office with your desk at one end and the crowds of people waiting to see you at the other. Often the same problem arose in relation to both the Army and the Navy, and I would first see Secretary Baker and then come across the hall to see you. I must have made literally dozens of such trips, and I shall never forget the deep personal interest which both you and Baker gave to the work of the two commissions. It didn't make any difference how trivial the question was. I could always claim the attention of both of you. In the Navy Department Frank Roosevelt was also a source of great strength to our work, and more than once when you were away I talked with him about some problem that had developed.

"When I went to Europe Admiral Wilson in Brest and Admiral Sims in London went out of their way to give our work every possible support. No finer coöperation could have existed than we had with the Navy Department, nor did I ever meet a finer set of men than I met in the American Navy in 1917, 1918, and 1919. Probably they are just as good today and perhaps better, but to my way of thinking the Navy personnel of those years could never be surpassed."

WINS FIRST BATTLE OF THE WAR

No branch of the military service was more forehanded than the Medical Department of the Navy. At the end of the war, the House Naval Affairs Committee officially declared, "The first battle of the war, that against disease, was won by the Medical Department of the Navy." When, before we had fired a shot, I was pressing before the House Appropriations Committee for a large appropriation for medical supplies and an increase in medical personnel, this colloquy took place:

Chairman Swager Sherley: "Mr. Secretary, do you really think there is proof of the absolute need for the whole of the large amount asked for by the Surgeon General?"

Daniels: "I do not."

Sherley: "Then why are you here urging the appropriation of so large a sum?"

Daniels: "For the same reason that will cause you to appropriate it."

Sherley, astounded: "Explain why you make that statement."

Daniels: "I cannot see into the future. Surgeon General Braisted is a very wise man. He has given careful consideration to these estimates. If the war is short with few casualties, the quantity of medical supplies will not be needed. If, however, it is a long and bloody war and there should be call for medical supplies and they were not forthcoming because I had not recommended and you had not granted the large sum asked, what would the mothers and fathers say of you and me for not having seen that there was an abundance? The country would not be big enough to hide us from their condemnation."

The big appropriation was made and there was not a call on this side or in Europe or on Naval ships or on the transports carrying the more than two million troops to Europe and back when there was lacking medical attention and medical supplies.

MEDICAL STATESMEN

At home and in the field Surgeon General Gorgas, of the Army, and Surgeon General Braisted, of the Navy, found wise counsellors and associates among the foremost men of the medical profession who gave their time to direction and to service at home and at the front.

Dr. Franklin H. Martin, of Chicago, was the medical member of the Advisory Committee of the Council of National Defense, and with him, to name only a few of the score of the most eminent physicians and surgeons of America, were Drs. Wm. H. Welsh, J. M. T. Finney and Wm. S. Thayer of Baltimore; Wm. J. and Charles H. Mayo, of Rochester, Minn.; Hubert A. Royster of Raleigh, N. C.; Frank Simpson and Frank Billings, of Chicago; Albert Vander Veer, of Albany; Fred B. Lund, of Boston.

The personnel of the Navy Medical Corps increased to 3,095 doctors, 485 dentists, 1,713 women nurses, 16,564 members of the hospital corps.

No history of war-time activities of men who served in the war is more complete and informing than Dr. Martin's of what the medical profession accomplished in war days.

THE GREAT DR. GORGAS

The Army was peculiarly fortunate to have the great Dr. William C. Gorgas as Surgeon General during the war. Goethals was justly honored for digging the Panama Canal, but neither he nor any other engineer could have succeeded in that monumental task if Dr. Gorgas had not discovered a way to rid tropical countries of disease-carrying mosquitoes as Dr. Walter Reed had ended the yellow fever scourge in Havana.

Admiring him at a distance, I felt my admiration increased by close association when he came to Washington as Surgeon General of the Army. As victory over yellow fever was his first and last service, in one sense his skill in its treatment brought him his greatest happiness. As a young medical officer on duty at Fort Brown, Texas, he was summoned to attend Miss Marie Doughty, who was visiting her brother-in-law, Captain William J. Lyster, and had been stricken with yellow fever. Her recovery was abandoned and her grave was dug. As there was no chaplain at the Post, Dr.

Gorgas was asked to read the burial service. But under the skill of the young physician, who even then gave promise of future success, she rallied. Before her convalescence, Dr. Gorgas was stricken with the terrible disease. Upon his recovery a friendship followed which ripened into love and into a perfect marriage. It had been a yellow fever epidemic that drove his mother from her home in Mobile to a near-by military post where she met Lieutenant Josiah Gorgas and became his wife. The father was a distinguished officer in the Confederate Army, General Joseph E. Johnston saying: "He created the Ordnance Department out of nothing."

The amazing triumphs of the medical men in the Army during the World War is in large part attributable to the genius and fore-sight of General Gorgas. A comparison of the remarkable record of the Army with Florence Nightingale's description of the hospitals at Sebastopol makes it stand out as an achievement to the glory of the American medical profession.

When war came, Surgeon General Gorgas of the Army and Surgeon General Braisted of the Navy coöperated to organize staffs of the most distinguished surgeons in America, who made sure that there was no lack of medical skill among the soldiers and sailors of our country. One of the most impressive memorial services in the history of the national capital was in honor of Dr. Gorgas, held under the auspices of the Southern Society, of which Dr. Gorgas was an honored member. It was fitting that the principal address was made by the Honorable Newton D. Baker, whose father, like the father of Dr. Gorgas, was a medical officer in the Confederate Army: It was a perfect tribute. Ambassadors and Ministers from Cuba and South America related the obligation their countries owed to the man who had rid their country of its greatest curse. In my address, after a heartfelt tribute, I remarked upon the small number of monuments erected in Washington in memory of distinguished men of the medical profession.

ONLY CRITICISM DISPROVED

During the entire war there was only one criticism as to medical efficiency. Early in the war Senator Calder, of New York, made a charge in the Senate that the Navy's hospital ship, the *Solace,* was overcrowded and sailors were neglected. It was based on a letter from an enlisted new recruit on the ship. The Surgeon General convinced the Senator that, while there was some overcrowding, there was no justification for the charges that had been made public in the Senate and broadcast in the press. Ordinarily the statement of satisfaction by the Senator after investigation would have been enough. However, I knew that as hundreds and thousands of youths were enrolling in the Navy, the story of lack of care for the sick would disturb the mothers, and nothing would satisfy them about the Navy but a clean bill of health. I therefore requested three of the most eminent men in America—Dr. W. H. Welch, Dr. Abraham Flexner, and Nathan Straus, a generous philanthropist who was interested in hospitals—to investigate and state the truth about the situation. They visited the *Solace,* found that the crowding had been remedied and gave high commendation to the doctors and nurses and the Navy administration. That satisfied the country, which owed a debt of gratitude to the three eminent men who rendered a real service.

MAKING OFFICIALS PHYSICALLY FIT

"You will certainly fall down in your war duties when you do not take regular exercise," was the warning I had from an authority on athletics. He added, "The condition of the Cabinet and advisers is as important as that of the troops."

Early in the war Walter Camp, the foremost athletic strategist in America, came from Yale to Washington and became Chairman of the Navy Athletic Commission organized in every Navy district. Its work in making and keeping the young men fit was a valuable contribution. He was not content with prescribing strenuous exercises for the young men. He rented a house in Washington and made it a place for athletic exercise for members of the Cabinet and others with responsible duties. A score accepted his invitation, and every morning at seven o'clock they repaired to his place for setting-up exercises, then a rub-down and breakfast with Camp before entering upon their duties.

"Report tomorrow morning," Mr. Camp said to me. "Orders is orders." I was grateful to him, but I had not taken any exercise since at the age of eighteen I was Captain of the Swift Foot baseball team. During the war, my working hours were from 9:00 A.M. to midnight. Except once a week, when the members of the Cabinet gathered for lunch to continue their discussion following a meeting,

I ate my lunch of a sandwich and a glass of milk at my desk. I often invited an Admiral to join me in the frugal repast as we continued discussion of some matter in hand.

"I cannot go," I said to Walter. "I need the sleep more than the exercise."

He scouted the idea and said, "You will fall down with your heavy duties unless you keep yourself hard and fit and you must follow my regimen."

I countered: "But I have taken no exercise in thirty years and am very well. It is getting hot weather, and I do not think I should begin at this time."

He thought I was a slacker and said it was his duty to order me to the morning setting-up exercises.

I almost felt like a slacker, but said: "I will consult the Surgeon General." Camp went to see him and told him I was endangering my capacity to carry on. Admiral Braisted advised me: "You violate all rules by taking no exercise, but as you are well with your habits, I would not advise you to undertake physical exercise in the warm days ahead." Walter Camp gave me up as hopeless and predicted that I could not keep up under the strain. Result: I did not lose a day from work during the whole war, while McAdoo, Lane, Franklin Roosevelt and two Admirals had to go to the hospital. I did not tell Walter Camp that his training did it. They would have had to go anyway, but it proved that as to myself my course didn't slow me down.

When I informed my Raleigh neighbor and surgeon, Dr. Hubert Royster, who was an officer of the Medical Reserve during the war, of my decision, he said: "Walter Camp is eternally right about everybody but you. I couldn't get along without my daily dozen, but as you have kept well over a quarter of a century without taking exercise, I put you down as a rare specimen, an exception to every rule."

When others taking exercise daily fell out, while I was going strong, Walter said, "I guess your Raleigh doctor is right in calling you a rara avis, but you'd live longer if you would follow my advice." Walter and his pupils have passed on, while I was strong and vigorous when I celebrated my eighty-third birthday.

Before coming to Washington to draft me and other officials into the strenuous daily dozen of physical training, Walter Camp wrote me that "every American had a stake in the country dependent upon you and your associates, upon whom *living* and *fit,* he is ready to blindly rely," and, as an argument why officials should give "three hours a week to a scientifically-tested schedule of combined out-door and in-door exercise," he asked a series of questions of which this was illustrative:

> "If you had a superintendent in a factory who doubled the number of hours he was running his automatic machinery and instead of doubling the amount of oil actually cut it in half and thus ruined the machines, what would you say of him?"

FIGHTING VENEREAL DISEASES

Among the earliest actions of the Council of National Defense, initiated by medical officers, was the recognition that alcohol and sexual promiscuity were the main causes of impairment of the efficiency of men in the armed forces. In April the Medical Board passed a resolution that "sexual continence is compatible with health and that it is the best prevention of venereal infections," that the use of "alcohol was a factor in spreading venereal diseases in the Army" and the President was asked to request Congress "to suppress the manufacture, importation, and sale of intoxicating liquors until after the close of the war," and the action of the Army and Navy to prohibit alcoholic beverages within military places was approved. These wise foresights by the most eminent medical men in America were greeted with approval and disapproval inside and outside the Council of National Defense, one member saying: "You shall not make the war an opportunity for so-called reformers to accomplish their nefarious work. When have fighting men been preached to on the beneficence of continence? The millennium has not yet arrived."

IMMORALITY UNDER BAN

Dr. Franklin Martin, Director of the Medical Board of the Council, records in his book:

> "When we [the Advisory Commission] marched into the meeting of the Council of National Defense, Secretary Daniels, who in the absence of Secretary Baker, was presiding, beckoned to me and said, 'Doctor, I understand that there is an organized opposition to your resolutions that were adopted Sunday. In

conversation with the President and the Secretary of War they have expressed their approval without change. I hope under this pressure you have not altered the resolutions in any way. If so, it is better to adjourn the meeting without action.' "

The resolutions as to action on continence, venereal diseases, and the exclusion of alcohol from military bases were adopted by the Council, and later Congress carried out the suggestion of the medical leaders and gave the country war-time prohibition. The great forward step proposed by the doctors was made the policy of the Army and Navy during the war, and carried out by the Commission on Training Camp Activities.

YOUTHS WERE SHIELDED

For the first time in the history of war, alcohol was taboo wherever men were trained or bivouaced for war, and the young men coming into the armed services were shielded from the houses of prostitution, which are the prolific source of spreading venereal diseases and rendering men unfit for combat duty.

The benefits of the order, excluding intoxicants in the Navy, with the inclusion of protection from lewd women, prevailed wherever men were in the armed forces. It gave America the soberest, cleanest, and healthiest fighting men the world has known.

It must not be supposed the only criticism of this moral code was in the Council. There were not wanting those in the Army and Navy who sneered at what they called, "Sunday School tutelage," but they were few in number. General Pershing, head of the Army, and Admiral Mayo, Commander-in-Chief of the Navy, approved the sensible steps taken.

"BY THIS CRAFT WE HAVE OUR WEALTH"

The most bitter criticism came from those interested in making money out of the weaknesses of human beings—liquor men and manufacturers of contraceptives. The latter on some ships made it a practice of getting some petty officers to hand out a package to each sailor as he went on leave and telling him it would prevent disease when he failed to practice continence. When I learned of what was really a suggestion to immorality to youths away from home for the first time, I forbade the practice and no more packages were distributed. This incident shows that ever since the days of

Demetrius there have been men who, influenced by the saying, "By his craft we have our wealth," are ready, in order to make money, to debauch even those men upon whom the country depends in war. I not only issued orders; I appealed to the youth to heed the wise counsel of the most competent physicians and practice sexual continence, and many a young man who heeded this advice returned home free from what often makes more wounds than the bullets of the enemy.

ATTITUDE OF ARMY AND NAVY

Secretary Baker stated his attitude in these words:

"Our responsibility in this matter is not open to question. We cannot allow these young men, most of whom will have been drafted to service, to be surrounded by a vicious and demoralizing environment, nor can we leave anything undone which will protect them from unhealthy influences and crude forms of temptation."

On June 20, 1917, I had expressed the thought of the Navy as follows:

"There lies upon us morally, to a degree far outreaching any technical responsibility, the duty of leaving nothing undone to protect these young men from that contamination of their bodies which will not only impair their military efficiency but blast their lives for the future and return them to their homes a source of danger to their families and to the community at large.

"These dangers are bad enough in ordinary times. They are multiplied manifold in times of war, when great bodies of men are necessarily gathered together away from the restraints of home, and under the stress of emotions whose reactions inevitably tend to dislodge the standards of normal life, and the harpies of the underworld flock to make profit of the opportunity. If we fail in vigilance under these conditions, the mothers and fathers of these lads, and the country generally, will rightly hold us responsible."

Speaking to the Clinical Congress at Chicago on October 22, 1917, I said:

"You, gentlemen of the medical profession, deal with life and death. You bring the babies into the world and you close the eyes of the dead. Yours is the ministering function, the intimate touch, and out of such relations you can exercise an amazing power of suggestion. It is this power that America calls upon you to use. Tell our youths the truth. It is a duty laid upon you, not by the moral law alone, but by the law of self-preservation that operates in nations as well as in individuals. That duty is imperative upon you now as never before. If you perform it, and our young soldiers and sailors heed your wise counsel,—and many of them will follow your teachings with lasting gratitude,—you will contribute more to the winning of the war than manufacturers of shells."

GORGAS AGAINST INTOXICANTS

General Gorgas was in Panama when the canal was dug and approved Colonel Goethal's orders requiring workers on the canal to refrain from the use of intoxicants. No pilot who drank liquor was permitted to carry ships through the canal. That experience and his observation in his long service in the Army caused him to oppose the use of intoxicating drinks on Government reservations as the Navy forbade their introduction on any Naval ship or shore station.

BIG STICK WHEN NECESSARY

The protection of youth in the Army and Navy was not always and everywhere easy. Most states and cities coöperated. The worst offenders were Philadelphia, where I sent Captain Hatch, an able Marine officer, to clean up the city of "Brotherly Love," and New Orleans, where houses of prostitution were licensed. I appealed to the Mayor of New Orleans to make his city fit for Naval trainees by securing the repeal of the century-old license of prostitutes. He came to Washington. I reviewed with him that when I became Secretary of the Navy, a Navy Yard at New Orleans had been closed, and in response to the earnest desires of the Mayor and other citizens, and to meet a real need of the Navy in the Gulf States, I had re-opened the Navy Yard. I said also that when war broke out I established a Naval training base in New Orleans, but I confided to him that the criticisms were so severe that I would not feel justified in continuing these Naval agencies unless the old French law that disgraced New Orleans was repealed. He promptly responded favorably and returned to New Orleans. The city authorities repealed the ordinance.

DISTINGUISHED PHYSICIANS WHO SERVED IN THE ARMY

Upper left, Dr. Charles H. Mayo, General. *Upper right,* Dr. William Mayo, General. *Lower left,* Dr. J. M. T. Finney, Brigadier General. *Lower right,* Dr. William H. Welch, General (all photos from U. S. Army Medical Museum).

Upper left, Charles W. Eliot, Harvard University, unofficial adviser of President Wilson. *Upper right,* Henry Van Dyke, of Princeton, chaplain in U. S. Navy during World War (Brown Brothers). *Lower left,* Edward Kidder Graham, President of the University of North Carolina, chairman of Southeastern Council of Education. *Lower right,* Frank Porter Graham, now President of the University of North Carolina, member of the U. S. Marine Corps during World War I.

NEWPORT NEEDED BITTER MEDICINE

All the people and officials in other cities were not as responsive as the Mayor of New Orleans. I can never forget that, though its good people wished Newport cleaned of festering places of ill fame, trouble climaxed in Newport when the only derelict chaplain of the Navy was found guilty of immoral conduct. His Bishop refused to believe the irrefutable evidence and persuaded Admiral Sims to go to Washington to intercede in behalf of the man who had disgraced the church. In order to give the Navy chaplain every opportunity, I directed Admiral Niblack, one of the best officers in the Navy, to investigate, and he was shocked at the evidence. Still the Bishop denounced the findings and upheld the minister. I, therefore, requested Assistant Secretary Franklin D. Roosevelt, an official in the Bishop's church, to go to Newport and look into the matter. When he found the conditions as reported and denounced them, he came in for the same condemnation of some church leaders that Naval officers and the Secretary of the Navy had received. The Bishop could not believe there was a Judas Iscariot in his church. He should have unfrocked him promptly.

The conditions of immorality were so disgraceful that I ordered Naval police to stand before houses of ill fame and prevent Navy personnel from entering the zones of rottenness. For this exposure of a bad situation I was not as popular as I deserved to be with some laissez-faire officials, and some who wanted a wide-open town for pecuniary reward. This caused the *Providence Journal* to make an independent investigation, and Editor Rathom telegraphed me (June 26):

> "Our investigation not only proves your charges were absolutely correct, but the houses of prostitution of the lowest type have been maintained under the patronage of city officials with police officers actually detailed to keep visitors in orderly lines before such places, awaiting their turn.... The peoples of Rhode Island owe you a debt of gratitude for your timely exposure."

The Navy exposure and denunciation of the authorities, backed by the *Providence Journal,* and the many good people of Newport, woke up the people and Newport was cleaned up. It was not only essential to the Navy as the site of the Navy War College and Torpedo Plant, but also as an important training station.

THE NAVY'S SKY PILOTS

The Navy was peculiarly fortunate in its Corps of Chaplains, headed by Chaplain Frazier, who had been Chaplain on Admiral Dewey's flagship in the Philippines when the Admiral and all in his fleet won renown. With the coming of war there was need of an increased number of the type of men who could win the hearts of the young and guide them in religious services. There is no more difficult task than that of chaplain in the Navy. He cannot succeed unless he secures the esteem and coöperation of officers and men, and the lack of access to them and often their aloofness fail to secure the desired close relationship. The Chaplain is less often to blame for this than the personnel, but a chaplain must be a regular fellow as well as a consecrated man, to fill the bill.

When I became Secretary of the Navy I found that the number of chaplains was the same as in 1841. The Navy personnel had increased from 12,000 men to 51,500, but there had been no increase in chaplains in all those seventy-three years. I secured an act allowing a chaplain for every 1,250 men, providing spiritual leadership for the young men of the service. When we entered the war, 175 more were commissioned, and Chaplain Frazier, of Tennessee, was made the Navy's first Chief Chaplain. He exercised the function of a bishop in the Navy church and deserved to have the rank of Admiral, which I proposed, and which was later granted. As Chaplain of Dewey's flagship at Manila Bay he was always beloved by the Admiral. During the battle he stood by Dewey's side on the bridge of the *Olympia*. At the Admiral's dying request Chaplain Frazier conducted the funeral of his great shipmate. He was a Methodist and the Chaplain of the Fleet was a Catholic—Chaplain Matthew Carlin Gleason. He was as eloquent as he was beloved, following in the footsteps of Father Chadwick, Chaplain of the ill-fated *Maine*. He proved that Catholics and Protestants could "work together for the glory of God." The Chaplains lacked nothing in measuring up to their holy office in that war, though no ballads were sung about "Praise the Lord and Pass the Ammunition."

I came in close touch with these men of God and can bear

tribute to the fidelity and consecration and high leadership of most of them.

THE CROSS LIFTED HIGH

As always, the Cross was lifted above the American flag during service on every ship. A congressman, who had a strong bias against Catholics and was on the lookout for some way to criticize, complained to me that he had observed in New York Harbor one Sunday morning that the Catholic priest had raised the emblem of the Catholic Church above Old Glory. He thought it an "outrage that Rome should thus claim to rank higher than America."

My answer to him was that on every ship in the American Navy during religious services the Cross was given the place of honor, and that if he had gone further down the river he would have seen the same Cross of Christ, which he called "the Catholic emblem," raised to the pinnacle of ships where Protestant chaplains were holding religious services. I arranged for a chaplain to be assigned to every dreadnaught.

COÖPERATION OF CHURCH LEADERS

During the World War an increased number of chaplains were appointed in the Reserve Corps to serve the expansion to 500,000 men in the Navy and Marine Corps, the most distinguished being Dr. Henry Van Dyke. Before making appointments I endeavored to ascertain how many of the enlisted men were Protestants, Catholics, and Jews, in order that each religion might be adequately represented in those who ministered to the men. The proportion of Catholic chaplains, when I came in office, had been less than was justified by the number of Catholic men enlisted. I conferred with Father Burke and Archbishop Hayes and asked them to name worthy priests as chaplains to give a fair proportion. They were glad to comply and suggested priests who proved their worth. With our entrance into the war, I requested the ablest leaders of each faith to nominate their best men for this holy work, with the result that the value of the service of these religious leaders was improved. I picked out a few myself, but they were selected as being acceptable to their church leaders also.

During the war Navy chaplains made full proof of their devotion. There was a "sky pilot" for every big ship and every important land base. They went with the Marines into the hell of fire in Belleau Wood, with Rodman's fleet of dreadnaughts in the North Sea, with the destroyers on their perilous journeys; they guided new recruits on sea and land. They were faithful, devoted spiritual leaders in days when men unafraid looked death in the face. These soldiers of the cross were comrades in battle, shipmates in storm, and comforters in death.

The chaplains not only held religious services, comforted the dying, buried the dead, but rendered every character of religious service and never shielded themselves from the discomforts and dangers inherent in war. Twelve were killed or wounded in action, and not a few died of illness caused by exposure and sacrifice.

In all the efforts of the two war secretaries, the chaplains, and the Commission of Training Camp Activities, they had the coöperation of President Wilson, who in a classic address to the fighting men as they went forth to battle said: "Let it be your pride to show all men everywhere not only what good soldiers you are, but also what good men you are, keeping yourselves fit and straight in everything, and pure and clean through and through."

CHRISTIAN SCIENTIST CHAPLAIN

We had appointed chaplains representing every creed except Christian Scientists. Inasmuch as members of that church were serving in the Army and Navy, leaders of the faith felt they should have spiritual advisers. The objection to that course came from medical officers. Finally on the 10th of January I named the first Christian Scientist chaplain, after first receiving assurances from church officials that there would be no conflict with the surgeons. That agreement was respected.

RELIGIOUS AND WELFARE ORGANIZATIONS

In addition to the work of the chaplains, the Red Cross, Salvation Army, the Catholic, Protestant, and Hebrew organizations volunteered the services of hundreds of well-trained men and women who in every part of the world added to the comfort and happiness of the men of the armed forces and were their moral and friendly mentors.

CHAPLAIN IN THE RANKS

During the war Chaplain T. P. Riddle called and told me he had resigned as chaplain because he could learn to serve the Navy by being an enlisted man without anybody in the Navy knowing he had been a chaplain. He was giving up a good salary and comforts and rank to fight in the ranks. I noted in my Diary: "This is the real spirit and I commended him warmly."

HOW CHAPLAINS WERE ASSIGNED

No officers have a more difficult and important assignment than Navy chaplains. Youths away from home are not always interested in religion and some are wholly indifferent. All chaplains cannot reach them. This was true at the Naval Academy as well as at training stations and afloat. As war drew near and the time came for the assignment of a new chaplain at the Naval Academy, I wished the successor to be a man who could reach and influence the midshipmen. Voyaging on a Navy ship in the Pacific, I observed the comradeship between the chaplain and the enlisted men. He entered into their spirit and they held him in esteem as a true shipmate. They thronged the ship chapel when he preached. His attitude alike to the enlisted men and officers convinced me he was the man needed at Annapolis. I therefore named Chaplain Sidney K. Evans as chaplain at the Naval Academy, though he did not rank that assignment. He was so popular and inspiring in his ministry that the officers and midshipmen insisted upon his remaining there until his retirement in 1935. He was called back to preach to the graduating class the next year. Upon his retirement Chaplain Evans wrote me (July, 1935):

> "You may remember that it was your good self who first sent me to the Naval Academy in October, 1915. At that time you told me it was as a result of a conversation which we had held when you were on the Pacific. You told me you were anxious to have a Chaplain at Annapolis who would join heartily in indoctrination with the proper ideas in regard to sailormen.... I have always considered myself appointed to duty at the Naval Academy by you for a special purpose. With affectionate regards for Mrs. Daniels."

I look back with satisfaction upon my association with the body of earnest chaplains in the Navy and my privilege of advancing their opportunities and their rank.

ADMIRAL MAHAN AND CHAPLAINS

Many stories are current in the Navy connected with differences between chaplains and commanding officers of ships. This one was told of Captain Mahan, a strict disciplinarian, who upheld every right of a commander. He was punctilious in his attendance upon religious services himself and expected officers and men to follow his example:

One morning he arrived late. The chaplain began the service before the captain arrived, and was saying: "The Lord is in his holy temple; let all the earth keep silence before him," as the captain arrived but before he had taken his seat. Addressing the chaplain, the captain said: "Chaplain, I would have you know that the Lord is not in His holy temple until I have taken my seat."

Here is another story, which was told of Mahan and another officer. Captain Mahan was very religious, a student of the Bible, and prided himself upon his orthodoxy. He opposed all innovations and any introduction of secular topics in the sermon. One morning, after the chaplain had preached a sermon that ran counter to the captain's theology and his social views, Mahan sent for him and rebuked him for his religious and social heresies. He concluded with the direction: "Hereafter you will write out your sermon and furnish me with a copy for my approval every Saturday, I will have no unsound doctrines uttered on my ship."

The chaplain declined, saying: "I will obey any order you issue that affects my military duty, but I am responsible only to God when I enter the pulpit. No officer has the right to censor my sermons."

Mahan was irate. "I will report you to the Secretary of the Navy for insubordination." He was as good as his word and requested the Secretary to direct the chaplain to submit his sermon to his superior officer. At the same time the chaplain wrote to the Secretary stating that as a servant of the Most High he owed allegiance in his religious messages to no human authority. Both waited for the decision of the Secretary. They are still waiting. It was a decision that no one with less wisdom than Solomon could make. Both officers have long been dead. That is one question no Secretary of the Navy has ever passed upon.

Admiral Mahan to the day of his death took great interest in the affairs of his church, and the only time I ever saw him after the war was when he visited my home city to attend a meeting as a trustee of St. Augustine School, a church institution for the education of Negroes, established by the Episcopal Church soon after the close of the war in the sixties. He took a keen interest in its work.

CHAPLAINS GIVE MEDALS

So far as I can recall the only medals given the President, Secretary of War, and Secretary of the Navy, were presented them by the Committee on Army and Navy Chaplains, the same awarded to all chaplains during the war. It was given to Wilson because of his leadership "in winning the World War and bringing to the world the ideals of the Word embodied in the League of Nations." In his letter of acceptance, Wilson paid tribute to "the sacrificial spirit with which the chaplains ministered to the troops, bearing their hardships with them and carrying the comfort and consolation of their ministry to the front line trenches where only the brave could survive."

XXI

COLLEGES IN THE WAR

W ILSON HAD TO decide many questions that called for Solomonic wisdom. One was the place colleges and universities and students should take in the war. The draft emptied colleges of youths of the age fixed by law. The President called on the heads of institutions to stick to their posts and give military training along with their academic instruction. Dr. Edward Kidder Graham, President of the University of North Carolina, was head of this duty in the South Atlantic States. Some British officers, who had been invalided by wounds, came over and gave military instruction to students.

WANTED TO SHOULDER GUNS

Dr. Graham was a Patriot with a big "P." He believed that others could do the teaching and that he must fight in the trenches. Long before either President Wilson or I had seen our way to think our country should enter the war, he had been insistent in urging that course. To the very marrow of his being he believed that civilization was at stake and that a German victory would turn the clock back to the days when Force alone ruled. After the sinking of the *Lusitania,* every time I saw Graham he wanted to know why Wilson did not take up arms against German frightfulness. We were close friends. I had placed him in nomination when he was elected President of the University, the youngest of presidents. Every now and then he would write me to urge Wilson to throw American influence into the scale against what he always called "German frightfulness." Not very long after the United States had declared that a state of war existed and was pouring its manhood into European battle-fields, Graham wrote that he must see me about "the most important decision of my life." I invited him to visit me. He came to Washington. We sat up half the night in a heart-to-heart talk. "You know," he said, "that from the first I have urged our participation in the great struggle. Now that the battle is on, I must shoulder a gun and cross the seas and bare my body in a struggle which I believe is holy. I cannot do otherwise."

I pointed out that as directing head of military training of youths in the Southern universities he was doing ten times more to win the war than if as one soldier he were fighting in the trenches. "That sounds good," he answered, "but it does not satisfy my sense of duty. Others can stay home and do that work as well as I can. The only way a man can make perfect consecration to the cause is to expose himself to the enemy in battle. I cannot sleep with myself until I am in the trenches in France."

We talked late into the night. I never saw a man more dominated by a conviction that actually offering his body and his life was essential to one who felt as deeply as he did the significance of the struggle. We finally went to bed, but neither of us to sleep. He was unchanged in his purpose in the morning. I had one more card to play. I went to the White House and told the story to President Wilson. He was interested and moved by Graham's sincerity and readiness to sacrifice. I told him that nothing but his orders to Graham to serve where the Commander-in-Chief knew he could do most for the cause would prevent Graham's enlistment as a private soldier and hurrying to France. He issued the direction.

Unwillingly Graham obeyed and was in the midst of organizing the collegians of the South for future participation in the war when a fatal attack of influenza ended his life. He was as truly a war casualty as if he had fallen on the battle fields of France, and yet he would have preferred to die with his face to the enemy where the fighting was fiercest.

I think at heart Wilson was more sympathetic with Graham than his formal direction indicated. Why do I say this? Later, in his Victory Message to Congress (December 2, 1918), Wilson said:

"Those of us who stayed at home did our duty; the war could not have been won or the gallant men who fought it given their opportunity to win it otherwise; but for many a long day we shall think ourselves 'accursed we were not there, and hold our manhood cheap while any speaks that fought' with those at St. Mihiel or Château-Thierry."

Edward Kidder Graham's young cousin, Frank Graham, who later became President of the University and received his mantle, entered the Marine Service as a private.

"Why didn't you come to see me when you were in Washington and let me know you were in the Marine Corps?" I asked him at the close of the war.

"I was afraid you might wish to do something for me and I wished to stand on my own. I didn't want to embarrass you or be embarrassed. All I wanted was to serve where the officers thought I could serve best."

That is the stuff of which the Grahams are made. It explains why they make great and popular Presidents of the University to which North Carolinians are devoted.

Frank Graham's service embraced both wars—as a Marine in 1917-18 and as head of a university in 1941-45 that has trained thousands for the armed services. As a trusted friend of President Roosevelt he served with conspicious ability on the War Labor Board and was a vital leader in all movements for broadening opportunities and securing a better world for all the people. The campus of his university extends to and includes the fishing folk, the farming folk, the workers in factories and in all lines of human endeavor, and is not limited to those who matriculate in the prescribed college courses.

YOUNG BOYS ANXIOUS TO ENLIST

A question, which pressed for solution early in the war was first brought up by me upon the request of Professor Abbott of Yale, who wished to be advised whether boys should leave college to enlist in the Navy. President Wilson was clear that under the existing conditions the answer should be No. He said, "College boys should be drilling and getting ready for later service, but the best preparation is for the youths to stay at school." That was the opinion of the Cabinet and I so advised Professor Abbott. Like advice was given to scores of heads of colleges and high schools and to numerous boys who were eager to get into the war. By the thousands there were earnest and intrepid youths who wished to take

> "The khaki and the gun
> Instead of cap and gown...."

As time went on, and well-grown boys of fifteen saw their brothers, who were no bigger, donning the uniform, they applied for enrollment. Not a few gave incorrect statements, saying they were "over eighteen." I recall the story of a strapping fifteen-year-old boy, determined to get in, who when asked his age replied that he was "over eighteen." When chided for his untruth, he said he had made no false statement. "Before I went in to enlist I took off both my shoes and put a slip of paper in the sole of each on which I had written 'over 18'—I was literally truthful."

In my own family my oldest, Josephus Jr., early enlisted as a Marine and my second son, Worth Bagley, was a midshipman in the Naval Academy. My third son, Jonathan, aged fifteen, felt that he was big enough to fight as well as his older brothers. I quoted the law and the regulations to him and bade him wait until he reached the age fixed by his country for military service. I thought he acceded to my view when I told him that he could not enlist in the Navy or Marine Corps. Some time later Secretary Baker, as we were going to a Cabinet meeting, said to me:

"Joe, I had an important visitor this morning, your son Jonathan. He told me that he was as well-qualified to enlist for the war as his two older brothers, but that you would not permit him to enter the Navy or the Marine Corps, and he had come to ask me to waive his age and let him enlist in the Army. I used your argument, Wilson's public declaration and my own judgment in the effort to convince him that the public policy not to grind the seed-corn was wise. I said: 'Go to school, Jonathan. Nobody knows how long this war is going to last and the more you learn the better qualified you will be to serve your country, if you are called when you have reached the legal age.' But my argument did not convince him, and he went away feeling that I hadn't given him the chance he craved."

Neither his mother nor I had any idea that Jonathan had gone direct to the Secretary of War to make his application. If we had known it, he would have been forbidden. He was emboldened to go direct to Baker because he had formed an attachment for the Secretary of War and it was reciprocated. "What are you going to be when you are a man?"—Baker told me he had asked the boy one day, and he answered: "An editor." Baker said, "Good, Jonathan, and when you are editor of the *News and Observer,* I will become a subscriber." The boy got the best of him by his answer. "Why wait so long? Better subscribe now."

Many times parents appealed to Baker and me to release young sons who in their patriotic zeal had mistated their age and enlisted.

In every case their request was granted, but there were times when the enlisted youngster strenuously objected to being separated from the service. There were some instances brought to my attention where the youths upon their return home ran away to another recruiting station and reënlisted under an assumed name.

WILSON'S APPRECIATION OF YOUTH

In England in the darkest hours of the war it was said—and said truly—that Lloyd George's enthusiasm and contagious faith was worth a whole division of armed forces. In America it was equally true that Wilson's trumpet call and patriotic addresses, particularly to youth, stimulated, as did no other influence, young men from college halls, country homes, and city dwellings and other men going to the front. In his classic address to the American troops—all youths and young men—at Chaumont, France, on Christmas Day, 1918, he said:

"I wish that I could give to each one of you the message that I know you are longing to receive from those at home who love you. I cannot do that, but I can tell you how everybody at home is proud of you; how everybody at home has followed every movement of this great Army with confidence and affection; and how the whole people of the United States are now waiting to welcome you home with an acclaim which probably has never greeted any other army. Because this is a war into which our country, like these countries we have been so proud to stand by, has put its whole heart, and the reason that we are proud of you is that you have put your heart into it; you have done your duty and done it with a spirit which gave it distinction and glory."

XXII

WOMEN IN THE WAR

MARS IS ALWAYS represented as a husky man. Except the fabled Amazons who buckled on the sword, women have stayed behind the scenes and kept the home fires burning. Of course, since Florence Nightingale they had gone to the front as nurses so that there has been no lack of woman's nursing. It remained for the year 1917 to see women serve on the boards of the Council of National Defense and to wear the uniform of the Navy and Marine Corps with all the rights of the enlisted force. In the Red Cross, Y.W.C.A., Salvation Army, and other organizations, they rendered the highest service.

"Is there any law that says a yeoman must be a man?" That was the question I asked the Admiral in charge of the Bureau of Personnel, who reported in the early days of the war that there was immediate need of hundreds and thousands of clerks, stenographers, and others to carry on the increased work the conduct of the war required. I passed that question on to the Legal Department, and it reported there was no law saying that a yeoman must be a man. I then said, "Go ahead. Enroll as many women as are needed in the Naval Reserve as yeomen, and we will have the best clerical assistance the country can provide." There were enrolled 11,000 yeomen (F), and 269 Marines (F), the only women serving during the war who were on the same footing as men with all allowances and pay and clothing outfits; and, with the exception of Army and Navy nurses, they were the only women after the Armistice who were eligible for membership in the American Legion. Not only did women serve as clerks and stenographers and in other clerical positions, but in making torpedoes and in many plants making munitions for the war.

The best type of young woman early applied for enrollment and there was no kind of service ashore they did not render and render with the highest efficiency. I have always prided myself as a designer of uniforms for women. There was much debate as to what

211

sort of uniform should be provided for these yeomen and marines. Several suggestions were made. The uniforms which were adopted (and having married into the Worth family, I claim to have been as good a designer of women's clothes as Worth of Paris) were so beautiful that afterwards they were copied by women all over the country. In the early days of enlisting I recall an incident. A lady' in Washington went to the recruiting office and said, "I wish to enroll as a yeoman but before I enlist I want to know what ship I am to serve on." It was explained to her that women were not to go to sea. "But I want to go on the *Nevada*," she said in a tone of disappointment. Investigation revealed that her fiancé was a sailor on the *Nevada*. She was told that in war times there was no place for honeymooners on battleships.

After the Armistice, the yeomen (F) and marines (F) were demobilized, and when the Rainbow Division was reviewed by President Wilson on their return from France, they were the guard of honor to the President. The country owed them a lasting debt of gratitude, and the efficiency of those women in World War I was responsible for the induction of many women into the armed forces in World War II.

WOMEN'S WAR COUNCIL

Early in the war, seeing the deep interest of the women in every line of war work, President Wilson appointed leading women as the Woman's Committee of the Council of National Defense, with Anna Howard Shaw as Chairman, Carrie Chapman Catt as Vice Chairman, and representatives of eleven leading women's organizations. The members were on duty throughout the war, organized the women in every State, and spoke to most women's organizations. There was little done in the war that did not get stimulus from these great women. Dr. Shaw gave her entire time and had planned large things to meet postwar needs. She was on a speaking tour to strengthen the organization when she became ill and her death soon followed.

THEY WERE MILITANT

I recall that when Dr. Shaw felt the women were not given the recognition they deserved and their fair allotment of war work, she made a vigorous protest and demanded equality with her male associates. When she and her associates felt they were like some church auxiliaries with no real work, she was irked and spoke out freely of what she regarded as lack of appreciation. Dr. Shaw thought agencies of the Treasury, Food and Fuel Administration should work with them. She announced bluntly that if she was not allowed to do real work, she would "take her doll clothes and go home." The Council appointed Lane, prince of diplomats, to represent to her that she and her women associates were needed and that the conduct of the war would be hurt if she withdrew. A few days later the members of the Council attended a session of the Woman's Committee, when Baker and Dr. Shaw made patriotic addresses and harmony and coöperation were achieved.

PATRIOTIC WOMEN AT THE CAPITAL

With the coming of war, all social activities came to an end in Washington, and the women in official life, as well as all others in the country, gave themselves fully to works that would contribute to the comfort of the men in the armed forces. Mrs. Woodrow Wilson initiated a sewing room in the White House and organized war gardens; Mrs. Newton Baker was head of the Army Red Cross; Mrs. Josephus Daniels and Mrs. Franklin Roosevelt were officers in the Navy Red Cross; Mrs. Thomas R. Marshall and Mrs. Champ Clark organized the women in Congressional circles for war work. The women were abundant in labor and carried joy and cheer to the young men making ready for the great adventure.

XXIII

JEWS IN WILSON'S ADMINISTRATION

T HE FIRST SPEECH I attempted after being inducted into office was at a banquet given by B'nai B'rith, a welfare organization of Hebrews. I told to my Jewish audience this story, which fitted the spirit of the gathering:

"In the town of Wilson where I lived as a boy, there was a fine citizen, Emil Rosenthal. One day as the business men were gathered at the post office—the civic center and meeting place of the town—(My mother was post-mistress and I was clerk; so we knew all that was going on in the village) the news came that the home of a farmer had been burned. Every man expressed sorrow for the farmer who had lost his home on which there was no insurance.

" 'How sorry are you?' asked Mr. Rosenthal, adding, 'I am sorry twenty dollars.'

"As a result, all who sympathized with the farmer expressed it in dollars and helped him to rebuild."

In a way it was fitting that my first appearance in Washington was with my Jewish fellow citizens who were meeting to further charitable purposes. On the day that the President's Cabinet was announced, two Jews were on the train en route to Washington. One, looking up from the paper, said to the other: "I am glad that President Wilson has appointed one Jew in his Cabinet."

"Is that so?" asked his companion. "Who is he?"

"Josephus Daniels," was the reply.

To be sure my given name is of Jewish origin, and during all my term of office I was the member of the Cabinet to whom the Jews turned whenever they wished the administration to do something. During the campaign I had been in touch with such leaders of the Jews as B. M. Baruch, Nathan Straus, Henry Morgenthau, Abram I. Elkus, and Herman Bernstein, and had formed ties of strong friendship. I was more intimately associated with Mr. Morgenthau. He was ambitious to hold high position in the administration and the

Secretaryship of the Treasury was his choice. However, from the first, McAdoo was Wilson's selection for that post, and no Morgenthau held that important position until Henry, Jr., was appointed in the Roosevelt administration. This made the Senior happier than any personal honor that could come to him. There was recognition by Wilson as President, as when he was Governor of New Jersey, that all American citizens stood equal. He leaned on good friends of every race and creed. Among his earliest supporters for the presidency were B. M. Baruch, Henry Morgenthau, and Abram I. Elkus, to mention only three who were active in the days when victory seemed doubtful. In the White House he relied on these and other friends of that great race, and many, particularly after war began, were called to high posts of responsibility.

AMBASSADOR TO TURKEY

The name of Mr. Morgenthau was considered for an ambassadorship. I think he preferred Germany or Japan. Wilson offered him Turkey. He declined, moved thereto because the leading Jews declared they resented limiting a Jew to the Mohammedan court. They thought it looked like a sort of segregation when no Jew was considered for other countries. They virtually demanded that Morgenthau decline to be shunted off to Turkey. He was in a mood of disappointment and resentment when he told me of his unwillingness to accept. I undertook to persuade him that it was his duty to go where the President asked him to serve. I offered as an inducement to accept the Turkish post that he would be the only Ambassador with a yacht at his disposal. The Navy kept the *Scorpion* at Constantinople at the service of the Ambassador to Turkey. Later, when it was clear to him that Wilson had no such thought, as Morgenthau's Jewish friends supposed, they assented to his acceptance. It turned out to be one of the most interesting and important posts in all Europe and Mr. Morgenthau won international reputation by his wise diplomacy. When he resigned to take part in the 1916 campaign, he was succeeded by Abram I. Elkus, who had served as Judge and in other important posts in the State of New York and who added to his reputation at Constantinople. The President had no racial feelings and had, as Governor of New Jersey, named a Jew as a member of the Supreme Court, not because he was a Jew but because he was the best qualified lawyer available.

T. R. CAUGHT WITH THE GOODS

As a result of his appointment of the first Jew to the Supreme Court of New Jersey, Wilson had no such mortifying experience as irked Theodore Roosevelt when he appointed Oscar Straus as a member of his Cabinet. The history of Teddy's later confusion was thus related to me years afterward by a friend who vouched for it. He said:

"The Jews were greatly gratified at the elevation of one of their race to the exalted station by a president for whom most of them had not voted. Wishing to give a dignified expression of their appreciation, the dean of New York Jewish bankers went to Washington and invited Roosevelt to a banquet to be given in his honor. The invitation was accepted. The night arrived and the banquet was elegant in every way. Mr. Schiff, very deaf, presided. In his address Mr. Roosevelt said nothing had given him more satisfaction than having Mr. Straus as one of his trusted advisers. He added: "I named him because of his ability and devotion to high ideals. I did not name him because he was a Jew. I would despise myself if I considered the race or the religion of a man named for high political office. I would have named Mr. Straus if he had been a Methodist or of French blood. Merit and merit alone dictated his appointment."

The audience was enthusiastic and voiced its approval. Mr. Schiff's deafness had prevented his hearing a word the President said. He arose to speak and said:

"Before making up his Cabinet President Roosevelt sent for me and informed me that he wished to appoint a Jew as a member of his Cabinet, and asked me to recommend the ablest Jew who would be most acceptable to my race. I recommended Oscar Straus. He was appointed, and he has more than justified the recommendation."

That disclosure embarrassed Teddy, but the incident passed without comment from him. He took his medicine with a straight face.

BRANDEIS A GREAT MAN

No two men outside the Cabinet possessed without a break the confidence of Wilson in a higher degree than two distinguished Americans of the Hebrew race—Brandeis and Baruch. Wilson elevated Louis D. Brandeis to the Supreme Court bench and depended on his wise counsel from the day he entered office. He was a great judge and a greater man than he was a jurist.

BARUCH—ADVISER EXTRAORDINARY

Preferring the post of unofficial adviser, Bernard M. Baruch, was ready for any war service. He was named Chairman of the War Industries Board, but not without opposition. The President consulted the members of the Council of National Defense. One member said that it would be a mistake to name Mr. Baruch because he had no business except that of a Wall Street speculator and the country would resent it. "If that was all," I answered, "you would be right, but Mr. Baruch is an able man whose study of industry and knowledge of business make him an ideal man for the position. He will sever connection with all money making and consecrate all his abilities to serving the country in its need of a man with his ability." I had tested his devotion to the Wilson policies and felt that his Wall Street affiliations would in no way affect this public service. I may unconsciously have been stronger for him because a colleague was inclined to place his Jewish blood as a disqualification.

The result of the great work of the Board, carried out under Baruch's wise direction, justified those who favored his selection. Later in Paris he was a tower of strength to the President when all his associates were not coöperative or helpful. Loyalty to Wilson was Baruch's first name. Admiration of Wilson was a passion with him. Agreeing or disagreeing with this or that policy, Baruch was the soul of loyalty to Wilson. He wished no office, and declined the suggestion that he become Secretary of the Treasury. "I was willing to be drafted for war work," he said to me, "and that could not hurt Wilson or the party, but to name a man who had made a fortune in Wall Street as Secretary of the Treasury might open the administration to criticism from many quarters." Upon assuming the chairmanship of the War Industries Board, Mr. Baruch divested himself of all the stocks that might be affected by war purchases and withdrew from all private business, thus cutting off his large sources of income and dedicating himself wholly to serving his government.

ROSENWALD, MERCHANT PRINCE

When the Council of National Defense got down to the business of preparedness in earnest, an Advisory Commission of eminent men of all parties was appointed, among them Julius Rosenwald, the Chicago merchant prince, head of the Sears-Roebuck house. I use the phrase "merchant prince" advisedly, for he was a prince among business men and philanthropists. He gave his great business experience during the World War to the Army, and Secretary Baker found his assistance invaluable. He was the type of Republican who put country first and refused to go along with his party, when party politicians were not patriotic. I came to know him well. He and my wife became the best of friends. I felt enriched by his friendship and helped by his example of broad tolerance and noble generosity. A Jew, he gave liberally to establish Y.M.C.A.s for colored youth. He built three hundred schools for Negro children in the South and was generous to many worthy institutions and objects.

On a visit to Raleigh, when he had come to the State at the dedication of a Negro school building his money had helped to build, Mr. Rosenwald noticed on my desk a bronze tablet of the Ten Commandments given me by the Jewish Centre of Brooklyn. It interested him and he made this jocular comment: "Sears, Roebuck & Company sell everything except the Ten Commandments. Why not? Because we have broken most of them."

HELP FOR JEWS IN THE NEAR EAST

Early in 1915 I received a call from a committee of Jews asking aid in getting food for starving men and women of their race in the Near East. Herman Bernstein had written me of their desperate condition, and I was eager to give any possible aid. The committee reported that they had raised the fund necessary and had purchased supplies for these needy members of their race cut off by war conditions, but to their dismay were unable for love or money to secure a ship. In their extremity they appealed to the Navy to transport the supplies. I found no authority of law to send a Naval ship on such a mission of mercy. I took the matter up with the President and found him eager to help. I suggested that I knew of but one way. I told him that the Navy was sending colliers into that zone to supply coal to American Naval ships in the Mediterranean, and I could reduce the amount of coal in the next two colliers and give the space to food and other necessities which the Jews wished to send to the starving people of their race. He approved. The supplies were delivered, and the suffering was reduced when the *Vulcan* arrived with its welcome food. Some months later the collier *Starling* carried medicine to Palestine. It also carried matzoth to Jews in that country. As the war progressed, and relief organizations could obtain no ships, the Navy continued these humane services whenever possible. Long after my term of office had expired, and I supposed these acts of mercy rendered by stretching authority had been forgotten, my heart was warmed at a dinner given me at the Jewish Centre in Brooklyn. Speakers voiced gratitude, and I found every humane act of President Wilson and mine was remembered and treasured by the race which never forgets the suffering of its people. I was presented with resolutions of appreciation and a bronze plaque with the Ten Commandments. It too often happens that when officials render a service which is not easy, the people whose requests are granted accept it as their due. Not so the Jews. Wherever I have gone from coast to coast I have found them eager, even years afterwards, to give evidence that in the hours of their sore need they had a sympathetic friend at the head of the Navy.

LIBERATION OF PALESTINE

If Jewish blood had flowed in my veins (although I bear a Jewish name, no family tree records it), I could not have rejoiced more than I did when it was cabled that General Allenby had liberated Palestine. I rejoiced that the land, for all time the beloved of three great religions, cradle of civilizations, had emerged to take its proper place in the world. It seemed a fulfillment of prophecy.

When a Zionist patriotic demonstration to celebrate the victory of the Allied Armies in Palestine was held in New York in 1918, President Wilson requested me to represent him when Rabbi Stephen Wise urged his attendance or that of a representative who could speak for the government. Wilson said to me:

"The promoters wish you to go and speak the administration's interest in not merely the rebirth of the Jewish people, but the birth also of new ideals, of new ethical values, of new conceptions of social justice which shall spring as a blessing for all mankind from that land and that people whose lawgivers and prophets and sages, in ancient days, spoke those truths which have come thundering down the ages, and from which modern civilization has drawn inspiration."

In all my life I have never seen deeper spiritual fervor. The great hall was crowded with Jewish men and women who felt that Zion was being rebuilded. Two of the speakers, wearing long black beards and looking every inch as if they had stepped out of the Old Testament, had lately arrived from the Holy Land. In religious and patriotic ecstasy they frequently broke forth in song as of old. No one without a heart of stone could have been unmoved as members of a scattered nation looked to the building up of the old homeland. As I witnessed a scene that moved me I asked: "Who knows but what in modern Judea, whose every hill and valley rings with the imperishable utterances of an Isaiah and a Jeremiah, of a Micah and an Amos, there may be born some new truth to bless the world and lead mankind to even greater heights than it has already attained?" The words were scarcely spoken when the thousands of devout Jews began a song of deliverance. I could not catch the words, for they were in the tongue of the days of David and Solomon, but I was transported to the heights upon which the singers stood.

Critics of the Jews have no comprehension of the depths of Jewish devotion to their religion or their appreciation of the opportunities in the New World, whose doors were opened to them by Thomas Jefferson, and to whose highest stations they had been called by Woodrow Wilson, the intellectual successor of the sage of Monticello. The critics probably do not know that it was a Hebrew banker who came to the financial aid of Washington in the Revolution, a Jewish Naval officer who saved the home of Jefferson, and another Jew who preserved it in its original stately setting until Jews and Gentiles together could dedicate it as the sacred shrine of Liberty in America. It was much later that the generous gift by the *New York Times* in memory of its distinguished editor, Adolph Ochs, an honor to the Jewish race and to America, provided for the collection of all the writings and letters of Thomas Jefferson to be permanently embodied in fifty volumes.

XXIV

PUBLIC INFORMATION, NOT CENSORSHIP

Before the United States entered the first World War American journalists, who had covered the war in England and France, reported upon censorship as practiced. I recall one story that illustrated the dumbness of the censorship: An American correspondent writing from France, wishing to give a literary touch to his story and relieve the sort of dullness imposed by censorship, quoted the words of Kipling, "The Captains and the Kings depart." It chanced that on another part of the front King George had visited British troops. The meticulous officer, who couldn't recognize style or literature, ruthlessly cut out "the Captains and the Kings depart." Indignant and astounded, the writer asked why that noble line had been deleted. The censor replied: "Under Rule X no mention can be made of the movements of Kings."

That story and others illustrating the stupidity of some censors, plus my inherent belief in the freedom of the press, created hostility in me, and when the United States entered the World War, I opposed following the practice of European nations. As the first destroyers were sent across the seas, I secured a conference with representatives of the press associations and Washington correspondents, seeking an understanding and coöperation. I informed them in strictest confidence of the sailing of the ships—told them that if printed on either side of the Atlantic, the man giving it currency would be responsible for deaths resulting from U-boat action. I found my fellow journalists as keen not to give publicity to any news that might aid the enemy as they were zealous to score scoops. Their response justified my confidence and, during the war, it was abused only two or three times.

Early I discussed with Secretaries Lansing and Baker the question of war censorship, and on April 13, 1917, we wrote a joint formal letter to President Wilson recommending the creation of a Committee on Public Information, to deal with "censorship and publicity." I had previously talked with the President about handling war news fully and promptly and correctly, and found he had been giving it thought. On April 14 he issued an Executive Order in accordance with our joint recommendations, naming as members the Secretaries of State, War, and Navy, and naming George Creel as civilian chairman. Though named first because of rank, Lansing was not in harmony with the views of Wilson, Baker, Creel and myself. He approved the British policy of strict censorship, which amounted to suppression, and soon withdrew from active participation in the work of the Committee. As the heavy responsibilities of organizing and directing the operations of the Army increased, Baker left the directing chiefly to me, saying: "As you are an editor, this is in your line. You should be the active member," but his counsel was invaluable. The vital initiation and carrying out of the policies were furnished by the versatile, able, and dynamic Chairman Creel, whose genius and enthusiasm showed that he measured up to qualifications recommended to the President—"A man of proved courage, ability and vision." Creel incarnated these qualities, in addition to his journalistic experience. The President had an affection for Creel, who had won his heart, while his brilliancy compelled his admiration. Wilson loved good writing. He was himself a master of style, and Creel's ability to write with elegance and vigor intrigued him. Their common devotion to real liberalism cemented the regard. Wilson took the deepest interest in the work of the Committee, making valuable suggestions from time to time. As the war drew to a close, he was keen about carrying his "Fourteen Points" to the people of Germany and was pleased when Creel caused leaflets to be dropped over Germany carrying Wilson's ideals of a just and permanent peace.

When it was decided to put armed guards on the Merchant Marine, I sent Wilson a copy of the tentative instructions of the armed guard and wrote him, "We are trying to cover the whole field and so word the instructions that if they should ever be published there would be no regulations contrary to the splendid spirit of our policy." In his own handwriting Wilson wrote back,

"Dear Mr. Daniels:
"This is all right; but I hope Creel will remind newspaper men of their agreement not to publish news of the movement of Naval vessels."

NAVY PRESS SERVICE

As the Navy gave out news instead of bottling it up, there was no need of a large public relations staff. Only two regular ones were on duty—John Wilber Jenkins, who had shown marked newspaper ability on the Raleigh *News and Observer* and the Baltimore *Sun,* and Marvin McIntyre, of Tennessee, who had demonstrated the ability as a journalist that later caused him to be requisitioned as secretary by President Roosevelt. Both maintained close relations with the Committee on Public Information. They furnished the press with news and served the Navy with efficiency in other ways.

PASSAGE OF ESPIONAGE ACT

As the war proceeded and a few widely circulated papers violated voluntary censorship by printing news regarded as endangering military operations, President Wilson felt that he ought to have legal power to punish such unpatriotic publications. Senator Overman and Representative Webb, both of North Carolina, piloted legislation through Congress which was called an Espionage Act. As originally introduced, life imprisonment was ordered for everyone who in wartime and without lawful authority should "collect, record, publish, or communicate" certain broadly defined types of military information "of such nature as is calculated to be, or might be, directly or indirectly, useful to the enemy." It had hard sledding. The press was violent in protest. One paper called it, "The Russian method," another "Kaiserism," a "gag-law," a "muzzling of the press." While this discussion was going on, the presence of spies and enemy aliens became known, and sentiment for the measure grew. Representative Webb said that the papers had created the mistake "that somebody is undertaking to unduly abridge the freedom of the press and the freedom of speech." President Wilson told Senators he wanted "a mild form of censorship which would impose more than a moral obligation upon any newspapers that might tend to print news by which the enemy might profit."

He got what he asked, the measure requiring the President to determine the character of information published, but the teeth in the bill was authority to impose heavy penalty on any "who shall willfully make or convey false reports or false statements with intent to interfere with the operation or success of the military or naval

forces of the United States, or to promote the success of its enemies" and punish those who "attempt to cause insubordination,
disloyalty, or mutiny." This was a Big Stick behind voluntary censorship. Later in May, 1918, Congress enacted a more drastic law,
imposing severe punishment on "the wilful writing, utterance or
publication of any disloyal, profane, scurrilous, or abusive language
about the form of government of the United States," etc. Wilson
did not avail himself of the act to muzzle the press, and Creel continued, with my approval, to carry on by asking voluntary coöperation of the press. The Big Stick provision, however, was favored by
some to hold in check the few recalcitrants. Wilson had expressed
his convictions in these words:

> "I cannot imagine any greater disservice to the country than
> to establish a system that would deny to the people in a free
> republic like our own, their indisputable right to criticize their
> own public officials. While exercising the great powers of this
> office I hold, I would regret in a crisis like the one through
> which we are passing, to lose the benefit of patriotic and intelli-
> gent criticism."

I took no part in the long-drawn-out controversy over the Espionage Act. I believed the inherent evil in such legislation carried
real danger. I trusted voluntary censorship and coöperation. It
was unfortunately invoked by the Postmaster General to deny the
mail privileges to some small newspapers without trial. I protested to
that honest official that if a less wise man possessed his power, he
might suppress papers advocating policies he did not like, thereby
anulling the constitutional freedom of the press.

THE MOBILIZATION OF THE MIND

The purposes of the Committee on Public Information as President Wilson conceived them were two: the mobilization of the
mind of America, and the fight for the "verdict of mankind." Inevitably, therefore, the Committee grew into a world organization
reaching deep into every American community and carrying America's war aims and peace terms to all parts of the civilized globe
through the press, films and posters.

Just as it fought apathy, ignorance, and disaffection at home, it
also fought prejudice and falsehood abroad. While the achievement

of national unity was a primary task, another important task was to stimulate Allied morale, win the friendship and support of neutral nations, and get the truth to the deluded peoples of the Central Powers.

Never at any time or in any degree was the Committee a machinery of concealment or repression. From the first, the censorship of the press was based on voluntary arrangement, for while the Army and Navy asked the newspapers to maintain secrecy with respect to military policies, plans, and movements, the request carried this explicit statement: "These requests are without larger authority than the necessities of the war-making branches. Their enforcement is a matter for the press itself."

A TYPICAL AMERICAN IDEA

A typically Amercian idea, but it *worked*. It was the first time in history that a government during war had tried the experiment of giving information to press and public instead of shutting up news sources. Its work was open and positive, for at all times it was President Wilson's insistence that national unity came only with national understanding, and that a sound, steadfast public opinion could not be formed until it had been *informed*. The war, he insisted, was not the war of administration nor the private enterprise of military chieftains, but the grim business of a whole people, and every man, woman and child must be given a feeling of partnership.

Trained men, placed in every war-making branch, gave a daily record of progress to the people; not "press agenting," but an honest, unvarnished factual report on construction and production, the good along with the bad. In no other country was there such absolute frankness on the part of the government, and it was a policy that paid dividends in popular confidence. And its total cost to the taxpayers was less than five million dollars. The Four-Minute Men commanded the volunteer services of 75,000 trained speakers, operating in 5,200 communities. Under the leadership of Charles Dana Gibson, the artists of America were organized on a volunteer basis for the production of posters.

TRUTH CARRIED ABROAD

Beyond America's borders there was a triple task. First, there were the peoples of the Allied Nations who had to be told of the magnitude of America's war effort and the certainty of speedy and effective aid; second, the truth had to be carried to the neutral nations, poisoned by German lies; and third, there were the peoples of the Central Powers who had to be reached with the facts and figures of America's determination and invincibility. Opening an office in every capital of the world outside of the enemy countries, the government wireless and the cables were used to pour forth a daily stream of American news.

Through the press of Switzerland, Denmark, and Holland, an enormous amount of American news was filtered into Germany, and Russia was also a firing line for CPI propaganda. Mortar guns, loaded with "paper bullets," planes, carrying pamphlets, bombarded the German front, and balloons with a cruising radius of 500 miles carried our printed matter deep into Germany.

It was the pride of the Committee that no dollar was ever sent on a secret errand, no paper ever subsidized, no official ever bought. From a thousand sources we were told the wonders of German propaganda, but original determinations were never altered. Truth was the Committee's one weapon, and with it the neutral nations were won to understanding and support, the Allied Nations lifted to new heights of enthusiasm and courage, and the morale of enemy peoples sapped to the point of collapse.

I believed then, and have since had that conviction strengthened, that no man was ever born wise enough to be a censor, and that censorship digs up more snakes than it kills.

VOLUNTARY CENSORSHIP WORKED

Voluntary censorship of the press was one of the early proofs that Baker and Creel and I were right in opposing Lansing's clamping down on the press as was done by European governments. Here is proof from my Diary (March 18, 1917):

"Ships went out yesterday under armed guard, saluted by every ship in the harbor, including German interned ships. Examining New York papers found no reference to it though it was the best news story of the week—all by voluntary acquiescence in censorship."

WANTED MORE NEWS

The problem of how much war news to print was difficult. Nothing that might give information to the enemy but everything else, was the policy of the administration during the war. It was not easy to draw the line. My Diary (January 27) records:

"Richard Hooker, of the Springfield, Mass. *Republican,* is well-posted as to Naval affairs, particularly on Naval construction. He thinks more intimate news about what our soldiers are doing for publication in home papers would make stronger sentiment for the war; shut off criticism and nerve the people to make greater sacrifice."

CONGRESSMAN POU SAVED CREEL

George Creel was a downright and forthright liberal, not always wise in his public expressions. In fact, he was a scrapper and did not accept criticism in silence. He replied in kind and in stinging and effective style to his numerous critics. They came from two directions: first, those like Lansing who wanted the censorship to be like that of Europe and shut off all the news; and second, from those who wished everything printed—even the sailing of ships carrying soldiers to Europe.

Creel came very near losing his job and would have done so if Wilson had not been willing to go to bat for him and found a champion for Creel in Honorable Edward W. Pou, Chairman of the Committee on Rules in the House of Representatives. When Creel was speaking in New York at an open forum meeting someone in the audience asked him whether he thought all Congressmen loyal. Without hesitation Creel answered: "I do not like slumming, so I will not explore into the hearts of Congress for you." If he had spit in the face of every member of Congress, more indignation would not have been created. Claude Kitchin voiced the excited feeling in Congress when he said, "Creel is unworthy of the respect of any decent citizen."

I was absent from Washington when the fire of denunciation of Creel broke out in fury. Upon my return there was a message that the President wished to see me at once. He was greatly disturbed and acquainted me with the situation that existed in Congress. He said: "Our friend Creel is in trouble and we must save him." He added that he had told Creel: "If necessary, I will go up there myself as your counsel."

When a group of Senators called to ask for Creel's head, Wilson replied, "Gentlemen, when I think of the manner in which Mr. Creel has been maligned and persecuted I think it a very human thing for him to have said." His attitude was another proof of Wilson's loyalty to an appointee who was honest and capable. The resolution that not only censured Creel but endangered the work of the Commission was pending in the Committee on Rules. "It is fortunate," I said to the President, "that Edward W. Pou, member from my district and close friend, is chairman of that committee, and I will see him at once." I did so. Pou told me that I knew any request from Wilson would enlist his best efforts, "but," he added, "never since I have been in Congress have I seen the members of that body so incensed and so angry over anything as against George Creel. If that resolution had been put to a vote at once, it would have had an almost unanimous 'aye' vote." Pou said he must play for time and let the anger cool and he would then try to prevent its passage. "But," he added, "frankly, unless action is postponed, George's condemnation cannot be averted." He bade me tell Wilson he would leave no stone unturned, but he added, "I can do nothing unless Creel withdraws his unjust reflection upon members of Congress and offers a straightforward apology."

When I told George he must apologize, he at first bluntly refused to do so and said enemies of the administration were making "a mountain out of a mole hill" to hurt Wilson. It was all the President and I could do to persuade him to accept Pou's advice. He finally and in a frank manner made the amende honorable, and Pou saved his official head. Nobody else in Congress could have done it, and Wilson and Creel were always grateful. How did he do it? My recollection is that he was called to his home in Smithfield and stayed until the cooling off process had been given time to work. I know I advised that course. I never knew all the strings he pulled, but he was a master strategist and persuaded his colleagues to leave the honor of the House in his hands.

I relate this as typical of the skill of Pou as a legislative strategist. The incident illustrated Pou's devotion to Wilson. But he early formed a like attachment for Franklin Roosevelt. During the first part of 1913 when Pou called at the Navy Department, I introduced him to Franklin Roosevelt. They became friends at once. Upon leaving the Department Pou said to me, "Joe, you and I will live to see that young man elected President." He was a prophet, and we both had some part in seeing that the prophecy was fulfilled.

WILSON'S WARM APPROVAL

There was very strong criticism of George Creel in Paris as there had been in the United States, but Wilson always stood by Creel and on March 20, 1919, wrote him:

"I wanted to tell you in person but I must now do so by letter how deeply I have appreciated the work you have done as Chairman of the Committee on Public Information. The work has been well done, admirably well done, and your inspiration and guidance have been the chief motive power in it all. I have followed what you have done throughout and have approved it, and I want you to know how truly grateful I am."

PARTISAN CRITICS REBUKED

Fear sat on every doorstep of homes from which sons had gone to fight in France as the first transports carrying troops sailed. That fear was based on dread of assassination of troops by U-boats. When the news came that, though attacked by under-sea assassins, all the soldiers got across safely, there was joyous thanksgiving on July 4th when the news was announced by me. The statement prepared by George Creel, Chairman of Public Information, was based on cables to the Navy by Admiral Gleaves, head of the Transport Service.

The rejoicing that the first troops had arrived safely, though attacked by submarines, caused me to give the announcement in terms of happiness that "lifted the shadow of dread from the heart of America." George Creel, who wrote the news story, admitted that "the spirit of thanksgiving insensibly took charge of phraseology" but there could be no denial of two attacks by U-boats. A reporter at Queenstown, as the result he said of "casual conversations with a couple of officers and some men on the docks" whom he did not know, sent a "confidential" wire to the AP, London office, that "Daniels' story was made out of whole cloth—that there was no submarine attack whatever, no torpedo and no gunfire from destroyers." Creel thought Sims was responsible for the denial of a proved attack.

When that cable seeking to discredit Admiral Gleaves' official report reached Washington Senator Penrose said the announcement by Creel and the Navy Department was "a submarine lie" and a colossal fraud perpetrated by the "committee on misinformation." He demanded an investigation, which the Senate refused to grant after Senator Swanson's excoriation of Penrose's attack in the course of which Swanson said:

"I should like to know, in the beginning of this war, if every time the Navy does a gallant act, it is to be the subject of petty, partisan ridicule which will please Germany and commend itself to the consideration of the Kaiser."

The Americans in Paris were greatly disturbed because there was no freedom of the press in Paris. Everything was excluded which the authorities did not wish printed.

TAX ON DISSEMINATION OF INFORMATION

The censorship which came in for the most criticism was the exclusion of papers regarded by Postmaster General Burleson as pro-German or subversive. He issued his orders—they were legal—ex parte without hearings. His motive was the most patriotic, and most of the papers he condemned were against national war policies. But Burleson came in for the greatest criticism when he urged a large increase of postage on newspapers and magazines. He said that they were being carried through the mails at a loss. He was supported by Claude Kitchin, leader of the House, and both came in for severe roastings from the press. I thought, maybe because I am a publisher, Burleson was going too far. President Wilson was not in accord with the increase in the rates, but his respect for Burleson and confidence in him were so great that he refrained from giving him directions. Long after, as showing Wilson's consideration of trusted assistants, in his home at Austin, Burleson said to me, "President Wilson suggested to me, after my report, that I do not insist on the increase in second-class postage rates on newspapers and magazines. The President offered the argument against such action that it was a tax on the dissemination of information. But he would not direct my actions when I could not consistently retrace my steps."

When bitter denunciation of Burleson's exclusion of papers from the mails and other matters of censorship reached Wilson in Paris, he wrote him from there (February 28):

"My dear Burleson:

"This is tough enough in all conscience but I cannot believe that it would be wise to do any more suppressing. We must meet these poisons in some other way."

There were many demands on the President to put a stop to all censorship by the Post Office Department.

BURLESON'S HARSH CENSURE

Early in the war my family spent Sunday on the river on the *Sylph*. My Diary records:

"In the afternoon the Burlesons and the Cranes came on board the *Sylph* and we had a delightful sail. Burleson talked about his course in denying the use of the mails to disloyal newspapers. He had in mind shutting up some big newspapers. He said he was going to advise W. W. to give a Garden Party and invite members of Congress who had stood by him and leave out men like Weeks, LaFollette, and others, so the country could see they were not trusted. He was full of the idea, and that it would pillory those not invited before they could go out to the country and speak against the plan before the second draft was called."

In vain did I argue with Burleson that it was contrary to the American ideals to deny the mails to newspapers unless it had been established that they were convicted of treasonable utterances and that social proscription by the President of men who did not see eye to eye with him would injure Wilson more than the Congressmen; that Weeks was with the President on the war question, while La Follette was militantly with Wilson on domestic policies but violently against war.

From my Diary of August 7:

"Gag Tom Watson: Burleson wanted something done to Tom Watson, editor of a paper in Georgia who was writing bitterly about the policy of the Government, particularly against the draft. 'It is a Socialist paper and should be suppressed.' Wilson listened to B's blast, and answered: 'We can not go after all the Damn Fools. Everybody knows Watson is a fool. We have better and more important things to do.'"

CRITICAL OF ENGLISH CENSORSHIP

The most dynamic of all the distinguished British visitors who came to Washington in the spring and summer of 1917 was Lord Northcliffe, the able and egotistical publisher. It was at the time when there was much demand for censorship in our country, and I asked Northcliffe about British experience.

"My country has been stupid. Every day we are told, 'Don't print this,' and 'Don't print that.' They would not permit us to print anything about Serbia." He added that he thought officials ought to give out for publication the names of vessels sunk by submarines and the list of submarines captured. He believed the people were entitled to the news, both good and bad, and that knowledge would stimulate patriotism and sacrifice.

The next day I went to a luncheon given by Tardieu, French Commissioner, in honor of Northcliffe, where Northcliffe spoke his mind with great frankness. He was greatly interested in the South and asked me many questions about the days of Reconstruction and the racial problems.

Northcliffe was the new type of Englishman. He had none of the hesitation that, for instance, marked Balfour, but spoke with a sort of American directness and emphasis. He was sure that Lloyd George (he almost admitted that he turned out Asquith) "will lead toward the most effective carrying on of the war and that now the United States is enlisted the victory will eventually be won, but he does not underestimate the difficulties in the way."

GERMAN PROPAGANDA

The anti-German sentiment had grown and on all hands there was talk of suppressing German propaganda. That was the main subject discussed at the Cabinet meeting on August 16. My Diary records:

"The President asked: 'Should all German newspapers be excluded? Should they be compelled to print in parallel columns the translation in English?' Baker gave strong reasons against such a course. W. B. Wilson thought very few people read German papers and he felt there was more danger from English newspapers. Burleson said there was great danger from the new Peace organization which was calling a convention in

September to try to compel statement of peace terms. He thought there should be drastic action. The President asked: 'What action?' He closed the discussion by saying: 'Better let them show their impotence than by suppression, as long as they keep within the law.'" ·

CENSORSHIP ENDED

Immediately after the war Wilson directed Lansing to "ask French and British authorities to entirely remove the political censorship upon American press dispatches." Within the week Creel issued an order that ended what censorship had been practiced in the United States during the war.

MAY NEVER BE EQUALLED

Dr. Beam, professor of History in the University of California, who made a study of the work of the Committee on Public Information, concluded with this just appraisal:

"One of the most remarkable things about the charges against the Commission is that, of the more than 6,000 news stories it issued, so few were called in question at all. It may be doubted that for honesty the CPI's record will ever be equalled in the official war news of a major power."

XXV

PROFITEERING IN WAR DAYS

M OBILIZE AGAINST PROFITEERS" ought to be the first order when war is declared. If it could be issued and executed it would save many worries and much money. Lincoln recorded that profiteers were the harpies that disturbed him, and the Spanish-American war was disgraced by scandals in furnishing supplies for the Army. With these object lessons in mind, early steps were taken to prevent their recurrence, and they were in the main successful. But the guards were not strong enough to keep the hands of some profiteers out of the public crib.

SHOULD WEAR LETTER ON BREAST

It is to be hoped that if there is a future war all men and all money will be drafted, and any who profit upon the exigencies of their country will have to wear a letter P, representing PROFIT-EER, on their bosoms as Hester Prynne was forced to go through the world displaying the red brand of A (proclaiming her adultery). I know no other punishment that would perfectly fit the crime.

PROFITEERS NEEDED STRONG MEDICINE

Someone has said, "War is waste," and in Rome they had a saying, "In war laws are silent." I found, as to some concerns making war materials, there was no conscience about profiteering at the expense of the fighters.

STEEL TRUST GAVE IN

When the Shipping Board needed large quantities of steel plate, the trust quoted it a price much higher than the Navy was paying. Chairman Denman asked how we managed to get steel so much cheaper than the Shipping Board when it wished to buy in large quantities. It was a rate fixed before the war. When the company asked a higher rate, I had experts investigate. They reported that the old price gave fair profit. The president of the company refused

to furnish steel at the price I offered. We had to have the steel. I told him that, while I should dislike to take such a course, unless he met our needs at the price offered I would ask the President to issue an order for the Navy to take over his plants under an act of Congress giving such authority. I added that if cost of production increased, the price would be readjusted. He thought I was bluffing.

The next day I brought up the matter at a Cabinet meeting. Wilson was indignant at the very thought of the excessive price demanded. Though some members of the Cabinet protested that the Navy could not run the great industry and it was better to pay the increased price, Wilson approved what I had told the steel executive. The next morning when he arrived, I informed him of the President's approval and expressed the hope that his company would agree upon the fair proposition of the Navy. Within twenty-four hours, the Navy was assured there would be no advance in price except such as increased cost of production might justify.

THE NAVY ORDER

When the industrial leaders learned what had been done as to the price of coal and steel plate, they were more ready to accept what came to be known as "Navy Orders." The Naval appropriation act gave the Navy the power, when an agreement could not be reached as to an essential article, to commandeer it—whether ships or land or munitions or supplies—to pay 75 per cent of the appraised price, giving the owner the right to contest in the courts the reasonable compensation so fixed.

"Place a Navy Order" was the way the Navy prevented most profiteering.

As the war proceeded, the War Industries Board, headed by Bernard Baruch, rendered most useful and invaluable service in securing fair prices, and it was not often necessary to take over plants or use Navy Orders. Admiral Frank Fletcher, the Navy member, proved as wise in counsel as in command of the fleet.

DOLLAR-A-YEAR MEN

For the first time we had in the Army what came to be known as Dollar-a-Year men, quite a number of men from the ranks of business desiring to serve their country without compensation. As Uncle Sam could not accept them and give them official status without pay, a check for one dollar was issued. Most of them, men too old to enter the armed forces, framed their checks and kept them as evidence of serving their country in war times in much the same spirit as soldiers kept their decorations. The need of capable and experienced men in the first days of the war was so imperative, and Congress had not made appropriations, that Secretary Baker, with the best motives, accepted unpaid service. There were applications to the Navy by Dollar-a-Year men, but Franklin Roosevelt and I took the position that we would pay such men or enroll them in the Naval Reserve and have no Dollar-a-Year men.

Some of these Dollar-a-Year men, to mention only two of quite a number, like Daniel Willard, President of the Baltimore and Ohio Railroad, and Julius Rosenwald, head of Sears, Roebuck and Company, were so patriotically efficient that they deserved the Distinguished Service Medal. Unfortunately, when high-minded men forgot their personal affairs to serve their country, there were some Dugald Dalgettys. They could not forego the temptation to make money by giving big Army orders to their own companies at profiteering prices. They took advantage of the recommendation of officers to be so forehanded as to buy enough to fit out a million more soldiers than enlisted, in the belief that the war would last two years longer. I recall one day (February, 1918) that Julius Rosenwald, charged with buying what the Army needed, was greatly discouraged. Why? The Army officers demanded, when he was certain twenty-one million pairs of shoes for the Army were all that would be needed, that he buy ten million more. Army officers demanded, for example, enough bridles and saddles for ten times the number needed. They were as unwise as selfish Dollar-a-Year men.

DID NOT FOLLOW THE ARMY

One of the worst evils—unknown to Secretary Baker or the rest of us until the war was nearing an end—came to my attention in this wise. The Tobacco Dollar-a-Year expert ordered millions and millions of cigarettes for the Army and fixed a price that was excessive considering the quantity purchased. It was paid. At the same time the Navy placed orders for a large number, but small compared to the Army. Cigarettes were purchased on the basis of the "Navy Order." When manufacturers called for payment, Admiral McGowan said the price was too high and offered 75 per cent cash, and the balance to be held subject to reaching a fair price. Some of the cigarette companies refused to accept anything but the payment of the full sum at the prices paid by the Army.

"Are you an honest man here in Washington as you were in North Carolina?" was the question my old friend, Dick Reynolds, head of the Camel Company, thundered at me one morning in the Navy Department. The Navy had bought many cigarettes, but the company had sent the bill at the same price the War Department had paid. The Paymaster General felt the price was too high but offered to settle on a "Navy Order" provision. When Reynolds' subordinate reported this situation, Dick came to see me and protested that the Navy was not treating the cigarette companies right. He wanted the full amount in cash at the same price the Army had paid. I told him that representatives of tobacco companies had directed the Army's action and it was too favorable to the manufacturer. We declined to pay the price the Army had paid and offered what was deemed a fair price or we would withhold 25 per cent. He refused to agree. The Paymaster General, keen for saving dollars, reported that Reynolds did not then settle on our terms because if he had done so the country would see that the Army had paid too much.

A WRONG PRINCIPLE

That was not the only reason I opposed the Dollar-a-Year men. Early in the war I had told Wilson that Uncle Sam ought not to appoint any man to public position without paying him for his service. My second reason was that it would deny the government's calling poor men to places of usefulness. The question came to a head in the Cabinet when it was suggested that the members of the War Industries Board, comprised mainly of rich men, would gladly serve without compensation. I said, "I happen to know that Hugh Frayne, the Labor member, is not a rich man, and he could not come to Washington without a salary that would at least pay his expenses. It wouldn't be right to him to ask the financial sacrifice it would require or to decline the position," and I added that if men of patriotism and wealth like Baruch and Brookings and Willard did not wish compensation they could turn their checks over to the Red Cross or some other war agency, as Baruch and some others did.

PROMINENT JOURNALISTS IN THE WORLD WAR

Upper left, George Creel, chairman of Commission of War Information in World War. *Upper right,* Ray Stannard Baker, Wilson's public relations adviser and later his official biographer. *Lower left,* Edward W. Scripps, head of the liberal Scripps newspapers which earnestly supported Wilson, "horse, foot, and dragoon," and backed his League program to the limit. *Lower right,* Marvin H. McIntyre, special assistant to Secretary of the Navy in charge of public relations and later secretary to President Roosevelt.

GREAT EDITORS WHO SUPPORTED WILSON AND THE LEAGUE

Upper left, Adolph Ochs, of the *New York Times* (New York Times Studio). *Upper right,* Frank Cobb, of the *New York World. Lower left,* Richard Hooker, of the *Springfield Republican* (photo by Bachrach). *Lower right,* William Allen White, of the *Emporia Gazette* (Brown Brothers).

"You are right," said Wilson. "I had not thought of the principle involved."—And they were paid. No government ought to accept service without just compensation. It is wrong in principle and opens a door to self-interest through which too many men walked in and filled their pockets in war days.

AN EMBARRASSING MOMENT

In World War II the bad practice of Dollar-a-Year men was reintroduced into several agencies in Washington. One day at a luncheon given to an important official from Washington I was asked my opinion about the Dollar-a-Year-Man practice. I expressed strong condemnation of the system though some of the best men were secured through it. I was embarrassed when the guest of honor said: "I am a Dollar-a-Year man." He added that when asked to go to Washington to do a job for which his experience qualified him, he felt the patriotic compulsion to respond. "But," he added, "I could not live on the salary paid such officials. I continue to draw my salary from my company and Uncle Sam pays me one dollar a year." He could see no cause for criticism in the system in war days, and in his case there was none. But there were others who saw no wrong in securing big orders at profiteering prices for the company paying their salaries.

A PATRIOTIC LANDLORD

The pests of every war are the profiteers. The strength of a republic in war days is business men who are as ready to do the patriotic things as are their sons who don the uniform. I detested the profiteers and honored the latter, of whom there were many whose good deeds were never known. As the best example of the spirit of most business men with whom I came in contact, I recall an incident that—not large in itself—is illustrative and meant much to me in crowded Washington in war days when a place to live was at a premium.

Our lease on the house on Wyoming Avenue (rent $200 a month), which housed the family of the Secretary of the Navy, expired in the early part of the war. Our real estate friend informed my wife that the house had been purchased by J. S. Cullinan, a prominent oil man of Houston, Texas, who would move into it shortly. Again the house-hunting nightmare hung over us. I thought

I might have to go to sea—live in the *Dolphin,* anchored at the Washington Navy Yard.

One day Mr. Cullinan called at the Navy Department. I knew he was a prosperous man though I had never met him. He said, "I am your landlord." I expected he had come to tell me when to vacate. At that time it was almost impossible to rent a suitable place at a price within my means. Before I could say anything Mr. Cullinan added, "I know the strain you are under in these days, the great service you are rendering your country, and the high rentals charged for houses in Washington. I have come to tell you that you may continue to live in the house as long as you desire at the same rental you have been paying." That removed a load from my shoulders, even a greater one from my wife's, who was used to taking the laboring oar in looking for houses in which to live. Such consideration and generosity by the owners of buildings and apartments in Washington were rare. It showed, as he did in other ways, the patriotic spirit of Mr. Cullinan.

THE GOLD DUST TWINS

Large credit is due to Admiral McGowan, Paymaster General, for the business efficiency of the Navy which was widely commended, particularly during the World War. There never was an order for supplies to go to any Naval base in Europe that was not filled instantly, and when the war was over th. officers serving in Europe were loud in their praise of the Bureau of Supplies. No suggestion was ever heard of favoritism in awarding contracts. McGowan was so careful that there should be no appearance of favoritism that he made it a rule during the war not to accept any courtesy, even a lunch, from any person having financial dealings with the Navy Department. That example might be wisely followed by all officials who have power to make contracts. We were fortunate also that he had as his chief assistant Admiral Christian J. Peeples (he was made head of an important department by Roosevelt when he became President). McGowan and Peeples were inseparable. If Roosevelt or I should wish—as we often did—to consult the Purchasing Department, they would always come together, never separately. And we called them "The Gold Dust Twins." Certainly the whole Navy in all matters of supply let them do the work for us.

McGowan was a great friend, in fact a protégé of both Senator

Tillman and Admiral Dewey. Both relied upon him in a hundred ways, as I did. None of us was ever disappointed in his friendship or his efficiency.

I GOT THE BEST OF ADMIRAL MCGOWAN

When he called one day in the interest of a young man who was about to be denied graduation from the Naval Academy because of an impediment in his speech, Admiral McGowan urged that he be permitted to graduate and go into the Pay Corps. "I demurred," says my Diary, "because of the handicap to usefulness by reason of the young man's impediment." McGowan replied: "It would be better for the service if every paymaster was dumb."

"Including the Paymaster General?" I answered.

"You have one on me," said the Paymaster General as he and his assistant, Admiral Peeples, retired.

WHITE WAY ALMOST SECEDES

New York's population, its press and officials made a fine record for doing big things to help the Army and Navy in war days. They never failed except once, but the Great White Way and its backers almost seceded. New York will give up everything for the good of the country except its White Way, its night clubs, and racing. When shortage of coal required the closing of schools and churches in the worst winter known, it created inconvenience everywhere, but there was rebellion only in New York City.

"I am glad to know there is one man in Washington who has some sense. I had begun to think you were all damn fools." That was what Frank Cobb, the brilliant editor of the New York *World* said to me over the telephone in January, 1918. That day H. A. Garfield, Fuel Administrator, had issued an order that dimmed the Great White Way in big cities. New York responded with such howls and denunciations as can hardly be described. The coal shortage was so serious that manufacturing plants had to be closed for a week, and on certain days theaters and motion picture houses, and other restrictions on offices and schools were made. It was a drastic order and New York was ready to crucify Garfield.

Cobb had called me by telephone to ask what I thought of Garfield's order, which had placed New York in deepest gloom. "It is one of the most terrible orders ever issued," I replied. Then it was he paid me the compliment. Pausing a moment to drink in undeserved praise, I said: "It was a terrible order. Only one thing could have been worse." "What on earth could that be?" Cobb queried. "Not to have issued it," I answered and proceeded to tell him of the serious coal shortage that faced us. I added that Baker and I, convinced that the drastic order was essential, had gone with Garfield to the President and advised him to sign the order. Hardly letting me finish, Cobb said: "I see I was mistaken. You have all gone crazy in Washington." If Garfield had obliterated Fifth Avenue, the denunciation in the metropolitan press could not have been more severe. Cobb appealed to Wilson, who stood pat.

That incident proved what I had said in an address in New York when bankers and others were violent against the Federal Reserve plan. In some respects New York is more set in its provincialism than any "hick" town in America. Smaller cities obeyed the order to do without the White Way at night because of the exigency of war. Not New York. It raised such a row that coal operators doubled their energies to furnish enough coal so that the White Way could again blaze brightly and let New York City turn night into day.

SAME THING IN WORLD WAR II

Baker and I were not surprised at the criticism that followed Garfield's order. In fact, before going to the White House with him, we told Garfield that his proposal would let loose a whirlwind. It came. Congressmen joined the rebellion. While it raged, Wilson said, "There is nothing to do but return to the cyclone cellar." McAdoo was game. He told Garfield, "Go ahead. I'm with you."

In World War II I was to see a like threatened nullification of Byrnes's order to close night clubs at midnight. It created more heat in New York City than all the rationing and price-fixing regulations and would have been nullified but for orders by the Army and Navy to men in uniform not to be found in a night club after midnight. And—such is devotion to night amusement and worse—it was the first prohibition lifted after the victory in Europe!

GARFIELD GIVEN NAVY FACTS

My first acquaintance with Harry A. Garfield was when severe critics early in the administration had said the Navy was inefficient and he had written to ask a true picture. My detailed reply was printed and convinced those who wanted true information. Some years before at Wilson's invitation Garfield had become a member of the Princeton faculty.

SPLIT IN GARFIELD'S FAMILY

It was the acuteness of the coal situation that caused Wilson to ask Garfield to come to Washington (August, 1917) as Coal Administrator, and he did a difficult job efficiently. The bitter attack on Garfield by the New York press, following our call on the President, was the beginning of a cherished friendship. He confirmed a story—and so did his brother, James A. Garfield, later, when I related it to him in Mexico—that I had heard. It ran like this: James A. Garfield, II, leading lawyer of Cleveland, learned in 1912 that his brother Harry was going to vote for Wilson. He felt that as the Republican Party had given the highest honors to their father, his sons owed it to the party to support its nominees. When Jim could not influence Harry to vote Republican, he went on a visit to California to ask his mother to use her parental authority to prevent Harry's leaving the party of his ancestors. After presenting the case strongly, he thought his mother would accede and he was dumbfounded when his mother said, "Jim, I cannot do what you ask. As a matter of fact, if I were at home, I would vote for Wilson myself."

The friendship with both these Garfield brothers was one I shall always cherish. One day I told Harry I had almost forgiven his father for depriving my mother of the means of support. Shocked at so grave a charge against his father, whose memory he venerated, Harry asked for a bill of particulars. I told him:

"When your father was President, he removed my mother by executive order from the postmastership at the town of Wilson because her son—meaning me—was printing a red-hot Democratic paper. Of course your father never heard of my mother and only acted on the recommendation of the Postmaster General who appointed a Republican to the position. As a Jacksonian, believing 'to the victor belong the spoils,' I have no criticism. But I never thought then that I'd be an admiring friend of the son of the President who did so unchivalrous an act as to turn a good woman out of her official home."

WILSON REPUDIATED HIGH PRICE OF COAL

Early in the war the situation demanded fixing the price of coal. Secretary Lane agreed with the operators on a price that was so high that Baker and I refused to pay it for the coal needed by the Army and Navy. We had attended a meeting of coal operators and others, and I had called upon them to follow the spirit of a popular song, "Uncle Sam, Here I Come"; but as Lane had been appointed on a coal commission, he had without consultation permitted coal operators to fleece the government and the consumers. The commission said it recognized it was fixing the price "too high, but the motive was to increase production." Baker, who had been hot about the high prices fixed, and I brought the matter before the Council of National Defense and Baker took it up with the President, who wrote Baker saying the price agreed upon was "clearly too high and I do not think that the government departments would be justified in paying it." The Department of Justice was bringing charges against the coal dealers. Gregory said the price fixed by the conference and approved by Lane as a member of the Council of National Defense (but without authority of the Council) was "actually higher than the coal price which had been previously fixed in secret" and for which he had indicted the coal dealers. The President publicly repudiated the price. Lane, jealous of his authority, held that the price was justified and believed the law of supply and demand would reduce the cost. Baker and I did not agree and we won out for a time.

FIXING THE PRICE OF COTTON

There was serious criticism of the administration in the fall of 1918 because it had fixed the price of wheat grown by Western farmers while no price was fixed for cotton grown by Southern farmers. It was charged that this implied favoritism to the South because Wilson and Southern members of the Cabinet controlled action. My Diary of September 11 says:

"War Cabinet discussed fixing the price of cotton. Garfield said that inasmuch as the price of wheat and coal had been fixed, the price of cotton should likewise be fixed.

"Baruch said notice was given to farmers about wheat. Should wait another year. Government can buy for itself and Allies and thus stabilize the price and compel use of other than high grades—that is now the trouble."

At the next meeting of the Cabinet the whole time was taken up with a discussion about whether the price of cotton should be fixed. Western Senators were speaking publicly of the injustice to the growers of wheat, saying that they would be getting four or five dollars a bushel for their wheat if the price had not been fixed. A number of resolutions were pending increasing the price at which wheat had been fixed and demanding that a price-fixing policy be adopted as to cotton. The world was clamoring for all the wheat that could be grown to feed the soldiers and the civilian population of Europe. There was a limit to the consumption of cotton and there was danger of its falling in price, as Germany and her associates were unable to get it.

After the discussion Wilson asked us, "Shall we fix the price of cotton?" I said, "Yes, if this would not involve too great a strain on the Treasury for its purchase, and the conditions are identical with those affecting wheat."

Finally Wilson stated that he thought it would be well to appoint a committee representing all phases to make a thorough investigation. He named a committee composed of Baruch and Houston, a cotton grower from the Deep South, a cotton commission merchant, and a textile representative: men who would know the most about cotton.

A very few minutes after I had left and returned to the Navy Department, I heard someone walking very rapidly across the long office of the Secretary of the Navy. I looked up and saw Senator Ellison D. Smith, of South Carolina. He was not walking—he was running; and even before he reached my desk he cried out:

"I've just got only one minute! I've come to ask you a question!"

"Take a seat, Senator," I said.

"No—I've only one minute," he answered. "I've just heard, in the cloakroom of the Senate, a Senator say that at the meeting of the Cabinet this morning you voted to fix the price of cotton. I said he was a liar; that you were a true Southerner and would never favor such a course. Tell me—yes or no?"

"Sit down and I will tell you what I said," I answered him.

"NO!" he shouted: "Is it yes or no?"

"Let me talk to you a few minutes," I said. "After all, I'm not on the witness stand."

"I'm not going to sit down," he said. He seemed in a hurry to go right back and confront the Senators and tell them I had not favored fixing the price of cotton. But when he was calm enough to take a seat I related what had happened in the Cabinet meeting.

He was indignant. He said, "Even the suggestion will have a tendency to break the price of cotton and cause suffering to millions in the South dependent on that crop; any Southerner who would think of such a thing is an enemy to the South." With that he rushed out.

The committee made a careful investigation of the matter and reported to the President, who at the next meeting of the Cabinet said that it had advised against the fixing of the price of cotton because the drain on the Treasury would be more than it could stand whereas the government did not have to buy wheat. And with that the question of fixing the price for cotton came to an end.

Time passed, and the price of cotton went down, down, and down. It went down so low that it became almost a companion of McGinty at the bottom of the sea.

There came a day when Senator Smith called again at the office of the Secretary of the Navy. When he had finished the business that brought him, I could not resist the I-told-you-so inclination. I said: "Senator, do you remember the day you came in to denounce me as a enemy of the South because I was willing to fix the price of cotton?"

"Of course I remember," he blustered.

"If at that time we had fixed a price," I said, "it would have been around 30 or 32 cents—but it has, as you know, gone down to below 10 cents. Don't you think I would have been a great friend of the South if I could have kept the price up 20 cents more than it is now?"

He has not answered my question yet—and he never after that called me an enemy of the South.

WAR SCARE TO OPEN OIL RESERVES

"Oil has dogged you all your life but it has never bit you," a close friend telegraphed me when some oil companies were roasting me because I prevented their attempts to lease the Naval oil reserves. But oil companies never give up, and they took advantage of war conditions to try to force the government to lease the reserves in California; and, to effect that, in June, 1917, another leasing bill was introduced in Congress. At a hearing before the committee representatives of the California Chamber of Commerce, President Wilbur of Stanford University, Mark Requa, and other influential Californians testified that the California industries using oil would have to close down unless the Naval reserves were available. Wilbur said: "The immediate relief of California would come only if Naval Reserve No. 2 is used. We are up against an immediate emergency in this war, and we feel like it is keeping money in the bank for some future need instead of taking care of the pressing need." Senator Husting countered by saying that "if this reserve is drained we might as well give up having a permanent oil-burning Navy." He drew from Mr. Requa the admission that there was enough oil in California outside the Naval reserve to last twenty-eight years. Mr. Doheny, who in the Harding administration paid Fall $100,000 in a "little black bag" to exploit the Naval oil reserves, urged the leasing, saying there could never be a greater emergency.

I fought the attempt to use the war as an excuse, with all the resource in my power, and showed that the big oil companies in California were selling large quantities of oil to foreign governments, that if they would sell to California industries there would be no need to ask to exploit the Navy's reserves, and I added that I would never agree to the leasing until all the properties of the oil companies were made available; that if oil was taken out in 1917, the Navy would be short in the greater need in 1918; that I would favor opening up the oil reserves when the necessity arose for the Navy or for war industries when there was no other source of supply; the sacred setting-aside of the Naval reserves should not be departed from for the benefit of trespassers who were the real parties behind the propaganda which had fooled the university professor.

My testimony covered thirteen pages and gave a history of the long fight of the Navy against dummy entrymen and avid oil companies. I was backed by courageous Senator Husting and by Attorney General Gregory and Assistant Attorney General Kearful, but Secretary Houston, who had sided with me in the seven-year fight, joined Secretary Lane and the Western Senators except Husting in saying that the emergency was so great that I ought to yield. Even my good friend, Senator Key Pittman, felt that the California plea was valid and favored leasing. Finally, when I fought to the end, Pittman said, "The Secretary of the Navy is immovable in his stubbornness. But as long as he takes that position, he has the whip-hand, there is nothing we can do. He has the last say."

The attempt to lease these lands failed. Did war industries in California close down? They did not. There was plenty of oil for them in California, and Mexico was glad to supply all needed quantities. The war scare didn't scare the Navy and the oil was retained for Naval uses, but again in World War II the same influences worked up another war scare to get the Navy oil.

OIL MEN WANTED US TO BELGIANIZE MEXICO

The opposition of Acting Secretary Polk was aroused when big oil men tried to induce Uncle Sam to dictate Mexico's policy. Years after the Wilson era, recalling those days, Bernard M. Baruch, head of the War Industries Board, wrote me:

> "You may recall that at one time the oil companies made a desperate effort to get hold of the naval oil reserves. Failing in that, they tried to get us to go into Mexico and take over that part of the country in which the great oil wells were located. After carefully listening to all the arguments, the President said something to this effect—'You mean to say that unless we move into Mexico and take by force the oil properties located in her territory, we will not be able to conduct war?'
>
> "Someone answered, 'Yes.'
>
> "The President then said, 'Well, you will have to adjust yourselves to a war with what oil reserves you have or whatever you can buy in the markets. Germany raised the same point when she invaded Belgian territory. We cannot do the same thing.'"

COMPETITION NOT WAIVED

One criticism of the Navy by profiteers during the war was a compliment. They said that the Navy was insistent upon holding to competitive bids on all contracts, a principle departed from in only a few instances because of war exigencies. We stuck to the widest public competition in the open market. Throughout the war all formalities attendant upon the opening of bids were strictly adhered to. The proposals were opened every day and read out publicly, each bidder having ample opportunity to know his competitor's offer and also to be sure that his own was not overlooked. Even in those cases where military secrecy was obligatory, there was still genuine competition. The eight bidders, for instance, on the mines for the North Sea barrage were invited to meet each other and the purchasing officials in a locked and guarded room—even these confidential bids being strictly competitive. The principle was that every transaction must not only be right, but look right.

Scarcely had war been declared when requests, even demands, were made to "cut red tape" by doing away with competition. The so-called argument was advanced that deliveries could thereby be expedited and work accelerated. As a matter of fact, in obtaining most supplies, competition speeded up deliveries. At one time there was criticism that the beef standards were too high and should be lowered during the war; there was criticism of the rigid Navy requirements. They were not reduced. The head of Supply declared— and the Navy stuck to it to the end—"Only the best is good enough for our fighting men." Most of the great construction was done under contract, as, for example, the giant armor plate and projectile plant at Charleston, West Virginia, and the big dry docks at Philadelphia and at Norfolk.

When quick construction of 250 destroyers was essential, the Navy advanced the money and had to depart from competitive bidding. It became necessary to inspect every process and every expenditure, and Admiral Washington Capps headed this service. He was fair and just, but safeguarded the Navy from shoddy work and exorbitant prices.

It has been said—and is too often true—that officers in the military branch are eager to get the best war materials in the quickest time but are not strong for economy in public expenditure in war time. If asked to name the one man most zealous to protect the treasury, get the best work, and require a dollars worth of ships and ammunition for every dollar expended, I would name Washington Capps. He was fair and just in all decisions, but safeguarded the Navy from shoddy work and exorbitant prices.

One day a contractor with a "Navy Order" complained to me that his company could not meet the schedule by the agreed date because Capps and his inspection officers were too meticulous. Particularly he objected to one inspector at his plant whose rejection delayed completion. I happened to know that the man complained of was the soul of efficiency and fairness, but would not pass any work not first-class. After the shipbuilder had complained that this officer "slowed down completion of the ships," and suggested that if we wished delivery a man not so rigid should replace him, I said to him:

> "You are not as smart as I thought you were. If you expected me to change the inspector, you ought to have praised him to the skies. I would have then feared he was not as diligent to protect Uncle Sam as he was to please you. I would then have replaced him. But when your only complaint is that he is too meticulous and 'delays work' I know he is zealous to protect Uncle Sam. Your criticism makes it impossible to remove him."

He saw the point and knew I saw through his desire to put speed ahead of thoroughness.

Part Seven

FRANKLIN ROOSEVELT

XXVI

FRANKLIN ROOSEVELT, NAVY STATESMAN

I HAVE OFTEN been asked: "In what particular part of Naval activities was Franklin Roosevelt most interested and what were his largest contributions to the efficiency of the Navy which functioned so well in war?" Perhaps the real answer to that question was made by F.D.R. himself: "I get my fingers into about everything and there's no law against it." He was vitally concerned with all activities, from getting recruits to swim, up to the construction of the biggest dreadnaught and everything on shore and afloat, and was fertile in new ideas of advance. He was a skilled navigator and versed in ordnance lore as well as in Naval construction and operation. As he said, he got his "fingers into about everything," and generally to the good. One newspaper called him "the Navy's labor expert." The direction of Navy Yards was immediately under the Assistant Secretary of the Navy, and we both early favored the advantages to labor which came years afterwards in industry and the whole country under his "New Deal." Indeed, McAdoo, when he became Director of Railroads, complained that the Navy rate of pay was so high it stimulated demands from railway employees for "the Navy schedule." When profiteers in industry and in labor were making production difficult and strikes were threatened, the question was how to bring peace. Franklin Roosevelt proposed a central organization to look after all labor matters. It was vetoed by the Labor Department, which said it was a function of that department.

In many other ways than in the purchase of bonds, the slogan "Match the Navy" was evidence of its pioneering and leadership. Franklin pioneered in such Naval achievements as the construction of the North Sea Barrage and had an important part in planning the Navy's sending the first airplanes across the Atlantic. He visited all Navy Yards and Bases and stimulated training. He was twice in Europe to direct Navy operations.

F.D.R. DENIED AUTHORSHIP

When the Navy was charged with the duty of keeping Haiti and San Domingo out of German hands and helping those near-by nations to get on their feet, Roosevelt spent some time in each country with the Navy and Marine officers charged with important duties there. He took so much interest in the road-building and other improvements that for a long time the papers persisted in quoting Roosevelt as having said, "I wrote the Constitution of Haiti." Even President Harding quoted it, and then Franklin felt the time had come to deny that he had penned the imperialistic document. However, I think it was written in the State Department, which insisted on dominating Haiti after I had advised withdrawing the Marines and letting the Haitians govern themselves. The story of how General Smedley Butler by a virtual shotgun party—which he didn't relish but "orders is orders"—secured the adoption of the Constitution and the putting in office of the hand-picked president at the direction of the State Department, smacked of imperialism. Butler said: "I won't say we put him in. The State Department might object. Anyway, he was put in." That was when Lansing waved the Big Stick and before Roosevelt's Good Neighbor policy changed our attitude toward Southern neighbors.

F.D.R. AND MOTOR BOATS

There was an early scare that U-boats would attack New York, and Roosevelt shared it. He made a tentative contract to build 50-foot motor boats to patrol the harbor and later we built 110-foot boats. Neither I nor the construction officers were in favor of 50-foot craft and I made this entry in my Diary (March 21):

"Franklin Roosevelt urged more motor boats to be used for patrol. Will order many but are they valuable? How much of that sort of junk should we buy? Admiral Taylor, ablest naval construction officer in the world, and Admiral Rodman thought it money unwisely expended. Roosevelt was intent upon having many for use in harbors. In my heart I agreed with Taylor and Rodman. But suppose U-boats should enter our harbors and we lacked patrol boats, what then? Contrary to my belief in their worth I told F.D.R. to go ahead and buy a number."

DIDN'T AGREE WITH F.D.R.

F.D.R. was eager to enter the war before Wilson and I, and suggested what he thought was good strategy and wished a leading hand in directing it. In most matters we were in agreement but here is an exception:

The day after war was declared Franklin, zealous that the Navy should lack in nothing, requested me to sign an order to Admiral Winslow to come to Washington as his assistant. I told him that it would be unwise to detail Winslow for such service, that Winslow's rank and position were too high for such assignment, and that his adviser, whomever he desired, should be a man of business experience rather than a flag officer. When Admiral Benson, Chief of Operations, heard of Roosevelt's recommendation, he literally went up in the air. "This is aimed at me," he said. It was evident that Roosevelt wanted Winslow to share power in Operations. It would not work. I told Roosevelt that there should be no division of power in Operations where Benson had very able assistants and enough of them. If I had acted upon Roosevelt's suggestion and assigned Winslow as his assistant, it would have been embarrassing, for Winslow was not a man to be content as Adviser to an Assistant Secretary. He was shortly called to important service under Benson and his ability was utilized in the war.

NEEDED NO ASSISTANT SECRETARIES

When war was declared, the Chairman of the Naval Affairs Committee offered to provide for the creation of two additional Assistant Secretaries of the Navy for the duration. I told him that unless the Navy was organized so that it could function without change in war, it was inefficiently organized. No new office was created, and Franklin Roosevelt and I directed the conduct of the war with the coöperation of efficient Naval officers.

LABOR APPROVED F.D.R.

Franklin Roosevelt as Assistant Secretary of the Navy gave evidence of his interest in better conditions for men who labor. The Navy in those years set the pace for fair pay and the best working conditions. As proof of appreciation of his early devotion to fair dealings, the *Federal Machinist* said, when Roosevelt was nominated for vice president: "No other Assistant Secretary of the Navy has ever gained as great a respect from the workers and their representatives as Mr. Roosevelt."

WHY SAILORS LIKED HIM

Roosevelt loved the sea. I think he would have been happy if the offices of the Navy Department had been located on a battleship. Every time he had the opportunity, even for a week-end, he would make for a ship and he loved to have part in its navigation.

The officers and enlisted men liked him and his friendly ways. He won the admiration of bluejackets by an act of personal courage at San Francisco in 1915. The submarine *F-4* had shortly before sunk off Hawaii, with all hands lost. Worried about the effect of this on Navy morale, Roosevelt went aboard a submarine himself and had the skipper take him down for several dives.

Here is a characteristic incident told by an Admiral:

"He'd come aboard a new ship, and say to me, 'See that electric clock there? That takes exactly so much money and so many feet of wire and so many man hours to build and install. If that clock hadn't been put there, we could have had two more guns.'"

But he was too progressive to wish to go back to the time when officers, minus clocks, reckoned time by the sun and were said to "make time."

A GOOD NAVIGATOR

As a boy Roosevelt learned navigation. It stood him and Wilson in good stead when Mr. and Mrs. Roosevelt were returning with them from Europe on the *George Washington* early in 1919. In the fog the captain had lost his reckoning. F.D.R. located the ship's position and put her safely on her way again.

PROOF OF FRIENDSHIP

In many ways Franklin Roosevelt showed his friendship and goodness of heart. I recall one touching my oldest son and namesake who had enlisted in the Marine Corps as a private. I quote from my Diary:

"When Franklin heard Josephus was enlisting as a private he came to me and said:

" 'You do not know how hard it will be for your son as a private—harder than for any other person in the service because he is the son of the Secretary of the Navy. Let me take charge of it and let him enroll as a Lieutenant.'

" 'It wouldn't be fair, Franklin,' I said, 'to him or to the Corps. He knows nothing about drilling or soldiering and could not therefore command men and train them to fight. More than that: I have declined to enlist men as officers unless they had special qualifications. How could I justify a different course with regard to my own son?'

" 'I understand,' he said. 'Leave it all to me and have nothing to do with it. If you appreciated what is in store for Josephus you would not think of letting him enter as a private.' "

I greatly appreciated his interest in the boy and his eagerness to help him, but could not feel that anyone ought to be given a commission when he had not earned it.

A RASCALLY ANCESTOR

"You must help my son who is being punished because he left ship," said a lady caller late in 1919. I asked, "Why do you say MUST?" Her answer was that her great-great-grandfather had signed a note for Franklin Roosevelt's like remote ancestor, and, to pay the note, her ancestor's utensils, etc., were sold. Therefore as F.D.R. was Assistant Secretary he ought to release her boy in payment of a Roosevelt debt. F.D.R. was out of the city. When he returned we had a good laugh when I told him I had been forced to pay the debt of his rascally ancestor. We made an agreement that he in return would take care of my "rascally ancestors" when and if they turned up.

FRANKLIN WISHED TO DON UNIFORM

From the first suggestion that the Navy send fourteen-inch guns to France, the boldness and possibilities of the new weapon intrigued Franklin Roosevelt. He was eager to go as Lieutenant Commander in Admiral Plunkett's specially chosen force after, early in the war, President Wilson had sat down hard on Roosevelt's application to don the uniform of a sailor and get into the actual fighting. He stuck to his big job at the Navy Department, sometimes restless to go across as a member of the American Expeditionary Force.

In October (1918) Franklin renewed his request to be enrolled as an officer. I told him that I could not conscientiously ask him to remain longer in Washington, and suggested that he make known his wish to President Wilson. He called at the White House. The President told Roosevelt that he had received what he thought was true information from Prince Max of Baden that an armistice was imminent. Wilson added, "You are too late. The war will be over before you could return to France."

F.D.R. SENDS MONROE MEMORANDUM

In the days before he crossed the Rubicon, Wilson pondered the history of events that preceded other wars and the attitudes of predecessors who sought to avoid war, as Madison did in 1812, Lincoln in 1861, McKinley in 1898, and as Wilson had done when there was persistent demand to wage war on Mexico in the Huerta days. Realizing that the President was reviewing history in the hope of finding guidance, Franklin D. Roosevelt sent Wilson a memorandum written by James Monroe, when the Congress of Vienna was about to meet. Roosevelt wrote: "It is in the handwriting of Monroe. I have been unable to discover that it was actually used in any official message or document." It had interest in 1917 and has interest now. The interesting part of Monroe's memorandum is as follows:

"A war in Europe, in which Great Britain with her floating thunders, and other maritime powers are always parties, has long been found to spread its calamities into the remotest regions. Even the United States, just and pacific as its policy is, has not been able to avoid the alternative of either submitting to the most destructive and ignominious wrongs from European Belligerents, or of resisting them by an appeal to the sword; or to speak more properly, no other choice has been left them but the time of making the appeal; it being evident that a submission too long protracted, would have no other effect than to encourage and accumulate aggression, until they should become altogether intolerable; and until the loss of honor, being added to other losses, redress by the sword itself would be rendered more slow and difficult."

REHABILITATION AND EDUCATION

At the meeting of the Council of National Defense on February 25, Franklin Roosevelt presented the report of the Committee on Rehabilitation and Vocational Education for wounded men after the war. That was wise foresight. Discussion followed as to who should be in control. The Treasury wanted it under the War Insurance Board. McAdoo wanted everything not nailed down to be put under the Treasury. It was decided to take it up with the President. It was proposed to make April 6—the anniversary of our entrance—as "Win the War Day."

F.D.R. CALLED IT "PARTISAN"

When a Congressional Committee, holding hearings on Naval affairs, asked Assistant Secretary Roosevelt and some officers to suggest any changes in the Navy organization which would be desirable, in his reply F.D.R. said:

"I do not believe the time has yet come. We are altogether too close to the war to understand its lessons. We are in the middle of a partisan campaign."

Behind the investigation, aside from partisanship, was the old desire of a number of Admirals to pattern the Navy after German organization, to give all power to an Admiral who would be chief of the operations, and make the Secretary a figurehead. When proposed early in my administration I opposed and defeated it. In his letter saying that no system was perfect, advising two assistant secretaries, F.D.R. gave this knock-out blow to the cherished desire of a coterie of Admirals advocating Nazifying the American Navy:

"It must be remembered that Congress in its wisdom, has from the earliest days of the Republic established the principle of civilian control at the head of the Naval Establishment. During only one period of our history has this been altered. That was the period after the war of 1812 when a Board of three Navy Commissioners, all of their high ranking officers, were given great power, thereby taking away much of the authority of the civilian Secretary of the Navy. That particular system fell of its own weight, the Naval service itself being thoroughly dissatisfied with what might be called the dual control. I feel perfectly confident that today, also, the service sees the folly of any such suggestion placing an officer as head of the Navy or Secretary. A little thought would convince anyone that it would be equally ridiculous to have a civilian Secretary of the Navy but to give him no authority and to give all the authority to the Chief of Operations."

NAMING DESTROYERS

With 350 destroyers under construction, the question of naming them presented a problem which I discussed with Franklin Roosevelt and officers of the Navy. The practice had been to give them the names of noted Naval heroes—men who had rendered service beyond the call of duty. That was easy when only a few destroyers were built yearly and some old ones were going out of commission. However, with the necessity of selecting names for 350 in a short time, there were not enough distinguished Naval heroes to go around. One day Franklin Roosevelt came in with the suggestion that in the future Indian names be given destroyers. He thought it would lessen the honor to give names of Naval men to the destroyers unless their service had been distinguished. As to Indian names, he had a list that showed, in tribes and chiefs, enough names to meet our schedule of construction. As usual, when he had an idea, he presented it with enthusiasm and confidence. I suggested that we were already giving certain types of ships Indian names and it would be somewhat confusing to give Indian names to other ships, and that it would be better to reserve destroyers' names for Naval heroes. "Where are you going to find heroes?" he asked, and added, "We have already sifted the list and given the honor to those who were worthy and certainly none should be given the honor just to find names." There was force in the argument, but I was not convinced.

"Already in this war," I said, "several of the Naval personnel have shown such courage—as for example, Osmond Ingram, hero of the *Cassin*—as to justify naming destroyers for them. I fear there will be many more who will be called upon thus to make a brave surrender of life, and we should reserve the names of destroyers for their immortality."

Fortunately, while there were losses, the number was not so large as we then feared, for the mine barrage and other agencies lessened U-boat encounters. When I was unwilling to adopt Roosevelt's suggestion, he and I and Naval officers all went to work to dig into

Naval records, and we found that there were more unrecognized Naval heroes than we knew of who had hitherto been born to blush unseen. Even so, it was not easy to find enough who qualified for the honor. We decided therefore to honor each former Secretary of the Navy who had passed on, by giving his name to a new destroyer. I thought and think, though none could qualify as heroes, that they had rendered a service to the Navy worthy of being commemorated. Still there were not enough names for all the destroyers. Who else should be honored? In the early days of the Republic there were audacious privateers who were as effective in upholding American rights on the seas as were Naval officers. As a matter of fact, around 1812, privateers were depended upon to seize British ships. I began a study of these privateers largely because I knew the history of one of the most successful, Ottway Burns, of North Carolina. An examination of his record showed that Burns had brought in prizes from as far north as the coast of Massachusetts. I therefore directed a destroyer be named *Burns* in honor of that privateer who had done so much for his country, who after the war was State Senator in North Carolina, and for whom the county seat of Yancey—Burnsville—is named. A few days after the papers had carried a statement that one of the new destroyers bore the name of Burns, Admiral Badger, head of the General Board, came into the office where Franklin and I were talking and asked:

"Have you abandoned the practice of naming destroyers for Naval heroes?"

I answered in the negative. He observed that a new destroyer had been named *Burns*. "I have been over the Naval Register," he said, "and I have not found the name of Burns. For whom, may I ask, is the new destroyer named?"

I told him that it was named for Captain Ottway Burns, a noted privateer from Beaufort, North Carolina, who had rendered distinguished service to the country around 1812. As Roosevelt was a connoisseur on ships, he knew all about Burns and related some of his captures on the New England Coast. "I think," I added, "that a privateer who captured so many ships is entitled to as much maritime honor as if he had been commissioned by the Navy. You know, Admiral, there was a time when such a distinguished man as John Paul Jones was advertised in Great Britain as a pirate and the same

may have been true of Burns. There wasn't much difference then
between an Admiral and a pirate."

He entered into the spirit of my badinage, and laughed when I
jokingly added that my experience as Secretary of the Navy had
convinced me that the difference between a Pirate and an Admiral
was the twilight zone. It became one of Franklin's prize stories.

OBJECTED TO MAURY

Naming destroyers brought criticism, as this extract from my
Diary (December 1, 1917) shows:

"In naming new destroyers I gave the name *Maury* to one
in honor of Matthew Fontaine Maury, "the path-finder of the
sea." I knew he had followed his State in 1861, left the Federal
Navy and joined the Confederate Navy, but the world owed him
a lasting debt for his primacy as path-finder and scientist. Speaking about it to Admiral McKean, Acting Chief of Operations
for the time, he said there would be objection in some quarters
because he had joined the Confederate Navy. I replied: 'We have
Camp Lee and Camp Jackson. Why not honor Maury, who did
most for the Navy?' His answer was that these camps named for
Confederate Generals were temporary and did not signify so
much, while the ship would keep the name for many years."

But the name was not changed. The war had been ended nearly
fifty years. Were the old sectional feelings and differences never to
end? Was the world to forget Maury's scientific contribution, his
studies on the Gulf Stream, his devotion to high ideals, and his high
standard of Christian living because in the war of brothers he felt
his highest allegiance belonged to the State that gave him birth?
I thought not, and resolved to give one of the largest destroyers
the name of an illustrious American whose contribution to the lore
of the sea makes him immortal. Invited to address the National
Geographic Society during the World War, I chose: "Maury, the
Pathfinder of the Sea," when all expected me to talk about the
pending struggle, though I prefaced my address by what I deemed
a tribute to Naval participation in those high and crucial days.

ROOSEVELT VISITS SEAT OF WAR

The strain on department heads in the first year of the war kept
Roosevelt and myself at our desks or visiting shipyards and munition

plants to expedite production. We depended on Naval officers overseas to keep us posted. The work easing up in the summer of 1918,
Franklin had the urge to go to the war zone. "One of us ought to
go and see the war in progress with his own eyes, else he is a chess
player moving his pieces in the dark," he said. Wilson wished me in
Washington for frequent conferences. I told Franklin, "You draw
the inspection trip. See Navy operations at first hand, send frequent
reports, and make recommendations as conditions demand." True to
his love of the sea he embarked (July 9, 1918) on a bucking destroyer
—the *Dyer* which was convoying transports carrying 25,000 soldiers
to Brest, the port of reception in France. He went everywhere, saw
everybody worth seeing, inspected every Naval base, Navy and
Marine unit, and cabled recommendations that strengthened our
forces in Europe. His letters and reports were informing and illuminating, based on his own keen observation and association with those
directing the war. He wrote of his visit to the front, and I quote
this characteristic extract from a letter (dated August 15):

> "Those Marines are simply magnificent and I am getting
> some material to bring back with us. They certainly do need
> more Marines over here. They are 2,500 short of being able to
> replace the losses in the original brigade. Of course, these losses
> have been very severe; we hope more so than ever will be again,
> but we haven't enough replacements in France yet."

General Butler's Thirteenth Regiment of Marines sailed for
France, which strengthened the Marine force there.

In his official report (October 15), writing of visiting the historic
spot where the Marines "had done such magnificent fighting a few
weeks before," Roosevelt added:

> "It requires a personal view of the region around Château-
> Thierry to understand how very important these actions in
> which the Marines took part were to the general plan of opera-
> tions, which has resulted not only in checking but in driving
> back the German armies. Belleau Wood formed a strategic
> position of enormous strength to the German line. Its complete
> occupation by the Marines after many days of fighting in the
> face of great odds and in the roughest country formed not only
> a brilliant chapter in the history of the Marine Corps but an
> event of high importance to the whole western front...."

General Degonta showed me the original of his Army order changing the name of Bois de Belleau to Bois de la Brigade de Marine."

Franklin's private letter, written after a visit to Italy, treated mainly of the Naval situation in the Mediterranean, where he found "the whole situation was up against a stone wall" with Britain and Italy in wide disagreement. He had talked with Sir Eric Geddes in London and found our Naval leaders backing up the British position.

F.D.R. HAD LANSING WORRIED

At a Cabinet meeting Lansing asked if Franklin Roosevelt, now in Europe, was authorized to tell Italy we favored the British plan of putting Jellicoe in command of Mediterranean forces. I said, "No." On the contrary, I had written him we earnestly favored Allied command but declined to say who should command. The French Ambassador was worried at news in Rome that F.D.R. had said this country wanted an English commander.

The next day Lansing saw me and repeated what Jusserand had heard—that Roosevelt had told the Italian Government that we desired a British Admiral for the Mediterranean. Sims thought Great Britain and France agreed on Jellicoe and wanted us to say yes. I said: "Allied Council must name the man." Roosevelt wrote me that he had talked with the Italian leaders in Rome and thought well of the solution that Italians remain in control in the Adriatic.

After detailed reports of the Naval activities, F.D.R. closed his letter with—"Quantities of people have begged me to get you over here in the Fall. You really ought to decide to come in October and you could get back again by the time Congress reopens."

NAVY BUILDED WELL

Roosevelt's official report, addressed to me, went into details about laying the mine fields in the North Sea, which he had early favored; told of "the enormous task which the Army has successfully faced"; told of visits to Paulliac, the great assembly and repair base for Navy aircraft with a Navy personnel of 5,000, practically erected by bluejackets, and of visits to all Naval bases overseas, with a commendation of Admiral Sims and Admiral Wilson. He concluded:

"In regard to our officers and men I can only add again that they have shown that in time of peace we had builded well for the emergency of war. The transition from peace to war went on at home as it had been planned and the transfer of the major operations from our shores to scattered fronts 3,000 miles away without friction and with true efficiency.... We have very good reason to be proud of what the Navy has done."

ACTOR KISSED WILSON

Franklin Roosevelt was fond of telling this story about an incident as he was returning to the United States with Wilson on the *George Washington*. He would say, "Wilson and others attended a party given below decks, and the leading lady kissed the President." When the listener expressed astonishment that she should take such a liberty with the dignified President, Franklin would wait a moment enjoying the effect of his story and then laughingly say, "You see the entertainment was given by the crew and the leading 'Lady' was a man, wearing a rope wig and a skirt."

F.D.R. USED FRENCH SWEAR WORDS

Franklin cabled me from France that upon his return, after he had reported at the Navy Department, he wanted to go back to Europe with an assignment in uniform to the Naval Railway Battery. When he reached Washington he told me he had talked to Admiral Plunkett about it at St. Nazaire, where the guns were being assembled and were nearly ready. I recall that in his report of his tour of inspection, he told me that Plunkett had asked him: "Can you swear well enough in French to swear a French train on the siding and let our big guns through?" Franklin said to Plunkett: "Listen!..." Thereupon with inventive genius he handed Plunkett a line of French swear words, real and imaginary, which impressed Plunkett so greatly that he said he would take Roosevelt on in his outfit with the rank of Lieutenant Commander if he could get the Secretary to give him a commission.

ROOSEVELT STRICKEN WITH PNEUMONIA

Though he thought he was robust and never spared himself, upon his return voyage he became ill. News came to me in September from the ship that F.D.R. had pneumonia. I communicated with his wife, who, with doctors and an ambulance, met him on the arrival of the ship in New York from Brest. "Flu" was raging in Brest when he arrived to embark for home. Franklin and his party attended a funeral before leaving in the rain. The ship on which he returned was a floating hospital—men and officers died on the way home and were buried at sea. All but one of his party were seriously ill but recovered. In her, *This Is My Story,* Mrs. Roosevelt relates:

"With them on the boat, coming to this country for a visit, were Prince Axel, of Denmark, and his aides. When they felt the flu coming on they consulted no doctor but took to their berths with a quart of whisky each. In the course of a day or two, whether because of the efficacy of the whisky or whether because of their own resistance, they were practically recovered."

The pneumonia left Franklin very weak and it was the middle of October before he could return to Washington and make the report in person of what he had seen on his trip of inspection. Even so, within a short time after he returned to Washington Franklin, and all five of his children, were down with flu.

ROOSEVELT'S TRIP TO DEMOBILIZE NAVY ABROAD

Roosevelt recovered in time to return to Europe after the Armistice, accompanied by Mrs. Roosevelt, to supervise the Naval demobilization. In my Annual Report (1919), I said:

"Upon the signing of the Armistice and the closing of Naval shore activities abroad, the Navy had a number of stations in Europe, and valuable material and equipment. In order that it might be sold, salvaged or brought to America, as in each case was most desirable, Assistant Secretary Roosevelt, accompanied by Commander John M. Hancock, who had shown high ability in the business side of the Navy in coöperation with the War Industries Board, and Mr. Thomas J. Spellacy, an able lawyer, as legal adviser, went to Europe in January and made arrangements by which the Navy's demobilization could be expedited and its property disposed of to the best advantage.

"The plans perfected and the negotiations completed have resulted in the disposition of Naval property in a way that has been wise and beneficial. The great high-power radio station in France was, through negotiations with the French Government, completed by our Navy, with the agreement that it be purchased by the French Government. Equipment and material that will be needed at home have been brought back and such as was not practicable or profitable to transport has been sold abroad."

COURAGE OVERCOMES INFANTILE PARALYSIS

In the summer of 1915 Franklin had to undergo an operation for appendicitis. When able to leave the Naval Hospital, I ordered the Secretary's yacht, the *Dolphin,* to take him to his summer home in Campobello, where the cooler air hastened his recovery.

When in the summer of 1921 the distressing news came that Franklin had been stricken with infantile paralysis, I recalled the three times he had to go to the hospital for operation and medical care while he was Assistant Secretary of the Navy, and that he had been kept out of the campaign in 1912 by an attack of typhoid fever. But every time he had come back strong and his courage and confidence enabled him, if not to overcome the handicap of weak limbs, not to let the loss of perfect locomotion prevent his arduous service in high posts in days that called for every ounce of strength and determination.

LOVING CUP ON RESIGNATION

When Roosevelt was nominated for Vice President in 1920, he felt that he should resign as Assistant Secretary of the Navy before entering upon his campaign.

When his resignation was announced, the Association of Master Mechanics, Employees of Navy Yards and Stations, and the Navy Department gave evidence of their regret and regard by presenting him a silver loving cup. Vice President Harry T. Morningstar made the presentation, through me, saying:

"I leave to you, Mr. Secretary, the honor of conveying to Mr. Roosevelt the kind thoughts and appreciation of every one connected with the Navy, and for the great work which he has accomplished, not alone for the Navy, but for the whole government of the United States.

"You must realize, Mr. Secretary, that this token is but a *half* token of the high esteem every employee holds for the *two* civilian heads of the Navy Department. We are looking forward, with gladness, to the fourth of March next, when we shall witness the inauguration of our beloved Assistant Secretary as the Vice President of the United States, in whose election we all hope to have a most welcome part."

In making the presentation I emphasized what Mr. Morningstar had said, told Franklin he had garnered the love of shipmates and co-workers which would endure as long as life lasts. Accepting it, Mr. Roosevelt said:

"Mr. Daniels and my other co-workers in the Navy, and through you the thousands all over this land and on the sea who are in the same great service, the day is a day of very deep emotion for me. It is a day that I have been looking forward to with real dread for a long time, not because it means leaving an official position, but because, as I think you know, there has been something deeper than mere employment in my work. I have had a kind of personal deep feeling from the heart that we were all of us working together in a common cause. And now at last the hour has struck, and with it I leave you with more than an ordinary feeling of parting; I leave you with the kind of affection that will always stay with me. Our work here for nearly eight years, in fact all of the work of this Department, I like to think, has been that kind of unselfishness on the part of all of us that goes deep down into the heart. And during those eight years, with every person that I have come in contact with, from our chief here down to the most recent comer in the ranks, we have a mutual trust, a mutual spirit of coöperation, and a desire to serve. And I feel very certain that when history comes to be written, it will write truly of the splendid work of Josephus Daniels and of every man and woman associated with him. And in this cup I will have something that will be a visible reminder, not only to me of my days—for I don't need a visible reminder—but it will be a reminder to my children and to every-one who comes to my house of the human side of working for Uncle Sam; of the human element, the fact that we have worked together with the right kind of spirit."

He then added he was sending Alnav messages in which he expressed pride in the Navy and his happiness in the privilege of service for nearly eight years, adding, "The Navy will carry on its splendid record," and in his longer message to those in the shore establishments to them he recounted the years of working together saying:

"When war finally came, a more terrible war than any one anticipated, one which called for our utmost endeavor, the Navy shore establishments met the crisis in a way which has earned the admiration of the country. It is the thing that I am most proud of in my life that I was able to help to bring this about. How much of our success was due to the coöperation of our civilian employees the country will never know or understand. Unswept by the search-light of publicity, which revealed the heroes of the battlefield, the men and women in our yards and stations and those attached to the Department at Washington worked with equal patriotism and with equal love of country to help win the war."

WILSON'S TRIBUTE TO F.D.R.

Shortly after his nomination as Vice President, after consultation with me, Franklin Roosevelt sent his letter of resignation as Assistant Secretary of the Navy to President Wilson who accepted it in the following letter written on August 30:

"DEAR MR. ROOSEVELT:

"Acknowledging receipt of your letter, tendering your resignation as Assistant Secretary of the Navy, I take occasion upon the acceptance of the same, to express appreciation of the able, efficient, and patriotic service you rendered your country in that responsible position during the seven and a half years of your incumbency embracing the period of the World War when the Navy's contribution won world appreciation.

"With congratulations upon the distinguished honor that has come to you and with cordial greetings and sincere good wishes, I am

"Faithfully yours,
"WOODROW WILSON

"HON. FRANKLIN D. ROOSEVELT,
"Hyde Park, New York."

I know this was a just appreciation of the service of Mr. Roosevelt by the President. How do I know? I wrote it myself. When Wilson received the formal resignation, he wrote me: "I will be very much obliged if you would formulate something for me to say in accepting his [Roosevelt's] resignation."

If Wilson and I could have looked into the future and seen Roosevelt as successor of Wilson in the White House, and the greatest strategist and promoter of peace in World War II, the note would probably have contained something like this:

"This honor that has come to you in recognition of your past distinguished service to your country, is but an earnest of greater honors that await you in the future, when you will win the gratitude not only of your countrymen but of free people in every part of the world."

We could not foresee that Franklin would be elected to the presidency four times; lift the country out of the depression and lead it to its era of greatest prosperity; see before others the menace of Hitler and prepare for the coming war; wage the war to the eve of victory; win the gratitude of all nations; plan the peace that has followed his blueprints; like Moses, die in sight of the Promised Land on the mountain top after delivering his people from the evils that afflicted them; write his name beside that of Washington; and say in his last speech, which he was not spared to deliver:

"We as Americans do not choose to deny our responsibility. Nor do we intend to abandon our determination that, within the lives of our children and our children's children, there will not be a Third World War."

I was at Hyde Park when Franklin Roosevelt was notified of his nomination and was happy at its reception and the enthusiasm of the great gathering. He was forced to quit speaking for a brief time when an aeroplane flew over Hyde Park. He received much applause when he changed his written word normal to "normalcy," a new word Harding had used to promise a backward march. It contrasted with Roosevelt's demand to go forward.

In his speech of acceptance he championed "a newly built merchant marine," a world peace pact and the progress foreshadowing his greater contributions to their achievement. Two brief extracts illustrate his convictions:

"1. Real peace must include a League of Nations. It is a practical solution of a practical situation.

"2. Some people have been saying of late: "We are tired of progress, we want to go back to where we were before; to go about our own business; to restore 'normal conditions'": They are wrong. We can never go back. Our eyes are trained ahead—forward to better new days. We must go forward or founder.

A TRIUMVIRATE OF THE U. S. NAVY, WASHINGTON, 1918

Left to right, Secretary of the Navy Daniels, Rear Admiral Samuel McGowan, U. S. N., Paymaster General, and Assistant Secretary of the Navy Roosevelt (U. S. Navy).

Above, Assistant Secretary Roosevelt on an inspection tour of the French Navy's strong-hold at Brest in 1918. With him are (*left to right*) Vice Admiral Moreau, Vice Admiral Schwerer, Rear Admiral Benoit, of the French Navy, and Rear Admiral Wilson, U. S. N. *Below,* Roosevelt inspecting a Naval Railway Battery in 1918, in the company of Rear Admiral C. P. Plunkett (on the left) and other officers (U. S. Navy photos).

WOODBURY SUCCEEDS ROOSEVELT

Looking for Roosevelt's successor, I turned to New England and talked to Senator Hollis and Congressman Stevens of New Hampshire about it, saying that I preferred to recommend as Roosevelt's successor a New Englander. They were greatly gratified and wanted New Hampshire to have the place. They recommended that Robert Jackson would be a suitable man. He was a member of the Democratic National Committee and was later prominent in the campaign that resulted in Roosevelt's election to the presidency. He informed the Congressman that he had accepted a business position which made it impossible for him to be considered, and I recommended to President Wilson the appointment of Gordon Woodbury to succeed Roosevelt. He had been editor of an important paper in Manchester and belonged to a distinguished family, his great-grandfather having been Secretary of the Treasury and Senator from New Hampshire. He was a worthy scion. When I wrote to President Wilson recommending Mr. Woodbury, he answered as follows:

"I am perfectly willing to accept your judgment about Mr. Gordon Woodbury and hope that he will justify your confidence in every way."

Mr. Woodbury held the office until the Wilson Administration ended and served with ability, loyalty, and devotion.

ROOSEVELT MEETS DEFEAT

When Franklin Roosevelt was nominated for Vice President in 1920 I little thought he was headed for a second defeat at the polls (the first was when he ran for U.S. Senator in 1914), which would have ended the political career of any man of less resiliency and less of what in a woman would have been called charm, which Franklin possessed from birth to death to the nth degree. It was that appealing quality which enabled him all unconsciously to win my heart at the Baltimore Convention and resulted in my recommendation that the President appoint him Assistant Secretary of the Navy. And it was that indefinable something in his heart, expressed in his innate courtesy, which held my affection until the end, and was not lessened in the few times—some deep-seated—in which we were not in agreement. My attitude toward him did not go as far as what Admiral Samuel McGowan related to me about friendship that knew no limit. One friend—let us call him David—facing a serious situation, asked Jonathan: "Will you stand by me to the end?" The reply was in the affirmative. "If the worse comes to the worst, will you go down with me to the very gates of hell?" Without a moment's reflection, this modern Jonathan said: "Yes, not only to the gates of hell, but I'll go in with you." I would not have gone that far with F.D.R., but I would have gone to the gates of heaven with him, hoping he would use his rabbit foot with St. Peter to get me inside the gates.

PROTESTED AGAINST KING PIN

Though Roosevelt was no longer in the Navy, his love and interest continued. He knew that there had always been some officers in the Navy who wished the Navy Department organized on the basis of the German General Staff. They held that the Chief of Operations should be the real director of all Naval matters, with the Secretary valuable only to get appropriations from the Congress. At one time a committee of Congress almost incorporated such a provision in the Navy Bill. I told the Chairman of the Committee, who had not appreciated its gravamen, that if the provision written by an Admiral was adopted Congress ought to abolish the office of Secretary of the Navy for he would have no power. I told him it was like putting the Secretary of the Navy at the top of the Washington monument without a telephone to the Navy Department.

My opinion that the Secretary of the Navy ought to be the head of the Navy and direct its operations, of course aided by experts in Naval lore, was shared by Franklin Roosevelt. Some months after he had resigned as Assistant Secretary, learning there was a renewed attempt to make the Chief of Operations the real head of the Navy, Roosevelt wrote me as follows:

"November 16, 1920

"DEAR CHIEF:

".... Of course it is just another case of going back to the old Navy theory that the Secretary of the Navy should be a rubber stamp who could always be used on convenient occasions to make him the goat in case any trouble came up in the service. However, there is real danger in all of this, for some fool administration may some day make the Chief of Operations the King Pin. I am glad that neither you nor I will be connected with the Department when that happens, even though it will hurt the Navy more than any other thing that has ever come to it. . . ."

Affectionately,
FRANKLIN D. ROOSEVELT

WILSON AND ROOSEVELT HAD SAME GOAL

Altough they were unlike in temperament, the similarity in the goals of Wilson and Roosevelt has often been commented upon. In 1920, though not as confident of victory as Wilson, the vice-presidential candidate, along with Cox, pressed only one issue, Wilson's "solemn referendum" on the League of Nations, when even New York City voted for Harding. In his forced retirement because of infantile paralysis, Roosevelt took little part in politics after 1920 until 1924, when he placed Smith in nomination for President. At that time neither Roosevelt nor Smith nor McAdoo stood with Newton Baker in his brilliant speech urging a League of Nations plank in the platform. I was one of a small minority in the North Carolina delegation who voted for Baker's plank. In 1928 there was no fight for the League and it was not until World War II that the great body of the people woke up to "the crime of 1919-20," which made possible the later holocaust. And then Roosevelt was the first to declare that America was entering the struggle in a war against war and died after having named delegates to the San Francisco Conference to fashion an instrument to insure lasting peace. Did the fact that in all the years at Hyde Park he used the same desk and chair that Wilson used aboard the *SS George Washington* en route to the Peace Conference in 1918 have any significance?

F.D.R.'s ATTRACTIVE PERSONALITY

In 1918 and again early in 1919, Assistant Secretary Roosevelt went to Europe on official duty. Of his trip to Paris and the impression he made, Webb Miller gives the best picture. He wrote:

"During the summer of 1918 I met Franklin Delano Roosevelt for the first time. He came to Paris as Assistant Secretary of the Navy in connection with the anti-submarine campaign. He received about a score of French journalists in a hotel on the Rue de Rivoli, and I was present. I recall particularly the excellent impression he made upon the French newspaper men and how he charmed them with his pleasant personality and unusual frankness. He was then about thirty-six years of age, slender, handsome, and prepossessing in appearance. He leaned against the mantelpiece and chatted with the newspaper men in fluent French; that alone won them to him, because he was the first American high official to reach France who spoke their language with facility.

"He astounded the French newspaper men by telling them that American Cabinet members received newspaper correspondents twice daily, something unheard of in Europe. Some time afterward, Roosevelt said that Clemenceau jokingly accused him of having almost overturned the French Cabinet. All the French newspapermen, Clemenceau told him, had rushed to the Quai d'Orsay and demanded that French Cabinet ministers receive the press daily, citing Roosevelt's statement that it was done in the United States. Roosevelt's famous charm of personality is no new development; he had it at least eighteen years ago.

"I met Roosevelt again briefly in 1932, but the next time I talked with him was at the White House in February, 1936, after my return from the Northern Italian Front in Ethiopia. He received me privately and asked many questions about the military and political factors of the situation in Ethiopia which revealed that he had a thorough grasp of them. I am not at liberty to go into the details of our conversation, but one of the stories he told me proved that the heavy burden of office had not affected his sense of humor. Of all the men in high places I have met, President Roosevelt possesses the warmest and most attractive personality."

XXVII

F.D.R. AND OTHER DUTCHMEN

A T ITS Thirty-Fifth Anniversary Dinner (January 15, 1920), I was invited to speak on Americanism by the Holland Society in New York. My shipmate, Franklin D. Roosevelt, welcomed me banteringly asking, "How did you manage to break into a Dutchmen's dinner?"

I surprised him by answering, "Wait till you hear me speak, and you will see I have as much right here as you have, and a little more."

In my introduction, after paying tribute to Judge Augustus Van Wyck, President of the Society, former Mayor Robert Van Wyck (they had a sister, wife of General Robert F. Hoke, living in my home city), Dr. Van Dyke, Franklin Roosevelt, and other Dutchmen of America, I disclosed that my great-great-grandfather was named Van Pelt, and I was hailed as worthy of membership in the Holland Society. I told Roosevelt that, so far as I knew, he never dropped the Van, though Roosevelt's forbears had dropped their Van and Americanized the name. He said, "As we are both Dutchmen, there is a new tie that binds us."

WHAT WE OWE THE DUTCH

In my address I recalled that Woodrow Wilson had, in summing up the contributions of the Dutch to America, credited them not only with founding the City of New York but with doing most to establish public education, free institutions, and liberty of conscience. When Englishmen were denied the right of free speech and to worship in accord with their conscience, Holland gave them welcome, and from the freedom of that little country dissenting Englishmen sailed to create New England. The only time I ever doubted the wisdom of making Holland a refuge to those denied residence in their homeland was when it extended welcome at Doorn to the Kaiser, who was compelled to leave Germany to escape the punishment or accept the fate of Napoleon—exile on a lonely island. When after the Armistice there was debate (this was before he was given refuge in Holland) of the kind of punishment that should be meted out to the German Emperor, I had urged that he should be sent to St. Helena, where the ghost of Napoleon could emphasize the futility of the ambition of world conquest. If Luke Lea had succeeded in his dash on Doorn to capture the Kaiser, as he attempted and nearly succeeded in doing, the German Emperor might have spent the balance of his life communing with the spirit of Bonaparte.

IF I HAD BEEN A PROPHET

If I could have looked into the future and seen the result of the election of 1932, I could have added this to my address at the Holland Society:

"Not only have the Dutch given America Martin Van Buren and Theodore Roosevelt as chief executives, but the day is not far distant when another Dutchman—my Assistant Secretary of the Navy, Franklin Roosevelt—will not only be elected to the Presidency but become so enshrined in the hearts of the people of America that he will break entrenched tradition and be elected to a third and fourth term and will become for all time a symbol of Domestic Progress and World Peace.

"Not only did this latest Dutchman in the White House foresee the danger of totalitarianism when Hitler wrote his *Mein Kampf,* but he warned his countrymen that they must vaccinate against Naziism if they would save democracy. Before he died it was his master strategy that relieved the Dutch from the blight of Nazi domination, so that they could look across the Atlantic, as when they came to found New Amsterdam, and plan a noble monument to Franklin Roosevelt, the American Dutchman whose vision liberated the land of his forbears."

DUTCHMEN

At this dinner of the Holland Society I was glad to see an old friend who had served in the Intelligence Department of the Navy during the World War, Mr. Warren C. Van Slyck. He was the only person I appointed to any place during the World War at the request of Mrs. Woodrow Wilson. He was an old friend of hers. She wrote me that Mr. Van Slyck, who was between forty and fifty, was so imbued with patriotic zeal when war was declared that, finding nothing at once available, he enlisted and was in training as a private sailor at Pelham Bay. He had been a lawyer of ability, and she thought his services could be utilized in some more important way. After talking with him I gave him a commission in the Intelligence Service and he more than measured up to all that Mrs. Wilson said of him.

This proved that military men and others are too much inclined to make an age deadline. They lose experience—the most valuable thing a man can bring to public service except, of course, physical strength in combat. A tendency toward putting men on the shelf while they were still vigorous and strong denied the service of many men who could have been most useful in civilian positions and thereby released thousands to active service afloat or in the field.

DR. VAN DYKE BECOMES NAVY CHAPLAIN

Next to Roosevelt my closest Dutch tie was with Dr. Henry Van Dyke, a relationship that brought a cherished friendship embracing my wife. One of Wilson's first diplomatic appointments was that of his former colleague in the Princeton faculty as Minister to The Hague. Dr. Van Dyke resigned before we entered the war. During the neutrality period he was a zealous advocate of our entrance; he urged Wilson in 1916 to take the plunge and lectured me because I was in accord with Wilson. A few days after war was declared, Dr. Van Dyke went to Washington to congratulate Wilson on belatedly following his advice, and called at the Navy Department. . .

"I am the most miserable man in America," he said. "For months I have been prodding Wilson and you to take the step, and now that war is on and my heart and soul are enlisted, I seem doomed to sit on the sidelines when I wish to have an active part. Isn't there some place you can give me where I will be enlisted?"

I replied that I could give him a commission as Chaplain in the Navy if he had not passed the age limit. "What is the age," he asked, "for a reserve chaplain?" I told him forty, whereupon he said, "I was forty once and my heart and pulsation are as young as ever." He said nothing would make him quite as happy as to wear the Navy uniform. I therefore sent for Chief Chaplain Frazier (he had been chaplain on Dewey's ship at Manila Bay), and introduced him to Dr. Van Dyke as an applicant for a commission as chaplain. The Chief Chaplain replied that he feared the doctor was beyond the age limit; otherwise the Navy would be proud to enroll him. Dr. Van Dyke was seventy.

I said, "Bishop (I called him that because he exercised functions like those of the episcopacy and was a brother Methodist), I will certify that Dr. Van Dyke is of the proper age. Please see that he is enrolled."

"The papers are under preparation," I said to Dr. Van Dyke, and added, "There is one more preliminary before you can be inducted." Asked, "What?" I replied, "You must stand an examination in theology."

"Who conducts it?" he asked, and was surprised when I said, "I do!" Beckoning to Bishop Frazier to stand beside me, I turned to the doctor and said as solemnly as if the procedure was not a farce, "The candidate will stand up."

The doctor stood as straight as a Marine on inspection. Addressing the candidate, I said, "The first question is: 'Do you believe in Calvinism?'" Without hesitation the Presbyterian divine answered: "I do not and never did."

That ended the examination of a Presbyterian applicant for chaplain conducted by two Methodists. I said to the doctor, "The examination is ended. You pass. But you ought to thank your stars that the examination was not conducted by Presbyterian elder Woodrow Wilson, or my Presbyterian wife. They would have flunked you."

CHAPLAINS OUT OF MOURNING

The new young-old chaplain was as pleased at his Navy uniform as a boy with his red-top boots, but soon registered a vigorous request that "Chaplains be taken out of mourning." At that time the uniform of a chaplain and other staff officers had a binding of black, was very sombre, and lacked the gold braid of sea-going officers. He told my wife—they had become good friends—that he had entered the Navy in the spirit of John Paul Jones, and had "just begun to fight," and it tended to dampen his ardor to be wearing black. His protest, backed by the advice of my Navy wife and afterward by "Bishop" Frazier, resulted, not only in changing the style of the uniform of the chaplains but also of all staff officers.

When I took chaplains out of mourning I issued orders that all staff officers in the Navy should have like rank and title as they enjoyed in our Army and in most navies. This is how Paymaster, Surgeon, Constructor, Chaplain in the Navy came to hold the title as high as Admiral. This recognition of their equal right to rank with all other officers was approved by the older and wiser officers who had Annapolis education, but some of the officers disapproved. To illustrate the almost fanatical zeal with which some of the line opposed the granting of rank to the staff corps, is the following remark, attributed to a respectable young line officer:

"I hold my rank dearer than life itself, and were any purser of the Navy to sign an official report above me, I would cleave him to the chin with my cutlass. I could never suffer my rank to be outraged in this way; I would rather die."

A SEA DOG ON LAND

"What assignment shall I give Dr. Van Dyke—he is too old to go to sea?" Bishop Frazier asked me after the doctor had taken the oath and been inducted into the service, and looked fit in his uniform. I asked the new chaplain. He wanted to be a "regular" and wished sea duty, preferably on the *New Jersey,* named for his State. Frazier did not approve, and so Dr. Van Dyke was given a roving assignment to visit and speak to midshipmen at Annapolis and the hundreds of thousands of young volunteers at all the Training Stations.

He entered into this service—he had been accustomed to association with youths at Princeton—and became the toast of the youth who flocked to hear his brilliant addresses and profound sermons. He was on fire to defeat "the Huns," as he always called them, and stirred to the heights of enthusiasm all of the youngsters eager to get to France before the fighting was over. His patriotic addresses and stimulating companionship with the young sailors more than justified the departure from a fixed age for chaplains in wartime. They loved his humor, his eloquence, his classical and otherwise denunciation of the Huns. He was pretty sure in his talks to the youths to ring the changes on the words, Rotterdam, Amsterdam, and all other places with the ending that had the sound of "damn." He said he was against all the "dams" that had German leanings. He possessed in large measure "righteous indignation," which is a Christian virtue, at times not far removed from the passion of hate for Huns and Nazis. There was only one apparent criticism, the publication by the Annapolis midshipmen had this paragraph: "No person in the Naval service is permitted to use the word, 'damn,' in public addresses, except chaplains and Y. M. C. A. secretaries."

On his first visit to Washington, proudly wearing his new gold-braid uniform, he paid a visit to his old Princeton colleague, President Wilson, who was intrigued by the commissioning of Dr. Van Dyke as a Naval officer. "I wanted the Prexy to see how handsome I looked," he said with a smile, "and Woodrow said he thought the Navy uniform became me more than the dress of a college professor."

VAN DYKE AND LA FAYETTE

One night at dinner at our home—(he had told my wife that his daughter was the inspiration of the word-picture of his Natalie in *The Master Passion,* saying, "Your playing the fife as you do war-work made me think you are another Natalie)—he spilled his soup on the table cloth. He was profuse in his apologies for what he called his "stupidity." However my wife soon put him at ease by saying, "When LaFayette visited my home city—Raleigh—he spilled the rich red wine on the table cloth. Did it trouble his hostess? Instead, she preserved the table cloth and handed it down to her daughters, telling them: "This red spot is where the great LaFayette spilled wine when he dined with me." And so my wife said, "I will have a like honor, in that I will hand this table cloth down to my descendants and say, 'This red spot is where the great Dr. Van Dyke spilled tomato soup.' "

A few days later she received autographed copies of all Dr. Van Dyke's writings, accompanied by a note saying: "I wish to be remembered by you by my writings rather than by my stupidity." He had marked the pen-picture of Natalie, and written that he had known three Natalies—the one he had created in his story, his daughter and my wife. Is it any wonder she cherished the books and kept the table cloth with the colored stains?

WENT BACK TO HIS BOOKS

The war ended, Dr. Van Dyke laid down his commission in the Navy in the same spirit in which he had donned the uniform, and in all America there was no man happier that autocracy had been defeated and that two Princetonians had had a hand in the victory—Woodrow Wilson guiding the war effort and Van Dyke praying and cheering the fighting sailors.

The pay which Dr. Van Dyke was required to draw was turned over by him to the Naval Academy as a trust fund, the income of which provides annually a gold watch for the member of the graduating class who submits the best original article on any Naval or equally patriotic subject.

After the war in a private letter from Dr. Tertius Van Dyke, who has written a worthy life of his scholarly father, he wrote:

"May I add that I always cherish the memory of the many kindnesses of yourself and Mrs. Daniels. In particular I recall the day during the war when my father was too sick to address the Poli Theatre meeting and you insisted upon doing it yourself— just as if you were looking for something to do! I remember your address with its interpretation of the 'Keeper of the Light'. Indeed, the whole incident is unforgettable."

PRIZED LETTER FROM VAN DYKE

My delightful personal association with Dr. Van Dyke ended when he ceased to be a chaplain, but not long after he wrote me a letter which made me happy that I had certified that he was young enough to be enrolled as chaplain in war days. He wrote:

"*Avalon, Princeton, N. J.*
"December 26, 1919.

"MY DEAR BAAS, (That's Dutch for Boss.)

"What Christmas gifts you have sent me! First, your heart-warming letter,—then your inspiring book! Two "thank-yous" are not enough. I send a bushel.

"These addresses of yours breathe through the printed page your fine, high, strong spirit which has been worth many a battleship to our Navy in the World War. In the delivery, (as I learned at Portsmouth and Boston as your comrade in service), they had the advantage of your ringing voice, your direct speech, your sympathetic presence. But even in this cold black and white they carry the weight of your thought, the warmth of your patriotism, the power of your faith. It is good to hear a man in high station bear testimony to religion, as you did to those boys at Portsmouth.

"You have done a fine work, my dear Secretary, and the country thanks you. I count myself lucky to have had active service under you. Yes, for your Dutch blood, I'll even forgive you for not sending me to sea to earn a cross or a ribbon.

"With affectionate greetings to you and yours,

"Your faithful chaplain and friend,

"/s/Henry Van Dyke
"U.S.N.R.F.

"To the
"Hon. Josephus Daniels
"Sec'y of the Navy."

Part Eight

POLITICS

XXVIII

COALITION CABINET AND T. R.

Not LONG AFTER the declaration of war, a Republican Senator demanded a coalition War Cabinet. Inspired articles appeared in the papers, calling it a "Super Cabinet," and saying that both the Secretary of War and the Secretary of the Navy were pacifists and that experienced Republicans—Root for War and Teddy Roosevelt for the Navy—ought to replace them. The propaganda, advocated by certain big newspapers, for what was called a "Super Cabinet" was partisan and was backed by some steel, oil, and shipbuilding companies. Wilson saw through the attack upon his leadership and declared:

"This is nothing more nor less than a renewal of the perpetual effort of the Republicans to force representation in the Administration on all hands. Republicans of the finest sort and of the finest capacity are working for and with the Administration on all hands and there is no need whatever for a change at the head of the administering departments. I am utterly opposed to anything of this sort and will never consent to it."

On February 17, Wilson wrote House:

"You notice the suggestion is being actively renewed that I call their crowd into consultation and have a coalition cabinet at my elbow. It is the *Junkerthum* trying to creep in under cover of the patriotic feeling of the moment. They will not get in. They have now no examples of happy or successful coalition to point to. The nominal coalition in England is a Tory Cabinet such as they are eager to get a foothold for here. I know them too well, and will hit them straight between the eyes, if necessary, with plain words."

Though he had none but Democrats in his original Cabinet and would not stand for a Coalition Cabinet, Wilson called many patriotic Republicans to high station such as ex-President Taft, Herbert Hoover, Harry Garfield, Julius Rosenwald, Charles M. Schwab,

Daniel Willard, Benedict Crowell, to mention only a few of the many. In what was called the Supreme War Council, as well as in the Council of National Defense, both parties were represented and worked for their country with no thought of party advantage. He believed in team work; he trusted the peace Cabinet to carry on war efforts without losing sight of upholding the New Freedom which was the heart of his Administration. In this he followed the wisdom of Jefferson, who relied on his Cabinet and found them a team with like principles and united for the policies the party incarnated.

T.R. URGED AS GENERAL

About the same time Wilson had to meet a demand from many quarters to grant the request of Theodore Roosevelt to recruit and lead a division of volunteers to the front in France. There was no lack of courtesy to the Rough Rider when he went in person to the White House to proffer his request. Before seeing the President (April 10), Colonel Roosevelt slapped Secretary Tumulty on the back and said, "You get me across and I will put you on my staff. Tell Mrs. Tumulty I will not allow them to place you at any point of danger." The interview was reported "very pleasant," by both Wilson and Roosevelt. Wilson, after Roosevelt left the White House, said to Tumulty: "Roosevelt is a big boy. There is a sweetness about him that is very compelling. I can easily understand why his followers are so fond of him." But the President at that time made no intimation to the ex-President what he would do. As Roosevelt left the White House he was surrounded by an army of correspondents, many of whom liked the idea of his raising a volunteer regiment as he organized the Rough Riders in the Spanish-American War.

Wilson reported the interview to the Cabinet. Lane, who had come to Washington as a member of the Interstate Commerce Commission appointed by Roosevelt and who greatly admired him, was enthusiastic for the idea. Before the meeting of the Cabinet, Senator Swanson, Chairman of the Naval Affairs Committee, called to see me and urged me to advise Baker and Wilson to accede to Roosevelt's request. I had a feeling that before seeing me he had discussed the matter with Assistant Secretary Roosevelt, who probably wished his fifth cousin's ambition gratified. But he never spoke to me about it.

WILSON DID NOT PLAY POLITICS

Great pressure was brought to bear to let Roosevelt raise a division with Leonard Wood as Commanding General. A New York banker (John H. Parker, a native of North Carolina) went to Washington as an enthusiastic friend of Roosevelt and bluntly pressed his point. When Wilson did not respond to his liking, Parker said: "I beg you, as head of the Democratic Party, at this crisis not to play politics." Wilson resented the suggestion and replied:

"Sir, I am not playing politics. Nothing could be more advantageous to me than to follow the course you suggest. I have made up my mind in regard to these matters very thoroughly. General Wood is needed here. Colonel Roosevelt is an admirable man and a patriotic citizen, but he is not a military leader.... As for politics, it is not I but the Republicans who have been playing politics and consciously embarrassing the Administration. I do not propose to have politics in any manner, shape, or form influence me in my judgment."

General March, Chief of Staff, in his book, *A Nation at War,* says that General Pershing explicitly, specifically, and insistently asked that General Wood be not sent overseas. In my Diary, reporting a Cabinet meeting, I wrote:

"Burleson said it made him hot to read Gen. Wood's fulmination. The President spoke strongly of the lack of loyalty by some Army and Navy officers. Said he came here without any prejudice against Wood, but his conduct had been most reprehensible."

WILSON AVOIDED CONTROVERSY

Wilson's action declining to grant the request of Colonel Roosevelt and General Wood brought a deluge of criticism. Every attempt was made to draw the President into public statements, which he avoided because he knew they might lead to acrimony. He made known his attitude in a letter to Tumulty in response to a suggestion by Arthur Brisbane that he make a statement which could go to the British press. Wilson wrote:

"I really think the best way to treat Mr. Roosevelt is to take no notice of him. That breaks his heart and is the best punishment that can be administered. After all, while what he says is outrageous in every particular, it does, I am afraid, keep within the limits of the law, for he is as careful as he is unscrupulous."

The proof that politics did not influence the selection of the Commander-in-Chief by Mr. Wilson and Mr. Baker was that they selected General John J. Pershing because they had tested his wisdom in the difficult situation in Mexico. The fact that he had married the daughter of Senator Warren, of Wyoming, a powerful Republican leader, in no way affected the situation though there were not wanting critics who incorrectly said the Administration acted to please the Wyoming Senator.

Before I knew that General Pershing, charged with the great task, had expressed his opposition to ordering Roosevelt and Wood to Europe in the way they wanted to go, I agreed with Baker and Wilson that no political generals should be commissioned. History proved Pershing's wisdom. It also proves the wisdom of the selection of Pershing, who was outranked by four generals.

Roosevelt felt very bitter at the refusal of his request to raise and command troops. He was quoted as saying that as he had been Commander-in-Chief of the Army and Navy while President— that was proof that he was well fitted. When one of his friends used that argument as a reason for letting him go to Europe, I replied that, by the same reasoning, as I was directing the operation of the Navy, I should take command in the case of a great Naval engagement. Speaking at Carnegie Hall in the campaign of 1918, Roosevelt thus ended his speech:

"When this war broke out, I, and all those who believed as I did, cast all thought of politics aside and put ourselves unreservedly at the service of the President. Of course if Mr. Wilson had really meant to discard politics, he would have constructed a coalition, non-partisan Cabinet, calling the best men of the nation to the highest and most important offices under him, without regard to politics. He did nothing of the kind. In the positions most vital to the conduct of the war, and in the positions now most important in connection with negotiating peace, he retained or appointed men without the slightest fitness for the performance of their tasks, whose sole recommendation was a supple eagerness to serve Mr. Wilson personally and to serve Mr. Wilson's party in so far as such serving benefited Mr. Wilson."

WILSON PROVED RIGHT

Time proved Wilson was right though I do not think T. R. ever forgave him. Later I learned that T. R. himself had admitted that he was not physically fit for high command, for in a letter he wrote to Pershing on May 20, 1917, he said, "If I were physically fit, instead of old and heavy and stiff, I should myself ask to go under you in any capacity down to and including sergeant."

SHOWED TEDDY EVERY COURTESY

Wilson did not hesitate to uphold Baker and Pershing in recommending disapproval of Theodore Roosevelt's request to go to France in command of a division which he would raise somewhat like the Rough Riders in the Spanish-American War. This showed Wilson's wisdom as well as his support of those entrusted with the direction of the Army.

Personally, I would have liked to see Roosevelt's desire gratified because of my admiration for his courage. Roosevelt had been a dynamic and able Assistant Secretary of the Navy and had done much to strengthen it, and every year I paid tribute to him on Navy Day celebrated on his birthday. Also, I appreciated that as we entered the World War he had said, "The Navy is the one Department of the Government that is ready for war." However, I felt that no man, however patriotic, ought to be called from private life to command the fleet or be Commander-in-Chief of the Army in the greatest war in history, and so stated to Senator Swanson, who requested me to urge Wilson to grant Teddy's request.

GENERAL SCOTT'S WARNING

I knew that General Scott had told Baker that to name T. R. would be to commit the same mistake Lincoln made in the early days of the War of the Sixties, of having political generals. Scott had said that T. R. "proposes to milk the regular Army of all its best officers for his one division, to form of this preferred stock the Rough Riders of this war, leaving the great Army of millions to be less well-instructed and on an inferior status." He added, "Our Army must be commanded by a trained soldier." He stated further in his note to Baker, "Consider what a ridiculous figure you would cut, attempting to punish Mr. Roosevelt by court-martial! No, it would never do. France and England would feel that you were not serious in this war and your promise to help would be disbelieved."

BAKER CALLS ON ROOSEVELT

Secretary Baker did Roosevelt the honor of calling on him at his daughter's home. Roosevelt presented his view and application. Baker listened, but made no commitment. In his refusal to name any except the regular officers of the Army for high command, Baker closed a long correspondence with:

> "It is, of course, unpleasant, to find myself at variance with you in a matter of opinion of this sort, but the earnestness with which you have pressed your views is a comforting assurance of the zeal with which you will coöperate in carrying forward unitedly, whole-heartedly, and effectively the operation determined upon."

WOOD TOO OLD AND INDISCREET

When urged to send General Wood abroad (he had been jumped over 596 officers for promotion by Theodore Roosevelt), President Wilson did not hesitate to express a "lack of confidence in Wood's loyalty and discretion." He had not forgotten how he tried to force the President's hand in 1913 and get us into war with Japan. Secretary Baker, in answer to a protest for keeping Wood in the United States when he wanted to go to Europe, wrote that he regarded Wood as one of the most gifted men in the Army and added: "I think General Wood has been indiscreet and I think the appearance of political activity which he has allowed to grow up about many of his actions has been unfortunate for his splendid reputation as a soldier."

CAMPAIGN AGAINST PERSHING

This is from my Diary of the Cabinet meeting (February 7, 1918):

> "Leonard Wood had sought to supplant Pershing by telling the French and English that if he were in command he would divide American troops in companies and have them united with English and French divisions. Reading (British Ambassador) expected to request Wood to go to Europe. 'If he does,' said W.W., 'I will not reply in diplomatic language.'"

WHY WOOD WAS NOT SENT TO EUROPE

Of the meeting of the Cabinet, May 28, my Diary records:

"W.W. began by quoting the prayer of the preacher beginning with 'O Lord, you have doubtless seen from the morning papers...' etc. He told members of the Cabinet that they had 'doubtless seen that Leonard Wood is here and I am to see him tonight. The papers will want to know why he is not sent to Europe.' W.W. then read a paper he had prepared setting forth that Wood was an agitator and it was better to let him agitate here than abroad—he could do less harm here for his agitation could be corrected in America. Most members of the Cabinet opposed W.W.'s saying anything. Baker said Pershing had not desired Wood and he had, therefore, told Wood so and would not send him."

DEMOCRATS AND DAMN FOOLS

In the early days of the war when millions of youths were to be trained in camps at home before being sent overseas, every city wished to be chosen as one of these locations. The plan was to locate camps in all sections so that the enlisted men could be trained in a climate to which they were accustomed. Southern boys in Northern Illinois and Massachusetts suffered and Northern recruits suffered in the Deep South. Up to June no training camp had been located in North Carolina, which had enrolled 106 men out of an expected 100. On June 30, Carey Dowd, editor of the *Charlotte News,* and Cameron Morrison, later to become Governor of North Carolina and United States Senator, went to Washington to press the claim of Charlotte for an army camp. They had made application to General Wood and had been turned down. That was bad enough, but they said he 'insulted us.' How? When a delegation from Charlotte presented the claims of Charlotte, General Wood had said: "There are two kinds of fools who never learn anything—Democrats and Damn Fools." The Charlotte people had told him he had promised to come to Charlotte to look over the situation and had broken his word. They said to him, "You have broken your word. An Army officer should keep his promises." It was only then that Wood had agreed to come to Charlotte. I, of course, was sympathetic with their plea for a camp in North Carolina and saw Baker. Later a camp was established near Charlotte—Camp Greene. It is doubtful if Wood would have recommended it, but for losing his temper. He got as good as he gave. Thousands of troops were trained there, and in the first few months the red clay was so deep and sticky that the troops carried off acres of soil on their boots.

When I informed Baker of the treatment General Wood had given the Charlotte Committee, and Senators Simmons and Overman had thrown themselves actively into the fight for a camp at Charlotte, Baker did not seem very much surprised. "You know, Joe," he said, "that Wood is another Fiske." That was enough. Wood was a pain in Baker's neck as Fiske had been in mine. Fortunately, I had gotten rid of Fiske, but Baker still had Wood to give him trouble.

On August 17 I saw General March and urged the location of a tank camp in Raleigh. I also talked to Baker and pointed out Raleigh's fitness for the camp. Later it was established and did good work.

FORT BRAGG A CENTER

Early in 1917, when the Army wished a training center in the East which was in near reach of Washington, an ideal site of 125,000 acres was selected near Fayetteville, North Carolina, which became one of the largest training camps in the country. Before World War II the wooden buildings were replaced with fine brick structures. Over a million men, trained at Fort Bragg, went overseas between 1941 and 1946. At one time 100,000 were at the Fort undergoing training.

XXIX

FORD DRAFTED TO RUN FOR THE SENATE

I S THERE A chance to elect a Democrat to the Senate from Michigan this year?" I asked the Democratic National Committeeman when I was in Detroit early in 1918 on a speaking tour in behalf of Liberty Bonds.

"As much chance as there would be to elect Henry Cabot Lodge from South Carolina or John Sharp Williams from Vermont," said the Detroit Democrat.

Destiny had clothed Michigan with unwonted dignity and power in 1918. On the vote of the Senator chosen to represent that State hung the destiny of the President's dream of world peace, and none realized it so keenly as did Wilson.

By that one vote would be determined the organization of the Senate, and also whether the Foreign Relations Committee would be packed with men hostile to the Wilsonian peace.

Democratic control of the Senate was shaky. Six seats in the Senate were in serious doubt. Five were conceded to the Republicans, but beyond that, control of the organization was hopeless. The loss of six meant disaster. In Michigan the President saw a glimmer of hope in the possibility of one man who was neither Republican nor Democrat, but who would stand by the League of Nations.

"Ford and Wilson are agreed in their desire for world peace," my Democratic friend said. "The automobile manufacturer supported Wilson two years ago and spent $200,000 printing advertisements saying why Wilson should be reëlected. Now, if Ford could be induced to run for the Senate—"

"But could Ford be elected?" I asked.

"It's a cinch," said the Detroit Democrat. "He would get the nomination of both Republicans and Democrats in the primary. He could be elected, and his desire for peace and his admiration of Wilson would give the President a Senator who would stand by the League of Nations and his other policies."

"But do you know whether he is a Democrat?" I questioned.

Ford was drafted to run for the Senate, but Republican money punctured his tires.

"He doesn't care a thing about politics, and it is doubtful whether he ever voted in his life before he voted for Wilson in 1916," was the answer. "Nothing interests him but making flivvers and making peace. He would give half his plant if he could stop the fighting in Europe."

PLOTTING TO MAKE FORD SENATOR

"Well, could you persuade him to run?" I inquired. "Can anybody persuade him to run?"

"Nobody in Michigan can do it. Nobody about here in politics has any influence with him. He thinks a lot of Edison—you remember they both supported Wilson in 1916—but no personal influence could make him run or even say he is a Republican or a Democrat."

"If you want a Wilsonian Senator from Michigan," my friend remarked, "you go back to Washington and tell Wilson he is the only man who can get Ford into politics. We will elect him, if Wilson can induce him to run."

Ford was oblivious to this plotting to make a Senator of him. Though I spent the whole day with him, I gave no hint of the thought. But he was our only hope of preserving the balance of power in the Senate. Upon my return to Washington I told the President that Ford was the only chance of gaining a vote from Michigan, and that he alone could induce Ford to make the race. I advised that he apply the Selective Draft to Henry Ford.

"We had better ask him to come to Washington, then," said the President. "You get him here and talk to him. You and he are friendly. If you fail, bring him over and I'll have a try at him."

WILSON ADMIRED FORD

The President had a real regard for Ford. He believed that his peace ship venture was chimerical, though born of fine impulses. His major impressions of Ford, however, were not based on the peace ship. On the night Bernstorff was dismissed, the President and Ford were guests at a dinner in Washington at my home. Turning to the President, Ford said, "I went to see the Secretary of the Navy today. I told him that if the Government needed it I would put the whole Ford plant at its disposal without profit." The Ford who had made that offer, and not the man who dreamed he could get the boys out of the trenches by Christmas, was the Ford the President wanted to run for the United States Senate to insure peace.

Setting the stage was vastly easier than inducing the leading man to mount the boards. Ford never liked the political atmosphere of Washington, and it was only in the most urgent situations that he could be induced to visit the capital. Several days later, in response to my urgent telegram, he came, entirely innocent of the causes that were behind his coming. He came direct to the Navy Department.

"What's up. What do you want with me?" he demanded.

"The President wants you to perform one of the greatest services that has ever been rendered this country," he was told.

"I'll do anything he wants me to do—what is it?"

WANTED NO SENATORIAL TOGA

"The President wants you to run for the United States Senate," I said.

Ford turned white, and the lines about his mouth tightened. "I can't do it. Not in my line. I thought he wanted my factory. I'll give him that. No, I can't come to the Senate. It's not in my line. I can't do that."

"The President has his heart set on your running to insure peace after the fighting," I said.

"What does a Senator have to do?" he went on. The argument that the President desired him to run I saw was having some effect. "Would I have to stay in Washington all the time?"

"Not at all; you can leave and go home every week-end," I said. "You will have to be here only when questions of major importance are under consideration."

Ford looked out the window that faced the White House for a few minutes. Then, "No, I can't do it. Not in my line. I can't stay here and listen to those fellows talk. I'll give you my factory. I'll do anything Wilson wants me to do but I cannot go into politics."

"This war is going to be over," I told him. "The President's plans for peace will be before the Senate that is to be elected this Fall. Whether he succeeds or fails will depend on the vote of the Senator from Michigan. With you we would have a majority of one vote in the Senate." He listened but was not influenced.

"No, I can't do it.—Hear all those fellows talk—no," he said with a note of finality.

"It will be the greatest opportunity of your lifetime to serve this world," I told him. "All sorts of problems of reconstruction and stabilization will need to be worked out. The President will need your tremendous experience. But most of all he will need your help in securing the ratification of the peace treaty and the League of Nations."

Ford seemed adamant. He would not agree but said he would hold absolute refusal in abeyance until after he had conferred with the President. It was apparent that only a personal appeal from the President would win him.

FORD CAPITULATES TO COMMANDER-IN-CHIEF

The following day we went together to the White House. I sensed that saying "No" to the President, for whom he had a profound admiration, for whose office he had a feeling akin to reverence and with whose peace and tariff policies he was in accord, would be infinitely harder than saying "No" to the Secretary of the Navy.

The President was straightforward. "Mr. Ford, I feel that it is your patriotic duty to come to the Senate from Michigan." Wilson understood. He had never been active in politics. He was drafted to run for Governor of New Jersey. He told Ford that the strain of war was so great that he would give anything to lay down his job, saying in substance:

"But the war is on and no man can quit. And then we must wage another war for peace—the goal that you and I wish above all things. I cannot follow my personal desire for the quiet of private life until both victories are won ... I would not stay here myself, and I would not ask you to make the sacrifice if Duty, with a big "D," did not compel the fullest consecration in this world emergency. We must carry on to both victories— an end of fighting to be followed by a war-less world."

That was not all. It was the most serious and eloquent appeal that could fall from the lips of a man ready to give his all. It transported me. It fell on receptive soil. Ford, a man not given to emotion, was stirred to the depths. I do not recall his words but they were those of simple dedication. He accepted the call to duty from the Commander-in-Chief as a good soldier.

FORD'S ANNOUNCEMENT

The automobile manufacturer left the White House enlisted for
the cause. The announcement of his candidacy was as unique and
different from the usual declarations as Ford was different from all
other candidates who had thrown their hats into the ring. He did not
say that he had responded to the call of the voters. He placed it
simply upon the feeling that duty compelled him to go with the
Commander-in-Chief. Here was his announcement:

> "The President has asked me to become a candidate for the
> United States Senate from Michigan. I know nothing about
> politics or party machinery, and I am not at all concerned about
> which ticket I am nominated on. They can use my name on all
> the tickets they want to; it is a matter for the people to decide.
>
> "I shall not spend a cent nor make a move to get into the
> United States Senate.... I would not walk across the street to
> be elected President of the United States. If I am elected, how-
> ever, I shall go to Washington and work with President Wilson
> with everything I possess, first to win the war, and then to help
> the Government develop ways of insuring against future wars.
>
> "A request from the President is to me a command. I believe
> that he was put into his present office to put an end to war. I
> hate war. I am a pacifist if it is to believe that war is the worst
> thing in the world."

HOW THE STRATEGY MISCARRIED

If the election had taken place the next week, Ford would have
been the unopposed candidate on both the Democratic and Republican tickets. The rank and file of both parties favored his election
and rejoiced in his announcement. If the stake in national politics
had not been so high—control of the Senate to give tariff bonuses to
campaign contributors and insure the defeat of Wilson's peace plans
—Ford would have been elected hands down. As soon as the Republican National Chairman saw that the vote of the Michigan Senator
would determine the control of the Senate, he hastened to New York
to plan the defeat of Ford.

A member of that political conference was Truman Newberry,
who held a commission in the Reserve as Commander in the Navy.
He coveted a toga. He had plenty of money. He wore the Navy
uniform in time of war. The Republican politicians backed his

candidacy and gave orders to Michigan Republicans to give him the nomination in the primary. That wasn't the only complication that upset our calculations. An old-time Democrat, who thought he saw a chance to win, came out as a candidate in the primary. The Democratic strategy was for all the Democrats except a handful to go into the Republican primary (the Michigan law permitted this). This would have insured Ford the Republican nomination. But when unexpectedly and foolishly this old Democrat became a candidate, it was necessary for enough Democrats to vote in their own primary to insure the nomination of Ford. This enabled Newberry by a narrow margin to obtain the Republican nomination and, because the Republicans poured out money so lavishly, it was estimated that for every vote cast for Newberry $1.00 was expended. In the general election Newberry won out by about 2,000 votes. It had cost $200,000 to nominate Newberry. It cost half a million to get him the paltry majority. Newberry was saved only by the Supreme Court's declaring the Federal Corrupt Practices Act unconstitutional.

FORD'S PATRIOTISM IMPUGNED

The senatorial toga was bought outright by the most corrupt use of money that had ever debauched American politics. Theodore Roosevelt, back in the Republican Party, entered the campaign in behalf of Newberry, his old Secretary of the Navy, and gave blistering denunciation of Ford who was, he said, making money out of the war; and his son, Edsel, of military age, was in a bomb-proof position having been exempted because the Ford works were making Eagle boats and munitions and material needed in war. Ford made no speech in the campaign and permitted no money to be spent to promote his election. In reply to Roosevelt he issued a statement in which he declared that if he had been a politician he would have put a uniform on his son, Edsel. Instead, Edsel was serving the country, by order of the War Department, where he was most needed. He said he and his son were directing the Ford plant, which was employed exclusively in war work.

THE FAKE NAVAL PICTURE

Even such appeals and the lavish use of money could not have defeated Ford if, in the last days of the campaign, the Newberry management had not perpetrated the cheapest fake and fraud known in politics. Only a few days before the election—too late to be exposed—there appeared in many weekly papers in Michigan a picture showing Newberry in Naval uniform, standing on the bridge of a ship, giving orders to sailors ready for duty. The ship looked as if it was stripped for action with its guns "ready and grim." Below the picture was a shrewd appeal to all voters whose sons or relatives were on the fighting front. It was substantially like this:

TRUMAN NEWBERRY
COMMANDER OF THE U. S. NAVY
ON BOARD HIS SHIP IN WORLD WAR

"When his country was in peril Truman Newberry responded to the call to duty, joined the Navy, and commanded a ship of the Navy.

"In those days when all patriots were fighting for their country, where was Edsel Ford, of military age? He obtained exemption from military service, and he and his father, Henry Ford, made millions while Newberry was baring his breast to the foe in command of a ship of the Navy."

The appeal was that Newberry was fighting on a ship in the war zone while the Fords were slackers. That canard, printed too late for the fake to be exposed before the election, "did the trick" and insured the certificate of election to Newberry.

THE HOAX EXPOSED

After the election the fraud was exposed. Newberry was never at sea. Here is the history of his Naval service:

Early in the war Newberry, who had been Secretary of the Navy under Theodore Roosevelt, went to Washington and told me he wished to serve in the war. As he was a licensed navigator and owned his yacht, which he could sail, I gave him the highest rank in the Naval Reserve. I felt that his experience qualified him to command a recruiting base and ordered him on duty at Boston. He asked a change because when he was Secretary he had reprimanded the commandant on duty at Boston. That was a reasonable request and was granted. I put him in charge of the Recruiting Base in New York City. He was zealous and efficient. In order to simulate life afloat and thus attract recruits, we built in Central Park a replica of a Naval ship—so to speak, "A painted ship upon a painted ocean"—

and it was operated exactly like a ship afloat, except that it was in the middle of Central Park and not on the ocean, and all Naval lingo and practices were insisted upon. When visitors or recruits came aboard they were received with all Naval ceremony by Newberry, the commanding officer. To make the similitude perfect, and attract youths, a Naval picture was made of Commander Newberry giving command to sailors as if the ship was going into action. It was the picture of that fake ship ashore which appeared in the Michigan papers. It proved you can fool many people.

At the time I gave Newberry the commission that made it possible for his campaign manager to perpetrate the campaign hoax, I never supposed I would be drawn into a senatorial campaign in Michigan. If I had not given Newberry the commission, he could not have run for the Senate wearing a Navy uniform and being paraded as the patriotic candidate fighting his country's battles. Again, if I had not induced Ford to convert his plant into a place to make Eagle boats and had not gone to Detroit, it is probable Ford would never have become a candidate for the Senate. A Navy friend, who knew all this history, said:

"You are in the hell of a fix. You got Ford to run and unintentionally you made it possible for Newberry to defeat him."

There was something in that.

FORD UNCOVERED THE FRAUD

Ford's defeat did not trouble him, but he was outraged at the corrupt use of money to control elections. After the Republican primary, the Grand Jury uncovered corrupt use of money, but as prosecution might look as if Ford was backing it to get a toga, he would have nothing to do with it. But when it was clear that the Newberry toga was tainted with rottenness, Ford was outraged. His indignation was heightened when Newberry's vote (while his seat was being contested) enabled Lodge to become Chairman of the Foreign Affairs Committee and Ford saw the danger to peace.

The *New York World* (January 14) said:

"The Republican Senators, who voted to sustain Newberry, voted to sustain political corruption in order to sustain the party record on the League of Nations."

His friend and attorney, Alfred Lucking, advised Ford to finance an investigation so that if it could be proved Newberry's seat was tainted, he could be deprived of it. Mr. Lucking told me that when he gave that advice, Ford asked:

"Will I be seated in the Senate if Newberry is kicked out?"

"No," Mr. Lucking replied.

"Then I am going to fight him. I don't want anybody to think that I am fighting for a seat in the Senate, but I am going to fight politics of the sort that seeks victory by the use of money. I authorize you to spend what money may be necessary to uncover the corruption you say debauched the election."

There was no bitterness in Mr. Ford's heart over defeat.

A few days after Ford had authorized Lucking to use all diligence to uncover the election wrongs that gave Newberry the soiled toga, Judge Lucking came to Washington. I had known him well through his connection with Henry Ford and his leadership in the Democratic Party in Michigan. He came to see me and acquainted me with the overwhelming evidence that had been secured—far more than sufficient to unseat Newberry.

Judge Lucking told me that not only would Ford not spend a cent on his campaign but he called together all in his organization and told them of his decision and demanded that none of them should spend any money to promote his candidacy. He added that if they did so it would be against his orders and he would not reimburse them. I gathered from what Lucking told me that some of Ford's closest friends did not wish to see him defeated and planned to finance the campaign supposing that after he was elected Mr. Ford would reimburse them. Lucking also said, "When a rich man runs for office he is expected to finance the campaign. When Ford refused, those politicians who always work for money grew lukewarm."

Judge Lucking asked my advice and coöperation as to how to proceed to have Newberry unseated in the Senate. I told him there were two men essential in the Senate. The first was Senator Pomerene, of Ohio, Chairman of the Committee on Privileges and Elections, and the other was Senator Reed, of Missouri, the most dynamic prosecutor in the Senate, who was also a member of that committee. He went to see Pomerene and presented the evidence he had. Pomerene was convinced that Newberry held a fraudulent certificate and ought to be expelled from the Senate. Then he went to see Reed, as he told me later. Reed was a strange man. You never could count on what course he would take, but you could always know that whether he was prosecuting a good man or a bad man, he regarded him as a heavy villain and prosecuted him in the Senate as if he were in a criminal court. Lucking saw Reed, and the next day came back to me much troubled.

"I saw Reed," he said, "and he gave me no encouragement. On the contrary, he said, 'Henry Ford made his fight and lost, and it is no use to bring it up in the Senate.'" Judge Lucking asked me what I would advise.

I said, "The Hearst papers have been making an issue of the Newberry election and they have printed vigorous articles exposing the frauds and lavish use of money. When they start a fight, they usually go all in for it. If you can get the head men of the Hearst papers to see Reed and assure him that they are going through with this fight, ask him to lead it, and say that the papers will back everything he does in fighting Newberry, I am sure Reed will come across."

Lucking went to New York, saw the Hearst manager, and in a day or two came in smiling broadly and said that Reed had sent for him saying that he "had his gloves off, Newberry was a grand rascal, and he [Reed] was going to drive him out of the Senate." And that is what he and Pomerene did. But the greatest damage had already been done. The Senate had been organized to sabotage the League, which it did later.

THROWN OUT ON THE PAVEMENT

The Republican Senators knew that $150,000 had been spent to get a senatorial toga, they knew the courts of Michigan would issue indictments to punish those guilty of corrupting the ballot box, and that Newberry might have to go to jail instead of occupy the senatorial seat. But they needed his vote to pack the Committee on Foreign Affairs to elect Lodge Chairman and sabotage the League of Nations. After that crime had been consummated, the Michigan Senator was forced to resign. But the investment of $150,000 to get the needed vote paid dividends to the isolationists, protectionists and hyphenates. After Newberry had done the deed for which a toga was bought for him, he was thrown out on the pavement.

AN INSIDE STORY OF FORD'S EARLY SUCCESS

At the time I went to Detroit to speak at a Liberty Bond campaign, I spent almost the entire day with Mr. Ford and Colonel Livingston, a prosperous banker. Both went with me to every place where I spoke and were deeply interested that Detroit should go over the top in its quota of bonds. Colonel Livingston was head of the largest savings bank in Detroit and head of the Lake Shipping Association. He regaled me as we went from place to place with many interesting stories.

During our travel over the city Ford rallied Livingston about his stinginess. A good story by Ford which I recall was that a man was driving a big car in the mountains of New Hampshire and ran out of oil. He could get none at the country stores until he found one proprietor who said he could sell him some castor oil and that would do the trick. He bought all the castor oil the man had and his car moved forward, and in a few minutes the big car passed a Ford.

One story that I told in all my speeches struck the funny bone of both Ford and Livingston. It was a quotation from a sermon on bonds by a Negro parson, who said:

"My brethren: There are four kinds of bonds. The bonds of sin from which you must get release by repentance; the bonds of slavery which have been broken; the bonds of matrimony which you must endure; and Liberty Bonds which you must buy."

But the thing that interested me most was the story that Colonel Livingston told of how Ford got financial aid when he was in a tight place. Livingston said:

"While Ford was trying to make his horseless carriage work he had a workshop in a small building which I passed every day. The thought of a buggy running without a horse was strange and as I saw Ford tinkering I became interested. Sometimes I stopped and talked with him. That's why he came to see me when in his perplexity he asked my advice. Ford's early partner had expected the car to be finished quickly and put on the market. He complained at Ford's long experiments and tinkerings and grew tired of putting up money with no results. His impatience at the delay in production grew to such an ex-

tent that it worried and troubled Ford. He could not go on without money and his partner had lost faith and threatened to
invest no more in a venture which did not look promising.
After hearing his story I advised Ford to make a proposition to
buy or sell. I said, 'Ask him to buy or sell and name his figure.'
Ford answered that the man might name a figure he would
take, but as he had no money he could not buy. The partner
might figure that as Ford had no money he would name a low
figure and get it cheap. Ford asked me, 'Suppose he offers to
sell? What can I do?' I said, 'Make an offer to buy or sell and
then come to see me.' Ford returned to the bank with the report
that the partner would sell for a given amount. It wasn't a very
large sum but Ford felt he couldn't raise it and suggested that
I buy and become his partner. I guess I ought to have done so.
If I had now I would be very rich. But I was a banker and interested in shipping on the lake and decided I'd better not go
into an experiment. I told Ford to close the trade and the bank
would lend him the money. I told him to have the papers drawn
up in legal fashion and he could then have the money. He
signed a note and then there arose a situation I had not foreseen.
The bank directors flatly refused to approve the loan, saying
Ford was a visionary tinkerer and it would hurt us if the de-
positors of our savings bank knew we were lending their money
to a crazy man who imagined he could perfect and sell a horseless carriage. I had faith in Ford and had gone too far with him
to draw back.

" 'Will you lend the money if I will put up my government
bonds as security for the loan?' I asked the directors.

" 'Certainly,' was the answer but they felt I was doing a foolish
thing.

"Ford got the money, bought out his partner, and it was not a
great while before he was the largest depositor in the bank. The
directors then thought better of my financial judgment."

PEOPLE LEAVING THE FARM

When I visited Henry Ford and Mrs. Ford in Detroit in November, 1919, I made this note in my Diary (November 22):

"Talked to Mr. and Mrs. Henry Ford. He says people are
leaving the farm—that with tractors and improved agricultural
machinery the day will come when farmers will work one-half
of the year on the farm and half the year in factories."

ELECTION OF 1918 FATAL TO WORLD PEACE

No off-year election has had worse consequences than that of 1918, when the Republicans elected a majority of the House and were enabled to organize the Senate by the purchase of a senatorial seat to which Henry Ford was honestly elected.

The Republicans claimed that Wilson's partisan appeal to voters, and not their lavish use of money was responsible for the Democratic defeat. Theodore Roosevelt wrote Lodge, "I am glad Wilson has come out in the open. I fear Judas most when he can cloak his activities behind a treacherous make-believe non-partisanship," and other Republicans spoke in like bitter vein. In many circles the Wilson letter of appeal to the voters was said to have been as fatal to its writer as was Henry Clay's letter written in Raleigh on the Mexican-Texas question. Wilson's letter breathed patriotism rather than partisanship, as these extracts show:

"If you have approved of my leadership and wish me to continue to be your unembarrassed spokesman in affairs at home and abroad, I earnestly beg that you will express yourself unmistakably to that effect by returning a Democratic majority to both the Senate and the House of Representatives.... I have no thought of suggesting that any political party is paramount in the matters of patriotism. The difficulties and delicacies of our present task are of a sort that the nation should give its undivided support to the Government under a unified leadership, and a Republican Congress would divide the leadership. The leaders of the minority in the present Congress have been unquestionably pro-war, but they have been anti-Administration....

"The return of a Republican majority to either House of Congress would, moreover, certainly be interpreted on the other side of the water as a repudiation of my leadership.... I am asking your support not for my own sake or the sake of a political party, but for the sake of the nation itself, in order that its inward unity of purpose may be evident to all the world."

While at the time there was a partisan and timid outcry against that greatest of patriotic appeals to voters, time has proved its wisdom. The Republican Congress elected effected a stalemate on domestic policies and enabled the Senate to sabotage the Covenant of peace. Wilson never admitted that the letter was other than a noble declaration (though his friend, Dr. Eliot, wrote him that he thought it was a mistake). The press began to ask, as is usual, "Who advised the President in his blunder?" Lane attributed it to Burleson, the leading politician of the Cabinet, but the Texan had an alibi. I was in New England campaigning. McAdoo was mad because he had not been consulted. Lansing said later it was "an injudicious and unwarranted attack upon the loyalty of his political opponents." Gregory said it had never been discussed in the Cabinet.

MC CORMICK GAVE THE HISTORY

Vance McCormick, Chairman of the National Democratic Committee, is the authority that Wilson himself was responsible for the appeal (1918) to the people to elect a Democratic Congress. The National Committee made a request that Wilson issue an appeal to voters to aid Democratic candidates. Mr. McCormick afterwards wrote:

"Tumulty and Bill Cochran brought me a letter which President Wilson had written, stating he wished my judgment. I felt very strongly that its publication in its present form would be misunderstood by the people and do great harm.... Tumulty thought the draft an excellent one.... Homer Cummings and myself proposed certain changes. Some were accepted but I was unable to bring about further modifications. I told the President if it went out as written, it would be misunderstood and react against him. I frankly told him my fears. He could not be made to see that it would be misconstrued....

"Subsequent events have proved that Wilson was right in his desire for a friendly Senate and House because the world has been thrown into chaos ever since the signing of the Versailles treaty, due to the action of an unsympathetic and bitterly partisan Senate."

There was much debate, some of it acrimonious, about this letter. William Kent said that Wilson, entering the Cabinet Room for the meeting following the election, looked at Burleson and said, "I have received the worst advice from one of the gentlemen present that any President ever got and I have acted on it." Burleson and Tumulty both denied this, and I am sure it was erroneous. In a note November 6, Lane called the election a "slap in the face for the President." Homer Cummings wrote Wilson after the election, "I am confident not only that the appeal was justified but that it had a very wholesome effect. It did not affect our vote adversely in any part of the country."

WILSON'S SUPPORT ELECTED WALSH

I was scheduled to speak in Hartford, Connecticut, the day that Wilson's appeal for a Democratic Congress appeared in all the papers. I had arrived late the night before from Massachusetts, where I had been campaigning for a Democratic Congress and in particular for David I. Walsh, who defeated Weeks for the Senate that year and has been continuously reëlected ever since. After the election, Mayor Peters telegraphed Wilson: "Your letter urging Walsh's election secured victory." One of the factors that made for Walsh's election was that many thousands were working for the Navy in Boston, at other places, and at Squantum, where the Navy had erected a plant which turned out scores of destroyers. The returns showed nearly all of the thousands so employed voted for Walsh. The Democratic Committee saw to it that I spoke in those districts, and always there were many Navy workers in my audience. I did not fail to stress the amount of money Uncle Sam was spending in the Bay State for war supplies and employment at high wages. Besides, the enlistments in the Navy for the war had been very large and the families of the enlisted sailors lent a willing ear to the appeals of the Secretary of the Navy. As I left the State I wrote the President that the voters would register a vote of confidence in the Administration and elect Walsh.

CONNECTICUT CHAIRMAN SAID IT SPELLED DEFEAT

I was roused from my bed early at Hartford (October 25) by the Chairman of the Democratic State Committee, who had a copy of Wilson's letter as he entered my room. I saw he was excited. He said: "If this letter had appeared a few days earlier, I would have called your meeting off. There is no use speaking now. Wilson's inept letter has insured a Republican victory." I asked him what he was talking about. He said, "Haven't you seen Wilson's letter, raising a party issue as we were winning in Connecticut by an appeal to let politics be adjourned until the war ends?" I had been away from Washington and had not known of anything except that Wilson had been requested to write a campaign letter. When I finished reading, the Chairman asked, "Don't you see that will defeat us everywhere except in the South?" I saw how it could be used—as it was—by Lodge, Theodore Roosevelt, and others to try to prove that Wilson thought "Republicans were only good enough to fight." But I did not admit that to the excited Chairman. I said to him, "Every statement in the letter is literally true and if the Republicans control Congress, they will stop all needed legislation and scrap the peace that lies nearest Wilson's heart. Don't you know that?"

"I only know," he said, "that we are defeated. We had the lines drawn and victory was certain in Connecticut. Now every independent Republican who was going to vote for our candidate on his war record will feel that his patriotism has been impugned and will vote for the Republican candidate." He added that there were some Democrats in Congress who had voted against the war and some whose support had been lukewarm. He said Wilson's letter would be construed as urging their reëlection and the defeat of Republicans whose war records were 100 per cent good. He sensed better than I did the effect of such a construction as that which flared in all the Republican papers and was stressed by the Republican speakers in the remaining days of the campaign. I spoke half a dozen times that day, mostly to factory war workers, and sensed no resentment among them to Wilson's letter. But when the Republicans carried the Congress, my Connecticut friend reminded me that he had correctly gauged public sentiment and held Wilson's letter as responsible for the defeat. In my speech that day and at other places in the campaign, I declared:

> "Every man who votes for a Republican for Congress votes for a debating society instead of a united, firm, and unmistakable pressing of America's fourteen demands plus freedom for the Czecho-Slovaks."

The only thing wrong about my statement was that what I called "a debating society" was a Congress that kept us out of the League and made possible World War II.

WILSON ANALYZED RESULT

Troubled that the Congress would be controlled by the opposition, Wilson took the result more philosophically than did his associates, though he said, "We are all sick at heart." He was grieved that the people had not responded to his appeal, mainly because it would make the attainment of peace more difficult. He said:

"Any party which carries out progressive and constructive policies is sure to bring about a reaction—there is apparently nothing in which the human mind is more inhospitable than to change and in the business world that is particularly true because if you get in the habit of doing business in a particular way and are compelled to do it in a different way, you think somebody in Washington doesn't understand business."

Replying to Dr. Eliot's statement that his appeal "was an un-necessary and inexpedient departure from the position you have previously held," Wilson said, "It distresses me that you thought I committed a mistake. If I erred, it was merely under the impulse to be frank with the people I am trying to serve."

When I visited the White House Sunday night to discuss some Navy plans I found that he was surprised at the criticisms of his appeal to the voters. He said, "I have no idea that the President is sacrosanct anyway. As the leader of his party he ought not to be dumb. He ought to appeal directly to the people." Wilson was in one of his moods of accepting the situation and said that under Providence it would work out better than it looked. I couldn't see it and said that I didn't believe Providence had anything to do with the Republican Party.

CRITICAL OF WILSON APPOINTEES

There had been considerable criticism of some of Wilson's appointments by old-time Democrats, and this cooled their ardor in the 1918 election. After the valued support Governor Glynn gave Wilson and his keynote speech at the 1916 Convention, which was a great vote-getter, I urged Wilson to call Glynn to an important post in the administration. He thought well of it, and when Red-field resigned I renewed the suggestion. But Wilson had already named J. W. Alexander, Chairman of the House Committee, whose leadership in creating a big merchant marine won him national gratitude. Glynn was greatly disappointed that no worthy recognition was given him, and one day, voicing his feeling, he said to me:

"Some of us [he meant Catholics] have about made up our minds never to favor the nomination of another Presbyterian for Chief Executive. We made possible the election of Cleveland, son of a Presbyterian preacher, and Wilson, whose father was a Presbyterian preacher, and neither of them has given us the positions to which we are entitled."

I reminded him that Wilson's closest associate was Joseph P. Tumulty, a Catholic. "Yes," he said, "but he is only a private secretary. He has named no Catholic in his Cabinet or as Ambassador, and there are among us men as able as he has appointed." He voiced this view, more because the recognition of Catholics would strengthen the party than from personal ambition, and went on to say that too many Republicans had been appointed, although he granted that most Republicans called to important posts during the war put country above party. While Glynn voiced the feeling of many Democrats, and with some cause, Republicans were critical because Wilson had not conducted the war by a Coalition Cabinet. Governor Glynn talked much about his *Life of Martin Van Buren,* for whom he was named, which he was then writing and which became one of the best biographies of the decade. He said he was glad I had spoken at the great Knights of Columbus meeting in New York on Sunday night.

Glynn was not the only Democrat who resented the appointment of Republicans. Mayor Spellacy, of Hartford, voiced a like feeling. He said that while Wilson had "adjourned politics" during the war, Republicans gave it first place. He added that the Republican Governor of Connecticut controlled all war work through Republican appointees and hardly one Democrat was on any war board.

GEOGRAPHY IN SELECTING CABINET

Before I made the recommendation of Governor Glynn for Cabinet membership, I had urged Wilson to name a New Englander to the Cabinet, seeing that his was probably the first Cabinet without a representative from that section. This was due to the fact that when Massachusetts politicians heard that Brandeis, a Boston lawyer, was scheduled to be Secretary of Commerce, they protested because he was not a registered Democrat. In effect Wilson said, "If you won't take Brandeis, I will look elsewhere." He named Redfield, of New York, who was born in Albany. Wilson highly esteemed Sherman Whipple and Homer Cummings, and I hoped that, as Cabinet changes occurred, I could welcome one of them as a colleague. But it was not to be.

One argument against long terms of office for a Chief Executive is that, though in his first term he gives consideration to geography, after some years the men near him get first consideration. It has been so with most presidents. Once when Wilson had no member of the Cabinet west of Iowa, I suggested he might name a Pacific Coast leader for the next vacancy, and intimated there was too much in-breeding. He asked me this strange question, "Do you suppose the people care about the geographical location of Cabinet members?" He added that they wanted the best man regardless of the section from which he hailed and they wouldn't care if they all came from one State provided they were the best qualified for the job. I told him that he could not convince States unrepresented that they had no men as able as those selected. I added, "In selecting your first Cabinet you gave consideration to every section except New England and it would be wise to stick to that policy and name a New Englander to the first vacancy."

But he did not take my advice and at one time had three from New York and two from Pennsylvania, half the Cabinet from one Eastern area. And toward the end of his term Franklin Roosevelt followed that and went further. He had in the last year five members from the State of New York and two from Pennsylvania, and not one west of Chicago!

XXXI

DID WILSON MAKE COOLIDGE AND HOOVER?

W ILSON'S APPOINTMENT OF Franklin Roosevelt gave the future President the chance to show the stuff of which he was made. That beginning as Assistant Secretary of the Navy was the first rung in the national ladder by which he ascended to the presidency and broke all precedents by being elected for a fourth term. Was Wilson not largely responsible for two other successors?

But for Woodrow Wilson's approval in the early days of their political life, neither Calvin Coolidge nor Herbert Hoover would have lived in the White House. But this was not premeditated on Wilson's part, and he did not vote for either. How, then, did they owe election to Wilson?

After Hoover had made a reputation in feeding the Belgians, as the representative of the Allies, on Wilson's recommendation the Council of National Defense elected him as Food Administrator. I voted for him. Previous to the meeting Secretary of Agriculture Houston said he thought all food matters should come under his department. That appointment opened the door through which Hoover entered the White House. Hoover went with Wilson to Paris to direct aid to starving Austrians and others. He early was an enthusiastic advocate of the League of Nations until it was clear the Republicans would win in 1920, when, stung by the presidential bee, Hoover joined Hughes and Root in telling the voters that the best way to secure entrance into the League of Nations was to vote for Harding. He went into Harding's Cabinet, and when later Coolidge said, "I do not choose to run" (Coolidge thought he would be drafted and was the most disappointed man in the world when the draft didn't come), Hoover became his successor, falling heir to the debacle begun in Coolidge's Frenzied Finance Jamboree.

It was in the gubernatorial election in Massachusetts in 1920 that Wilson's approval of Coolidge in the 1919 Boston police strike, reëlected Coolidge. The Democratic nominee was Richard H. Long, an excellent liberal, who deserved to win. I was interested in his campaign through my friendship with his upstanding brother, who was a General in the Marine Corps. The police strike in Boston in 1919 attracted the interest of the whole country. Coolidge was Governor and did nothing in every way in which, by doing nothing, he could fail as an executive in an emergency. Andrew Peters, Mayor of Boston, a Democrat, spoke out promptly. It was a hot potato and Governor Coolidge dodged responsibility, while people were calling on him to act. He did not intervene to prevent the strike, but on September 11, after rioting had ceased, he ordered out the entire State Militia to restore order and sent this telegram to Samuel Gompers:

"There is no right to strike against the public safety by anybody, anywhere, any time."

President Wilson was in Helena, Montana, when that message to Gompers appeared in the press and towards the close of his address on September 11 Wilson said:

"I want to say this, too, that a strike of the policemen of a great city, leaving that city at the mercy of an army of thugs, is a crime against civilization. In my judgment, the obligation of a policeman is as sacred and direct as the obligation of a soldier. He is a public servant, not a private employee, and the whole honor and safety of the community is in his hands. He has no right to prefer any private advantage to the public safety. I hope that that lesson will be burned in so that it will never again be forgotten, because the pride of America is that it can exercise self-control."

And that declaration from the White House insured Coolidge's election and the defeat of the Democrat who was the undeserved victim. Wilson acted impulsively. I expressed to him later that I regretted his statement. He did not know, what was afterwards proved by the findings of a commisison, that Coolidge did not deserve the commendation which was given because of his belated magnificent statement. Those praising him, including Wilson, knew nothing of the background before Coolidge was smoked out. All these facts were not known when the Republican National Convention, unable to induce Hiram Johnson to accept the vice-presidential nomination, nominated Coolidge on the slogan, "Law and Order."

When Coolidge was elected Wilson sent him this telegram (November 5).

"I congratulate you upon your election as a victory for law and order. When that is the issue all Americans stand together."

Did either Coolidge or Hoover acknowledge his debt to Wilson? I do not think so, and I do not think Wilson could take any satisfaction in their elevation or in his unintentional contribution to making both of them his successors.

COOLIDGE AND THE STRIKE

Coolidge did not claim he settled the strike, but he did not hesitate to accept the commendation of Wilson and others who placed the armor of a shining knight upon him. It was Mayor Peters who, while Coolidge pondered and quibbled, invoked an ancient law, called out the State Guard in Boston and put an end to the nightmare. In fact, when an early appeal was made to him, Coolidge said it was not his duty "to communicate with the commissioners on the subject." When the committee seeking a settlement next tried to see Coolidge, they were told he was "in the western part of the state." He was A.W.O.L. The honor of settling the strike was given to Mayor Peters in these big headlines in the Boston papers:

MAYOR ASSUMES COMMAND
CALLS OUT STATE GUARD
BRUSHES CURTIS ASIDE
ASSERTS AUTHORITY
CONFERRED ON HIM BY OLD STATUTE

The trouble began September 2. After all danger was passed the man of silence and procrastination spoke out on September 11. The committee of thirty-four citizens who investigated the matter, stated:

"On Thursday morning order had been generally restored in the city. On Thursday afternoon Sept. 11, the Governor assumed control of the situation."

HOOVER'S "FOOD WILL WIN THE WAR"

Hoover, crowned with national auras for feeding the Belgians, returned to the United States in the spring of 1917. I had followed as well as I could with a sentimental interest and admiration the reports of his humanitarian work as the Almoner for Woodrow Wilson and the Allied Nations in Belgium's distress. It was at first understood that Lane would draft him in the Interior Department. Both were Californians. At Brown University Commencement they both received the degree of LL.D., and they spoke the same language. Shortly after his arrival in Washington (May 8) Hoover called to see me at the Navy Department, and we talked briefly of the situation overseas and of how our country could help most in the war. I asked him to lunch with me the next day. He accepted. At first I thought of asking Franklin Roosevelt and Admiral Benson and others. Upon reflection I decided to invite nobody, wishing to learn at first hand the story of the holy work in beleaguered Belgium by the man who had been selected to represent the generosity of most of the world. I had learned that in getting at a man's heart "two is company, three's a crowd"—and I felt that Hoover would talk more freely in a quiet tête-à-tête than in a larger company. So we lunched alone and I looked forward to something of a thrill at the recital I expected to hear. I was never more disappointed. He told of the big work in Belgium as coldly as if he were giving statistics of production. From his words and his manner he seemed to regard human beings as so many numbers. Not once did he show the slightest feeling or convey to me a picture of the tragedies that went on while he was relieving the necessities. He related what had been done as coldly as if he had been measuring bushels of wheat. I take this from my Diary:

"May 8. Hoover said: 'No wheat or barley should go into intoxicants.' Ethically he believed in that course but advocated it also as part of the war plan. It was clear he wished to be Food Dictator but not under the Agriculture Department. He said, 'People fear bureaucracy and would wish dictatorship ended when the war closes.'"

I was disillusioned that the man who had been at the center of tragedy seemed not to have sensed the humanity of it nor had he been touched by the suffering he had officially relieved. He left me, with a cold shake of the hand, and I felt that I had been talking to a capable administrator who either had no heart, or whose heart had been atrophied by his experiences around so much suffering, or who deliberately concealed his deep feeling. I said nothing of my reaction, thinking he must be wearied after the big strain.

A little later when it became apparent that "food will win the war," and that America must increase its supply and conserve its food crops, Hoover was proposed as Food Administrator. The idea met a wave of approval all over the country. Though his reserve and cold manner had chilled my enthusiasm, I voted for him at the meeting of the Council of National Defense. Houston felt that everything that related to food was a function of the Agriculture Department and it would reflect upon its efficiency to establish an independent bureau to deal with food. Houston talked to me very strongly about his opposition to the plan. "How would you like it if the President were to put the destroyers in a separate bureau and deny you control of an important arm of the Navy?" he asked. I told him there was no similarity in the comparison. "The Food Commissioner must do a work that will not appeal to people, for they will not wish to deny themselves wheat and sugar," I answered. "If you or any other member of the Cabinet should ask people to give up food to which they are accustomed, they would resent it. But if the Almoner of starving Belgium, crowned with world praise, makes the request, the people will respond." Houston resented what he thought was the passing by of his department when it was equipped to do the only big work it could do in winning the war. I could see his point of view. Yet the need for a new man, with the Belgian aura, seemed to be so plain that I could not side with Houston. The President had a high estimate of Houston's ability, but realized that he lacked the popular appeal which was more essential at that time than practical efficiency. Houston had no popular gifts, and neither he nor Hoover could make a speech that would stir or delight or influence hearers. But Hoover needed to do nothing but let the papers glorify his Belgian record to open all doors to him. Houston had no imagination or eloquence and was not popular with the farmers or their leaders.

If I were asked to name two of the best-informed Cabinet members I have known, I would give places to Houston and Hoover. They had accurate knowledge, but I never knew two men with so much information who could, in their speeches and writings, so perfectly make the most interesting subject as dry as dust. Neither had style or even a suggestion of eloquence. Quite the contrary.

And yet they were authorities in the lines to which they had given their days and nights.

My admiration for Hoover waned when I began to suspect that his ambition soared so high that he was building up a strong Hoover organization—a suspicion strengthened by his clash with McAdoo over actions of the Director General of Railroads. McAdoo was so hot—and when he was mad his language was sulphuric—that I feared an open break and scandal. It was more than a clash—it raised serious issues which might have made an open breach in ordinary times. Wilson put his foot down upon letting differences between his appointees slow down war effectiveness. Few even in the administration knew how deep was the antagonism between McAdoo, who had Southern fighting blood, and Hoover, who was tenacious in carrying out his views but not willing to go fully to bat. Lane knew of the friction and thought Hoover nine-tenths right. I felt that Hoover had made a statement based upon incorrect information and he should retract. He had been the aggressor. On February 22, 1918, he gave an interview to the *New York Times* which created a sensation. He told the public that rail congestion had brought a serious situation on America and her Allies. He declared that of 130,000 carloads of potatoes ready November 1st only 28,000 had been moved and that transportation was not available for shipment where needed. The substance of his interview was that the Railway Administration was hopelessly swamped, that not only were the Allies in the utmost peril from lack of food, but that a desperate domestic food shortage was near.

McAdoo asked Hoover to inform him where food supplies were ready for shipment and promised prompt transportation. Hoover replied, thanking McAdoo, but he did not tell where food supplies were ready for transportation, and McAdoo demanded "the location of the supplies" so that he could provide transportation. Instead of answering, Hoover's attorney, Mr. Glasgow, asked for an interview for himself and Hoover. McAdoo thus recounts the interview:

"They came to my office. Glasgow did all the talking. Hoover sat with downcast eyes, like a diffident school-boy. Beyond the greetings as he came in, and his goodbye when he left, I do not

FRANKLIN DELANO ROOSEVELT

With him are Mrs. Roosevelt, his daughter Anna, his son James, and his mother, Mrs. James Roosevelt (U. S. Navy Recruiting Bureau).

CARDINAL GIBBONS DECORATES ADMIRAL BENSON

Commissioned by the Pope in 1921 to decorate Admiral Benson, Chief of Naval Operations, Charles James Gibbons performs the ceremony in the Cathedral at Baltimore. Secretary Daniels is on the left (photo by H. B. Leopold).

recall that he had anything to say. Glasgow told me on Hoover's behalf that the Food Administration wanted to coöperate with me in every possible way; that Mr. Hoover regretted his statement that had appeared in the *Times,* that the publication was a mistake and he hoped it would not interfere with our cordial relations. I said I had been giving the Food Administration preference all along and that I would continue to help, but that I thought Mr. Hoover should make his complaint to me and not to the public through the newspapers. Mr. Glasgow said, while Mr. Hoover made a minute examination of the floor, that Mr. Hoover would do that in the future."

That apology by proxy prevented a public explosion, but left a chasm between McAdoo and Hoover. At that time I did not suspect that Hoover was preparing to run for President and might be ready to give McAdoo a dig because it was generally recognized that the presidential bee had also stung McAdoo and stung him almost as hard as later it was known to have bitten Hoover. But I never suspected it until Hoover purchased the *Washington Times* and made it his organ. It was reported that he lost a lot of money in printing the paper and got out of it only when he realized that ownership of a paper at the national capital would not promote his candidacy.

HOOVER FAVORED REPLACEMENTS

The three Americans who had been abroad longest favored using American troops as replacements in French and British regiments when we entered the war. They were Admiral Sims, Herbert Hoover, and Ambassador Walter Page. Too often they sneezed when the British took snuff. It would have been fatal for Uncle Sam not to have had his own American Expeditionary Force. In a letter to Colonel House on February 13th, Hoover urged replacements and said that an American Expeditionary Force would require long preparation and much transport, and a large American Army in France would have "political difficulties in association." He proposed that the United States become a recruiting ground for "the French and other Allied armies," and he added that if our government "gave a stimulus by the provision of pensions, etc., I am confident that a large body of men could be recruited and sent simply as man-power to France. These men, put into the training depots of

Europe, would be ready for front line work within four or five months, and they would form a nucleus upon which a skilled army could subsequently be built if we desired to go further into the matter." He said that in this way we would be freed from all the impediments involved in an expeditionary force. However, Hoover went on to say that the United States should have a strong military force available for use in possible future emergencies. Then came the milk in the coconut, for Hoover always saw himself in the role of the big man. He suggested that the President appoint one man of Cabinet rank, with an expert staff, who would have direct access to every official and department in Europe. Who would that man be? Colonel House suggested Hoover, just as Hoover expected.

RED TAPE CUT TO FEED FRANCE

After the March drive, the situation in France was critical. Men and military supplies were rushed, but meeting any situation over and above the program was not always done with the promptness required. I believed in cutting tape, red and otherwise, and doing the necessary thing, and sometimes went out of my Naval sphere of duty to do so. An instance of this was told long afterward by M. André Tardieu in a signed article in *Gringoire* (Paris) upon the occasion of a visit by ex-President Hoover to Europe. Mr. Tardieu wrote:

"I knew Hoover after his return to the United States—(he had done a perfect job in feeding the occupied regions of Belgium and France)—in 1917 when he was Food Dictator and I was French High Commisisoner. He had two small, sunken eyes, but they were piercing and when he spoke he fixed them on his shoes. His Department worked like a clock. But his Chief's inflexible orders covering every detail would not fit well for emergencies of the war. In the spring of 1918 the British front gave way in Le Santerre and M. Clemenceau adjured me by touching cablegrams to send urgently some million tons of food, in addition to our monthly allowance, for the refugees who were pouring in to the rear. No, answered Mr. Hoover. There is a fixed quota.

"I went and found a kind old man who was Secretary of the Navy and was called Josephus Daniels. He immediately delivered the goods to me and the next day, using his power to make military requisitions, he levied the equivalent from Mr. Hoover's stocks."

The latter was enraged. President Wilson, who had a sense of humor, when he heard the story burst into laughter and said, "Fine joke!"

HERBERT HOOVER IN PARIS

The distress of the people of Europe after the Armistice and their hunger compelled Wilson to take steps at once to try to prevent threatened starvation. Herbert Hoover, who had made a reputation feeding the Belgians and who had done an excellent work as Food Commissioner of the United States during the war, was summoned to Paris to be Wilson's administrator in the matter of food. He told Wilson, "Every country that we have under relief is rumbling with social revolution. Without food there will be a total collapse." Hoover was met at once with the fact that there was no method of communication in Austria, where the lack of food was most severe and where the need of prompt action to save lives was necessary. The first thing needed was to get the telegraph, telephones, and radio working. Inasmuch as the Navy had entire control of radio and had experts in Europe on communications, Hoover asked the Naval advisers in Paris to undertake the matter of restoring and administering communications. Admiral Benson declined, saying that this land duty was a matter for the Army. Hoover, feeling that only the expert men of the Navy could do the job with celerity, cabled me the situation, and I answered promptly directing the Naval authorities in Paris to undertake the restoration of communications in Austria and any other part of Europe desired by Hoover in order to expedite the feeding of the people.

When I dined with Hoover in Paris, during the Peace Conference, he told me that without this assistance given so quickly he could not have carried on the process of preventing starvation so well. Hoover said, and said truly, in a letter to Wilson, "There is no right in the law of God or Man that we should longer continue to starve neutrals now that we have a surplus of food."

Before ambition to live in the White House dominated Hoover, he strongly supported the League of Nations and based his support of Harding on the disingenuous declaration that such support was the surest way to get the United States into the League. In 1919 he had said:

> "Opposition to the League at Paris arose entirely from the representatives of the old militaristic regime and from the reactionaries of the world in general. They had the vision to see and openly to state that it would mean the ultimate abandonment of military force in the world."

HOOVER—A DEMOCRAT OR A REPUBLICAN?

Even before the Armistice, Barnes and others of the Food Control Cabinet were grooming Hoover as the presidential candidate for 1920. Neither they nor Hoover cared on which party ticket he would be elected. In their adulation they hoped both parties might accept him on a "Feed the World" platform. I talked with him in Paris and found he was for the League of Nations. Returning from the Peace Conference, he wrote and spoke for the ratification of the League Covenant and most people believed that he would follow Wilson all the way.

DEMOCRATS OUT ON A LIMB

Early in November (1918) Hoover, who at that time didn't know whether he was a Democrat or a Republican, having been out of the country many years and having taken no interest in public matters, urged "united support for the President" and wrote:

> "I am for President Wilson's leadership not only in the conduct of the war, but also in the negotiations of peace, and afterwards in the direction of America's burden in the rehabilitation of the world."

He later wrote and spoke in support of the League of Nations and the ratification of the treaty, and the people of the country thought he was so much of a Wilsonian that the *New York World,* with its characteristic vigor when championing a cause or a candidate, set out to make Hoover the Democratic nominee in 1920. Hoover was, in 1919 at least, a "willin' Barkis."

"Why don't you have *The News and Observer* come out for Hoover?" asked Governor Bickett, of North Carolina, who believed Hoover was the party's big chance to win. I told him that I did not know whether Hoover was a Democrat or a Republican or Mugwump and that until he declared himself the paper would not declare itself.

Colonel John S. Cohen, editor of the *Atlanta Journal,* and Democratic National Committeeman, came to Washington to see Hoover and make plans to organize the South for him. He saw Hoover but got no satisfaction as to whether he would like to run as a Democrat or a Republican. I advised Bickett and Cohen not to come out for Hoover until Hoover put an X-ray on himself or they might find themselves out on a limb. Democratic papers and leaders called for Hoover's nomination, following the lead of the *World.* Hoover's friends were elated. They said the people en masse would draft Hoover. At that stage the Republicans became uneasy. They didn't want Hoover because he owed his appointment to Wilson and it was "pizen" to them that he had supported the League of Nations. But they saw something ought to be done to head off Hoover's nomination by the Democrats. Boise Penrose, astute politician, hated Hoover, but he saw that he was dangerous.

In the meantime the political director of the *World,* seeing that the primaries and conventions were coming on, decided that an organization should be effected to secure Hoover delegates from the States. This could not be done without Hoover's consent. Also, if Democrats were to go to work for Hoover, they must know absolutely that Hoover would not let them down.

"If Hoover will declare himself a Republican, he will be nominated and elected," was the word Boise Penrose caused to be gotten to Hoover's backers. They said, "This is a Republican year."

"If Hoover will declare himself a Democrat, he will be easily nominated and will carry the independent vote and win," said the *World* and those who seconded the *World's* nomination.

All the while Hoover made no declaration. The truth probably is that Hoover hardly knew the difference between the two parties and could be one as easily as the other.

A DINNER ENDING IN AN EXPLOSION

The *World* leader in the Hoover boosters wanted certainty. He invited Hoover to come to a small dinner to meet a few prominent Democrats who would finance the campaign and make plans for securing his nomination. Hoover accepted, but did not commit himself in any way. One hour before the time for the dinner the

World editor received a message from Hoover, through a third person, saying that he could not be in New York but that his friend and associate, Mr. Barnes, would come in his place. "I think what Barnes thinks and Barnes thinks what I think; talk to him as you would talk to me; what he says I say." Barnes went to the dinner. They talked of the war, of Hoover's acts as almoner in Belgium, of the Food Administration, of Hoover's great popularity in the country. After the salad course was served, the *World* editor said they should get down to their knitting, that if Hoover was to be nominated there must be organization and it would cost money. The two New York gentlemen said they had come to the conclusion that Hoover could be nominated by the Democrats and elected, and they would finance the pre-convention campaign. There was more talk of like character by the *World* man and the New Yorkers. Barnes listened and, they thought, approvingly. Finally, the *World* editor said that of course Hoover in some suitable way should indicate that he would accept the nomination by the Democratic Convention. Still Barnes sat dumb. The other gentlemen said that time was of the essence and asked him if Hoover would be ready to make such an announcement in a few days so that the organizing could begin. Asked a direct question, Barnes rose from the table and turning to the gentlemen said: "What in the hell are you gentlemen talking about? Herbert Hoover is a Republican and would not accept a Democratic nomination." It was a bomb-shell hurled in the camp. The party broke up. The *World* soft-pedaled, and the plan to nominate Hoover was abandoned by the Democrats.

PENROSE'S STRATEGY AS TO HOOVER

What else happened? Penrose put his agents to work to spread the word that all Hoover had to do to get the nomination was to say that he was a Republican. Hoover said the word, either because his Iowa parentage was Quaker-Republican, or he had been converted or was convinced that the road to the White House was to run on the Republican ticket, since the Republicans were in control of Congress and had the inside track for victory in 1920.

Everybody knows what happened. The big bosses in the Republican Party, who were to name the candidate in a smoke-filled room at four o'clock in the morning, were happy. One of the higher-ups said, "Hoover's tail is in a split stick. He says he is a Republican.

That makes it impossible for the Democrats to nominate him and we will never let him get the Republican nomination though the bait will be held under his nose until the man the leaders want is agreed upon." It went according to that schedule and Hoover was left high and dry. However, he declared for Harding and, along with Hughes and Butler and Root, who always put party first, signed a paper urging the people to support Harding as the surest way to get the United States into the League of Nations. The Republican idea was then to let Hoover fade away, but his ambition would not permit him to retire to private life. Moreover he had a strong hold upon a large element in the country. Obligated to put crooked friends in his Cabinet, Harding felt it essential to make a play to the better element. To appease them he appointed Hoover Secretary of Commerce. It is a matter of record that his service in that Cabinet post was so distinguished and had such popular approval that he held the position until he was nominated for President in 1928.

STICKS TO REPUBLICANS IN OFFICE

I rarely saw Hoover after he came out as a Republican and only a few times when he was President. Once, when he had to fill a vacancy on the Supreme Court Bench, I went to see him to urge him to appoint Chief Justice Stacy, of North Carolina. I pointed out that it had been nearly a century since North Carolina had been represented on the Supreme Court Bench and that it was entitled to the vacancy. He thought that was a good argument. Before I could urge Stacy, the President asked, "What do you think of Judge Parker of North Carolina?" I answered that if he was determined to appoint a Republican that Parker was the best appointment possible and personally I was a friend of Parker. "But," I said, "Mr. President, you ought to name a Democrat. All your predecessors have proceeded on the theory that both parties should have representation on the Supreme Court. Taft appointed White and Lamar. To have real representation now is the time to name a Democrat." Hoover interrupted, "There are now three Democrats on the bench." I asked him who they were. He said Brandeis, McReynolds, and Butler. I countered by saying that while Brandeis had been an independent in politics he was a better Democrat than most who registered as Democrats, and that McReynolds was a registered

Democrat but too reactionary. As to Butler, I said that though nominally a Democrat I understood that he had voted for every Republican candidate from McKinley to Hoover, and that his spectacles saw only big business interpretation of laws. I then told the President that if he had in mind naming a resident of the North Carolina district he should name a man who was representative of the sentiment of that section. I stressed Stacy's ability, that he had three times been elected as Judge and had become Chief Justice at the age of forty, and all because of proven ability and judicial qualities. "If the vacancy is to go to New England, your selection of a Republican would represent the prevailing opinion of that section. If you are going to North Carolina, you should name a man who could be elected by North Carolina votes."

The President came back to Parker. I told him that I was not familiar with Parker's decisions on the bench, that I had never heard anyone comment on them and did not know what leanings they showed, if any, but that Parker was a man of clean life, a lawyer of ability, and if only a Republican could be considered I preferred Parker to any other.

In the end, upon the urge of Republican politicians that the appointment of Parker "would strengthen the Republican Party in the South" and hold the States that had given their electoral votes to Hoover, the President appointed Parker. The Senate by a close vote rejected the nomination, because of opposition from labor and from Negro leaders. Later, when Parker's record was such as to disprove the charges against him, many regretted the rejection.

In all my association with Mr. Hoover our relations were cordial and coöperative and I would have been glad in 1920 to have supported him as a League of Nations and Progressive Democrat (as I thought him then) if he had decided to cast his lot with the Democratic Party. He owed the chance that made him President to Wilson and I believed in the early part of 1920 that Hoover could not go with the Republican Party, whose leaders had been as vicious in denouncing his administration as that of Wilson, his Chief.

Part Nine

"THUS THE WAR COMES TO AN END"

XXXII

THE DARKEST HOUR AND VICTORY

B Y LATE SUMMER of 1918 the submarine menace, which in the spring of 1917 threatened to win the war for Germany, had been decreased so much that we felt it would be made utterly ineffective when the North Sea barrage was completed. But neither our Navy nor that of our Allies ceased to increase their weapons and fighting ships. Our coöperation with the French and British navies was working perfectly after Britain joined us in convoying merchant ships, and in building the North Sea barrage.

Late in September I received a cable from London saying that Sir Eric Geddes, First Lord of the Admiralty, with his staff, wished to come to Washington for a conference with Naval authorities about a matter of such pressing and supreme importance that it could be revealed only in a face-to-face discussion. Of course I immediately cabled assent and an invitation to Sir Eric and his staff to be the Navy's guests while in Washington. No ocean voyages by air then!

Early in October Sir Eric, accompanied by Admiral Sir Ludovic Duff and other officers, were welcomed by the Secretary of the Navy, Assistant Secretary Roosevelt, Admiral Benson, and Admiral Mayo. That night, after dinner at my residence attended by all Naval chiefs and Mr. Roosevelt, we repaired to the large library of my residence on Wyoming Avenue and were in conference most of the night. If those walls could have talked, the Kaiser would have been happy and the Allies disturbed that night. The reason that had brought Sir Eric and his staff to Washington, as they explained, with a wealth of detail, was that a crisis had arrived which gravely threatened the Allies. Sir Eric was more like an American in the way he approached matters than were the other British officials. One Admiral said to him, "You are like an American." He replied, "I ought to know your ways—I spent some years in the employ of the Baltimore and Ohio railroad."

The substance of Sir Eric's statement was:

"We have the best intelligence service and we keep informed of every plan or movement of the German Navy and we know beyond a doubt that in the early Spring Germany will put on a U-boat campaign on the largest scale yet known. We know they are building many of the most powerful submarines and will be ready for a killing on incomparably the largest scale ever dreamed of and will carry out their plans as soon as their great building program is completed. Unless we can have an adequate number of destroyers and weapons and devices to defeat them, the war will go against us."

Admiral Duff and others elaborated on this statement which I have abbreviated. They were scared stiff and believed that the fate of the war depended upon our ability to meet the grave situation. They answered every question and convinced our admirals that the situation was grave in the extreme.

AN ALL NIGHT SESSION

Convinced that their information was accurate and that superhuman efforts must be concerted to meet and avert the crisis, the discussion turned on ways and means. Plans were perfected, all bureau chiefs instructed to use all diligence to hasten and to increase construction, and telegrams went out to every shipbuilding plant in the country to send a representative to Washington upon a matter of the greatest urgency at once. They responded promptly. Orders were given "Full Speed Ahead" to meet the demand. This conference of greatly disturbed Naval leaders perfected every detail of a big program of construction of destroyers and submarine chasers and detective and destructive devices by our Navy. We were assured by Sir Eric that before leaving London a speed-up program had been begun by the British Navy. Every minute of the stay of the British Naval leaders was employed to concert the preparedness to avert the immediate threat. All plans agreed upon, our British visitors sailed for home, gratified at our cordial coöperation, to press construction in their own plants. They had succeeded in imparting their scare to us. We could not doubt the seriousness of what had sent them across the ocean to impart.

A CONTRADICTORY REPORT

I had hardly reached my office in the War, State and Navy building, after the nearly all night conference, when there came this message to me from Secretary Newton Baker:

"A captain of our Army, who has been on duty in France, has returned with an important confidential message for you. He wishes to see you today, but because of the secrecy necessary, he prefers not to come to your office. Could you arrange to see him at your home?"

The answer was "Yes," and the result of the mysterious inquiry which intrigued me was that the captain, a trusted and able officer, made his statement to me substantially in these words:

"Shortly before leaving Paris, I had a talk with our Ambassador, Mr. Sharp, who asked me to bring a message to you as an old friend, of the highest import. It is: 'Tell Secretary Daniels, under a seal of confidence that he will impart the information to no one except confidentially to President Wilson, that I am sure the war will end before Thanksgiving. I have sources of information which are most trustworthy that make me confident that the Germans will sue for peace at the latest before the end of November.'

"The Ambassador was most serious—said he had been in France seven years and knew the difference between rumors and factual information—that he felt you and Baker and Wilson should be advised of his certainty that the end was near and that, of course, it must be held in confidence and his name must not be used."

The captain did not express any opinion as to the length of the war and I asked him for none. He said he was only a trusted messenger from one American official to another and must not be known in the matter at all. What was I to think? Which was right— the head of the British Admiralty leaving his post and crossing the Atlantic to try to stem the worst war effort the enemy had yet devised, or the American Ambassador in France? As I was under bonds to mention the message to nobody except the President, I could not even confide or discuss it with my Assistant Secretary, Franklin Roosevelt. There was but one course.

I went over to the White House proper, where there were no secretaries or stenographers, to see the President. I related to him the
object of the visit of Sir Eric Geddes, how the British were certain
that the worst was yet to come, and the preparations we had made
and were making to do our part and more.

Wilson was the best listener in the world. When I had finished
with all details of that disturbing situation, I then related the message the Army officer had brought from Ambassador Sharp. He
followed his custom of getting all the facts and opinions before
reaching a conclusion. Instead of saying what might be maturing
in his own mind, he asked: "What do you think, Daniels? Which
one is right, Geddes or Sharp?"

I told him that I had known Sharp well when he was in Congress; that he was a sound and unemotional business man with
vision, who kept his feet on the ground; that my first acquaintance
with him was when, in advance of other members of Congress, he
was urging a big program in aviation and was predicting that it
would take an important place in future warfare. I then said:

> "I have every faith in Sharp. I have a hunch he is right, but
> we dare not act upon it in view of the sincere stampede of the
> British Admiralty. We must act as if Geddes' fear was justified
> and be ready to meet the situation they are confident threatens
> us. If Sharp is right, we can stop our "Full Steam Ahead"
> building program. But if he is wrong, it would be fatal to let
> it slow down our action."

CIVILIAN SAW BETTER THAN NAVY LEADERS

Wilson agreed with that course and advised no let-up, but expressed the hope that Sharp was right. We reflected that Pershing
and other military leaders thought the late summer of 1919 would
be the earliest time we might hope for victory. Wilson said: "Military men must prepare for every contingency and not be over-
confident, but sometimes civilians can see further."

I did not know then—and neither did Wilson—for *Aftermath*
had not been printed—that Winston Churchill was to say: "The
governing minds among the Allies never expected the war to end
in 1918." He said, "They thought the Spring campaign (1919) on
the Meuse and the Marne would be the greatest campaign of all."

Our Navy went ahead—hammer and tongs—in October and the

first days in November on a 24-hour a day schedule to meet the call. And then on November 11, when thrilled by the news that the Armistice had been agreed to on his terms, I said to President Wilson: "Sharp was right."

And in Paris in the spring of 1919, as I went with Sharp when the French Society of Aviators gave him a distinguished honor, I told him that my hunch as to his message turned out to be well founded. He said of course he would not have felt impelled to send the message if he had not been perfectly confident that the Germans were near the end of their tether.

NO BRITISH EXPLANATION

Upon my return from Europe in the spring of 1919 I told Franklin Roosevelt what Sharp had said. He asked: "When you were in London and saw Geddes and Admiral Duff, what explanation did they make of their fright?" I told him that they volunteered none and I did not think they would have liked to admit that they thought the war was about to reach the worst stages as they believed and told us, when as a matter of fact it was within a few days of ending.

I did not follow the matter up in England or France or when I was in Germany in the early part of 1919. Admiral Benson and staff never could learn about the great German Naval construction which sent Geddes hurrying to Washington. Asked by Wilson afterwards what I thought, I said that I had no doubt the Germans had made blueprints of the big plans which so greatly disturbed Geddes, but that when the North Sea Barrage began to take toll of U-boats and when German sailors refused to go into the death trap, and mutinied at Kiel, the Germans saw the jig was up and did not build according to the grandiose plans of which Geddes had been informed.

NO HINT OF ALARM IN PRESS

No hint of the alarm of Sir Eric and his staff found its way in the papers of Britain or America, except of course that the heads of the British Navy had been in consultation with leaders of the American Navy in Washington on matters pertaining to the prosecution of the war. All that the *Encyclopaedia Britannica* says of it was that Sir Eric headed a naval mission to the United States in 1918.

WHAT IS A HUNCH?

Never since that experience have I dared to disregard a hunch. What is a hunch? A dictionary defines it as "a strong intuitive impression that something will happen, derived from the gambler's superstition that it brings good luck to touch the hump of a hunch- back." It is more than that. It is the logical unseen direction of the mind by inexplicable unerring influences which you disregard at your peril.

SCARED THE PILGRIM SOCIETY

After scaring us half to death—he was himself scared stiff—Sir Eric accepted an invitation to make an address at the Pilgrim So- ciety in New York just before his return voyage. He asked me if he might disclose the sore need of more weapons to meet the U-boat threat. I told him, "Yes, if you do not scare the people as much as you have disturbed the Naval officers."

Accompanied by Sir Ludovic Duff, he spoke at the banquet (October 14). He said he spoke with the approval of Secretary Daniels to appeal to Americans to hasten production of destroyers and other anti-submarine craft. He paid high tribute to the Ameri- can Navy saying, "America responded more quickly than any other nation to a call for quickened effort." Then he astonished his audi- ence by saying, "Submarines are a greater menace now than ever before, and a big German effort by undersea craft is to be looked for. We must not relax the muscles of our fighting arm."

He praised the work of America's "fast offensive mine-layers," said the results of the mine barrage "were very large," and this had "provided a situation highly satisfactory." Wilson wrote me: "I don't like the speech of Sir Eric Geddes a little bit."

CAME AS A SHOCK

In its leading editorial (October 16), the *New York Times* said the statement of Geddes "comes as a shock." It quoted Geddes as saying six months ago, "The submarine has been held in check." Jellicoe now said, "It no longer gives Allies grave concern," and Lloyd George had assured that the "U-boats are being sunk faster than Germany can build them." The *Times* said Geddes "has never been an alarmist," and all must take at face value his statement that

Above, left to right, Secretary of the Navy Daniels, Sir Eric Geddes, First Lord of the British Admiralty, and Rear Admiral E. W. Eberle, Superintendent of U. S. Naval Academy, at Annapolis (Bureau of Navigation). *Below, left to right,* Admiral Benson, Secretary Daniels, Sir Eric Geddes, and Admiral Duff in Washington (U. S. Navy).

Upper left, Admiral Sir David Beatty, Commander in Chief of the British Fleet. *Upper right,* Admiral Hugh Rodman, Commander in Chief of the American Fleet in the North Sea (both Brown Brothers). *Below,* Admiral Sims and Staff at Admiralty House Grounds, Queenstown, Ireland. *Left to right,* Commander Orlebar, R. N., Admiral Sims, Commanders Babcock and Daniels (U. S. Navy).

the danger from U-boats "is greater today than it ever was." The conclusion of the *Times,* based on the startling statement of Geddes was: "The war may go on another year or longer."

Twenty-eight days later, the Armistice was signed, and we were celebrating the victory.

The coming end of the war was in the October air. Upon my return from Raleigh I found a message to go at once to the White House, where I found Lansing, Baker, House, and the President in consultation over the answer to the German note. My Diary (October 14) had the following:

"All agreed that until German submarines quit sinking passenger ships and killing noncombatants, we could have no armistice and no peace with Germany without explicit acceptance of W.W.'s Fourth of July address—no autocratic government in Germany was accepted and put into practice. I urged to express these views but not to close the door to peace."

I read the following extract from a letter written to me by Governor Bickett, of North Carolina, which the President said was "fine":

"Respectfully suggest that the President's reply to Germany should be that no peace terms can be considered until Germany shall actually evacuate all territory she has seized anywhere during this war. Germany has no more right in Belgium, France, Russia, and Rumania than a burglar has in your house and no conference should be held until she gets out of all conquered lands...."

CELEBRATION OF REAL ARMISTICE

The news of the signing of the Armistice came over Naval wires at 2:45 A.M., November 11. Soon the news boys were crying "Extra" on the streets. Holiday was ordered by the President. Rejoicing beyond description. I felt the first thrill of joy in years—in fact, I had not been without distress and anxiety and strain since the beginning of the fighting in 1914. If I had followed my inclination, I would have climbed up to the top of the Washington Monument and shouted in excess of happiness and satisfaction and confidence. The glad news meant, to my optimism, not only that war was over and no more men would be killed, but also that it would usher in an era of permanent peace through a League of Nations. Shortly after the news of the Armistice came, my Diary records that Admiral Grant, of the British Navy, liaison officer at Washington during the war, called to express thanks for what the American Navy had done to bring victory.

At one o'clock President Wilson made an address before a joint session of Congress. It is impossible to describe the feeling of rejoicing that surged through the thronged capital or the effect of Wilson's historic address, "Thus the war comes to an end."

But that was not the end of the glad day. At 3:30 P.M., I went with the President when he reviewed a parade of the United War Workers. It had been planned before the good news came, and, instead of lessening interest, the excitement and rejoicing gave a chance for the celebration that was in all hearts. That night I attended a banquet given by Bernard M. Baruch to the members of the State Councils of National Defense, who had gathered to plan increased activity for war and remained to celebrate. Speeches were made by Baruch, Baker, Redfield, Hurley, Hoover, and myself. The day closed—a very full and happy day—when we attended a reception at the Italian Embassy given for us by my friend, Ambassador Cellari.

PERSHING AND FOCH DIFFERED

When the Germans asked for an Armistice, there was wide difference between Marshal Foch, Commander-in-Chief of the Allied Armies, and General Pershing, Commander-in-Chief of the American Expeditionary Force. Asked whether he would rather the Germans would reject or accept the Armistice that had been drawn up, Marshal Foch replied:

"The only aim of war is to obtain results. If the Germans sign an Armistice on the general line we have just determined we shall have obtained the result we seek. Our aims being accomplished, no one has the right to shed another drop of blood."

When General Foch visited Camp Bragg and other North Carolina places in 1921, he confirmed to me that position and enlarged upon how indefensible it would have been to have continued the war after the Germans accepted Wilson's terms.

Per contra, General Pershing, when overtures were received from the Central Powers for an Armistice, contended that a cessation of hostilities short of capitulation would postpone, if not prevent, the imposition of satisfactory peace terms. He added in a letter (October 30, 1918) to Colonel House:

"I believe that complete victory can only be obtained by continuing the war until we force unconditional surrender from Germany; but if the Allied governments decide to grant an armistice the terms should be so rigid that under no circumstances could Germany again take up arms."

Pershing continued that the Allies were gradually increasing in strength,

"through American assistance and the Germans were weakening; morale was high on the Allied side, low on the other; the Germans might use an armistice to revivify their army, and the Allies might lose the chance to secure permanent world peace....

Pershing estimated that the Allies on the western front had an advantage of 37 per cent over Germany in men and 35 per cent in guns. He commented:

"Germany's morale is undoubtedly low.... As the apparent humility of German leaders in talking of peace may be feigned, the Allies should distrust their sincerity and their motives.

"The appeal for an Armistice is undoubtedly to enable the withdrawal from a critical situation to one more advantageous."

In this opposition Pershing was voicing his personal opinion. Wilson and Baker in Washington, and Clemenceau and Lloyd George agreed with Foch.

"ON TO BERLIN"

From the time they disembarked in France the slogan of the American fighting men was "On to Berlin." In my addresses to men in the Navy and Marine Corps I always found a hearty response when I declared:

"We will not come back until it is over over there, and until our triumphant fighters enter Berlin led by the Marine Band."

But I found myself in agreement with Foch. "Our aims being accomplished, no one has the right to shed another drop of blood." Not a few agreed with Pershing when the Senate by its action defeated "our aim being accomplished," and others held with him "that the only way to convince the Germans that they had been defeated was to occupy their capital."

THE PREMATURE ARMISTICE

I had inside information, over a month before the premature or the real Armistice, from the American Ambassador in France, that Thanksgiving Day would be celebrated by a world free from war. On November 4, Colonel House cabled the State Department to announce to the American Press that "the terms of the Armistice to be offered Germany have been agreed to and signed by the Inter-Allied Conference unanimously." The Germans were to be told to sign on the dotted line without debate. On November 6, the German delegates had left to meet the Allied Commission. It was in the air that they would sign. But they had not actually signed on November 7, when Roy Howard from Brest, France, sent this message:

> "United Press
> "New York
> "Urgent. Armistice Allies Germany signed Eleven S morning. Hostilities Ceased Two Afternoon. Sedan taken, S morning by Americans.
>
> "Howard"

The hour was approximately 4:10 P.M. in Brest, and approximately 11:20 A.M. New York time.

"The Armistice has been signed," was the startling statement by Admiral Henry B. Wilson, U. S. Navy, in charge of Naval activities at Brest, when Howard, with ears trained for news, entered the Admiral's office in the afternoon of November 7 to arrange for transportation to New York. Within an incredibly short time the world, in a very riot of unconfined joy and enthusiasm, was celebrating the end of war. I was in Philadelphia and the cheering and marching and joyous shouting kept up far into the night so that I could not sleep. It never occurred to anybody that the Armistice had not been signed, even though the Associated Press and other organizations had not carried it. The people were on tip-toe expecting the good news, and celebrated as if Thanksgiving Day, Memorial Day, Labor Day, and Christmas had been rolled into one. Nothing like it had ever been seen. What I saw and heard in Philadelphia was duplicated in every city, hamlet, and village from coast to coast and from the Great Lakes to the Gulf. Roy Howard, later to become editor of the *New York World-Telegram,* and globe-trotter and correspondent plenipotentiary and extraordinary, furnished a graphic account in Webb Miller's book, *I Found No Peace,* of how he pulled off the Premature Armistice. This is his story condensed:

"As we entered the Admiral's office we were greeted by Ensign James Sellards, Admiral Wilson's personal aide, secretary, and interpreter. Sellards immediately ushered us into the inner office where Admiral Wilson was standing by his desk holding in his hand a sheaf of carbon copies of a message. The bluff old sailor's greeting to Major Cook, even before I could be introduced, was: 'By God, Major, this is news, isn't it?' and without waiting for a reply or giving Cook an opportunity to make an introduction, the Admiral barked at a young orderly who had followed us into the room:

"'Here, take this to the editor of *La Dépêche* and tell him that he can publish it—and tell him to put it on his bulletin board. And here, take this copy to that bandmaster; tell him to read it to the crowd—both in English and French—and then tell him to put some life into that music!'

"As the sailor saluted, reached for the copies of the dispatch, and started for the door with a single movement, the Admiral called after him, 'And tell the lieutenant on duty to break out the biggest flag we have, across the front of the building.'

"With this the Admiral turned to me with an outstretched hand, as Cook made the somewhat delayed introduction, followed by an inquiry as to what the big news was.

"'The Armistice has been signed,' replied the Admiral, as he handed a copy of the dispatch to Cook.

"'Is this official?' inquired the Major. 'Howard and I have been chasing this rumor all day, but haven't been able to get anything that was authoritative.'

"'Official, hell,' snorted the Admiral, 'I should say it *is* official. I just received this over my direct wire from the Embassy—from Jackson. It's the official announcement. I've given it to *Dépêche* and told the bandmaster to—. He's evidently done it.'

"At this instant a roar came up from the packed square five stories below, a dozen lorry motors started backfiring, and the Navy Band broke into 'There'll Be a Hot Time in the Old Town Tonight.'

"'I beg your pardon, Admiral,' I inquired, 'but if this is official and you've announced it to the base and have given it to the local newspaper for publication, have you any objection to my filing it to the United Press?'

"'Hell, no,' replied the Admiral. 'This is official. It is direct from G. H. Q. via the Embassy. It's signed by Captain Jackson, our Naval Attaché at Paris. Here's a copy of what I have just sent to *Dépêche*. Go to it. By the way, unless your French is okay, perhaps I'd better —. Here, Ensign Sellards, I'd like to have you take Mr. Howard over to the cable office. See that he gets this message through the censorship.'

"'Thanks, Admiral,' I replied. 'If this is quite okay with you, I'm going to take it on the run, and I'll be seeing you a little later.'

"'Okay, come back when you get through, and, Sellards, stay with Mr. Howard until he gets his message through, then bring him back here.' . . .

"When Sellards and I reached the cable office with the re-typed message, the censor room was deserted, the entire personnel having poured into the streets to join in the mass celebration which was on in the Place du President Wilson. Suggesting that I remain in the censor's office, Sellards alone went directly to the operating room at the cable head. Due to his being known by all the operators as Admiral Wilson's confidential secretary, he was able to expedite the sending of my dispatch and remained alongside the operator until the brief bulletin with its momentous potentialities had cleared into New York.

"Though I did not know it at the time, I learned afterwards that no French censor ever passed on the message. The impossible had happened. A fantastic set of circumstances which could not have been conceived of in advance combined unintentionally and unwittingly to circumvent an air-tight military censorship which no amount of strategy and planning had ever beaten.

"The surprising result was produced by a combination of extraordinary elements. The censors were, to a man, in the street celebrating, with the rest of the populace, what they too believed to be the official announcement of the end of the war. The dispatch, not by design but by the purest accident of my being unable to use a French typewriter, resembled in all its physical appearance an ordinary United Press bulletin passed by the American press censor in Paris, and relayed via the United Press—*Dépêche* leased wire to Brest. Furthermore, its authenticity was vouched for by the highest American naval commander in French waters, through the medium of his own personal and confidential aide, Ensign Sellards. The combination was more perfect than if it had been planned, and it resulted in the enactment of one of the most dramatic events of the entire war....

"By dinner time the streets were a solid mass of cheering, singing, good-natured humanity, and it was only with the greatest difficulty that we were able to make our way through the crowd to La Brassière de la Marine, Brest's liveliest restaurant. The scene inside would have put to shame the jazziest Broadway restaurant at one o'clock on New Year's morning. We had not yet ordered our dinner—not even the drinks which were to precede it—when a naval orderly, who had missed us at the Continental and had been told he could find us at the restaurant, made his way through the crowd to our table. He had a message for me from Admiral Wilson, in which the latter stated that a second message, which he had received via his direct signal-corps wire to Paris, had stated that the first dispatch was 'unconfirmable'. The Admiral expressed his regret at not having been able to get in touch with me personally, as he had to leave the city for the evening.

"Accompanied by Lieutenant Hornblow, I went immediately to the office of *La Dépêche,* where I wrote another dispatch, stating that Admiral Wilson's first bulletin had been followed by a second stating that the original statement was now held to be unconfirmable.

"This dispatch was filed at Brest approximately two hours after the first one. Had it been delivered with the same dispatch as the first, the correction would have been in the United Press office in New York sometime after one p.m. However, for reasons which to this day never have been satisfactorily explained, this second bulletin, which would have enabled the United Press to correct the original error within two hours, was not delivered to the United Press in New York until shortly before noon on the following day, Friday, November 8."

WANTED HOWARD REBUKED

On my return from Philadelphia, the early report having been shown to be premature, Melville E. Stone, manager of the Associated Press of which I was a member, called at the Navy Department indignant at the "fake message," as he called it. He wanted Howard and the United Press punished for the fake news that had set off the celebration.

Admiral Wilson and Roy Howard were both disturbed when they learned that a false report had gone out. Howard said to Admiral Wilson, "I would not have had it happen for $250,000. It has gone to all the four hundred papers covered by the United Press both in the United States and South America." Wilson told me later Howard was distressed because he felt he had acted too hastily.

"What are you going to do?" Stone asked, insisting upon some condign punishment. My reply was that I had cabled Admiral Wilson at Brest for the facts and would do nothing until I received his answer. While Howard was being roasted at home by some news agencies as a faker, forthright Admiral Wilson gave him and the United Press a clean bill of health by this statement:

> "The statement of the United Press relating to the signing of the Armistice was made public from my office on the basis of what appeared to be official and authoritative information. I am in a position to know that the United Press and its representatives acted in perfect good faith and the premature announcement was the result of an error, for which the Agency was in nowise responsible.
>
> "/s/ HENRY B. WILSON"

That didn't satisfy Stone, who insisted that the author of the false "scoop," which had made the American people delirious with joy, deserved censure, to which I replied, "See here, Mel Stone, you and I have been reporters eager for scoops. If you had received the news as Roy Howard did and had not rushed to give your papers the scoop, you would be no reporter and ought to lose your job."

That did not mollify him but there was nothing he could do about it until the Associated Press boasted that it awaited the official release of the true Armistice on November 11th and printed the best story of that historic event. But Roy Howard's "fake story" had

Upper left, Admiral Henry B. Wilson, Commander of Naval Forces at Brest, who received from the Embassy in Paris the news of the false armistice. *Upper right,* Roy W. Howard, representative of the United Press, who sent the famous telegram which brought announcement of the armistice three days before it was signed. *Below,* Scene of Pershing's reception in Washington, with Arch of Triumph on the right.

PERSHING LEADING TRIUMPHAL PROCESSION IN WASHINGTON

taken the bloom off the peach. And in time Stone and the others who had said the United Press was "a nefarious, soulless outfit, trafficing with the emotions of American patriots; the government should suppress it; its officers should be jailed," etc., when they had cooled off became good sports and admitted that in like circumstances they would have done what Howard did.

Admiral Wilson's full report to the Navy Department did not confirm all the details related by Howard. He said he did not send his aide to the censor's office with Mr. Howard but to the office of the Brest newspaper. He wrote, "Had I realized that the news was to be sent to America by reason of information received by me, I would not have authorized it."

It has never been ascertained who deceived Captain Jackson at the American Embassy in Paris by sending him the false message. Howard believes a German secret agent working in Paris, who hoped thereby to precipitate a soft peace, had caused the fake report to be sent to the Embassy. But the author remains as hidden as the old question: "Who struck Billy Patterson?" or "What caused the loss of the *Cyclops?*"

DOES HISTORY REPEAT ITSELF?

In 1918 the premature announcement of the Armistice was celebrated with so much enthusiasm on November 7 that when the official news came that the Armistice had been signed on November 11, while the celebration was genuine and general, it lacked the enthusiasm that prevailed when Roy Howard pulled off a celebration ahead of time.

Something of the same sort occurred on May 7, 1945, when Edward Kennedy, of the Associated Press, in Europe sent this message (dated Rheims, France): "Germany surrendered unconditionally to the Western Allies at 2:41 Rheims time Monday."

Everybody was looking for the Germans to surrender, and as a matter of fact what Kennedy sent was true. However, Brigadier General Frank Allen, Jr., Chief of the Public Relations Division in the ETO not only repudiated the message and prevented the filing of similar reports by other correspondents for twenty-four hours, but declared that Kennedy had been guilty of breaking faith not only with the Army officials but he had scored a scoop on all other associations and correspondents in a way that called for denying him further credentials with the armed forces in Europe. The General made a drastic ruling that:

"The Associated Press is suspended from filing copy by any means in this theater [European Theater of Operations] effective 1640 hours this date until charges are investigated in connection with the filing of a story under Rheims dateline that SHAEF had announced officially surrender of all German forces at 0241 hours this date."

The punishment of the whole Associated Press and its hundreds of newspapers was regarded as undeserved punishment to the papers and to the millions of readers who depended on Associated Press papers for their news. The incident created the greatest consternation possible. When the facts were known there was no defense for Mr. Kennedy, although he said he did what he considered was his duty.

The officials of the Associated Press disclaimed that they had any knowledge of the breaking of faith by their correspondent and printed his story as they printed other news about the war which the correspondent had been accustomed to send. The ban on the Associated Press was lifted seven hours after it was imposed though Mr. Kennedy was sent home and the war authorities continued the ban upon his attendance at any sessions when correspondents were given the news about the situation in Europe.

Prior to the Kennedy dispatch, the country, and the Nation's Capital in particular, were in a great state of expectation occasioned by an unscheduled trip of President Truman to the Pentagon Building for conference with high military leaders. Following this trip of the President, the rumors built up to a sort of crescendo which brought White House officials to their offices late one Saturday night and occasioned an extra edition being published by a Washington newspaper stating that the war had ended. It was necessary for the President to get in touch with General Eisenhower and obtain his official denial of the rumored peace agreement before the correspondents in the White House Press Association would depart from the White House Press Room, and the Capital could settle down to await official announcement.

In 1945, as in 1918, these preliminary and unofficial bulletins of the end of fighting had the effect of breaking into the well-matured plans for the solemn observance of VE Day, but in 1945—as in 1918—they did not minimize the thanksgiving of the American people that the fighting in Europe had ended.

SIMS SAID PERSHING UNABLE TO BREAK THROUGH

In October, when talk of an Armistice was in the air, Senator Glass and Representatives Byrnes and Whaley visited the war zone, London, and Paris. In a later address in Congress, Mr. Byrnes (afterwards Senator and Supreme Court Justice, now Secretary of State) said:

"On October 30th, with my colleagues, I saw Admiral Sims, who was then in Paris. I shall never forget that interview. The armistice had been requested by the enemy. Sims told us of the magnificent progress made by the British on the English front, and as we listened he proceeded to tell us that the armistice would have to be granted because Pershing had been unable to break through the German lines owing to the absolute breakdown of transportation behind the American lines. With pathos in his voice he told us how unfortunate it was that this breakdown occurred at so critical a moment. . . .

"When we informed the commanding officer and Chief of Staff of our desire to secure information with reference to this matter they were amazed. They advised us that it was the first time they had heard of it. They showed us records where General Pershing, after the St. Mihiel drive, had thanked the Services of Supply for its wonderful service, and again, just a few days prior to our visit, had written congratulating the Services of Supply upon its continued success in supplying our forces in the field. Wishing to avoid friction between our officers, we refrained from disclosing the source of our information.

"When told that our statement must be mere gossip in Paris, we advised the commanding officer that our information came from an officer of high rank in the service of our government, and in response to that statement an officer present said:

" 'That is nothing but British propaganda, and the only American officer who could have told you gentlemen this story is Admiral W. S. Sims.' "

ENDED SOONER THAN EXPECTED

None of the allied leaders believed the war would end as soon as it did. Marshal Foch said: "The decisive year of the conflict will be

SOMETHING THE ENEMY NEVER DID.

Admiral Sims Trying to Shoot Holes in the Navy's Great Record.

1919." Pershing thought it might end in the summer of 1919. When Austro-Hungary asked for peace in mid-September, 1918, it was manifestly at the suggestion of Germany. The food situation in Germany was critical. I was told, while in the occupied portion of Germany, that one of the compelling causes of Germans' seeking peace was not that the Army had been defeated so decisively that they could not carry on, but that the people at home were writing to the men at the front asking them to send them food. In the early days of the war German people at home sent food and gifts to their relatives and friends at the front, but in 1918 it was the reverse and soldiers denied themselves to send aid to the people back home. Dr. Bassett, the historian, says: "Up to November first it was not possible to say that Germany was defeated. Her lines were heavily bent but they still held."

In the spring of 1918 Secretary Baker was planning to have an army of five million men in France by the spring of the following year. On July 24 Foch dictated his famous memorandum:

"The Allied Armies have reached the turning point of the road. The moment has come to abandon the general defensive attitude and to pass to the offensive."

Ludendorff said that when the second battle of the Marne ended (August 8), "It was the blackest day of the German Army in the history of the war. It put the decline of our fighting force beyond all doubt."

Allied successes in the Balkans and Turkey's quitting on October 30 hastened Germany's suing for peace although the mutinies by the German submarine crews at Kiel had caused disaffection to spread to Hamburg and Bremen, where the sailors organized soviets and refused to obey orders. These two events—the victory at the Second Battle of the Marne, August 8, and the mutinies at Kiel caused the Kaiser to flee and the German military men to throw up their hands. The final German peace move came on October 4, 1918, five days atfer the surrender of Bulgaria, when the German Chancellor, Prince Max of Baden, appealed to President Wilson for a cessation of hostilities. Preliminary exchanges of notes continued for more than a month, but on November 8 German delegates were given safe conduct over the Allied lines. The Armistice was signed at Marshal Foch's headquarters in a railway car in the forest of Compiègne, five o'clock in the morning, Paris time, November 11, 1918, to take effect six hours later.

"Hostilities will cease on the whole front as from the eleventh of November at eleven o'clock."

Foch telegraphed his generals that the Allied troops were not to go beyond the line reached at that date and that hour.

Part Ten

PEACE THE GOAL IN PARIS

XXXIII

OUGHT WILSON TO GO TO PARIS?

AFTER THE Armistice there was much division of opinion as to whether the President ought to head the Peace Commission at Paris. There was a tradition that the Chief Executive ought not to set foot on any land outside the domain of the United States. When Taft met the President of Mexico, he went to a strip of land between El Paso, Texas, and Cuidad Jaurez, Mexico. Some Congressmen said it was unlawful for the President to go out of the country. Lansing told Wilson he thought it would be a mistake for him to go, and wrote in his book: "The President listened to my remarks without comment and turned into other channels." Lansing, who himself wished to head the peace commission, induced Vance McCormick to persuade Wilson not to go to Paris. When McCormick gave that advice, Wilson asked him, "Who can head the Commission if I don't go? Lansing is not big enough. House won't do. Taft and Root are not in sympathy with our plans. I must go." House had recommended Root and Taft. Among others, Jesse Jones, H. A. Garfield, Gavin NcNab, and the *New York World* and the *Times* advised against it. Congressman Adamson, who thought he should not go, said that he was empowered to go by a provision in the Navy bill. An old schoolmate, Frank Glass, who was in London, cabled Wilson that Balfour said, "Great Britain has no single leader able to grapple with Clemenceau." Balfour asked Glass if Wilson was a fighting man. Assured that he was, Balfour "pounded the table and said, 'Then by all means the President should go to Versailles. With the great prestige of his country behind him, he is the very man to cope with Clemenceau.'"

Replying to a telegram from House (November 16) Wilson cabled:

"I infer that French and English leaders desire to exclude me from the Conference for fear I might there lead the weaker nations against them.... The programme proposed for me by

Clemenceau, George, Reading, and the rest seems to me a way of pocketing me. I hope you will be very shy of their advice."

George Creel, discussing whether Wilson should go to Paris, reports Wilson as saying:

"Mr. Taft? ... A fine man and an honest one, but the very amiability that constitutes his charm makes it impossible for him to stand hitched. As for Mr. Root, the peoples of Europe look upon him as the principal exponent of the Dollar Diplomacy that has always been their sneering complaint against us. I sent him to Russia at the head of our mission, and the failure of that mission, as you know, was partly due to Russian distrust of Mr. Root."

Judge John H. Clarke, William J. Bryan, S. H. Bertron, John Franklin Fort, Cleveland Dodge, Cyrus McCormick, and many others advised him to go. While the debate was going on, Lane and I were invited to address the Governors' Conference at Annapolis, and Lane brought applause when he declared that the success of the Peace Conference depended on Wilson's heading the delegation. All the members of the Cabinet except Lansing felt that the President should go.

WILSON'S PRESENCE NECESSARY

Liberals all over the world wished Wilson's attendance at the Peace Conference. C. P. Scott, editor of the *Manchester Guardian,* sent this message (December, 1918) to the *New York World*:

"The presence of the President at the Peace Conference appears to me to be necessary.... He is the only statesman of the first rank who has concerned himself seriously to think out any policy at all."

SELECTING THE PEACE COMMISSION

There was not such unanimity as to his associates on the Commission. It was accepted that Lansing and House would be named. Not a few advised sending Root and Taft so that Republicans could take part. Republicans in Congress demanded that he appoint Lodge, Chairman of the Foreign Affairs Committee. That was, as Josh Billings would say "2 mutch." I said to Baker, who agreed: "To appoint Lodge would be to convert the American delegation at Paris into a debating society." Leading papers urged that Republicans be named. Wilson would have appointed liberal Republican Governor McCall, of Massachusetts, but that would have given mortal offense to Lodge and Weeks. He turned to Henry White, an able Republican diplomat, who for many years had lived in Europe by appointment of Republican Presidents. When I learned that White was being considered as the Republican member, I called at the White House to suggest from information that had come to me that the appointment of White would not please the Republican leaders, White having been away from the country too long to be regarded as a true representative of the party in 1919. As Wilson was not at the White House, I wrote him a note saying that while White was an able diplomat, he has "long worshipped at the shrine of Root and Lodge and is, therefore, less satisfactory than an appointee regarded as an orthodox and active Republican." Wilson replied: "Confidentially, I had already asked Mr. White." Results proved that I was wrong. No better or abler Republican could have been chosen. As to the fourth member of the Commission, General Tasker H. Bliss, a learned statesman as well as distinguished soldier, was appointed. I had learned to have the same opinion of General Bliss as was held by Newton Baker, who later said:

"I had the profound satisfaction when the President returned from Paris, of having him say to me that from the beginning to the end there was no shoulder so solid to rest his weary head upon as that which he always found when General Bliss was near."

NO SENATORS SHOULD ACT

Wilson's failure to appoint any Senator on the Peace Commission was based on a matured conviction that as it was the duty of Senators to vote on the treaty, they should not frame one which could go into effect only by their action. They would be voting twice—once as Peace Commissioner and then as Senator. There is much to be said for that in principle, but experience has shown that Senators have a brotherhood which inclines them to stand together, and they resent exclusion from negotiation in framing treaties.

It was said at the time that Wilson could not tolerate Lodge—a feeling that was reciprocated. But Wilson did not appoint the Chairman of the Senate Foreign Relations Committe, as McKinley did after the Spanish-American war, as Roosevelt did in 1945, because to do so would require him to name Lodge as a colleague. That may have influenced him to some extent, but as he appointed no Senator, the truth is that he acted from a principle he had long entertained.

WHY BRYAN WAS NOT ON PEACE COMMISSION

I felt at the time that Bryan and Taft deserved to be on the Commission because of their long and devoted advocacy of world peace. I wrote Wilson the following letter urging the appointment of Bryan:

> "THE SECRETARY OF THE NAVY
> "WASHINGTON
> "Nov. 14, 1918.

"DEAR MR. PRESIDENT:

"You will recall that some days ago, in discussing the personnel of the Peace Commission, I expressed the hope that you would name Mr. Bryan. He is in perfect accord with the spirit and letter of your declarations and your large purposes. His convictions as to the means to make permanent peace are in line with those you entertain. It is true that many regard him as a pacifist, and in a sense he is, but during the entire war his support of every measure for its prosecution has been generous and sincere, and in the early days it was helpful when ultra-militarists were criticizing and hindering the programme.

"Mr. Bryan, as you said in your speech in Washington in 1912, has rendered lasting service in pointing out deep rooted evils and in fighting them when many others did not see and warn. As a stout champion of the rights of the people he is a world figure and his devotion is appreciated by those who labor.

"It is the consuming ambition of his life to have the opportunity of rendering this service and I trust you will feel that you can name him as one of the commissioners. I know there are thousands—very many—who would be gratified at his selection.

"With the earnest hope that this suggestion (and you know I would not make it if I did not feel deeply it would strengthen the principles for which you stand) may meet your approval,

> "I am
> "Sincerely yours,
> "JOSEPHUS DANIELS"

In answering my letter Wilson said:

"I am sure you know my own cordial personal feeling towards Mr. Bryan, but I would not dare, as public opinion stands at the present moment, excited and super-heated and suspicious, appoint Mr. Bryan one of the Peace Commissioners, because it would be unjustly but certainly taken for granted that he would be too easy and that he would pursue some Utopian scheme.

"As I have said, this would be unjust, but I am sure you agree with me that it would be thought, and the establishment of confidence from the outset in the processes of the Peace Conference on the part of our people, now too much in love with force and retribution, is of the utmost importance."

Not being appointed on the Peace Commission disappointed Bryan. Some time before he had written Tumulty: "Acting on the theory that I may be honored with a place on the Peace Commission, I am devoting all my time this winter to study of European politics of the past century." As matters turned out in Paris, it would have been wiser if Bryan and Taft had been named instead of House and Lansing.

WANTED TO KEEP POSTED

As he was leaving for the Peace Conference Wilson wrote me on December 7: "I know you and all my colleagues will keep your eyes skinned against anybody getting the better of us while I am on the other side of the water," and signed the letter "Affectionately."

XXXIV

WILSON IN PARIS

I T WAS A shell-shocked and expectant Europe that awaited Wilson
when he was piped down the gang-plank of the *George Washington* as the ship landed in Brest on December 13, 1918. From that
day until the League was ratified in Versailles on June 28, except for
a short visit home in February, Wilson packed into these months
more work that touched the world than perhaps ever fell to the
lot of any other statesman. In addition to the day and night meetings with the Big Four and conferences with statesmen of all the
countries of Europe, he was besieged with invitations. He visited
Britain, Belgium, Italy, and other countries where his speeches set
the pace for such enthusiastic approval of the goal he had in view
as heartened and cheered him.

Fearing that Wilson might not favor as harsh a peace as the
French wished, Clemenceau and his associates urged him to visit
the devastated regions so as to see with his own eyes the ravages of
German frightfulness. When Wilson demurred and said that he did
not wish to have his mind shaped by vengeance, there was considerable resentment in Paris.

HAD SEEN DEVASTATED REGIONS

Oliver P. Newman reported (December 14) a talk with President
Wilson as to visiting devastated regions. Wilson said:

"I don't *want* to see the devastated regions. I was reared as a
boy in a devastated region—right in the heart of the region
through which Mr. Sherman marched to the sea. I grew up
on the bitterness, the hatreds, the animosities and the prejudice
caused by that devastation, and I don't want to see another
one. . . .

"You know, the reason I'm not going to the devastated regions
is that I don't want to get mad. I think there should be *one*
man at this peace table who hasn't lost his temper. In fact, if
I had *my* way, the first motion I would make would be to

adjourn this conference for a year and give everybody a chance to go home and get the bile out of his system."

DID NOT GO WITH WILSON

Evidently House and Lansing did not go with Wilson on Memorial Day when in the cemetery of Suresnes he made a prophecy which had literal fulfillment:

"I look for the time when every man who puts his council against the united service of mankind in the League of Nations will be just as ashamed of it as if he now regretted the union of the States."

MANY HISTORIES OF PEACE CONFERENCE

The story of Wilson and his leadership at the Peace Conference has been adequately told by Ray Stannard Baker, the authorized biographer of Wilson, and by others who were in Paris in those crucial days. All the members of the Peace Commission have written books, or inspired them, of the Peace Conference, and historians have given their appraisements of the Big Four.

In the end, all the Americans appended their names to the Convenant of the League of Nations.

TRIBUTE OF SMUTS

When the League was signed, Jan Christiaan Smuts, who had collaborated with Wilson in the peace pact, predicted that the name Wilson in the assize of the ages would stand higher than that of any other American. Washington, he said, had secured the independence of one country, while Wilson had brought a benefaction to the whole world. Of his own contribution Smuts later said to his friend, Minister Ralph Close:

"All else I have done in my life-time is as nothing and as dust and ashes compared to the small efforts I have been able to contribute toward the building of this organization."

The two men who were in the best position to tell the story of their chief's leadership were Lansing and House. In all their talks with him they had convinced him (until he was in the United States in the spring of 1919) that their minds ran in the same channel and that they saw eye to eye with the leader who had given them their seats on the Peace Commission. It was believed their memoirs would give the high place which history accords Wilson. Instead, the books they wrote and those they inspired are largely devoted to self-adulation, with lack of just appraisement of Wilson's ideals and accomplishments, which have been acclaimed among the highest in modern history.

WILSON WAS COMMISSIONER FOR THE WORLD

Historians and others wishing the best story of the Conference by American members of the Commission must look to Henry White, named as the Republican representative, and General Tasker Bliss, named for his distinction as military statesman, for the truest inside pictures of Wilson at the Peace Conference.

Better than any other appraisal of the greatness of Wilson at the Peace Conference is that given by General Bliss. He wrote:

"No man who was with Wilson at Paris, and probably no man in this generation will be able to give an accurate and balanced picture of the Peace Conference.

"Many books have been written. They are all special pleadings, written from the viewpoint of some man who accompanied him to or encountered him in Paris for a particular purpose. It is a tremendous pity that Wilson could not have himself written a comprehensive study of the Conference. He alone had a detached perspective of all that was done there.

"No man living could have accomplished the things he accomplished in those weeks in Paris. He could not have himself accomplished it if he had followed plans other than those he did follow. He carried the burden of the world on his shoulders during those months.

"The President's knowledge of conditions in Europe, military, political, ethnological and economic was tremendous. Brief memoranda were enough for him on any subject, apparently. We never had occasion to amend or amplify any memoranda submitted to him at his request. He grasped details instantly and assimilated them into his general picture of the situation in the world.

"My connection with the conference was purely military. He had other experts. He had Josephus Daniels there for naval matters, and because of their long association together in the Administration, perhaps the Naval Secretary's reactions are of a more personal nature. I have always understood that they were in close agreement.

Above, the American Peace Commission in France. *Left to right,* Colonel E. M. House, Secretary of State Lansing, President Wilson, Henry White, and General Tasker H. Bliss. *Below,* "The Big Four," *left to right,* Vittorio Emanuele Orlando, Premier of Italy; David Lloyd George, British Prime Minister; Georges Clemenceau, French Premier; Woodrow Wilson, President of the United States (both pictures, Underwood & Underwood).

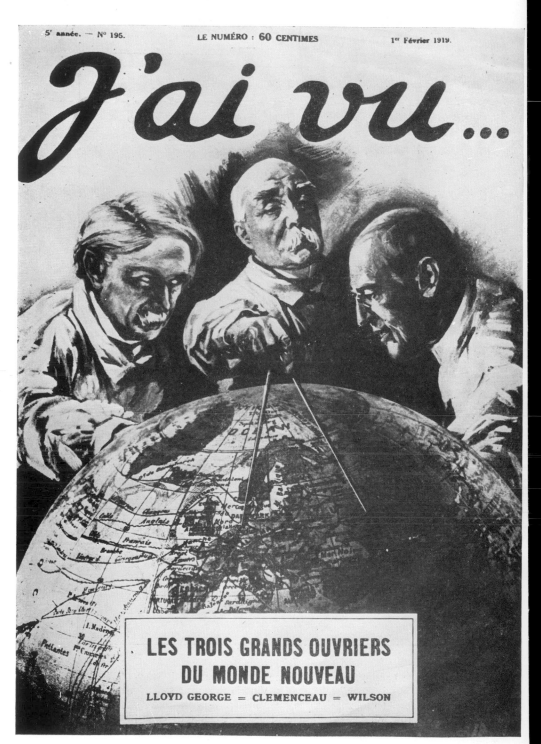

J'ai vu...

LES TROIS GRANDS OUVRIERS DU MONDE NOUVEAU

LLOYD GEORGE = CLEMENCEAU = WILSON

A Contemporary French Cartoon from *Le Numéro,* February, 1919.

"Other experts saw the conference from their particular angles. No man save Wilson himself saw the conference from an angle wider than his own interests, I think. Lloyd George perhaps saw from the British viewpoint entirely; Clemenceau saw it from the angle of France's special interests; Orlando saw it from the vantage of Italy's point of view."

General Bliss concluded:

"Other commissioners, with only their own interests at stake, could give themselves unstintingly but Wilson could not. He was the Commissioner for the World. That is the one fact that so many of his critics do not see. He claimed nothing for himself. He has never advanced a claim for himself. He had no interest save the world's interest."

Ray Stannard Baker gives the best picture of the Peace Conference in this sentence:

"At Vienna a hundred years ago, they danced their way to peace, but in Paris in 1919 no one danced. At Paris they worked and the councils were constantly agitated by cries of hunger."

AIDES PRACTICE NEPOTISM

The first intimation Wilson had that House and Lansing were not ready to accept his judgment was when he was several days out on the ship bound to the Peace Conference. At a real heart-hurt, he had vetoed the desire of his son-in-law, Francis Sayre, to go to Paris as a member of the body of advisers. Sayre had prepared for it at the suggestion of some of the college professors selected. Wilson's hostility to anything like nepotism compelled him to disappoint Sayre, who would have been a strength to him. Imagine how Wilson felt when he found that, repudiating the administration's opposition to nepotism, both House and Lansing had brought a number of their close relatives on the staff. Wilson disclosed his disapproval to a close friend, but it was too late to say or do anything about it. He had no question as to their ability, but naturally when both Lansing and House agreed to scrapping the League, their kin on the staff went along with them. The longer I live the more I am sure Jefferson and Wilson were eternally right in telling their relatives and in-laws if they wished a public position the only way was by the process of election.

RELIED ON BARUCH AND MCCORMICK

In the large staff at Paris, Wilson relied for information on a score of men who rendered service for which he was always grateful. Outside the experts, and some other valued friends and counselors, he leaned most on two friends whose judgment and affection were an abiding rock—Bernard M. Baruch and Vance McCormick. Both had declined seats in his Cabinet. They were among his earliest political friends and supporters for the presidential nomination and were true and tried and generous and steadfast until the end. Baruch was Chairman of the War Industries Board and McCormick was Chairman of the War Trade Board in the war days and both were advisers on these and kindred matters in Paris. But beyond official relations they were affectionate and loyal friends whose wisdom and constancy gave Wilson strength and happiness to the very end of his days, and the consciousness of his esteem has been an heritage they prized above all other possessions.

SECURING APPROVAL OF THE LEAGUE

Wilson was not long in securing approval of the League, for at the second plenary session (January 25, 1919) a resolution was passed providing that a League of Nations should be "an integral part of the Peace Treaty" and Wilson was made Chairman of the committee to draft it. His troubles came later, particularly from the French, and were increased when news of Lodge's Round Robin reached Paris.

The willingness of House and Lansing to exclude the League from the Treaty was equivalent to sabotaging world peace—though House, having ceased to be a "Me Too" and having become a Mr. "Smooth-It-Away," did not see its importance, and Lansing believed it was a dream. David Hunter Miller, an authority, truly said:

"If not written in 1919 as a part of the Treaty of Versailles, no Covenant would have been written at all, no League of Nations would have lasted in our time. The wisest of Wilson's many wise decisions was to put and keep the League in the Treaty of Peace."

When in April the negotiations bogged down and the Paris press, always voicing governmental opinion, was critical of Wilson and his insistence upon the League, which Clemenceau never desired, Wilson almost stunned Paris when he directed me to send the *George Washington* to Brest to take him to the United States. It not only stunned Paris but shocked the people in the United States. Acting Secretary of State Polk understood Wilson better than Private Secretary Tumulty and cabled, "Papers playing up order signifies President's determination to end peace delays." Tumulty had cabled Admiral Grayson that it was accepted at home "as an act of petulance and impatience. . . . withdrawal would be desertion. He should remain until the very last demanding an acceptance of his Fourteen Points. . . . Any necessary sacrifice should be made to get League." Dr. Grayson replied, "The French are the champion time-killers of the world. The *George Washington* has had a castor-oil effect on them all. More progress has been made in the last two days than in two weeks, and if the President's health holds out I am confident he will win handsomely."

IT WAS NO BLUFF

"You may tell Oulahan that I have ordered the *George Washington* to Brest, but ask him not to send it to his paper until tomorrow morning. I shouldn't want it printed until the orders have reached Admiral Benson," was what Wilson had said to Admiral Grayson when Paris and the world were stunned at the thought that Wilson was ready to quit the conference. Oulahan, able representative of the *New York Times,* sent the news early next morning. I was in Rome, and there, as in every hamlet in the world, people held their breath. Even the man in the street understood that it was Wilson's ultimatum that the American delegation would withdraw unless the dilatory tactics were ended.

The long delays only accentuated Wilson's disappointment when Lloyd George postponed the work of the conference after the Armistice until he could get carte blanche in what was called "the Khaki election." It wasn't necessary for the *George Washington* to go to Brest. The *mañana* policy ended. All recognized what Ray Stannard Baker put in words when he said that Wilson was *THE* Peace Commissioner at Paris." When others doubted, Wilson was as ready to fight for peace after the Armistice as he had been for victory when war was on.

Though critics at home said that ordering the *George Washington* was a bluff, nobody in Paris did. They knew it was an ultimatum for a treaty including the League of Nations. It worked.

Clemenceau and Wilson looked at matters from different angles. Wilson had gone to Paris to get the League of Nations. Clemenceau cared only to secure French immunity against future attack on France. But this difference in attitude did not prevent Clemenceau's saying there had never existed such beautiful friendship for the same length of time as between the French and the Americans. He said (February 11):

> "Inspired by the highest ideals, I may say transfigured, they had all the spiritual purpose of the old-time Crusaders.... Without American help France might have died. She would not have surrendered."

The "Old Tiger" thought he got the best of Wilson and Lloyd George in a notable conversation. It is thus recorded in the autobiography of Lincoln Steffens, who was in Paris during the Peace Conference:

> "It was the morning of the third day of the peace meetings of Clemenceau, Wilson, and Lloyd George, at the close of World War I. M. Clemenceau was speaking:
>
> " 'I desire, before we go any further, to make clear one essential point: I have heard something about a permanent peace. There has been a great deal of talk about a peace to end wars forever, and I am interested in that. But I would like to know whether you gentlemen meant it, the permanent peace?'
>
> "Wilson and Lloyd George nodded.
>
> " 'So,' Clemenceau said, 'you really mean it! Well, it is possible we can do it; we can make permanent peace—but we French cannot quite believe you mean what you say. Do you Mr. President?'
>
> "Mr. Wilson did.
>
> " 'And you, Mr. Premier?'
>
> "Lloyd George did.
>
> " 'All right,' Clemenceau muttered. 'We can make this permanent peace. We can remove all the causes of war. Have you counted the cost of such a peace?'
>
> "There was some hesitation. 'What cost?' they asked.
>
> " 'Well,' said Clemenceau, 'if we give up all future wars, if we are to prevent war, we must first give up our empires and all hope of empire. You, Mr. Lloyd George, you English will

have to come out of India, for example. We French will have
to come out of north Africa. You Americans, Mr. President,
will have to come out of the Philippines and Puerto Rico, and
leave Cuba alone. We can go to these and other countries as
tourists, traders, travelers. We cannot any more govern them and
exploit them, or have the inside track in them. We cannot longer
possess the keys to trade routes and the sphere of influence.

" 'We must also tear down our tariff walls and open the whole
to free trade and traffic. There are also other sacrifices we, the
dominant powers, must make. But first, are you willing to pay
these prices?'

"The premier and the President protested that they did not
mean all that, not all at once, anyhow. No, no, they did not
mean exactly that.

" 'Then,' said Clemenceau, sitting up straight and fisting the
table sharply, 'then you don't mean permanent peace. You
mean war!' "

DOMESTIC PROBLEMS PRESSED WILSON AT PARIS

Wilson had no release from the domestic situation while in Paris.
Daily there came messages from Washington, from and through
Private Secretary Tumulty, about every imaginable matter for
Wilson to pass upon. This, added to the great tasks in the Peace
Conference, was a severe tax on his strength, and more than once
he was ill for some time, and peace conversations had to await his
recovery.

Matters of appointment pressed particularly when Gregory resigned as Attorney General, and it was necessary for Wilson to
appoint his successor. Cables flew to him. Tumulty stressed that the
appointee ought not to come from the South, telling Wilson that
there was great dissatisfaction because it was alleged that the South
was in the saddle and had too much voice in the administration.
Baruch, stout partisan then, advised Wilson that in the selection of
the next Attorney General due consideration should be given "to
the selection of a candidate from a district where we can hope to
receive added strength rather than from one from which we cannot
hope for any results." Vance McCormick in Paris told Wilson that
Palmer's appointment would be the most popular "so far as the
organization is concerned." To the same effect advised Homer
Cummings, Postmaster General Burleson, and other men who had

been active in pressing Wilson's nomination and election. I wrote Wilson on February 23 expressing the belief that he would strengthen his administration and the public would be served by the appointment of Mitchell Palmer. I added, "In addition to his recognized ability and high character, his appointment would be pleasing alike to the bar and to the Old Guard Democrats, particularly those who won the fight at Baltimore and conducted the campaign." Palmer was appointed. Hardly a day passed that Wilson did not have to turn aside from making peace to making appointments, and people cabled him peremptorily demanding that he follow their directions. This is a sample: Twenty Democrats in the Massachusetts legislature cabled: "Come home and reduce the high cost of living, which we consider far more important than the League of Nations."

In February, 1919, cables to Wilson requesting him to renew diligence in urging the passage of the women's suffrage resolution were insistent. The women in Washington were militant. On February 10 Polk cabled, "Suffrage demonstration Sunday to influence vote on eve of elections resulted in the arrest of 36 members of the National Woman's Party for burning an effigy of the President in front of the White House." Wilson telegraphed to several Senators asking them to vote for the bill, but John Sharp Williams, Senator from Mississippi and a great friend of the President, replying to his request to vote for the women's suffrage, having in view the action before the White House, wired Wilson that he never could vote for that until the women "stopped making fools of themselves."

Not even at Paris did Japanese matters fail to flare up. April 4, 1919, Senator Phelan, of California, informed Wilson that Governor Stevens had used all his power to prevent bills denying Orientals the right to own or lease land in California and prevent immigration of so-called Japanese "picture brides," who were coming into California in great numbers in the guise of wives. Phelan said, "It is a political trick of a Republican legislature to embarrass the President, and we wish the President to say that the legislature should act on its own responsibility." He added, "The Japanese have devised a marriage between a resident Japanese and a woman in Japan who has never met the man until her arrival. I believe the object is to breed a race on our soil, because, born on our soil, the children are citizens and the alien father can then buy land in the child's name and thus circumvent the state law."

One of the thorns that pricked Wilson in Paris was the insistence by many correspondents that Eugene Debs, the labor leader who had been imprisoned during the war, should be released. He was bombarded with telegrams pro and con. Wilson telegraphed Tumulty on March 26, "If the Attorney General consents, I am willing to grant a respite in the case of Eugene Debs and the others suggested by Walsh, Benson, and Russell, but I doubt the wisdom and public effect of such action and hope you will go over it in the most serious way with Palmer and let me know the results of the conference before I act."

Answering (April 4), Tumulty said, "The Attorney General says 'I am opposed to granting any respite or clemency in the case of Eugene Debs. He was convicted on a charge of inciting the wage earners to refrain from aiding their government in the war. In his speech Debs said to them, "I have been accused of obstructing the war. I admit it. Gentlemen, I abhor war. I would oppose the war if I stood alone." The Attorney General added that he had been given 'eminently a fair trial and his attitude of challenging and denying the administration of law makes it imperative that no clemency or respite be shown at the present time.' " Tumulty added, "I agree with the Attorney General."

No action was taken then, but when Wilson returned home in March the matter of Debs's release was taken up in the Cabinet, and there was quite a discussion. Secretary Wilson and I and some other members expressed the opinion that Debs had been sufficiently punished and that further punishment would be cruel and that the petition signed by many fine men ought to be acted upon favorably. By that time Wilson had made up his mind and with the rigidity of the old Calvinism, which sometimes appeared, he turned to me and said, "Suppose every man in America had taken the same position Debs did. We would have lost the war and America would have been destroyed. No, I will not release him."

I felt strongly about it and so did nearly all of the labor people and many others. Perhaps I felt more strongly in favor of releasing Debs because, away back in the Cleveland Administration—in which I had held a small post—I had felt outraged when Cleveland sent the troops to Chicago and used them to override the State authority and punished Debs beyond what I thought the attitude of the strikers demanded. Debs never asked Wilson for pardon. Neither did he ask Harding after the 1920 election, but Harding granted the petition, and I was glad he did, for I thought Debs had suffered enough and ought to be freed.

PREDICTION OF GERMAN AND JAPANESE UNITY

In April, I sent to Wilson from Washington, through Benson, a cable from Naval Attaché Gillis at Pekin, in which what happened in 1941 was foreshadowed. He said:

"A Japanese mission is leaving immediately for Germany, ostensibly to investigate postwar conditions and look out for Japanese prisoners.... Japan is not now, and never has been, loyal to us or other Allied powers. I recommend we establish immediately a powerful fleet in the Eastern waters in conjunction with the British. Japanese newspapers are conducting anti-American propaganda campaign both in China and Japan."

On the other hand, Captain Vogelgesang, just returned from China and Japan, said, "Japan cannot fight us. We need fear no danger from that quarter."

COMING HOME WITH THE BACON

It was a gala day (July 8) when Wilson landed at Hoboken bringing home the League of Nations framed by the free nations and signed at Paris. On the Fourth he had made a patriotic address to the sailors on the *George Washington,* all of them from Captain McCauley down regarding him as a real shipmate. He was a proud and happy man, feeling that he had accomplished the high mission that carried him overseas, and he was confident his countrymen would ratify the treaty. At that time 80 per cent of the people favored it.

As his ship anchored, the members of the Cabinet and a great crowd welcomed him. I recall that Wilson began by expressing his delight at being home, creating a laugh when he said, "Jersey man that I am, this is the first time I ever thought Hoboken beautiful." He also said, "Though I have tried to conceal it on the other side of the water, I have been the most homesick man in the American Expeditionary Force," as he began his appeals for the ratification of the treaty against a strong opposition, which he did not think could sabotage world peace.

PRESIDENT AND MRS. WILSON WITH THE KING AND
QUEEN OF BELGIUM

Front row, left to right, Queen Elizabeth, President Wilson, Mrs. Wilson, and
King Albert (Brown Brothers).

PRESIDENT AND MRS. WILSON VISIT CHATEAU-THIERRY

XXXV

SEA BATTLE OF PARIS

W HAT HAD SENT the First Lord of the Admiralty and his staff
to Paris when they learned I was to arrive to attend the
Naval Conference? It was the published report in Britain that the
United States was bent upon immediately carrying out a policy
of building the greatest Navy in the world. Nothing could have
aroused the British so much as the fear that some day another nation
would have superiority on the sea. British papers had printed that I
recommended, and the House of Representatives had adopted the
Wilson plan to carry out the Three-Year Program of construction
which would have made the Navy of the United States stronger than
that of Great Britain. When I appeared before the Naval Affairs
Committee, Chairman Butler suggested that I ought to visit the
big Naval nations in Europe and learn the lessons, if any, the war
had taught. It was in pursuance of that suggestion that I set forth,
accompanied by Admiral David W. Taylor, Chief of the Bureau of
Construction, Admiral R. S. Griffin, Chief of Engineering, and
Admiral Ralph Earle, Chief of Ordnance, the three men who would
direct the technique of new Naval construction.

PARIS WITNESSED SEA BATTLE ON SHORE

Wilson went to Paris resolved that the ancient ambition, from
the first tiremes of Rome to the dreadnaughts of Britain, that one
powerful nation should rule the waves must no longer prevail.
Every warlike nation had aspired to be mistress of the seas. Spain
long ruled in both hemispheres until Nelson gave Britain supremacy
of the seven seas.

Control of the seas and imperialism have always been twins, while
democracy and the right of all peoples to self-government and free
commerce look to unrestricted water navigation. These two opposing
ideas on the use of the seas now ran into a head-on collision. When
I reached Paris, I was soon immersed in a controversy that at one

time threatened to end the friendly Naval relations cemented during the war and checked for a time the forming League of Nations.

Because of the near-fight between British and American Naval officers, and the great issue involved, I have often said that I spent a whole year in Paris in one month. The day after my arrival I attended a conference of officers of the British and American Navy on duty in Paris. I found that the British, headed by Admiral Wemyss, and the Americans headed by Admiral Benson, Chief of Operations and the Naval Adviser to President Wilson in Paris, were waging a battle with great vehemence. I soon learned that this meeting was the culmination of a number which had gone before.

"CAN'T SPIT IN MY OCEAN"

As the old sea-dogs—Benson and Wemyss—barked at each other, I was reminded of a story current on both sides of the Atlantic of an exchange between a British and an American sailor cruising on the same ship in the war zone. The American was provoking in his denunciation of all things British.

"I don't like your King," he said.

The British sailor said nothing.

"Your Navy has failed and all your boasting about being masters of the sea is bunk," prodded the American, who, continuing to voice every insult he could imagine, got no rise out of the British tar. Pausing for breath, he expectorated into the sea. That was the crowning insult, and the British sailor turned to the American and said, "You can abuse His Majesty if you choose, and you can deride our Navy and our country, but, by God, you shall not spit in our ocean." Then fists flew.

DECLINED BRITISH PROPOSALS

Immediately after the signing of the Armistice, with the approval of President Wilson, I had urged Congress to complete the three-year program of construction which as to large ships had been interrupted during the war by the necessity of utilizing all shipyards for the construction of destroyers and other craft suitable for U-boat warfare. The completion of the three-year program would have made the American Navy stronger than the British Navy, a situation the British regarded as unthinkable, even if it carried no threat to Britain's Empire.

Admiral Wemyss made the direct proposal that Admiral Benson and his Naval associates recommend to the President and Secretary of the Navy that they agree to a fixed ratio of Naval strength, conceding to Great Britain continued primacy. To effect such agreement, Wemyss insisted that the ships authorized by Congress to strengthen the American Navy should not be constructed. That suggestion irritated Admiral Benson, who plainly and with deep feeling told the British conferees that the United States would never be content with a Navy that was not equal to that of the British Navy. They did not swear, in their heated controversy, like the Army in Flanders, but they were dangerously near it; certainly there was a verbal collision. I had to step in to restore the urbanities. It was no personal difference. It was born of fundamental aspiration of the two countries whose Navies they represented.

Wemyss felt strongly that the far-flung British Empire was entitled to be mistress of the seas while Benson was equally determined that the Navy of the United States should not be outranked by that of Britain. I told Admiral Wemyss that the question was one to be settled by the two highest representatives of the governments, and Mr. Walter Long had agreed that it should be referred to Lloyd George and Woodrow Wilson. That closed the red-hot debate for the time being. But it was only transferred to another forum, where it was debated without any agreement's being reached.

BRITISH NAVY SHOULD NOT DOMINATE

Admiral Benson did not stop with his fight in the Council against British superiority. He wrote strong notes to Wilson, fearing that the unity between Lloyd George and Clemenceau might slip something through. It is well he did, for without realizing its far-reaching consequences, Wilson had to recall one agreement. On May 5 in a long letter to Wilson Admiral Benson wrote:

"It must be quite evident to you that in practically all questions that have come up, Great Britain has been able to maintain her position and carry through her claims largely through the dominant influence exerted in consequence of her tremendous naval superiority. It is quite evident to my mind that if this condition of inequality of naval strength is to continue, the League of Nations instead of being what we are striving for and most earnestly hope for, will be a stronger British Empire.

... American aims and ideals were entirely foreign to those of other powers. The alliance between France, Japan and Great Britain, together with their interests, is so intimately connected that any addition to the naval strength of the former two powers will be so much more added to the strength of Great Britain. Everything should be done to increase, or at least prevent an increase in the naval strength of Great Britain, France and Japan. In order to stabilize the League of Nations and have it develop into what we intended it to be, the U. S. must increase her naval strength to such a force as will be able to prevent Great Britain at least from dominating and dictating to other powers within the League."

NO INTERVIEW WITH SIMS

Wilson was fortunate in having so level-headed a Naval adviser in Paris as Benson, one whose Americanism was undiluted. I did not know until I reached Paris that Admiral Sims had aspired to be Naval adviser to the President. It was gall and wormwood to him when he learned that Wilson had named Benson, whose mind ran more nearly along with the President's and in opposite direction to that of Sims, who, asking for an interview, wrote the President:

"As I have in the past twenty months continuously and quite intimately associated with the naval people of Great Britain and our Allies, and also with many of the civil authorities, on terms of considerable intimacy, I think it possible that the knowledge I have thus acquired not only of their point of view but particularly of their *real attitude* and *feeling* regarding the United States might be of interest to you."

Wilson wrote he could not see him. He believed Sims only echoed the views of the British Admiralty. This was borne out by the following incident.

WHAT SIMS TOLD CONGRESSMEN

In October, 1918, Representatives Carter Glass, Byrnes, and Whaley visited Admiral Sims in London, as previously told. Upon their return, Mr. Byrnes in his report in the House said:

"Sims expressed the hope that we would not be led astray by the agitation for a merchant marine. He declared that England, because of her geographical location, must necessarily control the seas, and that we could rely upon her at all times providing a merchant marine to transport our goods to foreign markets. When I took issue with him, he stated that even if we entertained the view that it would be desirable for the United States to possess a merchant marine, it was impossible, because we could not compete with Great Britain; that it would be necessary to pay subsidies, for which our people would never stand; and that it was the part of wisdom for us to develop the great West and leave the sea to Great Britain. With that Government, he said, we would never have any trouble, and Great Britain could be depended upon at all times to care for our business upon the seas."

DIFFICULT AND DELICATE SITUATION

When our party reached Paris, I was informed that Mr. Walter Long, First Lord of the British Admiralty, and all his staff had arrived a short time before. "How long will the First Lord of the Admiralty be in Paris?" was the question my aide, Captain Foote, asked the aide of Admiral Wemyss when I had called by appointment to confer about the differences which had arisen between the officers of the American and British Navies.

"As long as Mr. Josephus Daniels is in Paris," was the answer.

This presaged the battle royal that lasted several weeks, and was confirmed in my first conversation with Mr. Long, who expected his stay to parallel that of "Mr. Josephus Daniels." In that first talk he told me that Lloyd George would not support the League of Nations if the United States accompanied it with a big Naval building program, for Great Britain could not consent for any other nation to have supremacy of the seas.

I didn't sleep much that night, even though Paris beds were comfortable. I knew that what carried Wilson to Paris was to secure the League. Was it so important that the Naval program must be scrapped to secure Lloyd George's support? Wilson was in one of the most delicate stages of the Conference. It looked as if the British Naval leaders had staged their demand at a time of all times when it would embarrass Wilson most. Clemenceau had always been inclined to alliances and force more than to a world league. He favored the league only when Wilson and Lloyd George agreed to recommend to their countries a solemn treaty to come to the relief of France if invaded. Lloyd George and Britain were the hope. If the British Premier failed him, how could Wilson realize his heart's desire and the hope of the world?

It was my duty to aid my chief—not alone from loyalty but because I shared his zeal for the cause and his faith in it as mankind's only hope. If because of Naval ambition for strength, the service of which I for the time being was the head should stand in the way of agreement upon the Covenant, how could it be justified in an appeal to history? I assured Mr. Walter Long that my country had no dream of supremacy, that it had taken its stand for equality, and it could not abate both its right and duty.

"It would not be difficult for us to reach an agreement," he said, "but public sentiment in Great Britain is very much alarmed by your building program." The interview was concluded by his saying that he, perhaps, was not fully informed as to the length to which the Prime Minister was ready to go—that he would see him and we would have a future conference.

DIVISION OF GERMAN SHIPS

The flare-up over the size of the British and American navies was not the only subject that was discussed after my arrival in Paris in the Allied Naval Council. The disposition of the ships of the German Navy, which had been interned at Scapa Flow, caused serious division. Admiral du Bon, of the French Navy, insisted that these ships should be divided among the Allied Nations in proportion to the losses sustained during the war. Such a division, of course, would have caused the United States Navy to come out the small end of the horn. Our Naval officers had tentatively agreed upon a division.

If the German ships were distributed on the basis of losses of men-of-war during the war, Great Britain would get 13 dreadnaughts; France—4; Italy—3; Japan—1; U. S.—0; and the other ships would be divided in proportion. During the war Britain lost 13 battleships; France—4; Italy—3; Japan—1; U. S.—0. The ships available for distribution from Germany and Austria were: dreadnaughts—21; Battle-cruisers—5; light cruisers—20; torpedo boat destroyers—111; T.B.'s—101; and monitors—12.

When I arrived, upon being asked what I thought of the plan of division of German ships, I said, "The American Navy does not wish to participate in any division of the German ships, and as the

European nations were first in the war and wish these ships, our country does not desire any and will permit the other Navy nations to divide them as may seem fit."

This surprised our Allies and they thought I was being generous. As a matter of fact, after talking with Griffin, Taylor, and Earle, I was sure that none of these German ships would fit into the organization of our Navy, and it was not generosity at all but a recognition of a situation. I was very willing for the European Allies to take these ships if they wished them. That night when I was dining with Admiral du Bon, he expressed his gratification that I had taken that course, and I frankly told him that we were not being generous but practical. The German ships were not built on the same pattern as the American ships and would be as much of a liability as an asset. He said, "You are right. If I could act on my own judgment I would not wish any of the German ships added to our Navy, but the French have lost so much in this war and the civilian leaders are determined to get from Germany everything possible. These ships as scheduled are worth so many million francs that the French people believe they are getting something big when these ships are turned over to us."

On March 30 I sent a note to President Wilson in which I said:

"The more I think about it the more I am impressed by the conviction that it would be a mistake to divide the ships between the nations, and for Great Britain to sink the portion that comes to her and for other nations to keep their portions. The most tangible evidence of faith in reduction of armament would be the impressive act of eliminating this great fleet as one whole. I confess that at first the idea of sinking them did not appeal to me, but when I reflect that it is not sinking many millions of dollars that would be useful, and they could not be used by any nation without large investment of money to produce ammunition to fit the German ships, it would really constitute a liability rather than an asset."

LLOYD GEORGE FAVORED SINKING OSTENTATIOUSLY

A little later when I was talking with Lloyd George about the Navies of Britain and America, he asked me what I thought ought to be done with the German ships in captivity. I replied that if I had my way I would sink them all as an object lesson to the future.

Lloyd George smiled his approval and said, "That's what I would like to do, but you know the British—particularly the Navy—like the French people, would not stand for it now. They think getting some of the ships compels Germany to pay for the cost of the war." Lloyd George added, "What I would like to see would be to tow all these German ships at Scapa Flow into the middle of the Atlantic and to surround them with ships of all the Allied countries, and to the music of all our national airs sink them ostentatiously."

A few days later an American newspaper printed a paragraph that I had said the United States did not want any of the German ships and commented, "Generous Secretary Daniels—He is very free in giving away what does not belong to him!"

What Lloyd George and I wanted came to pass without our having anything to do with it when later the Germans scuttled all their ships and they now lie at the bottom of Scapa Flow.

ALL SUBS SHOULD BE SUNK

On March 4 I wrote Wilson:

"I believe all submarines should be sunk and no more should be built by any nation, if and when the League of Nations becomes a fact. At the best they are stilettos and, like poison gas, should be put beyond the pale.... No nation should be dominant in military strength on land or sea.... In the League each nation should furnish the necessary force in proportion to its wealth and commercial importance to maintain peace.... The destruction of Heligoland is the best guard against German sea power. It should be destroyed."

WILSON WAS DISTURBED

During a luncheon with Wilson he told me that Lloyd George had discussed with him whether the United States had intended to build the ships in the three-year program. "Lloyd George wishes you to see Mr. Walter Long, First Lord of the British Admiralty, and discuss with him fully the building program," the President told me, and added, "Mr. Lloyd George is very much disturbed about the matter and the British Admiralty even more so. I wish you would see the representatives of the Admiralty here in Paris, talk over the matter fully and see if we can reach some real understanding." He did not say in so many words that the League of

ON THE BRIDGE OF THE GEORGE WASHINGTON

President Wilson's return from Paris after signing the Treaty of Peace was marked
by a tremendous ovation which began as soon as his ship reached Quarantine and
continued his progress up New York Harbor (Brown Brothers).

AT THE ST. GERMAIN CONFERENCE

The Chief Executive arriving at the Castle of St. Germain, where the terms of the Allied Peace Treaty were handed to the Germans. The President is accompanied by Rear Admiral Cary T. Grayson, his personal medical adviser (Underwood & Underwood).

Nations was being held up because the British insisted upon America's willingness to suspend its program and agree to have a Navy second to Great Britain, but he said that Lloyd George was pressing upon him that the Naval authorities of the two countries ought, before anything else was done, to confer upon the Naval strength of the two nations and agree upon it.

In pursuance of this request I had a conference with Mr. Walter Long. There had been a Walter Long in Parliament without a break in any generation for more than two centuries. I found him a typical, forthright Englishman, and after seeing much of him in Paris, and again in London, I would have held the same opinion of him that A. G. Gardner wrote: "I could not be a Conservative, but if I could be one I would wish to be one so downright and honest as Walter Long."

He was deeply disturbed in his first conversation, and even more so in our later conversations, about the differences that made almost an impasse between the Americans and British in the Allied Naval discussion in Paris.

I later reported to President Wilson the sharp division between the officers of the British and the American Navy and Walter Long's telling me that Britain could not be satisfied if we carried out our big building program. Wilson saw the dangerous implications if Lloyd George should back up British Naval demands and said, "Do not leave this matter in the hands of Naval officers. Take it up with Lloyd George. You and he are both civilians and will understand the situation better than men who belong to the profession of arms." He arranged a conference between Lloyd George and myself.

"That night," says Captain Foote, my Naval aide, "we were dining at Ambasador Sharp's. Immediately after coffee I departed on urgent business. As I went into the coatroom a British Naval officer entered. He was visibly in a hurry. On seeing me he inquired, 'Are you by any chance Captain Foote?' "When I replied 'Yes,' he said, 'Thank God! I've been chasing all over Paris for you.' "

He then told Captain Foote that the matter had been arranged, that Mr. Lloyd George had sent him to invite the Secretary of the Navy to have breakfast with him the next morning.

BREAKFASTING WITH LLOYD GEORGE

At breakfast with the British Premier the next morning, I found him quite as vigorous and determined as Walter Long or Admiral Wemyss. That was a good breakfast the British Premier served to the First Lord of the Admiralty and the Secretary of the Navy. Lloyd George was in the best of humor. What a charming and captivating manner the Welshman possessed! He was so agreeable and so entertaining that I feared he would capture me and the dreadnaughts by his engaging and winning ways. I never understood until that morning why he was so irresistible.

The sea-fight then began. Lloyd George brought up the subject at issue. He said if there was to be dependence upon reason and not war in the world, the lead should be taken by the English-speaking nations with reference to their Navies. "We have stopped work on our cruisers," he said, "and you ought to stop work on your cruisers and dreadnaughts if you really believe in the League of Nations." He asked, "What's the use of organizing the world for peace if the United States, the propounder of the League of Nations, insists upon going on with the construction of a big program of capital ships?" I pointed out that he would find the United States quite ready to lead in reduction of armament when the League was in action, and it would be eager to do so, but until permanent peace was assured the United States could not stop its construction program. I then asked him the pointed question if the agreement he proposed—that the United States abandon its Naval program—was a condition precedent to his support and the support of his country to a League of Nations. That had been the clear purport of what Wemyss had said to Benson and Long had said to me.

"Of course not," said the Premier, "but it would be a mere piece of rhetoric if you continue to build."

I told him that I could not consent to such an agreement in advance of setting up of the League. "Nothing can be done by us here in Paris that could not be presented to Congress—it must be done in public."

"I had no thought," he said, "of any agreement that could not be submitted to Congress and Parliament. But if we agree here I am quite sure our countries will approve."

"If I interpret it aright," I said, "the attitude of the United States is that when the League of Nations is a going concern, it will be able to undertake reduction in armament. We will go to any proper length to end Naval competition. In advance of setting up the League, we could not stop work. After the League is functioning, we think all nations should agree, and that there should be a Naval force only large enough to enforce the policies the nations agree upon. The United States will furnish its share. We do not wish to have superiority over any other nation. We cannot accept inferiority in power and size to any."

Lloyd George came back to the fact that England had stopped building and said that we should agree to do the same. To which I countered by saying, "When our three-year program is completed, the tonnage of the British Navy will exceed that of the United States." I had the figures with me and went over in some detail the standing of the two Navies. Great Britain had in 1915 in all 736 ships with a tonnage of 2,273,781. The United States had 259 ships with a tonnage of 1,001,533. The ships building and projected at that time would give the British 219 ships with a tonnage of 498,761, and the United States 349 ships with a tonnage of 1,116,389. I pointed out to Lloyd George that if all these ships were constructed by both nations the Navy of the United States would have 608 ships with a tonnage of 2,117,922, and the British would have 955 ships with a tonnage of 2,772,542.

Lloyd George waived that all aside by saying that tonnage was not the determining factor but guns, and that if America should complete its 13 battleships and 6 battle cruisers with their 16-inch guns, those ships would be superior to those of any other nation. That fact was the milk in the coconut. It was because of this fact that members of the British Admiralty and the First Lord had come to Paris and were putting pressure on Lloyd George to prevent the building of the ships.

"Why does Britain need a bigger Navy than the United States?" Lloyd George inquired, and answered his own question by saying that the British Empire reached into all continents and that it must have a greater Navy to protect its far-flung empire. "The United States," he continued, "between two oceans has no empire to protect and therefore it ought to be satisfied with a smaller Naval force." When he stressed the fact that the United States had less need for a Navy because it lacked colonies, I was ready for him. That same argument, not so well stated, had been urged by Walter Long, and I apprehended that Lloyd George would take the same position. Before going to see him I had gotten the Naval officers to draw two maps of the world—one showing the extent of sea lanes to be covered from London and the other from Washington. I was undoubtedly influenced in having these maps drawn and in telling Lloyd George we had the longest sea lanes, by a statement made by President Wilson in St. Louis in 1916. In that statement he was urging that the "American Navy ought in my judgment to be incomparably the greatest Navy in the world." In that speech Wilson said, "Have you ever let your imagination dwell upon the enormous stretch of coast from the Canal to Alaska, from the Canal to the Northern corner of Maine? There is no other Navy in the world that has to cover so great an area of defense as the American Navy." I pointed out that the United States was committed to the protection of such widely separated countries that we really needed a Navy stronger than Britain. He rose and said, "That is preposterous. You are a self-contained republic with no large empire." I pointed out from the map that we had to protect the sea lanes from the northern coast of Maine all the way down the Atlantic Coast to and including Patagonia, and then up the western coast of South America, Central America, and North America to Puget Sound; then, skipping Canada, the great territory of Alaska. Besides those, I said we had to protect Hawaii, Guam, Samoa, and the Philippine Islands, not to speak of Cuba, Puerto Rico, San Domingo, Haiti, and the Virgin Islands. To fulfill this obligation it was essential that we have a Navy second to none.

Lloyd George went up in the air. He asked, "Do you mean to say that your country dominates Mexico, Central America, and all South America?" I replied in the negative, that we did not control or wish to dominate those Pan American nations but that the Monroe Doctrine in which Britain had acquiesced—in fact had claimed to suggest —required that we protect those countries against any attempt to invade their sovereignty or acquisition by a foreign country. I added that we had once been compelled to warn Britain that we would send our fleet to Venezuela if she insisted upon dictating to that American nation.

This wide division of opinion brought Lloyd George and me to

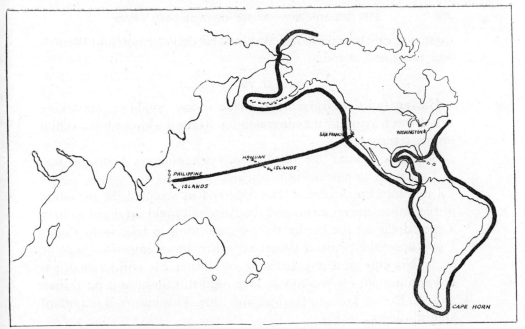

UNITED STATES

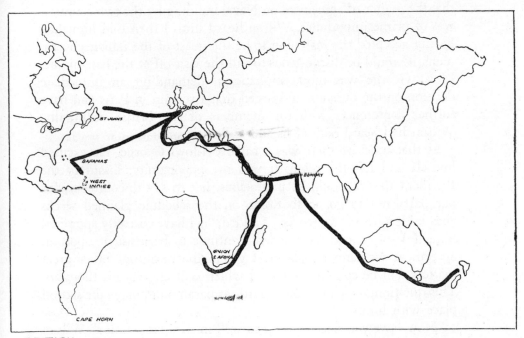

BRITISH

Maps illustrating Woodrow Wilson's statement, "There is no other Navy in the world that has to cover so great an area of defense as the American Navy."

quite as great an impasse as had existed between Benson and Wemyss and Long and myself.

APPEAL TO WILSON

Having failed of agreement, I rose to say good-bye, remarking that I was leaving in the afternoon for Rome and hoped to see him on my return.

"Going to Rome?" he asked. "No, you cannot go. You must stay in Paris until an agreement is reached."

I told him the American Naval party had accepted the invitation of the Italian government, and the Admiralty had arranged to have a special car on the border the next morning to take us to Rome. I was upon the point of departure, when in an imperious way he said, "No, you must stay. Let's go see Wilson. He will see that it is more important for you to stay here until this business is fixed than to go to Rome. You can go there any time. This matter is important and imminent."

We walked over to see Wilson. Lloyd George was most insistent that the matter of agreement on Naval building by the two countries was of prime importance. Wilson heard him. I then told him that, having accepted the invitation to be the guest of the Italian government, it would be discourteous to call the visit off at the last minute. Lloyd George was most emphatic in demanding an immediate decision on the question and urged that I remain in Paris and have further conferences with the members of the British Admiralty. Wilson had heard both of us and said nothing.

At that juncture there was a call for Lloyd George. He excused himself and left the room. It was my opportunity. I said to the President that it would be ungracious, not to say discourteous, for our party not to go on to Rome on the schedule planned weeks ahead. He agreed. "Moreover," I added, "if I have correctly appraised him, if I stay Lloyd George will continue to be insistent upon an agreement we cannot make. If I go, in the meantime other great matters will be coming to a head which will engross his thoughts. This question, which he now regards as paramount, may take second place with him."

"How have you sized him up so well in so short a time?" Wilson asked me. Lloyd George returned and turning to me said, "You cannot leave Paris until this question is settled. Nothing can be done until it is out of the way." Wilson reminded him that I had accepted the invitation and must leave for Rome but that I would hasten my return. He added, "You see, Mr. Prime Minister, the Italians in this present acute situation would regard it as an offense if Secretary Daniels and his staff did not keep their engagement. He must go and I will ask him to return early so this matter can be taken up again." Lloyd George protested but saw that protests were in vain and pretty soon withdrew—evidently not satisfied that the matter must go over.

The afternoon of the day Wilson had informed Lloyd George that there could be no decision of the Naval controversy until I returned from Rome, I left Paris with the members of our party to visit Rome as the guest of the government. Lloyd George may have been encouraged in his insistence by House's having early expressed his willingness not to press for approval of Wilson's demand for freedom of the seas. Discussing Point Two, Colonel House later stated that the position of Britain was thus expressed by Lloyd George: "Great Britain would spend her last guinea to keep her Navy superior to that of the United States or any other powers, and that no Cabinet officer could continue in the Government in England who took a different position." Wilson had written House (October 30, 1918):

"I feel it my duty to authorize you to say that I cannot consent to take part in negotiations of a peace which do not include the Freedom of the Seas, because we are pledged to fight not only Prussianism but militarism everywhere."

As usual, Colonel House weakened this vigorous statement in his talk with Lloyd George and accepted instead that the British "must reserve for themselves complete freedom" on the point of freedom of the seas. He did this after Lloyd George had said: "Were we to accept [Point Two] it would only mean that in a week's time a new Prime Minister would be here. . . . The English people would not tolerate it." Therefore, Colonel House (the "yes-yes-man") modified the position, saying all that was wanted was "the principle that the question could be discussed," a position totally at variance with Wilson's plain instructions, which Churchill called "a formula in a matter of life and death."

TWO OPPOSING VIEWS

On March 30, I talked separately with Colonel House and Admiral Benson. These extracts from my Diary show how wide apart were two of Wilson's advisers:

"Long talk with Col. House. In that, as in all his whispered conversations, he prefaced what he thought was important with his stock phrase—"Between you and me and the angels"—I never heard any fluttering of angel wings! He thought we could afford to have no program of Naval construction now if others would do likewise.

"Long talk with Benson who thought we could not agree to any limitation on building. If any nation has preponderance of Naval strength, it will have undue weight."

WILSON WOULD MAKE NO AGREEMENT

Within a week I was back in Paris. When I called upon the President to ascertain the status of the situation, he was clear in his position, and after a brief discussion said—and I wrote the words down in his presence to be sure of no error: "Please say you have seen the President and have found him deeply concerned about the whole method with which the entire peace program is being handled and that you have been instructed by the President to say that he cannot make any sort of agreement until he sees what the outcome is going to be."

That was the afternoon of Monday, April 7, 1919. The American-British Naval battle of Paris was ended. It had been nerve-racking while it lasted. Soon to be the guest in Great Britain of the British Government, I found Long gracious and courteous. And no reference whatever was made again in our talks of any agreement upon Navy building. It remained for a future administration to scrap the capital ships Wilson refused to scrap. Thereafter in a pleasant interview with Long I told him the determination at which the President had arrived. He said, "The matter being in the hands of our chiefs, we have no other duty in connection with it." We turned to a discussion of the time when the American Naval party would reach England in pursuance of the invitation tendered by the Government.

April 13. 1919

My Dear Mr. President:—

I cannot leave the city without a word which is the result of my impressions after seeing people from half a dozen countries. In Paris one is apt to forget that the people of the world are as sincere and as eager for a settlement will prevent future wars as they seemed this feeling when you first came over. But back home, though now unexpressed, they are looking to you with a dumb faith. I have felt this atmosphere though sometimes enwrapped in an atmosphere of covet, grab and defiing to hold on to old order. I know your devotion to the ideal that brought you over cannot waver, but thought you would like to know that I have sensed the feeling of hope in you — a hope not of today only but of all the future. That knowledge must give you comfort and strength for the last days of the ordeal. Our people at home, in spite of lack of vision and small politics and junkerism are in accord and grateful for your righteous leadership.

With my warm regards to Mrs. Wilson.

Sincerely,
Josephus Daniels

I hope a high court will try the Kaiser and let it fix the punishment

Admiral Benson has my address and you can reach me any time before I sail if desired.

Facsimiles of letters written in Paris
by Josephus Daniels to President Wilson

Apr. 14. 1919.

My dear Mr. President :—

If it finally determined to sink or beach the German Navy I earnestly hope it may be agreed that the action will be joint and that there will be no division of the spoil, leaving one nation to sink or the other to keep as may be decided. The moral lesson, much more than Lloyd George's "ostentatious sinking" will be of tremendous significance to the whole world. I happen to know that able French naval leaders believe the ships that would fall to France would be a liability instead of an asset. To divide and then debate whether to sink or not, or for some to hold and some to sink, lessens the dramatic lesson of the Peace Conferences resolve to reduce armament. The more spectacular it is made the better. Division is bad. Unified action is the answer.

Sincerely yours,

Josephus Daniels

THE SOUL OF HOSPITALITY

Mr. Long then told me of the arrangements made for our party in England, and invited any suggestions that would be agreeable while he was our host. He outlined the plans of the visit and, from the moment I had given him the message from President Wilson until he bade us a cordial good-bye after a week of royal entertainment in England and Scotland, no reference was made by word or attitude to our rather hectic controversy in Paris. I was received, and our party, with as much courtesy as if I had followed Sims in playing second fiddle to Britain as to the merchant marine and the strength of our Navies.

THE BATTLE WAS A DRAW

The Navy Sea Battle in Paris over Naval strength was a draw. John Bull did not get from Uncle Sam his recognition of Britain's primacy or agreement to cease the construction of a Navy that would be the equal of the greatest in the world, or any let-up in the construction of a merchant marine which Wilson believed was essential both to enlargement of markets for American goods, and to the international trade that lay near his heart. And Wilson was unable to secure an acceptance of the second of his Fourteen Points by Britain which, with the aid of France and Italy, put it in cold storage.

However, with bull-dog tenacity, the British held on to their national religion—domination of the seven seas—and later in the Harding Administration, by pulling the wool over the eyes of American leaders who did not lead, won in Washington what they could not extort in Paris. By the terms of the inept Washington Conference the United States obtained a fake equality by scrapping giant dreadnaughts on the way to completion—exactly what Lloyd George vainly demanded in Paris—while it naïvely scrapped some blueprints. As if that backward step was not enough surrender, the succeeding administration quit building ships and let the American Navy fall into a poor second place and abandoned the American doctrine for which it went to war in 1812 and to secure which the Sea Battle of Paris was fought to procure acceptance of the second of Wilson's Fourteen Points, framed in these all-embracing words:

"Absolute freedom upon the seas, outside territorial waters, alike in peace and in war, except as the seas may be closed in

whole or in part by international action for the enforcement of
international covenant."

FREEDOM OF THE SEAS—SINE QUA NON OF PEACE

Aside from the Declaration of Independence and Bill of Rights,
the doctrine of Freedom of the Seas is the oldest and most cherished
American policy. The War of 1812 was waged against "the senile
arrogance of the English ruling classes of that day" because of British
impressment of American seamen. The main reason why we entered
the World War in 1917 was to uphold the Freedom of the Seas
denied by the Germans, whose Emperor assumed to lay down lanes
of the sea where American ships might sail without U-boat attack.
Our country had protested against British interference earlier with
its export commerce. But ruthless sinkings by U-boats and the
German assumption to be Lord of the Seas carried Uncle Sam into
the war. The right of free seas could not be surrendered, and Germany found in defeat that her disregard of that cherished doctrine
proved her undoing.

The difference between the two English-speaking nations is and
has been that Uncle Sam demanded Freedom of the Seas for himself and all others, while the British have sought for Command of
the Seas. In January (1917) when Wilson was looking for "peace
without victory" he placed its basis on free peoples and free seas.
He was voicing the supreme purpose of America before we entered
the war and he declared for "an universal association of the nations
to maintain the inviolate security of the Highway of the Seas for
the common and unhindered use of all nations." He added, "the
paths of the sea must alike in law and in fact be free. The Freedom
of the Seas is the *sine qua non* of peace, equality, and coöperation."

From that conviction Wilson never departed. It was the second
of his Fourteen Points. Britain accepted all the others but wished
that to be deleted. When British leaders opposed Wilson's second
point, Sir Henry Wilson's Diary had this: "Everyone angry and
contemptuous of Wilson."

Lloyd George in his Memoirs says that Britain did not regard any
of Wilson's Fourteen Points as being at variance with the Allies
except in respect to the Freedom of the Seas, and "it constituted
no part of the official policy of the Alliance." Not only did Lloyd
George and the British Admiralty resolve that Wilson's "Freedom

of the Seas" should not prevail, but Winston Churchill took the same position. Shortly after the Armistice, Churchill said he favored the League of Nations "but it was no substitute for the supremacy of the British Fleet." Viscount Grey (December 12) made the delphic utterance that the League "would afford the solution of the freedom of the seas question."

Not only did Britain, aided by an agreement with European Allies, oppose Wilson's belief that the "Freedom of the Seas is the *sine qua non* of peace," but she was able to sidetrack it at the Paris Conference.

BRYCE ON DANIELS' STATEMENT

Admiral Sims had written me I was not very popular in England because of my advocacy of a great American merchant marine and the most powerful Navy in the world. In December (1918) this attitude was expressed by James Bryce to M. Storey. He said, in part:

"Some little feeling has been aroused here by what has been said, partly by newspaper correspondents, purporting to represent his views, and partly by indiscreet utterances on the part of Daniels and an Admiral. British opinion is naturally sensitive on the subject of the Navy. There is no reason why the relative strength of the United States Navy and ours should be dragged into this question at present. We have no sort of suspicion of the American Navy, nor need America have any suspicion of ours, so that the question ought to be settled without any friction. . . ."

THE POSITIONS CONTRASTED

In their authoritative work, *Freedom of the Seas,* Lieutenant Commander Kenworthy, M.P., and George Young, said:

"At the Washington Five-Power Conference in 1921 and the Geneva Three-Power Naval Conference in 1927, the British protagonists of sea domination adopted a pose which, if taken literally, means that only the British Empire has an interest in the Command of the Seas for its commerce and that no other nation's maritime interests are of any account. In the third decade of the twentieth century this position is untenable. In short, today, however loudly the British Lion may roar that Britannia rules the waves—

" 'Yet I have heard upon a distant shore
    Another Lion give a lordly roar,
    And the first one thought the last—a bore.' "

Per contra, Admiral Benson and the American Naval Advisory
Staff in Paris in an elaborate, confidential report setting forth the
American position of equality of Navies of Britain and the United
States, prepared for President Wilson, closed with:

"It is not believed, however, that any competition in arma-
ments is necessary. Once the principle of two equal naval
Powers ... is made clear to our own people and to the British
public, a means will be found to maintain a parity of the fleets
with the minimum of burden to the tax-payer."

UNCLE SAM OUT-TRADED AT WASHINGTON AND GENEVA

I have always thought that Hughes and others who acclaimed at
the Washington Conference (1921) the 5-5-3 ratio as a long step to
peace (fatal error!), believed that if equality in dreadnaughts was
obtained between the two English-speaking nations a great advance
was made. There was no restriction on total tonnage or numbers
as to cruisers and auxiliaries though their size was limited to 10,000
tons and their calibre to 8-inch. The ink was hardly dry on the pact
before some of the parties began rapidly to build cruisers and auxiliary craft, while the United States, holding to the spirit of the agreement, saw itself slipping back in Naval strength.

When Uncle Sam agreed to a fake "parity," Britain got what it
sought in Paris, and Japan was well pleased. Lieutenant Commander
Kenworthy truly wrote in 1928:

"Lord Balfour stretched his legs. Lord Beatty closed his eyes,
and Admiral Kako looked mo:: than ever like a benign Buddha.
The Japanese were allowed to keep their darling *Musto* for
whose construction patriotic Japanese ladies had sacrificed their
jewels. The British were allowed to build their *Rodney* and
Nelson, the most powerful the world has ever seen."

No wonder satisfied Balfour said the Conference had established
"a landmark in human civilization" and Beatty said it had "made
idealism a practical proposition," and Lord Lee rejoiced that "it
had changed the prospect of naval war into a promise of naval
peace." And President Harding and his associates believed they had

wrought better for peace than at Versailles, and Harding predicted that his much-vaunted "association of nations would meet yearly to make war impossible."

Uncle Sam's Navy had scrapped its *North Carolina, Washington,* and *West Virginia,* far advanced to completion. It remained for Franklin Roosevelt to build greater ships bearing the names that were sacrificed to a parity that was not achieved. While Uncle Sam took a recess in building, having lost his Naval shirt, "the British Admiralty embarked on an extensive building program" and Japan did likewise. The British believed that "by the grace of God and President Harding Britannia may still rule the waves."

Later, seeing they had been out-traded in Washington, our Navy people sought at Geneva (1927) for equality in cruisers, and Lord Cecil favored it, but the conference "broke down." President Coolidge said, "We were granted much coöperation by Japan, but we were unable to come to any agreement with Great Britain." Kenworthy commented that Winston Churchill was "the villain of the piece," and Lord Cecil "the victim," and Uncle Sam returned home empty-handed. When far-sighted men in Britain and America, like Cecil and Wilson, sought to unite the two English-speaking nations by recognizing equality on the seas, narrow British propagandists were preaching: "The Yanks are plotting to rob us of the Command of the Seas that is the Bond of Empire, the bulwark of our liberties and the basis of an economic existence." And in the United States similar isolationists were pulling the lion's tail and whooping up hatred in Britain.

BRITAIN DEMANDED PERMANENT SUPERIORITY

In his admirable book *The Drafting of the Covenant* David Hunter Miller has a chapter, "A Proposed Naval Agreement," containing correspondence between Robert Cecil, Colonel House, and Lloyd George, which throws light on the attempt of Britain to secure American approval of Britain's demand for recognition of its right to supremacy of the seas. In Cecil's letter to House he said that "recent utterances by high officials of the United States Navy have produced a very unfortunate impression." He was referring to my statement and that of Admiral Benson that the United States would not consent to conceding that any nation should have a stronger Navy than Uncle Sam. Cecil said:

"It has been now for centuries past an article of faith with every British statesman that the safety of the country depends upon her ability to maintain her sea defense. If I were British Minister of the Navy and I saw that British Naval strength was being threatened even by America I should have to recommend to my fellow countrymen to spend their last shilling in bringing up our fleet to the point I was advised it was necessary for safety."

Directed by our Peace Commission to draft a reply, Mr. Miller after giving statistics as to Naval strength said:

"As a result of the war, the enormous increase in the British fleet and the ending of the German fleet has created a situation where the British naval strength is out of proportion to any question of defense. That strength is now greater than the strength of all the other navies of the world together ... That situation is not healthy."

And Lloyd George was not only demanding acquiescence in Naval superiority in the future, but was trying to trade for our acceptance of it Britain's willingness to have the Monroe Doctrine inserted as an article in the League Covenant!

The British proposition, which Benson and I fought in "the Battle of Paris" was that the United States should scuttle its program of construction already authorized by Congress and leave Britain with a Naval strength "greater than all other navies in the world." I thought, and told President Wilson, that the proposal was "the impudence of impotence and the impotence of impudence." We never lowered our flag of equality. Our proposal that, with the smooth working of the League of Nations, we would stand for equality of the Navies of the English speaking nations, was rejected by the British spokesmen. They demanded an agreement of superiority for their country and inferiority for us—something we would not even consider for an instant.

XXXVI

NAVY OFFICIALS IN EUROPE

WITH MY WIFE, the three Admirals, Griffin, Taylor, and Earle, Chiefs of Engineering, Construction, and Ordnance, my Aide, Captain P. W. Foote, Secretary John B. May, and the ever-faithful butler Robert Gaines, we sailed from New York on the *Leviathan*. The only time I ever felt an obligation to the Kaiser was when my wife and I were quartered in the luxurious suite which he had ordered built on that ship. There was nothing like it on any liner in the world for magnificence. Having been under a long strain without a day's vacation for nearly two years, I did not realize that I was nearly all in until the ship left the dock in New York. Immediately after an early dinner I went to sleep in the Kaiser's quarters and didn't wake up until the next afternoon at five o'clock! I slept twelve hours a day on the voyage and caught up on much loss of sleep. The ship was taking Ambassador Morgenthau, Dr. Welch, Dr. Best and other distinguished physicians to Europe, and that company and the ship's personnel made the voyage more than agreeable. There was no part of the ship I did not inspect and no quarters of the crew I did not visit. I found a brief sea voyage better than a long vacation.

"ON THE BELL"

En route to Europe I was interested in every part of the great ship and one day took my turn heaving coal into the bunkers. It was a coal burner and consumed so much coal that I was drafted as a stoker. As my reward I was presented with a mammoth shovel like the one I used, bearing this bronze tablet:

> U. S. S. LEVIATHAN
> Hon. Josephus Daniels,
> Secretary of The Navy,
> Covered this Fire "On the
> Bell" on the 12-4 P.M. Watch

18 Mar. 1919, Making Passage
Hoboken, New Jersey, To
Brest, France

As I tried my prentice hand on every Naval activity I was glad to be "On the Bell." I still have the shovel, but as Navy ships now use oil, I am not called upon to coal ship.

FIRST SALUTE TO STARS AND STRIPES

As we neared Brest it was pointed out that we were not far from Quiberon Bay where the American flag received its first salute from a foreign power. It was on February 14, 1778, and John Paul Jones's U.S.S. *Ranger* received a salute of nine guns from Admiral La Motte Picquet, after Jones had fired a salute of thirteen guns to the French fleet in the Bay. This was the first acknowledgment of American Independence in Europe. The historic incident is commemorated in a famous marine painting by Edward Moran and is in the National Museum in Washington. As our nearness recalled the salute, we turned our faces toward the Bay and felt like saying, "We are here, Rochambeau."

NO BATHTUBS IN BREST

Arriving at Brest (March 23) I felt I had sailed out of one century into another. We were entertained by Admiral Moreau, Prefect Maritime, and gracious Madame Moreau. The building occupied by Admiral Moreau had been little changed since the days of Napoleon, and, while the entertainment was elegant, modern conveniences had not been installed. It was necessary to walk through a long hall to get to the bathroom, the tub being set up in the middle of a large room. I heard a story indicating the difference between the French and the Americans. Upon his arrival to enter upon duty in Brest, where he knew he would be for some time, a Naval officer rented from a Frenchman a house which contained no toilets or baths. He asked the owner if he might install these facilities, which he regarded as necessary comforts. "Yes," said the owner, "you may install them at your own expense, but it must be denominated in the lease that you shall remove them when you leave." When the time came to return to America, the officer, having spent a large sum in installing the plumbing, said to the owner, "I will make you a present of this installation." To which the owner replied, "No, you will not. You remove them every one from my house."

IT RAINED EVERY DAY AT PONTANEZEN

The moment of our arrival, the strenuous and entertaining trip to Europe began. First of all, of course, we visited the camp at Ponta-nezen, commanded by General Smedley Butler, where my son was on duty. This camp was the center through which most American soldiers entered France and embarked from France for the United States after the war. Through Pontanezen there passed 225,000 men per month. This fort had existed from the days of Napoleon. It early got a bad reputation with the troops. It was small. General Butler enlarged it and did a monumental work in making it as near ideal for its purposes as possible. It rains every day in Brest and when Butler arrived at Pontanezen the walks and roadways were nearly knee-deep in mud. He introduced buckboards, which were placed in lieu of pavements all over the camp. When these were being placed in position, with General Butler in the lead doing the actual work of placing the temporary makeshift for pavements, a visiting officer asked, "What is going on? I want to see the General." Butler, leading the working force, said, "I am the General." The man replied, "The hell you are. Nobody ever saw a General doing any work." But he did not know Butler. We went to a reception at the Naval Officers' Club in Brest; I spoke at the Y.M.C.A. hut; and in the evening we attended an official banquet given by Admiral Moreau.

FIRST DAYS IN PARIS

Reaching Paris on March 25, my wife and son were very much astounded when, as we entered the Ritz, a tall and distinguished gentleman welcomed me as if I were a long-lost friend, giving me what the Mexicans would call an *abrazo*.

"Who is your old friend?" my son asked.

"That is Lord Balfour," I replied. We had been much together when he visited Washington upon our declaration of war, and Balfour having been the First Lord of the Admiralty we had many things in common. I had heard much of his cold dignity and was astounded and gratified at the warmth of his greeting.

I was not long in Paris after paying the courtesy calls to the Minister of Marine, M. Georges Leygues (he had married a South

Carolinian), and Admiral du Bon, before I was rudely awakened to a situation in the American Peace Commission which was to have many unpleasant repercussions in the days to come. Going to the Hotel Crillon, where the American Commission and officials were housed, I made my first call on Colonel Edward M. House. I was greeted by his son-in-law and secretary, Mr. Gordon Auchincloss. He said that Colonel House would be in later. After a short chat I asked Mr. Auchincloss where I would find Secretary Lansing as I wished to call on him. I was greatly disturbed, and perhaps annoyed, when he replied, "Why call on Lansing? Nobody in Paris pays any attention to him. Wait and see Colonel House. He is the man that all Paris looks to in the peace negotiations." At that time I interpreted this remark more as a son-in-law's admiration than as a statement of how Colonel House might feel. House invited me to luncheon. The conversation was chiefly about my contemplated trip to England, and he spoke about the necessity of carrying on in peace times the same close coöperation with the British that had characterized the two Navies during the war. He gave no intimation that he was not in harmony with Wilson on the League of Nations.

LANSING NOT IN ACCORD WITH WILSON

I was to have another shock a little later when my wife and I were invited to dine quietly with Secretary and Mrs. Lansing, and the Secretary told me—I thought confidentially—that President Wilson was making a great mistake in not negotiating a peace treaty and leaving the matter of an organization of the League of Nations to some future time. I had not then seen Wilson, but I knew just as well as if I had talked with him that he put the League first of all. I told Lansing I thought Wilson was right.

That night I wrote in my Diary:

"Lansing discussed at length upon his fear that Wilson was making a big mistake. He said:

" 'You will not be here long before you will find much intrigue and conflicting interests between the representatives of the allied nations. The longer the conference goes on, the deeper those differences and the more difficult it will be to effect an agreement. Wilson insists that the League of Nations shall be incorporated as an integral part of the Treaty of Paris. He is wrong. The wise policy is to agree upon the terms of a peace treaty and postpone the consideration of the League to a more convenient season.'

"Lansing elaborated that suggestion and showed he was at wide variance with what I knew was the heart's desire of W. W. I expressed the opinion, saying I had just arrived and my knowledge was limited, that unless the League of Nations was made a part of the Peace Treaty there would never be any League."

These two incidents, showing a situation of disharmony beneath the surface in the Peace Commission, did not at that time indicate the future rupture between Wilson and his two appointees. Regarding these statements as confidential I passed them over. I knew in Washington that while Lansing and House might not always agree with Wilson, they made him think they did and I did not suppose they would take any action in any matter except in accordance with the known wishes of the President. I thought this would be repeated in Paris. I had not then learned that there was a disease prevalent in Paris to which people gave the name "Parisitis," meaning that many heads swelled at that Peace Conference. It proved that Wilson's old maxim was right, to wit:

"Something happens to every man who is called into public position—his head either grows or swells."

I learned in my first days in Paris what had happened to Lansing and House.

ONE-EYED ADMIRAL AND OPERA

Having never really seen Grand Opera my wife and I were pleased to accept an invitation from the French government to attend the opera *Henry VIII,* escorted by Admiral Andrew Long, of North Carolina, who was our Naval Attaché in Paris. He was a bachelor, and the next day an American lady said, "I see that you went to the opera last night with your one-eyed Admiral." I replied that I went with Andrew Long who had two perfectly good eyes. "You may think so," she replied, "but in Paris they all call him the one-eyed Admiral. Why? Because when he takes one lady out to dinner, he only gives her one eye using the other eye to try to charm a good-looking lady at an adjoining table. So we call him the one-eyed Admiral."

At the opera Admiral Benson, who would have been called straitlaced in Paris, was so shocked at the near nakedness of the actresses and the risqué remarks, that he expressed his condemnation in most vigorous terms to my wife and myself and urged all our party to leave the opera. He said it was a disgrace for respectable people to remain to be offended by such indecency. I quite shared his feeling but told him that as we were the guests of the French government we could not do anything that would show discourtesy.

CALLED "GUZZLER" BY PARIS MAGAZINE

I found when introduced to Navy men that I was better known as the Secretary who had made the Navy dry—"run on water"— than as the Secretary who had secured legislation to make the American Navy the strongest in the world. Why did I issue the Wine Mess Order? A Paris magazine purported to give the answer. It said that someone asked the Secretary of the Navy why he had issued it, and he replied, "Well, you know, when I was a young man, I was a great soak!" It said that I knew the evils of drink from experience! And that therefore I had issued the order to save men from my own fate! And in a footnote there was appended the French for "wine-bibber, guzzler and drunkard."

I sent the article to my son at the University of North Carolina saying, "Here's an article written by somebody in France about your father. I wish you would translate it and send it to me." He did so and wrote an indignant letter suggesting that I write to the editor of that paper and threaten him with a libel suit unless he retracted his statement! And I wrote back to the boy and told him that many worse things had been said about me, and some of them true. I showed a copy of my son's letter to Ambassador Sharp, who had served in Congress and was an old friend of mine. He called it to the attention of the editor. Shortly I received a handsome letter from the editor saying that in the next issue he would correct the error. It proved that I was not as great a "soak" as I was supposed to be.

LUNCHING WITH PRESIDENT AND MRS. WILSON

When, not long after I had talked with House and Lansing, my wife and I lunched with President and Mrs. Wilson, who made their home in Paris at Prince Murat's residence, the President told me of some of the delicate situations that had arisen in the Peace Conference, but if he knew the real feeling of House and Lansing he did not disclose it. I, feeling that Lansing had spoken in confidence, did not feel at liberty to warn Wilson that Lansing might not be loyal in his support.

As usual, Wilson interspersed serious talk with quaintness. He was still on a diet, following his serious illness, and telling us with a hearty laugh of the rigid regimen he had been on, he said that a lady who lived near by, hearing that he must have fresh eggs every day and knowing they were not easy to obtain in Paris, very kindly agreed to supply the need. "I will come over and lay a fresh egg on your table every morning," she said.

Before the luncheon, Wilson said, "While Mrs. Wilson shows your wife the establishment, let me show you where I live." Taking me to his bedroom he said, "Here is the big refrigerator where I sleep." It was very cold. "And now let me show you the strangest bathroom you ever saw." It was large, evidently built many years ago. Around it was a gallery. "Do you suppose the bathers had an audience who were placed so they could see the movements of the party in the tub?" he asked. I suggested that perhaps it was for an orchestra so that the bather might be lulled with sweet music while the ablutions were performed. I remarked that I had recently read that a distinguished writer of his time had been said to spend much of his time in his bathtub because he could think better there than anywhere else. "Perhaps getting nearer to the naked truth," Wilson said.

At the luncheon he told us some of the highlights of the Peace Conference, and graphically appraised the characteristics of the Big Four. He said he asked Lloyd George why in the December elections he had promised that if his government was returned to power he would hang the Kaiser and make the Germans pay the entire cost of the war, shilling for shilling. "Mr. Lloyd George's answer was characteristic of him," Wilson remarked. The Welshman had replied: "It was well for me that the election came as early as it did; otherwise I might have had to promise more." He liked Lloyd George, particularly the quickness of his perception, the sprightliness of his mind, and his fund of quips and stories. "He is more like an American than any other man in Europe," he remarked.

MEETING OF PEACE CONFERENCE

Attending a plenary session of the Peace Conference (April 11) we were struck with its world composition. Lloyd George, pointing out the varied costumes, some in the style before Caesar, said the languages were as different as the dress. I quote from my Diary:

"Session held in magnificent chamber of the Foreign Office. Clemenceau presided. Wilson and Lloyd George on either side. Mr. Barnes, Labor member of British Parliament, prefaced resolutions by an address depicting conditions and menace to men who labor who had never had their rights. He said better conditions and steady employment must be provided. Among other speakers a Belgian delegate said the choice is between the quick method of Russia or the slower method of Britain and his country had chosen the latter.

"Wilson, expressing regret at the enforced absence of Mr. Gompers, said the Labor Committee's Regulation depends on the Peace League and is fashioned on League of Nations lines. He invited the labor conference, of which Gompers is President, to hold its first conference in Washington in October."

THE DYNAMIC "OLD TIGER"

In Paris I had my cherished desire of a talk with M. Clemenceau, head of the French government and President of the Peace Conference. The "Old Tiger" had all the vigor and charm I had expected to see after following his dynamic course during the war. Of course, he did not confide to me any of the inside discussions of the Peace Conference, but he did not hesitate to speak of the necessity of keeping Germany down if we expected no future wars with that country. He spoke in the highest terms of Wilson and his ideals, but I did not fail to gather that he thought Wilson was too idealistic. This attitude called to my mind what a friend had told me the day before. He said that somebody asked Clemenceau how he was getting along in the Council of the Big Four and he replied, "What can a mere French Minister do when associated with Lloyd George who thinks he is Napoleon Bonaparte and Woodrow Wilson who thinks he is Jesus Christ?"

Clemenceau said to Wilson: "Why do you insist upon your Fourteen Points when the good God gave only Ten Commandments?"

Wilson answered: "If you will guarantee that we can carry out the Ten Commandments at the Peace Conference I will be only too willing to give up my Fourteen Points."

Though the "Old Tiger" could not share Wilson's vision and faith in universal peace, he expressed the same appreciation of American valor in France's darkest hour, as he later said in his quaint fashion to Stephen Bonsal:

"I love Americans better than any other people save my very own. 'Why?'—Because you are so very young and amusing."

"And then he added very seriously,

"And because when we were within two fingers of disaster you came and saved my gray hairs from knowing defeat and disaster."

After he was eighty-two years old Clemenceau wrote his voluminous autobiography and a philosophical book to be published after his death as his "literary legacy to posterity." He wrote in his own handwriting explaining his plans and how he worked after the French ungratefully retired him. Clemenceau said:

"I shall spend two years redrafting the first volume, then work eight or ten years on two other volumes. After that I shall rest and grow old....
"I am in bed every night before eight o'clock. I wake up about three or four in the morning, do some light gymnastic exercises, such as I have done all my life, then go to work by the light of the kerosene lamp. This morning I got up at one o'clock and worked until half past four, then went back to bed again.
"How do I keep so well? I eat little and exercise moderately. I sleep as much as I need, work no more than I want to, and, above all, I don't worry. I am one of the few men in the world who is free—absolutely free. I see only the people I want to see. I don't read newspapers any more and pay little attention to the world."

Webb Miller, who exacted a promise of an interview when Clemenceau was a hundred, quotes him as saying: "That's a definite promise. And I am going to live that long, too. I am too tough to die." Miller appraised him:

"He died an embittered old man with a canker in his breast because his enemies had snatched from him the presidency of the republic, upon which he had set his heart. Among all the figures produced by the war, Clemenceau was to me the most colorful and picturesque. His whole life had been stormy, and the tranquillity of his last years did not suit him. There was none of the post-war, mealy-mouthed hypocrisy in him. He knew there were no morals in international relations and did not pretend that there were. A grand character, but one I should not like to have had for an enemy."

After seeing Clemenceau I made an official call on President Poincaré and visited the Chambre des Députés. Previously in the day my wife and I lunched with Ambassador and Madame Jusserand with whom we had formed friendly relations in Washington.

NEVER HEARD OF PASTEUR

The Minister of Marine assigned, as our guide, philosopher, and friend, a delightful Naval officer who seemed to take pleasure in showing us everything in Paris that he thought we might like to see. He said, "Tomorrow morning I will take you to see the tomb of Napoleon. Is there anything else you are particularly interested in that I have not shown you?" I told him that I would like to go to the tomb of Pasteur. He had never heard of Pasteur and said he would have to look into it and find out if there were a tomb and if so, where it was. I reflected that there was nothing he did not know about Napoleon, his tomb, his history, the glory of his conquest. This was an evidence that in spite of its republicanism, the worship of military genius stood far higher in France than the appreciation of the greatness of one who had saved lives. Finally, he found the location of Pasteur's modest tomb. We stood reverently before it reflecting that whereas Napoleon was honored because he had conquered by killing men, Pasteur was enshrined in the hearts of men all over the world as a great healer.

TOMB OF IMMORTALS

Next to my desire to see the tomb of Pasteur was my wish—perhaps greater—to see where John Paul Jones was buried and the tomb of LaFayette. No mark showed where Jones was buried. When we visited the tomb of LaFayette and his son, George Washington, I found that Wilson had sent a wreath having on a card these words:

Above, Secretary and Mrs. Daniels en route to France on the *Leviathan.* With them, *left to right,* are Admirals Taylor, Griffin, and Earle, and other members of the Secretary's staff. *Below,* First Salute to the Stars and Stripes. En route to France, the Secretary of the Navy's party sailed near Quiberon Bay, where, on February 14, 1778, the first salute was given to the American flag in foreign waters, and, looking toward that historic spot, they saluted and said, "We're here, De Grasse and Rochambeau!" (National Geographic Society).

LEAVING BREST FOR PARIS
Secretary and Mrs. Daniels and their host, Admiral Moreau, French Naval head at Brest.

"To the great LaFayette
"From a fellow servant of liberty.
"Woodrow Wilson"

PADEREWSKI AND POLAND

In some respects Paderewski, because of his personality and his mission, was a leading figure in Paris during the Peace Conference. I shared with Wilson the hope for an independent Poland.

I never saw Ignace Paderewski until he called at my office in the Navy Department during the World War to request coöperation to help his suffering countrymen in Poland. With eloquent words on his tongue and tears in his eyes, he related the story of the dismemberment of his country as if it were a fresh tragedy, and the present hopes and needs of his countrymen. With an audience of one, he was as much moved as if he were speaking to a multitude. He opened his heart to me and from that moment I was an ardent advocate of the ambition of the Poles. Again I saw him at the White House when he was entertained by the President and Mrs. Wilson. His playing moved Wilson—he played nothing but Chopin—and his presentation of his hopes for his native land converted Wilson to the cause of Poland.

At the President's request in 1916, Paderewski had worked steadily thirty-six hours to prepare a memorandum of the Polish question. Two weeks later, having fully digested the memorandum, in a speech to Congress on January 22, 1917, the President made his first declaration of what should follow the close of the war, saying: "I take it for granted that statesmen everywhere are agreed that there shall be a united independent and autonomous Poland."

When Wilson announced his Fourteen Points, the thirteenth called for a reunited Poland. In Paris he obtained from a commission of special experts data to strengthen his case. And he needed all the resources to aid Poland, for Lloyd George was cold to the proposition at first. But Paderewski's charm won the Welshman. Clemenceau was not favorable. Wilson took the laboring oar and but for his determination the autonomous country of Poland might not have been reborn.

"The long-haired man who embraced you must have been your long-lost brother," said my Aide, who had never seen such an affectionate meeting between men as when Paderewski and I met for the first time in Paris. "Our hearts and hopes are united in hope for an independent Poland," I replied, "and we have had a common dream since 1916. He loves music but he loves his country more than his mastery of melody."

Paderewski had been commissioned by Pilsudski to become Prime Minister, Foreign Secretary, and his country's delegate to the Peace Conference in Paris. He poured out his money freely to feed his people until his speech to Wilson caused the President to send Hoover with food to the Poles. When I lunched with him, Wilson said:

"I wish you could have heard Paderewski's speeches for his country. They compared with Patrick Henry's famous 'Give me liberty or give me death,' and I could understand how the self-contained Jefferson was so moved as to light a fire of liberty in his heart that was never extinguished. I knew Paderewski was a master of harmony, but as we heard his eloquent appeals for his country I felt that it was in victory that he had touched chords more sublime than when he moved thousands as he commanded harmony from the piano."

When the Versailles Treaty was signed on June 28, 1919, I wondred which was the happier—Wilson, who had inspired it and led in securing it, or Paderewski, who saw in it the rebirth of his homeland.

Years afterward—when Paderewski was entertained by me in my home—I learned the story of how differences of opinion between Paderewski and Polish leaders had caused him to resign. The terrible days of 1920 in Poland had so distressed him that for a time he had no heart to return to his art. After representing his country in the first session of the League of Nations at Geneva and seeing Poland rise from its ashes, he responded to the call of music lovers. In 1923 he made a tour of the United States. It was on such a tour that he came to Raleigh. We invited a group of one hundred of the teachers and lovers of music to meet him. Before the evening closed, I requested him to favor the company on our piano. He did so with great courtesy, but I learned afterwards that he had to break a rule that he would play only on his own instrument. My wife always afterwards felt that because Paderewski's fingers had evoked almost divine harmony from its keys in music of his own composition, "The Polish Fantasy," among other selections, our piano had a sacredness.

TABLET TO JEFFERSON UNVEILED

During my stay in Paris I had the honor of taking part in the Jefferson Day Centennial exercises, April 12, at the corner of the Rue de Berri and the Avenue des Champs-Elysées. The Overseas Alumni of the University of Virginia had placed a tablet of marble and bronze on the site where Jefferson resided between 1785 and 1789 when he served his country as Minister Plenipotentiary to France.

General Jefferson Randolph Kean, a lineal descendant of Jefferson, presented the tablet which bears this inscription:

On This Site Resided
THOMAS JEFFERSON
United States Minister to France
1785-1789
President of the United States
1801-1809
Author of the Declaration of American
Independence
Founder of the University of Virginia
Placed, April, 1919, by
University of Virginia Alumni
Serving in the World War
Commemorating the Hundredth
Anniversary of the Founding
of the University.

Lieutenant Commander Charles O. Maas, Assistant Naval Attaché of the American Embassy, was the Master of Ceremonies, and addresses were made by General Kean; M. Chassaigne-Goyon, President du Conseil Municipal; Major Armistead H. Dobie, Professor of law, University of Virginia; M. Lucien Poincaré, Vice-Recteur de l'Université de Paris; William G. Sharp, Ambassador of the United States to France; and Josephus Daniels, Secretary of the Navy. It was an impressive occasion. The biting cold of that afternoon could not affect the evidences of patriotic emotion by Americans and Frenchmen who thronged the avenue. The addresses, which almost made those present—a large gathering—forget the cold, have been preserved in the *Bulletin* of *the University of Virginia,* July, 1919. In part I said:

"When Mr. Jefferson reached Paris in 1785 as the newly accredited Minister to France, he was presented to Louis XVI by the Minister of the Foreign Office in these words: 'Mr. Jefferson comes to take the place of Mr. Franklin.' Before the King could extend greetings, Mr. Jefferson quietly said: 'I have come to succeed Mr. Franklin in the office he filled with such ability, but no man can take the place of Mr. Franklin.' This high and just appraisement and appreciation of his predecessor, friend, and co-worker in science as well as in public affairs, in keeping with the courtesy which ever marked the Sage of Monticello, was the beginning of a career in France which meant more for the understanding and sympathy between the French and American people than has been accomplished by any other American in all our history. Franklin and Jefferson set the high standard for American diplomats which many evidences show has been sustained by the distinguished Ambassador, Mr. Sharp, who returns to his own country after high service in this centre in these epoch-making days...."

FOUR COUNTRIES CLAIMED JOHN PAUL JONES

Shortly after we arrived in Paris I had called upon my old friend, Mr. Sharp, our American Ambassador to France. While I was visiting him at the Embassy, he spoke of the necessity of getting our troops home. He said that they were restless; that there were 40,000 men and 1,000 officers in Paris without leave. Many of the French had forgotten that but for us, the Kaiser and his nobles would be ruling France.

I was to learn of a modern application of the old saying that "When living, Homer begged his daily bread, but seven cities claimed him dead." It occurred this way. Ambassador Sharp gave a dinner for our party to which he invited the Minister of Marine of France and distinguished Naval officers and officials of allied countries. Lord Balfour was invited, having been Britain's First Lord of the Admiralty. Called upon for a toast in a speech at the dinner I expressed our great pleasure on being in France, and said that the whole world had been stirred by Pershing's statement on his arrival, "LaFayette, we are here." I recalled that it was Rochambeau's French ships which won a notable victory in the American Revolution; that we not only held LaFayette in lasting gratitude but quite as gratefully remembered Rochambeau. All the talk of French help in the Revolutionary War was of the illustrious LaFayette. I called attention to the fact that it was the French Navy under Rochambeau which insured the victory at Yorktown and that Washington had written Rochambeau:

"We have been contemporaries and fellow laborers in the cause of liberty, and we have lived together as brothers should do in harmonious friendship."

I related that when Sir Harry Lauder visited Washington during the war he told this story, which might interest Mr. Balfour:

"I was passing through Baltimore. An American who recognized me asked, 'Are you Mr. Harry L-O-W-D-E-R of Scotland?' I replied, 'I have no such damned German name. I am Harry L-A-U-D-E-R.' The gentleman then asked me, 'Mr. Lauder, what do you think the English Navy will do in this war?' I replied, 'Damn the English Navy. *Damn* the English Navy.'"

As I quoted that sentence I saw our Admirals sensed I had made a faux pas. Mr. Balfour showed astonishment, and I think my wife agreed with the Admirals because she gave me a wifely look of disapproval, and then after a pause I continued:

"But Mr. Lauder added, 'If you will ask me what the British Navy will do in this war, I will tell you they will make the same great record that has given the British Navy glory ever since the days of Nelson.'"

That relieved the tension. I then went on to say that the greatest thrill upon reaching France was to sail near Quiberon Bay, where in 1777 the French Navy had given the first salute to the American flag when John Paul Jones commanded the *Ranger*. I added that John Paul Jones was one of the greatest of American Admirals; he found a friendly home in France after his retirement, and his sepulchre was there. At that point Mr. Balfour interrupted me to say, "But, Mr. Secretary, you must remember John Paul Jones was an Englishman." I made no reply to Balfour but that incident furnished me with conversation when later I breakfasted with Lloyd George and visited Sir John MacLeod in Edinburgh.

When I told the story of Sir Harry Lauder and my reference to

John Paul Jones at the dinner at Ambassador Sharp's to Lloyd George he interrupted me, asking, "Did Mr. Balfour claim that John Paul Jones was an Englishman?" I said that he did. "Well, he is wrong," Lloyd George said, Welsh pride in his voice. "John Paul Jones was a Welshman." I replied I knew Balfour was wrong but it was far from me to correct a former Prime Minister of Great Britain.

That was not the end of a story of national claiming. When we were entertained at Edinburgh by Sir John MacLeod, I told him of my reference to John Paul Jones which caused Balfour to claim him as an Englishman, and how Lloyd George had proudly called him a Welshman, while I was insisting that he was a good American. Sir John exploded. With Scottish burr in his voice, "Do you mean to tell me Balfour claimed he was an Englishman?" "I do," I said. "And that Lloyd George claimed he was a Welshman?" "I do," I said. "Well, they were both wrong. John Paul Jones was born in Scotland. He was a Scotchman, sir," said Sir John with emphasis. I replied, "Sir John, I knew all along he was born in Scotland but did not feel called upon to correct two Prime Ministers of your country. You are right." And then I added, "It is very interesting and delightful to me to see that Balfour claims John Paul Jones an Englishman, Lloyd George claims him as a Welshman, and you claim him as a Scotchman, whereas when he was alive and pouring hot shot into the British Navy, all of your three countries united in calling John Paul Jones that 'damned American pirate.' I am glad to have lived to see the day when all the world hails John Paul Jones as a great Naval captain." And I added to Sir John that I had particular reason for gratification because this great Naval officer, born in Scotland, was named simply John Paul. But when he became an American he added the name of "Jones" in honor of a North Carolina friend who gave him refuge when the authorities were seeking him on the charge of killing a seaman.

FIUME DISRUPTED AMITY

On the day that Wilson, Lloyd George, and I were discussing the Naval problem, and the day on which I left for Rome in the afternoon, the Big Four were in the throes of the Fiume discussion. Wilson told me that Italy had no just claim to Fiume. When Italy made a condition of its going into the war on the side of the Allies, it did not ask for Fiume, and Wilson said it had no right, at this late day, to make a demand that threatened the amity of the Allies. Wilson was even more emphatic in saying that the peace of that part of the world demanded that Yugo-Slavia should have a port and that Italy should not object to Spalato's going to that new country. It was only a few days after this conversation that the papers announced Orlando would quit the conference and return to Rome.

On the afternoon of the day I left for Rome, returning to my hotel, I found Count Cellari, the Italian Ambassador to the United States, awaiting me. Our relations in Washington were on an excellent basis and he correctly regarded me as a good friend of his country. "I am glad you are going to my country," he said. "You will be received by our officials and government with every honor. A special car will be ready for you and your party at the border and you will be an honored guest of our government."

After an interchange of mutual regards he grew very serious and said that he feared something was about to take place which would disturb the friendly relations between our two countries. I have never talked to any man more moved and troubled. Literally with tears in his eyes he pleaded with me to see President Wilson and urge him to agree to Italy's claim to Fiume, and he made the appeal with genuine eloquence. He also stressed the necessity of the Big Four's giving Spalato to Italy and the wrong of awarding it to the new country of Yugo-Slavia then being born. "When you reach Rome," he said, "you will find how tense the situation is there. This is the only question that could separate our countries." He remained long with me, and his emotion and deep interest moved me. I asked myself whether Wilson was right in the rigid attitude he had taken.

Shortly after the Count left, Admiral Bullard, of our Navy, called. He had represented the Navy in Spalato and had just returned from Italy. I asked him about the situation. He described it, and was strong in criticism of the Italian position and deeply sympathetic with the aspirations of Yugo-Slavia. Admiral Niblack wrote (April 5) a long report on the situation to Wilson, agreeing with Admiral Bullard, and in his report he stated, "Italy is unfitted to be entrusted with the enslavement of the 750,000 Yugo-Slavs in Dalmatia. Fiume should be made a free port under allied control. The Italian intention is to kill it in a business way. The Yugo-Slavs have demonstrated their fitness for self-government."

I therefore went to Rome feeling that, backed up by the Navy men who had been on the job, Wilson could not recede from his position and fearing that Orlando would carry out his threat to leave Paris. I did not talk about Spalato or Fiume with any of the Italian authorities while in Rome, but when I went with Ambassador Page to call upon King Victor Emmanuel, the King referred to the Yugo-Slavs but not by name. "There are people in this part of the world," he said, "who have strange ways and I fear your President does not understand them. They will get angry today and kill a man in their ferocity. When they realize what they have done, they will be very sorry. Their sorrow will be genuine, too. They will weep over the tragedy. But in a week they will murder somebody else and again have real contrition. But it will not last." At the time the King was talking, I was not clear of whom he was speaking when he said "some people," but afterwards Ambassador Page told me, saying that the Italians held the people in the hinterland beyond Spalato in no high regard—quite the contrary.

In Rome Ambassador Page told me that the situation in Fiume was very serious, and later (April 17) he wrote to Colonel House:

"I question very much if Orlando's government would stand 24 hours after the Chamber meets here if he remains in the peace conference after Fiume's status should be settled unless it be given to Italy. Situation demands careful handling and handling that is sympathetic to Italy. Otherwise there will come a situation that will not be only serious but very serious indeed. The Italians will say that we have fought and suffered with others and have won with our arms a great victory. Now why should our allies side with our enemies against us and snatch the one chance that may ever be had to restore to Italy elements of the Italian race who have looked to us through the generations and have suffered so much because of their continued demand to be free? This is their argument and they are applying it to Fiume. I have heard Italy will not give up Fiume no matter what the conference in Paris should decide about it."

VISIT TO THE ETERNAL CITY

When our party reached Turin (April 2), we were received by an Italian Senator and Lieutenant Commander Sansoni, who escorted us to Rome on a special train. One of the anticipated pleasures of visiting Rome was to renew an old-time friendship with Thomas

Above, unveiling of plaque placed on Jefferson's Paris residence by University of Virginia, headed by Captain Charles O. Maas, seated at extreme right. Secretary Daniels is speaking. Ambassador Sharp sits next on the left. *Below,* Secretary Daniels in Paris, with Admiral Niblack (in background) in command of the Naval forces at Gibralter, and J. J. Jusserand, long-time Ambassador from France to the United States.

DYNAMIC PERSONALITIES AT THE PEACE CONFERENCE

Left, Ignace Jan Paderewski, who obtained for Poland official recognition by the various Powers. *Right,* David Lloyd George, who insisted on Britain's need for a larger Navy than the United States (Underwood & Underwood).

Nelson Page, the American Ambassador to Rome. This master of letters and charming raconteur, who embodies the best of what I love to think is Southern, early said to my wife, myself, and our party, "Do not let any guides take you in hand. My wife and I want to give ourselves the pleasure of showing you the things in Rome you will want to see." I don't suppose any visitors to Rome ever had such distinguished guides, who took us to every place worth seeing and wasted no time in general sight-seeing. Best of all, Page introduced us to Senator Lanciani, an Italian who was the greatest archaeologist and authority on the restoration of places of antiquity. With them we visited the Forum, the Coliseum, the Baths of Caracalli, St. Paul's and St. Peter's, and the National Museum. He arranged for us to take flights over the city and introduced us to the many friends he had made in Rome in his distinguished diplomatic service.

SOUTHERNERS FOREGATHERED

It gratified my wife and myself to see in what esteem Ambassador and Mrs. Page were held. At the Embassy he gave a banquet to which were invited the great officials of Rome. At the end of the very formal banquet after the other guests had left, he said to Admiral Taylor—a Virginian—and my wife and myself, "Mrs. Page and I have been pleased to have you tonight as the guests of the American Ambassador to Italy. Tomorrow night you three are to come and have dinner alone with Mrs. Page and me, and we will forget Rome, forget Europe, forget the United States, and think only of that God-given part of the world which we call Virginia and North Carolina. And we will have some old Virginia ham and hot biscuits, and as we talk about the things that are dearest to us we will be transported back home, forget there ever was a war, and fall back into Southern ways and Southern talk." That was the way in which he invited us, and if I should live a thousand years I can never forget that dinner or the charm of his conversation and that of his wife. She was born a "damnyankee" but you would never have believed it from the way she entered into the talk of "Old Virginia" led by Page and Taylor, both being F.F.V.'s.

BANQUET BY MARINE MINISTER (ADMIRAL DEL BONO)

The next night the Marine Minister gave a formal banquet at which I spoke, paying particular tribute to the Italian Naval constructor Cuniberti, who had designed the first dreadnaught. I was able, thanks to Admiral Taylor, to tell the Italians some things about the contribution of the Italian Navy to the war which pleased them greatly. At this dinner my wife had the place of honor next to the Minister. The next morning Ambassador Page asked my wife, "What did you do last night to charm the Marine Minister? His wife is of the most aristocratic of all the ancient Roman families. Her friends are exclusively of the old Romans. I have never known her to entertain any American visitor, but she is inviting you—the first American —to whom she has ever been hostess. Why? When the Minister went home last night and told her he had met the most charming woman who had ever visited Rome, she departed from her exclusiveness to meet the lady who had so attracted her husband." This pleased Page very much, and he often spoke about it. Afterwards when he returned to America he said, "Neither you nor I made so great an impression as Mrs. Daniels in Rome."

WHEN WILSON THREW KISSES

When we reached Rome the people were still talking about the triumphal welcome when Wilson visited it earlier in the year. I was told that the triumphal arches erected to honor him were emblazoned with texts from his writings that raised him almost to the heights of Deity itself. When with Mrs. Wilson he stood on the balcony of the Quirinal, uncounted thousands of Italians massed beneath them, he was lifted out of himself by the enthusiastic reception. He threw kisses to the multitude. "He will speak to us in front of the Victor Emmanuel monument," was the word which passed through the throng. A dense crowd of humanity ranged four deep to keep open the narrow lane for the coming of the President. All day the common people waited to hail him who they felt would be their deliverer.

But there was no speech and no opportunity for the eyes of the hungry to look into the face of the man they believed was their deliverer. The King and the leaders resented the fact that the President would be speaking over their heads to the people, and so the orders were given and the procession clattered past. There was a gasp of disappointment. But a few days later—Mr. Page did not tell me how it was arranged—Wilson went over the heads of the men in power with an appeal to the people not only of Italy but of the whole world in which he made a final restatement of the principle of self-determination against the methods of the old machinery of international negotiation, the give and take of the balance of power and the enslavement of little peoples.

When I reached Rome, there were only the echoes of that day in Rome when the enthusiasm of the people flamed highest in honor of the American President. American correspondents who witnessed it said that old Romans told them nothing comparable had been seen in Rome since Caesar and his legions returned after the conquest of Gaul. But now a great change had taken place. Wilson had opposed giving Fiume to Italy. Clemenceau and Lloyd George had side-stepped that responsibility. Wilson was willing to take the laboring oar, and from having worshipped him almost as a god, the Italians turned on him and forgot the day on the Quirinal. Italy, which had long been rent with factions, was again reunited. The nation responded to the cry against Wilson, and the massed thousands again stood in the plaza, this time to denounce him as the betrayer of Italy. Another example saying that the people always crucify their deliverers.

PRECEDENCE OF CHURCH OR STATE?

When our party reached Rome I was armed with two sets of letters of introduction which, if I had used upon the first day of my arrival, might have created an incident reminiscent of the time when Theodore Roosevelt was refused an audience with the Pope—presumably because before asking to visit the Vatican he had gone to the Methodist School in Rome. My letters looking toward a visit to the Vatican were from Cardinal Gibbons, of Baltimore, who as a young priest had lived in North Carolina and with whom I had long enjoyed friendly relations, and from Cardinal Hayes of New York, who had acted for the Catholic Church in selecting chaplains for the Army and Navy. I had also been commended to the Pope by Admiral Benson, Chief of Naval Operations, the most influential leader of the Knights of Columbus in the armed services. My other letters to church authorities were from Bishop Cranston, Resident Bishop of the Methodist Church in Washington, to the head of the Methodist School in Rome.

When Ambassador Thomas Nelson Page met our party and saw

us safely installed in the hotel, I informed him that I had these letters of introduction. The Ambassador said:

"Keep the letters to the Vatican in your pocket until day after
tomorrow. If you present them and the Pope gives you an audience, the King will not see you. It is an invariable rule that if
any visitor in Rome makes the first call on the Pope, the King
will not receive him. I have made an engagement for you to see
the King day after tomorrow, but if you send these letters to the
Pope and he gives you an audience the engagement for you to
see the King by that very act will be cancelled."

He said the feeling between the Vatican and the King was more inherited and more formal than real. At that time the theory was that
the Pope was a prisoner in the domain of the King, but, as Mr. Page
informed me, that was only on paper. Of course I followed the suggestion of the Ambassador and did not present my letters to the
representative of the Church before my audience with the King.

TEDDY AND THE METHODISTS

In the meantime, though I knew I might be denying myself the
opportunity of being received by the Pope, I presented my letter
from Bishop Cranston to the head of the Methodist School. My wife
and I visited it and had the pleasure of seeing some hundred young
children and hearing them sing the American and Italian national
airs. I made a brief address to the children in the Methodist School.
Fortunately for me, my position was not as distinguished as that of
Theodore Roosevelt when the Pope refused to see him. He was notified that the Pope would not receive him unless he cancelled his
acceptance to address the Methodists. That created a great sensation
in America at the time. Roosevelt replied that he would not permit
his activities to be restricted, and did not see the Pope.

At that time a Cardinal at the Vatican was reported to have said,
"The Methodists are now carrying on the most offensive campaign
of calumny and detraction against the Pontiff." My paper had said,
"The country will applaud Mr. Roosevelt," and had commented on
the statement of the Cardinal: "This means only that the Methodists
are engaged in a characteristic revival in Rome and are reaching
the people."

The probabilities are that the Pope's refusal to see Roosevelt grew out of the "My dear Maria" letters. President Roosevelt, through the wife of American Ambassador Bellamy Storey—she being a devout Catholic, the sister of Nicholas Longworth—had interested himself in seeking the promotion of Archbishop Ireland. The Archbishop was one of the few distinguished prelates in America who had been active in Republican politics, and Roosevelt thought that, through the Embassy in Rome, he might elevate his friend. That was an unforgivable sin.

JOAN OF ARC CANONIZED

I followed Ambassador Page's advice and kept my letters of introduction to the Vatican until after I had seen the King. Then, through Father Mahoney, an audience was arranged for the following week. In the meantime President Wilson wired me it was important that I should be in Paris two days before the date set for the audience at the Vatican, and I left Rome without seeing the Pope. However, Father Mahoney had arranged something better than we hoped. It was that our party would be invited to the Vatican to the very solemn service preliminary to the Canonization of Joan of Arc, and my wife and son and our Admirals attended that historic ceremony. At the conclusion of the service, Father Mahoney turned to my wife and said, "The Holy Father wishes to speak with you." Not having ever been received by a Pope, she asked, "What shall I do?" and Father Mahoney said, "Treat His Holiness as you would any other gentleman," and so he conducted her to the Pope, who shook hands and talked with her. Admiral Griffin, a devout Roman Catholic, showed the customary obeisance to the head of his church and kissed the Pope's ring. My wife said to me later, "The President's order to return to Paris denied you the privilege of being present at a service which would have given you great gratification since all your life the Maid of Orleans has been one of your historic heroines." We had visited Domremy and almost felt that we had been in the aura of the influence of the Maid of France.

The Italians had arranged an itinerary for our party which included visits to Venice, Naples, Pompeii, Vesuvius and other points in Italy. After I returned to Paris my wife and party visited all these places. At Venice they were welcomed by Prince Udine, cousin of the King, who had been in Washington on a mission. The party stopped at Hotel Danielle in Venice, and the Prince said, "There is

no doubt that the hotel was established by one of your kinsmen."
A cousin no doubt—far removed.

GREATEST THRILL IN ROME

"What historic place in Rome gave you the greatest thrill?" was
a question asked me when I was relating to Wilson the acute situation I had found in the Eternal City. My answer was, "My visit to
the prison where Paul was incarcerated." Why? Because from that
prison went letters that have outlived all the victories of the Caesars
or the eloquence of the Ciceros or the manifestoes of the Vatican.

VISIT TO CHAUMONT

As the members of our party left Italy, the countryside was abloom
with cherry and peach blossoms, and when they reached the Alps on
their way back to Paris, they met snow. Having completed the business which had called me back to Paris, I rejoined our party and we
motored to Chaumont, the headquarters of General Pershing. As
Pershing had gone to Brest to meet Secretary Baker, our host was
General Liggett, one of the greatest soldiers of the war, about whose
service too little is known. En route to Chaumont we passed through
lines of hundreds of German soldiers dressed in working clothes
who were mending the roads. I shall never forget the proud look
on the face of a Southern Negro soldier, the tallest man I ever saw,
who was in charge of the working brigade. As we passed he gave a
salute and in his eyes he as much as said, "White folks, ain't it grand
that here I am a Southern Negro directing the work of these German
soldiers?"

After dinner, as I put my hands in my pockets, General Liggett
heard coins rattling. He said, "You haven't got any honest-to-God
money, have you?" I pulled out three quarters. He said, "Please give
me one. I haven't seen any good money in so long." A year or two
later when I visited him in San Francisco he said, "Look here. The
quarter you gave me in Chaumont I am keeping as a lucky coin."

VISITING BATTLEFIELDS OF FRANCE

The next morning our party started out on a long tour of visiting
the battlefields of France. One of the unofficial reasons why I
wanted to go to France during the war was to visit the battlefields
and stand on the soil where Americans had won immortality. I

had followed those battles in the press and in the official bulletins with absorbing interest and looked forward to viewing the trenches, dug-outs, and entanglements, and walking over the ground hallowed by the sacrifice of our troops.

Naturally the first battlefield I visited was at Château-Thierry and Belleau Wood, where the Marines halted the Germans on what they thought was their triumphant march to Paris. Every spot had interest for our party. General Feland, of the Marine Corps, and Major Charles M. Busbee, of the Army—from Raleigh, North Carolina—both of whom had won honor at Belleau Wood, accompanied us and pointed out the various stands and positions. We also went to Meaux, Rheims, where the gaping wounds in the cathedral gave mute testimony to German vandalism; to Soissons, and passed through Tardenois and Dormans in the Valley of the Marne.

The worst sight I have ever seen was the land around Verdun, where more than 500,000 men on each side had been killed. It had literally been churned up and looked as if it could never be restored. I had followed the fighting there, and had been thrilled by the magnificent resistance of the French, when the tide of battle seemed going against them and they nerved themselves to make good the slogan: "They Shall Not Pass." Until I saw with my own eyes the destruction in Verdun and the devastation in the adjoining terrain, I had no conception of what making good that pledge meant in human lives. It was in the Meuse-Argonne near by that the Americans saw some of their worst fighting, but while there was wreckage reminiscent of that bloody battleground, the blight loomed nothing like as terrible as around Verdun. As we walked through the wreckage and saw the result of the bombing, it was difficult to understand how any had survived. The people, before the German invasion, had, some of them told us, felt they were secure because after the Germans took it in 1871 it was strengthened by modern defense methods which they thought would withstand the heaviest German assaults. Its defense was helped by the Meuse heights, which overlooked Verdun. We were shown "The Sacred Way," over which 6,000 vehicles rolled daily.

VISIT TO ARMY OF OCCUPATION

After visiting the battlefields (incidentally, my wife took home with her shells from every battlefield visited and afterwards had marked on them the names of the battlefields and used them as bases for table lamps), our next objective was the visit to the men of the Army and Marines of the Second Division who were in occupied Germany. They had been ordered there to see that the Germans carried out the terms of the Armistice. Passing through Luxembourg, we felt how small the world was because, as we sat down to luncheon, seven North Carolinians shared the table with us.

As we entered Germany en route to General Dickman's quarters, we passed along the Rhine and were impressed with the terraced farms going up on to the hills and mountains. General Dickman was occupying the palace of Count von Oswald. Our officers in Coblentz, and in all that section of occupied Germany, were quartered in the old German palaces. While in that section we were the guests of General John A. Lejeune, Commander of the Second Division.

A POOR SECOND AT HONNENGAN

Easter Sunday was spent at Honnengan with the 18th Company of the Fifth Regiment of Marines. I quote from my Diary:

"At service with the Marines, a Catholic and a Protestant chaplain officiated, the Protestant preaching the sermon. The field kitchen on which the dinner was cooked had wound stripes painted on it because it had been shot through twice. That was one of the many times when I ran second. My wife, who at Quantico had been elected 'Mother of the Marines,' was guest of honor, though I made the longest speech. Private Tucker presented her with flowers and an insignia, colors of their shoulder piece, painted on satin. She created enthusiasm by her talk, 'Outranking the Secretary of the Navy.'

"We dined with General Lejeune and staff and later visited the Y.M.C.A. and at night I spoke in the theater at Neuwied.

"The day before rode in tractor when the Sixth Marines simulated trench warfare. They demonstrated an attack on a machine gun nest. It looked more like Indian warfare than any other fighting, as men would rise up from places not visible to the naked eye. Went to the bridge-head over the Wied River to see the patrol. 'No further' was the order. That was the limit of the territory of occupation. No American crossed over the river."

The next day we visited Ehrenbreitstein, which for centuries had been the military "Rock of Gibraltar" of Germany. There the Americans had raised on the highest flagpole, the biggest American flag I have ever seen. It dominated all the country at the confluence of the Rhine and Moselle rivers.

"TALK ABOUT GOING HOME"

Not far from the heights of Ehrenbreitstein was the celebrated German drill ground of Vallendar, where for a thousand years German soldiers had been trained. On a bright day of Easter week, in company with General John A. Lejeune, I reviewed the forty thousand American troops who made up the army of occupation. They were seasoned troops and made a fine appearance. The formalities over, I was hoisted on a table to speak. Looking into their faces, older by reason of hard service, I turned to the troops and asked: "What shall I talk about?" In unison the forty thousand replied, "Talk about going home. Talk about going home." I answered: "The last man I saw before coming overseas was Secretary of War Baker, and I am glad to inform you he is making preparation to grant your heart's desire." Again, as if in a great trained chorus, they cried out: "How soon? How soon?" And I replied in the only French I knew, "Tout de suite." These men had hoped for a return trip upon the signing of the Armistice, but there they were in Germany, an Army of Occupation, without any idea how long they must remain.

GENERAL MANGEN PROVED AN ALIBI

After we spent Easter Sunday with the Marines, we decided to take a trip on the Rhine to Mainz, on a boat manned by the Marines, and pay our respects to General Mangen, who commanded the French troops in that area. General Mangen, who began the offensive at Soissons in 1918, was quartered at the Palace where Napoleon's room was preserved. Of course he alluded gratefully to "LaFayette, we are here," and invited us to lunch. In the course of the meal, someone referred to the low birth rate in France, with the consequent lack of the ability to put as many men in the field as Germany, and that the large numbers of the German troops were responsible for the early victories of the Kaiser.

"There may be something in that," said the General, "but I can prove an alibi. I am the father of seven children and would be the father of more in my family except for the fact I was on a continuous duty in North Africa for fifteen months." I told him that he would make a good North Carolinian, for my State had a high birth rate and it was a proud boast that "we raise our own immigrants."

When I learned that we were not far from Bingen, I gratified a long cherished desire to pay it a visit. Admiral Taylor asked why I had rather go to Bingen than some German cities. I replied, "When I was a school boy there was a rule that children should give recitations. I do not know why, but I was intrigued by a poem by Caroline Norton, "Bingen on the Rhine"—committed it to memory, recited it, and had never forgotten the words which ran something like this:

"A soldier of the Legion lay dying in Algiers,
    There was lack of woman's nursing, there was dearth of woman's
        tears. . . .

Take a message, and a token, to some distant friend of mine,
For I was born at Bingen, dear Bingen on the Rhine.

That poem was retained in my memory two score years and caused me to visit Bingen. I didn't see any German soldiers, but if I had, I doubt if they would have been of the type pictured in the poem.

HAD NEVER SEEN A NEGRO

One incident occurred that day which our party could not forget. Leaving the car to make a trip in the city, we left Bob Gaines, my Negro servant, with the chauffeur. Upon our return a strange sight met our eyes, particularly strange for Southerners accustomed to live where Negroes make up a large portion of the population. The car was surrounded by hundreds of German children, who had never before seen a Negro. They flocked to see this strange man. Bob, who had a keen sense of humor, took in the situation and was not troubled by their curiosity. He had never before thought that, being a Negro, he would appear strange to any people. As we were leaving he called out to the curious children and waved his hat, saying "Good-bye" in English because he could not speak German.

Relating the incident the next day while lunching with General Bell (he had married a daughter of General Robert Ranson of North Carolina) I told him that Bob was never at a loss and never lacked a sense of humor, and related this incident:

"Our house on Wyoming Avenue in Washington was separated only by a narrow yard from a large house occupied by an organization that called itself the 'House of Truth.' Returning from church one Sunday morning, Bob was all grins as he opened the door. To our inquiry of the cause he said: 'About an hour ago some people came to our house, rang the door bell, and when I opened the door, asked—"Is this the House of Truth?"

" 'I was quick to reply: "No sir, this ain't no House of Truth—there ain't no truth here." ' And Bob fell to laughing at his own disavowal that he lived in a House of Truth."

That story, when later I related it to President Wilson, greatly pleased him and he thought so highly of Bob Gaines that one of his last acts was to give him civil service status by an executive order when I recommended it. Result—when I went out of office Bob remained and was an efficient messenger at the Navy Department until he retired for age.

I was glad, also, that our well-liked Negro chauffeur, John Pye, was continued by the new Secretary of the Navy and later was on duty at the White House. When Roosevelt became President he was glad to recognize Pye as formerly with us at the Navy Department. I think my wife's strong recommendation had most to do with the retention of their places by these two Negro friends.

WARNING AND PROPHECY

Shortly after our visit to the towering fortress on the Rhine opposite Cologne, there was printed in the *Stars and Stripes* a poem by Captain Joseph M. Hanson. "The Flag at Ehrenbreitstein." It intrigued me. The last verse had this warning to the Germans and a prophecy:

> "Ye may bask you in your legends
> Of Niebelungen lore;
> Of the mighty sword of Siegfried
> And the hammer strokes of Thor:
> But drink no more the potion
> Of gods and supermen,
> Or the flag on Ehrenbreitstein
> Will cross the seas again."

The warning was not heeded. Twenty-six years later, March, 1945, a mammoth American flag waved again on a flagpole on that high eminence. The prophecy, "Will cross the seas again," was fulfilled.

MARINE BAND DID NOT GO

In one way I rather over-spoke myself on that Eastertide, promising the men before me that the Marine Band would escort them into Berlin when the Kaiser made his formal capitulation. It did not turn out that way for, taking advantage of the century-old Holland policy of giving a home to political refugees, Holland permitted the Kaiser to find a home where he lived in retirement until death came.

BRINGING AMERICAN FORCES HOME

Upon my return to the United States I set about to find ways to bring American soldiers home. Half of the men had been taken to France on British transports, and these were now all engaged in carrying New Zealand, Australian, South African, and Canadian troops to their homes. We could not expect to receive the first call. We were short of transports. How could we accelerate their return? I directed that all the older battleships and cruisers be fitted out and hurried to France to bring the troops home. Admirals strenuously objected. One said, "They are not suited for transport duty. The men will be uncomfortable and will come home critical of the Navy." I had seen our troops in France, England, Italy, and occupied Germany, and having safeguarded their trip to France, I felt the duty of aiding the Secretary of War to arrange for their early return. We brought back 340,948 in one month, the battleships and cruisers bringing 140,000. We had carried 911,047 men to Europe in Navy transports. In all, the Navy, going and coming, with British aid, transported one million of the armed forces.

NO AMERICAN VENGEANCE

The days spent with the Army of Occupation in Germany showed that there was no spirit of vengeance in the armed forces. German children, some of them very anaemic and hungry, gathered about the soldiers who gave them food. I am sure that no foreign soldiers quartered even temporarily in a conquered country ever behaved themselves in such a way as to win so completely the esteem of the conquered and to illustrate the high spirit of the American fighting man as the men in this Army of Occupation. From time immemorial conquering soldiers have plundered their victims. Here we were feeding them and bringing succor to children.

Nor was there any spirit of vengeance in the White House. When some Americans, out of resentment for German atrocities, withdrew coöperation for raising funds for starving children in Germany, General Allen appealed to Mrs. Wilson. Her letter, characteristic of both Mrs. Wilson and the President, is recalled as the spirit that should actuate Americans toward children. She wrote her first and only letter that went to the public:

"DEAR GENERAL ALLEN:

"The information contained in your letter of February 10 with respect to the starving children of Germany causes me genuine distress. As a private citizen I will not venture to comment on the official aspect of the recent flag episode; but I am so convinced the feeling of my husband on the phase of the matter presented by you would so entirely accord with my own that I do not hesitate to express the hope that your fund in aid of helpless German children may continue to find generous support.

"I am sure Mr. Wilson would not have the devotion of the American people whom he so loved take on the guise of resentment which might cause suffering if not death among innocent children.

"Faithfully and sincerely,
"EDITH BOLLING WILSON"

GUESTS OF BRITISH ADMIRALTY

En route to London and Scapa Flow we stopped at Belgium and visited the site of the Battle of Waterloo. We also stopped at Zeebrugge, visiting the moat and docks which were the scene of the British Naval attack under Sir Roger Keyes in 1918, and seeing the break made in the dock by the British submarine. Later we visited Nieuport, which was completely destroyed by fire. We passed through that part of Belgium which the Belgians had flooded by opening the narrow locks in 1914, thereby stopping the German advance on Calais. I never saw any land that looked so utterly destroyed, except around Verdun, and yet when I returned in 1937 I found there—as at Verdun—land which I thought had been swept by the besom of destruction had been made into what looked like the richest of gardens.

Reaching Calais we prepared to cross the Channel. At that ancient French port we were met by Commander J. S. Barlion, Commander of the U. S. destroyer *Wakes,* and, escorted by three British destroyers, we entered Dover Harbor to the salute of nineteen guns—the first gun salute since the war. It was good to see Admiral Lowther Grant, of the British Navy, who had been Naval Liaison Officer in Washington during the war. He was our gracious host during our stay in Britain. I found that a week of Naval battle in Paris over the relative size of the British and American Navies, had left no scars, and British hospitality was as gracious as if we had consented to let Britain be mistress of the seas.

After a brief stay in London with the Naval officers, we left on a special train to Thurso, en route to carry out the chief purpose that took us to Britain, to visit Scapa Flow, which had been the headquarters of the Grand Fleet of Britain and our dreadnaughts during the war. We were all entertained on various British ships. There were eleven German battleships, including the *Baden* and *Rayern,* six battle-cruisers, two mine layers, six light cruisers, fifty destroyers and torpedo boats. General Admiral von Reuter was flying his flag on the *Emden.* The ships looked rusty, dirty, and defeated. Sailing around these German ships in Scapa Flow, we passed near the spot where the German submarine, *BU-116,* was sunk in a minefield November 9th, two days before the Armistice was signed. We learned there at first-hand something of the daring of the Germans. The officer who passed over the minefield when the submarine was destroyed had a chart wrapped around his body which gave all the information that the Germans might wish.

The welcome by Admiral Pendergast and his party, and the hospitality and dinner given by Admiral Keyes and other officers on the *Lion* were two of the highest points in our stay at the northernmost central Naval Base, where our ships and ships of the British Grand Fleet were given protection during the war. I noticed that the *Lion* still had many scars received at the Battle of Jutland. On the port side aft was the imprint of a complete shell—evidently made by a ricochet. In the Battle of Jutland the roof of the forward turret of the *Lion* was blown off.

NO INSPECTION OF GERMAN SHIPS

What mainly caused us to make the journey to Scapa Flow was to enable our Construction, Engineering, and Ordnance Chiefs to visit the German warships interned there. The Battle of Jutland had shown that in some respects the Germans were ahead of the British. We wanted to learn if German ingenuity had devised machinery or apparatus that could wisely be put into our big Naval building program.

Admiral Benson shared my hope that an examination of the interned German ships might be valuable in showing us any advance they had made in efficiency. "I hope," he wrote me, "that you will take Taylor and the others with you to Scapa Flow and they can get aboard the German ships, and be able to tell us something about them in case they are divided up." But when, as the guest of Admiral Roger Keyes on the *Lion* (the sailors joked about a Daniel in the Lion's den), I told him that I wished our Naval experts to go over the German interned ships and examine their construction, I was astonished when he said, "No British officer has gone below decks. The poor devils would feel we were spying on them. All we do is to sail around them every day to make sure they do not get away." And so the chief object of our trip to Scapa Flow was thwarted. We could not demand a privilege the British denied themselves. I doubted the wisdom of not keeping the German officers, crews, and ships under better surveillance, and asked the Admiral if he could be sure they would not try to get away or scuttle their ships. He thought the "poor devils" were too cowed to do damage to their ships. Recalling my experience, when we narrowly escaped the blowing up of the Philadelphia Navy Yard by German officers on their ships interned there, I felt the British were taking heavy risks. That suspicion was well founded when not long afterward the Germans, in order to prevent Allied possession and operation of their ships, secretly scuttled them and sent them to Davy Jones's locker to keep company with the inhabitants of the bottom of the sea.

VISITING SCOTLAND

We had the opportunity of visiting the old cathedral, St. Magnus, at Kirkwall, and many other places of historic interest. One of the chief objects of our trip was to visit Inverness, the headquarters of the Division under Admiral Strauss which laid the barrage across the North Sea. Admiral Grant told me a good story as we passed Glen Albyn Distillery. It was one of the largest distilleries in Scotland. It had been used during the war to store mines which were later used to construct the barrage. He said, "This big distillery and a number of others in Scotland having been taken over by the Americans, the story was invented—and had wide circulation—that you, being a strong prohibitionist, had commandeered these distilleries and shut them up, not merely because you wanted a place to store mines, but because you wanted to put an end to the distillery business in Scotland." I heard this again from several sources. We were entertained at the residence of the Marquis of Linlithgow, Hopeton House, near Edinburgh. Coming from a State having a large population of Scotsmen, I was very much interested in our visit to Scotland and particularly Edinburgh.

My wife and son did not go to Scapa Flow with us but were in Edinburgh when we arrived. I expected to find them in the hotel. However, upon their arrival in Edinburgh they were invited to be the guests of Sir Lord John MacLeod and his sister, Mrs. Wigham, Lady Provost. Sir John was the greatest linguist in Europe. I was told that he welcomed all important visitors to Edinburgh with a speech in their native tongue. He was equally at home in Japanese, Chinese, Hindustani, and all of the languages spoken in Europe. He had the Scotch directness. He and his sister took my wife and son to church at St. Giles Cathedral on Sunday morning and then had luncheon with them at the hotel. After the lunch he ordered his carriage and said to my wife, "I knew the Secretary of the Navy of the United States, but I did not know you. Now that we have met you, my sister and I claim you and your son as the guests at our home."

Quite a number of American soldiers were taking a course at the University of Edinburgh following the Armistice. I visited with them and spoke at the Officers Club and the Y.M.C.A. and decorated the grave of Corporal Templin of the American Army with the Croix de Guerre. My Presbyterian wife was much interested in that Presbyterian country and particularly in the house of John Knox.

THE BRITISH LIKE PRAISE

Previously while we were in Paris I had accepted an invitation of Mr. Walter Long to a dinner in the House of Commons in London

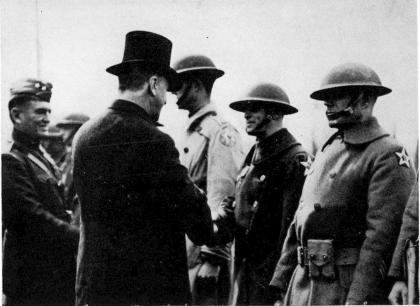

With the Army of Occupation. *Above,* Secretary and Mrs. Daniels, General Lejeune, and Naval Staff on the reviewing stand at the Heights of Vallendar in Occupied Germany. *Below,* Secretary Daniels conferring a medal upon Major Foertmeyer, Regimental Surgeon, 2nd Engineers.

Left, Brigadier General Smedley D. Butler, Commander of Camp Pontanezen at Brest, France. *Right,* Major General John A. Lejeune, Commander of Second Division Marine Force in Occupied Germany, and afterward twelfth Commandant of the Marine Corps of the United States (both U. S. Marine Corps photos.)

as guest of the British Admiralty. I wrote the address while in Paris, and recounted the long and close coöperation between the American and British Navy, high-lighted before the war in Mexico and the Philippines and reaching its crescendo in the World War when the ships of both countries served under common command. When I reached London, and just before going to Scapa Flow, while the guest of Ambassador John W. Davis, I asked him to do me the great kindness of reading the speech I had written and make such suggestions about it as he thought wise. I told him that I would hate to say anything that might embarrass him or that would not strengthen the ties between the two English-speaking nations. He replied:

" 'Leave your speech. I will look over it. I do not think there will be any occasion for me to make any suggestions. I can only give you one piece of advice. If you have not done so, lay it on heavy. Give the highest praise your conscience will allow you to the British and the British Navy. They think, or think they think, they do not like praise. In fact they pride themselves on their understatements. They resent it if they think anybody is trying to gain their favor by flattery, but no people in the world love commendation more than the English, if it is administered in such a way as not to offend their sense of thinking they do not like it. They can swallow more of it in comparison than any people in the world, but they do this thinking they are immune to what all people like. I advise you to spread it on thick. They can swallow it like a hog swallows slops—just like most human beings.'

"And then he laughed, saying, 'Of course I am putting it too strong. They are a great people and we have much in common. All I wish to say is praise them and praise them some more, but do it with artistic skill.' "

As I was leaving after handing him the manuscript, he said, "If you ever tell anybody what I have said, I will swear you are a liar. I could not stay in London a day longer after it was printed."

DINNER AT HOUSE OF COMMONS

The banquet at the House of Commons was attended by pretty much all the great and near-great in England—Lord Curzon, Winston Churchill, Walter Long, Rudyard Kipling, the leaders of Parliament, the Bench, and the Bar, distinguished Generals and Admirals including General Haig, who was the toast of the city. Lord Curzon made the address of welcome to the American visitors, in the course of which, turning to me, he said: "Mr. Secretary. We understand that you have filled this great office in your country for six or seven consecutive years. That is not understandable with us, for in that time we have had five or six First Lords of the Admiralty, none of whom have held the office except for a brief period. They would like to know how you managed to hold on so long. I see them scattered about tonight at this table." He called them "wrecks of politics." In the course of his address he spoke of his close relation with Americans and his admiration for them and appreciation of the American Navy. He said his friendship for the Americans began when he was a young man just out of the University. He voyaged with a party of Yale students in the Mediterranean, and because of my name he recalled after all the years a song these Yale boys sang on that summer voyage. He said it ran like this:

> "There was a farmer had two sons,
> And these two sons were brothers,
> Josephus was the name of one—
> Bohunkus was the other's."

I was later shown the bust of Sir Josephus Hooker, who is said to have introduced the rhododendron which covers in profusion the Great Smoky Mountain Park in North Carolina.

In the week in London our party was entertained at luncheons given by the Anglo-American Society, Sir Eric Geddes, who had been First Lord of the Admiralty, Ambassador Bryce, Admiral Knapp, Lord Astor and Nancy, Sir Robert Hadfield, Admiral Roslyn Wemyss, Sir Robert Perks at a dinner, and at a luncheon given by the King and Queen and the Royal Family at Windsor Castle.

BIRTHDAY AND WEDDING DAY

From my Diary (May 1):

"On my wife's birthday (May 1), lunched with the Anglo-American Society, where a birthday cake was cut. The Duke of Connaught was her partner. It was the anniversary of his birth too, and they both stood up to greetings and the Duke said: 'We are birthday children.' Ambassador Bryce spoke of his delightful visit to Raleigh and said he little thought that when we were talking about Sir Walter Raleigh in the city named for him that our countries would be allies in a great war and we should be celebrating victory in London.

"Dinner at House of Commons. Visited House of Lords also and heard speeches on budget and taxes—same subjects Congress is talking about."

From my Diary (May 2):

"On our wedding day, we had luncheon with Sir Eric Geddes who had visited us in Washington—met the gloomy dean at St. Paul, and he was gloomy—paid homage at Westminster to John Wesley and other notables. Gladstone's back was turned on Disraeli. Mrs. Dreybus, hotel proprietor, sent beautiful wedding cake. Wedding day dinner by Ambassador and Mrs. John Davis, who were interested in what we saw and heard on trip to Scapa Flow. Duke of Connought sent telegram of congratulations on wedding day."

DINNER WITH THE WESLEYANS

Sir Robert Perks, a leading Methodist layman, member of the British Parliament, tendered me and my staff a dinner with the Wesleyan Society shortly after we arrived in London, at which addresses were made by the distinguished Rev. Dr. Jowett and others. I sat next to Lord Fisher and talked with him after the dinner. He was one of the most entertaining men I ever met—full of zest, sparkling and with delightful stories. "Do you ever go to church?" he asked me, prompted no doubt by the presence of distinguished ministers. My reply was that from my early youth I rarely missed a Sunday service. "I have learned more from hearing sermons than from any other single source," he said. "These preachers know a lot in and out of the Bible, and if you'll listen to them, they'll help to educate you."

Among the men of whom I had heard much before reaching England was Lord Fisher, who had been Britain's most virile First Sea Lord. It was Fisher who conceived the construction of the dreadnaught, and completed the first one in twelve months. The dreadnaught virtually scrapped every battleship in every Navy in the world, and demonstrated that Fisher had the boldest creative mind among Naval statesmen. He had been called back to duty in the World War, when, as he phrased it, the Navy of his country, merely "waited to be kicked and wondering when and where." At the age of seventy-four he had "enough of the old fire to make the lumbering mechanism of the Admiralty fairly tremble under his unflinching determination to get things done." He was a doughty fighter, a breaker of precedents, and a good maker of phrases that sometimes carried a sting. He believed so much in himself that he excited jealousy in less daring officers. Fisher's career attracted me before I had the opportunity to know him in the flesh.

LORD FISHER'S WIT AND WISDOM

The Admiral related incidents grave and gay, in connection with his command of the North American stations when he was in association with Admiral Mahan, whose books on sea power broadened his thinking, and with Admiral Sampson and other American Navy statesmen. He told of some of his experiences in verbal battles with ultra-conservatives of the British Navy.

"How would you feel if your President should tell you that he had suffered more in popular estimation by appointing you to high office than by any other act of his administration?" Lord Fisher asked me. I replied that it would give me serious pain to have embarrassed my chief. Whereupon, after relating what I had already heard, that for years he and King Edward VII had been intimate associates, he said: "One day while lunching with the king, he said to me, 'Fisher, do you know that of all my acts since I came to the throne the one that has brought me most criticism was my appointment of you as First Sea Lord?' Fisher repeated the king's question with a grimace and asked: "How would you have answered such a remark from your superior?" In the Yankee way of answering questions, I asked, "How did you reply?" He said he paused a few minutes, being somewhat stunned by the king's remark, and "then an inspiration came to me and I answered, 'I congratulate your Majesty upon your wisdom in picking a winner.' "

We talked about speeches, and some good speeches were made at Perks' dinner. Lord Fisher asked me what was the best speech I had ever heard. That was a poser. I had only that week heard half a dozen of the greatest speakers in Great Britain and had hardly finished applauding a remarkable speech by Fisher. I hesitated. He loved to talk—and how entertaining he was—and he continued:

"The best speech I ever heard was made by an American Admiral, who, as I understand, did not think he could make a speech. It was in Philadelphia at a dinner, attended by many big men. I was called upon to speak and gave warm praise to the achievements and standing of the American Navy, praising its officers in terms they deserved, and expressing the sentiment that the Navies of the two great English-speaking nations were doing much to strengthen the friendly feeling between the two countries. The audience applauded me—and my speech was worth applauding, I can assure you [this with an inimitable smile], and then I sat down. Your Admiral Sampson was the ranking officer of your Navy present. He did not rise and evidently did not intend to speak until several Naval officers by nudges and suggestions conveyed to him the information that he ought to respond to the speech of the British Admiral. Finally he rose, looked about him for a period as if not knowing what to say, and then without preface, Sampson made this brief and brilliant speech: 'Well, all I have to say is this: It was a damned fine bird that hatched the American eagle.'"

And as he told me this Admiral Fisher's eyes fairly beamed with enthusiasm over what he repeated was the best after dinner speech he had ever heard.

ARE DREADNAUGHTS DOOMED?

When I talked with the breezy and unconventional Lord Fisher, he seemed proud he had built the first dreadnaught. I was therefore surprised to learn that a few months before he died he declared that the submarine had scrapped all dreadnaughts just as the dreadnaughts had put all the ships previously constructed on the scrap-pile. And that was before bombs from the air were doing their deadly destruction.

A PRESS INTERVIEW

While no official of any government referred to the Sea Battle of Paris, that was not true of the vigilant press. Almost every day in England I was met with an inquiry about America's Naval policy. I quote from an interview reported in the *Pall Mall Gazette* (May 1, 1919):

"... It was pointed out to Mr. Daniels that the British man in the street was asking why the United States had an estimate of 600,000,000 pounds for the Navy, which seemed rather a large sum for police work.

"'Perhaps the man in the street has not read the Bill,' suggested Mr. Daniels. 'The Naval Bill, with a 600,000,000 pounds estimate for new construction, has a provision which I helped to draw up providing that if the League of Nations is established it is in the discretion of the President to say that all the new ships may not be constructed. When the estimates were drawn up the Armistice had not been signed, and it was a question for each country to decide independently what it should do. I remember when Mr. Winston Churchill advocated a vacation in Naval buildings in 1913, I approved of it in our country and added—Why a vacation? Why not an international agreement which would be of permanent assistance by agreements for such Navies as would be sufficient to guarantee the world's peace?

"'It is unthinkable that any nation under the League should undertake competitive Naval building based on suspicion and distrust. I think that the day when the League of Nations was agreed to unanimously—which is the greatest event which any generation has witnessed for centuries—will make unnecessary the tremendous expenditure of money by each nation. Of course, we must have in the League of Nations a mobile police force. We must follow the example of that great American soldier in the Revolution who advised his soldiers to—"Trust in God and keep your powder dry." The greatest pressure, of course, will be economic and social, but there must be behind that, certainly in the early days, a sufficiently mobile Navy of free nations to see that we are not going to have any more wars like the last. When nations realize the fate of Caesars, Napoleons, and Kaisers they will not be so ready to enter into the idea of dominating the world.'"

CAME HOME ON "MT. VERNON"

Our party spent a week-end at Warwick Castle, owned by an American—Mr. Marsh—and met "Babbling Brook"; a visit to Stratford-on-Avon; a night at Checquer's with Lord Lee, whose wife was an American. We returned to London and after luncheon at the American Club with Ambassador Davis acting as Chairman, and Admiral John Fisher making an amusing speech, our party bade good-bye to our British hosts. We spent the day at the Portsmouth Navy Yard, visited Nelson's flagship *Victory;* then a day at Plymouth where we went aboard the *Corsair* and set sail for

Brest. After entertaining Admiral Moreau and other French and American Naval officials, we went aboard the USS *Mt. Vernon* en route home. The *Mt. Vernon* was bringing 5,800 troops, principally of the Thirty-third Division, a Congressional Committee, and other Americans. The ship was commanded by Captain McDougall. A short time before, en route to the U. S., it had been seriously damaged after distinguished service. Quick repairs made it as good as new.

It gratified me to receive a message while in mid-ocean from Captain E. E. McDonald that the History Committee wished to dedicate to me the book on the *Leviathan,* which they were preparing. The story of the ship the Germans built, which our Navy employed to transport thousands of American troops to defeat the German armies, has permanent value. If that ship could speak it could a tale unfold!

After a smooth voyage the *Mt. Vernon* reached New York Saturday, May 17, in time for me to reach Washington to celebrate my birthday, May 18.

XXXVII

WALKING WITH KINGS AND KEEPING THE COMMON TOUCH

I N MY experience (I was reared in a community where democracy, with both a little "d" and a big "D" was exalted), the King business was regarded as a hang-over from the days before Thomas Jefferson convinced us that all just governments rest upon the consent of the governed. Nevertheless Tennyson's "Idylls of the King" had intrigued me with the glamor of the days of King Arthur, when knighthood was in flower. If kings in the modern world had won their crowns by deeds of valour and chivalry, as in poetic fiction, instead of by the accident of birth, royalty might not have fallen from its high estate.

The first King with whom I "walked" in Washington, without losing the "common touch," looked every inch a king. He was Albert, of Belgium, who was the guest of the Wilson Administration in 1919. This was not long after the Armistice and the writing of the Peace Covenant at Versailles. His visit came not a great while after Ambassador John W. Davis had attributed to him the immortal words, "Belgium is a country and not a road," in reply to request for permission by the Kaiser that his troops might be permitted to pass freely through Belgium on their mission of unprovoked war against France.

King Albert came to Washington to honor Woodrow Wilson, then an invalid, stricken while pouring out his all in a taxing swing to the Pacific in behalf of the ratification of the League, and to express to the uncrowned leader of a peaceful nation the gratitude of Belgium and all the countries delivered from German tyranny.

As the members of the Cabinet, headed by Vice President Marshall, welcomed him to the National Capital, the figure of King Albert loomed head and shoulders above all of his hosts. He indeed seemed sun-crowned. He looked every inch a King. You felt that he measured up to the divinity that "doth hedge a king." Physically, he looked down on all of us, but there were dignity and friendliness

SECRETARY AND MRS. DANIELS AND PARTY AT THE PRINCE OF
WEID'S CASTLE, FRIDAY, APRIL 18, 1919

Upper left, Secretary Daniels in front of Rheims Cathedral after German bombing. *Upper right,* Interior of Cathedral as it looked to the Daniels party. *Lower left,* Secretary Daniels' colored Butler, Bob Gaines, an object of interest to German children in Bingen, who had never seen a Negro. *Lower right,* Secretary and Mrs. Daniels, with General Liggett, on steps of Pershing's Chateau at Chaumont.

that won all. I was not at the White House when, propped up in bed, Wilson received him as a comrade of the high days of war. In a few words that came from the heart the King spoke to members of the Cabinet of his call on Wilson as the first object of his visit to America.

I was with him and Queen Elizabeth at Old Point Comfort when he embarked on the *George Washington,* and his parting words to my wife and myself were a tender message to the President, and he sent one written with his own hand to Wilson, by wireless, in which he said: "It is with great regret I leave the hospitable shores of America. I am glad at the pleasure of seeing you and it is comforting to feel that you will soon be in full health and vigor and able to continue your great work."

THE QUEEN SET THE FASHION

On the last day in America the Queen gave the signal that sent the water of the Elizabeth River flooding two great dry-docks. As our guest on the voyage of the *Mayflower,* the Queen formed a friendship with my wife which had begun when we were guests of the King and Queen in Brussels. She was an inverterate photographer and snapped hundreds of pictures of places and people. She was the first woman to wear the small hats no larger than a bird's nest and probably set the fashion for the excuse for hats that became the universal fashion. That is the only thing I hold against her.

I heard Albert address the Congress—frank, sincere, and without eloquence, evidently finding it not easy to be fluent in English, if, indeed, being a man of few words, he could be fluent in any language. The King gave evidence of pleasure--Kings like praise like "us ordinary folks"—when Secretary Baker in words of eloquence conveyed America's admiration and gave him the highest decoration that America confers. He spoke no words when he laid the wreath on the grave of Washington at Mount Vernon. Asked why, an aide said: "He made no address at Louvain." There are times when words are not in order. Standing on the deck of the *Stockton,* before embarking on the *George Washington,* commanded by Captain McCauley, the King in his good-bye message said to Lansing and all the officials and officers and their wives gathered: "The Queen and I are very grateful for the kindnesses extended us everywhere we have been. We bear away a lively admiration for the genius, so varied and resourceful, of the American people."

A DELPHIC ANSWER

"That story is too good to be true."

These were the exact words used by Albert, King of Belgium, to me on a beautiful October morning in 1919 as we were riding in an automobile from Washington City to Annapolis. The King and his son, Prince Leopold, who became the object of so much controversy before and after World War II, visiting Washington as the guests of the nation, had expressed a desire to visit the Naval Academy. As Secretary of the Navy, I had invited them to pay a visit to the institution where Naval officers were trained.

Early that morning I was called to the Capitol to confer with the Chairman of the Naval Affairs Committee. As the conference ended, one of the oldest and ablest, and best informed of the corps of Washington correspondents joined us and said, "Mr. Secretary, I understand that you are to take the King of Belgium down to the Naval Academy to-day."

I replied that he had been correctly informed.

"Did you know," the correspondent asked, "that when King Albert was a boy he spent several months incognito in the United States?"

I had never heard that incident in the life of the King and I so informed the correspondent.

"Well, he did," went on the correspondent, "and it is a very interesting story about the time when he lived and worked in a western newspaper office, when not even his employer knew that he was entertaining a king-to-be unawares."

"You are kidding me," I answered. "It is not so easy for a prince of a royal family to lose his identity even for a few months."

"It is true, I assure you," he replied, "and I got the story from an entirely trustworthy party."

"Tell us about the incident or fairy tale," I said, still skeptical. He therefore related the alleged incident as follows:

"King Leopold and James J. Hill, both empire builders in different ways, were good friends. They exchanged views freely when Mr. Hill was visiting King Leopold in Brussels. They talked about railroad construction and all the big things that interest men who talk in terms of empires either by the conversion of the Northwestern part of the United States or in the Congo. In the course of the conversations, the King remarked that he wished that his son Albert, who would succeed him on the throne, could, before entering upon his kingly duties, know life as it really exists for those who are not brought up in the environment of royalty and power and comfort. He told Mr. Hill that he felt if Albert could go to America, for example, under an assumed name, get a job, and come in contact with people of all conditions of society, the knowledge gained by such experience would fit him to rule more wisely when the office of state fell to him by succession. The King enlarged upon the fact that most young men who came to kingship had never really known what life was. They were tutored and petted and coddled and treated as if they were superior beings, born into the world to be waited upon and receive salaams, the King went on, so that they could hardly be expected to enter into the feelings and aspirations of the mass of their subjects. Therefore they made mistakes, they had to rely for information upon their ministers, and often they acted without the first-hand knowledge which all rulers should possess.

"The King showed so much zeal in elucidating his desire that Albert should know how the average man lives and how he acts, that Mr. Hill was convinced of his sincerity. He agreed with the King that he could give his son no better preparation for the duties that would devolve upon him when he ascended the throne than for him to live in America and have the feel of the man who has to make a place for himself.

"The upshot of it all was that Mr. Hill told the King that he would be glad to take Albert, a youth of, I think, around eighteen, to the United States, introduce him to America as it was, get him a job where he could learn how American youths win a place in the world, and let him see for himself the agencies and influences which had developed the wide expanses, particularly of the Northwest, where the Hill railroads had opened up a section long remote and unsettled. The King was glad to have so capable a chaperon and guide for the adventure of his son, for it is a great adventure for a prince to shed all the trappings of royalty and emigrate to America as a Belgian youth to see how deep the water was. Albert loved the idea. It appealed to him as romance and adventure appeal to all youths. He had heard his father and Jim Hill talk of the greatness and big future of the United States. Compared to his little country, he felt that he would be exploring illimitable space, and the enterprise would give him a glorious time.

"So Albert sailed for New York, he was met by a friend of the great empire builder, and taken to St. Paul. During the trip and his stay in Minnesota, his young eyes opened at the miracles of development and industry that faced him at every turn. After being instructed in many things, Albert took the train for a small city in the Northwest to enter upon his duties in the advertising department of a newspaper which was illustrating the American motto of the era: 'Don't knock; boost.' He knew nothing about newspapering or advertising. Jim Hill had told the publisher who had been set up in business by Hill, that Anthony King—that was the name Albert went under while in the United States—was the son of a Belgian friend who wished the boy to learn journalism as it was practiced in a breezy and new American city. The publisher put him to work as an understudy to an advertising solicitor, who was instructed to give the boy an opportunity not only to learn newspapering but to see life as it existed and deported itself in that young city. And Anthony King, who said little but kept his eyes and ears open, was an apt pupil. He learned something about how a newspaper is made, heard reporters and printers talk in idle and busy hours, found out how they lived, how much they earned, and how far a dollar would go. In a few months Albert was an encyclopaedia of the city where Jim Hill had placed him. Then he resigned and went by St. Paul to see his father's friend and sailed for Belgium, knowing more about life in a bustling Western American city than all the princes and kings-in-the-making in the whole world."

The Congressman and I listened, intrigued by the story, which the correspondent told so graphically, and which if true was illustrative of Jim Hill's skill as an educator of young royalty and of Albert's adaptability. If a fairy story, it was a good one and was told in such a way as to give a thrill to those of us who heard it.

When the story ended, still somewhat skeptical in spite of the skill of the narrator, I said:

"That is an enchanting story you have told us, but, while you have clothed it with seeming verity, it sounds more like Baron Munchausen than a writer of facts."

The correspondent averred it was every word true, that he had it from undoubted authority, and when some of us smiled the smile of the unconvinced, he turned to me, and fired this shot:

"There's a way of testing my story. If you doubt it, ask King Albert about it as you ride over to Annapolis today. That will convince you that what I have told you is as true as preaching."

That seemed a fair challenge, but I hesitated, not having much association with royalty, to address so personal a question to him. Not accepting the challenge of my friend, I said, "I think you are romancing but I will think it over."

Shortly after this conversation we were on the way from Washington—the King of Belgium and the Secretary of the Navy of the United States. He was not a fluent conversationalist, though he spoke English well. He talked of his visit to the White House and his admiration for President Wilson, and of his desire, after going to the Naval Academy where he would see Naval officers in the making, to go to West Point to see the processes of training Army officers. I promised to furnish an airship to take him from New York to West Point when he reached that metropolis. Then conversation lagged. I suggested several topics about which he would say "Yes," or "No," or "Quite," or make some crisp and brief comment. But he introduced no new topic, and, after exhausting all my initiative, we drove along in silence, the King smoking and looking off into the distance.

I felt that I was not entertaining His Majesty. In sheer desperation, I was tempted to put the truth of my newspaper friend's story to the test by asking him the bald question: "When you were young, did your father send you to the United States to learn its ways? And did you work on a newspaper in Montana or some other mountain State?" That did not seem to be quite the way to treat royalty. I therefore dismissed the idea of asking him that direct question even in the face of the challenge hurled at me that morning in the Capitol. I essayed some other topic, with no better result. Finally I screwed up my courage and said: "Your Majesty, I heard a very interesting and intriguing story about you at the Capitol this morning."

"So?" he said in monosyllable, but his eyes displayed an interest his question did not reveal.

Seeing that I had his attention, I proceeded to tell the story, almost word for word as I outlined it above. I added several thrills. He listened intently, betraying genuine interest, interrupting me now and then with a comment that gave no indication as to how he felt about the story. When I had finished my narrative, telling how graphically the Washington correspondent had told it that morning, I looked to see how he had received it. Not a flicker indicated his response. He had a far-away look in his eyes, as if he were looking across the wide expanse of wheat lands that stretch west from St. Paul, or over the wide stretch of the Atlantic which separated him from his country. Nothing more. He took out his package of cigarettes, put one in his mouth, struck two or three matches before the wind permitted him to light it. He smoked on in silence, flicking off the ashes now and then.

I was sitting quite as silent, wishing to ask: "Is the story true?" but hesitating to urge a committal unless he should volunteer one. The car moved on. The silence began to grow oppressive and as his host I felt I ought to say something. However some instinct kept me silent. The King lighted another cigarette. Finally, he turned to me his immobile face, and said gravely:

"That is a very good story. It is too good to be true."

That was all. He then lighted another cigarette, and returned to his inner contemplation. A little later I asked him some questions about the stories of war atrocities, about the German Army's mistaking Belgium for a road instead of a country, about Cardinal Mercier, about the part Herbert Hoover took in feeding the Belgians in their distress. He answered all my questions, adding additional information and giving some sidelights.

By that time the dome of the Naval Academy (the midshipmen at Annapolis call it an iced cake) hove in sight (to use a seaman's phrase) and soon we were within the gates, welcomed by Superintendent Scales and his staff, standing attention as the gun boomed the salute to the King; and before starting about the grounds for inspection, we awaited the arrival of his son, Prince Leopold, who in another car had driven down from Washington with my son Frank. These youths were about the same age, more interested in football than anything else. As we were walking through the grounds, observing the objects of interest, the Superintendent of the Academy and the Commandant with the King and the Secretary, and the young Naval officers escorting the Prince and my son, a secret service officer touched Frank on the arm, saying: "You are giving us lots of trouble. Change your position. You are walking on the right side and Naval officers are worried because the Prince ought to have the position of honor." Both the boys were so engrossed in talking football and sports neither had given thought to rank or precedence.

"We have Kings in the United States," I said to the King as we stopped before the figure of Tecumseh, where we were surrounded by photographers who were shooting the party.

"So?" said King Albert in a tone of surprise.

"Yes," I answered. "Did you not hear that photographer order us to face the camera this way and then that, and we all obeyed him. The only Kings in America are photographers."

That amused King Albert. He spoke in warm praise of the Naval Academy, the bearing of the officers, and the perfection of the whole place, so well adapted for its purpose, accepted the hospitality of the Superintendent, and then we travelled back to Washington. There was more conversation, bearing particularly on naval and military training and the problems growing out of the war.

He made one remark that I recall. "I must be getting back to my country shortly. It is not wise for a ruler to be away long in these times of changing conditions." Did he mean it was possible that there might be any shaking of the throne in Belgium or any uprising? Or that, devoted to the welfare of his people, he was moved by duty to them to return to lead toward prosperous days? I did not ask him. I think he meant the latter.

A little later I had the pleasure of placing a seaplane at the disposition of King Albert, which he used for morning flights around New York, including the trip he had said he desired to make to visit West Point and see how Army officers were trained.

Query: A quarter of a century has passed since King Albert said, of the story that as a youth he had spent some months in the United States studying the country, "It is too good to be true." I have often asked myself: What did he mean by that delphic answer?

A VISIT TO THE BATTLEFIELD OF WATERLOO

My wife and I never forgot our visit to Brussels, to which the King and Queen of the Belgians referred during their sojourn in Washington. Knowing that Ambassador Brand Whitlock, whom I had known in the days when we were both Bryanites, must be over-burdened with welcoming officials and other Americans (they flocked over after the Armistice), we planned only a day in Brussels, where we were welcomed by the King and Queen at their palace. No intoxicants were served. The King said he was what Americans called "a tee-totaler," and added, "like you." A visit to the Battlefield of Waterloo, with a strenuous climb up 252 steps, where a guide pointed out the places of conflict in the battle that unhorsed Napoleon, was followed by a visit to the towns where the Germans wrecked churches and monasteries in their march to the Marne. The devastation in these places was terrible to behold, particularly at Louvain. Its forts, which Brialmont thought impregnable, fell before German guns like a house of cards. Anything that man has made can be destroyed by man.

LEOPOLD REMAINED WITH HIS COUNTRYMEN

These brief visits with the King added to the universal sorrow at his mysterious death. Later, in World War II, when Leopold remained with his people while Belgian officials hurried to England to escape the Germans, I confess to a feeling of admiration (perhaps because I had found the lad attractive when he visited Washington in 1919, and he and my young son Frank became good comrades) that Leopold alone of the high officials whose country was overrun by the Nazis elected to take the same treatment that was meted out to his countrymen. He was severely criticized, but I felt that the doctrine of noblesse oblige had governed his course.

THE TWO GREATEST

At the time of our visit, the two towering figures of Europe in popular admiration were Cardinal Mercier and King Albert, because when thrones were tottering and religious and other leaders lacked stamina, that quality shone in these two great Belgians. A later visit in 1937 to have a part in the dedication of a monument to American soldiers of World War I, who had been buried in Belgium, increased my admiration for the Belgians and their ability to wipe out the scars of war.

DISTINGUISHED BRITISH NAVAL LEADERS

Upper left, Sir Rosslyn Wemyss, First Sea Lord of the Admiralty (Underwood & Underwood). *Upper right,* Walter Long, First Lord of the Admiralty upon whose invitation Secretary of the Navy Daniels and party visited England. *Lower left,* Lord Jellicoe, who commanded British ships at the Battle of Jutland. *Lower right,* Admiral Keyes, British Commandant at Scapa Flow, where German ships were held captive.

SECRETARY AND MRS. DANIELS AND PARTY WITH BRITISH NAVAL
OFFICERS AND THEIR WIVES AT WHALE ISLAND, ENGLAND, MAY, 1919

My Diary (April 23) contains:

"Lunching with the King at Brussels, the Queen told my
wife that she was using their silver for the first time. It had been
given by Queen Victoria when they were married. It had been
kept in a cistern during the war.

"In a pleasant talk, Albert said the French were too imperialistic. He spoke of the broad spirit which must be shown
by all nations to preserve the peace of the world. Said much land
in Belgian had been destroyed. 'You can rebuild cities, but
when land is destroyed and machinery removed, it takes time
to get back into production. Many Belgians have no work. You
cannot put mechanics to farming or mill men to building roads.'

"Visited Antwerp, stopped at Ghent to see where 1814 treaty
between Britain and the United States was signed—then a hotel
and now a Catholic place for brothers. Spent night at Brugge
in Hotel Flanders. Germans had taken away all mattresses because Belgians make mattresses of wool. Good supper. Delightful night.

"Previous day through Belgium. Visited Liège from which all
machinery in factories had been taken to Germany and no work
can be done until machinery can be obtained from America.
Destruction awful at Louvain."

It was not long after the visit of King Albert before the arrival
of Edward, Prince of Wales, who visited Washington as the guest
of the Republic. Slight of figure, debonair, affable with the charm of
youth, courtesy, and tact, he walked into all hearts, and set quivering
those of the young belles with whom he danced. He gave evidence of
enjoying his visit and seemed to like people. As he stepped from the
train the only persons in the party to receive him that he knew
were my wife and myself. We had been luncheon guests of the King
and Queen at Windsor when the charm of my wife had attracted
his admiration. He turned to speak to us after being welcomed by
the Vice President and Cabinet members. To my wife he said:
"Mama and papa wished me to give you their regards."

There was an incident at the train that didn't set well with
Americans—a British custom as old as royalty—but not witnessed

before in Washington. The Prince shook hands cordially with all
the Americans, but not with Sir Edward Grey, the British Ambassador at Washington. I observed with wonder and astonishment
that as the Prince reached the line where Sir Edward stood, the
Ambassador had his hands folded behind him and bowed with a
sort of attitude toward Edward that indicated the gulf that separated
royalty from subjects. I couldn't understand, not familiar with court
practices, but was told that royalty did not shake hands with subjects.
There Edward was shaking hands cordially with the Hoosier Vice
President and me, a country editor, but by custom he could not
shake hands with a subject even though he was one of the ablest
statesmen and scholars in the world, towering in intellect above any
king or prince. When I spoke of it to a British Navy officer he seemed
to think it was one of those ancient customs whose observance
called for no feeling such as the Americans had. It would have riled
Americans, who believe in the equality of all men and hate the
spirit of caste. Of course no criticism was due Edward. Old customs,
however archaic, persist in Britain.

At all of the many receptions and social functions, except some
informal dances, which the Prince loved, the Vice President had
been delegated by Wilson to be the host of the royal visitor. Nothing
quite so dazzling had been seen in Washington as the banquet at
the Congressional Library. The beauty and chivalry of Washington
officialdom were gathered there. The younger man's attitude of
deference and respect toward Vice President Marshall, his host, was
the acme of courtesy. As the evening wore on, the Vice President,
somewhat tired because of many functions, wanted to go home, as
Mrs. Marshall told my wife. He asked the Prince something about
how long he would be staying. He deferred to the Vice President,
saying he would be saying good-bye shortly, and asked Marshall
how long he would remain, to which Marshall answered: "I will
follow you very quickly, Your Majesty." It was while at supper
that Edward (I can call him Edward since he has married an
American and has lived on this side of the Atlantic) asked my wife
if we would be good enough to arrange for him to call on Mrs.
Dewey, whose husband he greatly admired. The next afternoon we
took him to see the widow of the hero of Manila Bay, who was glad
to welcome him. He was interested in the many magnificent tokens
that had been given to the Admiral by his admirers. They filled

most of the lower floor of the H Street home. Mrs. Dewey gave the Prince a flag which England had taken from Spain. It had been presented to the Admiral.

Another day on the *Mayflower* we were his hosts when the Prince and his party voyaged to Mount Vernon for the customary placing of the wreath on Washington's grave, a ceremony nearly all the members of the visiting missions observed when they came to Washington.

One of the happiest days he spent, I think, was when Franklin Roosevelt and I accompanied him to Annapolis. On that occasion he discarded the uniform of the Welsh Guards and wore a uniform of a Captain in the British Navy. He said to the midshipmen, "I have had four years' training in the British Navy and feel that I can speak to you as a comrade. I would like particularly to express my appreciation for the splendid service which the American Navy performed in the war—both in the North Sea and elsewhere." He told midshipmen he thought their quarters were palatial. "When I was at naval school I lived in a trunk and preferred that to fine quarters if I could get more leave."

When Edward was en route to the White House, an aged woman was introduced to him, and she said that she met his grandfather when he was in Washington, "and he kissed me, too," she added.

The Prince was interested at the White House to find in one of the rooms a picture of his grandfather. He asked, "Did grandfather wear a high hat while he was here?"

EDWARD, THE SYMBOL OF GIVING ALL FOR LOVE

Little did we think then that the day would come when the debonair young prince, though evidently susceptible to the attraction of the young women who made much of him, would become the world symbol of "giving all," even a throne, "for love." If he had given his heart to a lady of his own country, or even of the effete royalty of Europe, Edward would today be wearing a crown and living at Buckingham. Cupid has a way of playing pranks, and when it sent the dart that made a King love a charming untitled American woman, the old order in England was aghast at the thought of an American's becoming Queen and successor to Victoria's title of Empress of India. Love paid the price and Edward lost the crown.

I never could understand it, but a crown is cold and glittering and love is warm and comforting!

During the excitement—that is the word—that ended in the marriage in the face of official threat of dethronement, I recall talking to the wife of a British diplomat who was scandalized about it all. My wife and I were shocked when she said, "In England we do not object to our sovereign's having affairs with other women than their wives (it has often occurred), provided it is not flaunted in the face of the Empire." She even referred to affairs of Edward's grandfather. "But," I said, "My dear lady, this young Prince has no wife. He is not having what you call an 'affair' with another man's wife. She is a widow, unattached, of good family and fine standing. It is a case of love on both sides and you do wrong to attach a wrong meaning to it. If they want to marry, it is nobody's business but their own."

The old archaic genuflection ingrained in her—and many of her countrymen—brought no condemnation for royalty, present or past, who violated their marriage vows. The crime in her opinion was that an American woman, by wiles and fascination, had hypnotized the young Prince because of her towering ambition, and so had brought scandal on the Empire.

LUNCHEON WITH KING AND QUEEN

The first King and Queen with whom I broke bread abroad were King George and Queen Mary in Windsor Castle at London in the spring of 1919, when, upon the invitation of Walter Long, First Lord of the Admiralty, my Naval staff, my wife and son, Captain Josephus Daniels, Jr., of the Marine Corps, went to England as the guests of the Government. The King and Queen invited my wife and me, "accompanied by one Admiral," to luncheon at Windsor. As I was accompanied by three Admirals, I thought the King ought to have included all of them, and as his three sons were at the luncheon, it would have been fitting to have asked my son. But perhaps the King didn't know there were so many in my party, and perhaps he wished a more of *en famille* luncheon. As I could take only one Admiral I departed from my principle of selection and practiced seniority, and Admiral R. S. Griffin, head of Engineering, accompanied us.

The luncheon was held in a small room. As it was informal, we could talk freely. My wife, who had a genius for attracting youths because she had four sons of her own, talked mostly with the boys, while my conversation was mostly with the King and Queen. After the first course was served, the King said: "I wish to ask you a question, Mr. Secretary, but you need not answer it if you prefer not or if it causes you any embarrassment." "What is the question, your Majesty?" I asked. "I have heard," he said, "that while your President was in Paris you sent him a remarkable cable which may become historic if the report that has reached us here is true." I replied that I sent the President a number of cables while he was at the Peace Conference, but I could recall none as important or historic as his question implied. The King said: "I will quote the cable you are said to have sent: It was, or as nearly as I can recall:

"President Wilson,
"Peace Conference, Paris.
 "Come home at once. If you do not this country will become a republic.

"Daniels."

As he finished, the King leaned back in his chair and laughed long and heartily, showing he enjoyed the story which he said had been told often in his country. My wife and I and his sons joined in, but the Queen was not greatly amused.

The King showed perfect familiarity with all Naval matters and asked me what the feeling was in the American Navy about the Battle of Jutland. Fortunately for me, I had brought Jellicoe's book with me on the *Leviathan* and had read his story on the voyage coming over. I told him that my feeling as to Jellicoe's account of the Battle of Jutland was that it was, as a lawyer would say, "a plea of confession and avoidance." I said that his book acquitted Jellicoe, the Commander of the Fleet which did not come off victorious, by convicting Jellicoe, the First Sea Lord, whose duty it had been to see that the ships were made ready for battle. I added that the first news of the battle that reached us belatedly was from German sources—no information was given out by the Admiralty—and they reported a victory for the German Fleet.

"It was a great mistake," said the King, "not to have announced at once that the battle had been fought, giving all the facts. As it was, the people were demoralized at the reports of a German victory, whereas it was a drawn battle even though our losses were the greatest. The German Fleet hastened to their home waters and have never sought since to try conclusions with us."

The Queen spoke of her interest in the movement then under way to provide better modern houses for the people, but otherwise her conversation and my wife's were on topics mothers talk most about—their children.

The King was not as tall as his wife. He looked not a bit as Kings have been pictured, but he talked interestingly and had a quiet humor. He showed that he was abreast of current events, including the affairs of the Peace Conference.

As we were driving back to our hotel my wife said to me, "Captain Siler was right." I could not imagine what she was talking about and asked what brought up Captain Siler, an old Confederate soldier school teacher at Holly Springs in Wake County, North Carolina. "Don't you remember how Captain Siler introduced you when in 1889 you delivered the commencement address at his school?" Captain Siler in his introduction had said:

"The highest honor of an Englishman is to introduce his Wellington; a Northerner, his Lincoln; a Southerner, his Lee, but a greater honor is mine, that of introducing the young statesman, Josephus Daniels, who is known on both hemispheres —or will be."

At that time I was unknown outside of my home section, and my wife meant that since being a guest at Windsor, I had become known on two hemispheres.

The next day my wife and I were invited to be present on the reviewing stand when the King reviewed the Anzacs, the tall soldiers from Australia and New Zealand who were honored in England as they were en route home from France after winning glory in the World War. The review ended, the Queen introduced us to "mama," the widow of Edward and mother of the King.

"HE DOESN'T LOOK LIKE A KING"

"I thought we were to see the King," said my disappointed son as we were leaving the palace in Rome where all my staff had been presented to King Victor Emmanuel before Ambassador Thomas Nelson Page and I went into his inner office for a forty-five-minute talk, in which we discussed the relations between our two countries, and other matters growing out of the differences that had developed at the Peace Conference.

In answer to my son's remark, I said, "You met the King when we first arrived." He wasn't wearing a crown but was dressed in the uniform of an officer of the Italian Army. My son asked, "You mean that little man?" When I answered in the affirmative, he said, "He doesn't look like a King." And he didn't, and later history proved that in him the House of Savoy had run down so low that he became an agent of Mussolini and instead of protecting the people when Mussolini marched on Rome, he hastily made terms with him and became his puppet until Mussolini was driven out.

On that day in March, 1919, the King was troubled about Fiume, Durazzo, and particularly about the Yugo-Slavs. He did not impress me as having great qualities, and subsequent events proved my impression was correct.

LOOKED THE PART OF A QUEEN

After seeing the King of Italy, my next visit to royalty was in Paris during the Peace Conference. Learning that Queen Marie, of Rumania, was in my hotel, I asked my Naval Aide to call and "request an audience." That is the correct procedure to get an appointment with royalty. It must always "grant an audience," even when it turns out to be nothing more than talking with a lady. Marie looked queenly—tall and stately and handsome, with the charm which was in evidence when later she made a tour from coast to coast in the United States.

I recall one part of the conversation which showed I was a real commoner. She was talking about the difficult days of readjustment ahead in her country and said that one of the problems was the restoration of agriculture and industry. The Queen said, "Rumania must be helped, else who will wish to be virtuous?" When I suggested that the crown lands ought to be divided among those who till it, she said, "The King was very wise in that he took the step early before it was demanded. But it isn't easy. Yesterday I could look over great stretches of corn and say: 'It *is* mine'; now I can say, 'It *was* mine.'" But she doubted if it would work well, and added that many tillers of the soil preferred to be retainers of the King than to work without direction. She spoke of Wilson's confidence in a world of peace when she talked with him. She said, "I hope, but I look with one eye behind me because I fear selfishness."

I was later to see in Mexico, when Cárdenas was dividing up the large estates under the slogan: "The land belongs to those who till it," how the old hacendados and plutocratic Americans living there said: "The peons will not like it; they prefer to be guided by the rancho grandees." The Queen was as ignorant of the ambitions in the breasts of Rumanian farmers as the old Spanish hacendados were of Mexican tillers of the soil."

ROYALTY FROM HAWAII

I was in Washington in the Cleveland days when Queen Liliuo-kalani from Hawaii arrived to make a fight for restoration to the throne from which she had been evicted by means that reflected no credit on Uncle Sam. Mr. Cleveland denounced the methods employed, but the Queen died an "ex." One of the most queenly-looking Princesses seen in Washington in the Wilson days was Princess David of Hawaii. She was as tall and stately as an Amazon and had the kindliness characteristic of Hawaiians. She had no illusions of the return of royalty and never expected to wear a crown. She was none the less devoted to her country and first visited me to request that a fighting ship of the American Navy be named the *Honolulu*. She was gratified when the promise was made. A friendship between Princess David and my wife caused us to be received in Hawaii by the members of her family and to be introduced to Hawaiian hospitality and Hawaiian food.

PRINCE AXTEL OF DENMARK

Denmark was not in the war, but in September Prince Axtel of that country, cousin of the King, and a party of leading men from his country made a pilgrimage of friendship to Washington. He was a Commander in the Navy. My Diary of September 22 says:

"Lunched at the White House with Prince Axtel. W.W. in fine spirits and full of anecdotes. He told of playing golf with two secret service men—a maid called them 'silver service.' Four little boys came out of the bushes and, pointing to W.W. and then to the secret service men, one of them said to the other: 'Them's his keepers.'

"The Prince referred to the King of Bulgaria as 'a nasty King.'

"Lunched with the Minister from Denmark to meet Prince Axtel. Dinner by Admiral Benson to the Prince. Naval Attachés from foreign countries present. On Sunday I took the Prince and his party on the *Mayflower* to Mount Vernon and, of course, he placed a wreath on the tomb of Washington."

CAROL NOT ADMITTED TO THE UNITED STATES

The next and last King I met—but had little converse with—was Carol of Rumania, who, when he "skeedaddled" out of Rumania, with his lady love—not his wife—Madame Lupescu, found refuge in Mexico. That country, like Holland, prides itself on being a haven for political refugees. When he arrived in Mexico it was suggested that I invite them to the American Embassy. It was not done. Later when he sought the privilege of coming to the United States, presumably to lay claim to the eighty million dollars of Rumanian money held here when his country entered the war, I advised that the United States be not the haven for discredited kings. He did not get permission to enter.

THE KING BUSINESS GOING OUT

It looks as if the trade of Kings is playing out. The war disclosed that most of them were inefficient, a costly and wasteful extravagance, responsible for the lack of ability of their nations to defend themselves, and the worst Kings deserted their people in the critical days of war. Those who remained have been shorn of power and remain only as "symbols of empire."

AN AMERICAN PRINCESS

I must conclude this walking with royalty by saying that of all the great of the earth who have hereditary titles, whom I was privileged to meet, the Princess who in my opinion ranks higher than any is the descendant of Pocahontas, Mrs. Edith Bolling Wilson. In her charming, *My Memoir,* she tells a story of how this royal descent from Pocahontas won her a place among royalty when she and President Wilson were in Europe at the time of the Peace Conference:

"... M. Vesnitch had headed the Serbian Mission which had come to America after our entry into the War. On our arrival in Paris I felt we were already good friends, but could not imagine what he wished to see me about, in such haste.

"He arrived, and, with many apologies and real embarrassment, told me the following: 'I was at a large dinner night before last and had the honor of taking in the Duchess of R. I asked her if she had met the President and Mrs. Wilson, and to my great surprise she answered: "No, and I do not want to meet them. Paris has gone mad about President Wilson and I am sick of hearing about them. What are they? Only ordinary Americans with no claim to aristocracy or title." "Oh," I said, "Duchess, there you are wrong, for Mrs. Wilson is directly descended from a Princess, and of the only aristocracy in America; her grandmother seven times removed was the great Princess Pocahontas. I have just returned a short time ago from the United States and there I read all of this in a paper which I kept and can show to you." "Why," said the Duchess, "this is very important and I knew nothing of it at all. Of course I must go and call on Mrs. Wilson at once and give an entertainment in her honor." 'So,' said M. Vesnitch, 'that is the reason I begged that you see me at once that I might tell you about this....' "

Part Eleven

EPIC LEAGUE OF NATIONS FIGHT

XXXVIII

THE SENATE SABOTAGES THE LEAGUE

WHEN HE arrived in America with the League of Nations Treaty signed at Versailles June 28, Wilson left no stone unturned to win ratification. In August he held a three-hour conference with the Senate Committee on Foreign Relations, whose chairman (Lodge) carried a concealed dagger to the conference and sought some statement that would enable him to drive the dagger into the heart of the Covenant. The report of that discussion covers fifty-six printed pages and discloses that Lodge and other opponents were not seeking light but some way to trap Wilson.

FINANCIERS HAD FIRST LOOK

The Peace Treaty was signed at Versailles, June 28, 1919. On July 4 a copy was in the hands of the House of Morgan, and there was a premature release. Wilson telegraphed from Paris: "Anyone who has possession of the official English text has what he is clearly not entitled to have or communicate." How did this document, held so secretly, get into the hands of Morgan partners? Thomas W. Lamont gave a copy to H. P. Davison, who gave it to Ehihu Root, who showed it to Lodge. Here was the arch enemy of the League in the Senate with the text, while no advocate or any member of the Cabinet had been furnished with it. It turned out that Admiral Sims, who had somehow obtained a copy, had given it to a member of the Morgan firm. A pipe-line seems to have run from Sims in close connection with the partisan foes of Wilson. In this case Lodge had the treaty before the State Department. This leak created the greatest indignation, but nothing was done about it.

LODGE HOSTILE FROM THE START

Some of the opponents of the League wanted to see the treaty before joining their forces with those who had early opposed it. Not Lodge. Though in 1914 he had been one of the earliest advocates of a league to secure peace, he began his fight against Wilson even before the war ended. He was an original advocate of entering the war, but, except for his consistent support of the Navy, he was critical of the policy of the administration, never losing an opportunity to criticize almost every move Wilson made. He denounced the Fourteen Points, opposed Wilson's going to Paris, saying later that Wilson should have followed Lansing's advice not to go, and, when in Paris he should make peace and postpone action on the League. He wrote the Round Robin designed to tell members of the Peace Conference and Wilson's enemies that the President had been repudiated at home, and he accompanied it by the signatures of thirty-nine Republican Senators, who indicated they would kill the treaty that embodied the League.

After Wilson's Boston speech (March, 1919) urging ratification, Lodge made no secret of his plan to "create a situation" in which, if the treaty were beaten, "Wilson's friends should be responsible, and not the opponents of the treaty." This was along the line of the Round Robin he had caused to be sent to Paris. Lodge went further. He wrote to the London *Tory Review* that Wilson had been repudiated; the editor took off post-haste to see Clemenceau and asked him,

> "As the Republicans are now masters of the situation in Washington, and will decide the fate of any Peace Treaty that may be drafted in Paris, could you not establish some liaison with the Republican Party so that you may know how far they will go in approving what is done here?"

The Frenchman didn't bite and asked, "Is it to be open or secret liaison? How can it be open in the face of Wilson's attitude toward the Republican Party? How could it hope to remain secret seeing that no secret is ever kept in Washington?"

In addition to this attempt to weaken Wilson in Paris, Lodge, in December, 1918, had given Henry White a memorandum to be shown to Balfour, Clemenceau, and Nitti. Undoubtedly Lodge presumed upon White's Republicanism to aid him in undermining Wilson. But he was mistaken in his man. White did not show the papers.

In marked contrast with the biting hate in their war over the League of Nations, when Wilson finished his war message to Congress, Senator Lodge had been among the first to give hearty accord, saying, "Mr. President, you have expressed in the loftiest manner possible the sentiments of the American people."

THREW DOWN THE GAUNTLET

In his Boston speech Wilson threw down the gauntlet. Replying to the report that Lodge and others were whetting their knives for the treaty, he said:

"I should welcome no sweeter challenge than that. I have fighting blood in me and it is sometimes a delight to let it have scope, but if it is challenged on this occasion, it will be an indulgence."

In his New York speech, he said:

"When the Treaty comes back, gentlemen on this side will find the Covenant not only in it, but so many threads of the treaty tied to the covenant that you cannot dissect the covenant from the treaty without destroying the vital structure."

WORST AND GREATEST

Wilson's speech, when he took the Treaty to the Senate (July 10), was praised and criticized. John Sharp Williams said: "It is the greatest thing ever uttered by any President since Lincoln died." Brandegee said of it: "Soap bubbles of oratory and souffles of phrases." Henry Watterson called Senators against the League: "Cravens and crooks, hypocrites and liars because of broken promises to Allies." Bryan called opposition to the League "the most colossal crime in all history."

BRITISH VIOLATE DIPLOMATIC USAGE

The files of the papers of that day bear out the opinion expressed by Senator McKellar that Lord Grey's influence helped Lodge to win his fight against the League. In addition there is abundant evidence that British leaders injected themselves into the situation at the suggestion of Colonel House and at the request of Lodge and others who were antagonistic to any alliance or agreement with foreign powers. The first proof of this is in a letter from Colonel House in London, written to Wilson (July 30, 1919), in which he detailed that he dined with Haldane and Grey "to settle" (Grey later suggested the word "settle" should be changed to "discuss") "the League of Nations, and also the naval program and the Irish question. He quoted Grey as ready to come to the United States "for the purpose of discussing these questions."

Wilson had a high opinion of Grey and said he would "look forward to being associated with him," never dreaming that so astute a statesman would inject himself into an American contest, particularly taking sides with those trying to defeat and humiliate the Chief Executive of the country to which he was accredited. Wilson was on his Western trip, speaking for the ratification of the treaty, when Grey arrived (September 26, 1919), and was too ill to see Grey when he returned to Washington. While Grey was in Washington (he was there four months during the crucial League fight in the Senate), the *New York Times* said that he talked with both Republican and Democratic Senators, and added:

> "It can be stated that to some Senators he has exhibited at least one telegram from Premier Lloyd George in which the latter indicated that Lodge reservations as voted on in the Senate on the closing day of the special session, would be accepted by the British Government."

Grey returned to England in January, and shortly thereafter wrote a letter to the *London Times* in which he said it would be "the greatest mistake to refuse that coöperation because conditions are attached to it.... The difficulties or dangers which the Americans foresee in it will probably never arise or be felt by them when they are once in the League," he added, which had no meaning except taking sides with Lodge and against Wilson. The Springfield *Republican* commented:

> "Lodge cannot conceal his pleasure over Lord Grey's acknowledgement that Great Britain would now favor the admission of the United States into the League with almost any reservations rather than have this country stay out entirely; and the acknowledgement undeniably weakens the President in the struggle for a treaty as nearly as possible like the treaty which he signed and which the other powers have ratified.
>
> "Viscount Grey, it must be admitted, acting unofficially for the British Government, and in consequence of a kind of desperation, has become in effect an ally of Lodge, for the senator can now say that reservations to which the British government

Above, Returning from Europe on the *Mt. Vernon. Left to right, seated,* Captain Douglas A. Dismukes, Mrs. Daniels, Secretary Daniels. *Standing,* Rear Admiral Ralph Earle, Admiral R. S. Griffin, Rear Admiral D. W. Taylor, Commander Percy W. Foote. *Below,* Secretary and Mrs. Daniels, Captain Dismukes, officers and fireroom crew when the *Mt. Vernon* was torpedoed. Taken on return trip from France.

POST-WAR AMBASSADORS

Upper left, John W. Davis, Ambassador to Great Britain. *Upper right,* William G. Sharp, Ambassador to France. *Lower left,* Thomas Nelson Page, Ambassador to Italy. *Lower right,* Pleasant A. Stovall, Ambassador to Switzerland.

no longer objects ought no longer to be objectionable to any portion of the American people."

The publication of Grey's letter, following his personal intimate association in Washington with Lodge and other opponents of the League, outraged the sincere advocates of ratification without nullifying reservations, and there was resentment that a British Ambassador should come to Washington on a "special mission" to take sides against the President. There was demand that he be given his papers and sent home. But that demand found no favor in the State Department, where Lansing, like House in London, was glad to have the British interfere in American affairs. With the exception of Lansing, the Cabinet members were incensed at the violation of accepted diplomatic policies. Wilson was astonished and if he had been well would have withdrawn the recognition of Grey as Ambassador to the United States. But there is no doubt how he felt. In the Wilson Papers, drafted in Mrs. Wilson's handwriting, is the following statement:

"When comment was asked for at the Executive Office upon Viscount Grey's extraordinary attempt to influence the action of the President and the Senate it at once became evident that the Executive had been as completely taken by surprise as the general public itself by Lord Grey's utterance.
"It may safely be assumed that had Lord Grey ventured upon any such utterance while he was still at Washington as an ambassador (a post which he has just left with the intimation that he was on leave) his government would have been promptly asked to withdraw him."

In the annals of diplomacy there is not a more flagrant violation of an age-old rule that diplomats to another country must not inject themselves into the affairs of the country to which they are accredited.

SELF-SELECTED ARBITERS

There is no evidence that Viscount Grey sought to discuss "the Naval building program," or "the Irish question," which House had written he and Grey and Haldane and Curzon had gathered in London to "settle." House's letter has a flavor of the tailors of Tooley Street who called themselves "we, the People of England."

Such assumption over a roast-beef dinner in London by self-selected arbiters to dictate to the American Senate and defeat the American President has no parallel in history.

"A PESTILENT ASS"

When a trusted friend informed Wilson that a British officer, General Brancker, was in secret conference with Republican leaders and approving Lodge's annulling reservations, Wilson characterized General Brancker thus: "He proved himself a pestilent ass while he was here and I have sent word to the British Government that we don't want to see him again. We are quite willing to see representatives to the government but not representatives to the press."

No one can read Winston Churchill's excoriation, in his *Aftermath,* of Wilson's attitude as to the Peace Conference without understanding that Wilson was justified in resenting foreign meddling with American affairs. It was in marked contrast with the attitude of Sir Robert Cecil and most British leaders, whose devotion to the League won world commendation.

NO FRONTAL ATTACK ON LEAGUE

Before the Pittsburgh group and other high protectionists had raised a slush fund for propaganda and sabotage, public sentiment favored ratification. Senator Borah, a forthright and downright isolationist, fought the Treaty in the open. Lodge told him he knew that most of the newspapers, the educators, those accustomed to write and speak, and the man in the street favored the League, but Lodge said when they were educated as to the need of reservations (meaning by the Frick money bags and alien organizations), its ratification could be prevented. Lodge played for time for the costly propaganda to get in its work and kept the Treaty in virtual cold storage for long months before he applied the deadly stiletto.

The Republican "whip" of the Senate, James W. Watson, of Indiana, records in his autobiography this conference with Lodge:

"Senator, I don't see how we are going to defeat this proposition. It appears to me that 80 per cent of the people are for it. Fully that percentage of the preachers are advocating it. Churches are very largely favoring it, all the people who have been burdened and oppressed by this awful tragedy of war and who imagine this opens a way to world peace are for it, and I don't see how it is possible to defeat it.

"Lodge then went on to explain how, for instance, we would demand a reservation on the subject of submitting to our government the assumption of a mandate over Armenia, or any other foreign country, 'We can debate that for days and hold up the dangers that it will involve and the responsibilities we will assume if we pursue that course, and we can thoroughly satisfy the country that that would be a most abhorrent policy for us to adopt' ...

"Senator Lodge then went on for two hours to explain other reservations and went into the details of situations that would be thus evolved, until I became thoroughly satisfied that the treaty could be beaten in that way."

A poll of 17,000 Protestant, Catholic, and Jewish clergy gave all but 800 favoring entry into the League of Nations.

Taft sincerely wanted peace and in many ways he and Wilson fought together. But Taft once said: "Wilson thinks he is running the whole show himself. Sometimes I feel like bursting; as Theodore does the bursting, perhaps I can pursue some other function."

THREE LITTLE ELEPHANTS

Throughout the contest, the cartoonists were busy. One of the best was by Harding of the Brooklyn *Eagle*. It was entitled "Three Little Elephants" with their arms cupped, one over the ears, another over the eyes, and another over the mouth:

> "Lodge—'Hear No Good of the League.'
> Knox—'See No Good of the League.'
> Borah—'Speak No Good of the League.' "

PROTECTION PROPAGANDA KILLED LEAGUE

It was not until the early autumn that the cloven hoof of the high protectionists was seen in the organizing to scrap the League. It was plain that money was supplied to the inspired organizations of various groups active in opposition, travelling all over the country. Where did it come from? There was secrecy about it for a time.

One day my wife, who had been at luncheon with the wives of some of the very rich, confided to me that they were against the League because they feared it would result in tearing down the tariff walls by which they had their wealth. She said she had not talked with the wife of a high protectionist who was not opposed to the League. That opened my eyes. Except some big concerns with foreign connections, and some who put patriotism above pelf, those who had secured high tariff laws and wanted them continued, including the Home Market Club of Boston which backed Lodge, were all lined up to kill the League. Pittsburgh supplied the boodle.

DESIRED RESERVOIR FOUND

In his book, *Frick the Man,* Colonel George Harvey, who was the "eager propagandist" among the conspirators to stab the League of Nations to death, records that on May 11, 1919, the group opposing the League met at the home of Senator Brandegee at the time when the campaign against the League was "seriously endangered." The outlook was "lamentably gloomy" when Senator Knox of Pittsburgh suggested "as a last resort" that an appeal should be made to Mr. Frick and Mr. Mellon to put up the money to carry on the fight. Harvey was sent to "pull the leg" of Frick first. Mellon came across next. Harvey says: "The desired reservoir has been found and it was deep and full." After investing in the fight Frick said, "Put up a good fight. Now that we are in, we must win." Knox wrote that he obtained the same amount from Mr. Mellon that Frick contributed. Harvey shows that the money furnished by Frick and Mellon—others, too, put up money—killed the League. He writes:

> "All anxiety respecting the sinews of war was dispelled. Rejoicing prevailed in the camp of the Irreconcilables. Efforts were redoubled all along the line and the redoubtable little band pushed on to victory which, whether desirable or not, presently was won in the Senate and was ultimately ratified by the people. Mr. Frick's interest became intense and never lagged for a moment."

In his book Colonel Harvey does not state the amount contributed by Mellon and Frick, but he was quoted as saying there was a guarantee fund of five million dollars by Frick, and Knox wrote that he "obtained the same amount from Mr. Mellon" that Frick contributed.

Not only did Frick and other steel men finance the fight against the League, but some profiteered in war contracts. When the war began, the Navy was paying 01.90 cents per pound for ship plates. When the Shipping Board ordered large quantities, the steel men made a charge of four cents for the same plates. William Denman, Chairman, came to see me and asked what the Navy was paying. He felt outraged that he was asked more than double. Wishing to ascertain what it cost to produce ship plates, B. M. Baruch, Chairman of the War Industries Board, went to see Mr. Frick and told him that President Wilson wished to know what it cost to produce the plates. Frick said, "It costs us $2\frac{1}{2}$ cents." Baruch asked, "Including a profit?" Frick answered, "Only sufficient to safeguard the manufacturer against loss." After much higgling as war went on, Uncle Sam paid 03.41 cents a pound. But Frick's biographer says that Frick would have no part in profiteering!

LODGE ACCEPTED RESPONSIBILITY

After the Treaty was formally presented to the Senate on July 10, 1919, Lodge stretched out the hearings in his committee for forty-five days, and scores of destructive amendments were introduced. During this waste of time Lodge was trying to round up the solid Republican vote for his so-called reservations, which Wilson called "nullifications."

During the dawdling, running into months, when press, people, and pulpit were demanding action, Lodge in his committee report declared it was "unfitting to suggest that if the Senate adopted amendments or reservations the United States will be excluded from the League," and added emphatically: "That is one thing that certainly will not happen." And yet that was "certainly the one thing" that did happen, and years later Lodge virtually accepted responsibility, saying:

"I will frankly confess that in the time which has elapsed since the Senate's discussion of the League I have become more and more satisfied that the final decision of the Senate was correct."

When in the studied delays, destructive amendments including rejection of Article 10, were approved by a Senate majority, Wilson said:

"That is a rejection of the Covenant. That is an absolute refusal to carry any part of the same responsibility that the other members of the League carry. This (Article 10) is the heart of the Covenant."

Lodge attributed the utterance to "pride of authorship."

On November 19 when Lodge called for a vote of ratification of the Treaty with the reservations, thirty-nine voted "aye" and fifty-five "nay." Five Democrats voted with the thirty-four Republicans, and thirteen Republicans voted "nay."

Finally, when Senator Underwood proposed a resolution to ratify the Treaty as sent to the Senate by Wilson, it was rejected by a vote of thirty-eight yeas to fifty-three nays. One Republican voted "aye" and seven Democrats voted "nay." And then the Sixty-Seventh Congress adjourned.

Before the votes, Senator Hitchcock, who was the leader in the fight for ratification, had asked Wilson's counsel. In a letter (November 18), Wilson said:

"In my opinion the resolution in that form does not provide for ratification, but rather for the nullification of the treaty. I sincerely hope the friends and supporters of the treaty will vote against the Lodge resolution of ratification.... I understand the door will then probably be open for a genuine resolution of ratification."

There followed attempts to recall the killing of the League.

After the rejection of the League of Nations, a gentleman of high character in Pittsburgh, explaining the Republican victory, wrote me that it was brought about as the result of a five-million-dollar-propaganda campaign financed by Republican capitalists to defeat the League of Nations. He said:

"The Irish Free State advocates were stirred up while the Poles were angered with reports that Wilson was responsible for the failure to give East Prussia to the Poles and to evacuate the Germans from that region; the 30,000 Lithuanians in Chicago were agitated with reports that Wilson favored the Poles with Vilna; the Hungarians were told that Wilson was an accomplice in the slicing of Hungary; the Yugo-Slavs were told that Wilson, despising Slavs, had given Dalmatia with the Croatian population to Italy; the Italians were told that Wilson, plotting with Lord Cecil and Clemenceau was responsible for cheating Italy of its fruits of victory in the division of the colonies; the Norse, essentially pacific and resentful of being drawn into war, being generally favorable to Germany, were told that Wilson had dragged them into war; the Austrians were educated to blame Wilson for the delimitation of Austrian boundaries, and, in fact, a cause of resentment was found for every nationality, whether favored by the Treaty of Versailles and, in this adroit work, Harvey had the assistance of such master propagandists as George Sylvester Viereck, the leading German spokesman in America prior to the World War (II), Daniel F. Cohalan, Surrogate of New York, who sounded the tocsins for the Irish Free State, and others.... The conflicting rivalries and claims of racial antagonists were aroused to a boiling point, yet adroitly fired at one objective: the destruction of the League of Nations as a Wilsonian creation, as a tool of British diplomacy."

Wilson said of the Lodge forces: "They have poisoned the wells of public sentiment." The Frick money was used to scatter the poison, particularly with hyphenated Americans.

TREATY NOT RETURNED

The saddest hours in the Cabinet meetings were in the days after the Senate killed the League of Nations Treaty. I recall the President sitting and speaking critically, even bitterly, about the men who had killed the Treaty. "It's dead and lies over there," he said one day, pointing to a place. "Every morning I put flowers on its grave."

One day Burleson suggested that Wilson send the Treaty back to the Senate and say what reservations he would accept. "Otherwise," said Burleson, "people will think Wilson's stubbornness killed the Treaty." Burleson said if the President sent it back and the Senate refused to accept what Wilson proposed, the people would blame the Senators. Wilson replied:

"The devils had taken me up to high mountains to be tempted of them, but I had forced British and French statesmen (I do not trust them) to sign an Americanized treaty. I am compelled to be sincere if they are not. I can stand defeat. I cannot stand retreat from conscientious duty. I may not talk as well but I can still use the English language and if the people do not see the issue clear, I will put it so plain they must see it."

Burleson thought other issues in the campaign would outweigh the Treaty, among them the cost of living and taxes. Meredith and Palmer both agreed with Burleson and advised that sending the Treaty back with statements of acceptable reservations would be good tactics.

"I will not play for position," said Wilson. "This is no time for tactics. It is time to stand square."

"I said, "If the treaty is sent back, Borah will use an axe to cut it to pieces, and Lodge will use poison gas and the issue will be between reservations instead of upon the principle of a peace treaty."

Newton Baker and W. B. Wilson took the same position with regard to reservations.

CONCILIATION FAILED

The Treaty, though ratification had been defeated in November, was brought back to the Senate in January, and a Committee on Conciliation was appointed which sought to secure such reservations as would be "interpretative and not destructive." There is evidence indisputable that Lodge's program was to induce mild reservationist Republicans to agree to reservations so destructive that the Democrats would not accept them. His tactics were to make mild reservationists and Democrats believe he wished ratification, while all the time Borah and his irreconcilables knew Lodge would not vote for anything that would not insure the defeat of ratification. Lodge played a double game, making Senator Colt, a sincere Republican in favor of the League, and Democrats believe he wanted a compromise that would result in ratification, while his attitude was what a Republican newspaper said in big headlines: "Republicans Willing to Compromise But Will Concede Nothing." He held meetings with advocates of ratification with clarifying amendments. Thirty Democratic Senators met at the home of Senator Owen (January 12). They declared for "interpretative and against destructive reservations." On the 23rd the Associated Press predicted an agreement along that line. Mr. Taft went to Washington to urge compromise and most Democrats were in agreement with his proposal. Some believed that Lodge might accept the "interpretative" reservations discussed in the Bi-Partisan Conference. Then two things happened that killed the hoped-for agreement:

1. Lodge asked to leave the conference to lunch with Sir Edward Grey, the British Ambassador. Senator McKellar said: "I have always believed but for Senator Lodge's luncheon engagement with Lord Grey on that particular day, we would have brought about a ratification of the Treaty, including the League." There is no doubt Grey was in close association with Lodge, so much so as to make Wilson feel he had violated the accepted diplomatic code.

2. The Bitter End Republican Senators—the irreconcilables who had gone along with Lodge on the assurance of Borah and Watson that Lodge would make or find a way to scrap the League—were disturbed that Lodge was consorting with the friends of the League. They called a meeting (January 23), and the *Post* printed that the indignation of these outraged statesmen "grew and grew" and the meeting seethed with "threats to repudiate Lodge's leadership." They summoned Lodge to the office of Hiram Johnson, who was fired by an aroused temper. They would stand for nothing but the original Lodge nullifications camouflaged as reservations. The Bi-Partisan Conference held an expiring session when Lodge told the members he would not accept what had previously virtually been agreed upon. Lodge was well content. He had persuaded many that he was not an irreconcilable opponent of the League at the same time that he had maneuvered its rejection, and he declared its death was due to Wilson's insistence upon it with un-American provisions. He said the Democrats must accept his original reservations—with Article X in its exact language—or the Treaty would fail, and its failure would be laid at Wilson's door. But history written by fair-minded men lays the killing to Lodge, and his own later statements and those of his close friends show that he felt proud of his leadership in keeping America out of the League and thereby repudiating the country's pledge that World War I was waged as "a war against war."

RATIFICATION AGAIN DEFEATED

The resolution of ratification finally came before the Senate (March 19, 1920). When the vote was taken, Burleson and I were in the Senate Chamber hoping against hope. The papers next day said we were "button-holing waverers." The resolution received forty-nine affirmative to thirty-five negative votes. Twenty-three Democrats voted or were paired in favor of ratification, and twenty-five

Democrats and fourteen Republicans voted or were paired against the ratification with the reservations. On March 19 Lodge moved to return the Treaty, which had been kicked about and maimed for many months, to the President, and this action was taken by a vote of forty-seven to thirty-seven, all the Republicans and six Democrats favoring that action. The League was dead and Lodge, gloating that no United Nations could prevent war, closed his record with a vain attempt to lay at Wilson's door responsibility for his own failure to embrace the opportunity he had envisioned in his Union College address.

BURIAL OF THE LEAGUE

The League of Nations was dead. Lodge preached its funeral. The pall-bearers—the Penroses, the Reeds, the Brandegees, men of the earth earthy, who had never entertained a vision splendid—had no qualms as they interred the corpse in the sepulchre provided in the Senate Chamber for the repose of the victims of the One-Third dagger. To the high protectionists it was the burial of a potential enemy, and they paid for the funeral robes and rites. To the aliens, who had fattened on American residence without giving allegiance to the country that gave them sustenance, there was the comfort that comes to those who love vengeance. To the partisans, who felt that the very hope of regaining power was the elimination of Wilson and his ideals, the interment removed the only obstacle to obtaining the spoils of victory. To the congenital isolationists there was the dream that, living unto itself, America could be freed from the duty of sharing its faiths and obligations with the millions who looked out of darkened windows in hope that the rays of liberty from the New World might brighten their lives.

Put the seals on the coffin so that there can be no resurrection, said Lodge as he read the "dust-to-dust" ritual. The immovable stone was placed over the grave. Guards were stationed to keep away those who might roll it away. Yes, it was dead beyond resurrection, "as dead as Hector," said Jim Reed. "As dead as Marley's ghost," cried Lodge. Americans were told they could turn undisturbed to selfish money-making, gloating, "Let Europe stew in its own juice." But it would not stay dead. You cannot permanently inter a principle that had caught the radiance coming from the Prince of Peace. While the pallbearers and the isolationists held their wake, an uneasy conscience would not let Brutus and Cassius and Casca and the other murderers sleep.

Yes, the League was dead and officially so proclaimed when Wilson's "solemn referendum" was rejected in the November (1920) election and the candidate of the nullifiers was elected president. However, Secretary of State Hughes advised that it be taken out of the archives and sent to the Senate. Harding agreed at first, but recanted. Hughes had told the voters that the surest way to get into the League was to elect Harding. He wished to keep his word but was overruled by the isolationists who nominated Harding. An uneasy conscience could not be deadened. "Let us have an association of nations to promote peace," said Harding, who had held the clothes of those who stoned the League. He called the Washington Conference, which, believing peace was advanced, strengthened Japan for its treachery at Pearl Harbor and surrendered supremacy in Naval power to Britain.

Yes, the League of Nations was dead. Even a Democratic National Convention was deaf to the eloquent and inspiring call of Newton Baker to revivify it. When John H. Clarke put off the judicial robes to lead the people to another battle, he was ridiculed as a visionary dreamer. However, on the banks of the great lake at Geneva, the League was functioning, but in a limping way without the participation of the two biggest nations. Russia and the United States were absent without leave. Important nations lacked the Wilson vision, but Uncle Sam's conscience compelled some little participation without obligation. And in 1945, to the consternation of those who had worn funeral robes in 1919, Wilson's League, only changed to meet changed conditions, was approved by fifty nations. This generation has lived to see the truth of the immortal doctrine of the Resurrection.

WHO KILLED COCK ROBIN?

As I saw them, the Senators—one by one—send their poisoned arrows hurtling into the body of the League, I could but paraphrase the rhyme of "Who Killed Cock Robin?"

> "Who Killed Cock Robin?
> 'I,' said Cabot Lodge,
> 'You never saw me dodge
> I killed Cock Robin.'

"Who gave the funeral rose?
'I,' said Boise Penrose,
'I gave him the dose
I killed Cock Robin.'

"Who killed Cock Robin?
'I,' said Albert Fall,
'I shot best of all,
I killed Cock Robin.'

"Who killed Cock Robin?
'I,' said Steel Magnate Frick,
'My money did the trick,
I killed Cock Robin.'

"Who killed Cock Robin?
'I,' said William Borah,
'I did not him adore
I killed Cock Robin.'

"Who saw him bleed?
'I,' said Jim Reed,
'I did it with my snead
And am proud of my deed.'

"Who saw him die?
'I,' said Gerald Nye
'With my little eye,
I saw him die.'

"Who knocked off his block?
'I,' said Philander Knox,
'I put his body in a box,
He's safe under the rocks.'"

WHY LODGE HATED WILSON

"I am fighting President Wilson; that I am willing to acknowledge," said Henry Cabot Lodge at Boston during the battle over
the League of Nations in the Senate. He made no secret of it. It
was the man he was fighting. The League, and its destruction, was
the weapon he used against Wilson.

Why did Senator Lodge embitter his own life and reap repudiation
by hate of Woodrow Wilson? At the Republican Convention in
1920 Lodge with bitterness used these fighting words:

"Mr. Wilson and his dynasty, his heirs and assigns, or anybody that is his, anybody who with bent knee has served his purposes, must be driven from all control, from all influence upon the Government of the United States. They must be driven from office and power."

What actuated Lodge's hate? I once said in an address on "Two Scholars in Politics," that it had its origin in the difference between the article "a" and "the." Before Wilson became President writers referred to Lodge as "*the* scholar in politics." With the advent of Wilson Lodge dropped to "*a*" scholar in politics.

No longer could Lodge chant unchallenged as "the scholar" in the realm of politics. He could not declaim a bit of doggerel he liked:

> "My name it is Benjamin Jowett,
>   I'm master of Baliol College,
> Whatever is known, I know it.
>   What I don't know isn't knowledge."

However, the basic reason was that Lodge thought if he could cause the rejection of "Wilson's League," as he always called it, his party would make him President. He believed if the League was ratified the glory that would be accorded Wilson would give him a third term. That would be fatal to Lodge's soaring ambition.

In 1916, when Theodore Roosevelt deserted the party he had headed in 1912 (that party died, according to Dr. Eliot, because "the one-man idol was not a good foundation"), and returned to the Republican Party, seeing that he could not get the nomination himself, he volunteered to be active in the campaign if the party would nominate Lodge. The basis of their revived friendship (Lodge had supported Taft) was hatred of Wilson. This hatred went back to 1912, when Wilson had thwarted Theodore Roosevelt's ambition to return to the White House (no man since Old Hickory ever voluntarily left it). Hatred of Wilson was an obsession with Lodge and Roosevelt and cemented the bitterness both manifested as long as they lived.

By all the rules of the game, Lodge deserved the nomination he coveted in 1920. That failure was gall and wormwood to him. He had created the issue, "Let Europe stew in its own juice," which enabled the profiteers, protectionists, and isolationists to elect Harding. He had even forgotten in his obsession that at Union College in 1915 he had said:

"The great nations must be so united as to be able to say to a single country, 'You must not go to war,' and they can only say that effectively when the country desiring war knows that the force which the united nations place behind peace is irresistible."

Lodge had also conveniently forgotten that at the dinner of the League to Enforce Peace in Washington in 1916, he had said:

"It is the vision of a perhaps impossible perfection that has led humanity across the centuries. If our aspirations are for that which is great and beautiful and good and beneficent to humanity, even when we do not achieve our end, even if the results are little, we can at least remember Arnold's lines:

"'Charge, then, and be dumb,
　　Let the victors, when they come,
　　When the forts of folly fall,
　　Find your body at the wall!'"

Later Newton Baker was to remind the people that Lodge was AWOL when the time came to charge against the "forts of folly."

THEODORE ROOSEVELT JEALOUS OF WILSON

Theodore Roosevelt gave early strength to the opponents of the League. He had done so many good things in his day that his word attracted thousands where the cold and scholarly Lodge would not have been heeded.

Wilson won the gratitude of all mankind when the Treaty of Peace was signed at Versailles. But the jealousy and hate of Roosevelt and Lodge would not let them give him the acclaim he had won.

VENOM OF LODGE AND THEODORE ROOSEVELT

The opposition to the League by Lodge and Roosevelt was not against that document. It had been fashioned on lines they had long advocated. As far back as 1915 T. R. wrote Lodge approval of the "force" they decried in 1919 when Wilson stressed "moral force," for T. R. had written then: "Nothing can be truer than the folly of making treaties which have no force and no intent of enforcement behind them."

And when he received the Nobel Peace Prize at Christiana in 1910, Theodore Roosevelt said:

"It would be a master stroke if those powers honestly bent on peace would form a League of Peace, not only to keep the peace among themselves, but to prevent, by force, if necessary, its being broken by others. . . .

"The ruler or statesman who should bring about such a combination would have earned his place in history for all time, and his title to the gratitude of mankind."

Wilson did that very thing—he "brought about the combination," but Roosevelt conspired with Lodge in keeping the United States out of the League. They could not prevent Wilson's securing "the gratitude of mankind."

The publication of the letters that passed between Lodge and Roosevelt are proof positive of their personal venom toward the Wilson administration. Here are some extracts of letters from T. R.:

January 15, 1916: "Wilson is astute and conscienceless. His motives have been base. Wilson and Daniels lied about the number of ships."

February, 1917: "Wilson is responsible for Germany's wrong to us. If Wilson does not go to war, I will skin him alive."

May, 1917: "The only arch offender is Wilson. If our people were only really awake, he would be impeached tomorrow. Daniels, Baker, and the General Staff are merely his tools."

August, 1917: "I cannot run around slopping over an administration which I despise and distrust. The whole attitude of the administration has been really infamous."

October 9, 1918: "I sympathize with the Western gentleman who said: 'If Wilson had the chance, he would double-cross his creator.' "

In like vein Lodge wrote to Roosevelt:

January 15, 1915: "If I had let go about Daniels as I should have liked to do, my speech would have been called partisan. But Daniels is intolerable.

February 9, 1916: "All that is told us about the Navy Department is one long issue of misleading statements. Daniels has got about him officers who hold their position solely on condition that they say what he wants them to say. Daniels reports he is following the General Board. He is doing just the opposite." [This after the Wilson big building program had been urged in Congress by Wilson, the General Board and myself.]

November 15, 1918: "Daniels came to Massachusetts and substantially told all the workers at Fore River that they had to vote the Democratic ticket."

November 26. "The League should not be attached to the Treaty of Peace. We should deal with it first and by itself."

When Roosevelt was asking to be allowed to raise a Division in the Army, he wrote Lodge: "I say nothing about Wilson in public now as I have applied for leave to raise a division. I doubt the propriety of doing so.... The President is backing away from duty."

Referring to Lodge's statement in a political talk in Massachusetts, I said: "I did not give any such instructions. Before I went to Massachusetts, Lodge and his son-in-law, speaking in Maine, had told the voters that the South was in the saddle and was running the government. Answering that statement, I told the voters of Massachusetts that the Navy was spending more money in Massachusetts and employing more men than in all the South Atlantic States. I then contrasted what the Navy was doing for Massachusetts and all New England in dollars and numbers with what had been done when a Massachusetts man was Secretary of the Navy, and I showed that dollars had gone to Massachusetts under a Democratic administration compared with pennies under a Republican administration.

BITTER WORDS SPOKEN

George Harvey, who was to get his reward by wearing knee pants in the American Embassy in London, employed a particularly vindictive and vicious pen against Wilson. This extract is from what he called "The International Hymn" sung by advocates of the League:

> "Our foreign countries,
> The lands of Chimpanzee,
> Thy name we love."

A Texas writer of that period said: "To follow the trail of Lodge would have broken the back of the most supple rattlesnake."

Wilson experienced what Gibbon saw was the portion of leaders of vision: "The first moment of public safety is devoted to gratitude and joy; but the second is diligently occupied by envy and calumny."

REVENGE WITHOUT REWARD

Lodge got his revenge, but not the reward he expected when his party elected Harding. Gloatingly and venomously he said: "Wilson's League of Nations is dead by the verdict of the great tribunal of the people."

Though early in the administration Lodge had stood by Wilson in the matter of the Panama tolls, and had congratulated him on his speech declaring war, the break between them later was complete. Speaking in war days at Boston, Lodge stated that Wilson's strong words to Germany were not meant seriously, and that Germany was destroying American rights because she knew or believed the United States would not defend those rights. He charged that Wilson had sent a straightforward message to Germany over the sinking of the *Lusitania,* which was made public, and then had given intimation to the German government that a proposal for arbitration would be acceptable. Wilson declared, "The statement made by Senator Lodge is untrue. No postscript or amendment of the *Lusitania* note was ever written or contemplated by me except such changes as I, myself, made which strengthened or emphasized the protest." Lodge claimed that the information came to him from a friend. Lodge's venom caused him, without investigation, to broadcast a false and slanderous charge against the President.

Is it any wonder that Wilson fully reciprocated Lodge's animosity? Invited to speak at the 100th anniversary of St. John's Church, Wilson wrote to the rector (December 19, 1916):

"I find upon examining the program Senator Lodge is announced as one of the speakers. Senator Lodge's conduct during the recent campaign makes it impossible with self-respect to join in any exercises in which he takes part or to associate myself with him in any way."

Lodge spoke. Lansing and Lane (neither loved Wilson) were the only members of the Cabinet who attended. I felt that loyalty to Wilson should keep me away. My Diary said:

" 'I am afraid I will not have on the proper wedding gar-
ments, i.e., I will not have a ticket of admission.' I related a
story attributed to Lincoln. Shortly after his inauguration an old
friend from Illinois was an applicant for an appointment. He
secured a trunkful of letters recommending him and took them
to Washington to file in the appropriate departments. However,
Lincoln, knowing him well, did not care anything about recommendations and made the appointment without seeing
them.

" 'What shall I do with all the recommendations I have
brought, Mr. President?' asked the new appointee who got the
job on his own.

"Quizzically Lincoln said, 'Keep them. Some day you may
wish to join St. John's Church and then you will need recommendations.' "

OPPORTUNITY KNOCKED ONLY ONCE

Opportunity knocked at Lodge's door. He was deaf to the summons. In his Memoirs he sought to lay the crime of the century
at the door of Wilson, alleging that the President had lost "the
greatest opportunity ever given to a statesman," and quoted as
applicable to Wilson:

> "it is the hour of fate,
> ... but those who doubt or hesitate,
> Seek me in vain and uselessly implore.
> I come and I return no more."

Lodge was unwittingly writing his own condemnation.

MRS. WILSON'S DIAGNOSIS

Mrs. Wilson, years later, made the best diagnosis of Lodge's policy:

"My conviction is that Mr. Lodge put the world back fifty
years, and that at his door lies the wreckage of human hopes
and the peril to human lives that affect mankind today."

If she had written this in 1944 she could truthfully have added:

"His fight against the League has cost America over a million
casualties in World War II and hundreds of billions of dollars.
It has put mourning on thousands of homes."

IMMOVABLE NOT STUBBORN

There was a concerted attempt to make people believe that Wilson was stubborn and would accept no changes in the draft he brought from Paris. That was far from the truth. In fact, on February 7, he wrote Senator Hitchcock about the explanatory and constructive reservations, saying, "I have once more gone over the reservations proposed by yourself and am glad to say that I can accept them as they stand."

When urged by some of his closest friends to compromise and accept reservations which he knew were destructive, Wilson stood unmoved. He yielded everything in his letter to Hitchcock that was possible without cutting the heart out of the covenant. Even Ray Stannard Baker, who had been close to Wilson at Paris and was his authorized biographer, was stampeded into urging Wilson to accept undesirable reservations. Baker wrote and in person advised him to "get something done quickly, some going organization to meet the problem of the world—get the spirit, a real League will grow."

When she saw how his travail was hampering his recovery, even Mrs. Wilson advised compromise. "And you too, Edith!" But she was moved only by devotion to him and all else was secondary. She and Baker and other friends who were carried away by the desire to "get something done" later realized that the "something" they advised meant nullification and not compromise. Baker later came to see that Wilson was right and said, "Wilson is about the only immovable thing left"; and of his last visit to Wilson (late in February, 1919), he wrote:

"I shall never forget the sad finality of the President's words regarding the situation. He said: 'These reservations (that is, the reservations demanded by the Lodge group) are not made by thoughtful men to improve the Covenant; they represent a dishonorable attempt, on the part of leaders who do not speak for the people, to escape any real responsibility, so far as the United States are concerned, for world peace in future years. They are essentially partisan political devices. If I accept them, these senators will merely offer new ones, even more humiliating. These evil men intend to destroy the League."

And Wilson was right!

"I AM NOT HIS KEEPER"

Wilson's last known reference to Lodge was when the sun shone on the earthly Valhalla of the nation on the day at Arlington when America buried the sacred ashes of its unknown soldier. The sun shone on the carriage of a citizen, tired and gray, in the long line that had come to pay tribute to the nameless hero.

There was a delay in the procession, and a young army officer rode down the line in search of Senator Lodge, who was to take part in the ceremony. Before the carriage of the citizen who waited in the line, he halted.

"Can you tell me where I can find Senator Lodge?" he asked.

The man in the carriage looked at the officer for a second in resentment before seeing his youth. Then he spoke.

"I am not his keeper," said Woodrow Wilson.

WHEN WILSON DIED

Lodge appeared only once again in the Wilson period. When (February 4, 1924) Senator Robinson announced the death of Wilson and offered fitting resolutions, Lodge rose and spoke in favor of their adoption. The highest tribute in his speech was that Wilson was "a chief figure" in the days when truth to history should have caused him to call Wilson "THE chief figure" in all the world. He made no reference to Wilson's achievements as President or to his masterly strategy in war and devotion to peace. Lodge was appointed on the committee to attend the funeral, but a slight cold prevented.

Lodge was to live long enough to feel what he regarded as the ingratitude of his party as he was passed by at the next Republican Convention. He died without a single great measure bearing his name, though he had served in Congress many years. He is remembered chiefly as the leader who, after praiseworthy service during World War I, afterwards "Kept us out of peace."

In the historic duel between them, these questions have been asked: Did Lodge Win? Or did Wilson?

The answer is that in 1945 fifty countries organized the United Nations in a peace pact shot through with the spirit and zeal of Woodrow Wilson's League of Nations.

NOBEL PRIZE AWARD

It was after the rejection of Wilson's solemn referendum on the League that in December, 1920, the Nobel Peace Prize was awarded to him. That was the court of world opinion overruling the act of the United States Senate in 1919 and foreshadowing the reversal by that body in 1945.

XXXIX

A COVENANTER FIGHTS FOR THE COVENANT

WILSON BEGAN HIS fight for the League of Nations even before
he called on Congress to carry "this great peaceful people
into the most terrible and disastrous of wars," so that by "the concert
of free people" victory would bring an end of war and "make the
world safe for democracy."

He made it one of the Fourteen Points—"a general association of
nations"—when he secured acceptance by the Allied nations and the
Germans before he would agree to an Armistice.

Wilson went to Paris to secure the League as in integral part of
the peace treaty. The story of his unyielding and successful victory
over open and secret enemies at the Peace Conference is an epic of
the crusading Covenanter who could "do no otherwise." Returning
to the United States to sign acts of Congress in March, he opened his
campaign for the League when he landed in Boston, the locale
of the Home Market Club and the State of Henry Cabot Lodge, who
had sent a poisoned dagger to Paris in the shape of a Round Robin
seeking to undermine Wilson's influence with Lloyd George and
Orlando and Clemenceau. Wilson was strongly supported by Senator
Murray Crane and tepidly by Governor Coolidge. Again, before
sailing from New York on his return to Paris, introduced by Governor Al Smith, he threw down the gauntlet. He said the opponents
of the League had "a comprehensive ignorance of the state of the
world,"—that the American people understood what he was talking
about even "if certain politicians don't." In that March, Boston and
New York favored entrance into the League. Their backsliding came
later.

On July 10, when Wilson spoke to the Senate urging ratification,
only one Republican applauded his speech—McCumber, of North
Dakota, later to be the only Republican Senator to vote for it without
reservations. He knew as well as Wilson that the reservations were
nullifications.

476

"TIME FOR SENATORS TO SPEAK"

At that time, in spite of the lack of applause by Republican Senators, Wilson's confidence was perfect that his country would accept the leadership in world organization to outlaw war. The load of anxiety of the waiting months in Paris was gone, and he was supremely satisfied as he looked to the United States' taking its seat at the head of the table at Geneva. He was in a happy and contented mood on the night of July 14, 1919, when, uninvited and unannounced he and Mrs. Wilson appeared at a Bastille Day dinner and celebration at the home of Ambassador Jusserand. He had but a few days before returned from Paris with the League and had been welcomed enthusiastically in Washington. This is taken from my Diary July 15:

"Bastille Day was celebrated at the French Embassy with a dinner to Cabinet Members and other Officials and Senators and their wives and a large reception afterwards. While we were seated at dinner, suddenly the Marine Band struck up the national air. Ambassador Jusserand and his wife, showing surprise, hastily rose from the table and went into the drawing room where to their surprise they found President and Mrs. Wilson. Invited into the dining room, President Wilson in a brief talk said that as he and Mrs. Wilson were sitting on the White House porch, she remarked that as this was Bastille Day, the French Ambassador was celebrating it with a large reception. Wilson said, 'Let us go and join with these friends in their patriotic day.' When Mrs. Wilson replied, 'We have not been invited,' he pushed that aside and they came unbidden. Briefly and illuminatingly he touched upon the Peace Conference and how it had cemented the ties with France. Turning to the Senators, he said, 'But this is the time for Senators to speak,' the reference being to the coming fight over ratification. That allusion made a big hit."

ILLUMINATING DOME OF CAPITOL

It was the custom in Washington in the early part of 1919—it still is—to illuminate the dome of the Capitol upon notable occasions. Observing that it was not illuminated the night the cheering population welcomed President Wilson back from Paris, my wife said to the President, "I think it is a shame that Congress did not order the dome of the Capitol illuminated tonight."

"Do not let that trouble you, Mrs. Daniels," he replied. "There are domes underneath the Capitol building that need illuminating more than the physical one."

THE COVENANT WRITTEN ON HIS HEART

To Wilson the League of Nations was as sacred as the Holy Grail, and he bore it home with a deep sense that Americans had been privileged to keep the pledge made when youths shouldered their guns—that they were fighting to win peace. In his passion for peace, it could be said of Wilson and the Covenant what Queen Mary said of her heart's desire: "When I am dead you will find Calais written on my heart." His heart beat high when the people welcomed him with their support, as he bore the Covenant to Washington, and as, in an early White House Conference, he outlined the chart of entrance into the haven of lasting peace. In the first hours of almost universal rejoicing over the victory at Versailles, the people, the press, and the pulpit hailed the League as the long sought deliverance from the pestilence of war. That was in July and August, 1919. That was before partisan Senators, backed by a five-million-dollar-propaganda fund, had begun the campaign to sabotage it.

CARRIED NEXT TO HIS HEART

I always knew that the League of Nations was close to Wilson's heart but I did not know that he literally carried the document next to his physical heart until I learned it from Ray Stannard Baker. Writing of the trip from France to Boston (February, 1919) on the *George Washington,* Baker says:

"During all the stormy voyage the President carried that precious document—the first tentative draft of the League of Nations Covenant—in the inside breast-pocket of his coat. Once when he was climbing the stairs to the ship's bridge and his coat flew open, I saw it there. It was the most cherished thing in his life."

HE GOES TO THE COUNTRY

When Wilson saw in the early fall the organized and well-financed opposition to ratification, he felt that the only way to win was to go to the country. He believed the people would build such a backfire against them that Senators could not betray the pledge made to the armed men who believed they were fighting in "a war against war." He left Washington on September 3, spoke in seventeen Western States and travelled 8,000 miles. The complete text of these masterly arguments covers 370 printed pages.

ADVISED AGAINST THE TRIP

Secretary Baker advised Wilson not to undertake so strenuous and taxing a campaign. His physician, Dr. Grayson, vainly tried to induce him not to go. Wilson felt it a call to a holy duty and said that though it might cost him his life he would "willingly make the sacrifice to save the Treaty." In his autobiography Editor Kohlsaat, who had been in Paris during the Peace Conference, writes that, learning Wilson was planning to make a swing around the circle as far as the Pacific to arouse the people to whole-heartedly support the League, he went to the White House to try to dissuade him from so severe a tax upon his strength. He found Wilson determined on the trip and quotes him as saying: "I don't care if I die the next minute after the Treaty is ratified," and Kohlsaat adds: "We were alone. Wilson indulged in no heroics. He meant it."

In his address at Spokane Wilson said: "I am ready to fight from now until all the fight has been taken out of me by death to redeem the faith and promises of the United States." The League was written on his heart.

I was on the Pacific Coast inaugurating the beginning of the Two-Ocean Navy at that time. I met him at Seattle when he spoke there. I heard him twice as he thrilled his hearers. I sensed after his second speech that he had put into it his last ounce of strength. He could not sleep that night and when my wife and I called the next day we found that he had a splitting head-ache. Mrs. Wilson was anxious. Afterwards, though proud of his courage and eloquence, she called the western trip "one long nightmare." To him it was a consecration.

The swing around the circle in behalf of ratification was the high-water mark of Wilson's consecration and eloquence. Great crowds thronged all his meetings and he had the assurance that the heart of the country beat in unison with his own. If a vote could have been taken, uninfluenced by party or boodle, eighty per cent of the people would have voted for ratification—the same proportion Borah and Watson said favored it when Wilson brought it from Versailles.

PROPHECIES FULFILLED

Most of the addresses were impromptu and fitted the spirit of his audiences, though they had a universal appeal. We have lived to see that he was a true prophet as he uttered this warning at Omaha:

"I can predict with absolute certainty that within another generation there will be another World War if the nations of the world do not concert the method by which to prevent it. . . ."

And a few days later, at San Diego, he prophesied:

"I do not hesitate to say that the war we have just been through, though it was shot through with terror of every kind, is not to be compared with the war we would have to face next time. . . . What the Germans used were toys as compared with what would be used in the next war. . . ."

APOLOGIES TO ARMED MEN

One of Wilson's most significant and best remembered statements was at St. Louis when he said:

"I would like to get together the boys who fought in the war and I would stand up before them and say: 'Boys, I told you before you went across the seas that this was a war against wars, and I did my best to fulfill the promise, but I am obliged to come to you in mortification and shame and say I have not been able to fulfill the promise. You are betrayed. . . .' "

The breakdown foreshadowed by his throbbing headaches at Seattle came on September 26 as he was reaching Wichita, Kansas, for an address. He returned to Washington a broken man with a partial paralysis from which, though he was able later to hold Cabinet meetings, he never recovered.

WILSON NEVER GAVE UP

Wilson never gave up the fight even after he was stricken. Nobody felt like telling him that the cards were stacked against ratification. Senators Simmons and Swanson, who were ready to go down the line for what Wilson wanted, told me that the fight without the Lodge reservations was hopeless. I advised them to so inform

Wilson. They said in his state of health they feared the effect upon him, as his heart and soul were fixed on ratification. However, always frank with him, I told him one day that we were headed for defeat in the Senate. He could not bear to hear it. He rather rebukingly replied: "My information is exactly the reverse of what you have been hearing."

When the Senate twice defeated ratification of the Treaty, Wilson had supreme faith that the people would react favorably in a "solemn referendum," which he advocated and which was incorporated in the Democratic National platform in 1920. The defeat of Cox and Roosevelt, standing on the platform for the United States to enter the League of Nations, came to Wilson as a surprise and serious shock.

VOICED DISAPPOINTMENT AND INDIGNATION

In retirement Wilson at times brooded over America's failure to join the League and in his last two public appearances gave expression to his disappointment that his country had lost its golden opportunity, and did so in strong language. In his last Armistice Day address to a crowd that thronged the street in front of his entrance, leaning heavily on his cane, in the spirit of a prophet of old, Wilson said:

"I have seen fools resist Providence before and I have seen their destruction, as will come upon these again—utter destruction and contempt. That we shall prevail is as sure as that God reigns."

The year before, speaking to a gathering of friends, who bemoaned the lapse by the Senate, Wilson said:

"... the stimulating memories of that happy time of triumph are forever marred and embittered for us by the shameful fact that when victory was won—won be it remembered chiefly by the indomitable spirit and valiant sacrifice of our own unconquerable soldiers—we turned our backs upon our associates and refused to bear any responsible part in the establishment of peace, and withdrew into a sullen and selfish isolation which is deeply ignoble because manifestly cowardly and dishonorable."

As the shadows lengthened and this greatest casualty of the war moved toward the sunset, his old-time confidence that mankind would not be defrauded of the warless world he had envisioned, Wilson to more than one friend expressed his faith that his country-men would reverse the adverse decision rendered in a period of partisanship and disillusionment.

Part Twelve

SMEARING THE ARMY AND THE NAVY

XL

SMEAR INVESTIGATIONS

W HILE THE WORLD was ringing with the plaudits of the achievements of the Army and the Navy in the World War,
partisan politicians and a few disgruntled officers were coöperating
to try to find or invent some flaw in the great work of the armed
forces in the direction of the war. As a result of their conspiracy,
investigations were begun by Congressional committees controlled
by Republicans.

"HELL AND MARIA" KNOCKED THEM OUT

Following the attempt to smear the Navy, which turned out to be
a dud, a Republican Congressional Committee started out to smear
the Army and the conduct of the war, thinking they could make
political capital in the next campaign. It was alleged that millions
were wasted, and muckrakers made reckless charges of waste and
extravagance. But the "best laid schemes of mice and men gang aft
agley." Honorable Charles G. Dawes, who had been Chief of the
A. E. F. Supply Procurement and had been in France with Pershing
two years, like all men who had done a great job in a masterly way,
was outraged at the attempt to tarnish the greatest adventure in the
history of the country. His testimony consumed seven hours and
three sessions, and his "Hell and Maria" indignant denunciation of
the muckrakers was heard in a hall where there was standing room
only. The great crowds gathered and approved when he said, "Hell
and Maria, of course there was some waste," but that a war could
not be won without some loss, and there was no wrong-doing, no
scandal. He declared the investigation had been undertaken "to
blacken the American military achievement for political and partisan purposes." The substance of the speech that demolished the
muckrakers and compelled that Committee shortly thereafter to go
out of business was an enlargement of this opening:

"As I thought over the work we had done in France, my indignation that it should be attacked steadily increased, and I sud-

PAGE MR. von TIRPITZ — HE KNOWS

denly decided that so far as I could bring it about either the Committee or I would go out of business—that after all it was not my work which was being attacked but that of the splendid army our country had sent to France—that it was not at the service of particular men that mud was being slung but at the glorious banner of American achievement—that we, coming home, were now only meeting that which had confronted our great war President and his Secretary of War, who had been faithful to our army—a pitiful, detestable effort to exploit political and partisan purposes through our recent national calamity."

When he showed his righteous indignation, Mr. Dawes used vitriolic language, which was deserved by the detractors, but it was deleted in the published report because the stenographers said his remarks were "replete with profanity," an overstatement of the denunciations by a participant in the war who refused to speak softly when the use of a Big Stick on muckrakers was the medicine they needed.

THE COMMITTEE WENT OUT OF BUSINESS

The testimony of Mr. Dawes put a quietus on the smelling committee and it soon folded up, with the condemnation of the American people. If any thought the language of Dawes was too much interlarded with profanity, the people thought he had ample justification. Instead of condemning him, the Committee was repudiated, and Dawes—a courageous Republican who had won the confidence of the people—was later elected Vice President.

HE BROKE DOWN IN TEARS

The Republican Congressional Committee tried to fix profiteering on Mr. Schwab. Some of his companies did make big profits and if the Committee had been really investigating there were courts to compel profiteers to recoup. But they were smelling to hit the Wilson administration and all its officials. Mr. Schwab had been one and his driving force had turned out ships "to win the war." In his book, Mr. Dawes thus refers to the attitude of the Committee toward Mr. Schwab:

"Only a week or so before my appearance, when Charles M. Schwab was a witness before the same Committee, their brutal and unjustified reflections upon his integrity had broken him down into tears."

The *New York Times* gave the story under these headlines:

SCHWAB ON STAND
WEEPS AS HE TELLS
OF MEETING MORSE

HEARING HALTS AS CONGRESSMEN
CONGRATULATE STEEL MAN ON
HIS WAR WORK

TEARS FILL WITNESS'S EYES
VOICE CHOKES WHEN HE AGAIN
DENIES GOVERNMENT PAID A CENT
OF HIS EXPENSES

When Schwab had finished his testimony, Representative Foster, amid general applause said:

"I can't help making this reflection at this time. As a member of this committee I want to express on the record my appreciation of the manner, Mr. Schwab, in which you have introduced evidence concerning this voucher; and aside from my membership on the Committee I want to express my appreciation as an American citizen of the service you have rendered in the recent war."

And that ended the scheme to smear Schwab and the Emergency Fleet Corporation, as "Hell and Maria" had ended the attempt to smear the Army.

SCHWAB'S POLITICS NO DETERRENT

When Wilson started the big ship building program he called in men he believed the most capable, regardless of politics. Some Democrats were not pleased when Charles M. Schwab, steel captain, was given an important post. He did a great job and threw his whole soul into production.

For a time Mr. Schwab was the chief money raiser for the Republican party in Pennsylvania. Years afterwards he made this revelation to Senator Guffy:

"I used frequently to come to Washington. I never received a telegram from the late Senator Penrose without dropping everything and coming to Washington. He never asked for less than $250,000 on each visit, and sometimes more.

Secretary of the Navy Daniels and Admiral Sims, critic of the Navy in World War I.

"I reached the maximum in one presidential campaign when I raised the sum of eight million dollars, and, as Max Leslie, the former city leader of Pennsylvania would say 'most of that was free money'—that is, money that does not have to be accounted for."

When Schwab was appointed to rush the construction of merchant ships he called to see me and said:

"I have made all the money that I want or ever will want. For the balance of my life, particularly while this war is on, I wish nothing except to serve my country. I never want to make another dollar."

Perhaps he saw doubt in my eyes and asked, "Do you believe me?" I did not say "yes," but replied: "I am very glad to know that you, like all good Americans, are patriotically volunteering to serve your country and put that above all private interests."

A Congressional Investigating Committee is put out of business.

XLI

CHARGES AGAINST THE NAVY DISPROVED

IT HAD LONG been the fixed policy of the United States to permit no public official to accept a decoration or medal from a foreign government. It was a proper precaution against the possible over-agreements with such governments by diplomats and others to obtain a coveted piece of ribbon supposed to be an insigne of distinction. That wise policy was sometimes evaded by permitting a decoration to be tendered and placed in cold storage in the State Department to be given to the recipient when he became a private citizen. On July 31 I sent a confidential telegram to Admiral Sims in London saying, "The State Department has been directed to diplomatically inform all European governments that this government does not desire any decorations conferred upon American officers, either Army or Navy."

ONLY DECORATION RETAINED

President Wilson and members of his Cabinet declined decorations which Allied Nations desired to give them. I did not accept those informally tendered. When I reached Raleigh, after my term expired, I found that Poland had sent a beribboned decoration. I did not send it back, assured that Paderewski was responsible for what he regarded as an honor to an early and real friend of Free Poland.

I knew Wilson entertained the same idea about foreign decorations as I did and had declined all tenders, enough to have covered his breast twice over. I did not know, however, until I read Mrs. Wilson's *My Memoir,* that he, like me, had accepted only the Polish decoration. She wrote:

"The only foreign decoration my husband ever accepted was the Order of the White Eagle of Poland. During the war he could decline such honors by saying that under our laws a special authorization by Congress was necessary and Congress was engaged with matters more important to the common cause.

492

GERMAN
NAVY

OUT AT LAST.

ROLLIN
KIRBY

In 1922 when the Polish Government asked to present Mr. Wilson this medal, he could think of no polite reason for refusing and the Polish Minister brought it out to the house in November. The only time he wore the decoration was on January 5, 1923, at a family dinner in honor of my dear mother's eightieth birthday."

When American armed forces for the first time served with Allied European nations, France and Britain tendered medals to American comrades-in-arms. Should they accept them? When Britain tendered such decoration to Admiral Sims, the reaction of Wilson was against changing the old practice. He said, "No," and I thought properly. In August (1918) I had a conference with Wilson about our people accepting decorations or medals. He said France ought to be asked not to give decorations to Admiral Wilson, though Britain did give one to Sims. He asked me to convey his wish to the State Department. When we learned of the decoration to Sims, I was inclined to tell him not to accept, but he had already accepted and we could not embarrass our British allies by ordering its return.

SIMS'S AMBITION DISAPPROVED

Before the tender of this medal by the British, when a letter came from Ambassador Page saying that the King of England and the Admiralty wished to make Sims an honorary member of the British Admiralty, Page added: "It is a compliment without precedent. No member of any other Navy ever having been so honored."

Wilson wrote me the following letter:

"31, January, 1918

"MY DEAR MR. SECRETARY,

"I appreciate fully the spirit in which this honour is offered Sims, and I wish he could accept it; but I am afraid it would be a mistake for him to do so. The English persist in thinking of the United States as an English people, but of course they are not and I am afraid that our people would resent and misunderstand what they would interpret as a digestion of Sims into the British official organization. What do you think? ...

"Faithfully yours,

/s/ "W. W."

"THE SECRETARY OF THE NAVY."

I agreed with the President and informed Page and Sims that no American Admiral could accept a position—honorary or otherwise—in the British Admiralty. A Naval officer to whom I talked said: "You have won the everlasting enmity of Sims. He would rather be a member of the British Admiralty than to have the highest honors the United States could give."

CONGRESS APPROVES ACCEPTANCE

Later when officers of our Army in battle were awarded medals of honor for bravery, Congress enacted a law permitting acceptance. At first I opposed Naval acceptance, but when Congress opened the door for the Army, I agreed that if one branch of the service could be decorated it should apply to all. In the beginning, medals and decorations were given only to men of high rank who led their men to battle or for bravery beyond the call of duty. They were prized as were like distinctions conferred by their own country.

DECORATIONS WERE CHEAPENED

As time wore on, some Allies, particularly the French, gave decorations so profusely and indiscriminately as to cheapen them. After the Armistice any influential American in Paris who had rendered no greater service than buying bonds was decorated. Some had their breasts covered with almost as many medals as General Pershing could worthily wear. I recall that when King Albert, of Belgium, visited Washington, he decorated almost everyone that rendered him a service, giving a medal to the chauffeur who drove his car.

AWARDING AMERICAN MEDALS

Like Wilson I believed a medal or decoration should connote some achievement above regular efficiency. Therefore, at the close of the war I appointed a Board of Award to study and pass upon all recommendations. When the report came to me for action, as I went over it carefully, I found that desk service, far from danger, had been given recognition beyond that awarded to men who showed ability and courage under fire. On the first report, 140 officers were recommended for Distinguished Service Medals, and of these 68 per cent were for those serving on shore and only 32 per cent for those at sea in the war zone. I did not approve such awards, as I

could not give the same honor to the commander of an old battleship in the Chesapeake as to the officer commanding a battleship in
the North Sea. I insisted on awards for men engaged in the hazardous duty of laying mines in the North Sea Barrage. I could not approve omissions of Navy guards on perilous duty. I held that duties
ashore in war times were of second importance to duty in the war
zone. And there was scant recognition of enlisted men who had
braved the enemy. Out of 500,000 enlisted men, only 119 were recommended for medals. I added the Distinguished Service Medal to 13
and the Navy Cross to 68 more enlisted men. Thirty-two of the
Armed Guard deserved medals but only six were recommended. I
awarded thirty-two. I thus stated the policy of the Navy in awarding
medals:

> "Those officers and men who served in the actual war zone,
> and particularly those who in this service have come in contact
> with the enemy, should come first in the recognition of their
> services. Those in positions of great responsibility on shore duty,
> etc., should have recognition for their services also, but it is my
> belief that service in the active war zone should have paramount
> recognition. The Navy exists on the sea."

FEUD BETWEEN SIMS AND WILSON

Admiral Sims, who was the highest officer in the European area,
recommended a Distinguished Service Medal to his capable Naval
Aide who only trod the deck in a sumptuous office in London, and
reommended only a Medal of Honor to men who, under fire and in
the perils of torpedo attack, bore themselves with courage beyond
the call of duty, and no recognition whatsoever of Admiral Henry B.
Wilson, who was commanding officer at Brest, the most important
shore duty in Europe, in which Wilson won gratitude and honor
from his French comrades and appreciation by his country. The
reasons: When Sims removed the first officer at that post and recommended to succeed him an officer I had tried and found wanting, I
named Wilson, whose excellent qualities had been tested in command afloat of forces in the important Caribbean area. Sims didn't
like him and passed him over while recommending too high honors
to some in his London office. When Sims visited Brest and in Wilson's presence berated President Wilson and the Secretary of the
Navy, he was sternly reprimanded by Wilson, who threatened to

inform the White House of Sims's insubordination. They did not come to blows but Sims never forgave Wilson.

Commander-in-Chief Mayo, however, had recommended a Distinguished Service Medal to Admiral Wilson and it was approved.

ARCHAIC BRITISH PRACTICE

Worse than all, although Mayo, Gleaves, and other Admirals recommended the Distinguished Service Medal to officers who bore themselves with ability and signal courage when their ships were torpedoed by under-sea assassins, Sims advised only a Medal of Honor. This non-recognition was in line with an archaic British Naval doctrine that if a man lost his ship, no matter if he showed as much heroism as Nelson, he was "done for." Not even Britain, in the World War, stood for such a doctrine in the new secret warfare by under-sea assassins. But there were a few American Naval officers with eyes in the back of their heads, as well as some in Britain, who with Sims held to that inhuman old crucifixion of brave men. I answered the worm-eaten doctrine by citing a dozen illustrious precedents, six in the war of the sixties, for my attitude. Among those cited in the early days of the Navy were:

> "There are plenty of men like Lawrence and Sigsbee just as deserving of high honor as officers and men whose ships, through no lack of deathless valor, could not be saved. Commodore Bainbridge lost the frigate *Philadelphia* off Tripoli in 1801, but that did not stand in the way of later high honors. Captain James Lawrence lost the *Chesapeake* in the fight with the *Shannon,* but that did not deter Congress from honoring him. Captain David Porter lost the frigate *Essex* in a fight with a British sloop in the harbor of Valparaiso, and upon his return to America was ordered to command a large frigate, building at Washington, the name of which was changed to the *Essex,* in compliment to the ship sunk under command of the brave captain whose ship was lost in spite of his courage. Captain Charles Morris abandoned and burned his ship in 1814 to prevent its being captured by the enemy."

I declined to approve the Board's full list of recommendations. Some Admirals, who were overruled, felt their recommendations should be final and the civilian Secretary should sign "on the dotted line." Naturally there were some differences of opinion. I gave time to the consideration of each case, seeking a uniform policy to make the recommendations of different Admirals harmonize so that a D.S.M. should not go to a man at a desk, as recommended by one Admiral, and a Medal of Honor to a like officer, recommended by another Admiral. A howl went up from some desk officers, who had been preferred above fighting men at sea, and their backers and some others. Certain Republican Senators, always alert to attack the Wilson administration, prompted by Admiral Sims, secured an investigation by the Naval Affairs Committee which was barren of beneficial results, only affording a sounding board for the airing of real or fancied grievances, and culminating in an outlet for ridiculously false charges against the Navy in the World War by Admiral Sims. The House Naval Affairs Committee, headed by Honorable Thomas S. Butler, Republican, of Pennsylvania, declined to join in the investigation, saying, "We are of the unanimous opinion that the matter of Naval awards should be left to the Secretary of the Navy and his assistants."

TEMPEST BORN IN POLITICS

It was not long after the sensational announcement that Sims was "going to blow the Navy's conduct of the war out of the water" before everybody in Washington understood that it was the first gun Penrose had primed for the 1920 campaign. Honorable C. C. Carlin, member of the House of Representatives from Alexandria, Virginia, quoted Republican members of the House Naval Affairs Committee to that effect. I quote this extract from my Diary (February 27):

> "Representative Carlin recalled that when he was in London Sims said to him: 'The United States does not need a big Navy. We have always depended on England and can do so in the future.' Carlin added that I ought not to be worried about Sims' charges. They had brought out in the open what was being whispered, and as his statements were being refuted, my position was strengthened. The whole tempest was started as a political move to hurt the Democratic party. Carlin's opinion was that instead of hurting, it would help."

WARNED SIMS TO BE CAREFUL

In his bill of indictment Sims had said that Admiral Benson had given him this admonition:

"Do not let the British pull the wool over your eyes. It is none of our business, pulling their chestnuts out of the fire. We would as soon fight the British as the Germans."

Admiral Benson said because of the known fact that Sims was pro-British he was warning him as a friend not to follow the course that later brought down on Sims's head the condemnation of President Taft for saying in his Guildhall speech:

"If the time ever comes when the British Empire is seriously menaced by an external enemy, it is my opinion that you may count upon every man, every dollar, every drop of blood of your kindred across the sea."

Benson testified that he did not recall the exact words that he used, but probably used very forcible language to impress upon Sims the seriousness of the situation and the importance of being very careful that his "feelings toward the British did not lead him into any indiscretion." Benson added that his statement as to the Germans was "merely as a figure of speech to impress upon him the delicacy of the situation."

All of this was in March and the United States did not enter the war until April 6.

SENSATIONAL CHARGES DISPROVED

The great fuss about medals was only a feint to introduce a long-planned more serious attack on the Navy, as Senator Hale intimated when I was called to testify on awards. They would call me, he said, "at some future time in regard to the other matters." The first I heard of other matters was when a sensational muckraker printed that Sims—and he could have gotten it only from Sims or one of his co-conspirators—had charged that "failure of the Navy Department to immediately send its full force of destroyers and anti-submarine craft prolonged the war four months and occasioned the loss to the Allies of 2,500,000 tons of shipping, 500,000 lives, and $15,000,000,000."

That reckless charge and scores of others had been foreshadowed by partisan charges in the Senate by Senator Penrose, a bitter partisan critic of the Wilson Administration. What Sims charged was almost exactly what Senator Penrose, speaking in the Senate (August 22) said: "The Navy lost at least three months and it cost this country and the Allies $100,000,000 a day and $15,000,000,000." When Senator Pittman protested against the useless investigation, Sims said: "I just sized it up that there was some political flavor about it." He and Penrose knew the inspiration.

As a result of the desire of Republican Senators to second Sims's purpose to smear the Navy because the President and the Secretary of the Navy had not accepted British Naval policies and had refused to let Sims accept honorary membership in the British Admiralty, the Senate Naval Affairs Committee began hearings March 9, 1920, and continued them until June, the testimony covering 3,445 pages printed in two large volumes. The House Committee was invited to join in the investigation but refused to be a party to it. A dozen of its members, at home and in the war zone abroad, composed of both Republicans and Democrats, had testified through Chairman Padgett to the Navy's remarkable record of achievement and efficiency and gave their report of its activities in the war zone as follows:

> "The magnitude of our Naval operations overseas, on the water and in the air, reflects credit upon the American people, and commands the respect and admiration of our Allies. When the war is over and the full history of our Naval operations abroad may be given in detail, it will be a source of pride and honor to the American people, and the fidelity, patriotism and devotion of our Naval officers and enlisted men, embracing as a part of the Navy the Marine Corps officers and men, will form a bright part in the world's history."

CHARGES RESENTED

The charges made by Sims were resented most by those whose distinguished service had won world praise for the Navy. Among them was Admiral Rodman, who had commanded the American vessels in the North Sea. He wrote me from San Pedro, Feb. 5:

> "As a matter of principle, I feel that you should know my views in reference with Sims's investigation. I wish to combat his statements and help preserve the deservedly good name which the Navy earned during the war, not only with the public, but which we of the service honor and hold in the highest esteem. It is up to us, who have spent our lives in the service to do all in our power to preserve the good name which the Navy has always held, not only in this war but in all others."

ADMIRALS CALL CHARGES UNFOUNDED

Though a number of officers with a grievance pointed out an instance which they thought was not perfect, after a drag-out and calling of every officer who thought he had not been given all the good assignments which he thought he deserved, not one was found who testified that any lives or shipping or millions were lost by the latches of Navy administration, and though the Republican members of the committee signed a report critical of some phases of Naval administration, they did not uphold the grave indictments. The Democratic members of the committee, headed by Key Pittman, examined in detail the allegations and the evidence and showed the falsity of the charges. The Admirals who held the most responsible posts and knew at first hand the Naval direction of the war repudiated Sims's attempt to "smear the Navy." Here are their statements:

"Admiral Badger, President of the General Board: 'The statement is utterly unfounded.'

"Admiral Benson, Chief of Operations: 'It is an outrage to the American people and an outrage to the honorable record of the United States Navy. If it is allowed to stand, it will be to the everlasting disgrace of the Navy.'

"Admiral Mayo, Commander-in-Chief: 'I consider that this assertion of Admiral Sims is a wild statement, not at all susceptible of proof, and is an unwarranted attack upon the Navy Department and the Navy.'

"Admiral Hugh Rodman, Commander of the Battleship Division in the North Sea: 'I do not believe there is a particle of truth in that statement.... There are three kinds of lies—lies, damn lies and statistics.'

"Admiral Wilson, Commander at Brest: 'I do not believe this to be true. On the contrary I believe our naval force materially aided in shortening the war, saving untold life and property.'

"Admiral Niblack, Commander of Gibraltar Base: 'Statement indefensible historically. I would be glad to help my friend Sims out but I cannot.'

"Admiral Strauss, in charge of Mine Barrage Force: 'As to Sims's charge of losses, my answer is NO.'

"Admiral Frank F. Fletcher, former Commander-in-Chief

and member War Industries Board: 'The delays charged did not prolong the war for a single day.'

"Captain W. V. Pratt, Acting Chief of Operations: 'If all our anti-submarine craft had been sent over immediately, it would not have shortened the war a single day.'

"Admiral McKean, Assistant Chief of Operations: 'The charge is monstrous and an insult to the Navy. Had it been invented by the inflamed, exaggerated, diseased ego of a patient at St. Elizabeth's (the institution for mentally ill patients in Washington, D. C.) no one would have been surprised. . . . Made by an officer of the Navy it is an insult to every officer and man now in the Navy.' "

"GIVE THEM HELL"

Admiral McGowan brought me a message from Mrs. Dewey who, when she learned that I was going before the Naval Affairs Committee to reply to Admiral Sims, said to tell Secretary Daniels, "Go after them. Give them hell. That is the messsage George Dewey would give you if he were here, and go with your staunchest friends with you."

COMPLETE HISTORY OF THE NAVY

After the weeks and months in which I told the complete story of the Navy during my administration, fortified by comprehensive statements by the officers detailing every activity, the evidence of Naval efficiency in peace and war was conclusive. It was so full that Chairman Hale, whose role was more of a prosecutor than a seeker after knowledge, in an aside asked me, "Are you writing a story of the Navy?" I replied, "You asked for it, and I am putting in the record the complete report that disproves every allegation reflecting upon the efficiency of the Navy."

SIMS NOT COMMANDER-IN-CHIEF

There was a misconception on the part of both Admiral Sims and the public as to his status abroad. In testimony before the Senate Naval Affairs Committee, Admiral Pratt, Assistant Chief of Operations, thus correctly gave his status:

"Admiral Sims in his office in London was not the Commander in the field or afloat, in the sense indicated by Mahan. This was a war of logistics and the tactical operations of our naval forces at the front were the preliminaries to the great effort being carried on elsewhere. Nowhere had our great naval fleet assembled in one mass ready to come to grips with the enemy. Admiral Sims was the commander of the divisions in the advance, but he was not the general that commanded the whole army. The similarity of his position with that of General Pershing, which he has remarked upon in his testimony, only continued for such time as our army was distributed among the Allies. When the army united as an individual army under our own leaders, with Pershing in general command, then the position of Pershing and Sims became different. He was the Assistant to the Chief of Naval Operations, at the front. He was not the Chief of Naval Operations, nor the Commander-in-Chief of the Fleet."

MAKING NO MARTYRS

In most administrations the charges broadcast to the world by Sims would have called for a court-martial of the officer making them. Certainly the accusation that Admiral Benson, charged under the law with Naval Operations, lacked "the will to win" and was hostile to an Ally would have resulted in a trial and conviction. The high-ranking officers of the Navy thought as a matter of procedure that course would follow.

From my Diary (February 8):

"Admiral McGowan said Sims should be relieved of duty and put on waiting orders. Admiral Coontz, Chief of Operations, and Admiral Washington, Chief of Navigation, strongly urged me to remove Sims from his assignment and court martial him because he made false charges reflecting on the entire Navy. They pressed this course. 'I can assure you,' said Coontz, 'that there would not be the slightest doubt of his conviction for the older officers of the Navy feel strongly that he has been guilty of such false charges that he should receive the punishment to fit his offense.' I didn't doubt that he deserved to be court-martialed or that any court would fail to convict him."

I declined, however, saying that I had always invited discussion and criticism even if destructive; that I knew I had the power which, set in motion, would bring a verdict of guilty for Sims, but I would not invoke it. One officer, so resentful of the attempted slur, said he was sure President Wilson if consulted would make the punishment fit the crime and urged me to take it up at the White House. I did so, prefacing it with the statement that I thought it would be an unwise course and would give Sims a chance to pose as a martyr, and opponents of the administration would say it was persecution. Wilson said, "You are right. We want to make no martyrs. Since Sims has ruined himself, why not let him stay in the hole he has dug for himself?"

WHEN SIMS WAS SAVED

Admiral Sims had quickness of mind, a certain charm that won youth, possessed style as a writer, but lacked high Naval loyalty, particularly to officers of higher rank. He had soaring ambition and was regarded as an able officer who never imagined that his course could be wrong or that "the mother country" (he was born in Canada) did not possess superior wisdom.

I had known of his looseness of statement and little regard for accuracy from Admiral Frank F. Fletcher, who in an official report, after maneuvers of the fleet before the war, charged Sims with falsehood. That was a serious accusation from the Commander-in-Chief of the fleet. With much difficulty I persuaded Admiral Fletcher to lessen his charge to a virtual statement that Sims lacked accuracy of statement. I wished to avoid friction or a court-martial for Sims, feeling that his cock-sureness was responsible for his lack of veracity. Years afterwards, when as a co-worker with Penrose and other Republicans, Sims sought, from the high assignment I had given him, to charge me with the crime of being responsible for "the failure of the Navy Department to immediately send its full force of destroyers and anti-submarine craft [which] prolonged the war four months and occasioned the loss to the Allies of 2,500,000 tons of shipping, 500,000 lives, and $15,000,000,000," and attempted to smear the record of the Navy in the World War, Admiral Fletcher asked me: "Are you not sorry now you persuaded me not to press my charge that Sims was guilty of falsehood?" Fletcher added: "You have now learned what all of us in the Navy have long known—the statements of Sims cannot be depended upon, and loyalty to superiors is not in his make-up."

CONGRESSMEN REPUDIATED REPORTS OF SIMS

When, as the World War was drawing to an end, Representatives Carter Glass, Byrnes, and Whaley made their call on Admiral Sims at his hotel in Paris and presented the letter of introduction I had given them as they were leaving Washington, he astounded them by telling them that the Armistice would have to be granted "because Pershing had been unable to break through the German lines, owing to the absolute breakdown of transportation behind the American lines." This caused them to investigate, and they learned that there was no foundation for such an attack upon Pershing or the Services of Supply.

Returning to the United States, Mr. Byrnes told President Wilson the substance of what Sims had told him, and said that at the approaching Peace Conference the President would need Naval advisers and "if Sims advised him he would be incorrectly advised."

Afterward, speaking in the House of Representatives, Mr. Byrnes said:

"In October, 1918, with two of my colleagues, Representative Glass, of Virginia, and Representative Whaley, of South Carolina, I went to France, and among other places visited Tours, the headquarters of the Services of Supply of our Army, and was thrilled with pride at the marvels worked by this branch of the service. On October 30, with my colleagues, I saw Admiral Sims, who was then in Paris. I shall never forget that interview. The armistice had been requested by the enemy. Sims told us of the magnificent progress made by the British on the English front, and as we listened he proceeded to tell us that the armistice would have to be granted, because Pershing had been unable to break through the German lines, owing to the absolute breakdown of transportation behind the American lines. With pathos in his voice he told us how unfortunate it was that this breakdown occurred at so critical a moment. In amazement we listened, and in the monologue he delivered he proceeded to tell us that while Americans believed their Navy was working wonders, as a matter of fact we had but three per cent of the antisubmarine craft in English waters; that Great Britain had brought over two-thirds of our troops and had escorted one-half of them. I left him not only depressed at the failure of the American Army, but humiliated at the small part played by the American Navy. Believing that this disaster to the American Army, which, according to Sims, made necessary our granting the armistice asked by the enemy, was destined to be a national scandal, Mr. Whaley and I determined to again visit the headquarters of the Services of Supply in order to ascertain the details of this disaster. Because of Sims's statement we traveled 150 miles or more to Tours. When we informed the Commanding Officer and the Chief of Staff of our desire to secure information with reference to this matter they were amazed. They advised us that it was the first time they had heard of it. They showed us records where General Pershing, after the St. Mihiel drive, had thanked the Services of Supply for its wonderful service, and again, just a few days prior to our visit, had written congratulating the Services of Supply upon its continued success in supplying our forces in the field. Wishing to avoid friction between our officers, we refrained from disclosing the source of our information.

"When told that our statement must be mere gossip in Paris, we advised the commanding officer that our information came from an officer of high rank in the service of our Government, and in response to that statement an officer present said: 'That is nothing but British propaganda, and the only American officer who could have told you gentlemen this story is Admiral W. S. Sims.'

"While in London visiting the naval headquarters to secure information as to the departure of ships, we again met Admiral Sims. He courteously invited us to his office, and evidently forgetting that he had delivered his lecture to us in Paris, he again proceeded to impress upon us the small part our Navy played in the war, reciting the figures stated above, and which I have proved to be false. Not satisfied with telling us how small a part we played upon the sea in time of war, he proceeded to tell us that in time of peace we should seek to play no part at all."

Byrnes then proceeded to tell Congress Sims's arguments against the United States' ever attempting to develop a merchant marine of her own. These arguments have already been quoted in another connection. Sims believed that England, because of her geographical position, must necessarily control the seas and that the United States could always rely on Britain to provide a merchant marine. When Byrnes disagreed with him, Sims asserted that it would be impossible for the United States to possess a merchant marine, even if it were desirable, because the United States could not hope to compete with Great Britain. This, he declared, would involve paying subsidies, and our people would never stand for it.

In testimony before a Congressional Committee Carter Glass confirmed the statement of Byrnes and added that two British statesmen in London had told him there had been a breakdown in the American Communications and the Services of Supply; and Representative Whaley, now a Federal Judge, wrote a letter confirming in every respect what Glass and Byrnes had said and reënforcing it by additional evidence.

A NAVY LIMERICK

A man in the Naval service, knowing his fondness for limericks, sent this limerick to Wilson:

> "THERE WAS AN OLD ADMIRAL NAMED SIMS,
> WHO WAS CHUCK FULL OF CROCHETS AND WHIMS,
> SAID HE, 'IF THE SEC
> DON'T OBEY ME, BY HECK,
> DEAR OLD LUNNON FOR ME IF I SWIMS.' "

COURSE WAS CONSISTENT

With Wilson, Benson, and Daniels, in Paris, who with William G. McAdoo, had fought to secure a strong American merchant marine, it was logical that the Americans should stand firmly for its continuance. Before I arrived, Admiral Benson had opposed the British idea, endorsed by Admiral Sims, that Britain should be foremost on the seas. When I arrived, I backed him up and Wilson stood by us. Benson's creed was in these words: "Constant protection can come only from an ample Navy and a permanent merchant marine under our own flag."

As far back as 1916 I had written Senator Fletcher that "by lack of adequate merchant marine, upon which all other nations look for a supply of auxiliary vessels in time of war, the United States Navy would be seriously handicapped if we should go to war under conditions which now exist in our merchant marine." Senators Fletcher, Newlands, and Simmons strongly supported that position.

Part Thirteen

SEEKING TO OUST WILSON

XLII

DIAGNOSTICIANS DISILLUSIONED

W HEN WILSON on December 2, 1919, for the first time since his inauguration sent his message to Congress to be read instead of delivering it in person, Fall and others took that as a sign that Wilson was incapacitated, and they wished to have him ousted. These self-appointed diagnosticians declared Wilson's illness constituted "inability" and urged that the Vice President assume the duties of the office. The most prominent was Senator Moses, of New Hampshire, and he was given the title, "Doc Moses." It stuck. Several bills to oust Wilson were introduced but all "died a-bornin'." The one by Madden was to "define the meaning of 'inability' as used in Article II, Section 1, Clause 5 of the Constitution." He would oust the President "whenever for any reason whatsoever" he became "unable for a period of six consecutive weeks to perform the duties devolved upon him." Who would "bell the cat?" Madden's bill directed the Secretary of State to call a meeting of the Cabinet to make "official inquiry." If their findings were that his "inability to discharge the powers and duties of the office," the Vice President should take over, but he provided the bill should not go into effect until March 4, 1921. Senator Fess proposed to change the Constitution so as to give the power to determine "disability" to the Supreme Court, when authorized by a concurrent resolution of Congress. Mr. McArthur wanted the Vice President to succeed, "Whenever the President shall leave the territorial limits of the United States."

None of these measures pleased "Doc" Moses or "Petroleum" Fall and other Wilson haters. As diagnostician extraordinary "Doc" Moses wanted Marshall to step in and told him Congress would recognize him as the lawful Chief Executive. It was in the hope of getting first-hand evidence that Fall made a motion that two Senators, one Republican and one Democrat, visit Wilson and discuss in person Fall's resolution to end relations with Mexico. The Mexican resolution was only an excuse for Fall to get into the White House, feel Wilson's pulse, and report that he was too ill to transact public business.

I was the only member of the Cabinet except McAdoo who knew the President had suffered a partial stroke of paralysis. At the end of the meeting I said to Dr. Grayson, "If you would tell the people exactly what is the matter with the President, a wave of sympathy would pour into the White House whereas now there is nothing but uncertainty and criticism." Grayson replied, "I think you are right. I wish I could do so and state that the paralysis is partial and he will probably get over it or get over it enough to return to his full duties. But I am forbidden to speak of it. The President and Mrs. Wilson have made me make a promise to that effect. You are the only person except his son-in-law that knows his condition."

Such was the attitude of those close to Wilson of devoted loyalty and friendship that I never even told my wife what the trouble was until when he was better she saw him limp as he walked.

Because the people did not know what was the matter with Wilson, all sorts of rumors circulated. Members of the Cabinet had not seen him. When he received King Albert in his bedroom the King had told me that the President had a full beard and it was white. No member of the Cabinet had seen him until he was clean-shaven. A British labor leader, on trip on the *Mayflower* to Mount Vernon, said he was told by a rich American lady: "Wilson is not sick—his reception in the West was a frost, and he has taken to his bed—is just shamming."

Neither Fall nor any of the people who were trying to find a way to drive Wilson out of the White House supposed that Wilson would receive them. They expected the answer would be, from his physician, that Wilson was not well enough. Nobody was more surprised and astounded than Fall when Dr. Grayson and Mrs. Wilson expressed willingness for the conference.

When Lansing knew that Fall and Hitchcock were going to see the President, on December 5, 1919, he wrote the President saying that he "knew the vast amount of material collected by the Fall Committee," and told Wilson he "ought to know Carranza's past record of hostility towards this government," and added that he "thought the Jenkins case could be handled without endangering our relations with Mexico." He added that he did not think that case would cause intervention in Mexico.

PETTICOAT GOVERNMENT

One day before he had decided to inject himself into the sick chamber in the White House, Senator Fall is said to have pounded the table with his fist in a frenzy declaring, "We have no President. We have petticoat government. Wilson is not acting. Mrs. Wilson is president." It was Mrs. Wilson who received him with studied courtesy when he called at the White House with Senator Hitchcock. No one could have told from her manner that she had heard and resented the imputation. Those who saw her that day, as she led the way for the Senators to her husband's bedside, said, "She looked like a Queen." It recalled the remark made of her by an American as Mrs. Wilson and the beautiful Italian Queen stood side by side in Rome, "Well, I don't think the Italians have got anything on us."

PETTICOAT PRESIDENT

From the day the President suffered a partial paralytical stroke at Wichita, and even before, when his severe headaches presaged the breakdown, until the end when "the old machine was broken," Edith Bolling Wilson had no thought and interest in life but to nurse him back to health, guard against overtaxing him in his convalescence, and be not only his lover but his guide, philosopher, and friend. She stood between him and a nation calling for his active leadership when she knew the hope of activity lay in the regimen the doctors had prescribed and of which she was the executor. For weeks no member of his Cabinet saw him and no visitor entered the White House. She kept vigil—as strict as it was loving—and had to deny admission to some who insisted on seeing him.

This closing the White House to even Cabinet members laid heavy responsibilities on Mrs. Wilson, which she discharged with the best judgment, permitting very few matters in the early days to be brought to Wilson's attention and enlarging this as his strength returned. Between his skilled physicians, who were also devoted friends, and the company of his wife, he was able to resume his activities in the early spring. However, there was not lacking criticism at her taking responsibility, and vicious opponents said, "We have a President in Petticoats."

Upon the insistence of the doctors, who said that Wilson's resignation would have "a bad effect upon the patient and the country," Mrs. Wilson, in the days before he could see members of his Cabinet, recorded the following:

"I studied every paper, sent from different Secretaries and Senators and tried to digest and present in tabloid form the things that, despite my vigilance, had to go to the President. I, myself, never made a single decision regarding the disposition of public affairs. The only decision that was mine was what was important and what was not, and the *very* important decision of when to present matters to my husband."

And that statement answered the cruel gossip of a President in Petticoats. She protected and saved him, but in matters of policy it was Wilson who gave the decision, even when oil interests sought to get leases, thinking he might depart from his long opposition to despoiling the Navy oil reserve.

Wilson's appreciation of the wisdom of Mrs. Wilson, as well as his affection, was expressed in a book on Government he had hoped to write when he retired from the presidency. When he knew that this long-cherished hope would never be realized, he wrote the dedication to the never-to-be book on a single sheet of paper on his typewriter and gave it to her. It was in these words:

A DEDICATION
to
E. B. W.

"I dedicate this book because it is a book in which I have tried to interpret life, the life of a nation, and she has shown me the full meaning of life. Her heart is not only true but wise; her thoughts are not only free but touched with vision; she teaches and guides by being what she is; her unconscious interpretation of faith and duty makes all the way clear; her power to comprehend makes work and thought alike easier and more near to what it seeks."

"WOODROW WILSON"

FALL GIVES WILSON CLEAN BILL

When it was announced that Fall and Hitchcock were to be received by Wilson at the White House, the gates of the White House, for the first time since the beginning of the war, were swung open and free entrance accorded. The grounds swarmed with newspaper correspondents. They had come from New York and all near-by cities. They waited on the White House lawn. Fall and Hitchcock were with the President from 2.35 P.M. until 3:15 P.M., and when they emerged from the White House the reporters gathered around, all asking—not "What does Wilson think about the Fall resolution," for they recognized that was only an excuse to see ·Wilson— but they all asked, "How is Wilson?" "Is he able to talk?" "Was he well enough to confer with you?" Hitchcock was smiling broadly and suggested to the press that Senator Fall should give the account of the conference and of Wilson's condition. He added, "We had a splendid chat with the President. Senator Fall did most of the talk-· ing. The President looked much better than when I last saw him. He was sitting up, wearing a dark brown sweater. He was clean-shaven. I understand he now shaves himself." He then turned to Fall, who said:

"In my opinion, Mr. Wilson is perfectly capable of handling the Mexican situation. He seemed to me to be in excellent trim, both mentally and physically, for a man who has been in bed for ten weeks. He was lying in bed flat on his back. His shoulders were propped up slightly. His bed was in a shaded portion of the room. He greeted us pleasantly, and, while his articulation was somewhat thick, during the conference I could understand every word he said. I think he was covered up to the chin, with his right arm out. I sat a little to one side and slightly below him, near a table, and he frequently turned his head to talk to me. He also reached over the table several times to secure a paper on it. He does not seem to have lost any weight."

Fall added, "The President after discussing the Mexican resolution very lucidly and clearly expressing his views, stated he would prepare a memorandum which he would send giving additional expressions concerning not only the Fall resolution but the whole situation." Then Fall became facetious and said, "As a result of this visit Senator Moses (he was the Senator who had diagnosed Wilson's condition as being mentally unable to attend to public duties), would be assured although he might be disappointed." Fall told the President he would send him a memorandum of his views.

At this point Hitchcock broke in and said, "At the end of the conference President Wilson told us some stories, one of which was that he said the discussion of the Mexican situation reminded him of Mr. Dooley, quoting Hennessey, who, upon being asked whether he thought the United States should intervene and take Mexico, replied: "Mexico is so contagious to us that I am thinking we will have to take it."

Senator Hitchcock also informed the reporters: "While we were in the midst of our talk, Dr. Grayson brought a message from Lansing that Jenkins had been released."—It was quite dramatic. In fact, the stage was so well set that the dramatic effect was perfect.

When Fall's testimony (he was the President's worst enemy and would not have made the statement unless he had seen Wilson with his own eyes, like the disciple in the Bible who wanted to be assured by a touch) that Wilson's mind was working normally and that he was able to discuss clearly and intelligently a question of great moment, was published, the conspiracy in the Senate to oust Wilson ended. They might not accept Grayson's statement, thinking he was Wilson's friend, but when Wilson's severest critic testified to his physical fitness the diagnosticians were silenced.

In a brief time President Wilson sent a formal statement, in response to the Senators' request, which was as follows:

> You ask an indication of my desire with regard to the pending resolution which you and Senator Hitchcock called to my attention last Friday, and I am glad to reply with the utmost frankness that I should be gravely concerned to see any such resolution pass the Congress. It would constitute a reversal of our constitutional policy which might lead to very grave confusion in the guidance of our foreign policy.
>
> "Only one of the Houses of Congress is associated with the President by the Constitution in advisory capacity and the advice of the Senate is provided for only when sought by the Executive in regard to explicit agreements with foreign Governments, and the appointment of diplomatic representatives who are to speak for this Government in foreign capitals.
>
> "The only safe course, I am confident, is to adhere to the prescribed method of the Constitution. We might go very far afield if we departed from it."

Wilson defeated every move made by Senator Fall toward Mexico. With the coming of the new Administration Fall was placed in fields more fertile to his hand. They were oil fields. The Teapot Dome investigation has now disclosed the character of the enemy of Woodrow Wilson in the Mexican situation. Wilson knew him then as the world knows him now.

There was an unconfirmed rumor coming from that conference in the sick chamber that Wilson, lying white and tired at the White House, greeted Fall as he entered with the query:

"Well, Senator, how are your Mexican investments getting along?"

FALL AS DIAGNOSTICIAN

"Why should Senator Fall wish to queer me with the Almighty?" That was the question President Wilson asked me the first time I saw him (December, 1919) after Senators Fall and Hitchcock had spent three-quarters of an hour with Wilson ostensibly for the purpose of asking his views on the resolution Fall had introduced into the Senate to bring about war with Mexico. Wilson continued:

"Fall came to see me thinking I was crazy, but I think I convinced him that I was as sane as he was, which wouldn't be saying much. When the discussion about his resolution had ended, and Fall and Hitchcock rose to go, Fall leaned over me (I was still confined to my bed) and pressed my hands between both of his and said in an unctuous tone, 'Mr. President, I am praying for you.' Why should Senator Fall wish to queer me with the Almighty? Don't you think Fall knew the Almighty would be inclined to do just the opposite of any request he should make?"

FALL PLAYING POSSUM

Strangely enough, on the very day when Wilson was passing into his last sleep, another Senate Committee was sending a delegation of Washington physicians to examine Fall and see if he was really sick or merely malingering in order to avoid appearing before the investigating committee to give an explanation of the $100,000 he had received from Doheny and others to turn over the leases of the Naval oil reserve to greedy oil men. One of Wilson's physicians, Dr. Sterling Ruffin, was one of the number who were called by the Senate to examine Fall whose lawyers were trying to excuse him from testifying on the ground of illness. Dr. Ruffin and his associates testified that Fall was well enough to go before the Committee. That convinced the people that Fall had been playing possum.

Fall, who was said to hold large properties in Chahuahua in Mexico, had seized upon every possible pretext to involve the United States in war with Mexico. Before that, Fall had declared in the Senate, "I favor the immediate organization of an army of 500,000 men ostensibly for the policing of Mexico or for the invasion of that country in order to protect our citizens if necessary. Our supine policy has made us looked upon as cowards by the Mexicans." He was to rejoice when Lansing made the demand for the immediate return of Jenkins, and there was gossip that he was in collusion with Lansing in the hope of bringing about war with the neighbors across the Rio Grande, but no proof of it.

When Fall was a candidate for reëlection to the Senate a voter in New Mexico, remembering that in Fall's early days before he became the spokesman of the oil people he had gone to New Mexico as a Democrat, wrote Wilson and asked whether he thought Fall ought to be reëlected and whether Wilson could depend upon him. Wilson answered:

> "Your question whether I would be willing to depend upon Senator Fall's support in settling our foreign relations is easily answered. I would not. He has given such repeated evidence of his entire hostility to this administration that I would be ignoring his whole course of action if I did. No one who wishes to sustain me can intelligently vote for him. If that is the issue the voters of New Mexico wish to vote upon it is easily answered."

Naturally the members of Wilson's Cabinet were gratified when Fall was compelled to testify that Wilson was sane. They had not forgotten what Fall had said about some of Wilson's advisers, to wit:

> "I have no confidence in the President's Cabinet members. They have proven themselves absolutely inefficient. I will vote to clothe the President with absolutely autocratic power but he shall not hide behind the skirts of Hoover, or Wilson, or Baker."

APPLES MEANT FALL

At that time Ira Bennett had not disclosed that in the Department of Justice code used by Edward B. MacLean in the Teapot Dome investigation, the word "apples" meant Fall. It was an apple that figured when Adam and Eve were driven out of the garden. When Fall was convicted and imprisoned some paraphrasists said:

> "In the fall
> We sinnèd all."

XLIII

WHY DID LANSING RESIGN?

W HY DID Wilson call for the resignation of Secretary Lansing (February, 1920)? In the President's letter he gave as the reason that Lansing had called meetings of the Cabinet without his knowledge or authority. Does any man ever give the real reason for any important action? Or does he actually know, from a culmination of events, which determined his course?

The Cabinet met at the call of the ranking member only after the approval of his associates. If that reason was sufficient for the dismissal of Lansing, all of us participating were guilty. I know I favored regular meetings when the President was too ill to direct affairs. The only meeting of the Cabinet when Lansing took a course that should have caused the President to feel a sense of condemnation was the one when Lansing called upon Dr. Grayson and Private Secretary Tumulty to say that Wilson was by "inability unable to discharge the powers and duties of the office." They declined emphatically. When Wilson learned that at a Cabinet meeting Lansing had taken the same position as Fall, "Doc" Moses, and other Republican Senators who assumed to give an absentee diagnosis and declare his inability, he had a right to feel that such action by one in whom he had placed confidence and to whom he had given high position deserved censure. It was disloyalty in the political family.

INCENSED AT BULLITT AND LANSING

There is no doubt that Wilson was outraged when, on the Western tour that had broken his health, he learned that Lansing had agreed with Bullitt's criticism of the pending Treaty, saying if the people understood what it let the country in for they would reject it. Here is what Lansing said to Bullitt: "The League Covenant is thoroughly bad and it is my opinion that if the Senate understood it, it would reject it." When Lloyd George read Bullitt's statement purporting to quote him, the British Prime Minister characterized it as "a tissue of lies." When Wilson received Lansing's telegram sent in response to a demand for a statement, Wilson, with a deep show of feeling, according to Private Secretary Tumulty, said:

"Read that, and tell me what you think of a man who was my associate on the other side and who confidentially expressed himself to an outsider in such a fashion? Were I in Washington I would at once demand his resignation! That kind of disloyalty must not be permitted to go unchallenged for a single minute. The testimony of Bullitt is a confirmation of the suspicions I have had with reference to this individual. I found the same attitude of mind on the part of Lansing on the other side. I could find his trail everywhere I went, but they were only suspicions and it would not be fair for me to act upon them. But here in his own statement is a verification at last of everything I have suspected. Think of it! This from a man whom I raised from the level of a subordinate to the great office of Secretary of State of the United States. My God! I did not think it was possible for Lansing to act this way. When we were in Paris I found that Lansing and others were constantly giving out statements that did not agree with my viewpoint. When I had arranged a settlement, there would appear from some source I could not locate unofficial statements telling the correspondents not to take things too seriously; that a compromise would be made, and this news, or rather news of this kind, was harmful to the settlement I had already obtained and quite naturally gave the Conference the impression that Lansing and his kind were speaking for me, and then the French would say that I was bluffing."

Mr. Tumulty records: "I am convinced that only the President's illness a few days later prevented an immediate demand on his part for the resignation of Lansing."

WILSON DEEPLY WOUNDED AT PARIS

The course of Lansing in Paris had deeply wounded Wilson and, though he saw other members of the Cabinet after his return, he rarely saw Lansing and never trusted him after what he regarded as his betrayal at the Peace Conference. He never spoke of his hurt that the two men—House and Lansing—he had trusted had failed him, but it was a wound that could not be healed. Lansing once said that Wilson told him that the reason he was appointed was because he felt their minds ran together. Of course they never did on the question of vital democracy, for Lansing was a Big Stick diplomat who believed in Dollar Diplomacy and in Force and had no part in Wilson's idealism and faith in real democracy. Colonel House was always to Wilson a yes-yes man until he was given position beyond his merits or his ability.

Before Americans knew that Lansing was not in accord with Wilson in Paris the European members knew his attitude. Orlando said: "Lansing did not show any too great admiration for his chief, who had bewitched with his eloquence many foreigners. It was understood that Lansing disagreed with Wilson on Italy."

THE LAST STRAW

All these reasons operated in Wilson's demanding Lansing's retirement, but the immediate cause was, in my judgment—strengthened by what I learned later when I was Ambassador to Mexico—Lansing's ultimatum to the Mexican Government to restore Consul Agent Jenkins, of Puebla, who was said to have been kidnapped by bandits. Lansing's ultimatum was followed so closely by Fall's resolution for the severance of diplomatic relations as to cause some people to think that Lansing and Fall were in agreement. I am confident Jenkins kidnapped himself in order to bring about war between Mexico and the United States, something which Lansing and all the imperialists and concessionaires wished. Wilson repudiated the "immediate" ultimatum and ordered an investigation. When I read in the morning paper the drastic demand of Lansing on President Carranza, I asked Lansing if the President had authorized that drastic course. He said he "did not wish to trouble the President." He had consulted no members of the Cabinet. The exploiters of Mexico applauded it because they had been denouncing Wilson for years when he did not use the Big Stick and send the Marines to drive Carranza from power. While the investigation ordered by Wilson was in progress, Jenkins was released on a bond given by J. Salter Hansen, an American who said he took that course to prevent hostilities between the two countries threatened by Lansing's ultimatum. That ultimatum outraged Wilson and he repudiated the act.

That was the "last straw that broke the camel's back." It was the culminating reason for saying to Lansing, "Here's your hat—what's your hurry?" There was sound reason for not publicly avowing it.

No President would like to make an issue of a matter touching our intercourse with foreign nations.

Lansing wrote Wilson that he and certain members of the Cabinet felt that "in view of the fact that we were denied communication with you, it was wise for us to confer informally together"; he did not think it "unconstitutional, contrary to Wilson's wishes," and there had been "no intention to assume the power and functions exclusively conferred on the President."

LANSING WANTED WAR

The Jenkins case threatened trouble with Mexico. I quote from my Diary (November 28):

"Talked with Lansing about Jenkins case. Had talked previously with Baker who asked: 'Did you hear what Lansing said at cabinet meeting today? "If we go into Mexico it will settle our difficulties here." ' Baker thought that sentiment was at the bottom of much talk of 'straightening out Mexico.' As he was going away Baker urged me to try to prevent our doing what Lansing seemed to favor. Said Lansing was fanning the flames of war. I urged upon Lansing thorough investigation of Jenkins case. I pointed out that we had been unable several times to grant demands of other governments because they had demanded that our Federal Government do what was in the exclusive right of a State (when Japan demanded that Uncle Sam coerce the State of California to change its land laws).

"Burleson wanted us to go into Mexico. Said conditions there very bad. . . . Lane agreed. W. W. said when an American elected to go into a country like Mexico, buy land and oil cheap because of conditions, he had no right to call upon his country to send the Army and Navy to make his property more valuable."

W. W., NO WAR WITH MEXICO

From my Diary (December 4):

"Had talk with Tumulty. He told Lansing that W.W. would not go to war with Mexico and we ought not to make the issue acute. If there is war, let the Republicans wage it.

"Saw Lansing. He said Mexican Embassy in Washington was headquarters for red literature. Received letters from Lansing enclosing one from Justin McGrath asking that ships be sent to Mexico and telegram from William Randolph Hearst urging such course. Lansing requested ships be sent."

WILSON'S SOUND REASONS

People who criticized Wilson's action forgot that, independent of the Paris and Mexican and other incidents, he had sound reasons, as expressed in his second letter to Lansing:

"While we were still in Paris, I felt, and have felt increasingly ever since, that you accepted my guidance and direction on questions with regard to which I had to instruct you only with increasing reluctance, and since my return to Washington I have been struck by the number of matters in which you have apparently tried to forestall my judgment by formulating action and merely asking my approval when it was impossible for me to form an independent judgment because I had not had an opportunity to examine the circumstances with any degree of independence."

Wilson added that the resignation would relieve him "of the embarrassment of feeling your reluctance and divergence of judgment," and to "select someone whose mind would more willingly go along with mine."

CABINET REJECTS LANSING'S PLAN

While Wilson was in the early stages of his illness, with doctors and nurses in the White House, Secretary Lansing called a meeting of the Cabinet (October 6) to discuss calling upon the Vice President to assume the duties of President. When we were gathered Lansing quoted this section of the Constitution which he thought applied:

"In case of removal of the President from office, or his death, resignation or inability to discharge the duties of the said office, the same shall devolve upon the Vice President."

There was suppressed indignation among loyal Cabinet members that Lansing had brought up the question in the early illness of the President. Dr. Grayson and Private Secretary Tumulty were asked to express their views. Dr. Grayson declined to give a diagnosis of the case, indicating his belief that improvement of Wilson's condition could be expected. His statements gave no aid to those in Congress and others who wished to oust Wilson. That was about all that could be drawn from him except that no physician could predict the course of illness. "His condition is encouraging but we are not yet out of the woods," and Dr. Grayson added that the President wanted to know why Cabinet meetings were held and did not like it. He said, in answer to a suggestion by Lansing, that he would not sign a certificate of "inability" of the President. Tumulty, his Irish up, showed hostility and said nobody could induce him to sign such a statement as opposition Senators wished to use to oust Wilson from office.

Houston, who voiced opposition to Lansing's plan, said: "Garfield was shot early in July and no disability was said to exist."

Lane said: "Wayne MacVeagh ran the government."

Lansing made no comment upon the protests of Grayson and Tumulty but looked guilty and baffled. The guarded expression of Dr. Grayson and his firm statement that he would not give a certificate of inability, and the notification by Tumulty that he would fight any attempt to secure the retirement of the President, and the remarks of members of the Cabinet, convinced Lansing that his suggestion had no support. That ended the attempt within the Cabinet to oust Wilson. Disturbed and loyal to their chief, and anxious, the Cabinet took no action. Wilson's restoration to ability to carry on, even though never strong again, justified their refusal to accept Lansing's point of view.

WHAT TUMULTY SAID TO LANSING

Before the Cabinet meeting was called, Private Secretary Tumulty relates:

"Mr. Lansing came to the executive office October 3. He informed me that he had called diplomatically to suggest that in view of the incapacity of the President, we should arrange to call in the Vice President to act in his stead as soon as possible, reading to me from a book which he had brought from the State Department, which I afterward learned was Jefferson's Manual, the following clause of the United States Constitution:

" 'In case of the removal of the President from office, by death or resignation, or inability to discharge the duties of the said office, the same shall be devolved upon the Vice President.'

"I turned and said,

" 'Mr. Lansing, the Constitution is not a dead letter in the

White House. I have read the Constitution and do not find myself in need of tutoring at your hands of the provision you have just read. I will be no party to certifying to the President's disability.' Dr. Grayson came in just at that time and left no doubt in Mr. Lansing's mind that he would not do what Mr. Lansing suggested. I told Lansing that if anybody outside of the White House should attempt to certify to the President's disability, Grayson and I would stand together and repudiate it."

LANSING NEVER A WILSONIAN

"O that mine adversary had written a book," was the prayer of a man who preferred that an enemy should destroy himself with his own pen than to be compelled to use the sword.

If Secretary Lansing had not written a book he would have retained the early advantage over President Wilson in the matter of his resignation. Proof that Wilson labored under a misapprehension that Lansing was in accord with him, when he was appointed to succeed Bryan, is furnished in Lansing's "Memorandums." Wilson could not have seen the one in which Lansing says he urged war in 1915, when Wilson thought he was with him in trying to keep out of war. The memoranda and correspondence were removed from the State Department by Lansing when he went out in 1920. After his death in 1928 his relatives returned them and they were printed by the State Department. This publication, plus Lansing's Memoirs, discloses that he was a disciple of his father-in-law, Secretary Foster, and Root, whose views as to foreign affairs were as far apart from Wilson's as possible. But Wilson never knew this while Lansing was writing letters at the instruction of the President—though I sensed it in 1917—until Paris.

In this matter as in most other fundamentals of democracy and Americanism, Lansing was not in sympathy with the President. When there was an exchange of notes with Britain about the right of American ships to carry goods to neutral ports, Lansing wrote the President: "The present controversy (over American rights to freedom of the seas) seems here, where we are all close to the question, academic."

"SUBMERGED IN VERBOSITY"

Wilson did not know till long afterward—it was not revealed until years later—when in his Memoirs Lansing said that in all correspondence between the British and American governments relating to trade, "everything was submerged in verbosity." Why? He answered:

"It was done with deliberate purpose. It insured continuance of controversies and left questions unsettled, which was necessary in order to leave this country free to act and even act illegally when it entered the war."

Lansing's justification for "verbosity" was that we would "ultimately become an ally of Great Britain, and it would not do, therefore, to let our controversies reach a point where diplomatic correspondence gave place to action."

Twenty-two years later, when Lansing's imperialistic record and Big Stick diplomacy had been revealed, Charles Fisher wrote: "Lansing was acting in a manner which would have driven him out of office in a fury of protest had his program not been kept secret."

As further proof that Wilson was wrong when he thought Lansing's mind and his functioned alike, Lansing in his book shows how wide apart they were upon the most fundamental principle. Here is how Lansing defined his position as diametrically opposed to that of Wilson, Franklin Roosevelt, and Thomas Jefferson:

"Self determination is as right in theory as the more famous phrase 'the consent of the governed'—The more I think about the President's declaration as to the right of self determination, the more I am convinced of the danger of putting such ideas into the minds of certain races. It is bound to be the basis of impossible demands on the Peace Conference and creates trouble in many lands. What effect will it have on the Irish, the Indians, the Egyptians, and the nationals among the Boers? The phrase is literally dynamite. What misery it will cause."

There have been many reasons assigned for Lansing's defection. The underlying one was that he had no faith in liberalism or genuine democracy or sympathy for the aspirations of the neglected of the earth. Wilson mistakenly believed that their minds ran in the same channel when he made him Secretary of State. Lifted out of technical drafting, where he revelled in protocol and legalistic writings, Lansing soon saw himself a second Root. He wished to head the Peace Commission to Paris and for that reason advised Wilson that the President ought not to go. At Paris he resented the superior place taken by House. Dr. Bell, in his *Woodrow Wilson and the People,* thinks that if Lansing had been "appeased" and "taken more into the President's confidence" his testimony before the Foreign Relations Committee would have been different.

WHY COLBY WAS NAMED TO SUCCEED LANSING

When Lansing was forced out (every other Cabinet officer who left the family did so on his own volition), there was much speculation. Most Washington people thought Under Secretary Frank L. Polk, able and esteemed, would succeed. If not, Baker was the chief prediction, and the next favorite was Alderman. The Cabinet was surprised when out of a clear sky came the appointment of Bainbridge Colby. What influenced Wilson in that selection? Wilson was giving much attention to strengthening the merchant marine and he turned often to Colby, of the Shipping Board. When in Washington and when he was in Paris, Colby always had at command the very information Wilson wanted or could further Wilson's plans promptly and efficiently. That impressed Wilson most favorably, particularly at Paris. Colby had tact and Wilson came to rely on him and to feel that their minds were in agreement. In that assumption, in some matters, he later found he was as mistaken as when he told Lansing that he had been selected because he felt that they thought alike.

One other thing that influenced Wilson was that he regarded Colby as a man who had shown devotion to liberal principles. With Theodore Roosevelt, Colby had left the Republican Party in 1912 and was one of the most eloquent leaders in the Progressive Party. In 1916 when Roosevelt threw his party to the wolves because in 1912 and 1914 it had elected so few sheriffs, Colby refused to abandon the new party. Instead, seeing that the hope of real liberalism lay in the reëlection of Wilson, before long Colby was rallying the Progressives to the support of Wilson.

In the short time he held the office, when Wilson needed a strong right arm in foreign affairs, Colby was personally devoted to carrying out what Wilson wished, and his record embraces important if not distinguished service. I always liked him, even when as in his Mexican policies I was in disagreement with him. I later learned that he lacked the martyr-to-liberal-principle blood that Wilson attributed to him.

In Wilson's closing hours in the White House he, who even in sickness had guided great affairs, hated to look forward to inactivity in private life. Enter the engaging Colby to open a door to save him from the boredom of inaction. A fellow member of the Cabinet who loved Wilson, when the announcement was made that a law firm of Wilson and Colby had been formed, said: "Bainbridge has vamped Wilson." We all knew that Wilson could not engage in the practice of law, and some said Colby was going to trade on his name. The truth was that Wilson suggested the partnership. Colby did not initiate it.

Colby opened an office in New York and came to Washington for conferences with his senior partner. There were plenty of clients proffering large fees, but Wilson turned down those that had any relation to government.

Colby said to Mrs. Wilson, "Day after day I see a procession walk through—thousands and thousands of dollars—and not one put in our pockets." He added, "It is a sublime position on the part of your husband, and I am honored to share it as long as I can afford it."

Wilson realized that he ought not to stand in Colby's way of representing clients who had matters pending in the Departments (something Hughes, McAdoo, and other ex-Cabinet members thought proper).

The partnership soon terminated. One day Colby came to Washington to consult with his law partner. He informed Wilson that he had accepted a fee as retainer for a big oil company. This fee was $500,000. Wilson put his foot down on accepting the retainer. He felt the fee was not for legal service but for the use of his name. He had seen how some big oil men retained lawyers to get special favors. His name could not be so used. The fee was not accepted. The partnership came to an end.

Speaking of the incident to a beloved friend Wilson said: "The very size of the fee was an insult." He held his name so dear that it could not be used by those who were in the habit of retaining great lawyers whose names brought them prestige. Like Lee, who declined a big salary to head a legitimate enterprise, his name was not on the market.

XLIV

DID JENKINS KIDNAP HIMSELF?

T HOUGH WILSON gave another reason, I am sure that the immediate cause for his demanding Lansing's resignation was the
Secretary of State's ultimatum to Mexico which threatened war with
that country.

Jenkins was consular agent of the State Department at Puebla,
and the news came to the State Department that he had been kidnapped by bandits. Without waiting to investigate, Lansing sent a
peremptory demand for his immediate release "or else." That was
so contrary to all of Wilson's dealings with Mexico through the
tortuous years that he was incensed that such a demand should have
been made without consultation with him. Did Jenkins kidnap
himself?

STATEMENT BY J. SALTER HANSEN

Mr. J. Salter Hansen, an American, who was in Mexico on business
in the Carranza days and afterwards during the time I was in Mexico, talked with me frequently in Mexico about the Jenkins case. I
asked Mr. Hansen to tell me the facts, as he was responsible for the
release of Jenkins from jail. Mr. Hansen, in response to my questions,
gave me the history of the case, as follows:

"I paid little attention to the so-called kidnapping of W. O.
Jenkins and to Jenkins' refusal to furnish bail in the sum of 1,000
pesos until I realized that this incident was being used by certain
reactionary elements in the United States and some public officials to bring about a war between the United States and Mexico
which euphemistically was called 'intervention.' I realized that
there were powerful elements outside of Mexico eager for an
opportunity or an excuse to overthrow and destroy the liberal
government under President Carranza and reëstablish the form
of government, or rather dictatorship, which had existed for
decades under Porfirio Diaz.

"On December 2 certain information reached me so disturbing that I realized that steps must be taken immediately to have

Jenkins released from jail, where he had been incarcerated for several weeks. Jenkins' refusal to furnish the bail himself after he and his lawyer had asked the court to fix the amount was due to the fact that certain officials in the State Department in Washington were working in collusion with some oil and banking interests and others in the United States to create a situation that would make war between the United States and Mexico inevitable.

"On Thursday, December 4, carrying out this desire to use the Jenkins arrest as the excuse for war with Mexico, Lansing had given an ultimatum for the immediate and unconditional release of Jenkins by the Mexican Government under President Carranza. Knowing all the inside facts, I left for Puebla on Thursday, December 4, at four P.M., arriving at Puebla at 9:00 P.M. and had W. O. Jenkins out of jail by 11:15 P.M. When the Attorney General of Puebla, Mr. Mitchell, Judge Guzeman, the Puebla correspondent of the Associated Press, and the Chief of Police of Puebla went into the well furnished room in which he was incarcerated, Jenkins pleaded not to be shot, stating that he had asked Matthew Hanna, assigned to the case by the Department of State, to be allowed to furnish bail required by law for his release.

"On the following morning, Friday, December 5, I observed Matthew Hanna having breakfast at the Hotel Del Pasaje. He greeted me very cordially and informed me that Jenkins had been released unconditionally through diplomatic pressure on the Mexican government by the Department of State. On his table were two newspapers published at Puebla; one, *El Democrata,* a pro-Carranza government paper, gave the correct facts, namely, that I had furnished the bail. The other, *La Tribuna,* a paper hostile to the liberal government, announced that it was the ultimatum from Secretary of State Lansing which brought about the unconditional release of Jenkins. Mr. Matthew Hanna had read the statement in *La Tribuna* but failed even to glance at the headlines of *El Democrata.* I told him that I hoped that he had not informed the State Department at Washington of that version of the case. He stated that he had cabled the Department that the release was upon representations of the State Department, whereas Jenkins was released solely because I had put up the bond. Anxious not to have the State Department give out the wrong information, I asked the Attorney General of Puebla, Mr. Mitchell, to try and have Hanna's wire stopped if it had not yet been sent. We went together to the cable office, were informed that Hanna had sent a wire half an hour previously and when we asked what it contained, we were told that the cablegram was in code.

"The newspapers in the United States received the news of Jenkins' release on bail correctly through the Associated Press correspondent in Puebla. The State Department officially informed the public that Jenkins had been unconditionally released due to Secretary Lansing's ultimatum.

"Senator Fall and Senator Hitchcock were in President Wilson's sick room on December 6 in order to ascertain Wilson's views on the Fall resolution to sever diplomatic relations with Mexico when a dramatic incident occurred. Dr. Grayson was called to the phone and announced to President Wilson that Jenkins was released. Wilson said, 'That is wonderful news!' "

Asked about the bond, Mr. Hansen said the bond had been fixed at a very nominal sum, the Mexicans expecting that Jenkins would give it as he was a rich man and could have put up the bond easily, and they did not think but that he would avail himself of it, but neither he nor the State Department wished his release, feeling that his continued confinement in jail would make a casus belli. The amount of the bond fixed was about 1,000 pesos, which was then about $500 in American money. "I put up the bond myself and here is a photostatic copy of it," said Mr. Hansen as he handed it to me.

On December 9, the *New York Tribune* contained the story sent by the Associated Press, as follows:

HANSEN PAID JENKINS BAIL ON OWN INITIATIVE

"Mexico City, Monday 8. J. Salter Hansen, who furnished the bail upon which W. O. Jenkins, the American Consular Agent at Puebla was released Thursday night, disclosed in a statement tonight that he had acted on his own initiative. Mr. Hansen said:

" 'I wish to say the following: Tuesday morning last, on account of certain facts that came to my attention, which I am in no position to disclose, I suddenly realized that war between the United States and Mexico was inevitable unless one of the two governments was ready to sacrifice its honor, prestige and dignity by receding from the dangerous position into which it had been forced. I therefore took all the steps necessary to effect the immediate release on bail of W. O. Jenkins and relieve the tension. I did so spontaneously and on my own initiative. And I am ready and willing to take upon myself the full responsibility or credit according to the point of view.

" 'It was a source of infinite pleasure to me to hear that the news of the release of Jenkins cheered our President and I ardently hope that his complete recovery is near.' "

I asked Mr. Hansen why the Attorney General, who did not know him, accepted his check. He said, "The Attorney General told me that Louis Cabrera, Secretary of the Treasury of the Mexican Republic, wired him that I was a good friend of his. 'Therefore,' said the Attorney General, 'I accept your check, knowing it is good.' "

I asked Mr. Hansen if the check had been cashed, and he said, "No." "Why?" I asked. "Because," said Mr. Hansen, "Jenkins did not run away and the bond, only for his appearance, was not forfeited. May I add that I look upon this check as a very valuable instrument as it prevented the possibility of war between two countries which within the last ten years have become the closest friends and associates."

Mr. Hansen gave me a photostatic copy of the check he had given to get Jenkins out of jail on which was written in Spanish and the translation is as follows:

"Cheque for $500.00 Dollars on the Guaranty Trust Company of New York,' deposited December 5, 1919, by the Secretary of the 2nd Criminal Court by order, and at the disposition of said court."

XLV

STRANGEST FRIENDSHIP AND ITS END

ONE OF THE strangest intimacies in history was that between Woodrow Wilson and Edward M. House. It began and ended with suddenness. They had never known each other until House, after first advocating the nomination of Mayor Gaynor, espoused the cause of Wilson. It was nothing new for Colonel House to make himself serviceable to men prominent in public life. He had inherited a small fortune and was free to follow his desire without engaging in any business or profession. Politics interested him. Though never holding any office except member of the Austin (Texas) Board of Aldermen, he loved, behind the scenes, to be near public favorites, ready to advance their causes. His first adherence was to Governor Hogg when that vital figure was a favorite in Texas. When William Jennings Bryan was the idol of Texas Democrats, Colonel House invited him to visit Texas on hunting trips. In 1912, possibly 1911, Colonel House saw in Wilson a winner. He tendered his support and his good offices to Wilson who saw in him—or thought he did—a selfless man who was attracted to him from common progressive beliefs.

Colonel House told me in Paris, where he was a member of the Peace Commission, that the only difference between a meeting of the Board of Aldermen in Austin and the Peace Commission in Paris was that in Austin differences were about purely local matters while in Paris the questions had world application. "But," he added, "there are the same jealousies, rivalries, and personal problems to be adjusted, and if you lost sight of the bigger issue at Paris I could almost think I was back in Austin debating which street should be paved first."

I first met Colonel House during the 1912 campaign, when he was behind the scenes seeking to promote Wilson's election. House was in Europe when the fight at the Baltimore Convention which gave Wilson his chance was won. He was not an original Wilson man, but when Burleson, Tom Love, Henry, Ball, and Cone

Johnson organized Texas for Wilson, they had the long-distance hearty coöperation of House. However, in the early spring he lost hope and wrote Wilson, "The fight seems to be going against us," predicting that "the opposing candidates might be Bryan and Roosevelt," and went to Europe.

When to his surprise the men who stayed at home nominated Wilson, the Texan returned to New York, and Wilson was glad to rely upon him in the campaign, and as adviser when he was selecting his Cabinet, and as a sort of roving ambassador-at-large. The public got the idea that House played a large part in nominating and electing Wilson and the Colonel encouraged that fiction.

After Wilson's inauguration, Colonel House was always at his command. He had a talent for acquainting the President with what was going on. When it became known he was close to the President, many who wished to reach Wilson sought out Colonel House. Before war was declared, Wilson sent Colonel House to Europe to confer unofficially with the rulers of Britain, France, and Germany in the hope of bringing about peace. The mission failed. Ray Stannard Baker, close to Wilson and his chosen biographer, sums up the result: "It is significant that House travelled about Europe for two years, finger on lips, in an atmosphere of mysterious conferences and secret codes, with no result whatever."

The war ended, Wilson sent House to Europe as his representative to make arrangements for the Peace Conference and named him a Peace Commissioner.

Early in his administration Wilson told me that what he liked about House was his perfect unselfishness, wishing no honor for himself, happiest when he could advance the administration's policies. He did not know that all the time, almost from the beginning, House was, in his Diary, writing of himself as the power behind the throne.

Not long before his death Albert Burleson, of Texas, Postmaster General in Wilson's Administration, who had Wilson's regard and confidence and who was the soul of loyalty, candor, and truth, requested me on my way to Mexico to stop and spend at least a day with him at Austin. His message was: "You must stop. I have something important to say to you and to point out a duty you owe." My wife and I, glad to renew associations with old friends, visited Mr. and Mrs. Burleson. This was the mission he entrusted to me:

"You must write the inside story of the Wilson Administration. You are a writer. We both loved him and followed him to the end and know, perhaps better than any others his true greatness. There is one thing you must do. You must tell the true story of Ed House and his supposed great influence over Wilson. I cannot do it. I am a Texan. Ed House and I were friends. Therefore, it is your duty to correct a false impression. Ed House never influenced Wilson. He never carried Texas for him as has been believed. He never inspired any of his great policies; he was a capable emissary, and was ready, until Paris, to do whatever Wilson suggested. But it was Wilson who thought out policies, and House never differed from any view Wilson expressed. How did he manage to make Wilson think he was wiser than he was? I will tell you. When House would come down from New York to see Wilson he would arrive on the early morning train. Before going to the White House he would come to see me and ask, "Albert, what is the President thinking about?" or "What is his attitude on this or that policy (naming it)?" I would tell him. He would sometimes ask McAdoo, or you, or some other member of the Cabinet. By that means he would acquaint himself with what was in Wilson's mind before he reached the White House. And then, before Wilson could ask any questions, House would suggest the very policy I or others had told him was in Wilson's mind."

That was the substance of the conversation that ran on a whole afternoon as we sat and talked in his Austin home. When I was leaving, in characteristic earnestness he repeated: "Joe, you must do it. You owe it to Wilson and to the truth of history." What Burleson enlarged upon bore out what Dr. Grayson said: "House is a 'Yes' man."

If I were to obey Mr. Burleson's command to "tell the truth about Ed House," it could be compressed into giving him the name of Mr. "Smooth-It-Away," and that would accurately describe his status in his close and intimate association with Woodrow Wilson from 1912 until he ceased to fill the function for which he was qualified—the behind-the-scenes guide, philosopher, and friend of greater men. Relatively inexperienced in the ways of practical politics when he entered upon the national scene, Wilson accepted House, who placed himself by his readiness to be a selfless go-between at Wilson's disposal. He was rich enough to be independent. He was wise in the ways of politicians. He loved to confer and to conciliate. He had ability and a certain genius for finding out trends which Wilson lacked and for which he had no taste. House complemented Wilson and he gave House the opportunity to come in touch with men who had power, an association which became, as it enlarged, the very breath of his nostrils. To be the ambasasdor from Wilson first to political leaders, then to other Americans whose names were famous, and then to the titled and the premiers of the Old World— this opportunity was heaven on earth to Colonel House. It was his balm in Gilead. And Wilson found his reports, made in his hush-hush way, interesting and relied upon his advice, which was not always good—often quite the reverse. But Wilson did not doubt that it was given without the least thought of personal ambition or desire for fame. "Colonel House is the most selfless man I have ever known. He wants nothing for himself. His only desire is to serve those of us charged with guiding the administration." That was Wilson's opinion and estimate of House until—Paris. And Wilson was right so far as House's wishing to profit by his association. He had no lust to take advantage of his favored position, which gave him access to the rich and powerful, in order to gain anything of money value for himself, as has too often been characteristic of men who feathered their own nest by closeness to the White House. There was nothing of the profiteer or money-seeking in House, though he often, in his desire to make things smooth, played that game, as when he quietly sided with the exploiters in Mexican problems.

Colonel House knew his Texas and his New York and his way about Washington. However, early in the privacy of his Diary, he saw himself a leader while Wilson saw him as a selfless guide to officialdom. But it was not until war when he was thrust into the world terrain to report to Wilson unofficially on the world field that he found himself at sea without a life-preserver or a rudder. By that time he had come to believe himself a world figure and able to advise as to changing the course of world affairs and indeed make a new map of the world. And Wilson believed in him as a political astrologist and sent him to spy out Europe, to sound out the Kaiser, to walk with kings and princes and report what was in their minds.

With the acceptance by the Allies and the Germans of Wilson's Fourteen Points and the Armistice founded on them, Wilson sent his Mr. Smooth-It-Away to Europe to make easy the way to peace negotiations. House was a world figure. "See Colonel House" was the order in the Chancellories of Europe for those wishing to get in touch with Wilson in the United States. Suave, affable, agreeable, compromising—even giving away the Point calling for Freedom of the Seas—House was Wilson's trusted agent to make all Peace Conference arrangements in Europe. Such things irked Wilson. They were House's delight. Wilson was glad to have a friend to make arrangements, one who was thoughtful, sympathetic, and helpful.

And then came the Peace Conference, and House was lifted out of the role as confidential ambassador extraordinary from the Chief Executive to the Peace Commission. He was no longer Wilson's alter ego. He was, as he saw himself, "Fashioner of Treaties." He continued to be accessible to everybody and the center of information, but now as principal and not as agent. The metamorphosis was complete. Now as Peace Commissioner he essayed a role. He put on the robes. They did not fit. And, when his mentor, the great man who made him, was called to Washington, he failed in the crucial testing hour. He agreed with Lansing and Clemenceau to cut the League of Nations out of the Peace Treaty—to destroy its very heart, bone and sinew, blood—to make it a copy of the Treaty of Vienna without a promise of independence and peace. And Wilson was forced to see that the man he had given first place in his confidence had sacrificed the one thing that had caused him to lead his country into war and had carried him to Paris—a World League to Secure Lasting Peace. It cut Wilson to the heart. But there was no word of blame, no scene, no condemnation of an old friend. Between his life's goal and master passion and a cherished friendship he had no choice. In the spirit of, "I can do no otherwise," Wilson took steps to uphold the League. There was an end of the association upon which he had so long relied and in which he had trusted.

WHAT CAUSED THE BREAK?

"What caused the break between Woodrow Wilson and Colonel Edward M. House after nine years of an intimacy in public matters almost without precedent?" That was a question that nobody could answer and neither man would speak about it.

Wilson never told House in words that he had lost confidence in him, though they never met after they returned from Paris. He just never saw him again, made no answer to his letters. He was sorely wounded when House deserted in the fight for the League of Nations. And the wound was so deep he never spoke of it.

While the Senate was having hearings on the Treaty, House wrote a letter to Senator Lodge, Chairman of the Foreign Relations Committee, offering to come before the committee and give his views about the pending treaty. It was understood he favored accepting the Lodge reservations if necessary to secure ratification. That a trusted member of the Peace Commission would be ready to compromise the vital principle was too much for Wilson.

It was always an anomalous position which Colonel House occupied in the Wilson administration. He had no official status. The fact that he held such a relationship made him and the President the targets for criticism. I once heard Colonel House say that it was unfortunate that our Government does not permit the President to have advisers free from departmental duties so that they might devote themselves wholly to the study of large problems.

HOUSE COULD NOT EXPLAIN

One incident told me by one who knew and vouched for its accuracy may throw light on the beginning of Wilson's separation from Colonel House. One day during the Peace Conference, Colonel House called on Wilson, who was not feeling well. He excused himself and House was received by Mrs. Wilson. In the course of the conversation House said: "I wish you would say to the President I enjoy the closest and most friendly relations with Mr. Wickham Stead, the able correspondent of the *London Times*. He will be glad to do anything I ask him. If the President has anything he would like to be given to the world that might help in the matters in which he is interested, I can get Mr. Stead to give it journalistic wings."

The hostess asked to be excused for a minute. Upon returning, she held a clipping containing an article Mr. Stead had written while Wilson was in Washington. It was to the effect that Wilson would be wise not to return to Paris, but to entrust the continuation of the conferences and the agreements touching the peace treaty to Colonel House. The article stated that the negotiations had stalled but, while Lloyd George was in England and Wilson in the United States, Colonel House had brought them back "from the brink of failure to relatively safe ground." It added: "The improvement was due to the fact that Colonel House has placed his savoir faire and conciliatory temperament at the disposal of the top-most peace-makers." The article concluded with the highest praise of House, who was acclaimed as the fittest man to complete the negotiations and could complete them better than Wilson, who should have remained in America and let House take his place.

"If you are such a good friend of Mr. Stead," said Mrs. Wilson after Colonel House had read the article, "perhaps you can explain this."

The Colonel, confused, said he had not read the article and took his departure. He never returned.

FIRST STATEMENT OF BREAK

The first statement about the causes of the break was contained in an article by Louis Siebold, an able writer, which appeared (December, 1919) in the *New York World*. He quoted foreign officials as attributing the break to the embarrassment which House caused Wilson when he agreed to the exclusion of the League from the Treaty. Siebold said that the reasons for House's incurring Wilson's disfavor were:

> "First, that Colonel House had overstepped his authority and had been the cause of leaving out of the Armistice terms and the Peace Treaty draft the "freedom of the seas" clause favored by President Wilson. In this respect he was represented as having been used as an innocent catspaw by British diplomats.
>
> "Second, that he espoused the Orlando cause in the Fiume dispute and assured the Italian premier he could win the President over, when the President's determination to see that the Yugoslavs got justice, according to his understanding, was reported to be unwavering.
>
> "Third, that he had forced the unwilling consent of the allied diplomats to Paris as the seat of the Peace Conference by representing that the French capital was the choice of the President, when in reality Mr. Wilson first learned from the Colonel himself that some spot more agreeable to the majority of the conference was not to be selected."

SECRETARY BAKER ON HOUSE

When the *Papers of Colonel House* appeared long after Wilson's death, those closest to Wilson knew that the impression they would make on those who did not know the real situation would be as misleading as were many ex parte statements printed about great men after their death.

Secretary Newton D. Baker, who had Wilson's complete confidence, was shocked and indignant at the implication of the House letters. He wrote me on March 12, 1926:

"DEAR JOE:

"The House letters have offended me more than anything that has happened within my recollection. To have him make matter of vulgar merchandise of the intimate confidence which President Wilson gave him is bad enough, but for him to attempt to create the impression that Wilson had a dependent mind is false to the facts.

"The time may come when you and I will have to say for the public information that in our long contacts with the President, House was rarely within a thousand miles and that the President was perfectly able to reason with the precision of a Swiss watch and decided with the firmness of a trip-hammer, without having any assistance from House, or anybody else to guide him.

"I never knew House very well, which, of course, is a part of the general good fortune which has attended me through life. All told, I probably had no more than three conferences with him, none of which, so far as I can remember, were about the War Department, so that I am relieved from any anxiety lest he should claim in the remaining two volumes that he selected Pershing, planned the strategy of the Meuse-Argonne offensive, wrote the Selective Service Act, and organized the services of supply. Did he design any of the battleships or have anything to do with the selection of Benson, Sims, Wilson or Rodman? I really would like to have an affirmative statement from you on this subject, because there must be some limitations to his colossal genius and industry and I am trying to collect a few instances, at least, which will authoritatively show that he did not do everything that was done throughout the whole period of eight years.

"Affectionately yours,
"NEWTON D. BAKER"

RELATIONS WITH COLONEL HOUSE

While I saw Colonel House only occasionally after the 1912 campaign, our relations were always on a friendly basis, and I was disposed not to dispute what Wilson had said to me: "House wants no reward in office, nothing for himself." These extracts from my Diary indicate our relations:

September 15, 1917:

"The Boston Transcript a few days ago printed a story to the effect that Woodrow Wilson and Colonel E. M. House were at odds because he had advised Wilson to get a new Secretary of the Navy. I had not seen the Transcript article until Colonel House called my attention to it in a letter referring to the publication and saying he had denied it, adding 'but these things have to go a certain length after once begun. I regret it beyond measure because of my friendship and high regard for you.'"

October 11, 1917:

"Colonel E. M. House called at Navy Department. He said to me: 'You may say with a certain Governor of Texas: "I have made no mistakes."' I replied that I could not truthfully say that. He goes to Europe at direction of the President for conference with the powers on our side. An Army and a Navy officer will go with him. We talked of what the Navy had done and the work of offensive ahead of it."

January 28, 1918:

"Colonel House called. 'In all this talk and criticism,' he said, 'the good condition of the Navy has saved the day. This makes nobody so happy as W.W.' He said everybody abroad praised the alertness of the men of the Navy. Benson was easily the first man of the Military Council—towered over Jellicoe and told them what to do and put them to doing it."

HOUSE DIED WITHOUT SPEAKING

In 1923, when I was writing my Life of Wilson, I went to New York to see Colonel House and told him I thought it was due to Wilson and to himself and to the truth of history for him to give the real cause of the break. Though House declined to answer my question, the New York Times (July 26, 1934) quoted House as saying: "The bedroom circle kept him apart from me and kept me apart from him. My letters never reached him; no messages were ever sent to me."

Part Fourteen

AFTERMATH OF WAR

XLVI

CABINET MEETINGS RESUMED

W HEN WILSON was somewhat improved, Cabinet meetings were resumed. I recall that those members of the Cabinet who had not seen him in his illness were distressed at his appearance and were shocked at the way he limped when he walked.

The plan of holding the first meetings was that the President would be seated at his accustomed place in his library. Cabinet meetings were held in the White House and not in the Executive Office, and as each member would come in separately Usher Hoover would speak very plainly and say, "Mr. Baker, Mr. Burleson," etc. At first I did not know whether this was necessary while I feared that Wilson's eyesight was impaired, but it was an extra precaution, for later this course was abandoned.

At the first meeting it was painful to see that Wilson would repeat himself, telling at successive meetings the same stories and the same jokes, and that made us all anxious. However, in a little while he improved so much that the meetings went along as in the old days—or nearly so. He was always as clear as a bell on any topic or matter that he had considered before his illness but as to most new matters, he wished to postpone them or to refer them to some member of the Cabinet. I think this was at first upon the advice of his doctor.

WILSON SAID, "DO NOT SEE RED"

At the first Cabinet meeting there was a red-hot debate between Attorney General Palmer and Secretary Wilson over Palmer's complaint that certain aliens, declared by him to be anarchists, had not been deported as he had advised. He said to Secretary Wilson, "If Acting Secretary Post had deported them, the strike would have ended." Secretary Wilson thought such act would aggravate it. About this time Mrs. Wilson and Dr. Grayson appeared in the doorway, anxiety written on their faces. "Holding this Cabinet meeting is an experiment, you know," said President Wilson, "and I ought not to stay long."

It was at this meeting that, referring to the fact there had been some criticism of Burleson, Wilson said, "This seems to be an open season for criticizing Burleson." Then, turning to the Attorney General, the President said, "Palmer, do not let this country see red." It was a needed admonition for Palmer was seeing red behind every bush and every demand for an increase in wages.

SERIOUS RUPTURE IN CABINET

There was one rupture that threatened a resignation in Wilson's Cabinet. I had been absent from Washington several days. Upon my return Secretary Lane came to me and said, "Secretary Wilson is determined to resign. He is in disagreement with Palmer and Garfield, he feels that most of his associates have taken sides against his position, and he is under the impression that the President has been persuaded that he is wrong. In fact, he has written his resignation. It is unfortunate that the President is not well enough to hear all sides of the matter. You were in agreement with Wilson in the main and we think if you would add your request to ours he may be persuaded not to send his letter."

The break between W. B. Wilson and Garfield, backed by Palmer, over wages of the miners came to a head when Attorney General Palmer made a public announcement that the Cabinet had unanimously agreed to his proposal to enjoin the miners. This came as a surprise while W. B. Wilson was holding conferences he believed would result successfully. Secretary Wilson was incensed when he heard the Attorney General had decided to use the writ of injunction under the Lever Act to prevent or break the impending strike, without providing means to determine the merits of the controversy. Wilson protested with all the vigor he possessed, and that was five hundred horsepower. He gave the argument against the use of a writ of injunction that neither the operator nor the government had any property right in the labor of the mine-workers and could not therefore invoke an injunction. Moreover, he declared that an injunction would not stop the strike, and more, that it would not mine any coal. In taking this position, Secretary Wilson was relying on the statement President Wilson made to Mr. Gompers and the

Secretary that the Lever bill would not be used to secure an injunction.

Palmer was mistaken in supposing the Cabinet approved the injunction. One member told him, "if you have determined on that course, we are without authority to direct your action." Garfield told the Cabinet that unless his figures, which he said would protect the consumer, were approved, the Cabinet would have to ask the President to remove him.

At the request of members of the Cabinet, Secretary Wilson resumed his efforts to bring about a settlement, the injunction having failed to end the strike. He secured an agreement between the mine-owners and miners upon a wage rate that would keep pace with the increase in the cost of living, the operators conditioning their agreement upon the approval of the Fuel Administration of making the selling price of coal conform to the new wage scale.

Later it was agreed by all parties to submit the question to a commission of three—one operator, one miner, and one person not connected with mining. When the award was made, the increase in wages ranged from 20 to 27 per cent. This award showed that the members of the Cabinet who refused to side with either W. B. Wilson or Garfield and favored an adjustment were right. But I never saw a man so immovable and so cocksure he was right and so determined to admit no change in his figures as Dr. Garfield. The difference between Garfield and Secretary Wilson almost reached the point of estrangement. But both were so honorable, sincere, and patriotic that they restrained themselves from anything more than an unyielding position.

It took all my power of persuasion to induce Secretary Wilson to withhold his resignation, pleading that he owed it to the President, who was not well enough to go into all the ramifications. He was particularly incensed that Palmer—from his own State—should take vigorous action against the labor unions without giving him a hearing. I do not think that estrangement was ever healed.

A well Wilson would have nipped the injunction in the bud. At a later meeting of the Cabinet (President Wilson was improved), when Palmer suggested an injunction in a strike in New York Harbor, the Secretary of Labor protested and said it was not the remedy.

"Every lawyer knows that is an abuse of the writ," President
Wilson quietly said, turning to the Attorney General.

That ended the suggestion of an injunction.

As we left the Cabinet meeting, W. B. Wilson was a happy man.
"The President's declaration that an injunction would be an abuse
of the writ was balm to my soul," he said to me. "And I am glad
now that the letter I wrote resigning was never sent." I felt repaid
for my urging him not to resign.

I often wonder if President Wilson would have been so successful in the labor and fuel administration if he had lacked able men
like William B. Wilson and Harry A. Garfield.

W. B. WILSON A SOLID ROCK

The country never really knew the stuff of which Secretary
Wilson was made or his ability and worth. Modest, quiet, devoted
to reading and with none of the arts of getting in the limelight, he
was one of the wisest of President Wilson's counsellors. He was born
in Scotland, came to this country when a very small boy, worked
in the mines when he was eight years old, became a leader of the
miners, went out on a strike, served as national labor official and
represented a Pennsylvania district in Congress before he became
a member of Wilson's Cabinet. He had even published a volume of
poems, though I hope nobody will hold that against him. Some
of them were good, particularly those in his native tongue. He had
no formal schooling, but he was a well educated man.

In the many problems affecting labor that came up in the eight
years, the President counselled freely with Mr. Wilson and found
him always fair and just. A devoted member of labor unions, and
believing in them as beneficial to the country, he knew they made
mistakes and he never hesitated to say so when it became necessary.
Labor had a seat in all the councils of the Wilson administration.

LABOR A ROCK OF DEPENDENCE

It was a matter of pride that at no time in the stress of war, with
its great strain on man-power, did Labor fail to measure up equally
with the men in uniform. In my 1920 report I said:

"Labor was the rock upon which preparation and supplies
depended. It was mobilized and efficient. . . . The day of giving
to skill and toil a mere living wage has passed. It is entitled,

after a fair day's work, to a fair day's wage, sufficient for comforts and some luxuries as well as necessities. Without the skill and industry and fine spirit of men in overalls, our men in arms could not have been furnished the required munitions and supplies.

SUPERIOR RIGHTS FOR CAPITAL

With Wilson ill, the trend in the Cabinet was away from his attitude toward Labor. My Diary (October 14, 1919), has this:

"Cabinet discussed strike. Labor offered to arbitrate. Lane said proclamation should be made that the Government would send troops wherever there was disorder. I said this would be regarded as the Government's advertising it would side with capital and be resented by Labor. Lansing said: 'If a man owns a plant, the right of property gives him privilege to conduct it as he pleases.' Not so. The public has rights which he must consider. Public rights apply to both employer and employee. Labor had offered to arbitrate and we should insist that Judge Gary do the same. No action taken, but Woodrow Wilson to urge agreement."

"THAT IS AN IMPERTINENCE"

I do not recall at any Cabinet meeting that words were used with intent to denounce a Cabinet officer except once in all my eight years. It was a tense session when Judge Payne, Chairman of the Shipping Board, by word and manner excoriated Lansing, Secretary of State, who made no reply to a bitter denunciation more bitter in manner than in matter. It is thus recorded in my Diary (October 21, 1919):

"Long Session. Lansing brought up detention of Standard Oil tankers by England and Shipping Board's retention of ships leased from England to bring troops home. Lansing said we had agreed to return them after troops were brought home and Great Britain was very much excited because we had not done so. He said it was not keeping faith and Shipping Board had no right to act on the question at all in any way. He was very indignant, and most of the Cabinet seemed to agree. I said: 'Let us hear the Shipping Board's side before we act.'

"Judge Payne came over and Lansing, after repeating what he had said in the Cabinet (but somewhat modified) asked

Payne if the Shipping Board's action was not for the benefit of the Standard Oil Company. Bitterly and scornfully Payne looked Lansing in the face and contemptuously said: 'That is an impertinence.'

"Another question by Lansing brought from Payne another withering: 'That is an impertinence.' Payne said Britain was trying to prevent a merchant marine and he could not take any other course except at the direction of the President. Lansing and Payne are to send briefs to Woodrow Wilson.

"Palmer saved the situation by asking tactful questions. I have never heard more contempt in any voice than Payne employed in his scornful 'That is an impertinence.' Lansing's only act was to keep his eyes on the paper where he was, as usual, drawing a picture of some member of the Cabinet, and he had talent in drawing."

XLVII

THE ELECTION OF 1920 AND AFTER

JACKSON DAY DINNER

THE TWO Jackson Day Dinners which stirred the people most were the one in the year preceding the Baltimore Convention of 1912 and the Jackson Day Dinner of 1920. The latter dinner was held at a time when issues were shaping up for the presidential campaign of 1920 and Wilson was urging only one issue—a referendum on the League of Nations. There were so many people attending this dinner that it required the big dining rooms in two hotels to accommodate them, and most of the speakers cut their speeches in half and delivered part to one set of diners and part to the other.

I got into more or less trouble over my speech, because most of the Wilsonians were anti-Bryan and Wilson was not very well pleased with Bryan's attitude. I was not in agreement with Bryan when he said,

> "We cannot win the next time on the same arguments that failed to convince the voters in 1918. . . . I stood with the Senators for ratification; our plan was rejected, and we must face the issue as it is. We must either secure such compromises as may be possible or present the issue to the country. We cannot go before the country on the issue that such an appeal will present. Neither can we go before the country on the issue raised by Article 10."

Wilson did not attend the dinner but wrote a fighting letter which upheld the League of Nations and called for the Democratic Party to make it the sole issue in the campaign of 1920. He said, "If there is any doubt as to what the people of the country think, the clear and sensible way out is to submit it (the League) for determination at the next election to the voters of the Nation—to give the next election the form of a solemn referendum." He resented, though he never said so publicly, Bryan's criticism of Article 10 and Bryan's opposition, which was shared by a number of others, to making the League of Nations the sole issue in the campaign.

In my speech I praised Bryan for his devotion to peace and declared that the Bryan treaties foreshadowed and were the foundation of the Covenant, saying, "The Declaration of Independence and the Covenant of the League are the two living light fountains of liberty and peace. It is the glory of the Democratic Party from Jefferson to Wilson that we have given charts for all time for safe navigation upon all seas."

It had been hoped this dinner would usher in victory in 1920 as the Jackson Day Dinner in 1912 foreshadowed the Wilson election. It failed of that expectation.

As Bryan began, voices cried out, "Stand by the President." Bryan's eyes flashed and in a voice of resentment he shouted, "If you can guarantee victory, I will not speak."

SAN FRANCISCO CONVENTION

The Democratic National Convention of 1920 is memorable for two incidents:

First, that the two Wilsonians—McAdoo and Palmer—candidates for the nomination, met defeat at the hands of Cox, whose main support came from delegates who were anything but Wilsonian, including nearly all the city political leaders or bosses. The anti-Wilson men did not know that Cox would, as he did, risk his campaign on an ardent advocacy of entrance into the League. He not only did that, but he made able and eloquent addresses stressing the truth that entrance into the League was the only way to avoid another World War. He did not win but lived to see the people of his country come to his way of thinking, when they ratified the same kind of convenant he upheld as the only hope of ending war.

Second, the near-fight in the New York delegation when a demonstration for Wilson and Wilson ideals became the most spectacular event of the Convention. Some of the leaders from the Empire State determined that its delegation should voice its silent opposition to the "solemn referendum" on the League which Wilson urged. So in the first stages of the demonstration, New York was conspicuous by its sitting posture. There was a vibrant young man in the delegation who never did like inaction and was always ready to stand up and be counted. With him, to decide was to act, and so forty-year-old Franklin Roosevelt, his tall and lithe form towering over those who preferred a sitting non-participation, grabbed the New York banner and marched around the convention hall of enthusiastic shouters. But before he got the New York standard, Roosevelt and others with him had a battle-royal with those who grabbed and held the State standard in its socket. There were scrapping and scuffling and maybe blows before Franklin Roosevelt emerged victorious, holding aloft the banner in what was an enthusiastic demonstration during the otherwise rather listless convention. Roosevelt won out as he had done in the New York Legislature when he forced the election of Progressive Judge O'Gorman to the Senate over Tammany Hall's William F. Sheehan, attorney of the big utility corporations then seeking to monopolize water power for their enrichment.

That dynamic, seemingly unimportant incident, had two aftermaths. One was that it caused Bainbridge Colby to think that the Convention was ready to nominate Wilson for President, a proposal that died when Wilson's Cabinet and Wilson turned thumbs down on the suggestion that Wilson's name be presented for the nomination. The other was the nomination of Franklin Roosevelt for Vice President. That ticket would have won in any campaign except that year, when the American people, imitating the Greeks when they turned on their greatest man because they were tired of hearing him called "Aristides the Just," turned their backs on Wilson's ideals and worshipped materialism and isolation under the banner of normalcy.

The contest for the nomination was between Secretary of the Treasury McAdoo and Attorney General Palmer and Governor Cox. If the Wilsonians had united on either McAdoo or Palmer, he would have been nominated, but when they split on the two Cabinet members, the convention chose Cox. The general opinion was that while Wilson was taking no part, he favored McAdoo. Naturally McAdoo expected Wilson to look with favor on his candidacy, but Wilson never spoke to him about it and McAdoo did not open up to his father-in-law. Wilson kept hands off. Shortly after the November election (1918), according to Burleson this conversation had occurred: Wilson asked, "Do you think Mac has got it in his head to run for the presidency?"

"I believe he has," said Burleson.

"He is not fit for it," said Woodrow Wilson.

THE PLATFORM FIGHT

Wilson wanted nothing in the platform except the referendum on the League. Bryan wanted prohibition. Others had other planks for which they pressed. I called to see Carter Glass, chairman of the committee, to urge some policy that I felt ought to be stressed in the platform. He was not in agreement, and with characteristic vigor spoke his mind and got "het up." When I saw he was riled, I said: "Good-bye Carter. I came here for light and not heat." He said, "Come back, come back, and let's talk it over."

The convention, urged thereto in the speech by Chairman Homer Cummings, unanimously adopted the "solemn referendum" incorporated in the platform by Carter Glass's Committee.

PINCH-HIT FOR F. D. R.

It is an unwritten law that candidates nominated for the presidency or vice-presidency must await their acceptance until notified by a committee, and time is given to prepare an acceptance speech to be used as a campaign document. That precedent came near being broken when Franklin Roosevelt was nominated for Vice President. He was sitting in the New York delegation when the nomination was made, and he beat a hasty retreat as calls were made for him to go to the platform. He had not then become so great a breaker of precedents and tradition as when he became President. As he departed, I pinched-hit for him, being called upon, and said, as printed in the Proceedings of the Convention:

"Mr. Josephus Daniels of North Carolina: Ladies and Gentlemen:

"Sharing the faith of the millions of Democrats in America that it is to our party that men and women who believe in social justice must turn, we rejoice at the conclusion of this Convention that we have adopted a platform consonant with Democratic achievement and Democratic aspirations, and that we have nominated a ticket of young, able, and efficient men, who will lead this party to victory, upon the principles of the great party to which we belong.

"I wish to say that to me, and to five hundred thousand men in the American Navy, and to five million men in the Army, it is a matter of peculiar gratification that this Convention unanimously has chosen as a candidate for Vice President that clear-headed and able executive and patriotic citizen of New York, the Assistant Secretary of the Navy, Franklin D. Roosevelt. And I wish to add that his service during this great war, in the capacity where he had much responsibility, was chiefly executive, only because, when the war began and he wished to go to the front, I urged him that his highest duty was to help to carry the millions of men across and to bring them back and make a great record of it.

"I congratulate us all that we leave this Convention with a confidence of victory, and we shall meet in Washington on the 4th of March to inaugurate these candidates and carry forward the great work that has been begun."

TWENTY-FIVE-YEAR-OLD SECRET

As sometimes happens, in spite of the vigilance of ubiquitous reporters, the biggest piece of news in San Francisco, which would have made front page in every newspaper in America, happened behind closed doors, and no hint of it got into the press. In fact, the secret has been kept for twenty-five years. Some gossip about it leaked out some years ago by those who had an inkling, but no correct account appeared of the early morning meeting. Now it can be told.

WANTED TO DRAFT WILSON

After the enthusiastic Wilson demonstration and the seeming deadlock in the balloting for nomination of a candidate for President, Bainbridge Colby, Secretary of State, conceived the idea that, having resolved to make "the solemn referendum" on entrance to the League the issue in the campaign, the logical thing to do was to name Wilson, who incarnated the issue, the standard bearer, even though Wilson's illness would prevent any active campaign. And, without consulting other members of the Cabinet or close friends of Wilson who were in San Francisco, Colby sent a message to President Wilson telling him that the Convention was in a mood to draft him as the candidate on the platform for entrance into the League, and that unless forbidden by Wilson, he (Colby) would the next day rise in the Convention and present his name for the nomination with the certainty that the Convention would draft him to head the ticket.

The first thing I knew of Colby's suggestion or had any hint of it was when about midnight I reached the *New Mexico,* lying in San Francisco harbor (having come up in it from San Diego; I was living on that dreadnaught during the Convention), I was given a message called "urgent," requesting me to be present early next morning at a meeting of the members of the Wilson Cabinet present in San Francisco at a given room of a certain hotel. It said it was "of the utmost importance" and was "imperative." When I arrived, I found my Cabinet associates, Senator Joseph E. Robinson and a few other leading Democrats. They had been summoned to meet from the White House. We were informed, and Secretary Colby confirmed it, that he had advised Wilson that unless he directed otherwise, Colby would place his name in nomination. The message from the White House was to request those friends at the Convention to discuss the Colby suggestion and give the result of their conference to President Wilson. I never saw more indignation and resentment in any small gathering. All present felt that Colby ought not to have sent such a message without conferring with other members of the Cabinet in San Francisco, and some of his colleagues told him it was a cruel thing to have done in view of the state of the President's health. I think we were all agreed that, if Wilson had been in robust health, the people would have drafted him to run as the incarnation and embodiment of "the solemn referendum" on the League of Nations. But we knew that Wilson's physical condition would not make his candidacy advisable, and moreover we were all agreed that Colby had misinterpreted the attitude of the delegates. We all felt that if Wilson's name was presented, the result would be to embarrass and humiliate the great soul to whom we were devoted. I remember that I said to Colby: "You had no right to send such a message without consultation with your associates who had shown their devotion through the years to Wilson. Your representation of the sentiment of the Convention is not correct and your message might have greatly disturbed our ailing chief."

COLBY'S SUGGESTION FAILED

I knew—and so did all the others—that Wilson would have freely given his all, even his life, to secure the entrance of his country into the League. If the Convention had unanimously drafted him, we felt he would regard it as a command, even if it meant it would kill him. I do not recall the words of the reply we forwarded to Wilson but the substance of it was that, being on the spot and knowing the situation, we felt that Colby's suggestion should not be carried out, and that was the end of the hasty and dangerous proposal made in the best of faith and born of admiration of Wilson by his Secretary of State.

The matter was never referred to by the President after we returned from San Francisco, and I never reported what had caused the action we had felt constrained to take.

FAVORED NOMINATING COLBY

When Mitchell Palmer withdrew, and most of his delegates went to Cox, there was a movement to nominate Colby. The California delegation and Charlie Murphy's New York delegation were ready to vote for him. But the trend to Cox had set in too strongly to be checked.

In his good-will tour to South America on a Navy ship Colby's charm and eloquence made a deep impression. In his book on the Monroe Doctrine, Dr. David Thomas wrote: "There can be no doubt that the visit of Mr. Colby had a wholesome effect, and that it accomplished more than the visit of Mr. Root fourteen years earlier."

THE WHITE HOUSE INTRIGUES THEM ALL

Why do I think Wilson, even though partially paralyzed, would have felt constrained to have accepted if nominated? Because he would have regarded it as a command with a vital principle as the issue, and his views were so well known that personal campaigning would not be necessary. There is another reason based upon some acquaintance with Presidents and some knowledge of politics and history. It is my deliberate judgment that, since Andrew Jackson returned to the Hermitage after having hand-picked Martin Van Buren as his successor and paved the way for Polk, his political protégé, to carry on his policies—since Old Hickory's day, no President has willingly left the White House. There is something about the office and place that intrigues the least ambitious of its incumbents, that makes all after-life lack that something which only the White House gives. If Wilson had been a well man, he would, in my opinion, have been willing to break the old three-term jinx in devotion to the League. It is well known that Theodore Roosevelt expected to resume residence after one term for Taft, and that he never lost the *animus revertendi,* even bolting the Republican Party in 1912 and organizing a new party which he thought would lead to the White House. Most people believe if he had lived he would have been given the Republican nomination in 1920. When Cleveland's term expired in 1889, he declared he was happy to be relieved of the duties and retire to private life. But if he was fooling himself and the public, he did not fool his wife. As she was leaving the White House she told a faithful Negro who had long been there, "Keep everything as it is now so that we will find no change when we return in 1893."

Taft felt that Teddy had "done him wrong" when he sought to oust him in 1912 but was somewhat consoled when made Chief Justice. He wanted a second term and felt he was entitled to such an encore when Wilson won. When Coolidge said "I do not choose to run," he thought that delphic utterance would cause the people to break the third-term tradition for him without his initiating it. No man was ever more disappointed when his statement was construed to mean that he did not desire the nomination.

Hoover has never really found himself since his ejection from the White House. No President ever worked harder than Hoover, or, in his own peculiar way, enjoyed being President more than Hoover. It was not all his fault that the depression came to make his re-election impossible.

Franklin Roosevelt loved the great office to which he added distinction. He did not need great persuasion to accept nominations that gave him the unprecedented honor of being elected four times.

THEY ALL HATE TO LEAVE IT

They love to go into the White House, and they all hate to leave it. Perhaps Old Hickory might have been willing to stay longer (and he could have been reëlected) if Rachel had lived.

DO NOT LOSE THE HOPE

This lure also affects all men, or most of them, who aspire to the presidency and whose aspirations do not carry them to the White House. Henry Clay, James G. Blaine, and William Jennings Bryan, to name the three most famous who came within a few steps of

Upper left, Truman H. Newberry, Republican candidate for United States Senator from Michigan in 1918 against Henry Ford (*Detroit News*). *Upper right,* Henry Ford, who reluctantly yielded to President Wilson's personal request that he become a candidate for the U. S. Senate (Brown Brothers). *Below,* Democratic nominees in 1920. *Left,* James M. Cox, nominee for President; *right,* Franklin D. Roosevelt, nominee for Vice President.

DISTINGUISHED LEADERS IN INDUSTRY AND WAR

Upper left, Daniel Willard, president of the Baltimore and Ohio and chairman of the Advisory Commission of the Council of National Defense. *Upper right,* Julius Rosenwald, member of the Advisory Commission and adviser of Secretary of War Baker. *Lower left,* Charles M. Schwab, chairman of board Bethlehem Steel Corporation, head of Emergency Fleet Corporation. *Lower right,* Charles G. Dawes, with Pershing in France, and afterwards vice president.

entering the White House, tried again and again. All three served as Secretary of State—an office which in the early days of the republic was the sure stepping stone to the presidency, as seen in the elevation of Thomas Jefferson, James Madison, James Monroe, John Quincy Adams, and Martin Van Buren. That method of advancement seems to have gone into innocuous desuetude.

I have often said that no man stung by the Presidential bee ever quite recovers. This was markedly true, in recent years, of William G. McAdoo, Mitchell Palmer, Al Smith, Alf Landon, and Thomas E. Dewey, and everybody knows that Wendell Wilkie died in the belief that he would some day hang up his hat in the White House.

THE PRO-GERMAN VOTE

During the campaign I spoke many times, mostly in the Middle West. I sensed the situation and said to a friend before leaving Washington: "I am like the man in Maine who said to a neighbor, 'I am going down to Boston to get drunk, and Lord, how I hate it.'" I soon saw that the tide was running so strong against us that the Democrats could not win. For the first time I learned that resentment of the wartime draft would cost us votes. In one county, with large German population, nearly always Democratic, a county official told me two things would defeat us: (1) Not a few parents, who dared not say anything during the war, had resented drafting their sons and would get even by voting the Republican ticket; and (2) Democrats who had at heart sympathized with Germany would do likewise. As he predicted, the old Democratic county gave a big Republican majority.

A GERMAN PAINTED YELLOW

Speaking in a county in the Middle West in behalf of Liberty Loan bonds, I learned of this incident. There had been difficulty in raising the Liberty bond quota in war days. A remote township in which a German merchant resided was badly behind. He was the richest man in that section. He was rabidly pro-German, and when a committee asked him to buy bonds he not only declined but gave expression to his pro-German sentiment in bitter abuse of the President for "being fool enough to carry the country into war against the invincible shock troops of the Fatherland." That night a group from the county seat took him out of his home, carried him to the Court House, stripped him naked, and painted him in yellow from head to toe and marched him back to his home. The next day when the bond committee again called on him—still yellow under his clothes—the merchant asked to be permitted to buy a big block. And others with like alien views, fearing a similar coat of paint, hastened to buy. But they got their revenge in 1920 by voting against Wilson's "solemn referendum," supported by Cox and Roosevelt.

PROGRESSIVES FOLLOWED ROOSEVELT

I soon learned that the Progressives had followed Teddy Roosevelt back into the Republican Party, even though Wilson had given them most of the reforms they had demanded when they quit the party. At Rock Island I was introduced by a college president who said, "I am a Bull Moose." I told the crowd that it had been reported the Republicans had swallowed all Bull Moose. "If so," I said, "they will have more brains in their belly than they have in their head."

MILITARY USED TO COERCE

The saddest day I had was in speaking at a number of points from Bluefield to Huntington, West Virginia. There had been a strike by mine workers and in the cold fall days, with a sprinkle of early snow, the miners and their wives and children had been evicted from company houses and were suffering. Worst of all, men in the Army uniform were being used by the mine-owners under the pretense of "preserving order." When I saw shivering children living in shabby tents it aroused my indignation to the boiling point, and at Matewan I voiced it in such denunciation of the operators as to arouse their hostility. Most of my audience were evicted miners and their wives. When I finished, the irate wife of a mine official gave me a tongue-lashing saying: "I have always been a Democrat and proud of it until today. You make me ashamed by your speaking to these murderers."

When I reported how men in the Army were being used by mine operators, Newton Baker was as indignant as I.

BONDS OR BAYONETS

In a later period I recall that Franklin Roosevelt is reported to have said at a meeting of his Cabinet: "Every crisis must be solved with bonds or bayonets. I will never call out Americans to shoot down Americans." And he never did, and neither did Wilson nor Baker, but some militarists under Baker used armed forces to help coal operators and did it in a cruel and un-American way.

WILSON COULDN'T BELIEVE IT

When I reported to Wilson what I had learned on my campaigning trip and told him Cox and Roosevelt didn't have the ghost of a chance, he could not and would not believe me. He could not conceive how the people who had responded so patriotically in war could be seduced into rejection of the solemn referendum of the League. He believed Cox would win, until the election returns staggered him.

A DIVORCEE IN THE WHITE HOUSE

One day as Judge Payne, my wife, and I were waiting for lunch at a famous inn on our visit to the Yellowstone, learning that two members of Wilson's Cabinet were in the waiting room, an irate woman brushed in and in tones of high pitch that made her heard all over the inn, asked, "Are you Democrats going to disgrace America by voting to put a divorcee in the White House?" I was shocked at her manner and astounded at her question. I did not then know that there had been a divorce in the Cox family, or, for that matter, in the Harding's. But Judge Payne, did and with the courtesy and sting of which he was past master, he said to the irate lady, "If nothing else about the presidency concerns you except the fear of having a divorcee in the White House, you cannot vote for either Cox or Harding." Infuriated, she replied, "I could not vote for Cox because he is a divorcee." Payne: "Then you cannot vote for Harding either if you are dead set against having a divorcee in the White House, for Mrs. Harding is a divorcee."

"That's a Democratic lie," screamed the bitterly partisan woman, and she was so mad I thought she might strike Judge Payne. Calm and judicial as usual (only once did I know him to get "het up") Judge Payne—as scores of tourists listened—turned her anger into dumbness by saying: "I happen to know all the circumstances about the divorce Governor Cox obtained, and the circumstances are such that no blame can attach to him. I know the present Mrs. Cox well. She has every grace and virtue that would make her an ideal First Lady in the White House."

The irate lady snorted: "But why does your political bias make you slander Senator and Mrs. Harding?"

The crowd listened eagerly for Payne's reply. He said: "I know Mrs. Harding well—as fine a lady as lives. Her first marriage was unfortunate and by every standard she was entitled to the divorce which she obtained. Later she married Senator Harding, a happy and ideal marriage. I am a Democrat and will vote for Governor Cox, but I assure you that if Harding is elected, the country will find his wife fitted in every way to preside in the White House."

The lady retorted: "I do not believe Mrs. Harding is a divorcee." Then an Ohio gentleman spoke up and said: "I am a Republican living not far from Senator Harding's home. All that Judge Payne has said is true. Mrs. Harding ought to have obtained the divorce and all Buckeyes hold her in high esteem."

And so in 1920, no matter which candidate won, there was a divorcee in the White House. Nothing else was heard about divorcees in the campaign. It was not an issue.

CITIES FOR AND AGAINST COX

Politics has many curious quirks. The Convention was in high gear as it enthusiastically cheered Chairman Homer Cummings' great passionate League of Nation speech and hailed the solemn referendum. And then it refused to nominate either McAdoo or Palmer who incarnated the Wilson consecration to the League. The cities succeeded in nominating the candidate who in the first stages had received most of his support from big city delegations hostile to a referendum of the League. And in November those big cities turned against the candidate they had named. For the first time in history New York City gave a Republican candidate for President a majority. Not even the popularity of Franklin Roosevelt in his native State availed to overcome the tidal wave that rolled up unprecedented majorities for Harding, or rather for "Normalcy."

AL SMITH TELLS HOW HARDING CARRIED NEW YORK

I never heard, until 1928, the true inwardness of the Harding campaign of deception which enabled the Republicans to carry New York City for the first time in history. I was the guest of

Governor Al Smith, the Democratic candidate for President, having gone by his invitation to discuss some matters connected with the campaign. It had been said that the Irish, who have always had powerful influence in the metropolis, had voted against their party as a rebuke because Wilson had not made Ireland independent at the Peace Conference.

After we discussed the strategy of the 1928 campaign, we fell to talking politics. The Governor said New York and Massachusetts were in the bag because of the certain big majorities Greater New York and Boston would give him. Becoming reminiscent, he said that in Greater New York the vote for Harding surprised him and Tammany leaders who were loyal to the Democratic ticket as much as it did Cox and Roosevelt, who lost the city. As proof he told me this story:

"A few days after the election I had occasion to call on a business man and arrived at his office sometime before the hour of my appointment. I told his lady secretary I would wait for him. Shortly she asked me: 'Are you Governor Al Smith?' I told her I was and she then said: 'I am glad to see you. We are both Irish Democrats and can talk freely and in confidence. I am Chairman of the Democratic Organization in my precinct. It is predominantly Irish and almost solidly Democratic in elections. The reason I am so glad to see you is that I want to ask you a question about a matter which interests me more than anything in the world.'

"I saw she was deeply sincere and anxious. I told her I would be happy to answer any question if I had the information. She then asked: 'How soon do you think it will be after Harding is inaugurated before Ireland will be a free republic?'

" 'Never,' I answered. 'He has not the power. Ireland can only gets its independence through the Irish or the British Parliament and no American President can bring about that desired independence of the old country we both love.'

"If I had knocked her down she would not have been more stunned. It was a blow that blanched her cheeks and brought tears to her eyes. She was so shocked her whole body shook. When she had recovered from the shock of my plain reply to her question, which I now see had about it the brutal frankness of truth, she told me this story, but in much more detail than I can repeat. 'You astound me. They told us in the campaign, but said that we should not make it public, that Harding had promised if elected he would make Ireland free. It would be his first act. Believing it, I and all my Irish friends were active in his support and nearly all the Irish Democrats voted for Harding. It will break our hearts if the promise that caused us to support him is not carried out. I only live to see Ireland free.'

"By this time the gentleman with whom I had business had arrived and I bade her good-bye, telling her that somebody in the campaign had sold her and her friends a gold brick. I was never so sorry for any disillusioned person in all my life."

WILSON'S LAST POLITICAL TALK

When Wilson left the White House he refrained from participation in political life, even so much as imparting through friends his views and suggestions. He declined invitations to write his recollections even before he was stricken, but in the early days of the war he had said to my wife one night: "When I get out of this job I intend to write a book and it will deal with some men in a way that turns the true light on them." But after his affliction that purpose, if seriously entertained, was abandoned. The only thing he wrote for publication was an article in the *Atlantic Monthly* (August 1923) on "The Road Away From Revolution," which was his confession of political and religious faith.

He said the Russian Revolution was "due to the systematic denial to the great body of Russians of the rights and privileges which all normal men desire and must have." He asked: "Is the capitalistic system imperishable?" and said that "Capitalists have often seemed to regard the men whom they used as mere instruments of profit." He added:

"The world has been made safe for democracy. But democracy has not yet made the world safe against irrational revolution. The road is clearly marked; it is the maintenance of the highest and purest standards of justice and right dealing. . . .

"Our civilization cannot survive materially unless it is saved only by becoming permeated with the spirit of Christ."

NO SENATORIAL TOGA

James Kearney, editor of the Trenton *Times,* who had been an early and late supporter of Wilson, visited him in the latter part of

1923 in the hope of inducing him to become a candidate for the Senate in New Jersey. It did not appeal to Wilson though he said: "There is only one place where I could be sure of effectively asserting leadership," and he added, "if I were to go to the Senate, I should get into a row with the old Lodge, who no longer counts for anything. As I have remarked before, I'd rather be a dead dead man than a dead live man." Kearney closed his recollections of Wilson's last chat with an old Jersey friend: "And he got a lot of fun out of repeating the revised version of the old Massachusetts limerick about where the 'Lodges speak only to Cabots and Cabots speak only to God.'

" 'You recall,' he said, 'how that family of Kabotskis in Philadelphia tried to change the name to Cabot, and how the Cabots went to court for an injunction, and so the limerick had to be made over.'

"And then, with a merry twinkle, he repeated the revision:

> " 'Here's to Massachusetts,
> The land of the bean and the cod,
> Where the Lodges can't speak to the Cabots
> Because the Cabots speak Yiddish, by God!' "

SUGGESTED TUMULTY FOR SENATOR

A short time before, Tumulty had delivered an unauthorized message, supposedly from Wilson, at a testimonial dinner to James M. Cox; this irritated Wilson, who publicly declared that he had not authorized any letter. This was not because he was unfriendly to Cox, but because he did not wish to appear to be committed to any candidate at the time. On the contrary, he said to Kearney about that time: "Cox was a very brave man to take up the League of Nations fight in 1920." Wilson always spoke for himself and resented Tumulty's assumption after he had twice told him that he would send no message. That made a rift between Wilson and his old private secretary, which friends deplored. But it did not prevent Wilson later (October 30, 1923) from writing to Kearney that he thought Winthrop Daniels "would make a serviceable member of the Senate," and he added:

"Let me say also when you are canvassing the field as a whole I don't think you ought to overlook Tumulty, whose political training has been more varied than that of any other man I know, and who—when he was in the New Jersey Assembly—proved himself a redoubtable debater. He would make some of the reactionary senators sit up and take notice of the arrival of modern times and circumstances."

Kearney, commenting on this letter, said to Wilson: "That was a handsome thing you said about Tumulty in your letter," to which Wilson replied: "It's the way I felt; Tumulty would make them all sit up and take notice; he could render the country fine service in the Senate."

PLANNING FOR THE FIRST FLIGHT ACROSS THE ATLANTIC

These men, with Secretary of the Navy Daniels and Assistant Secretary Roosevelt, took part or advised in the initial trans-Atlantic crossing. Those visible in the picture, with the ranks they held at the time, are, *left to right,* Ensign H. C. Rodd (behind Roosevelt's shoulder to the left); Assistant Secretary Roosevelt, Lieutenant Commander M. S. Mitscher (behind Roosevelt's shoulder); Lieutenant Commander Richard E. Byrd; Commander Holden C. Richardson (face covered); Lieutenant Commander Albert C. Read (who commanded the NC-4, first to complete the crossing); Marvin H. McIntyre (face blurred), who later became President Roosevelt's secretary; Lieutenant (jg) Walter Hinton; Lieutenant David H. McCulloch; Captain John H. Towers (in command of the flotilla); Secretary Daniels. (International News photo).

Secretary of the Navy Daniels and Assistant Secretary Roosevelt with the crew of the
NC flight on the steps of the War, State and Navy Building. *First row, left to right,*
Lieutenant Commander A. C. Read, Secretary Daniels, Captain John H. Towers,
Assistant Secretary Roosevelt, Lieutenant Commander P. N. L. Bellinger. *Second row,*
Ensign H. C. Rodd, Lieutenant (jg) H. Sadenwater, Lieutenant L. T. Barin, Com-
mander H. C. Richardson, Lieutenant D. H. McCulloch. *Third row,* Lieutenant J. L.
Breese, Lieutenant C. R. A. Lavender (face not showing) (official U. S. Navy photo).

XLVIII

NAVY PLANES FIRST TO CROSS THE ATLANTIC

To the Navy goes the honor of the first flight across the Atlantic Ocean. I took the deepest interest in furthering this adventure. In May, 1913, I had been the first head of any Navy to fly and the plane carried the flag of the Secretary of the Navy as it rose over the Severn river at Annapolis.

Naval leaders—backed by the Secretary of the Navy and Assistant Secretary Roosevelt—conceived the pioneering of crossing the Atlantic by aviators. One day in September, 1917, Admiral Taylor sent for Constructors Westervelt and Hunsacker and gave them this instruction: "We want a plane designed that will fly across the Atlantic." That daring idea aroused my enthusiasm. No flying planes of anything like that size and power had been produced and skeptics doubted. But the Naval experts went to work with faith and skill to be ready with machines as soon as the war ended. The N.C. 1 was completed a few days before the Armistice. It was made jointly by the Navy and the Curtis Aircraft Company. It flew from Rockaway to Washington, thence to Hampton Roads and back to Rockaway. Taylor said N.C. stood for Navy-Curtis. I contended it also connoted North Carolinia in honor of the fact that the first flight in the world had been made by the Wrights in North Carolina. The dream of conquering the upper air and bringing Europe and America within a few hours of each other was near to realization. Early in the Spring of 1919 the hope of centuries was gratified by the Navy of the United States. Five Naval airships crossed the Atlantic Ocean and charted the way of those who were to follow in the full conquest of the air.

The route selected was from Rockaway to Halifax, Nova Scotia; Halifax to Trepassy Bay, Newfoundland; Trepassy to the Azores; Ponta Delgado to Lisbon, Portugal; Lisbon to Plymouth, England. Prior to the flight destroyers left port and took their positions along the route to act as guide-posts, furnish weather reports and connection by radio, and render any assistance needed.

Commander John H. Towers was placed in command of Seaplane Division No. 1 with N C 3 as his flagship. Lieutenant Commander Albert C. Read was given command of N C 4, and Lieutenant Commander N. L. Bellinger of the N C 1.

AVIATORS GIVEN ENTHUSIASTIC WELCOME

On the morning of May 8, 1919, the three giant planes took off from Rockaway Naval Air Station. They met thick fog and rough weather and they were delayed at Horta for three days. Lisbon gave an enthusiastic welcome when Commander Read of the N C 4 landed and departed for Plymouth, England. The long flight of 4,500 miles across the Atlantic and up the European coast ended at the port from which the *Mayflower* started three centuries before. In England they were feted by the King, Premier, and people, and then flew to Paris, where a royal welcome was given them. The flight of the N C's across the ocean—the first trans-Atlantic flight, caused me to say in my 1919 report: "This emphasizes the necessity of developing aviation as an integral part of our military and naval forces. When an airship can fly from America to Europe in a few hours, the ocean is no longer a dependable protection against possible attack."

NEED FOR A SOLOMON

The aviators were welcomed in Europe as modern world discoverers. Spain likened their crossing the Atlantic to the voyage of Columbus from Spain to the New World. When they reached Paris, they were enthusiastically received and given the highest honors in a country which was air-minded. Soon a question arose that would have given pause to Solomon. The American Ambassador at Paris cabled and asked to whom the honors should be given for first crossing the Atlantic. The Acting Chief of Operations, using the analogy of a surface Naval fleet, advised, "To Towers because he was in command of the expedition." I answered, "But aviation is a new arm and new conditions call for new policies. Towers organized and was in command of the expedition, but the ship in which he was flying was not the first to reach Europe. In aviation, fliers go on their own, and the honor ought to go to the officers whose ship was the first to land on European soil." I took that position, though I had made my first flight in a ship with Towers, had placed him in command of the expedition, and had admiration for his pioneering in aviation and confidence in his aviation knowledge. Admirals vigorously combatted my view, holding that as a commander of a fleet he should be given the glory of the achievement even if the flagship had not been first to land. I could not be governed by what seemed to me an outmoded Naval doctrine, not applicable in the new field of flying. And so I wired to Paris that as the ship commanded by Read had actually made the first flight across the Atlantic, the honors should go to him. The debate raged and was taken up by the House Committee of Naval Affairs, and I was gratified when its Chairman, Honorable Thomas S. Butler, called to congratulate me on what he called "a decision worthy of Solomon," and said his committee rejoiced in the action I had taken.

When Commander Read reached Paris he received this telegram from President Wilson:

Paris, 28 May, 1919

"LIEUTENANT COMMANDER A. C. READ.

"Please accept my heartfelt congratulations on the success of your flight and accept for yourself and your comrades the expression of my deep admiration. We are all heartily proud of you. You have won and deserve the distinction of adding still further to the laurels of our country.

/s/ "WOODROW WILSON"

Wilson also cabled me as follows:

Paris, 28 May, 1919

"SECRETARY OF THE NAVY
"Washington

"May I not join with all my heart in the expression of the deep gratification that I am sure all our fellow countrymen feel in the success of the arrangements made to safeguard the flight of the aeroplanes across the sea? The Navy is warmly to be congratulated for the effective service of the gallant men who carried it through.

/s/ "WOODROW WILSON"

NO NAVAL CONTROVERSY

It might have led to another controversy like the Sampson-Schley case if Towers had written the same kind of report as Sampson, who announced: "The fleet under my command," when he was not present at the engagement. The fleet was under Sampson's command, but at the moment of the attack, Sampson was absent on a perfectly legitimate duty elsewhere.

Towers made no such mistake. He reported the details of the flight in which a younger officer's plane was the first in crossing the Atlantic to land in Europe. The honor went to the officer who landed first. The Navy Admirals disapproving my decision, harked back to the time when most of them took sides with Sampson in a bitter controversy. At that time as an editor I had criticized the Navy's ruling, little thinking the time would ever come when in the new arm of aviation I would overrule it.

MOFFETT—A SACRIFICE TO DIRIGIBLES

After the war Captain W. A. Moffett was not satisfied with shore duties; he could not keep his feet on the ground, and so he became an aviator. He was one of the first captains to see the future of aviation as a first line of offense in war. He was made Chief of Aeronautics in the Navy Department. I did not see him for a long time, but met up with him at Roosevelt's first inauguration. He had become an enthusiast on the construction of dirigibles and tried to convince me that they were the airship of the future. I expressed doubts. He said: "I am going to take a trip in the *Akron* day after tomorrow, and I would like you to go up with me. It will be a great experience and will convert you into an enthusiast for the dirigibles." I accepted, but, the day after, President Roosevelt sent me a message saying he wished to see me on a certain day (it was the day the *Akron* was to fly). Regretfully I called Moffett up and withdrew my acceptance. He said: "I will take you up the next time you are in Washington." I accepted. The *Akron* departed on scheduled time with Moffett aboard. It never returned, and the Navy lost its aeronautical leader and I a dear friend. The victory of aviation has been won at the cost of the lives of the most daring.

XLIX

NAVY AND MERCHANT SHIPS AFTER THE WAR

I SOON LEARNED, after the Armistice was signed, that Mazzini was right when he declared, "The morrow of victory is more perilous than its eve." While the war was waging, every man was on his toes, ready to obey any order or make any sacrifice. It was not so when the order "Cease Firing" was given. Most men who had entered for the duration were eager to get home.

There was a feeling on the part of some younger Naval officers that with the warless world they thought would follow, there was no promotion or glory for them in uniform. A number received flattering offers in the business world and tendered their resignations. In every instance I talked with these officers—I advised against resigning, pointing out that Naval training did not fit men for business and counselling them to "abide in the ship." Most of them took my advice and thanked me for it. A few who resigned succeeded in business, but not many; and those who found themselves unfitted for the business world applied for reinstatement. The answer was, "You resigned because you loved money more than you loved the Navy and the promotions go to those who have only one love."

The Navy quickly practiced the rule, "The way to demobilize is to demobilize." In a comparatively short time the Naval strength was reduced from 500,000 to 132,000. Of the 8,000 Naval Reserve, all but 1,800 officers and 4,700 men were quickly released from service. The 67,000 in the Marine Corps was reduced to 17,000. We got down quickly to a peace-time basis and put old ships out of commission.

A TWO-OCEAN NAVY

Shortly after the Armistice I carried out a plan I had contemplated since my inspection on the Pacific in the first year after becoming Secretary of the Navy. I gave the country a Two-Ocean Navy. On my visit to the Pacific in 1913, I sensed the feeling of the people on that coast. They felt neglected by the Navy and they were right. The fleet was divided, one based on the Atlantic, with Admiral

Henry B. Wilson in command, and the other on the Pacific ports. Upon the inauguration of the Pacific Fleet, I accompanied Admiral Rodman, in command of the Pacific Fleet, and the fleet paid visits to all the seaports from San Diego to Seattle, everywhere welcomed by people who rejoiced that at last the Pacific ocean was no longer being neglected as a "red-headed step-child of the Navy." At every city, where we were given enthusiastic receptions, I told the people: "We have not come to make you a visit. We have brought our bed and board and have come to make our home on the shores of the Pacific."

As the climax of this historical inauguration of the Pacific Fleet (it is unfortunate that later it was not continued), President Woodrow Wilson reviewed the fleet in Puget Sound. Standing on the historic *Oregon,* recommissioned for the gala day, President and Mrs. Wilson, Secretary of the Navy and Mrs. Daniels, and Admiral Rodman received the salutes of the greatest fleet that had been seen in the Pacific.

FOREIGNERS AVID FOR OUR MERCHANT SHIPS

When I learned after the Armistice that the British had a deal on to buy from their American owners fifty-seven of the finest ships ever built, constituting the best fleet in the world, I resolved to try to prevent it. This threat to the merchant marine of our country was brought to my attention first by friends in Newport News, Virginia, and second, by Honorable Sherman L. Whipple, able, public-spirited lawyer of Boston. I asked Mr. Whipple, the best-posted man in the country, to put in writing what he had said so I could show it to the President. Here is what he wrote:

"We have just expended rising three billions of dollars in order to get ships. Those we have built are costing us from $175 to $200 per d.w.t. Some we have purchased have cost us much more. Free ships have been selling in the open market as high as $300 per d. w. t.

"But here are 57 ships,—all finer than any that we have built, most of them better than any that we shall build for years, constituting the finest fleet in the world, owned by American citizens, paid for with American money,—it is proposed to sell *for less than $90 per d. w. t.*

"How can we justify the expenditure of our billions, with so little present result, while we let this magnificent fleet go out of American ownership, when we could save it by the expenditure of some seventy millions?

"The main objection is that the ships, being under the British flag, are under British control; that the American owners cannot use them as they please; that the Government has prior and dominating rights which make their value much less than if they were free ships,—which in its last analysis means merely this, that Great Britain so restricts and heckles American owners by drastic and harsh legislation that she makes ships which are really worth $300 per ton actually worth only $90 per ton, and then buys in what she has made of such little value.

"I very much doubt whether she would take such an attitude if our Government should make the purchase. But if she did, this course is open to us: The British companies could go into liquidation and offer the ships for sale. If Great Britain purchased them, she would have to pay their fair value; if she waived her option on them we could then purchase and hold them by a title free from restricted legislation. I do not believe that Great Britain would dare to refuse the request of the American Government that these ships be transferred to our flag after the war emergency is over.

"But the most suggestive thing about the situation is this: Our Government is not moving in the matter; England is the one that is disturbing the situation. She is reaching out to get something which she has not now got. She is trying to acquire from American citizens the complete ownership of the finest fleet in the world. We are satisfied with the *status quo;* she is not. Under such circumstances is it not perfectly proper for us to say that we cannot allow our citizens to part with this fleet, which belongs to this country, and that if it is necessary, to save it to its present ownership the Government itself will intervene and acquire it?

"I fear that when we are held to account by the American people for the expenditure of the billions which have been put into our shipbuilding program, we shall not find it easy to explain why for such a moderate sum we let slip out of our hands the finest fleet of ships now sailing the ocean anywhere in the world."

Wilson was both astonished and indignant at the prospect of the defeat of his long devotion to building up a merchant marine big enough to carry American commerce. He expressed himself strongly that we ought to exert every pressure to prevent the transaction and I notified, by Wilson's direction, the Americans who were conducting the negotiations, that our Government could not permit so heavy a blow to be struck at American shipping at the time it was essential to restore peace-time water-borne commerce.

The compelling reason why Wilson stressed freedom of the seas in Paris was that it had cost him one of his hardest struggles to induce Congress to provide for the building of many merchant ships. He believed that the hope of increased world commerce depended upon carrying American goods in American ships. During the war he had backed the Fleet Corporation in spending billions to construct the greatest fleet in the history of his country. He looked forward to insuring enlarged markets after the war. In Paris he had as advisers Edward M. Hurley, head of the Shipping Board, and Bainbridge Colby, member of the Board.

NORWEGIAN COMPANY WISHES SHIP PLANT

This was not the first time foreign interests had looked forward to denuding Uncle Sam of strength on the seas and securing ships from the United States by purchase or construction in this country. This is shown by my Diary (August, 1918):

"It was reliably reported to me on August 10th that a Norwegian Company wished to buy the Newport News Ship Building Plant. If necessary, the plans were to commandeer it for the Navy rather than let it go into foreign ownership. The owners were told of the Navy's strong feeling in the matter and the President's opposition. The deal was not consummated."

FOLLOWED MAHAN

In all my early and late advising of a strong merchant marine under the American flag, I was strengthened by the wisdom of the great Admiral Mahan, authority on *The Influence of Sea Power*. I kept in mind that he had said:

"A nation's sea-borne trade is the lifeblood of its power, the assurer of its credit, the purveyor of its comfort, and commercial enterprise is never so secure, nor so untrammeled as under its own flag."

In 1902 he warned, "the United States in her turn may have the rude awakening of those who have abandoned their share of the common birth-right of all people—the sea."

Every American shipbuilder who looked ahead put Freedom of the Seas in the same category as did Wilson. In 1810 Robert Fulton wrote: "The Liberty of the Seas will be the happiness of the earth." And John Ericsson, who gave us the *Monitor*, declared, "My only object is that of seeing the sea declared by all nations as sacred neutral ground. It is the highway of mankind." George Bancroft, Secretary of the Navy, writing of the position of the Andrew Jackson administration, said: "The Democratic party has ever contended for the freedom of the seas as the highway of commerce—for the rights of neutral nations—for the exchange of trade which should make all intelligence the common property of the world, should compensate the inequalities of climate, soil and mineral wealth, and interchange all products of peculiar skill."

L

HAWAII, "CROSSROADS OF THE PACIFIC"

I
N VIEW OF THE attack on Pearl Harbor by the Japanese on December 7, 1941, in which army planes on the ground and Naval ships unprotected in the harbor were destroyed—the worst blow ever dealt the American Navy—I recall with satisfaction the action taken by me as Secretary of the Navy to enlarge the Naval Base in Hawaii and my recommendation to develop Pearl Harbor and Kaneche Bay so that they could accommodate a fleet of any size. In my 1920 report I said:

"Hawaii is the key to the Pacific, its strategic location is well recognized; its possibilities have been carefully studied and set forth by naval experts and its development as a fleet operating base cannot be too strongly urged. There can be developed facilities for a fleet of a thousand vessels."

In the same report I recommended the development of Naval Bases in Guam and at Cavite in the Philippines.

THE DRY DOCK "SUNK UP"

In my first year as Secretary of the Navy, an event occurred that made me Pearl Harbor conscious. A previous Congress had authorized the construction of a dry dock in that harbor large enough to service our largest dreadnaughts. In the course of its construction, by the convolutions in the seismic foundations, an accident occurred that destroyed the work done and threatened the rebuilding. Literally the earth "sunk up" and destroyed the entire structure far advanced. Could a modern dry dock be built in that foundation— or lack of foundation—or must the Navy be satisfied with an unsatisfactory floating dock? These questions were debated. Admiral Harris said the dock could be built. I called in Alfred Noble, a distinguished engineer, and he and Admiral Parks went to Pearl Harbor. After studying the situation, they recommended a plan of construction by stages that resulted in a dry dock that still stands, in spite of the doubts of some Naval experts and some members of Congress.

When the dock was completed, I went out, accompanied by my wife, my two youngest sons, and Naval officers. We journeyed to Pearl Harbor on the U. S. S. *New York*, commanded by Captain W. V. Pratt. The visit to the Hawaiian Islands was the fulfilment of a long-cherished desire.

"LOOK UP TO GOD"

I was an official in Washington when Cleveland refused to approve the high-handed and imperialistic act of ousting the local government and taking Hawaii without the consent of its people. Though Cleveland was roundly denounced, I shared with him the feeling that we had no right to annex Hawaii by chicanery and force, without the consent of any of its people except those Americans who themselves or their ancestors obtained possession of the land of the Hawaiians. One had said: "The missionaries came here and told us to look up to God. While our eyes were turned to the heavens, their sons obtained possession of our lands."

GENEROSITY OF HAWAIIANS

Our reception was almost proof of what Secretary Lane told me before leaving Washington. He said: "When you visit most places, you will be told, 'what I have is yours,' but they don't mean it. However, in Hawaii, they really do mean it." They are the most generous of people. By no credit to me, I made a good impression. In my response to the addresses of the native Mayor and Judge, I pronounced the capital Ho-no-lu-lu. The Judge said, "You are the first official from Washington who ever came here who knew how to pronounce the name of our city." How did I know the correct pronunciation? I listened to the addresses of welcome. Both speakers called it Ho-no-lu-lu. I thought the people who lived in a place knew best how to pronounce it and visitors ought to accept their pronunciation. But I made a hit even though until that morning I had always put emphasis on "Hon."

HOSPITALITY EXTRAORDINARY

I was surprised to see that there were more nationalities represented and people of more colors than I knew existed at the reception given by Governor McCarthy, Japanese, Portuguese, Chinese, Americans, outnumbering the native Hawaiians. My wife was entranced at the rare flowers in great abundance, the fish of many colors, and the sweetness and beauty of flowers, trees, and birds. When she spoke of the many shades of green, the Irish Governor answered: "When asked my favorite color, I always say, 'It makes no difference just so it is green.'" Every element of the population and nationality vied with each other in hospitality and gifts, which proved Lane was right and knew what he was talking about. My wife, with a genius for friendship, had in Washington won the regard of Princess David, who wrote to her relatives of the royal family—"ex's" then— and we saw the first real Hawaiian dinner at the home of the descendants of Queen Liliuokalani. There were native dishes of old Hawaiian style, with raw fish and the like served when we sat down. Since they might not appeal to the American palate, almost immediately another dinner, such as is served in America, was brought on, all to the accompaniment of the delightful Hawaiian music. The next day the Mayor served in picnic fashion a real Hawaiian dinner with roast pork, barbecued in a manner handed down from old times. There were native music and dancers dressed in ancient Hawaiian style. The Chamber of Commerce, the Chinese, Portugese, the Hawaiians, and others entertained so that the visit was one round of pleasure. Nearly all gave presents to my wife. On the last day, dressed in lovely silk, the leader of the Japanese colony called at our hotel with the largest and most beautiful vases we had seen. A gentleman, not fond of the Japanese, said: "It is just like the Japs. They wait till the last and surpass others in the magnificence of their gifts."

JAPANESE SCHOOLS

Since the Americans assumed the government of the islands, English is taught in all the schools and all children must attend. As we drove out through the sugar and pineapple plantations, my wife observed that across from every school house in the Japanese settlement, on the opposite side of the road, there was another schoolhouse. Why? The answer was that all Japanese children attended the public schools where only English was taught, but when that school closed in the early afternoon, all Jap children walked across the road and attended a school maintained by the Japs where they were taught in that language and indoctrinated in Japanese ideals and ways, thus keeping them separate from others on the island. The Japanese were industrious and frugal, and some Americans expressed real fear that they were so prolific they would come to outnumber all others and would then wish Hawaii dominated by the Japanese. Others scoffed at the suggestion. I saw nothing that enabled me to have an opinion.

APPEASED THE SHARK GOD

The big event which took us to Hawaii, of course, occurred at Pearl Harbor. With the experts of the Navy, we made a thorough examination of and then attended the formal exercises of the opening of the dry dock. A more perfect day (August 21, 1919) the world never saw, and the people came from all over the island of all nationalities. With very formal ceremonies my wife broke the bottle of champagne and pressed the button which turned the waters into the dry dock amid the shouts and acclaim of the people, and I made a brief speech about the importance of Pearl Harbor and necessity of making it an important Naval Base in the Pacific, of which the completion of the dry dock was but the beginning. When it was all over, the Mayor said to me,

"Then the Shark God didn't get you, after all."

This was so much Greek to me, and he related the story which was current in the Island that when work was begun on the first dry dock in Hawaii, the natives went to the Admiral and warned him against trying to build a dry dock on the site he had selected, and he said, "Why ought I not to build it here? It seems to be the best place."

"You cannot build it there," they said, "because that is the home of the Shark God and if you build it there, some day the Shark God will rise from his slumber and lift his mighty tail and destroy your dry dock for the impiety of disturbing his home." This seemed ridiculous to the Admiral and engineers, and so they went ahead and had it almost completed when the dry dock "sunk upward." Whereupon the Hawaiians who had foretold that something would happen to the dry dock went to the Admiral and said: "You see, it was as we told you. You disturbed the Shark God and he rose up and flirted his tail and see where your dry dock is."

Afterwards, when it was determined to rebuild this dry dock on the same site, this story was widely told, and some of the Hawaiian priests and priestesses went to see the new Admiral who was then in charge and recalled their former prediction, saying it was dangerous to try to build the dry dock at the home of the Shark God. Instead of laughing at them, this wise Admiral asked, "Is there no way to appease the Shark God? I have always heard if you will treat a Shark God with reverence and consideration, his wrath may be averted. Is there no way we can do this in Hawaii?"

The priests and priestesses of the Hawaiian religion conferred among themselves and perhaps communed with the god and then returned to the Admiral and said, "Yes, there is a way to appease the Shark God. If you will turn over to us the religious ceremonies, we will hold them on the spot. You have to have a bottle of wine and pour it on the ground. You have to kill a chicken and pour its blood on the ground. . . ." And there were some other things which were a little vague, then. "And with incantations you must pray to the Shark God to give his permission for the dry dock to be built on what has been for ages his home."

The Admiral seemed to agree that this was necessary, furnished the chicken and wine and other things the priests and priestesses had declared essential, and then they added: "Also it is necessary that in the construction of this dry dock Hawaiians shall be engaged to help with the work."

The wise Admiral did all they suggested and immediately there grew in the faithful Hawaiians the confidence that the dry dock could be built and the Shark God would seek another home because he had been appeased. However much truth there may have been in this religion, certainly on the day we were in Hawaii the Shark God did not flirt his tail, the waters came into the dock, and everything went off as perfectly as could be desired. The incantations seem to have taken effect, for up to this time the Shark God has never indicated that his repose has been disturbed.

VISIT TO THE VOLCANOES

"Move back quick or you'll be killed," was the command of the expert in Hawaiian volcanoes on the day we visited Mauna Loa. When we arrived, we saw a black and undulating plain, which soon became a lake of red liquid lava heaving as the waves of the sea. The volcano was throwing up burning lava which looked like delicate glassy fibres called "Pele's hair" by the Hawaiians. It is spun by the wind from the rising and falling of the drops of liquid lava, and blows over the edge or into the crevices of the crater. Pele, in idolatrous times, was the dreaded goddess of Kilauea. "This is the first eruption in a long time," said our Hawaiian guide. "It is celebrating in honor of the visit of the Secretary of the Navy and the completion of the Pearl Harbor Dry Dock." One thing I distinctly remember: we had to move fast to avoid the red-hot liquid lava, and one lady's dress was scorched. My wife brought home some of Pele's hair.

ALOHA AND LEIS

Bedecked with leis by young Hawiian girls and weighted down with flowers that lasted to the shores of California, we left Hawaii, amid farewell "Alohas," saying that if at the end the gates of heaven should be shut to us, we would love to come to Hawaii.

LI

LAST DAYS IN WASHINGTON

T HE PRICE IS too high for me to pay."
     That was the answer I gave to Honorable Thomas S. Butler, Chairman of House Naval Affairs Committee, who had said to me: "Mr. Secretary, we Republicans of the Committee wish you were a Republican so that you could remain as Secretary of the Navy for another eight years."

It was a love feast of friends who for eight years had coöperated to give the United States the most powerful Navy in the world. Shortly before the close of the Wilson Administration, the House Naval Affairs Committee invited me to attend a banquet in my honor. It was unprecedented that a committee of Congress should thus honor a retiring Cabinet member of an opposite party. In my eight years as Secretary of the Navy my association with the Committee had been most agreeable, both when the Democrats were in control up to the 1918 election and afterwards when the Republicans controlled the committee. To this dinner the Congressmen invited the heads of the Bureaus of the Navy Department and influential Admirals. Nothing in my life has warmed my heart more than this evidence of a cherished friendship. Cordial words of affection and confidence mostly by the Republican members of the Committee evidenced that there had been no politics in Naval matters. Responding to the friendly expressions in my speech of grateful appreciation, I told this story:

"I feel very much like a Negro preacher in North Carolina. On a Sunday morning at the hour of service a gentleman met him on the main street and asked: 'Isn't this the hour for preaching at your church?'
     " 'It is,' said the preacher.
     " 'Why, then, are you not at church?'
     " 'It is this way,' was the answer. 'When my congregation met last week and handed in my resignation, I found I must quit preaching there and seek another job.'

Upper left, Key Pittman, whose cross-examination confounded the critics of the Navy (Brown Brothers). *Upper right,* Samuel Gompers, President of American Federation of Labor, who was credited with being the most powerful civilian factor during the strenuous days of the World War. *Lower left,* Captain W. V. Pratt, Assistant Chief of Naval Operations, who, with other officers who held important posts during the World War, defended the great work of the Navy. *Lower right,* Judge E. Y. Webb, Chairman of House Judiciary Committee, who defended Claude Kitchin and piloted the Anti-trust Law through Congress.

At Pearl Harbor, when the Dry Dock "sunk up," a new dock (*below*) was constructed. It was completed in 1919 and was formally opened by Mrs. Josephus Daniels (*above*). With her are Secretary Daniels and the Governor of Hawaii, Charles J. McCarthy.

"When my congregation (the voters of the United States) met on the second Tuesday in November and handed in my resignation, I must return to my editorial sanctum in Raleigh."

ADMIRAL BENSON AND CARDINAL GIBBONS

I was gratified—and so was my wife—to be present on an occasion when a high distinction was given Admiral William S. Benson, whom I had named as Chief of Operations of the Navy, when that position was created by Congress. The Admiral received the Order of St. Gregory the Great, Military Division, First Order from Pope Benedict XV. The insigne of the Order was bestowed upon him by Cardinal Gibbons in the Baltimore Cathedral on April 1, 1920. It is the highest order given to laymen and was in recognition of his outstanding integrity and virtue as a Catholic gentleman and officer. It was worthily bestowed on Admiral Benson, prominent Knight of Columbus, devoted to his church and incarnating the best of virtues of the Christian religion. His mother was a Methodist and I once told him he illustrated the best qualities of both creeds.

I was not only gratified at the high honor to my chief adviser and friend, but pleased to be the guest of Cardinal Gibbons, a friend of long standing. Not long before, I think it was his eighty-second birthday, I attended a celebration in Washington when he was feted by men of all faiths. Called upon to speak, because the Cardinal had spent his first years as priest in Wilmington, North Carolina, after paying tribute to him as a distinguished religious and civil leader of righteousness, I said something like this:

"My State, North Carolina, has always had pride and a certain sense of ownership in the noble prelate because he spent the first years of his priesthood in our State. He left an influence that abides. He had the good fortune as a young priest to live in a state in which there were few communicants of his faith. Most of his friends were Protestants. He won them and they reciprocated. I wish that in their early ministry all Catholic priests and all Protestant ministers could associate much with people of other creeds. It would do both good and prevent misunderstanding and want of comradeship.

On one visit—for he followed St. Paul and rode a long circuit—Priest Gibbons was to preach in the then small river town of Greenville. He was the guest of the only Catholic in the county, an able surgeon and eloquent speaker—Dr. Charles J.

O'Hagan. Upon his arrrival, Dr. O'Hagan said: 'Father, you are invited to preach either in the Court House or in the Methodist Church—which will you choose?' The answer was: 'In the church.' It was crowded. The next day an old Methodist class leader, who had never heard a Catholic priest, said to Dr. O'Hagan: 'I never heard a greater gospel sermon and I don't believe John Wesley could have done better,' which was the highest praise a Wesleyan could give."

I recall at the breakfast, a Senator, turning to Cardinal Gibbons said: "Your eminence, I hope you will live to celebrate your nine-tieth birthday."

The Cardinal responded by saying that he felt like a certain Pope, who, when a friend expressed the wish that he "might live to be a hundred," replied, "Why place limitations on the goodness of the Almighty?"

BIGGEST NAVY IF NOT IN THE LEAGUE OF NATIONS

With the signing of the Armistice, there was a general belief that the League of Nations would insure a reduction in costly military establishments. The President was in Paris, and I wrote him express-ing the hope that, since the League of Nations was not yet in opera-tion, he would stress the Navy building program in his message to Congress. He answered, "You may be sure I will not forget the three-year program when I write my message." And he did not.

My last recommendation to Congress, made in January, 1921, was to urge the adoption of the program approved by the General Board of the Navy, and to ask for an appropriation for ten warships, air-plane carriers, cruisers, and other ships. In a hearing before the House Naval Affairs Committee on January 11, 1921, I said:

"With reference to the Naval program of the United States, there are just two courses, and only two, open:

"1. To secure an international agreement with all, or practi-cally all, the nations, which will guarantee an end of competition in navy building, reduce the national burden, and lead in the movement to secure and buttress world peace.

"2. To hold aloof from agreement or association with the other nations as to the size of armament. This will require us to build a navy strong enough and powerful enough to be able on our own to protect Americans and American shipping, defend American policies in the distant possessions as well as at home, and by the presence of sea power to command the respect and fear of the world.

"There is, of course, the third alternative of being content with a small navy in a world of big navies, exposed to certain destruction in case of war with a great power or powers. I dismiss that alternative without discussion because it is a waste of money to spend money on an agency of war which would be helpless if needed. Whatever else the American people may approve they will not approve such an ineffective policy. Equality with the greatest or an international agreement alone can be seriously considered.

"Of the only two plans for consideration I am here to press the first."

I called attention to the fact that all the Allied nations and Germany had signed this pledge: "The members of the League recognize that the maintenance of peace requires the reduction of national armament to the lowest point consistent with national safety and the enforcement by common action of international obligations." In response to questionings, I declared that if we did not enter the League of Nations or get an agreement for reduction by other nations, we should build unquestionably the largest Navy in the world. General Pershing and General Bliss both agreed with my position, General Pershing saying: "The safe policy of the United States would be to continue her program both as to the Army and Navy. It would not be safe for one nation to undertake disarmament unless all do." I also strongly opposed the suggestion pressed in certain quarters, and later virtually adopted at Harding's so-called Peace Conference, of an agreement between the United States, Japan, and Great Britain, as to Naval construction. It ought to be a world agreement, through the League of Nations.

At that time Admiral Sims took the position that we ought not to have a Navy the equal of or larger than any other country, and we need not have a Navy "as big as a Navy that is 3,000 miles away." He virtually advocated that if we had war with a nation 3,000 miles away from our coasts, we should wait for it to come and attack us on our coast. Mr. Oliver confounded him by pointing out that Dewey attacked in the Philippines.

Chairman Butler, sensing that we would not enter the League of

Nations, wished the United States to ask all nations to meet to agree upon a reduction of armament and there was much sentiment in favor of it, but Elihu Root wrote the Committee suggesting that no action be taken until Mr. Harding was inaugurated. His advice was taken and nothing was done. My slogan, "Enter the League of Nations or build the most powerful Navy in the world for the United States," was rejected. With the incoming of Harding we did neither. We did not take our seat in the League of Nations or build the greatest Navy. Worse than that, we scrapped the partly built dreadnaughts and let the Navy sink to a lower place than it had occupied. And we made no provision for preventing another war, as we would have done if we had entered the League.

INEPT CONFERENCE SCUTTLED NAVY SHIPS

When I was leaving Washington, I never dreamed that the great dreadnaughts I had sweat blood to get money to build would be scrapped when partly completed by the inept "Washington Conference," in which Britain and Japan scrapped blue-prints and old ships, and Uncle Sam was sap enough to scrap great ships in building, which would have given us the strongest Navy in the world. It was that knowledge and fear that induced other Big Navy nations to agree to the terms of the Washington Disarmament Conference in the early days of the Harding administration. It scrapped the League and then proceeded to scrap the Navy, when the only course for our country was to choose whether we would secure peace by international agreement or have a Navy so strong that the republic would be impregnable to attack.

MOST PEOPLE WERE HYPNOTIZED

I was in Washington when "the deep damnation" of Navy scuttling was done in the belief it would promote peace. On the day that distinguished speakers from Britain, the United States, and Japan eloquently hailed the scrapping as the dawn of a new day, I sat with fellow newspaper men in the Washington Conference. The atmosphere was permeated by a wave of both pumped-up and sincere enthusiasm for sinking ships as the route to peace. The speaking ended, there followed applause of long duration, nearly every person in the historic hall applauding what they had been hypnotized to believe was "a great day in the world's history."

DECLINED TO APPLAUD AT MY OWN FUNERAL

I kept my seat, apparently busily engaged in writing, while all the men around me were standing in an abandon of enthusiasm. A fellow journalist, observing my position, put his hand on my shoulder saying, "Get up, Josephus. This is the most notable day in our history. It connotes the end of war." I kept my seat, saying, "You may cheer if you please at scuttling powerful ships of our Navy; others may do so, but I decline to applaud at my own funeral. I sweat blood to get the money to build these ships that are being destroyed. I decline to applaud the worst blow aimed at the Navy."

THE BRITISH GOT THE LION'S SHARE

After the Conference, Admiral Benson, who had been Chief of Navy Operations, and was the Naval adviser of the Peace Commission in Paris, wrote me that he thought the Conference left us "from a Naval standpoint in a very dangerous position." He went on to say:

"I think the Conference was a sequel to the conference that was held at the Crillon (Paris) in 1919 between you, Mr. Long (First Lord of the British Admiralty), Admiral Wemyss and myself. I shall always feel that the British, being unable to accomplish their desired end of remaining supreme on the sea in any other way brought about this Conference, the result of which leaves them decidedly supreme on the sea.

"Great Britain will have three super-Hoods making 29 knots and carrying 12 sixteen-inch guns in addition to a number of battle cruisers, while we have no battle cruisers and our fastest battleships when completed will make only a little over 21 knots and carry 8 sixteen-inch guns, so it can readily be seen the Hoods could always be in a position either to engage the battleships or keep out of our way by superior speed and eventually destroy everything we had on the ocean by getting it in detail. In addition to this, Great Britain has 12 merchant ships capable of making twenty or more knots at sea, while we have only three."

FACES LOOKED LIKE FLINT

My last official association with President Wilson was on March 4, 1921, the day of the inauguration of his successor. With other members of his Cabinet, I was with Wilson as he sat on the last day of his term in the President's room in the Senate Wing of the Capitol. It was the custom for the Chief Executive to be near at hand to sign bills ratified in the last day of the session of Congress. Wilson looked worn and weary as he conversed officially with members of his Cabinet for the last time. He referred each bill presented for his signature to the member deemed best acquainted with the subject matter, and when it had been approved, gave it the signature that made it law. There was a poor attempt at cheerfulness, in which Wilson led.

At the end, the Committee headed by Lodge entered the room just before the time set for Harding's inauguration. The Senator, with a cold look as hard as the ice on the White Mountain in December, and in frigid tones said: "Mr. President, we have come as a Committee of the Senate to notify you that the Senate and House are about to adjourn and await your pleasure."

With studied politeness and the suggestion of a smile on his drawn mouth Wilson, whose speech had been impaired by illness, said, some thought icily: "Senator Lodge, I have no further recommendations to make. I thank you. Good morning."

The New Freedom went out of the door as Harding and Teapot Dome came in through the window in the spirit of, "The King is dead. Long live the King." As Wilson was leaving the Capitol, the Marine Band was honoring the new executive with "Hail to the Chief."

Wilson wished Harding "all the luck in the world" and painfully, with help, made his way to the elevator after telling his successor, "I am afraid I will have to beg off" attending the inauguration. "I understand," courteously said Harding.

AFFECTION AND FRIENDSHIP

As I was leaving Washington to return to my home in Raleigh, I gave, in person and by letter, expression to the President of the happiness it had given me to be associated with him in the great days. Replying to my letter, Wilson wrote me the following:

"March 14, 1921

"MY DEAR DANIELS:

"I have often had occasion to express to you my affection and friendship; but it is always a pleasure to renew the assurance, and I respond to your letter of March 5th with a very live feeling of gratitude that I have so entirely won your confidence and support.

"Our association has been very delightful to me, and I hope in the years to come we will ever be able to renew our personal friendship and remind each other of the days of service together and our genuine affection for one another.

"With warmest regards and best wishes for you all;

"Your sincere friend,

/s/ "WOODROW WILSON"

LII

BACK TO THE OLD LOVE

T HE PRICE IS too much to pay" even if by changing my political coat I could have retained the Cabinet portfolio or if there had been a drop of Dugald Dalghetty blood in my veins. The country had voted for a Republican administration, and I was glad to turn my face toward home. Eight years was a long time for a Tar Heel editor to stay out of his printing office. I had at no time thought of myself as an office-holder, but as Managing Editor of the Navy all the eight years. Returning, I was only taking on a larger field of operations, for a journalist feels he can advise all and several about world affairs. With cordial good wishes for my successor and fond adieus to associates and friends, and glad to get back to the "paste-pot and scissors," I and my wife and sons turned our faces toward Raleigh.

I was no richer in dollars, but had garnered many riches in the forming of cherished friendships. The most valued new possession I carried to Raleigh from Washington was the silver shaving cup which Admiral Dewey had always used. Our last week in Washington was spent as guests in the home of our dear friend, Mrs. Dewey, between whom and my wife a beautiful friendship had grown up. She gave me the Admiral's cup saying, "I wish you to have it because the Admiral loved you, and you loved him."

Our old-time friend Cliff Berryman gave us a good-bye in a *Washington Star* cartoon with "Miss Democracy" marked on a trunk, which my wife always prized. It had this caption: "Packing up is so hard when one doesn't know for how long a stay."

Reviewing the acts of the Cabinet, G. Gould Lincoln, in the *Washington Star* said: "Secretary Daniels... has sought ever to improve the condition of the enlisted men, and in his efforts has trod on the toes of the traditions in the old Navy. Under his regime, however, the United States Navy has been built up as never before."

NEAR THE END OF THE WILSON ADMINISTRATION

Secretary Daniels, Assistant Secretary Gordon Woodbury, and other officers on duty at the Navy Department near the end of the Wilson Administration. They are, *left to right: front row,* Rear Admiral McVay, Rear Admiral McGowan, Secretary Daniels, Assistant Secretary Woodbury, Admiral Coontz, Rear Admiral Badger, Rear Admiral Mayo, Major General Lejeune; *second row,* Rear Admiral Clark, Rear Admiral Peoples, Rear Admiral Griffin, Rear Admiral Washington; *third row,* Lieutenant Commander Warren, Rear Admiral Jackson, Lieutenant Colonel Lucas, Rear Admirals Parks, Stitt, and Taylor, Commander Metcalf, Rear Admiral Rodgers, Commander Foote (U. S. Navy).

THE HOUSE ON "S" STREET

Spontaneously on the last Armistice Day of his life, great crowds gathered before his home, and Wilson made a speech in which he declared: "I am not one of those that have the least anxiety about the triumph of the principles I have stood for. . . . That we shall prevail is as sure as that God reigns."

Going Home at the close of the Wilson Administration, "with a swelling in the throat."

HOMEY WELCOME BY OLD FRIENDS

It was Sunday morning, March 7, when we reached Raleigh to find a welcome so cordial as to warm our hearts and to make us feel that we were rich in the love of old friends. It was a homey welcome—no banquet with dress suits and evening gowns—but a gathering that afternoon of five thousand neighbors and friends, in the city auditorium which I had a part in building. They planned a reception that had the Tar Heel flavor of the real good neighbor, from country and city. Governor Morrison and the dignitaries were there, but an eloquent country doctor, Dr. J. M. Templeton, made the welcoming address—racy of the soil. City and country choirs held a real community songfest led by John Park, editor of the *Times*. The prayer was offered by a preacher born in Hyde County, my mother's birthplace (Rev. Dr. Barber).

War Governor Bickett, unable to be present, wired: "We all take honest pride in the way Mr. Daniels administered the great office in the biggest time of the Navy's history. We love them both because while in the seats of the mighty they never forgot nor neglected folks down home."

The choir rendered my favorite song, "Oh Love That Will Not Let Me Go," and my wife's favorite, "The King of Love My Shepherd Is."

No one understood so well as I that the chief welcome of homecoming was to my Raleigh-born wife, for I was never regarded as a real Raleighite until she vouched for me. My wife and sons shared with me the feeling expressed by Samuel Johnson: "To be happy at home is the ultimate result of all ambition."

The story of our homecoming, covered by Ben Dixon McNeill, in *The News and Observer,* gave these glimpses of a gathering that made the homecoming heart-warming:

"When the barbecue season rolls around out in Rhamkatte, the luscious melons are ripening out Garner way, when it is ''possum and 'tater' time out in the dark corners of New Light township and in White Oak township, where the tobacco worm dieth not, a welcome awaits the returning Secretary of the Navy to his native heath, Dr. J. M. Templeton told Josephus Daniels yesterday when the community got together to welcome him home...."

"Col. Albert L. Cox told Mr. and Mrs. Daniels how glad the people of the city were to have them back after eight years, of with what interest they had followed their careers in Washington during a period of so great stress, and with what pride they had witnessed their triumphant surmounting of the obstacles that stood in the way of achievement....

" 'I have not come home from a larger job, but I am back to take up again the greatest work in the world—fighting for the man who has unequal opportunity,' said Private Citizen Daniels.

" 'I lay down an office in which I was privileged to serve during the most critical years of our history. And I served under a great man, the most illustrious man living in all the world today'— The throng broke in with a tempest of cheers.—'I have come home to fight, to be your comrade, to stand with you for justice and equality of opportunity, to work with you, and to have your love, which I covet above all things.'

"Mrs. Daniels had not intended to speak. She was taken unawares when Mr. Park, master of ceremonies, called upon her, and she had not the words with which to begin. After a moment of hesitation, filled with a swell of applause, she came forward to the edge of the stage.

MRS. DANIELS RESPONDS

" 'When I entered the auditorium today,' she began, 'it was a feeling of almost dismay, a feeling that comes sometimes when one is ushered into the presence of kings. But I know now why it was that I felt that way—it was because you are the kings and queens of our hearts—you people who are our own people.

" 'I have been sitting there exulting over Mr. Daniels. He is the stranger and I took him in. It is so nice of you to approve of my judgment.' The audience laughed heartily with her. She expressed keen pleasure at being back home again. 'There is but one cloud on the horizon today,' she went on. 'The chariot has swung low many times in the eight years that we have been gone, and there are faces missing that we loved. We want you to feel that where there is one among you who has had sorrow, that the sorrow is shared by us, that where there is grief, we have grieved, too.' "

That was not the only time in my family that I came sixth. My wife and four sons were born in Raleigh and were on their native heath.

I was regarded in the eighties as an "outlander," having never lived nearer Raleigh than fifty miles until after I was twenty-one, when the dome of the State Capitol attracted me, and having been born on the broad Pamlico, with most of my life spent on the banks of Contentnea Creek. As a matter of fact, I lived in Raleigh a dozen years before some Negroes in our end of town knew I had any name except "Miss Addie Bagley's husband," and that was the highest rank I have ever attained or desired.

IN HARNESS AGAIN

The next morning found Editor Daniels back in the sanctum writing editorials in his own hand with a big black pencil, which only one printer could read. He resumed the journalistic know-it-all advice to the President and Cabinet officers, from the outside looking in, forgetful that for eight years he had been on the inside looking out. It is easier to tell an official what to do than it is to do it.

From the first editorial (March 7) this extract is taken:

"Upon my return home, writing to readers who are regarded as friends rather than patrons—talking out loud to the family so to speak—I wish to say that I never had but one ambition in my life. As a boy the goal of all my ambition was to become editor of this paper published at the capitol of my native state. . . . I think I was born to be an editor, and for the last eight years I have served a Managing Editor of the Navy. . . . My whole life and ambition is to do a man's part in making a better world for this generation and our children to live in. And my pulpit is the sanctum of this paper."

The next day The Old Codger (a fictional character) reappeared, and the Rhamkatte Roaster (a fictional paper) mentioned the Songfest, in which The Old Codger said, "I'd rather hear Larry Woodall sing 'Amazing Grace' than to hear Caruso," and he quoted a poem after Burns—considerably after—by W. S. Copeland, an old friend, "Jo Daniels, My Joe."

Part Fifteen

━━━━━━━━━━━━━━━━━

THE BLUE AND THE GRAY

LIII

MEMORIALS AT ARLINGTON

LOOKING BACK ON the eight years as a member of Wilson's Cabinet, I have the satisfaction of knowing that what I hoped to see come to pass was, the most part, accomplished. But there was failure of two things. One, and the greatest dream that ever possessed the mind and heart of a statesman of practical vision, was Wilson's League of Nations. The other was that the cherished complete and brotherly reunion of the Blue and the Gray was not proclaimed in imperishable marble in the white Amphitheatre at Arlington.

Almost in the first days of the time when Wilson's New Freedom blessed the country in advancements that burgeoned into larger fruition in the New Deal, the administration looked toward the end of war. Bryan's famous Treaties, which required nine-months cooling time before nations could go to war, with provision for the utilization of that period to find a substitute for the settling of differences by the arbitrament of war, had the approval of the executive and the legislative departments. In like vein, but more as an auxiliary, was my proposal for an agreement of nations to end competitive big navy building, while I pioneered in the legislation authorizing the construction of "the most adequate navy in the world," which would, however, cease construction if and when nations found a way to settle disputes without the arbitrament of the sword.

I was brought up, as were most Southern boys in the seventies and eighties, in the atmosphere of Father Ryan's poems. The spirit of those days, as reflected in the schools, was indicated by the character of the recitations. The favorite was "The Sword of Lee":

> "Forth from its scabbard all in vain
> Bright flashed the sword of Lee
> . . . .
> Defeated, yet without a stain
> Proudly and peacefully."

Another was "The Conquered Banner," which boys recited in the spirit of those who in the sixties 'hailed it gladly' and sorrowfully— these words in the last verse:

"Furl that Banner, softly, slowly!
Treat it gently—it is holy—
    For it droops above the dead.
Touch it not—unfold it never,
Let it droop there, furled forever,
    For its people's hopes are dead!"

My teacher (Cousin Ed Nadal), who at the age of sixteen had left school to join the Confederate Army, became a member of the Ku Klux Klan in Reconstruction, and thought his idol Stonewall Jackson incarnated every virtue, indoctrinated as far as he could all his students into his creed.

Among the highlight events that furthered the union of Blue and Gray were gatherings addressed by such eloquent men as General John B. Gordon and Corporal Tanner. As a young man I was present at those patriotic meetings in the early nineties, privileged to be the escort of General Wade Hampton, whose lameness permitted me to be his aide in Washington in 1893-94, and thereby I came into a relationship I still cherish.

Naturally, therefore, when I found myself, by virtue of my office, a member of the Commission to erect a stately memorial at Arlington to the heroes of "all wars," I had thrilled to think I might have a part in the realization of the dream of burying sectionalism in my country. When the cornerstone of that imposing structure was laid, in my address I had said:

"This memorial is erected in honor of all men of all wars in which Americans have engaged. It is erected at the home of Robert E. Lee, the brave young soldier who fought under the Stars and Stripes in Mexico, and afterwards fought with equal bravery for the Stars and Bars."

Every time I visit Washington, I drive out to Arlington and pause at the memorial to the "Men of the Maine," in the dedication of which my youngest sons had a part in memory of their uncle, Ensign Worth Bagley, the first Naval officer to be killed in the Spanish-American War; and the magnificent Memorial Amphitheatre erected by the Commission of which I was a member. I take off my hat in memory of Robert E. Lee as I stand in the home from which he went to lead the Confederate Army; and pause in tribute to the Unknown Soldier; and look across the Potomac to have an uplifting view of the Lincoln Memorial, the Washington Monument, and the new Jefferson Memorial—classic building. But it recalls rather poignantly an untoward incident showing that in 1916 the much-boasted perfect reunion of the North and South had not really arrived. Why? Because, though erected to the heroes of "all wars," the same honor is denied Robert E. Lee and Stonewall Jackson and the other leaders of the Southern Army that is given to the names of Ulysses S. Grant, Thomas, Sherman, Sheridan, and other heroes of the Federal Army. And thereby hangs an unpublished story.

COMMISSION GIVEN WRONG STEER

In view of the fact that Fred Beall, a Confederate veteran, had been placed on the Commission, I felt that the Memorial was to be in honor of all American soldiers. When the time came to select the inscription and names of battles and commanders to be placed on the Memorial, the matter was referred to a committee consisting of the Librarian of the Military Academy at West Point and the Librarian of the Naval Academy at Annapolis. Their recommendations were submitted to a committee composed of the Presidents of Harvard, the University of Michigan, and the University of Virginia; the General Staff of the Army and General Board of the Navy were asked for their suggestions. The result was that these various bodies made the recommendations.

NO CONFEDERATE HERO HONORED

The omission of all who had served in the Confederate Army was a matter of deep regret to me when I was apprised that the various committees had recommended only those who had fought in the Federal Army. The Confederate members of the Commission made a vigorous protest, backed by Southern organizations. I asked President Alderman why the names of Lee and Jackson and other great Southerners did not appear in the list. He replied that he had been told suggestions were limited only to those fighting under the Stars and Stripes. I talked to Secretary Baker, whose father was a surgeon in the Confederate Army. He felt Lee and others should have been recognized, but did not advise vainly trying to undo what the various

committees had decided upon because it would arouse sectional bitterness. The question was brought up when the Commission met,
and there was a clash between the representatives of the Grand Army
and the Confederate Veterans who were heard. In the hearing the
Grand Army spokesman declared that the inception came from them
so that at Arlington there could be a suitable edifice for the celebration of Memorial Day on each Thirtieth of May, and they declared
with vigor that they would never consent that the Memorial should
contain the name of any except those who fought to preserve the
Union. They pointed out that no Confederate was on the Commission in the original act and that it was not until 1915, after the contract was awarded, that Congress had authorized the naming of a
Confederate Veteran on the Commission. The intimation was that
this was due to Southern Democrats in Congress, but that the act
giving this representation on the Commission did not change the
fact that the Memorial was in honor only of those who served under
the Stars and Stripes. Judge Howrie, of Mississippi, and others declared that the act contemplated honoring soldiers who had served
"in all wars," that the debate over the 1915 appropriation when a
Confederate veteran was added to the Commission showed it was the
clear purpose of Congress to honor Confederates as well as Union
veterans.

HEART WITH US BUT NOT HEAD

It was plain that the only hope of securing equal and deserved
honors for the Confederate great men was in persuading Captain
Charles W. Newton, the Spanish-American member of the Commission, to side with me. I had visited in his home at Hartford and
we had talked about how the Spanish-American war veterans had
bridged the chasm between North and South. I pointed out that
General Joe Wheeler and General Fitzhugh Lee had been his comrades and that his organization was the one body to wipe out old
sectionalism, and that the way to do it was to include Lee and Jackson among the illustrious names inscribed on the Memorial. He had
no sectional feeling. In his heart he was ready to vote with me, but
he doubted the wisdom of overruling the recommendations of the
various committees. Moreover, being a native of Vermont and a citizen of Connecticut, while regretting the attitude of the G.A.R., he
did not feel that he should vote contrary to the position they mili-

tantly maintained. He told me that the question troubled him greatly, and it did, but he could not vote against the views of the several committees which had omitted Southern leaders.

POLITICS ENTERED IN

Before that, I had talked with President Wilson. He thought it was unjust to omit Southern veterans but, like Baker, feared the effect of the precipitation of a bitter sectional controversy, which he foresaw if he and I and Baker should seek to override the G.A.R. and the committees which had made the recommendations. The election of 1916 was approaching, and we knew it would be close. Already Republican politicians were seeking a winning issue by saying that the Washington administration was controlled by men from the section which had "tried to destroy the Union." Some Southern Congressmen threatened to demand the insertion of the names of Lee and Jackson, but political consideration deterred such action. Still there was a deep undercurrent of feeling in the South which I fully shared. At the meeting, when votes were lacking to carry out my wishes, I said that I thought the Committees had misconceived the purpose of the Memorial, and that I hoped at some future time the names of the noble men of the South would stand with those of the North on the soil consecrated by association with the name of Lee. I still entertain that hope, and I never cease to regret that the representatives of the Grand Army of the Republic did not rise to the heights of devotion to a reunited country with "charity for all," by helping to make the Memorial truly one that honored veterans in "all wars."

NO SECTIONALISM IN PATRIOTISM

Still, Arlington then and now and always connotes the name of Robert E. Lee, the noblest of American soldiers since Washington fell asleep.

I do not know whether "The Unknown Soldier," who lies in the grave on the hill near the Memorial Amphitheatre was born in North Carolina or Vermont or Oregon—all were called "Yankees" in Europe and all were equally patriotic. But I rejoice that in the World War in which the "Unkown Soldier" made the supreme sacrifice, it was given to the South to furnish, as leaders of America, the three men who directed the armed forces of America in a struggle which brought glory to our country—Woodrow Wilson, born in Virginia, Commander-in-Chief; Newton D. Baker, born in West Virginia, Secretary of War; and Josephus Daniels, born in North Carolina, Secretary of the Navy.

HISTORIC DEDICATORY ADDRESSES

At the dedication of the $750,000 Amphitheatre (May 15, 1920), the Commander-in-Chief of the Grand Army of the Republic, Dan M. Hall, presided. He said, in part:

> "In the name of the Grand Army of the Republic, I now dedicate this Memorial shaft.... I dedicate it to the memory of those who on land or sea fought for the Union and fell in defense of the Flag."

President Wilson's illness prevented his attendance, but in his letter he literally breathed the spirit I had shared when I tried ineffectively to have the names of Lee and Jackson given deserved honor. Wilson's letter, read by Captain Charles W. Newton, contained this passage:

> "Time has thrown its softening influence over the controversy when men fought out the constitutional questions insoluble by other processes; time has eliminated from our memories the bitterness which that controversy aroused, but time has only served to magnify the heroic valor of the captains and the men who fought the great fight."

He concluded with:

> "reverent thanks to the God of Nations that He has made it possible for us in this day to show the world that America is still baptized with the spirit of her founders and builders."

Secretary Baker declared that the "War Between the States" laid to rest questions which fretted and vexed our national development, conluding with:

> "Some day it is planned that a bridge shall span the Potomac and couple up this Amphitheatre with the Lincoln Memorial on the other side, making a great composite monument, at one end the resting place of the heroic dead, and at the other the monument to the great, simple, patriot President. Perhaps it is not vain

to hope that the future may see another bridge, starting here and ending no one can tell where; at this end the exalted virtues of patriotism and loyalty and a willingness to die for the truth, and at the other a peaceful world, held together by its adherence to those ideals and living in harmony because these men of an earlier age have laid to rest the anxious causes of international discontent, and have first learned and then taught the rest of the world the processes by which liberty fruits in justice and peace."

Following Baker's eloquence I closed my address by saying:

"Arlington must no longer connote a mere resting place for our heroic dead; it must become a rallying ground for unselfish endeavor and whole-hearted consecration to national and international service. The world is sick, but it can find here the remedial influences that will heal it and restore it.

"Bring hither, then, your fading torches, my fellow countrymen, and relight them; bring hither the faltering purpose and reënergize it; bring hither the idle dream and put into it the iron of action and the faith of these high-hearted dead.

"We dedicate this Amphitheater not to those who have gone from us but—

> To those immortal dead who live again
> In minds made better by their presence.

"We dedicate it not to an irrevocable past but to an everlasting future; we dedicate it not to fame or to glory as isolated peaks of human effort but to fame found because not sought and to glory made more glorious in the service of mankind."

THREE HOPES DEFERRED

Writing in 1945, in view of the fact that Southerners in the armed forces in World War I and II did not object to being called "Yanks," and the closer unity of all parts of the country, and the promise of a warless world, I still hope to see three deferred hopes realized.

1. A League of Nations that will insure lasting peace.

2. An end of competitive Navy building, an efficient Navy, with powerful aircraft, united under the direction of one Department of National Defense.

3. Recognition of heroes of "all wars" in the Arlington Amphitheatre.

CONFEDERATE AND G. A. R. REUNIONS

"If we had possessed that many soldiers, we Confederates would have won the war," said my wife (daughter of Major W. H. Bagley) in answer to a remark of Vice President Marshall, as the President, Vice President and members of the Cabinet were reviewing the Confederate parade in front of the White House in June, 1917. That was in reply to the Vice President's statement that it looked as if there were "a million men marching by." President Wilson, with a twinkle, said: "We must have no renewal of the Civil War differences now that we are in a bigger war."

THE TOWERING CHIEF JUSTICE

Heading the Louisiana Confederates in the parade was Chief Justice White, head and shoulders above his old comrades. He was greeted with applause from the great crowds and those in the reviewing stand. A true American, he never forgot he was a Southerner or lacked comradeship with the soldiers of the South.

A RARE BANQUET

My wife, whose devotion to her Confederate father, and Miss Mary Lee, daughter of General Lee, devoted themselves to what I called "gracious Southern Hospitality." We gave a dinner on the *Mayflower* to the officers of the Confederacy attending the Reunion, to which Corporal Tanner, the most eloquent of Federal soldiers, General Sherwood, Congressman from Ohio, and other Northern officers were invited. It was truly a notable occasion, where the Blue and the Gray in mellow association unbosomed themselves in such moving patriotic eloquence as I have seldom heard.

RECEPTION AT PAN AMERICAN BUILDING

Under the rules no reception or entertainment could be given at the stately Pan American Building except by the Secretary of State. My wife thought, and Miss Mary Custis Lee agreed, we could do nothing so fitting as to give the Confederate veterans and their wives and the Daughters of the Confederacy a reception at the Pan American. When I visited Secretary Lansing, Chairman of the Pan American Union, and requested the privilege of holding a reception for the Southerners in the Pan American Building, he showed me a rule he could not change, that no official at Washington could be host at any gathering in the Pan American Building except the Secretary of State. Sensing my disappointment at not being able to do this honor in the best way to the Southern Veterans, Secretary Lansing said: "I will tell you what I will do. Invitations will be sent to all the Confederates and ladies of the Auxiliary you furnish, in the name of the Secretary of State and Mrs. Lansing. All we will allow you and Mrs. Daniels to do will be to receive them and—" he paused and smiled—"you may have the privilege of paying the bill." It was a notable event and the Southerners were happy to be entertained in that most beautiful of Washington buildings.

JOHNNY REB FORGOT HIMSELF

When it was announced that the Confederate Veterans were to hold their reunion in the Capital city, which General Jubal Early tried to take—and came near taking—in the War of the Sixties (the best name for the war of brothers), the members of the Grand Army in a large sense became the hosts of their former enemies in war. There were many gatherings and fraternal meetings of the commingling of the blue and the gray. Postmaster General Burleson told this story of how an old Johnny Reb from Texas, who had served under Burleson's father in the Confederate Army, came up upon Burleson's invitation. Talking one day with Burleson, the Texan said:

"Albert, before we left home we were told that we were to be welcomed and given hospitality by the members of the Grand Army. It warmed my heart to think we old fellows who fought one another are now good friends, all together working to strengthen our common republic. I looked forward to this brotherly love association more than anything else at this Reunion, and felt that we would together cement mutual unity. But (and he paused) I have been here two days and have not met a single son-of-a-bitch of them."

So saying he walked out, never realizing that he was using the language of the sixties instead of the friendly words in his heart in 1917.

G. A. R. ON OLD STAMPING GROUND

When the Grand Army held its reunion in Washington, the officials and citizens gave them the freedom of the city and every courtesy and every kind of hospitality. They were most interested to visit the marble memorial to the heroes of America erected at Arlington, one of the noblest memorials in the world. As was the habit, the Boy Scout organization appointed a Boy Scout to be the special courier and host to every veteran. It chanced that my young son, Jonathan, was assigned as guide, philosopher, and friend to a one-legged veteran from Kansas. There sprang up a genuine affection between the Federal veteran and the grandson of a Confederate Major. In fact, the difference in sections and attitudes of the sixties cemented a real friendship. My wife—a devoted Daughter of the Confederacy—invited the Kansas veteran to our home. On the day for his departure, Jonathan used the Secretary of the Navy's carriage to take his new-found Kansas friend to the train, saw him safely seated with ticket and baggage, and, as he said Good-bye, the soldier expressed his thanks to his young companion and slipped a bill into his pocket. "A Boy Scout never takes a tip. He loves to do a good deed to a good man and can accept nothing." In vain did the veteran say he was offering no tip but wanted the boy to accept a present from him.

This was not the first time the Grand Army of the Republic had held its meeting in the National Capital, but it was, I think, the first time the Confederate Veterans had made it their meeting place. Both felt at home and were made to feel at home by members of the Wilson administration and all Washingtonians.

LIV

"TOO MANY SOUTHERNERS"

REFERRING TO CRITICISM of the Navy by some of his Republican colleagues, Chairman Page, of Vermont, a charming gentleman who regarded my wife so highly that he was friendly to me—said one day (October 13, 1919), as my Diary reads:

"Page said sentiment was I had too many Southern Democrats around me—said Coontz (Chief of Operations) was a Southern Democrat from Missouri; Washington (Chief of Navigation) from North Carolina; Taylor (Chief of Construction) from Virginia; Griffin (Chief of Engineering) from Virginia; McGowan (Chief of Supplies and Accounts) from South Carolina.

"I pointed out that Mayo (Commander in Chief) was from Vermont; Sims (Chief of Naval Affairs in Europe) from Pennsylvania; Earle (Chief of Ordnance) from Massachusetts; Barnett (Head of Marine Corps) from Michigan; Butler (in command at Quantico) from Pennsylvania; Wilson (Commander of Atlantic Fleet) from Pennsylvania, etc., etc. and told him that he should give that information to criticizing colleagues.

"It is disheartening to see how even the best of Republicans seem to feel that no Southern man should have recognition. Sims and Benson would have been promoted as Admirals if they had been Northern Republicans. (Benson was from Georgia and the Senate could not confirm Sims without also promoting Benson, and both failed.)"

That remark by Senator Page, coming from a personal friend, was illustrative of a feeling that had been voiced in New England in the 1918 campaign where Lodge and other speakers stirred up bitter sectional prejudices which had more to do with Democratic defeat than Wilson's letter. This, too, when the Navy alone was spending more money and employing more men in New England than in all the South from Maryland to Texas.

THE SOUTH IN THE SADDLE

All during Wilson's administration, partisan opponents were bitter, alleging, "The South is in the saddle," as if it were a crime for the South, which had contributed most to Wilson's election, not to be excluded from posts of honor. That sectionalism was hurting Democrats in some parts of the North, and they advised that fewer Southerners be appointed. Wilson was unaffected by that clamor. He went serenely along, appointing as many men to high stations from Texas as from New York, and putting fitness first. Naturally, as the South was solidly Democrat and, though a citizen of New Jersey, Wilson was born and raised in the South, he would not discriminate against that part of the republic. And neither did I. It was the first Administration, except Cleveland's, where the South had been given a voice at the council table of an administration in Washington since the War of the Sixties. Along the same line I quote from my Diary (October 24):

"Went to see Senator Page of Vermont to urge him to support the nomination of John Skelton Williams, of Virginia, as Comptroller General. He had been poisoned by Senator Weeks. 'Temperamentally' not fitted was the word used by bankers. Republicans had held a conference and decided to vote against confirmation."

I was minded to go to see Senator Page because of friendly relations and my faith in his fairness. He and I together shared pride in Vermont's three great Naval officers—Dewey, Clark, and Mayo, and he appreciated the fact that I had named Mayo Commander-in-Chief of the American Fleet. He was not of the highest order of statesmanship, but a gentleman every inch. I was surprised that Weeks could influence him. I do not think of his own motion he would have had that sectional bias.

The real opposition was not because Williams was a Southerner, though that didn't help him with stand-pat New Englanders. It was because he didn't take orders from the big bankers, and Wall Street and made them obey the laws like the little bankers. Some years before, two members of the Cabinet had tried to poison Wilson's mind against Williams and he asked my view. When he was assured that Williams, though tactless, was able and courageous, Wilson stood by him as he did by all appointees who were true to the Wilson policies.

Again from my Diary (November 12):

"Chairman Page wanted me to agree not to take any steps on Charleston (S. C.) dry dock until Senate acted on Calder's bill not to build it. 'Nay, nay, Pauline' sectional animosity and partisan bitterness. I will be heard before action is taken.

"Nov. 15. I went before Senate Naval Affairs Committee in opposition to Calder's bill to withdraw appropriation to build dry dock at Charleston. Five were authorized—one at New York, Boston, Philadelphia, Norfolk and Charleston. All built except Charleston—no attempt to withdraw any in the North."

WILSON A SOUTHERNER

That attitude could find no favor with Wilson, any more than if some Southerner had sought special favor for his section. Though Wilson spent all his adult life teaching in Pennsylvania, Connecticut, and New Jersey, the early influences of birth and residence in the South left their permanent mark on him. As President, he was truly national and had no tolerance for professional Southerners or men in any part of the country who permitted sectionalism to influence their action. I sat under the spell of his eloquence, when, speaking on Lee, at the University of North Carolina, he made this profession:

"It is all very well to talk of detachment of view, and of the effort to be national in spirit and in purpose, but a boy never gets over his boyhood, and never changes those subtle influences which have become a part of him, that were bred in him when he was a child. So I am obliged to say again and again, that the only place in the country, the only place in the world, where nothing has to be explained to me is the South ... with all the old memories I know the region to which I naturally belong."

Part Sixteen

WOODROW WILSON

LV

WILSON IN SELF-REVEALMENT

VOLUMES HAVE been written about Woodrow Wilson, and a great moving picture, portraying illuminating events and family life, has been seen by thousands. They reveal on the printed page and to the eye phases of Wilson's life, traits, and trends. And of the making of books touching upon the Wilson Era there seems to be no end.

In almost every chapter of *The Wilson Era—Peace* and in this volume *The Wilson Era—War and After,* Wilson emerges on the world stage as the most distinguished figure of an age which has been depicted as the time when mankind must be "Looking Back to Glory." We have walked and talked with him as our country emerged from peace into neutrality; then entered World War I; and then received him in the culmination of his bringing home from Versailles the Covenant of Peace.

The portrayal of Wilson as President, as Commander-in-Chief in war and in the councils of the great at Paris, does not introduce us familiarly to Wilson in his own proper person apart from the dignity of office, the trappings of war, and as one of the Big Four commissioned to garner the fruits of victory into a lasting peace pact. To understand the man—the lights and shadows—I have selected a few illustrative sidelights and comments when he was "at home."

STORIES AT WHITE HOUSE LUNCHEON

It was in the circle of intimates or at his own table with a few friends that President Wilson was at his best. His conversation was without reserve. I have never known a more charming and delightful conversationalist or a more interesting story-teller. If his guest had some matter of importance to discuss, Wilson would give himself to it at once. When it was settled, he acted as if he was not directing the greatest war in history. He doffed the presidential garb and acted as if great matters of state were not on his shoulders. I recall one instance of this three weeks after the declaration of war, which I recorded in my Diary (April 30):

"I lunched with the President and Mrs. Wilson. We talked about sending ships to England and France and decided to send 36 at once and try to secure other small craft. Must act now. The President did not like the Committee Lane and W. B. Wilson had named. He said all of them had fought the shipping bill. It had been near his heart and as our need now was great he could not forgive the short-sightedness of those who had opposed it.

"Wilson told good stories apropos of topics as they came up. He spoke of a criticism that had been made of him because under provocation he had used the word 'Damn,' saying, 'I was guilty of profanity. My critic,' he said, 'was unaware of the fact that when some Democrats, wishing to impeach a Federalist judge, charged him among other things with profanity on the bench, specifying that he used the word Damn, the court held that Damn was not profanity but just a way of being emphatic. Perhaps I should not have let my temper get the best of me when I used that emphatic word, but at least that decision acquits me of being guilty of profanity.'

"We had waffles, with syrup, and I remarked on my love for them and told the story that my small sons were fond of repeating whenever waffles were served: A visitor was served waffles. He had never seen or tasted them before. They were so good he devoured them faster than the waiter could bring them to the table, finally calling out: 'Bring me more waffles. Don't stop to print 'em.' However, at this luncheon the stories were so good neither of us asked the waiter, 'Don't stop to print them.'

"I do not recall how the subject came up, perhaps all three of us being Southerners, we were interested in topics touching the South. Mr. Wilson told of having seen Jefferson Davis as he was being taken through Augusta to prison, and said: 'I saw him passing through the streets guarded by Federal soldiers, and later I was in the crowd that welcomed Robert E. Lee when that greatest hero of the Confederacy visited Augusta.' I recalled his classic tribute to Lee when he spoke at the University of North Carolina, in which he referred glowingly to 'the delightful memory of standing, when a lad, for a moment by General Lee's side and looking up into his face.' He said that it was out of such memories and late ones in the South and Washington that he had written *Division and Reunion*.

"Speaking about gifts for institutions of learning and how one big job of a college president was to secure funds, he related this incident out of his Princeton days: 'Dr. McCosh was one day entertaining the rich Mr. Garrett, and showed Mr. Garrett the plans of a new building for Princeton. Garrett gave the necessary money and the story got out that Dr. McCosh had asked Garrett for the money while entertaining him in his own house. Dr. McCosh resented the story as a reflection upon his hospitality. Mrs. McCosh explained that her husband had not asked Mr. Garrett for the money, but that after showing him the plans said to him: 'I have all the money except $10,000— What do you say?' "

WILSON GAVE TIPS

Very little went on in Washington that Wilson didn't know about. I knew, of course, that it is an American habit to write many letters about all manner of things to the Chief Executive, but it seemed at some times that he got wind of nearly everything that went on in Washington. He frequently sent Baker and me tips about matters relating to war and war material. I recall this as an example:

In November (1917) Wilson wrote me: "Some very dirty work is being done about the Liberty Motor, and I understand that the active man in it is one ———, who is frequently if not permanently here in Washington. He ought to be smoked out." That tip had the desired result.

NO FOOTBALL GAMES DURING WAR

Reading that a suggestion had been made that the Army and Navy teams have an exhibition game in New York for the benefit of one of the war funds, Wilson wrote me early in November (1917):

"I take it for granted that your judgment is mine in such a matter, that the Army and Navy game ought not to be used for that or any similar purpose, but my judgment goes further. It seems to me that the Army and Navy game ought to be omitted altogether this season....

"I need not say that I heartily approve of athletics for both academies and hope they will play all they please on their own grounds."

TOLD PRINCETON STORIES

At almost every Cabinet meeting some member presented the view of someone proposing a new program. Most of them were either already employed or were impractical. This caused Wilson to recall that he made a speech over at Princeton saying, "No novelties are wanted here." The reporters printed that he had said, "No new thoughts wanted here," which was the very thing Princeton wanted. W. W. added, "They are not always wanted at colleges."

This was only one of many times he regaled us with stories having a Princeton flavor. Another day he told the story of a professor of chemistry who said: "In my laboratories I am all mind; outside, I am all soul." The professor was given to big words. "Why did I have to take out to dinner that dessicated female?" As Disraeli said of Gladstone, he was "inebriated by his own verbosity."

COULDN'T TRUST YALE

The President told this: Some years ago he went to a stomach specialist who said, "What I am about to do you will find uncomfortable, but not intolerable." He tried to induce the doctor to talk, but he was economical in conversation. So Wilson told this football story: A Princeton football player went to see Dr. Janaway, who gave him a prescription for his ailment. The coach could read only one word: it was 'strychnine.' The coach said: 'Don't take it. Dr. Janaway is a Yale man and he may be trying to poison you.' The doctor did unbend then.

Wilson told this story about himself:

"When a young man I wore side-whiskers. One day in court, the Sheriff looked at me so hard I thought something must be the matter with me. Then the sheriff took his long legs from the table and walked over to me and asked: 'Did you know that you had left one side of your whiskers longer than the other?'"

AN UNLOVELY SIDE

The soul of courtesy, under severe provocation Wilson sometimes found it difficult to control his temper. He once said that trying to do so when he felt righteous wrath against wrongs or evil men was the hardest part of being President. Most of his denunciations were of those who had betrayed causes they pretended to favor or had tried to frustrate needed reforms. President Eliot, of Harvard, upon whom Wilson often leaned, but with whose views he did not always agree, in an article in the *Atlantic Monthly* (June, 1924) said of his fellow college president: "Woodrow Wilson, like most reformers and pioneering folk, had a fierce and unlovely side."

SOME UNIVERSITY PLAGIARISM

At a meeting of the War Cabinet, or Council (it was called both, and was usually held in the White House basement, as my Diary records), after passing on the matters in hand, Wilson said:

"It is too hot to bring up very serious questions. A Yale man read in a literary magazine the prize oration and found it was the one he had delivered forty years ago. He had not read a copy for 20 years, though taking it regularly except that issue. He exposed the young man.

"W. W. told of a man who, after graduation at Oxford, sealed his oration and hid it behind the oldest book in the library, thinking 100 years hence he would play a joke on posterity. He happened to be near Oxford at Exhibition nearly half a century later, the first time since he graduated. He was astonished to hear the first honor man deliver the speech he had delivered upon his graduation fifty years before."

IS IT A RICH MAN'S WAR?

At a meeting on November 2, 1917, Wilson said the criticism was made to him that in a sense this was a rich man's war. I quote from my Diary:

"It is being said that sons of rich men are being given commissions and bomb-proof jobs away from the firing line. 'This ought to be prevented,' Wilson said with emphasis. Lane said that he thought the report in error, and that the sons of rich men were going quicker than others. 'You cannot be too careful to see that there is no foundation for this report,' said the President. I reported that in early days of the war some Naval commanders had commissioned sons of men with pull as Ensigns and Lieutenants, who had no knowledge of navigation and had given them desk work, and I had summoned them to Washington and issued strict orders against it, but that while it was greatly reduced, it is an evil that must be combatted all the time.

"Tumulty sent over several gentlemen whose sons are serving in the Naval Reserve in France. They complained that commissions as Ensigns had been given young men who had not gone to sea and denied to their sons who were in the war zone. They wanted their sons sent to Annapolis to study for commissions. I sent for Palmer (Chief of Personnel) who pointed out that they could win commissions on ships by demonstrating ability, but we could not bring them from actual service in France to give them an opportunity for study at home. He explained that the trouble was due to the way the first class was selected. Orders were given that preference be given to men in service in the war zone."

OBLIGED TO VOTE FOR WILSON

A story told by a friend of McAdoo greatly intrigued Wilson, for, like most Southern men, he loved Negro stories. It was the best of many that were current after Wilson issued his proclamation establishing Daylight Saving Time for the duration of the war. It ran like this:

"At a primary election at which only county officers were being nominated an old Negro who had not voted since the days of Reconstruction, presented himself to the poll-holders and asked that he be permitted to vote. He was told that only regular Democrats could vote and his name was not on the books.

" 'But boss,' he said, 'I am just obleeged to vote in this election.'

"Asked why, not having voted in over a score of years, he was so anxious to vote, the Negro replied: 'I'm just obleeged to vote. I want to cast my ballot for Woodrow Wilson. He air the greatest man what ever wuz in the White House.'

" 'Why do you think he is greater than all others?' he was asked.

" 'Why, boss, you know he is, becaze he changed God A'mighty's time and tuck away all the railroads from the men what owned 'em and give 'em to his son-in-law.' "

That story didn't set well with Son-in-law McAdoo, when it was first told, but he came to like it.

WILSON AND THE IRISH

"I believe the way is provided in the League that the Irish and all countries not enjoying independence may be heard and the policy of self determination prevail all over the world."

That was Wilson's answer when criticized by many because he had not obtained Ireland's independence at Paris. If Wilson had been permitted to take the seat reserved for the United States at Geneva, the independence of Ireland would have been on the early agenda. He said that any member of the League had the right and duty to bring up the desire of the Irish or any people in like situation "and it becomes the business of the League." However, the U. S. Senate kept that seat vacant. Wilson's hopes came to fruition when on September 10, 1923, Ireland became a member of the League of Nations. Wilson said, before the Irish question became acute in war days and after: "English statesmen must realize that in the last analysis force never permanently settles anything. I have tried to impress upon Englishmen that there can never be full comradeship between England and America until this issue is definitely settled and out of the way."

Then, turning from grave to gay, he said: "You know I am half Irish and half Scotch." When there are hard problems to decide, the Scotch in me says: 'Punish him, make him pay.' Then the Irish begins a fight within me and says: 'No; don't punish him—what's the good? He's a fine fellow—let him off.' The battle goes on between the two, and me sitting in between."

IRELAND AND HOME RULE

At that same meeting Wilson, prefacing criticism of Senator Phelan for insisting at that time (January, 1918) that the United States demand Home Rule for Ireland, told this incident: "A gentleman, who saw Dublin after the destruction by a catastrophe of nature, said: 'I did not know Ireland had home rule.'"

As to Phelan's insistence upon fighting with Britain, Wilson said such pressure was both untimely and injurious, and my Diary records:

"Wilson said Phelan made him so mad he could hardly restrain himself. He added that he had been informed that Trotsky will ask all Allied nations to join in giving self-rule to Ireland, Egypt and India, along with Belgium and Serbia. That is playing into the hands of the Germans, but it is a shrewd move. He related the story of a preacher in Orkney Islands who prayed for 'the people of this land and the adjacent islands of England, Scotland and Ireland.'"

NO HATE OF GERMANS

A passion of hate of Germans and all things German affected large sections of the country. Directing the fighting with every ounce of power, Wilson refused to let the poison of hate of Germany corrode his spirit. I recall that discussing the spirit of vengeance Wilson said, "We must face such intolerance against Germans. I may have to become their advocate for justice against American Prussianism. We must never do the things we condemn." This extract from my Diary (October 16, 1918):

"Baker said that while in Europe he had heard many stories of cruelty and barbaric actions by Germans. Army men traced them down and found only two of many cases true. Generally a man had heard that it happened in another regiment. Stories of German cruelty and of our cruelty were exaggerated. One American soldier did shoot a German in the back, but they found he was crazy.

"Referring to action in some parts of the country forbidding teaching of German in the schools, W.W. said 'It is silly to forbid teaching German or tearing down statues.' In that connection he quoted Andrew Carnegie as having said there was no more reason to study Greek than Choctaw, and made this comment: 'Not to a man who couldn't understand there was literature in Greek and not in Choctaw.' Baker said the statue of Frederick the Great ought not to have been taken down at the War College.

"The President told of reports from the town of Aspinwall, Iowa, where many Germans live. They took no Liberty Bonds. A delegation from a nearby town went over, shut up every store, arrested the owner of the Town Hall because he would not permit its use for a Liberty Loan meeting. Wilson, after recounting the incident, asked 'By what authority did these people act?' and he answered 'None.' McAdoo thought their conduct in obstructing the Liberty Bond campaign justified what was done. It angered Wilson.

"Burleson told of pro-German papers. 'I sent for the editors,' he said, 'and asked: 'Have you printed that Germans dropped bombs on Red Cross hospitals? Have you printed any atrocities practiced by Germans?' On every case, such news had been deleted by these pro-German editors. They promised it would not occur again."

TOAST TO GERMAN "HEMPEROR"

On October 29 the President told of an English sailor who entertained German sailors at a banquet. After an English petty officer had proposed a toast to " 'is 'ighness, the German Hemperor," he asked a German sailor if he would not propose the health of the English King. No answer. He asked again. No answer. "Then up comes your Hemperor," says the British sailor, thrusting his hand down his throat.

GERMANY'S CHIEF TROUBLE

At a meeting on October 2, 1917, the chief discussion was over Germany's ability to carry on—what was its chief trouble. I quote from my Diary:

"Gregory said he had heard that Germany needed engines and would be glad to give one submarine for engines. That reminded W.W. of the man who said he would like to swap a falsetto voice for a false set of teeth. The President thought it would be well if Mrs. Dewey would give out the suppressed chapters of Dewey's book on the German attitude.

"There was discussion of exemptions in draft. The President said he had received a letter from a woman in Arizona who wanted her son exempted. Husband had two children and a wife dependent on him and his mother did not want him to go. President said the mother was President of a Wilson League and had been vigorous in his defence against the vile slanders upon him during the campaign. It was his first and only reference to the active whispering campaign against him in 1916.

"Returning to the German situation, whether its chief trouble was men, money, or munitions, W.W. related the story of the English ruler who couldn't speak English but wished to make a good impression. He was told to say: 'I have come for your good and the good of all.' What he actually did say was: 'I have come for your goods and all your goods.' Wilson said his father had used that incident when Louisville offered money if the Presbyterians would move their seminary to that city."

Shortly after that Cabinet meeting I called to see Mrs. Dewey about securing her consent to publishing Dewey's unpublished chapter about the German action at Manila, and how Dewey read the riot act to the German officer who came on board the *Olympia*. I told her the President thought it would be well to print it now. She said that after serious reflection the Admiral decided not to print it and if she gave it out now it might provoke controversy and she did not "think it would please him." This last reason was sufficient for her; as long as she lived, what might have pleased him in life was the law and gospel to her. Wilson understood and appreciated her point of view.

THE BRITISH MONOCLE

Wilson had genuine admiration for his English cousins but was fond of the jokes at their expense.

From my Diary:

> "At one Cabinet meeting Wilson told the story of a talk between Ambassador Spring-Rice and Captain Harts, Superintendent of Buildings and Grounds. 'What is the White House made of?' 'Virginia sandstone,' was the reply. 'That is not white?' 'No, it must be painted,' replied Captain Harts. 'Why,' persisted the Ambassador. 'To cover up the burns made after the fire,' answered Harts. 'What caused the fire?' inquired Spring-Rice. 'The British Army,' replied Harts."

EXCHANGE OF PREACHERS

I recall a discussion concerning an exchange of preachers between England and the United States. Advocates of the scheme wished the approval of the administration. Dr. Jowett had made a fine impression on our country by his ministry, as had the Archbishop of York on his short visit. Why not many exchanges? The President spoke of how most English preachers who came here regarded themselves as representing "the mother country" and added: "That is not pleasant. Some are condescending. Might do more harm than good."

FEARED HE WOULD HATE THE ENGLISH

I went to see the President (April 13, 1918) about the request of Mayo, Commander-in-Chief, who wanted to go abroad in command of the naval forces. According to my Diary:

> "The President agreed that the time was not ripe for a separate fleet and therefore Mayo need not go. We then talked about the situation and how Britain had seemed to object to

nearly every proposition this country made. 'I fear,' said Wilson, 'that I shall come out of the war hating the English.' "

OPPOSED PROPAGANDA ORATORS

Wilson gave no approval to the attempt to influence public senti-ment here by British speakers who came over to tell us what to do, and he was especially adverse to American stump-speakers going to England to interpret us to them and instruct them as to their duty. He doubtless thought that both could serve their respective countries better at home, and if they had any influence it should be exerted in their own country. When Creel suggested that James M. Beck, a Dugald Dalghetti in politics, should be asked to make a speaking tour in England, Wilson laid down a sound rule when he wrote:

> "I strongly disapprove of the English idea of having speakers come from the United States and make anything like a sys-tematic canvass of Great Britain. I think they have made a mis-take in sending speakers over here.... It is the idea I am op-posed to."

THE PRESIDENT WAS FOXY

At the Cabinet meeting on July 16, 1917, Wilson opened the meeting by referring to his letter telling Sims he had been disap-pointed at the inefficiency of the British Navy and at Sims's rejecting American suggestions for "shutting up the hornets in their nests." He said—and he knew I was happy to hear him:

> "I was more foxy in my letter to Sims than you may think. His friends would later say, if I had not written, that Sims is original and that if he had been given his way he would have proceeded along lines of such vigor as to win success. Now in his reply he has advised nothing except what the British have planned and has shown that instead of being original he follows the British slavishly."

THE DAMNEDEST FOOL

"I have reached the conclusion," said President Wilson to me one day when he was irked by Walter Page's pro-British attitude, "that Walter Page is the damndest fool we ever appointed." And he asked, "Don't you agree with me?"

I shook my head and answered: "No I do not. I am committed to Admiral Sims."

That was when Page was more in sympathy with the British Foreign Office than with the policy of the President whom he ought to have represented. However, the personal affection born when they were both at Johns Hopkins and kept up through the years was renewed in the years of their common devotion to winning the war and the peace.

THE VOGUE FOR SHORT SPEECHES

A member of the Cabinet congratulated Wilson on introducing the vogue of short speeches and asked him about the time it took him to prepare his speeches. He said:

"It depends. If I am to speak ten minutes, I need a week for preparation; if fifteen minutes, three days; if half an hour, two days; if an hour, I am ready now."

How did Wilson react as to making speeches? Once when the Methodist Conference was meeting in Washington and emphasizing Asbury—"the Prophet of the Long Road"—the first American Methodist Bishop in America, I urged Wilson to reconsider his refusal and make a brief address. I said, "You can go in the side door, make your ten- or fifteen-minute address, and retire. You will not be away from the White House more than thirty minutes." He replied:

"You talk, Daniels, like a man who never tried to make a speech. It isn't the thirty minutes. I'd be glad to give that. But, if I accept, the question of what I will say will be on my mind, and I will wake up in the early mornings with the sleep-killing thought that everything a President says is printed. I must keep that in mind. It isn't a matter of minutes but of days if I promise to speak."

But he did accept and did say things that deserved to live.

HAVING NOTHING TO SAY

One member of the Cabinet—I think it was Baker—asked Wilson what he thought of the speech of a certain public man which had been played up in the papers. Wilson answered:

"I think that Mr. X is a perfectly well-meaning man and would like to do the right thing and say the right thing. He reminds me of what Walter Bagehot said of the difference between the English and French languages. 'Which is the best language?' asked Bagehot. 'The French, of course. It has more delicate shades of meaning and the French can express themselves much better in that language. The trouble with the French is they have nothing to say.'"

A BUNGALOW MIND

It was of another public man that Wilson once said: "He means well. The trouble with him is that he has a bungalow mind."

"RATS," SAID WILSON

At a meeting (August 31, 1920) Wilson asked me if the report in the paper was correct that I had sent a ship to Danzig. "Yes, at the request of the Secretary of State," I replied. "Rats," said Wilson. "That is the excuse always given for sending ships that ought not to go. We have no right there. The French and British want us to help them."

Colby said he had requested it because American refugees there might need protection. He regretted making the request. I cabled recall of the ship, hoping to reach the captain before it reached Danzig. The State Department had a way, under both Lansing and Colby, of regarding the Navy as their police force to enforce imperialistic plans. I was glad when Wilson's "Rats" put an end to it.

WHAT TO DO WITH WHISKEY

There was hardly any matter that did not get Cabinet consideration, big and little, from prohibition to the disposal of intoxicants. My Diary (March 5, 1918) has the following:

"Gregory: 'What shall I do with whiskey seized by U. S. marshals?' No authority to dispose of it. Much merriment. W.W. told of whiskey put in buckets at Army canteen and a mule got its head in the bucket and drank and drank and drank. Became so drunk he kicked over everything, but did not 'kick the bucket.' Burleson said it would be a sin to pour out good whiskey, it was getting too scarce and too high. He suggested that it be given to hospitals."

YOUNG MAN TAKES PLEDGE IN WHITE HOUSE

I expect that taking the pledge at the White House was never done except on November 6, 1917. My Diary says:

"A young man who had been to Occoquan for drinking called and told me of a half-hour with President Wilson, in whose presence he had signed the pledge. The President had written below in his own hand: 'I will add this line to express my confidence that Morrison will keep this pledge so solemnly taken. Woodrow Wilson.' He had been a pupil of Wilson at Princeton."

MANY COUNTRYMEN "DAMN FOOLS"

At a meeting in March, McAdoo urged upon the President that he ought to make an address to the country on April 6, the anniversary of our entering the war. It was needed, he said, to strengthen the public morale. After discussing various classes who were standing in the way of victory, W.W. said: "Now, having proved that many of our fellow-citizens are damn fools, let us come to business." This was one of the five or six times I ever heard Wilson use "the short and ugly word."

WROTE LETTER FOR WEAVER

I recall in 1918, the year we lost Congress, that the mountain district of North Carolina seemed to be in danger for the Democrats, and I asked Wilson to write a letter urging the voters to reëlect Zebulon Vance Weaver. As evidence of his carefulness in such matters, Wilson wrote me this characteristic letter:

"I should be very glad to help Mr. Weaver but I would not dare to write a letter just off my own bat to him.... If someone in Mr. Weaver's district should address me a letter asking some pertinent question about his record, it would give me an opportunity to send an answer which I would be glad to send."

The letter was written and Wilson wrote a strong letter, which was widely circulated and insured Weaver's election.

WILSON NEVER FORGOT

There were people who said Wilson lacked the genius for friendship. The close comradeship of his classmates at Princeton and his loyalty to men who stood adamant for their principles never failed. He never broke with a friend except when a supporter had been ready "to sell the truth to serve the hour" or who had lost zeal for the cause he had favored. Early in his administration he was determined to secure anti-trust legislation fathered by Henry D. Clayton of Alabama. When Clayton resigned, Congressman E. Y. Webb, of North Carolina, led the fight that secured its passage. He also fathered important war measures as Chairman of the House Judiciary Committee. Wilson did not forget, and when there was a vacancy on the Federal bench in Western North Carolina Webb was appointed Judge.

Speaking of the Clayton anti-trust measure Webb told me: "The President and I, at his desk in the White House, drew the provision in the bill which declares 'the labor of a human being is not a commodity or article of commerce.' I offered this provision on the floor of the house and stated it was "Labor's Magna Charta." Samuel Gompers used that term as the slogan of organized labor.

CHARACTERIZED CLAUDE KITCHIN

Of a meeting in August (1918) my Diary had this entry:

"Claude Kitchin, Chairman of Ways and Means Committee, had made some criticisms in a rather dogmatic way. Wilson said the North Carolinian was a man who when he made up his mind would never open it. He loves to argue. Reminded W.W. of a certain Englishman (Jeffers) who loved to argue and never agreed with anyone. One night he was ill. Someone at the door called out: 'All is well and the sky is clear with the stars shining.' The man rose from his bed, saying: 'I doubt it,' and pointed out a small cloud in the sky."

NO ARMY PROPAGANDA

Wilson hated propaganda, particularly by the military. Hearing that army intelligence officers were interesting themselves in propaganda abroad, Wilson wrote Acting Secretary Crowell:

"I regard nothing more delicate or more intimately associated with the policy of the administration than propaganda, and if any agency of the army is attempting to organize propaganda of any sort, or to take a hand in controlling it, I would be obliged if you would call them off."

MILITARY MEN AS CANDIDATES

While the war was still on there were suggestions of choosing military men for public office. The Cabinet discussed this and my Diary discloses the attitude of Wilson and Baker:

"Shall men in military service run for office? Baker said they should be disenrolled when they accepted nomination. McAdoo agreed. 'Suppose Pershing should be candidate for President?' asked McAdoo. 'I would bring him home at once,' said Baker. I said that in the Civil War Garfield, Hayes, and others were elected to Congress. There are two sides to the question. President thought nothing should be done until after the election and then candidates should vacate military positions."

GOD INSPIRED WILSON

At one meeting Redfield told of a bitter dispute between Democrats and Republicans, the latter being bitter against W.W. Finally the Republicans had to admit that Wilson was right, but would not give him personal credit and said: "Wilson is making good only because he is inspired by Almighty God."

SEAMAN COULD TASTE FOG

The President told of a visit to Nantucket. A sea captain became stage driver to Sconsett. In dark nights in a fog he would stop his horses, drop the staff of his whip to the ground, draw it up, put it in his mouth. 'Why?' 'I know every foot of land hereabouts and can tell exactly where I am by tasting it.'

THE "P" IN COMPTROLLER

At the Cabinet meeting on October 19, there was talk of having a Comptroller General of Railroads, and someone raised the question as to whether it should be spelled Controller or Comptroller. The President related this story:

"Once upon a time a man built a small lumber railroad. He was a practical man, not well educated, but knew enough to keep his books. The railroad prospered and the owner employed an elderly man to keep books and he signed himself 'Controller.' When he died the business had grown and the owner employed a young efficiency expert. When he brought in his first report he spelled his title Comptroller, not Controller, as had his predecessor. The old man didn't like the change and said so very emphatically, and stormed out 'Since when was there a P in Controller?' The young man got even by quietly saying: 'I think it was the last time you watered the stock.'"

STEEL OR STEAL AND OIL

I recall in June, 1917, when I was making a fight to prevent the steel people from charging outrageous prices to the government and to prevent the big oil companies from getting legislation to drain the Naval oil reserves, I had two letters from Wilson. He said he had hoped we could find a way of relieving California "without going too far in opening the door to those who have been trying to get a foot-hold in the oil fields in a way we cannot approve or sanction," and with reference to steel on June 16, 1917, he wrote me, "Thank you very much for your letter about the steel prices. I hardly know how to spell the word. The prices they were charging the Shipping Board were so outrageous that I think they ought to have spelled it S-T-E-A-L."

When the California people were trying to secure oil from the Naval reserve, oil they planned on selling to Japan, I received some important information from Mr. Thomas Spellacy. I sent the letter to Wilson. He was pleased and said, "It is an interesting and unexpected light on the situation out there."

TRIBUTE TO SECRETARY HERBERT

Busy as he was, when I suggested he send a message of condolence to Mrs. Micou, daughter of Honorable Hilary A. Herbert, who was Secretary of the Navy in Cleveland's Administration, at the time of the death of her father, Wilson promptly sent this message: "The country has lost a servant who illustrated in the whole spirit of his service a very high order of patriotism as well as a great ability."

OLD FRIENDS MEANT MUCH

Old friends meant much to Wilson and no matter how engaged he was in Paris or Washington he always responded to any evidence of friendship. When Wilson reached Boston on his return from Paris he received a telegram signed by James Sprunt, J. A. Taylor, and H. C. McQueen, saying, "Your old friends in Wilmington

(N. C.) proud of your splendid achievements under God's guidance desire to welcome you home. Well done, good and faithful servant." To which Wilson replied promptly, addressing his letter to James Sprunt, who had been his father's closest friend while his father was Pastor of the Presbyterian Church in Wilmington,

"DEAR FRIEND:
I was greatly cheered by the message from you and Mr. Taylor and Mr. McQueen. Oldtime friendships grow dearer rather than dimmer and such a greeting from my old friends in Wilmington has cheered me greatly.
"Cordially and sincerely yours,
/s/ "WOODROW WILSON."

On February 18, 1918, Wilson wrote me that a young Presbyterian preacher in New York, Frank Latimer Janeway, desired a commission as Chaplain in the Navy, and said, "It is delightful to see such men turn to this service. He was a pupil of mine at Princeton and is one of the finest fellows I have ever known. If there is a vacancy available, I hope sincerely that he will get it."

Old friends meant so much to him that he would occasionally write a letter like this:

"MY DEAR DANIELS:
"Here is a really pitiful case. I wonder if the boy could not be released. The writer of the letter I send you is an old and intimate chum of mine of the University of Virginia, and what he says can be absolutely relied upon...."

Wilson rarely made suggestions as to any Navy assignments. I think only half a dozen during the whole eight years, and these were always of men whose loyalty he had tested. He became attached to Captain Berry, who was in command of the *Mayflower*, the President's yacht, and when we were commissioning the new destroyers in 1917 Wilson wrote me, beginning his letter as always,

"My dear Daniels: May I not express the personal hope that in assigning commanders to the best of the new destroyers, Berry will not be overlooked. He seems to me particularly qualified for service of the enterprising sort required in these particular craft."

APPROVAL BY COMPETENT JUDGES

After some controversy about Naval matters I had letters from Honorable John D. Long and Honorable William E. Chandler, who had been formerly Secretary of the Navy, approving the policies which had received criticism. I sent copies of these letters to the President and he wrote he was hoping they could be published and added,

> "I did not need to have anybody tell me how entirely correct and excellent your administration of the Department has been, but I want this evidence from the opposite party published. It gives me personally the greatest pleasure that you should receive such evidences of the approval of men competent to judge."

When I wrote Wilson expressing the gratification of the country that Congress had followed his advice and made provision for making our Navy the most adequate in the world, Wilson wrote me, "Your own part in this whole thing has been the central part and I think warm congratulations are due to you."

DOCTRINE OF ELECTION

At the Cabinet meeting (November 9, 1917) Wilson, returning from New Jersey, where he went to vote, expressed pleasure on the whole at the result of the election. From my Diary:

> "Wilson told a story of Senator Vance's trying to induce a Negro to join the Presbyterian Church. The Negro said he did not believe in the doctrine of election for eternity. 'I do,' said Vance. 'It is a sound doctrine.' The Negro answered: 'I hain't never heered of your being a candidate for heaven.'"

This story tempted Houston (born in the same county in North Carolina that gave birth to Andrew Jackson) to tell this anecdote of Vance, who said, "I am a Presbyterian and do not believe in falling from grace but am always falling. My brother Bob (member of Congress) is a Methodist, believes in falling from grace, but never falls."

The President said it was a good idea to watch how some men vote and then vote the other way. He told a story of Princeton days:

> " 'You fool, didn't you see how West voted?' asked a pro-Wilson member of the faculty who had voted against Wilson's

policy, and added: 'If you don't understand a question, never vote as West votes.'"

The President added that such a rule would be good in Congress—always vote against what certain congressmen vote for.

INTERPRETATION OF HIMSELF

These casual sidelights reveal phases of Wilson "off guard." Now let us see Wilson's appraisement of himself. Fortunately it is preserved. Asked by an old Massachusetts friend to interpret himself, Wilson wrote:

"MY DEAR FRIEND:

"You have placed an impossible task upon me.—that of interpreting myself to you. All I can say in answer to your inquiry is that I have a sincere desire to serve, to be of some little assistance in improving the condition of the average man, to lift him up and to make his life more tolerable, agreeable, and comfortable. In doing this I try hard to purge my heart of selfish motives. It will only be known when I am dead, whether or not I have succeeded.

"Sincerely your friend,
"WOODROW WILSON"

"I am content," said Wilson one day, "to leave my reputation to the verdict of history."

LVI

CRITICS WERE CONVERTED

As the wise policies of Wilson bore fruit for better government, many who had been doubtful of the "professor's" statesmanship gave support to his administration, and many more gave expression to their confidence in his greatness which in the early days they had doubted.

As one remarkable evidence of this (I could fill chapters with like expressions), I quote the following extract from a letter I received from Colonel Henry Watterson, who had early been an advocate of Wilson for President in 1912, but who, after the Harvey incident, opposed his nomination: -

"Well, didn't I tell you that Wilson needs no chaperon? If he were as broad as he is high—if his intellect had not been cultivated and sharpened at the expense of his affections—he would be ideal. Nevertheless, I think my lambasting on that side has done him good, and it may be that before he is out of the woods he will find that the intelligent support of an independent and disinterested man is grateful as well as valuable. I don't like him, but I believe in him; that is to say, a man may recognize another's genius and follow his lead without wanting to share his grub and bed with him!

"Go to, go to—you dashed old functionary!—I alone am beautiful and good! Except the Secretary of State I don't know a single one of your colleagues, and, as I am hardly likely to be in Washington ever again, I don't expect to. Presently I shall go abroad and forget all about you—Congress and Cabinets—even Woodrow Wilson and George Harvey—but not you, Josephus, not you!"

Early in the spring (1921) after my term of office expired, I made a trip through the Southern states in the interest of endowments for Methodist colleges. When I reached Louisville, I went to his country home to call upon my old friend and fellow editor, Colonel Watterson. We had hardly exchanged old-time greetings when Colonel Watterson said to me:

"Josephus, I did not like your man Wilson. I did not like him at all. I did not like many things he did, but I want to say to you—and this is not personal but my serious conviction—that long after you and I and all other actors on the stage are dead and forgotten, Woodrow Wilson will loom in history as the greatest man of our era."

FOR WILSON, AGAINST HIM, APPROVED HIM

I quote Watterson's prediction because it is typical of those frank and honest men big enough to correct earlier opinions. The Kentucky Colonel could revise his appraisement of Wilson because he was never influenced by selfish considerations. He had not remote kinship with the Wilson haters who were controlled by their selfishness. The Protectionists, profiteers, and the Boston Home Market clique foamed at the mouth because Wilson kept their hands out of the public treasury and out of the pockets of the people through legislation outlawing the methods that had made them rich.

In 1911 Watterson called Wilson "the moral and intellectual light of the Democratic situation; a scholar among politicians, a politician among scholars." That was when together we were advocating Wilson's nomination for the presidency. When, governed by intimate friendship for Colonel Harvey, he turned against Wilson because he felt he had not shown gratitude to a supporter, he then described Wilson as "the stalking horse of intellect and culture, which had, like a clothier's model, displayed showing resemblances of a leader." He devoted a whole column in the *Courier Journal*, to pointing out what he regarded as my inconsistency, as a Bryan man, in supporting Wilson, to whom he attributed genuflections to the rich, saying:

"It would be a vital question even with Josephus Daniels, whether a single year of recantation and apology, has destroyed, has eliminated and blotted out Wilson's conviction of a life-time exalting, the bankers of the East as the sole custodian of financier's wisdom."

That was in 1912. Colonel Watterson, however, thought consistency a hobgoblin of little minds and by 1922 was to tell me that my consistent appraisal of Wilson was the one that history would accept.

LVII

WILSON STILL LIVES

THERE MAY BE debate as to whether "The Wilson Era" ended when Wilson went out of office March 4, 1921, or when he died on February 3, 1924. But there can be no two opinions that from the day he emerged from academic life to become successively chief executive of his state and of the republic Wilson rose to be the commanding figure in American public life. It is equally true that from the day in 1917 when he carried "this peaceful nation" into "a war against war" he rose to heights which no contemporary dared to challenge.

Mankind in every hemisphere hailed him as the human savior when, out of the long days and nights of agony at the Peace Conference "the Wilson League" emerged bearing the signature of the representatives of all the Allied Nations. It was the long desired covenant of deliverance from war.

WILSON'S PLACE IN HISTORY

"Wilson is more alive than ever he was," wrote Bliss Perry after his passing. "The curtain does not fall upon such idealists as Woodrow Wilson; the play evolves into the eternal drama that makes up the life of humanity."

"No other American has ever builded so large in the affairs of civilization or wielded so commanding an influence in shaping their ends," was the *New York World's* appraisement.

"The world will look in vain for his equal as a statesman, philosopher, and humanitarian," declared Cordell Hull.

"Wilson will be held in everlasting remembrance as a statesman who, when others sought revenge and material gain, strove to bring nearer the day which should see the emancipation of conscience from power and the substitution of freedom for force in the government of the world," was the considered judgment of President Franklin D. Roosevelt.

In his historic memorial address at a joint session of Congress, Edwin A. Alderman declared:

"Even as death enfolded him in its shadows, men paused in their busy lives and came to comprehend that a man of great faith had lived in their era, akin in heart and blood to John Milton and John Hampden, Mazzini, and Luther, that a prophet had guided their country and stirred the heart of mankind in an hour of destiny, and that an incorruptible liberal aflame with will to advance the slow ascent of man had joined those whom men call immortal...."

As Wilson returned to private life, his co-worker for the Covenant at Paris, Jan Christiaan Smuts, who has lived to see his prophecy come true, gave him the highest place among all Americans, saying:

"The Covenant will stand as sure as fate.... And the day is not far off when all free peoples of the world will gather around it.... It is not Wilson that failed. It was the human spirit itself that failed....

"And the leader who, in spite of apparent failure, succeeded in inscribing his name on that banner has achieved the most enviable and enduring immortality. Americans of the future will yet proudly and gratefully rank him with Washington and Lincoln, and his name will have a more universal significance than theirs."

History was to repeat itself, for nearly always mankind has crucified its saviors or has stood by, holding the clothes of those who threw the stones. In succession Italy rejected Orlando; France threw Clemenceau into the discard; Britain, turning from Lloyd George, ended his leadership; Greece repudiated Venizelos; Poland ungratefully forgot Paderewski. And when the United States Senate "broke the heart of the world," it was proclaimed, "Wilson has failed."

But did Wilson fail? Was it not rather that the people failed and for a score of years wandered in a maze of isolation, corruption, frenzied finance, and depression?

As long as men seek independence, the name of Washington will be revered; as long as men looking out of darkened windows long to achieve government by the consent of the governed, the name of Jefferson will be their inspiration; as long as any man in any part of the world is held in slavery, Lincoln's emancipation will be their goal; and as long as men place reason and justice above strife and war, the name of Wilson will be enshrined in their hearts.

WILSON'S PROPHECY FULFILLED

The spirit of Woodrow Wilson brooded over the San Francisco Conference as the commissioners of fifty free nations on June 24, 1945, signed a pact fufilling Wilson's last prophecy. Shortly before his passing, calling upon him at his home in Washington I confessed to my beloved chief some depression and fear of the future, because our country was not a member of the League of Nations and his and my great dream of lasting peace had been shattered beyond repair. Though "broken at the wheel," he sought to cheer me up, because he never recognized defeat, believing that no man is ever defeated until he admits it.

"Do not fear about the things we have fought for. They are sure to prevail. They are only delayed."

> " ' 'Tis the sunset of life gives us mystical lore
> And coming events cast their shadows before.' "

And he added with the quaintness that gave charm to all his sayings, even when weakness was in his voice, "And I will make this concession to Providence—it may come in a better way than we proposed."

I am thankful to have lived to see the day that Woodrow Wilson's prophecy has been fufilled.

If Elizabeth Barrett Browning had known Wilson and divined his thoughts and heart's desire, she could not have better described him and his faith than in these lines:

> "A great man (who was crowned one day)
> Imagined a great deed;
> He shaped it out of cloud and clay,
> He touched it finely till the seed
> Possessed the flower: from heart and brain
> He fed it with large thoughts humane,
> To help a people's need.
>
> He brought it out into the sun—
> They blessed it to his face:
> "O great pure deed, that hast undone

So many bad and base!
O generous deed, heroic deed,
Come forth, be perfected, succeed,
Deliver by God's grace!"

Then sovereigns, statesmen, north and south,
Rose up in wrath and fear,
And cried protesting by one mouth,
"What monster have we here?
A great deed at this hour of day?
A great just deed—and not for pay?
Absurd—or insincere." . . .

But he stood sad before the sun
(The peoples felt their fate).
"The world is many—I am one:
My great deed was too great.
God's fruit of justice ripens slow:
Men's souls are narrow; let them grow.
My brothers, we must wait."

INDEX